REF
E
78
C2
E55
v.5

Encyclopedia of
indians of the
Americas

Encyclopedia of Indians of the Americas

Encyclopedia of Indians of the Americas

VOLUME

5

Scholarly Press, Inc.
19722 E. NINE MILE RD., ST. CLAIR SHORES, MICHIGAN 48080

ENCYCLOPEDIA OF INDIANS OF THE AMERICAS

Library of Congress Cataloging in Publication Data

Main entry under title:

Encyclopedia of Indians of the Americas.

1. Indians. I. Harry Waldman, ed.
E54.5.E52 970'.004'97 74-5088
ISBN 0-403-01795-5 (v. 5)

Printed in the United States of America
First Printing—1980

COLORADO, the state, is rich in remains of ancient history. Evidence of ancient men hunting ancient animals, found on the Lindenmeier and Yuma archaeological sites, goes back 10,000 years, and Mesa Verde National Park spans the development of the Anasazi culture (*q.v.*) from AD 100 to *c.* 1299.

When the Spanish entered the Southwest in the 16th century the Colorado mountains were the range of nomadic bands of Shoshonean-speaking Utes. The Utes acquired horses and managed to defend their mountain strongholds against invasions by warring Plains tribes. In the 19th century Comanche and Kiowa tribes settled along the Arkansas River until they were forced to the south by allied Cheyenne-Arapaho tribes who occupied territory between the Platte and the Arkansas. In 1840 these former enemies formed an alliance against their common enemy, white settlers, and during the turbulent 1860s and 70s were labeled "hostiles" by the U.S. government.

The discovery of gold in 1859 brought settlers swarming over the hunting grounds of the Cheyenne-Arapahoes with inevitable results. Mounting tensions between settlers and Indians culminated in the notorious massacre at Sand Creek (*q.v.*), a surprise attack in 1864 by Colorado volunteers under Colonel Chivington on the peaceful Cheyenne-Arapaho village of Chief Black Kettle.

A war of revenge for Sand Creek followed and continued intermittently for ten years. It spilled over the Colorado borders into all the neighboring states and involved all the allies of the Cheyennes. Wagon trails became impassable and stage stations like Julesburg were destroyed. The Comanche-Kiowas, satisfying an old grudge, unleashed their fury on the settlers of Texas. In 1868 the Northern Cheyenne suffered a defeat by Colorado troops at Beecher's Island. The great warrior Roman Nose was killed, but the tribe recovered to fight at Little Big Horn. In 1874 the Southern Cheyenne surrendered and were removed to Oklahoma.

The Colorado Utes, whose chief Ouray was a noted peacemaker, managed to stay out of serious conflicts until they were settled on the White River Agency. There the pressures of the agent Nathan Meeker to turn these stylish horsemen into farmers led to an attack on the Agency in 1879 known as the Meeker Massacre (*q.v.*). Ouray negotiated a peace that removed the Indian offenders, without further reprisals, to a reserve at Uintah, Utah.

Today the Southern Utes occupy a reservation near Ignacio along the New Mexican border where they hold individual farms. They also retain their language and tribal identity, the traditional Sun Dance and Bear Dance ceremonials, and the arts of basketry and leatherwork. Ouray rests in their cemetery. The Indians of the Ute Mountain reservation, bordering Mesa Verde Park, have clung more stubbornly to primitive tribal ways. They live communally as nomadic sheepherders and are unfriendly to visitors.

COLORADO. Before the arrival of the Spaniards in South America, the Colorado Indians lived in the lush Pacific lowlands between the mountains and the coast of western Ecuador. There they cultivated maize, chili peppers, cotton, and guavas, caught fish and extracted salt, all of which they traded with the highland peoples of Ecuador, even crossing the Andes to obtain fish poisons from the Canelo. The Colorado, whose name came from their liberal use of red body paint (*achiote*), are the southernmost extension of peoples speaking dialects of the Barbacoan division of the Chibchan language family. As such, they belong to a group of scattered Pacific lowland tribes ranging from the Chocó in northern Colombia and Panama to the

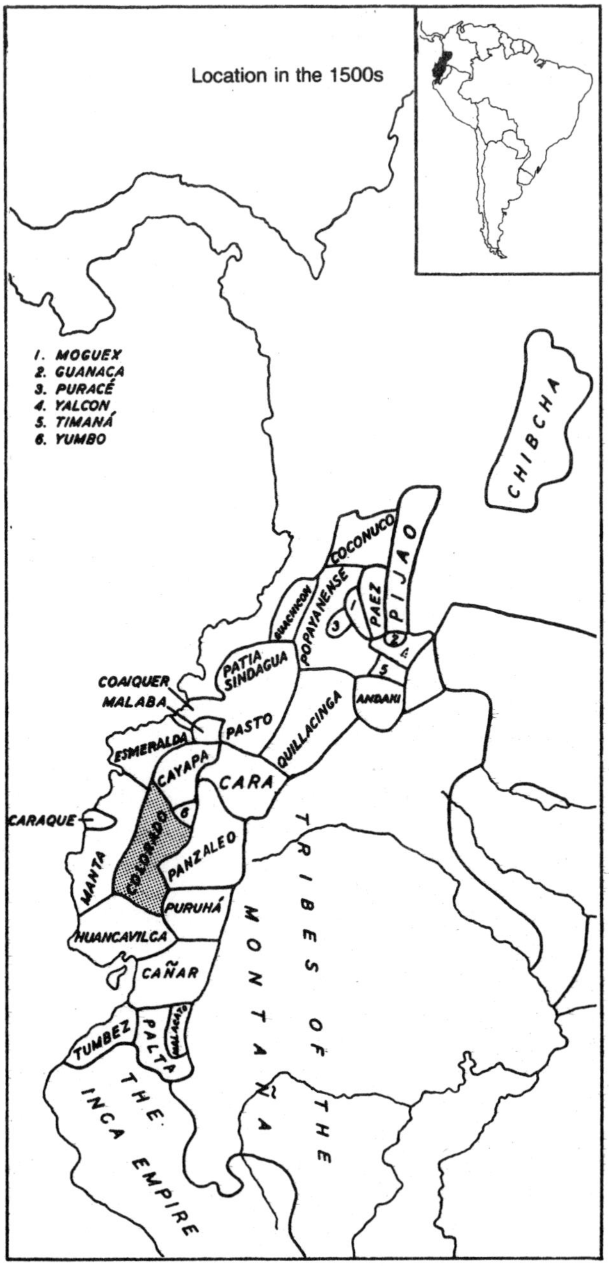

The Colorado and neighboring Highland tribes of Colombia and Ecuador.

Colorado Indians of Santo Domingo, Ecuador.

Cayapa and Colorado in the south whose tropical forest culture was far more consistent with the Indians of the Amazon than with those of the Andes.

Known also as the Campaz, and preferring to call themselves Tsatchela, the Colorado did not feel the impact of the Spanish conquest immediately for the climate of the wet lowlands did not attract the Europeans in the early part of the colonial period. Nonetheless, by the end of the colonial period, nearly every tribe west of the Andes was destroyed as the area was settled, as it is now, by *montuvios*, peoples of mixed white, Indian, and black ancestry who consider themselves Ecuadorians, not Indians. The only surviving aboriginal groups are the Cayapa and the Colorado who fled from their lowland home to the forested western slopes of the Andean cordillera, the Cayapa to the north and the Colorado just south of them. It is interesting to note that both the Cayapa and the Colorado by tradition believe that they originated in the highlands, moving from there to the lowlands sometime in the distant past. It is possible that this tradition made the adjustment from lowland to mountain slope more successful. Yet, they have been followed by the inexorable process of settlement. The Colorado occupy the upper reaches of the tributaries of the Esmeraldas and Daules rivers; and this area in the western part of Pichincha Province has been heavily colonized by Ecuadorians since the 1930s. During World War II, an all-weather road was opened and the end of Colorado cultural and social institutions was in sight. More and more Ecuadorians have since settled in this region and most of the Colorado have been incorporated into the highland plantation economy. By 1950 there were approximately 300 Colorado left in two centers, Santo Domingo de los Colorados and San Miguel.

The Colorado are known as excellent cultivators, growing plantains, sweet manioc, yams, peppers, and cacao in fields near their houses. They also clear fields in the forests and plant such crops as maize, rice, pineapples, and citrus fruits. They also raise their own medicinal plants and *barbasco*, a drug used in fishing. Men clear the fields, fish, hunt and make nets while the women cook, weave and tend their children and domesticated animals which include guinea pigs, pigs, chickens and dogs. Both men and women cooperate in cultivating and harvesting the fields and in taking the produce to Ecuadorian market towns. The Colorado fish in the tributaries of the rivers, using nets, traps, and hooks as well as *barbasco*. Hunting is not very productive in this region, but the men shoot monkeys, agoitis, and an occasional deer with muzzle-loading shotguns. Before the turn of the century, blowguns with clay pellets were the main hunting weapons for birds.

Like the Cayapa, to the north, the Colorado have no nucleated villages but live dispersed in the forest near their fields. There is a church which marks the center of a settlement and to which the Colorado come for Catholic ceremonies, baptism, marriage, masses for the dead, and so forth, which occur at infrequent intervals when the circuit-riding Dominican priest visits the region. Houses are large frame buildings without walls, the palm-thatched roofs supported by posts. There is often a separate sleeping section within the house. Platform beds are used for sleeping. Each household is economically self-sufficient in terms of the traditional system.

No real information is available about the traditional social and political organization nor is the exact composition of the multi-family household known. What might have existed as political leadership has long since disappeared. However, some descriptions of the rituals connected with life cycle events have been written. At birth, there is no specific ceremony save the parents observing certain food taboos until the infant's navel was healed. The influence of the church may be seen in the appointing of godparents for each child. A puberty ritual is noted for boys only in which the shaman conducts a nose-piercing ceremony for those ten to twelve years old. After this event, the boy may begin painting his body and drinking *nepe*. Girls are married soon after puberty but boys wait somewhat longer. Marriages are performed by the shaman and are occasions for great feasting with music, dancing, and drinking. Marriages are considered final when blessed by the priest.

Colorado funeral rites are a mixture of traditional beliefs and highland influence. The deceased is dressed in his best clothes and is guarded by relatives for one day during which time they weep loudly, drink, and sometimes dance. Special games of the types seen among the highland Indians are played with rubber balls or burning wood. These games serve a dual purpose: to keep mourners awake and more importantly to prevent the spirits which caused the death from attacking the survivors. The body is then placed in a shroud and suspended above the ground under the floor of the deceased's house. A platform is placed over the body and a string connected to the roof is tied around his neck. The string helps the soul to depart quickly from the body. After leaving some food and a candle, the relatives abandon the house. At each full moon, the oldest member of the family comes back and touches the string gently. When it breaks at the touch, the soul has left the body.

Colorado religious life shows the effects of the long period in the eighteenth and nineteenth centuries when they had resident Catholic priests among them. All formal ceremonies and rites of passage, with the possible exception of the funeral rite, show Colorado attachment to the Catholic ritual. However, in the process of day-to-day activities, the aboriginal Chibcha concepts as well as those of other highland Indians are evident. The traditional creation story gives an important place to the two major Andean volcanoes, Cotopaxi and Chimborazo. There is a strong belief in good and evil spirits as causes of good fortune and of disease. Shamans play a large role in Colorado society, especially in recent times as the Catholic priest has all but disappeared from the community and what political leadership there had been in the past is no longer evident. The shamans are held in such high regard that they are often called upon to journey up into the highlands to practice their curing prowess. It has been said that Colorado shamans treat not only Indians but mestizos as well. Disease was believed to be caused by sorcery and by evil spirits. Colorado share the montaña belief that disease is caused by the intrusion of sharp spikes which must be sucked out by the shaman. The Colorado practice therapeutic diet also to cure disease in which the patient, his relatives, and the shaman observe certain food regulations in order to facilitate the cure. During the actual ritual, *nepe*, a narcotic, mildly hallucinogenic drink, is taken by both the shaman and his patient. Brandy is also consumed, drums and rattles are beaten, trance dancing takes place, and finally the sharp spine is sucked out and displayed for all to pay witness to the shaman's great power.

L. C. AND S. R. FARON

COLORADO RIVER RESERVATION, in Yuma County, Arizona, and San Bernardino and Riverside counties, California, is 264,092 acres of land owned by more than 1,600 members of the Mojave and Chemehuevi tribes.

The Mojave and Chemeheuvi Indians, members of the Yuman family, have lived in the Lower Colorado area since recorded history. Both tribes controlled vast stretches of land until the arrival of the Spanish in the 16th century. The United States acquired this territory under the Treaty of Hidalgo in 1848, and agreed to preserve the rights of the Indians to their land. In 1865, the Colorado River Reservation was created to induce the Mojave and Chemehuevi to give up their war-like tactics, which they had embraced upon the arrival of the Spanish, and to adopt agriculture as a mode of living.

The Colorado River tribes approved a constitution in 1937 under the Indian Reorganization Act. It created a tribal council, the governing body which meets monthly. The council members are elected for two year terms. On the reservation, most Indians of the family work and pool their resources to increase their family income. The education level is high school. While there are no Bureau of Indian Affairs' schools, students attend public or private schools.

Farming is the economic backbone of the reservation, with the annual tribal income at $600,000. There are several companies located on the reservation, and several Indian-based concerns. The Indians belong to the Indian Development District of Arizona. In addition, mineral deposits of clay, gypsum, and gold provide additional income to the Indians.

The Colorado River area has always been a great natural paradise. In the past Yuman Indians produced such crops as corn, melons, pumpkins, beans, and roots, and hunted for wild game.

The Indians are rediscovering the wonder of this area, and are again hunting and fishing. The past for the Mojave and Chemehuevi was never forgotten.

COLOROW (White River Ute; ?-Dec. 12, 1888), was a Muache Ute chief who was a leader in the battle for the White River Valley, Colorado, in 1879.

As a small child, Colorow was seized from a Comanche camp during a raid. He was adopted into the Ute Tribe and given the name Too-p'-weets ("rock"). He excelled in all Indian games and became expert in horse racing. His initiation as a warrior was in a fight between the Ute and the Arapaho in Roaring Fork Valley, Colorado. Colorow escaped from the Arapaho and led a brilliant counterattack which resulted in a victory for his band. For his bravery and skill on this occasion he was made a chief of the Northern Ute.

In 1868 Colorow was one of the Ute chiefs who went to Washington to negotiate a treaty with the U.S. government. Following the treaty, he lived on a small, temporary reservation adjoining Denver. In 1875 this reservation was closed and Colorow took his Muache Ute tribe up to the White River Agency.

In the spring of 1878, Nathan C. Meeker became the agent at White River and immediately tried to convert the Indians from hunting to an agrarian way of life. He moved the agency to their favorite pasture lands and began constructing the agency buildings on a traditional racing strip where the Indians enjoyed their favorite sport of horse racing. When Meeker attempted to begin plowing a section of the pasture in 1879, some of the tribesmen stopped the plowing by force.

Troops under Maj. Thomas T. Thornburgh were dispatched, at the request of Meeker, and began to march from Ft. Fred Steele on September 21, 1879. Colorow learned of the soldier's approach a few days later, and on September 28 he met with Thornburgh, who agreed not to enter the reservation. When the soldiers nevertheless advanced, Colorow led one of the parties that fought the command and killed Thornburgh and several of his men on September 29. Others then attacked the agency, killed Meeker and the male employees, and made captives of the white women. At the Los Piños Agency, 150 miles to the south, the Ute head chief, Ouray (*q.v.*), heard of the fighting. He quickly sent a message that induced Colorow and the others to cease hostilities before the arrival of army reinforcements.

Colorow and his followers were eventually excused from punishment on the grounds that they were warriors engaged in a fair fight. The Indians who killed Meeker and the others were charged with murder. In September 1881 Colorow and the White River Ute were moved to the Uintah and Ouray Reservation in Utah, where he died in 1888.

COLOR SYMBOLISM is of primary significance to the Indian artists and their crafts. Both in their multiplicate forms of elaboration and widespread usage, the tribal systems of color symbolism traditionally have remained an integral part of the objects created by Indian artisans.

Each tribe had its own system of color symbolism. As with all visual symbolism of the Indians, color symbolism was developed in a structured manner which established specific color denotations. The colors most frequently used symbolically are black, white, blue, red, yellow, and sometimes green. Most often they symbolize localities; not only the North, South, East, and West of the physical world but also directions relating to the Upper, Middle, and Lower regions of the metaphysical universe. At the same time various tribes utilize these colors as symbols for other basic elements (such as day, night, male, female, earth, air, fire, water) and ceremonially communicating changing situations (strength, success, trouble, happiness, peace, victory, defeat, death, mourning). Assignment of colors varied between tribes, and even, as with the Navajo, within the tribe. Consistency was not overwhelming, as the meanings attributed to black and white can at times be interchanged.

Colors symbolizing the male connoted a greater preponderance of violence, noise, and largeness in size while the female colors symbolized warmth and gentleness. The assignment of "male" or "female" colors to the various directions infused into the directions the male or female characteristics symbolized by those colors.

Complexly developed systems of color symbolism appear in many forms of Indian life. Most visible are the warriors and dancers who painted their bodies with colors in the Southeast as well as the Southwest, and were thus symbolically imbued with the powers and attributes appropriate to their roles.

Among the Navajo, rival teams or players in games are given identifying colors symbolizing opposing forces in the universe, such as day and night. Hopi sand paintings used in oblutive and curative rituals not only utilize color symbolism in design but are created in ceremonial sequence following the directional pattern represented by the colors. Individual Hopi deities are symbolized by significant colors, and Hopi kachina dolls (carved wooden figures embracing the spirits of important ancestor figures) are painted appropriately.

Indian languages do not always contain words which distinguish between subtle shades of colors. Frequently Indians are called by names incorporating the word for a color whose symbolic characteristics are admirable.

The influence of white people, greater communication and inter-tribal trade led to a more widespread treatment of colors and a breakdown of the use of color symbolism as a distinguishing element of tribal individualism.

COLUSA RESERVATION, in Colusa County, California, is a reservation of 269 acres, and is home to 16 members of the Cahil Dehe band of Wintun Indians.

The rancheria was purchased by the Secretary of the Interior in 1907, and expanded in 1938. Located in central California, the rancheria has a topography which is hilly, mountainous, and sometimes flooded. The Sacramento River runs through the reservation, and at times overflows its banks.

Today, very little of the culture of the Indian tribe remains. The few Indians are served with water, gas and electricity. Sewers are outdoors only. The nearest towns, Colusa and Sacramento, provide commercial and medical services.

COLVILLE RESERVATION, in Ferry and Okanogan counties, Washington, is an area of more than 1,000,000 acres and is home to about 3,000 members of the Confederated Tribes.

The reservation was established by an executive order in 1872. At that time, the Confederated Tribes were a seminomadic Plateau Indian culture, who roomed over the lands of Idaho, eastern Oregon, and Eastern Washington. Today, the tribal members on the reservation are governed by the Business Council, which consists of 14 members representing the four voting districts on the reservation. The council represents all segments of the Indian people. The tribes are organized under a constitution which was approved in April, 1938.

The Confederated Tribe has an annual income of $3 million, and uses part of this money to provide scholarships for continuing education on the part of those interested. Today, about a third of the Indians remain unemployed and undereducated.

COMANCHE, a Ute word meaning enemy, is the name generally applied to a group of "nomadic" southern Plains Indians of Shoshonean linguistic stock and Rocky Mountain origin, who first appeared in the

Spanish documents of New Mexico a little after 1700. In the eighteenth century they were also known to the French and later to the Americans as Padouca or Pado, a name probably originally applied by the French to various Plains Apaches, whose country to the northeast and east of Santa Fe was taken over by the Comanches in the course of the eighteenth century. Early nineteenth century American documents also referred to the Comanches as Ietans. The Comanches' name for themselves is *Nemena* or "The True People" ("Human Beings"). The signs for Comanche in Plains sign language refer both to the Comanches' Shoshonean origin and to their separateness from other Shoshoneans, some of whom were called "Snakes." On the north Plains the sign for Comanche was indicated by a snake crawling forward or, after this sign was made, by flipping the hand over and again indicating a snake, signifying "another snake." On the south Plains the sign for Comanche was a snake crawling backwards.

Horses and plunder drew the Comanches from the mountains into raiding the Indian pueblos and Spanish rancherias of New Mexico, and the military and organizational advantages inherent in large horse herds permitted the Comanches to take possession of the south Plains and there establish the first "typical" Plains adaptation. Little is known of Comanche culture until about 1830, while most of the ethnographic descriptions of this group apply to the period of about 1850-1874, by which time the Comanches were a typical Plains tribe, little resembling their Shoshonean forebearers, contrary to statements by those who stress the "Shoshonean orientations" of the Comanches. On the south Plains, in the early nineteenth century, the Comanche homeland extended from the Arkansas River to the Nueces and from about the Pecos to the middle Brazos. Although various semi-sedentary tribes also hunted in part of this country, the Comanches and their Kiowa allies (with whom the Kiowa-Apaches were associated) regarded this land as theirs. Later the southern Arapahoes and southern Chey-

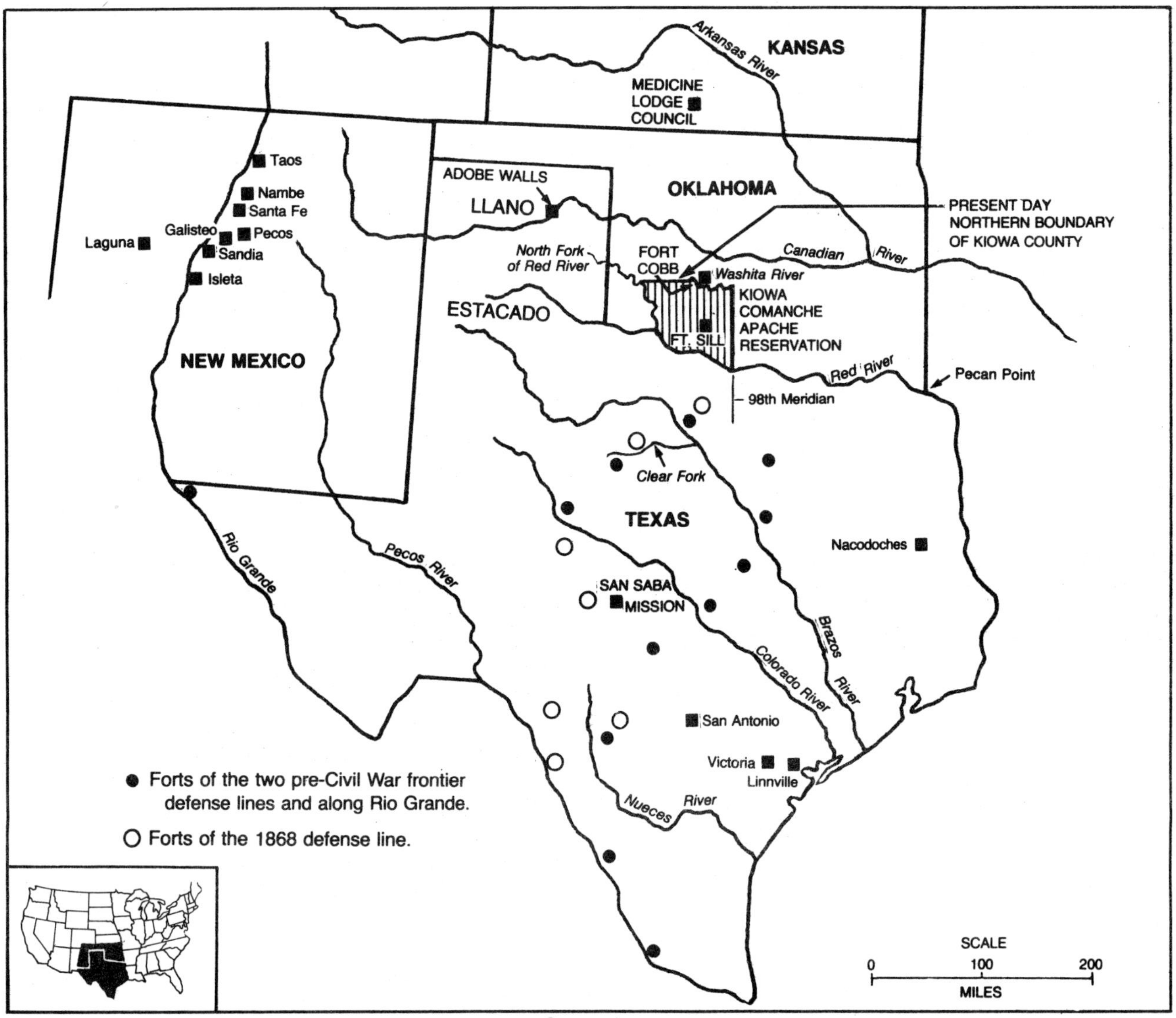

Comanche

ennes peaceably shared in the Comanche and Kiowa range. The Comanche language became the lingua franca or "court language" for the southern Plains.

Ecology

Horse nomadism on the Plains involved a number of complex ecological "trade offs," so that more than one set of choices could be found amongst a given Plains group at any given time. The increase in horse herds not only made pursuit of the buffalo more efficient, but also meant that more meat could be dried and carried to offset food scarcities engendered by the erratic movement of the buffalo, and especially to meet the common food scarcity in very late winter or early spring. But the increased size of horse herds also meant that a group would have to move more frequently through the exhaustion of forage for horses. Put simply, without considering numerous complications, the basic choice was between small groups with relatively long term residential stability and large groups that had to move frequently to secure horse forage. It is well known that large groups of Comanches aggregated in the summer, examples being Thomas James' estimate of 1,000 lodges and Catlin's of 600-800 lodges. Although there was a tendency to disperse into wooded bottomlands in the winter, it is sometimes forgotten that large aggregations did occur in the winter months, such as Jacob Fowler's (1821-2) report of Comanches in a multi-tribal camp of 700 lodges with a herd of 20,000 horses.

The Comanches were not merely passive participants in the Plain's ecosystem, but had developed techniques to help shape their environment. Although fire cycles are common in any grassland, the Comanches set fires in favored areas to insure more succulent grass next year. In addition, the Comanches were competent horse breeders who practiced gelding to build up their horse herd and select for the brave, fast and agile horses needed for buffalo hunting, an activity with a high horse mortality rate.

The frequent early references indicating that the Comanches ate only buffalo meat are assuredly wrong; ethnobotanists have identified more than twenty wild plants eaten by Comanches, but the early references do show how preponderant buffalo meat was in their diet. The techniques used by the Comanches in buffalo hunting were the surround, in which a mounted party caused a small herd or portion of a herd to move in a circle while the hunters on the edge of the circle shot the animals, and "running," where hunters chased individual animals. The Comanches, unlike most Plains Indians, frequently used a spear against buffalo. Only when the buffalo failed and famine threatened did a band resort to the magical communal antelope hunt. Horses were another emergency food.

Social and political organization

The extended family was the basic building block of Comanche society and, as a band chief's family was the core around which his band formed, large and powerful families often played important political roles. It was not by accident that there was a marked tendency for band chiefs to be sons of band chiefs. A band chief had to have a good war record and see that his followers were not lacking in the necessities of life, food and horses primarily. By producing wealth and giving it away, a band leader maintained his following and validated his own status. Hence, a large family which contributed wealth was a great asset to a social climbing Comanche. The principal familial prop to the chief was his "brother," which in the Comanche kinship system included not only a man's own siblings, but his male cousins as well. Comanche families created alliances with other families by marriage. As a man grew in importance he would attract followers from these allied families.

Bands composed of an extended family core and often a varying number of allied families were the basic subsistence units of Comanche society. In 1878, shortly after going onto the reservation, the subsistence band (which became the reservation "beef band" drawing rations together) averaged forty-seven people.

An important chief was the leader of his own subsistence band, but was also followed by a number of other band chiefs, often unrelated to him, and their subsistence bands, who looked to the great chief for guidance and support. Hence the number of people following a particular chief might range from a single subsistence band of no more than twenty people to a collection of subsistence bands of a thousand or considerably more people.

Confusion has surrounded the Comanche "divisions" because of substantial variations in their reported numbers. Late eighteenth century Spanish sources reported three divisions, "Cuchanecs" or "Cuchanticas" ("Buffalo Eaters"), "Yamparicas" ("Yap Eaters"), and "Yupes" ("Timber" or "Stick People"), as did David Burnet in 1819 (Comanches, "Yamparacks", and "Tenawas" or "Liver Eaters") and some American Indian agents in the 1860s and 1870s ("Quahadas", "It-chit-a-bund-ah" or "Cold Weather People," and "Penatekas"). Spanish and Mexican sources of the early nineteenth century (Padilla 1820, Berlandier 1829), as well as De Cessac in 1882, reported only two divisions. Late American sources, on the other hand, claimed a considerably larger number of divisions. In 1847 Butler and Lewis claimed six divisions, while agent Neighbors in the 1850s reported eight, and in 1861 Pike, the Confederate agent, mentioned five, as did W. P. Clark in 1885. In 1885, Ten Kate, who obtained information through a U.S. military interpreter, stated there were seven divisions. In late American documents "Nokoni" was a frequently mentioned division name, but other division names were sometimes given only once or twice by one or two writers ("Pohonim," "No-na-um" or "Noonah," which is reminiscent of the Comanche name for themselves, "Hai-ne-na-une," and "Par-kee-na-um").

There is reason to believe that the Comanche divisions corresponded to meaningful Comanche political groupings. The late increase in names does not indicate an increased knowledge of the Comanches, but rather a confusion of synonymous terms. For example, Neighbors recognized that "Hois" and "Penateka" were synonyms, but "Yupe" was also a synonym, as was probably "Tenawa." "Yamparica" can be equated with "Cold Weather People," and "Cuchantica" with "Nokoni" and "Quahada." At least from the late eighteenth century, the Comanches seem to have been organized into three divisions, each of which had a generally recognized pre-eminent chief. That one division sometimes made war while the other divisions were at peace with their enemy shows that the divisions were the highest level of effective political organization among the Comanches, although joint councils of divisions and, at least occasionally, a head chief of all divisions was sometimes recognized.

The conclusion that the divisions were important political groupings is supported by the meager data on Comanche soldier and medicine societies, which suggest that each Comanche division had its own societies. Table 1 collates the probable synonyms for the Comanche soldier societies with Lowie's information on the divisions in which the societies were found. The officers of each soldier society had various kinds of special paraphernalia such as lances and sashes, and each society appears to have owned the rights to a particular dance. The earliest (1820s) account of a Comanche soldier society reported that members of the Wolf society wore an untanned wolfskin strap and were pledged not to flee in desperate struggles. In addition to the lodges of the soldiers, there was a lodge for the old men.

Recognition of a head chief for all Comanches was the policy of the Spanish and American governments, a policy which before about 1840 seems to have received some Comanche support, but by the middle of the nineteenth century there was such a multiplicity of interests among the Comanches that no chief ever again attained enough prestige to be recognized by all Comanches. In 1786 the Spanish claimed that the leading Cuchantica chief had been elected head of all Comanches. Burnet stated that in 1819 "the three...[divisions] collectively acknowledge one head or grand chief...[the] extent of [his] authority...depending more on the force of his personal character than on the investments of office." Burnet reported that Parrow-a-Kifty, a Tenawa, was head chief. And in 1835 the United States Commissioners heard the Comanche Ichacoly (Catlin's Ee-Shah-ko-nee) say: "I will tell you the same thing I told you before. I am the only head chief of my nation."

Culture and life cycle

Comanches were very concerned with personal cleanliness and adornment. Adults bathed every morning, to the point of breaking ice on steams, and washed before eating. Young children of both sexes went nude, but older girls wore smaller versions of women's two piece (by mid-nineteenth century spliced together) leather dresses. Although men usually wore only a cloth breechclout in summer, they sometimes wore leather or cloth leggings and hide shirts. All ages and sexes wore hard-soled moccasins, and in winter wore buffalo robes, often decorated with beads and paint. After contact, silver and copper ornaments, especially

Table I

Comanche Soldier Societies

Comanche Division:	Lowie (1915):	Lowie (1915):	Clark (1885):	Ten Kate (1885):	Berlandier (1829):
Yamparica	Crow	Crow	Raven	Crow	
Quahada	Little Horse	Colt		Little Horse	
Quahada	Big Horse	Horse		Big Horse	
Nokoni and Penateka	Fox	Swift Fox	Swift Fox	Fox	
All Divisions	Buffalo	Buffalo	Buffalo Bull	Buffalo Bull	
				Turkey Cock	
	Drum		Gourd	Gourd	
			Afraid of Nothing		Wolf

brooches, were popular. From the middle nineteenth century, American manufactured clothes began to supersede native dress. Men wore their best clothes to war, often including spectacular headdresses, and frequently made tatoos around wounds as well as painting themselves. While women wore hair cropped at the neck, men wore long queues, often with horsehair spliced in to make them several feet long.

Transportation equipment was devèloped, although the travois, among most Plains Indians the most important accessory to the horse, may have been only an improvised affair (baggage packs tied to tent poles drug by horses). In addition to the horse travois, a few poor Comanches followed at the tail of a moving camp with dog travois. The lack of travois elaboration may have been due to Comanche horse wealth; a horse can pull more than it can carry. The horse rich Comanches were one of the few Plains tribes to use pack horses and pack saddles (made of rawhide pads). Riding saddles were of the Spanish type, with stirrups and a high pommel and cantel (less deep on women's saddles) made of rawhide-covered wood, cinched with a hide strap. Women seem to have used cruppers. Bridles were plaited hide or hair. Babies were carried in a fur lined pocket attached to a board equipped with straps for placement on the mother's back, the pommel of a saddle, or a tree or lodgepole in camp.

Comanche camps (and camp-life) were pretty much the same whether composed of only a few or five hundred lodges. There is no authenticated reference to orderly arrangement of lodges or the camp circle of the northern Plains. The only pre-reservation dwelling was the conical buffalo-skin (later canvas) tipi, using a "four pole foundation," which varied in size according to the number of inhabitants and wealth of the owner. Heating and ventilation was achieved by combination of a central fire pit, eared flaps around the vent, and a tipi liner. Tipis were often elaborately decorated with designs and drawings. Brush shelters were sometimes made by travelers and brush arbors were sometimes erected in camp. Comanche men might have more than one wife (often sisters) and important men had separate tipis for each wife (as many as ten) and her children, clustered around his principal lodge. It seems probable that such groups shared in food preparation.

Food preparation and utensils were simple. Fire was made by fire-drill. Meat was roasted on sticks or boiled. (Before traders introduced kettles this was accomplished by dropping hot stones into an animal skin or buffalo pouch.) Bear oil was used like lard. Corn was obtained through trade and used to make gruel, which was eaten with wooden spoons from bark bowls or, following European contact, tin or sometimes ceramic dishes. A kind of bread was made from locust pods. Pemmican, pounded dried meat and berries, stored in rawhide containers (parfleches), was eaten without further preparation. Solid food was eaten off a board or piece of leather. There is some evidence that the Comanches made a few baskets.

Activities were determined by sex and age. Women's work included: firewood and plant gathering; food, hide and container preparation; manufacturer of clothes and tipis; erection of the lodge; packing of camp equipment. Men were primarily concerned with: the procurement of meat; the manufacture of weapons, hunting and horse equipment; warfare. Children had a happy existence. There was a richly developed, formalized vocabulary, heavy in redundant syllables, used for talking to babies, which was gradually replaced as children learned adult speech patterns. The threat of supernatural (owl=ghost) sanctions was used to discipline, rather than corporal punishment. Children's play was mostly imitations of adult activities; girls, for example, played house and had dolls. Older boys, however, attended the horse herds.

Games, often involving adult gambling, were of considerable importance to adults as well as children. Individual competitive sports included archery and arrow throwing, and foot and horse racing. The hand game ("bullets" or "buttons"), played by two parties, was a leading gambling game, as were several forms of dice. Betting occurred on other games as well, such as the shinny and double ball games played by women. Other social gatherings included story and myth telling, and dances. Some games and all dances involved music by drums, rattles, whistles, and singing. (Flutes and the single-string violin, an example preserved in the Field Museum, were also apparently used.) Until late pre-reservation times these gatherings were never marred by drunkenness; the Comanches were noted for their sobriety.

Very little is known about Comanche communal dances (during which there were aggregations of subsistence bands). Lowie, in 1912, found that the Comanches were "... in part very unwilling..." informants. He thought the Comanches had a festival of several weeks duration in which all the soldier societies performed their dances. This would be reminiscent of the Cheyenne Massaum ceremony in which individual medicine societies participated. Only in the 1930s and in 1945, when few pre-reservation Comanches were alive, were further data obtained. One informant thought the Buffalo Hunting Dance (apparently Lowie's "festival") had been the most important ceremony, but no details were known. (The buffalo "society" of Table 1 may refer to this dance rather than to a particular society.) The report of a Green Corn Dance is based on a fraudulent source (Nelson Lee) and the misinterpretation of another (the novel *Matouchon*, in which "Melville," based on the real missionary Methvin, saw a dance at an unidentified, but apparently Caddoan, not Commanche, village.) It is often stated that the Sun Dance, generally the most important High Plains ceremony, appeared among the Comanches in 1874, but some anthropologists, notably Shimkin, have suggested a much earlier appearance. Be that as it may, at least by the mid-nineteenth century, many Comanches attended the annual Kiowa Sun Dance.

Other dances and ceremonies appear to have belonged to particular medicine societies. According to Hoebel, the "medicine" or "power" was obtained through a vision and then shared with less than a dozen others. The members of such societies had similar talismen and ritual paraphernalia. It is not known if the medicine men supervising the three most important rituals found in subsistence bands were members of specific societies. The three rituals were the Owls Spirit Seance, called to obtain information on lost objects or absent people, the Beaver Ceremony, a cure for illness from sorcery, and the Eagle Dance.

Public pipe smoking was the most common ritual among the Comanches. Sometimes this was a component of other ceremonies, sometimes it occurred by itself to mark solemn events.

Most Comanche religious practices were concerned with personal "medicine," but some things, such as the sun, had much more power than others. Any man could obtain "medicine" by presentation, through the "sharing" mentioned by Hoebel, or through a vision, usually during adolescence. At the time of a successful vision quest, a guardian spirit outlined the often onerous ceremonial requirements for maintaining the power given, and presented a talisman (or several objects) which was placed in a "medicine bag," and a power song (the so called "death songs" sung before battle). Shields, lances, and war bonnets almost all had ritual obligations attached to them. "Power" was manifest in its ability to protect its owner and entail his success. If a man was killed or unsuccessful in life, it was a sign that his "power" was false or that he had not carried out his ceremonial obligations.

The concern with "medicine" was exemplified at many life cycle crises. At birth a midwife attended, but if delivery was difficult, a man of special "power" was called in. While the camp was moving a woman might halt and give birth, then rejoin the band, but in camp a special lodge might be set up for delivery. There the mother stood upright, with legs apart, grasping a stake which had been driven in the ground near the edge of the lodge. In early days the baby was washed and painted in red ochre, then wrapped in furs. If twins were born, one was sometimes killed, as was the case if the child was born deformed. (Occasionally abortions were induced by the mother beating her stomach with stones.) Naming might occur any time after birth, but always by the time the individual had emerged from babyhood, and was important as names had the power to affect life success. Hence a medicine man or warrior, men of proven "power, bestowed the name at a public ceremony. The next important life passage was adolescence, marked for girls by menstruation and the vision quest for boys. At first menstruation, and monthly thereafter, a woman had to live in a separate hut, as the blood nullified all "medicine." Some boys obtained visions unsought, but others sought out lonely spots and fasted (but did not engage in the self-torture of some Plains tribes).

Marriage marked adulthood for young men and women, although pre-pubescent girls seem to have occasionally been reared in the lodges of their husbands. Men generally did not marry until they were established warriors, at age twenty-five or more. Premarital sex was not uncommon. Girls, not boys, could make sexual advances and some early reports called the unmarried women "very dissolute " to the point of some having intercourse with dogs, which Berlandier said was common among Comanche men, although homosexuality was rare. This Comanche "dissoluteness," however, was contradicted by Lehmann, a Comanche captive in the 1870s. Marriages were arranged in that horses and other gifts were sent by a suitor, through an intermediary, to the father of the woman, who could decide to accept or reject the gifts (and the marriage) without consulting the woman. Sometimes, however, lovers eloped. A man could have as many wives as he could support, but most men had only one. Women could not engage in extramarital sex, although a man might permit his classificatory brothers, especially when he was absent on the warpath, as well as trading partners visiting camp, to sleep with his wife. A woman's adultery was punished by beatings or cutting off her nasal septum, or sometimes by death, although a woman might escape punishment if her paramour was stripped of his property by her husband, who might whip the paramour in lieu of taking his goods.

War was viewed as a man's pre-eminent occupation; much care was lavished on war equipment and there were many social occasions where a man recounted his coups (war honors), the greatest being touching a live enemy. Scalps were taken primarily for the victory celebration at camp, which could only be held if no Comanches were lost. Most war parties were rather small and were organized to avenge the death of a Comanche or to take horses, but in summer very large expeditions of several were organized. The actual attack on the enemy was often at night, when, according to Dodge, the Comanche was "the most dangerous of all Indians." Adult captives were usually killed or taken back to the village for torture, especially by the women, although captive women were sometimes taken for sexual service. Captive children were often adopted, but young children were usually tortured to death. Special war equipment included poison made from rattlesnake venom for application to arrows (later to bullets), buffalo hide shields and shield covers, and warclubs (which had generally ceased to be used about 1860). Most war techniques (smoke signals, for example) and equipment (such as quivers for bows and arrows—weapons later replaced by guns, lances, and knives) had uses other than in war.

War losses were largely responsible for the disproportionate ratio of woman to men, but, if not killed by enemies, a Comanche, before the spread of European diseases, could generally look forward to a long life. The Comanches were expert in treating arrow and gunshot wounds and in setting fractures with bandages, as well as having an extensive knowledge of medicinal plants. Sweat lodges—closed domed structures in which water was sprinkled on stones heated outside—were also used in medicinal treatment. But medicines and magic could not prevent aging, and when the aged could no longer take care of themselves, they were abandoned.

Like most Plains tribes, mourning involved scarification by relatives and often by friends, and extensive destruction of wealth and horses, but unlike most Plains tribes, burial was by internment. Before about 1850 a man's favorite wife (and sometimes captives) was killed to accompany him. After about 1850, some Comanche bodies were placed in trees or on scaffolds, but the majority were placed in a flexed position in gullies or caves and covered with rocks. A place where a death occurred was abandoned, and a dead person's name was never mentioned.

History

The specifics of early Comanche history were determined by their resource needs and by logistics, while later Comanche history was a response to the challenge of Americans, at first martial and then political and social.

Only brief glimpses are caught in the documents of the Comanches during the first years after they came out of the mountains, in association with the Utes, to plunder New Mexico, but before the middle of the eighteenth century the Comanches had shattered the western Plains balance of power. In 1706 Comanches were first mentioned as a threat to Taos Pueblo and as having attacked the Jicarilla Apaches. Ten years later they were again mentioned after an attack on Taos. Then in 1723 and 1724 Jicarilla delegations unsuccessfully pleaded for Spanish support (a presidio), and by 1733 Jicarilla remnants from the Plains were settled near Taos and among the Pecos. Other Plains Apaches had also suffered at the hands of the Comanches; by 1739 the Farones had been driven from the Canadian, and in the 1750s the Paloma and Cuartelejo Apaches finally established near Pecos.

Guns permitted the Comanches to take the central and southern High Plains from the Apaches, but changed intertribal relations in other ways as well. Most guns they obtained (along with corn) from the horticultural Caddoan villagers of the eastern Plains (who got them from Mississippi Valley French traders); horses, buffalo meat and robes were given in exchange. In the 1740s, although the Comanches were still trading with the village tribes, they began to have direct access to French traders. By 1748 the Comanches, who wished to restrict others' direct access to French traders, were at war with their former Ute friends. This marks the beginning of the classic Plains warfare pattern—the northern tribes raiding the horse rich tribes of the south. Soon the horticultural Pawnees and Osages, two tribes which continued to war with the Comanches until almost reservation days, were raiding southward.

Dover Pictorial Archive.

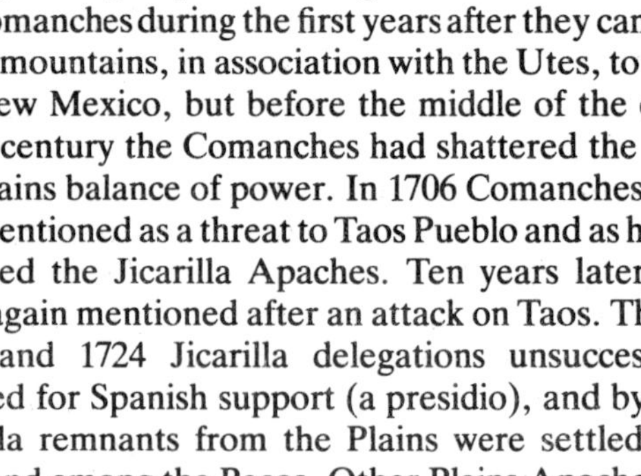

Comanche painted rawhide bag.

With a ready supply of guns the Comanches attacked New Mexico mercilessly and began penetrating deep into Texas as well. The New Mexican Spanish launched an unsuccessful expedition in 1742; Comanche plundering continued. Between 1744 and 1749 Comanche raids had caused the death of 150 at Pecos Pueblo alone. In 1748 the Spanish managed to halt a raid on Pecos and in 1751 they killed almost a hundred Comanches returning home from attacking Pecos and Galisteo Pueblos. Although this may have given New Mexico a short breathing space, the Comanches began appearing in the vicinity of the San Saba River mission and San Antonio. In 1758 they attacked the Lipan Apaches, their perennial enemies until the reservation period, at the San Saba mission, and next year chased a Spanish punitive expedition all the way from Red River back to south Texas. Within ten years the Lipans were driven from the San Saba country and the mission was eventually abandoned, as the Comanche threat grew in New Mexico as well.

The establishment of small Spanish garrisons at Pecos and Galisteo Pueblos and attempts to make peace did little to halt Comanche raiding; the Comanches penetrated even further into the pueblo country. In 1762 peace was established in New Mexico for a few years and reestablished for less than a year in 1771. The Comanche attacks were often only small raids but sometimes, as in 1772 when 500 Comanches attacked Pecos, were attempts to sack a pueblo. Galisteo, Taos, Nambe, Sandia, Laguna and Isleta Pueblos were raided through the next five years.

The Spanish introduced a peace policy in Texas in the early 1770s, making peace with all the raiding northern tribes except the Comanches. In 1777 an attempt was made to extend the peace to the Comanches, but serious steps were taken only in 1783, and it was 1786-7 before peace was attained. At the peace negotiations a head chief was recognized by most of the Comanches and his task was to deal with the Spanish. The Spanish goal was peace between the Comanches and Utes, both of whom they hoped to use in their war with the western Apaches and Navajos.

With the Comanches pacific, the Spanish undertook making them sedentary. It was reported in 1787 that a Comanche chief had asked Spanish help in establishing

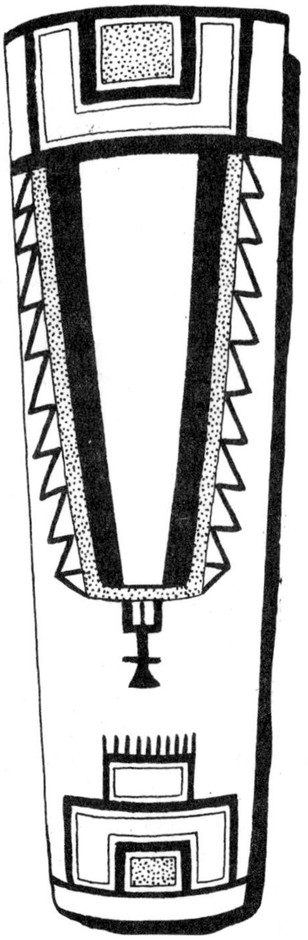

Dover Pictorial Archive.
Comanche medicine case.

Comanche war shield, 19th century.

a pueblo. Soon Spanish women built a number of houses on the Arkansas, but the pueblo was abandoned a few months later.

The 1787 peace was more enduring than Comanche occupation of the Arkansas pueblo, lasting until the unrest engendered by the 1810 Mexican revolution and penetration of the southwest Plains by Anglo-Mexican traders. The early nineteenth century raids on the Texas frontier were primarily to obtain horses for the American trade, a new source (or a replacement of the extinct French source) of manufactured goods in addition to the long established indirect trade through the eastern Plains horticultural villages. By the 1820s the Comanches had traded thousands of horses and mules to Anglo-Americans through three main channels: Nacodoches, Pecan Point, and the Kansas River.

The wave of eastern tribes which swept the Plains from the 1820s to about 1840 as a result of the federal relocation policy resulted in another realignment of Plains tribes. The Kiowas, who had come from the north, became allies and associates of the Comanches about 1790, but a portion of the Arapahos and especially their Cheyenne allies, who soon followed the Kiowas, fought the allied Comanches and Kiowas (with the Kiowa-Apaches). In the face of the emigrant threat, about 1840 or a little earlier, the Cheyennes and Comanches and their allies made peace, which strengthened the military position of all of them and assured the Cheyennes access to Comanche horses. And in the late 1830s and 1840s, the Comanches now free of a northern threat, tremendously expanded their raids on the northern Mexican states.

Even before the 1836 battle of the Alamo, the Republic of Texas sought to achieve peace with the Comanches, a task later hampered by the short tenures of Texas presidents and resulting fluctuations in national Indian policy. Throughout the period of the republic most Indian battles were fought by companies of Texa Rangers. Serious wars began in 1840, after Houston's 1838 peace, when more than thirty of the Comanches who came to negotiate at San Antonio were killed at the Council House. In retaliation about 500 warriors destroyed the town of Linnville and attacked Victoria. When Houston again became president (December, 1841) he sought to reestablish peace, but was unsuccessful, although a treaty was made in 1844.

During the 1840s the Comanches were again ravaged by diseases. In 1848 smallpox struck, followed by the 1849 cholera epidemic. The 1816 smallpox epidemic was also severe, but it was not known if the 1833 cholera epidemic made headway among them.

Soon after the United States annexed Texas, plans were made to make the Texas frontier secure. In 1848 the federal government began a chain of forts from Red River to the Rio Grande: Forts Worth, Graham, Gates, Croghan, Martin Scott, and Inge. Settlement had passed this line in less than two years and a second line of forts were built beginning in 1851: Forts Belknap, Phantom Hill, Chadbourne, McKavett, Terrett, and Clark.

With the annexation of Texas the Anglo-Americans of the east ceased to be a ready market for Comanche plunder and there was a great increase in the "Comanchero" trade (primarily thousands of stolen cattle) with the Mexican traders of New Mexico (even though New Mexico had also been annexed to the United States). The Comanchero trade persisted into the 1870s after reaching its height immediately after the Civil War (while the frontier was still ungarrisoned) with the establishment of the Loving-Goodnight cattle trail to New Mexico. As Comanches increasingly again frequented the approaches to Santa Fe, the federal government sought, by the 1853 Fort Atkinson treaty, to end the threat to the caravan trade. This treaty called for an annuity of $18,000 for ten years in exchange for promises of halting raids in the United States and Mexico.

The next year the Texas legislature, which controlled the public domain in Texas, provided minute reserves for the Comanches and other tribes, but few Comanches ever resided on them. These reserves were the Brazos Agency (4 leagues, later doubled) and the Clear Fork Comanche Reserve (4 leagues). Only a portion (about 400) of the Penatekas went to their reservation. In 1847 large numbers of non-reserve Comanches moved into the country between the Canadian and Arkansas, from which they launched unprecedented attacks on Texas, which were answered by state punitive expeditions. Meanwhile Texas citizens demanded removal of the reservations, which resulted in the relocation of the reserves to Indian Territory (Wichita Agency north of the 1868 Comanche Reservation) where Fort Cobb was built for their protection. The Penatekas stayed on their reservation even after the Comanche Reservation was established.

With the Civil War, federal troops were withdrawn from Texas, and although the Confederates made a treaty in 1861 and established an agent at Wichita Agency, the Comanches soon ignored the peace. Even the Penatekas took to raiding after Wichita Agency was destroyed by federal affiliated Delawares and Shawnees in 1862. Texas suffered greatly from the Comanches during the war and some counties on the northwest Texas frontier were depopulated to the point that county organization was abandoned.

In October, 1865, in attempting to reassert federal Indian control, the United States, in exchange for Comanche, Kiowa, and Kiowa-Apache assent to federation with the Cheyennes and Arapahos, offered the "federated" tribes most of the Llano Estacado (Staked Plains) and all the Indian Territory west of the 98th meridian as a reservation. The agreement floundered by the refusal of the Texas legislature to grant Texas land.

It was some time before effective control of the frontier was gained by the United States. By 1867 Texas was aflame from extremely heavy raids, while the northern and central Plains tribes were also at war. That year Hancock and Custer's central Plains campaign proved a fiasco for the army.

A new federal policy was introduced after the January, 1867, report on the "Conditions of the Indian Tribes," and in October, 1867, a peace commission met with the five "federated" tribes at Medicine Lodge Creek. This last treaty signed by the Comanches gave them a reservation in the southwest corner of the Indian Territory and annuity goods for thirty years, in exchange for their other land claims. The new direction in Indian policy became Grant's "Peace Policy" with the appointment of Quakers to positions of authority in the Indian Office.

The army did not rely only on the Quakers; by 1868 some of the old posts of the Texas defense line had been regarrisoned and new posts built, although active campaigning was necessary to enforce the reservation policy. A campaign with converging columns from Kansas, Colorado, and New Mexico, to drive in all absentee Indians ended with the Battle of the Washita (November, 1868) and the apparent acceptance of reservations by the south Plains tribes. In late December, 1868, the Comanches received their first annuity, and a few days later Fort Sill was begun to watch them, but within a year a large number of Comanches (including all the Quahadas) was absent. Mackenzie's fall, 1871, campaign against the recalcitrant Comanches was unsuccessful, but his destruction of their village in the summer of 1872 brought the Quahadas to the reservation.

The final extermination of the great southern buffalo herd was a time of social turmoil for the Comanches. From 1872 through 1874 almost four million buffalo were killed. Isatai, a prophet who claimed his medicine would drive out the Americans and restore the herds, led the Comanches in a Sun Dance, preparatory to the last great Comanche "uprising," but he was discredited when the first major attack (Adobe Walls, June, 1874) failed. Nevertheless, numerous raiders swarmed into Texas while the army campaigned on the Staked Plain. Quahada resistence became futile when Mackenzie, at the September battle of Palo Duro Canyon captured their horse herd and killed over a thousand ponies, although the Quahadas, the last "wild" Comanches, did not surrender until June, 1875. To prevent a future outbreak, the Comanche horses (over 6,000) were sold or killed on their return to the reservation and there were nine Comanches among the south Plains Indian "ringleaders" sent to prison in Florida. In addition, the agents prohibited dancing and set to work to break the authority of the chiefs. Though there were no more general outbreaks, there were occasional raids into the 1880s.

On the reservation, peyote use, which had been known among the Comanches since the 1860s or earlier, quickly became a focus of "nativism" and the Comanches (with the Kiowas) were the principal agents of peyote diffusion, but the Comanches, except for the Penatekas, had little to do with the 1890 Ghost Dance fervour. Through the 1880s and 1890s the Comanches leased large portions of their reserve for grazing (in 1893 almost a million and a third acres for over $200,000). A strange blend of idealism and land hunger brought about the General Allotment Act, which by 1901 led to the division of communal lands and the allocation of one hundred-sixty acres to each Comanche. The remainder (the largest part) of the reservation was then sold to non-Indians.

Population

Early nineteenth century population estimates run from Catlin's grossly inflated 40,000 to Burnet's commonly quoted 10 to 12,000. There are no compelling reasons, however, to believe that the Comanches ever numbered more than 6 to 8,000. By the 1860s they had been reduced to less than 2,000.

MELBURN D. THURMAN

COMCOMLY (Chinook; fl. late 18th and early 19th centuries) was a wealthy and powerful chief of the Chinook, a tribe that inhabited the northwestern U.S. at the mouth of the Columbia River. Although the existence of the Chinook had been known to white traders at least 12 years earlier, the first description of the tribe came from Meriwether Lewis and William Clark following their expedition (1804-06). Comcomly greeted the American explorers warmly when they entered Chinook territory late in 1805. He was friendly to the pioneers who followed, and his daughter married Duncan M'Dougal, the Canadian leader of the Astor expedition, which took possession of the territory for the U.S. in 1811.

When a British man-of-war appeared in 1813 to capture the Astoria outpost, Comcomly offered 800 warriors to fight the intruders. He quickly altered his allegiance when the Americans made a peaceful transfer of property and when the British plied him with gifts.

According to the Jesuit missionary Pierre-Jean de Smet, Comcomly took with him 300 slaves when he visited Vancouver. In addition, before he would walk from the gate of the fort to the governor's house (a distance of several hundred feet) he would have his path completely carpeted with beaver and otter skins.

COMECHINGON lived alongside their neighbors, the Sanavirón and others, in the Sierras de Córdoba in northwestern Argentina just south of the Gran Chaco. The Sierras de Córdoba are the most southeastern extension of the Pampean Sierras and are composed of three cordillera running north to south from latitude 29°S to 33°S near longitude 64°W. The Comechingon inhabited the fertile valleys and quebradas found between the cordillera where there were numerous streams which provided water for horticulture. Indeed, the Comechingon represented the southeastern limit of the Andean agriculture pattern into the land of the southern hunting peoples. Spanish explorers gave the name, "Provincia de los Comechingones," to this territory which today is included in the provinces of Córdoba and San Luis in modern Argentina. The Comechingon spoke a dialect of the Huarpe-Comechingon linguistic family, a classification covering many of the peoples in the northern part of Argentina.

Long extinct, the Comechingon in pre-Conquest times were fairly numerous, a reasonable estimate being some 30,000 with a density of 15 per $km.^2$. As so often happened in the days of exploration, the Indians were identified by their outstanding physical characteristics rather than by the names which they called themselves, and thus the Comechingon became known as "the bearded ones."

Information about the first Spanish contacts with the Comechingon is sketchy and what exists is found in the old chronicles which were written after the first expedition in 1546 and were based on testimony of the survivors. More details about Comechingon life is found in government reports issued after the actual conquest and occupation of the territory late in the sixteenth century, but these, too, leave much unsaid. Archaeological work in the area has revealed surprisingly little about this once sizeable population which was able to withstand the Inca onslaught but eventually succumbed to Spanish power and was assimilated into colonial society leaving little evidence of a former way of life.

The Comechingon were sedentary agriculturalists, growing the typical Andean crops of maize, beans, and quinoa on irrigated terraces. They tended large llama herds and raised barnyard fowl. Hunting guanaco, deer and rabbits was an important but secondary subsistence activity and fishing played no role in their economic life. Horses were not known to the Comechingon.

Many of these Indians lived in "stone houses," natural shelters of rock outcroppings which were modified by masonry work, a technique diffused from the Andes. Many such shelters are still used, at least on a temporary basis. There are also references in the chronicles to the fact that some Comechingon lived in partly subterranean dwellings which they dug themselves and which were said to be so constructed to protect themselves from the cold. A village was composed of several houses and was administered by a chief, possibly an inherited position. Each chief was independent of all others, a fact which caused the Spaniards no end of difficulty as they sought to place these Indians under the *encomienda* system. However, there was cooperation among villages in forming raiding parties. There is no concrete evidence on the nature of Comechingon social organization, but some scholars have assumed that they were partilineally organized because they were hunters and warriors.

On the subject of warfare the Spanish chroniclers were more verbose and described in detail the fierce and effective attacks by the Comechingon and the unusual timing of their raids. Warriors, sometimes numbering in the hundreds with their faces painted black and red, attacked by night, "carrying fire." In close formation, the archers in one position, the spearthrowers in another, they went forth against either the Spaniards or neighboring peoples. It was written that they killed an armored horse with only five arrows.

There is no information about any life cycle observances by the Comechingon. Graves have been located which contain bodies placed on their sides in flexed position. There were no signs of grave offerings. Some variation in the positioning of the body has been reported. There were no true cemeteries as never more than five bodies in one group have been discovered and graves were unmarked. All this indicates little emphasis on funeral ceremonies.

Archaeological remains of pottery fragments reveal coiled pottery with two types of decoration: incised or punctuated and net or textile impressed. Weaving was known and the early Spanish documents speak of both men and women wearing woolen tunics worked with beads to which long capes were added in winter. Some skins were worn also. But the most noteworthy legacy from the Comechingon are the remarkable rock paintings which exist on the walls and roofs of shelters as well as on appropriate rocks. These are varied and complex pictures, utilizing many colors but with red, white, and black predominent. They are of great artistic value and provide the only lasting ethnographic record of the Comechingon, depicting scenes of daily life, local animals, and battles between themselves and the Spaniards with realistic precision.

Again, the historical record reveals nothing about religious life of the Comechingon apart from a vague statement that they worshipped the Sun and the Moon, the former because it helped to grow their food and the latter because it aided them in their nighttime raids. This and a few grumbling and highly unreliable references by priests to devil worship, sorcery, and idols leaves us with no real information about Comechingon concepts of religion and morality.

L. C. AND S. R. FARON

COMMISSIONER OF INDIAN AFFAIRS. During the Revolutionary War period, and until the passage of the Ordinance of 1786, Indian relations of the United States were handled by a Committee of Indian Affairs; in 1789, the regulation of such matters was then assigned to the War Department as a logical responsibility of that branch of government. An Act of March 1, 1793 provided that the President appoint Indian agents and superintendents to live and work among the several tribes in order to assure a continuation of friendly relations; this was amended April 16, 1818 to extend their authority and to act as representatives of the nation. In 1806, recognizing the vital role of commerce with the tribes, the post of Superintendent of Indian Trade was created, but this was primarily a commercial rather than political post. Aside from this individual, there was no government official solely responsible for Indian affairs; and while this may be excused in view of the problems of settling a new country and the intervention of the War of 1812, it nevertheless affected the attitude towards Indian relations, creating a secondary level of importance which continues to the present day. This lack of a key administrator was not acknowledged until March 11, 1824, when Secretary of War John C. Calhoun came to grips with the problem of setting up a Bureau of Indian Affairs on his own authority, appointing Thomas L. McKenney, who had been serving as Superintendent of Indian Trade since 1816. In 1822, the latter office was abolished, consolidating those responsibilities within the new bureau; but McKenney's strong defense of Indian needs conflicted with demands for land and the self-righteous religious attitude of many whites; and jealousy and greed for the rich trade opportunities available in the Indian field—the result was political intrigue on a scale which caused his dismissal in 1830. The expansion of the frontier, the increased demands upon the War Department, the complexity of the Indian problem itself—and continued friction with the several states who insisted upon keeping autonomy over the various tribes within their borders—combined to lead to the establishment by Congress on July, 1832 of the position of Commissioner of Indian Affairs, appointed by the President with the consent of the Senate, and subordinate to the Secretary of War. The first appointee was Elbert Herring who, with Samuel S. Harrison, had carried out the duties of the Bureau following the departure of McKenney. The need for further change had become apparent by this time, and on June 30, 1834, a Department of Indian Affairs (so called at the time) was created, in an effort to reorganize the Bureau, but still operating within the War Department. This act authorized certain agencies and superintendencies, and the enabling statement under which it was organized remains with modifications the legal base of the Bureau of Indian Affairs to the present day. The duties of the commissioner were succinctly spelled out:

> "... to manage all Indian affairs and all matters arising out of Indian relations."

This broad power offered a remarkable opportunity to do good or evil, depending entirely upon the way in which that power was handled. Historically, by-and-large the appointees have been well-intentioned men, anxious to promote fairly the needs of the country in its relationship with the original inhabitants. Some have been capable individuals, working with imagination and integrity, who did their work well; others were weak, unable to defend their charges or their bureau against political or venal attack, and proved incapable of controlling the field agents who, at far distance, often became lords of their fields, regarding themselves as answerable only to a very far-away Washington, if at all. A few have been corrupt; but most of the charges of less-than-honorable practice have been more accurately aimed at lower-level personnel. After the conclusion of the War with Mexico, and the expansion of national boundaries to the Pacific and the Mexican border, the need to efficiently conduct the management of the many problems which would inevitably arise out of relations with the tribes living within this vast territory, caused another change. In 1848 Robert J. Walker, then Secretary of Treasury, pointed out that the duties of the Commissioner of Indian Affairs were too important to be ignored, and that the nation's expansion, even then underway, would cause collisions which should receive a peaceful solution rather than military conflict. Accordingly, he urged that the Bureau of Indian Affairs should no longer be continued within the War Department but should be placed in conjunction with the Land Office, since this involved a similar responsibility. Accordingly, on March 3, 1849, Congress created a Department of the Interior to manage the territorial problems of the nation, and transferred the Bureau of Indian Affairs to that body, where it remains today. Although the President had been impeded from appointing new agencies by the Act of 1834, this was remedied in 1851, when the number of agencies was enlarged to meet the needs of the new region. The approaching Civil War greatly moderated any progress with Indian affairs and frustrated much of the work of the commissioner: the bureau and its administration tended to exacerbate the touchy states' rights issue, which had always been a difficult problem for them; and since Indian loyalty in the coming contest was in sharp question in some of the states, the matter was, in effect, taken out of his hands by overriding national concerns. Little could be accomplished until the war ended, and it was not until the inauguration on June 3, 1869 of the so called "Peace Policy" under President Grant that any real resumption of various Indian problems was taken. This also introduced a serious challenge to the authority of the commissioner. Indian conflicts in the West had brought differing theories of how to handle them, even within the government; corruption was rampant—venal agents were defrauding the nation and the Indian—white settlers were being killed in increasing number in the insensate rush for land. In an effort to contain some of the problems, President Grant was importuned to place responsibility in the hands of persons who presumably could assist in achieving a politically nonpartisan, socially neutral, and beneficial solution of the increasing Indian problem. Thus the Board of Indian Commissioners came into existence, which is often confused with the actual Commissioner of Indian Affairs. The board was a group of "not over ten philanthropists with an interest in Indian affairs," who would serve without pay, acting jointly with the Secretary of the Interior to control the expenditure of Indian appropriations, to give special attention to the matter of Indian assimilation, and to provide better cooperation between the bureau and the public. At the same time the authority to nominate Indian agents and superintendents was handed over to the various religious organizations in the country, in the belief that they could clean up the national scandal. These two actions interlaced white religious interests with political concerns and combined with an unspoken rivalry for the domination of missionary activity. This policy, clearly doomed to failure, proved completely unworkable: inter-faith squabbling, unrealistic expectations, political rivalry, and selfish goals, all combined to bring out the worst in the program. And when many of the church appointments proved to be of extremely poor quality—some were even less able than the previously maligned agents—the policy was abandoned with the departure of the President in 1869. The board, however, continued until it was also abolished by President Franklin Roosevelt in 1933. For the first five years it had been fairly successful, in spite of continued conflict with the secretary and commissioner; but in 1874, it was deprived of funds with which to operate, and gradually declined to a point of impotence, and enjoyed only a limited social and political recognition after the turn of the century. Although the commissioner was able to ride out this challenge to his authority, the political attempt to interfere continued, as it does to the present day. The attitude of the political administrations toward Indian problems, incessant demands that the individual be "from the right party and the right state, with the right attitude," plus the general apathy of the public towards Indian matters, makes the commissioner's position an impossible one. He is placed in the position of basically serving two conflicting masters in almost everything he undertakes. As a result, many of the appointees have been political hacks less interested in the bureau and its charges than political ambitions, or else directed by social attitudes not always of lasting benefit to the Indian people. There have been many times when the office has gone vacant, with functions carried out by lower-level personnel. The inevitable result has been a bureau with relatively low morale, unable to command real attention to its needs and those of the people it is mandated to represent. Although there is an opportunity for tremendous good to be done, bureaucracy, non-Indian interests competing with the needs of the Indian, aggravated by the shortness of political appointments, all combine to make it almost impossible for any devoted individual to accomplish marked improvements. At best it is a thankless job, beset by Indians and whites alike—at worst, it has served to arouse distrust in Indians, and frustration or contempt among whites. There have been 42 Indian commissioners to date, one of whom has served twice; the average term of office has been 3.6 years. It will be noted that only eight men have come from states with sizeable Indian populations, and that several of the appointees have never enjoyed any experience whatsoever in Indian matters. Yet there are also several outstanding administrators who have made significant contributions to the alleviation of the difficulties of the Indian population; and a half-dozen are among the giants of Indian sociopolitical relations. The first commissioner of American Indian descent was Ely S. Parker, *Seneca*; the next, almost a century later, was Robert L. Bennett, *Oneida*. He was followed by Louis R. Bruce, *Mohawk-Sioux*; Morris Thompson, *Tanana*; and Ben Reifel, *Sioux*. The following list includes all Commissioners of Indian Affairs to date, their home state, and the date of their inauguration as can best be obtained from the record.*

Morris Thompson resigned as commissioner on November 3, 1976, and Mr. Reifel was appointed *in recess*. On July 12, 1977, Forrest J. Gerard, part Blackfoot, was appointed to a newly-created position of Assistant Secretary for Indian Affairs. At the time of this writing (fall 1978), there is no Commissioner of Indian Affairs. Suggestions have been made that the office be abolished, but no decision has been made one way or another.

FREDERICK DOCKSTADER

*Some discrepancies in dates are due to variant recordings of the time when the individual was appointed, actually took office, or was confirmed by the Senate. The record is not very clear on this point.

U.S. COMMISSIONERS OF INDIAN AFFAIRS

Elbert Herring	New York	July 10, 1832
Carey A. Harris	Tennessee	July 4, 1836
T. Hartley Crawford	Pennsylvania	October 27, 1838
William Medill	Ohio	October 28, 1845
Orlando Brown	Kentucky	May 31, 1849
Luke Lea	Mississippi	July 1, 1850
George W. Manypenny	Ohio	March 24, 1853
James W. Denver	California	April 27, 1857
Charles E. Mix	Washington, D.C.	June 14, 1858
James W. Denver	California	November 8, 1858
Alfred B. Greenwood	Arkansas	May 4, 1859
William P. Dole	Illinois	March 13, 1861
Dennis W. Cooley	Iowa	July 10, 1865
Lewis V. Bogy	Missouri	November 1, 1866
Nathaniel G. Taylor	Tennessee	March 29, 1867
Ely S. Parker	Washington, D.C.	April 21, 1869
Francis A. Walker	Massachusetts	November 21, 1871
Edward P. Smith	New York	March 20, 1873
John Q. Smith	Ohio	December 11, 1875
Ezra A. Hayt	New York	September 17, 1877
Rowland E. Trowbridge	Michigan	March 15, 1880
Hiram Price	Iowa	May 4, 1881
John D. C. Atkins	Tennessee	March 21, 1885
John H. Oberly	Illinois	October 10, 1888
Thomas J. Morgan	Rhode Island	June 10, 1889
Daniel M. Browning	Illinois	April 17, 1893
William A. Jones	Wisconsin	May 3, 1897
Francis E. Leupp	Washington, D.C.	December 7, 1904
Robert G. Valentine	Massachusetts	June 15, 1909
Cato Sells	Iowa	June 2, 1913
Charles H. Burke	South Dakota	April 1, 1921
Charles J. Rhoads	Pennsylvania	July 1, 1929
John Collier	Georgia	April 20, 1933
William A. Brophy	New Mexico	March 15, 1945
John B. Nicholas	New Mexico	April 14, 1949
Dillon S. Myer	Ohio	May 8, 1950
Glenn L. Emmons	New Mexico	August 10, 1953
Philleo Nash	Wisconsin	September 26, 1961
Robert L. Bennett	Wisconsin	April 13, 1966
Louis R. Bruce, Jr.	New York	August 11, 1969
Morris Thompson	Alaska	February 7, 1973
Ben Reifel	South Dakota	December 7, 1976

COMMITTEE OF ONE HUNDRED was a group of eminent Americans appointed in 1923 by U.S. Secretary of the Interior, Herbert W. Work, to advise on and review U.S. Indian policy. Among the Indian members was Henry R. Cloud, a famed educator who tried to improve the government's treatment of Native Americans, Charles Eastman, Arthur C. Parker, and Thomas C. Sloan. The Committee's main contribution was to pass a series of resolutions advocating changes in the approach to providing Indian health care and education. Despite the presence of other distinguished members—Bernard M. Baruch, William Jennings Bryan, Gen. John J. Pershing, Frederick W. Dodge, and Alfred L. Kroeber—the lot of the American Indian did not change much.

COMMUNICATION. Any attempt to treat the topic of American Indian communication must inevitably focus on issues of American Indian language structure and language use. Traditionally the vast topic of American Indian languages has been divided in accord with geographical criteria and scholarly conventions by distinguishing North American, Mesoamerican, and South American Indian languages. North American Indian languages are native languages spoken, or formerly spoken, in what is today the United States, Canada, and northeastern Mexico contiguous with the American border. Mesoamerican Indian languages are spoken, or were formerly spoken, in central, southern, and northwestern Mexico, Guatemala, British Honduras, El Salvador, and portions of Honduras and Nicaragua. South American Indian languages are located, or were once located, in the remainder of Central and South America and the Antilles.

American Indian languages are nearly as diverse as they are numerous. The original number of American Indian languages in North America is approximately three hundred of which almost two hundred still exist today. Approximately seventy American Indian languages are spoken today in Mesoamerica. In South America, which has enjoyed far less scholarly attention from linguists than either North or Meso-America, some six hundred languages have been attested by at least rudimentary documentation. Of these languages, approximately one hundred are extinct. These figures as well as possible lists of three times these numbers are surely inflated by counting the dialects of a single language as separate languages. A more precise estimation must await the refinement which only additional linguistic research can provide.

Though it is conventional to observe this distinction between North American, Mesoamerican, and South American Indian languages, it should be noted that these boundaries only imperfectly reflect the linguistic situation. Some language families have representative languages in more than one of these geographical areas.

Genetic classification

As previously mentioned, American Indian languages are not only numerous; they are also diverse. No structural generalization of any significance can be posited concerning these languages without noting many exceptions. Against this background of diversity, linguistic similarities stand out in clear relief. A major source of such similarities is common ancestry—two or more languages share a common parent language. Languages which are related in this manner typically show systematic resemblances in both vocabulary and grammar. In North America alone there are almost sixty of these language families. Approximately one third of these are located in California. California thus displays more linguistic diversity than in all of Europe. Mesoamerica adds another twenty some language families to this list. For South America some scholars have produced lists of over one hundred separate language families though these classifications are chiefly based on similarities in vocabulary not grammar.

The systematic genetic classification of American Indian languages received its first comprehensive treatment from John Wesley Powell in 1891. Based on vocabulary resemblances, Powell's classification grouped languages into minimal genetic units. Partially because Powell's conservative classification acknowledged only rather close genetic relationships (e.g. comparable to the relations between the Romance languages) it has endured almost without change. Far more ambitious was Edward Sapir's classification of 1929. There Sapir classified the languages of North America into six *phyla*, or maximal genetic groups, on the basis of general grammatical criteria. This classification, though amended slightly by such scholars as Mary Haas and Stanley Newman on the basis of their respective investigations of aboriginal southeastern languages and the southwestern language of Zuni, survives today and forms the basis for the mapping and classification of North and Mesoamerican Indian languages presented here.

As this table shows, several North American language phyla are also represented in Mesoamerica: Aztec-Tanoan, Penutian, and Hokan. Similarly, though on a lesser scale, the Mayan Family of Mesoamerica appears to have a South American member in the form of Uru-Chipaya, a language spoken in Bolivia. Clearly the conventional geographical distinction between North, Meso, and South America have proven to be no barrier to the migrations of speakers which account for why related languages are not always spoken in geographic proximity. Linguists term languages which have been so carried into alien cultural and linguistic contexts as *outliers*. Unlike outliers, which are separated from known families, *isolates* represent languages for which no genetic relations can be established.

continued on page 24

Table of American Indian Languages

PHYLUM, Family Language	North, Meso- or South America	Location
I AMERICAN ARCTIC-PALEOSIBERIAN		
A Eskimo-Aleut Family	North America	Coastal Alaska, American Arctic
1 Central Greenlandic Eskimo		
2 Alaskan Eskimo (Kuskokwim Eskimo)		
3 Eastern Aleut (Unalaskan)		
4 Western Aleut (Atkan, Attuan)		
B other families/languages in Siberia		
II NA-DENE		
A Athapascan		
1 Dogrib, Bearlake, Hare	North America	Northwest Territories
2 Chipewyan, Slave, Yellowknife	North America	Northwest Territories
3 Kutchin	North America	Yukon, Alaska
4 Tanana, Koyukon, Han, Tutchone	North America	Alaska
5 Sarsi, Beaver	North America	Alberta
6 Carrier, Chilcotin	North America	British Colombia
7 Tahltan, Kaska	North America	Northwest Territories
8 Tanaina, Ingalik, Nabesna, Ahtena	North America	Alaska
9 Eyak	North America	S. Central Alaska
10 Chasta Costa, Galice, Tututni	North America	Southwest Oregon
11 Hupa	North America	Northwest California
12 Kato, Wailaki	North America	N. Central California
13 Mattole*	North America	N. Central California
14 Tolowa	North America	Northwest California
15 Navajo	North America	Arizona, New Mexico
16 Western Apache	North America	W. Arizona
17 Chiracahua, Mescalero Apache	North America	S. New Mexico
18 Jicarilla Apache	North America	N. New Mexico
19 Lipan Apache	North America	Texas
20 Kiowa-Apache	North America	Southeast Alaska
B Tlingit		
C Haida	North America	British Columbia
III MACRO-ALGONQUIAN		
A Algonquian		
1 Cree, Naskapi, Montagnais	North America	Eastern Canada
2 Menominee	North America	Great Lakes
3 Fox-Sauk, Kickapoo	North America	S. Great Lakes
4 Shawnee	North America	Oklahoma
5 Potawatomi	North America	Michigan
6 Ojibwa, Ottawa, Algonquian, Salteaux	North America	S. Ontario
7 Delaware	North America	C. Atlantic Coast
8 Penobscot, Abnaki	North America	New England
9 Malecite, Passamaquoddy	North America	New England and Canadian Maritime Prov.
10 Micmac	North America	Montana, Alberta
11 Blackfoot	North America	E. Colorado
12 Arapaho, Atsina, Nawathinehena	North America	E. Wyoming
13 Cheyenne	North America	New York, New England
14 Mohegan-Peqout-Montauk*	North America	Northwest California
B Yurok	North America	Northwest California
C Wiyot		
D Muskogean		
1 Choctaw, Chickasaw	North America	N. Mississippi
2 Alabama, Koasati	North America	Alabama
3 Mikasuki, Hitchiti	North America	Northwest Florida
4 Muskogee Creek, Seminole	North America	Georgia, Florida
E Natchez*	North America	N. Louisiana
F Atakapa*	North America	SW Louisiana, SE Texas
G Chitimacha*	North America	S. Louisiana
H Tunica*	North America	N. Louisiana
I Tonkawa	North America	E. Texas

* = Extinct Language.

PHYLUM, Family Language	North, Meso- or South America	Location
IV MACRO-SIOUAN		
A Siouan		
1 Crow	North America	E. Montana
2 Hidatsa	North America	N. Dakota
3 Winnebago	North America	Wisconsin
4 Omaha, Osage, Ponca, Kansa, Quapaw	North America	Central Plains
5 Dakota	North America	N. Plains
6 Tutelo, Ofo, Biloxi*	North America	Gulf Coast
B Catawba*	North America	Carolinas
C Iroquoian	North America	
1 Seneca, Cayuga, Onandaga	North America	New York
2 Mohawk	North America	New York
3 Oneida	North America	New York
4 Wyandot* (Huron)	North America	SE Ontario
5 Tuscarora	North America	N. Carolina
6 Cherokee	North America	S. Appalacians, Oklahoma
D Caddoan		
1 Caddo	North America	Arkansas
2 Wichita	North America	Texas, Oklahoma
3 Pawnee	North America	Kansas
4 Arikara	North America	Dakotas
E Yuchi	North America	S. Appalacians
V HOKAN		
A Yuman		
1 Hualapai, Havasupai, Yavapai	North America	NW Arizona
2 Mojave, Kwitsaan (Yuma)	North America	Lower Colo. R.
3 Cocopa	North America	Colo. R. Delta
4 Dieguenо, Kiliwa	North America	S. California, Baja
B Seri	North/Meso-America	Sonora Coast
C Pomo	North America	NE California
D Palaihnihan		
1 Achomawi	North America	NE California
2 Atsugewi	North America	NE California
E Shastan	North America	NE California
F Yanan	North America	N. Central California
G Chimariko*	North America	NW California
H Washo	North America	E. Central California Nevada
I Salinan	North America	W. Central California
J Karok	North America	NW California
K Chumashan	North America	S. California
L Comercrudan*	North/Meso-America	S. Texas, NW Mexico
M Coahuiltecan*	North/Meso-America	S. Texas, NW Mexico
N Esselen*	North America	W. Central California
O Jicaque	Meso-America	NW Honduras
P Tlapanecan		
1 Tlapanec	Meso-America	Guerrero
2 Subtiaba-Maribio	Meso-America	Nicaragua, El Salvador
Q Tequistlatecan		
1 Huamelultec	Meso-America	SE Oaxaca
2 Tequistlatec	Meso-America	SE Oaxaca
VI PENUTIAN		
A Yokutsan	North America	S. Central California
B Maiduan	North America	N. Central California
C Wintun		
1 Patwin	North America	N. Central California
2 Wintu, Nomlaki	North America	N. Central California
D Miwok-Costanoan		
1 Sierra Miwok	North America	S. Central California
2 Coast Miwok, Lake Miwok	North America	Central California
3 Costanoan*	North America	W. Central California

PHYLUM, Family Language	North, Meso- or South America	Location
E Klamath-Modoc	North America	S. Central Oregon
F Sahaptian		
1 Sahaptin	North America	N. Central Oregon
2 Nez Perce	North America	W. Central Idaho
G Cayuse*	North America	NE Oregon
H Molale*	North America	N. Central Oregon
I Coos	North America	Southwest Oregon
J Yakonan		
1 Alsea*	North America	W. Central Oregon
2 Siuslaw,* Lower Umpqua*	North America	W. Central Oregon
K Takelma*	North America	Southwest Oregon
L Kalapuya	North America	W. Central Oregon
M Chinookan	North America	NW Oregon, SW Washington
N Tsimshian	North America	W. Central British Columbia
O Zuni	North America	W. Central New Mexico
P Mixe-Zoque		
1 Mixe	Meso-America	E. Oaxaca
2 Zoque	Meso-America	Tabasco, Chiapas, Oaxaca
3 Sierra Popoluca	Meso-America	Veracruz
4 Texistepec	Meso-America	Veracruz
5 Sayula	Meso-America	Veracruz
6 Oluta	Meso-America	Veracruz
7 Tapachultec*	Meso-America	Southeast Chiapas Coast
Q Mayan		
1 Huastec, Chicomuceltec*	Meso-America	N. Veracruz
2 Yucatec, Lacandon, Itza, Moplan	Meso-America	Yucatan, Chiapas, N. Guatemala
3 Chontal	Meso-America	Tabasco
4 Chol	Meso-America	Tabasco, Chiapas
5 Chorti	Meso-America	Honduras, E. Guatemala
6 Tzotzil	Meso-America	Chiapas
7 Tzeltal	Meso-America	Chiapas
8 Tojolabal	Meso-America	Chiapas
9 Chuj	Meso-America	Northwest Guatemala
10 Kanjobal, Acatec, Jacaltec	Meso-America	Northwest Guatemala
11 Motozintlec, Tuzantec	Meso-America	SE Chiapas
12 Teco	Meso-America	SE Chiapas, W. Guatemala
13 Mam	Meso-America	SE Chiapas, W. Guatemala
14 Aguacatec	Meso-America	NW Guatemala
15 Ixil	Meso-America	NW Guatemala
16 Uspantec	Meso-America	NW Guatemala
17 Quiche, Cakchiquel, Tzutujil, Sacapultec, Sipacapa	Meso-America	Central Guatemala
18 Pocamam, Pocomchi, Kekchi	Meso-America	East-Central Guatemala
R Uru-Chipaya	North America	Bolivia
S Totonacan		
1 Totonac	Meso-America	Veracruz, Puebla
2 Tepehua	Meso-America	Veracruz, Hidalgo
VII AZTEC-TANOAN		
A Kiowa-Tanoan		
1 Kiowa	North America	Oklahoma
2 Tiwa	North America	N. Central New Mexico
3 Tewa	North America	N. Central New Mexico
4 Towa (Jemez)	North America	N. Central New Mexico
B Uto-Aztecan		
1 Mono	North America	E. Central California
2 N. Paiute, Bannock, Snake	North America	Northeast Calif., S. Idaho
3 Panamint, Gosiute, Shoshone	North America	Nevada, Utah,, Wyoming
4 Comanche	North America	N. Texas
5 Kawaiisu, Ute, Chemehuevi, S. Paiute	North America	Calif., Utah, Nevada
6 Hopi	North America	N. Arizona
7 Tubatulabal	North America	S. Central Calif.
8 Luiseno	North America	S. California
9 Cahuilla	North America	S. California
10 Cupeno	North America	S. California
11 Serrano	North America	S. California
12 Pima-Papago	North America	S. Arizona
13 Yaqui-Mayo (Cahita)	North America	S. Arizona, Sonora
14 Tarahumara (Raramuri)	Meso-America	Chihuahua
15 Cora	Meso-America	Sonora

PHYLUM, Family Language	North, Meso- or South America	Location
16 Huichol	Meso-America	Sonora
17 Tepehuan	Meso-America	Sonora, Jalisco
18 Nahuatl (Central, Northern Aztec)	Meso-America	Mexico, Puebla, Hidalgo
19 Nahual (Western Aztec)	Meso-America	Michoacan
20 Nahuat (Eastern Aztec)	Meso-America	Veracruz
21 Pipil	Meso-America	
22 Pochutec*	Meso-America	Oaxaca Coast
VIII UNCLASSIFIED		
A Keresan	North America	New Mexico
B Yukian		
1 Yuki	North America	N. Central California
2 Wappo	North America	N. Central California
C Beothuk*	North America	Newfoundland
D Kutenai	North America	Montana, Idaho, British Columbia
E Karankawa*	North America	SE Texas
F Chimakuan		
1 Quileute	North America	NW Washington
2 Chemakum	North America	NW Washington
G Salish		
1 Lillooet	North America	Central British Columbia
2 Shuswap	North America	E. British Columbia
3 Thompson	North America	Central British Columbia
4 Okanagon, Sanpoil, Colville	North America	S. British Columbia
5 Pend d'Oreille, Flathead Spokan, Kalispel	North America	N. Idaho
6 Coeur d'Alene	North America	N. Idaho
7 Middle Columbia, Wenatchee	North America	E. Washington
8 Tillamook	North America	NW Oregon
9 Twana	North America	NW Washington
10 Chehalis, Cowlitz, Quinault	North America	W. Washington
11 Southern Puget Sound Salish	North America	W. Washington
12 Straits Salish	North America	SW British Columbia
13 Halkomelem	North America	SW British Columbia
14 Squamish	North America	SW British Columbia
15 Comox, Sishistl	North America	Vancouver Island
16 Bella Coola	North America	West-Central British Columbia
H Wakashan		
1 Nootka	North America	Vancouver Island
2 Nitinat	North America	Vancouver Island
3 Makah	North America	NW Washington
4 Kwakiutl	North America	WC British Columbia
5 Bella Bella, Heiltsuk	North America	WC British Columbia
I Timucua*	North America	Florida
J Tarascan	Meso-America	SW Michoacan (Mex.)
K Cuitlatec*	Meso-America	Guerrero (Mex.)
L Jicaque	Meso-America	NW Honduras
M Tucanoan		
1 W. Tucanoan	South America	Peru, Colombia, Brazil
2 E. Tucanoan	South America	Colombia, Brazil
N Quechumaran		
1 Aymaran	South America	Bolivia, Peru
2 Quechuan	South America	Colombia, Peru, Argentina, Ecuador
IX OTO-MANGUEAN		
A Manguean		
1 Mangue*	Meso-America	Nicaragua, Honduras
2 Chiapanec*	Meso-America	Chiapas (Mex.)
B Oto-Pamean		
1 Otomi	Meso-America	Hidalgo, State of Mexico
2 Mazahua	Meso-America	Michoacan, State of Mexico
3 Matlazinca, Ocuiltec	Meso-America	State of Mexico
4 Pamean	Meso-America	Hidalgo (Mex.)
5 Chichimec	Meso-America	Guanajuato (Mex.)
C Popolocan		
1 Popoloc, Choco	Meso-America	SE Puebla, NW Oaxaca
2 Ixcateco	Meso-America	NW Oaxaca
3 Mazateco	Meso-America	SE Puebla, NW Oaxaca

PHYLUM, Family Language	North, Meso- or South America	Location
D Mixtecan		
1 Amuzgo	Meso-America	E. Guerrero, W. Oaxaca
2 Mixtec	Meso-America	E. Guerrero, W. Oaxaca
3 Cuicatec	Meso-America	NE Oaxaca
4 Trique	Meso-America	W. Oaxaca
E Chinacantecan	Meso-America	N. Oaxaca
F Zapotecan		
1 Zapotec	Meso-America	Ixtlan, Mitla, Yatzachi
2 Chatino	Meso-America	SW Oaxaca
3 Papabuco*	Meso-America	Elotepec, Oaxaca
X MACRO-CHIBCHAN		
A Chibchan		
1 Abiseta, Boruca,* Bribri, Tirub	South America	Costa Rica
2 Andaqui	South America	Colombia
3 Atanque, Ijca, Guamaca, Tairona*	South America	Colombia
4 Bairira, Motilon	South America	Colombia, Venezuela
5 Betoi*	South America	Colombia
6 Cara,* Cayapa, Campaz, Pasto*	South America	Colombia, Ecuador
7 Catio,* Nutabe*	South America	Colombia
8 Chibcha,* Tunebo	South America	Colombia
9 Chimilia, Malibu*	South America	Colombia
10 Changuena,* Chumula*	South America	Panama
11 Coconuco, Guambiana, Moguex, Totoro	South America	Colombia
12 Corobisi, Guatuso, Guetar, Suerre	South America	Costa Rica
13 Cuna	South America	Panama, Colombia
14 Guayami, Move*	South America	Panama, Colombia
15 Panzaleo,* Paez	South America	Ecuador, Colombia
16 Rama	South America	Nicaragua
17 Sebondoy	South America	Colombia
B Esmeralda,* Yaruro	South America	Ecuador, Venezuela
C Itonama	South America	Bolivia
D Paya	South/Meso-America	Honduras
E Misumalpan		
1 Misquito	South/Meso-America	Nicaragua, Honduras
2 Matagalpa, Cacaopera	South/Meso-America	Nicaragua, Honduras
3 Sumo, Ulua, Tahuajca	South/Meso-America	Nicaragua, Honduras
F Xinca	Meso-America	Yupiletepeque, Jutiapa, Sinacantan
G Lencan		
1 Lenca	Meso-America	SW Honduras
2 Chilanga	Meso-America	El Salvador
H Waican (or Yanoaman)	South America	Brazil, Venezuela
I Warao	South America	Venezuela
XI ARAWAKAN		
A Amuesha	South America	Peru
B Apolista*	South America	Bolivia
C Arauan	South America	Brazil
D Chamicuro	South America	Peru
E Maipurean		
1 Achagua, Capite, Minanei, Maipure	South America	Colombia, Venezuela
2 Asorai, Mapidian, Wapishana	South America	Guyana, Brazil
3 Baniva, Yavitero	South America	Venezuela
4 Baure, Mojo, Muchojeone, Pauna	South America	Bolivia
5 Campa, Machiguenga, Piro, Cuniba*	South America	Peru, Brazil
6 Caripuna, Marawan	South America	Brazil
7 Chane,* Guana, Terreno	South America	Brazil, Argentina, Paraguay
8 Paressi, Sarave	South America	Brazil, Bolivia
F Taino*	South America	Antilles
G Morique	South America	Peru
XII CARIBAN		
A Carib		
1 Acawai, Waica, Taulipang	South America	Venezuela, Brazil
2 Apalai, Aracaju, Upurul, Oyana	South America	Surinam, Brazil
3 Apiaca,* Arara,* Pariri*	South America	Brazil
4 Atroahi, Quirixana, Waimiri	South America	Brazil

PHYLUM, Family Language	North, Meso- or South America	Location
5 Bakairi,* Nahakua, Yaruma*	South America	Brazil
6 Bonari,* Hiskariana, Parucoto, Waiboi, Waiwai	South America	Brazil
7 Cachuene, Mutuan,* Pauxi,* Salum Wayewe, Chiquena	South America	Brazil, Guyana
8 Carare, Opone	South America	Colombia
9 Caribe		Antilles, Guianas, British Honduras
10 Carijona	South America	Colombia
11 Colima,* Muzo, Pijiao	South America	Colombia
12 Cumanagoto,* Tivericoto*	South America	Venezuela
13 Keseruna, Macushi, Paraviyana*	South America	Brazil
14 Mariquitare, Yecuana	South America	Brazil, Venezuela
15 Mapoyo, Yauarana	South America	Venezuela
16 Motilon	South America	Colombia, Venezuela
17 Palmela*	South America	Brazil
18 Panare	South America	Venezuela
19 Patagon	South America	Peru
20 Pawishana	South America	Brazil
21 Pianocoto, Tliometesen, Trio	South America	Brazil
22 Pimenteira*	South America	Brazil
23 Ya[illegible]	South America	Fr. Guiana, Trinidad
B Choco	South America	Colombia
XIII MACRO-GE		
A Bororoan		
1 Bororo	South America	Brazil
2 Otuke	South America	Bolivia
B Botocudo*	South America	Bolivia
C Fulnio*	South America	Brazil
Ge		
1 Akroa,* Xakriaba,* Xavante	South America	Brazil
2 Apinaye-Kayapo, E. Timbira, Suya	South America	Brazil
3 Caingang, Xokleng	South America	Brazil
4 S. Kayapo	South America	Brazil
E Jeiko*	South America	Brazil
F Kamakan*	South America	Brazil
G Karaja	South America	Brazil
H Kapoxo,* Malali,* Maxakali*	South America	Brazil
I Ofaye*	South America	Brazil
J Puri-Colorado*	South America	Brazil
XIV MACRO PANO-TACANAN		
A Chon	South America	Argentina
B Mosetene	South America	Bolivia
C Pano-Tacanan		
1 Panoan	South America	Bolivia, Peru, Brazil
2 Tacanan	South America	Bolivia
D Yuracare	South America	Bolivia
XV TUPIAN		
A Tupian		
1 Tupi-Guarani	South America	Brazil, Fr. Guiana, Bolivia, Argentina, Paraguay
2 Cocama, Omagua	South America	Peru, Brazil
3 Guayaki	South America	Paraguay
4 Mawe	South America	Brazil
5 Siriono	South America	Bolivia
B Arara	South America	Brazil
C Arikem,* Kabishiana,* Karitiana*	South America	Brazil
D Arue, Digut, Monde*	South America	Brazil
E Guarategaya,* Tupari, Wayoro	South America	Brazil
F Kuruaya*	South America	Brazil
G Manitsawa,* Shipaya,* Yuruna	South America	Brazil
H Purubora	South America	Brazil

continued from page 16

In examining the accompanying table and map which respectively indicate the classification of American Indian languages and plot their geographic distribution, two observations are worth noting. One, the table represents the conventional classification of American Indian languages accepted by the majority of scholars of North, Meso, and South American Indian languages. As such it masks the controversies which surround some of the classifications and neglects some recent proposals which would alter the present classification. Among the latter are the following: one, a retreat from the problematic Penutian grouping, two, the proposal of a genetic relationship between the Uto-Aztecan and Chibchan Families, and, three, the creation of a Mesoamerican Phylum which would include Mayan, Zoquean, the Huave isolate, Totonacan, Lencan, Jicaque, and Oto-Manguean.

Another observation worth noting concerns the problematic nature of classifying South American Indian languages. Given the relative lack of knowledge regarding many of these languages, their classification must be regarded as more tentative and less comprehensive than other American Indian languages. While scholars of North and Mesoamerican Indian languages have amassed the prerequisite data—at least for the non-extinct languages—to enable a genuine classification of languages, scholarship on South American Indian languages, in many instances, remains insufficient to establish genetic relations at the relatively modest level of the family let alone more remote relationships. Rather than convey the impression of having a knowledge of South American Indian languages comparable to those of North and Mesoamerica, the map and table provide a more abbreviated treatment of South American Indian languages limited to the better established families and their component languages. While it is true that scholars of North and Mesoamerican Indian languages are not always unanimous in matters of classification, their occasional disagreements focus on the larger phylum-like groupings rather than on the more fundamental level of the language family (as is the case in South America).

Language contact

In addition to common ancestry an important cause of similarities between languages is language contact. Few, if any, Native American languages existed in isolation from other languages and their associated populations. In many cases this contact assumed the form of bilingualism, or multilingualism, in which some or all the members of a particular speech community include two or more languages in their linguistic 'repertoires'. Contact between two languages in this manner usually promotes linguistic *diffusion*—more commonly known as linguistic borrowing. This borrowing can occur at either or both of two levels: lexicon (or vocabulary) and grammar. Lexical borrowings, or loanwords, represent the incorporation of a non-native term into the vocabulary of a people. Grammatical borrowing, in contrast, reprsents the influence of one language on another in one or more subsystems of the grammar. These sybsystems include phonology (the sound system), morphology (word formation), and syntax (sentence formation).

In North America, patterns of language contact show considerable regional differences. In aboriginal times the Pacific Northwest once represented a location of significant linguistic diversity and a relatively high population density. These factors coupled with the stable location of tribes produced a language contact situation of widespread multilingualism. This stable multilingualism yielded, in time, linguistic borrowing in both its lexical and grammatical forms. In contrast, the American Southwest, despite comparable linguistic diversity, rarely displayed a comparable multilingual situation. Even on those occasions when one group did learn another's language it appears that native cultural values may have actually inhibited linguistic borrowing. Speech communities in the Pueblo Southwest, for example, have been particularly noted for their linguistic "conservatism" in this regard. As a linguistic consequence of such factors we find a general lack of readily recognizable borrowing—even at the relatively superficial level of the lexicon.

Unlike North America, much Mesoamerican linguistic borrowing is associated with the spread of the civilizations which flourished there. For example, Mayan languages have provided the sources of loanwords in Xinca, Lencan, and Jicaque while Nahuatl (the language of the Toltecs and the Aztecs) has provided loans for Mayan, Lencan, and other Mesoamerican Indian languages. In South America this pattern is reproduced by Quechua which was diffused first by the expansion of the Incan empire and later by the missionary efforts of the Spanish. As a result of contact with Quechua in this manner, many South American Indian languages located in the Andes and its eastern foothills have borrowed significantly from it.

In at least two instances in the Americas language contact has produced "pidgin" languages—compromise languages usually associated with trade which draw their grammars and vocabularies from diverse sources. These pidgins are acquired by individuals as second languages useful in facillitating intergroup commerce. Two such pidgins were Chinook Jargon of the Northwest Coast and Mobilian Trade Jargon of the lower Mississippi Valley of southeastern North America. Both of these pidgins were a blend of such indigenious languages as Chinookan and Choctaw respectively as well as such European languages as French and English.

Today and in more recent times the contact of American Indian languages with such European languages as English, French, Portuguese, Russian, and Spanish have resulted in extensive bilingualism and considerable lexical borrowing. Borrowing has not, of course, been one-sided. In addition to numerous placenames (e.g. Massachusetts, Chicago, Mississippi, Seattle), American Indian languages have provided English with a considerable quantity of loanwords. From various North American Indian languages English has borrowed such words as "squash", "raccoon", "moose", "succotash", and "abalone". Mesoamerican Indian languages, especially Nahuatl, have contributed many contemporary English words which were transmitted via Spanish. These loanwords include "chili", "avocado", "chocolate", "coyote", and "tomato". South American Indian languages such as Taino (Arawakan) and Quechua have also furnished such loanwords as "canoe", "tobacco", and "condor". In sum, many of the terms currently used for flora and fauna by non-Native Americans are loanwords derived from American Indian languages.

Grammatical characteristics

While many similarities between American Indian languages can be traced to genetic and diffusional sources, the overall impression of American Indian languages is one of marked grammatical diversity. Though related languages typically show an array of structural traits usually characteristic of their particular families, American Indian languages, in general, defy attempts to isolate such defining and distinguishing characteristics. Partially due to the genetic diversity which comprises them, American Indian languages display no invariant properties that could be defined as "uniquely" American Indian. But while many of the traits found in American Indian languages can be observed in natural languages elsewhere in the world, some can be identified as 'typical' in that they are common to a major portion of American Indian languages or in that they represent structural attributes rarely found in English and other Indo-European languages.

Two characteristics of Native American languages which came to the early attention of European and Euro-American scholars were *polysynthesis* and *incorporation*. Polysynthesis refers to the phenomenon of combining many sentence-like elements into the structure of a single word by adding prefixes and suffixes. An illustration of this characteristic is provided by the Shawnee example ni-pekw-alak-h-a, meaning "I clean it (a gun) with a ramrod." In this example which appears segmented into *morphemes*—minimal units of meaning—each morpheme contributes information that would typically be encoded by a separate word in an English translation (e.g. ni = I, pekw = dry space, alak = interior of a hole, h = by means of a tool, a = action performed on some object.) Yet the Shawnee example is really only one word.

Incorporation is the inclusion of a noun, typically the object, into the verb word. For example, in Tewa one would say "He has a toothache" or "His tooth aches" as na-wae-hee (na = he, wae = tooth, hee = be ill). Some eighteenth and nineteenth century linguists, eager to find evidence of a primitive mentality embodied in American Indian languages, interpreted these structural attributes as proof that these languages were reflections of a confused and irrational perception of the world by their speakers. In truth, an American Indian language is the equal of any other natural language both as a conceptual vehicle and as a highly complex structural object. Though American Indian languages do categorize the world somewhat differently than European languages, one could only regard them as inferior if one equates mere differences with inferiority—an ethnocentric notion long abandoned by serious scholars. Though of an equal complexity to

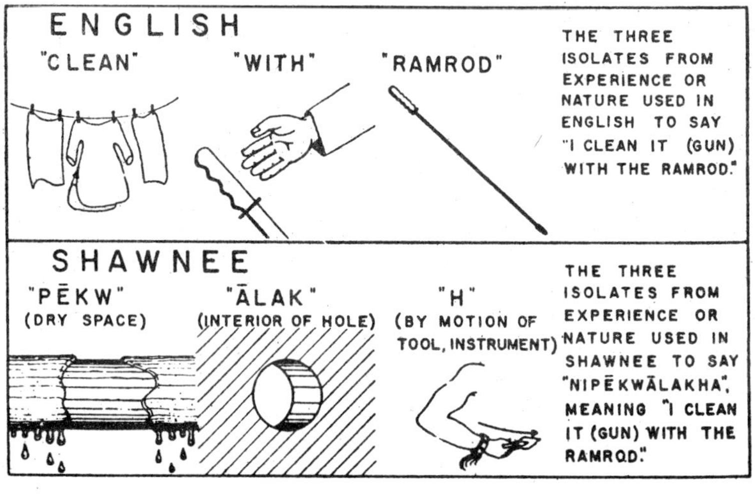

Languages dissect nature differently. The different isolates of meaning (thoughts) used by English and Shawnee in reporting the same experience, that of cleaning a gun by running the ramrod through it. The pronouns "I" and "it" are not shown by symbols, as they have the same meaning in each language. In Shawnee "ni" equals "I"; "a" equals "it."

languages such as English, many American Indian languages display their complexity in portions of the grammar that are somewhat less complicated in Indo-European languages. Thus where English has a relatively complex syntax and a comparatively uncomplicated morphology, an American Indian language like Shawnee has an intricate morphology and a rather straightforward syntax. This demonstrates the futility of comparing whole languages to each other. What success linguists have achieved in the comparison of languages has emerged not from the comparison of whole languages but rather from the detailed comparison of such parts of the grammar as phonology, morphology, etc. Any effort to suggest some of the structural features of American Indian languages must accordingly make use of such distinctions.

In terms of the phological, or sound, system—for example—great variation can be observed in the number of distinctive sounds, or *phonemes*, which each language employs. A language like Campa (Arawak) has only seventeen phonemes whereas as many as fifty-three can be discriminated for Rio Grande Tewa. Many American Indian languages do exploit certain positions and manners of articulation not regularly found in a a language like English. For example, many American Indian languages employ a *glottal stop* (the complete closure of the glottis as between the two syllables in the English exclamation oh-oh!) and glottalized consonants which must be recognized as distinct from the plain (non-glottalized) series of consonants. Many languages also make a larger number of tongue positions relevant in the articulation of distinctive sounds. Many American Indian languages, like Mono (a Uto-Aztecan language of central California), distinguish two types of velars—sounds produced with the back of the tongue: a *k* roughly comparable to English *k* and a uvular *q* produced further back in the mouth. In addition to these types of sounds, some American Indian languages use pitch, or tone, to distinguish words in much the same manner as Chinese. Thus for example, in Tewa p'ó means moon and p'ò means water. (High and low pitches are indicated with the acute and grave accent marks respectively while the apostrophe indicates that the preceding consonant is to be pronounced with glottalization.)

Morphologically most American Indian words—especially verbs—are characterized by a complex morphology. In many languages a pronoun-like prefix or suffix conveys information about the subject and/or object. Another type of information often included in the verb is supplied by *evidential* morphemes and by *tense-aspect* suffixes. Evidential markers such as those of Wintu (a Penutian language) indicate the evidential basis on which the statement or was it simply reported to him by another person? Tense-aspect suffixes specify the time and character of the action expressed by the verb. Many American Indian languages lack a well developed tense system which clearly distinguishes a present, past and future. Instead they display an elaborate aspectual system which details not the objective time of occurrence of the action but rather its temporal character—ongoing, finished, potential, intended, habitual, etc.

Two other common attributes of American Indian languages can be briefly noted. In many languages, such as many Oto-Manguean and Mayan languages, two forms of the first person plural pronoun (such as English "we") exist: one which encodes the speaker and the hearer and another which encodes the speaker and some third party. The final characteristic which will be mentioned here is the relatively conspicuous absence of the category of gender in American Indian languages. Speakers of English, who possess such gender encoding third person pronouns as "he", "she", "it" are often surprised to find that no comparable distinction is made in many American Indian languages.

Language and culture

While structural analysis permits some valuable insights into American Indian grammatical patterns, it does not address the problem of the relationship of a language to the thought or culture of its speakers. No simple one to one relation exists between the form of a language of a specific cultural similarity. For example, in the Kiowa-Tanoan Family of languages we find three languages associated with a Pueblo cultural adaptation (Tiwa, Tewa, Towa) but the fourth, Kiowa, with a Plains culture. The converse also holds true: among the culturally similar Pueblo Indians representatives of four distinct language families are spoken: Hopi (Uto-Aztecan), Zuñi (Penutian), Tiwa, Tewa, and Towa (Kiowa-Tanoan) and Keresan (an isolate).

But while such gross correlations between language and culture must be rejected, anthropologists can justifiably maintain that languages provide their speakers with a symbolic guide to their cultures. Since much of culture is verbally encoded, languages supply a classification of the culturally significant universes of their speakers. Since children must acquire the language spoken by their caretakers—parents and other adults—in order to express their increasingly complex needs, the very necessity of acquiring the language introduces them to a world pre-shaped by the cultural concepts encoded in the language.

The belief that the grammatical characteristics and vocabularies of particular languages equip their speakers with a unique world-view unshared by speakers of other languages has a long popular and intellectual history. In its most recent form, called the Whorfian Hypothesis (after the American linguist Benjamin Lee Whorf), we find this idea revived in both a strong and weak form. The strong form states, in essence, that languages determine the conceptual possibilities of their speakers whereas the weak form simply claims that language influences thought. Data from American Indian languages have been marshalled in support of each of these positions. In Nootka (Wakashan language), for example, several different words exist for what speakers of English term "snow" depending upon whether it is falling, on the ground, or being used as a building material In a similar manner Hopi Indians use two distinct terms for English "water" depending upon whether the substance occurs naturally or in a man-made container. But whereas English discriminates "airplane", "aviator", and "flying insect", Hopi generalizes these terms into a single word meaning roughly "flyer." Do such differences in how languages express certain concepts betray actual psychological differences between their speakers? Are Hopi Indians unable to tell the difference between airplanes and dragonflies? Certainly not. In much the same manner it would be foolish to argue that speakers of English are blinded to the distinctions regarding snow which guide the Nootka speaker in selecting the proper term. Speakers of English can express types of snow that are lexically distinguished in other languages by modifying the word "snow" ("falling" snow, "dry" snow), compounding (snow-drifts, snow-house, snow-covered), and employing other grammatical devices. It would appear then, as many linguists have contended, that languages differ not so much in the concepts they can express as in the relative ease of their expression. Because of such "codability" differences, certain statements in English and their translation equivalents in various American Indian languages will inevitably differ both in length and in specificity. English "I see snow" would find greater precision in Nootka as to the type of snow. English "There is a fly in my soup," on the other hand, would be (perhaps) humorously ambiguous in Hopi.

Languages classify items of experience differently. The class corresponding to one word and one thought in language A may be regarded by language B as two or more classes corresponding to two or more words or thoughts.

Though many of the obvious differences between languages are located in their vocabularies, grammatical evidence often provides a better source of support for a Whorfian notion of linguistic relativity. In a language like Wintu one must choose an evidential morpheme in the verb which conveys information as to the validity of the statement. Since this represents an obligatory choice it confronts the speaker with a consideration that speakers of languages like English—where it is not mandatory to include such information—need not face. Another example comes from Navajo where verbs of handling and movement must be selected from more than a dozen distinct possibilities depending upon the shape, texture, and other attributes of the object. Since the choice of an appropriate verb depends on such attributes, one could conclude that it directs the attention of the speaker to these characteristics and in so doing influences thought.

In addition to structural differences languages also exhibit differences in use. Members of various cultures differ in regard to what they consider appropriate behavior on a given occasion; American Indians are no exception. Among the Cuna of Panama, speakers of a Macro-Chibchan language, we find certain ceremonies where the curer talks to inanimate objects which are believed to be intermediaries to the supernatural. This shows that in some cultures and for some speech events the addressee need not be a human. Hupa (Athapascan) storytellers precede their stories by boasting of previous instances in which they displayed their skills to appreciative audiences. For the Hopi individual who seeks to voice his outrage over some injustice a traditional means is to expose his views via a roof-top chant rather than by directly confronting the suspected wrong-doer with an accusation. Speaking an American Indian language, like any natural language, means not only speaking grammatically but also speaking in accord with the prevailing ntions of appropriateness in the speech community.

Even silence represents a communicative commodity that is regulated by cultural expectations. Among the Western Apache, for example, many occasions that might, from the perspective of a Euro-American, invite verbal behavior are appropriately met with silence. Thus in the presence of the bereaved, in response to the verbal abuse of an enraged individual, and when greeting kinsmen after a long absense, an Apache finds silence an appropriate response where his Euro-American counterpart would supply words of condolence, a verbal retort, and general words of welcome, respectively.

No article on American Indian languages would be complete without some mention of one other type of non-verbal communication—sign language. Though today sign language is known to a comparatively few individuals who use it to communicate during inter-tribal ceremonies, in traditional times it provided an important means of inter-tribal communication in the

Great Plains of North America. By moving and shaping the hands and fingers into signs, Indians of diverse tribal affiliations could communicate without knowing each other's verbal language. This was particularly important on the Great Plains where the many different language families represented there, including Algonquian, Siouan, Kiowa-Tanoan, Uto-Aztecan, Athapascan, and Caddoan languages, posed great communicative problems for tribes who might meet only on an infrequent basis. Since these conditions tend to discourage multilingualism, sign language supplied the need for a common language.

A final remark on language and culture should be devoted to the relationship of language and ethnicity among American Indians. As elsewhere in the world, many Indians of the Americas view their distinctive languages as symbols of their ethnic heritage. For example, the Arizona Tewa, who have lived as a minority among the Hopi for almost three hundred years, have altered their social organization in numerous ways to adapt to the patterns of their Hopi neighbors thus diminishing the total number of differences which once characterized the two groups. Yet the Arizona Tewa have never forsaken their native tongue or the pride in the separate identity which it signifies. Likewise in the Vaupés territory of southeast Colombia—an area in which Carib, Arawakan, and Tucanoan languages are spoken—language and ethnicity are so intertwined that marriage is partially determined by the native languages of the prospective spouses. Another manifestation of the importance attached to language in this region is the persistence of many different languages spoken by only small populations which resemble each other in regard to virtually all other cultural possessions. Here as in the Tewa case previously cited one can only understand this persistence with reference to the function of language among many American Indian groups as a "badge" of ethnicity.

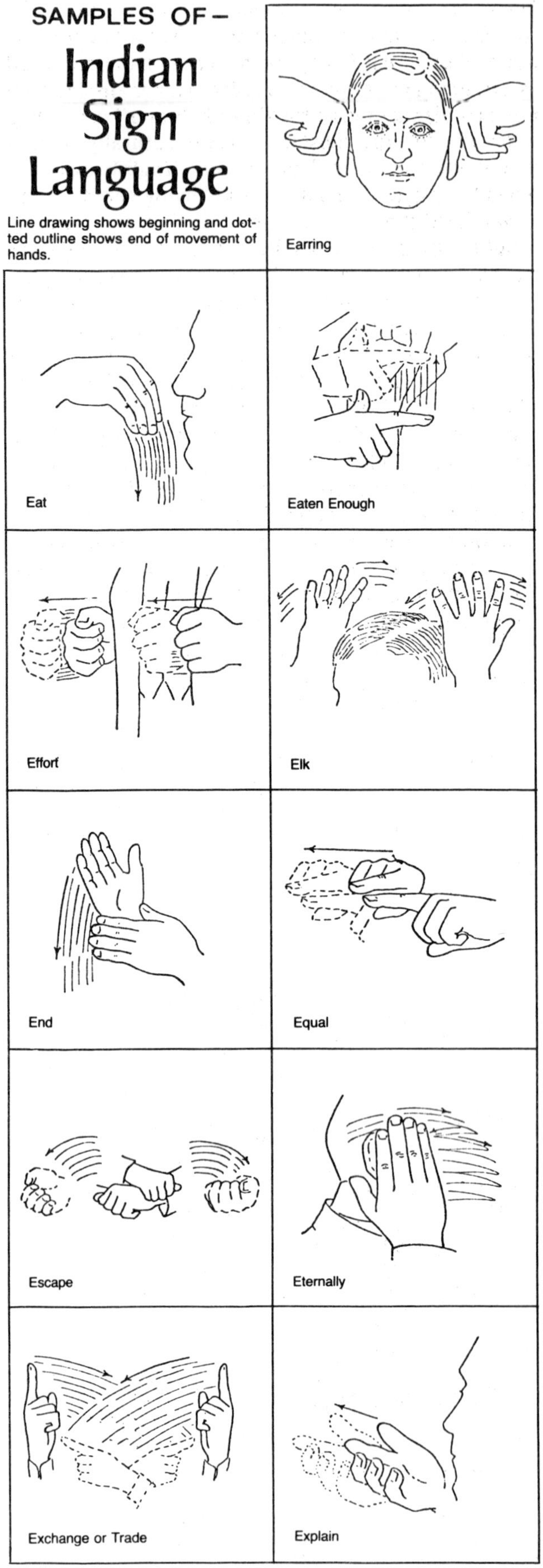

Writing systems and texts

While spoken language provides the primary means of communication for all American Indian groups, some groups do have their own writing systems. Mesoamerica represents the only area in the Western Hemisphere where some form of writing existed in pre-Columbian times. The Mayans invented a writing system which may have originated in the first century AD. While this Mayan system has yet to be completely deciphered, many of its general characteristics have been revealed through study of documents, written on paper of native manufacture, called *codices*. Most scholars maintain that this written language consists of a combination of ideographic and phonetic symbols. Ideographic symbols generally represent morphemes (words and their affixes) whereas phonetic symbols represent the sounds associated with pronunciation.

By the time of European contact a less elaborate form of notation had long been available to the Aztecs, Zapotecs, Mixtecs, Otomis, and perhaps other Meso-

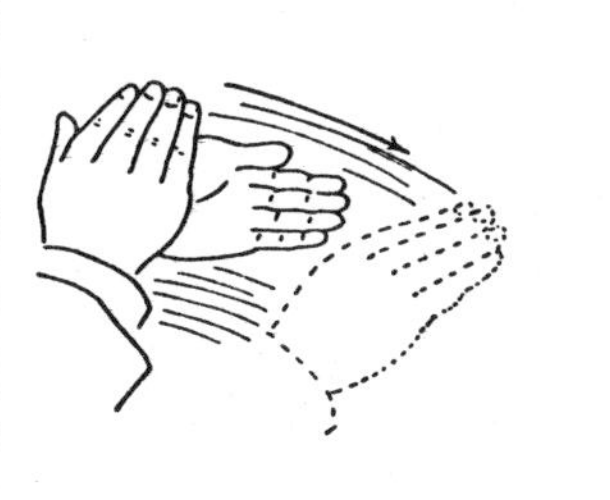
Exterminate

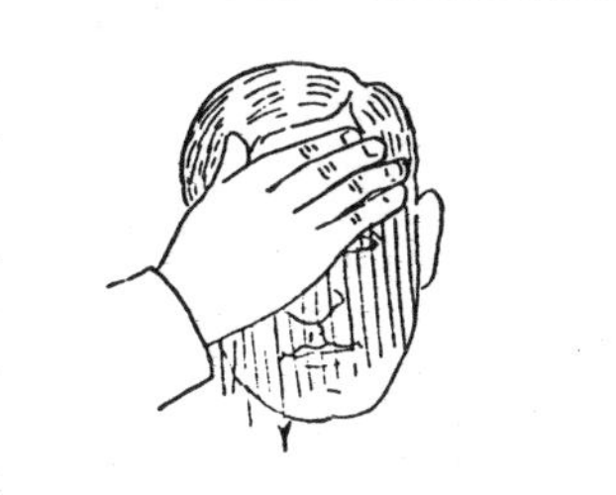
Face

Fall (of water)

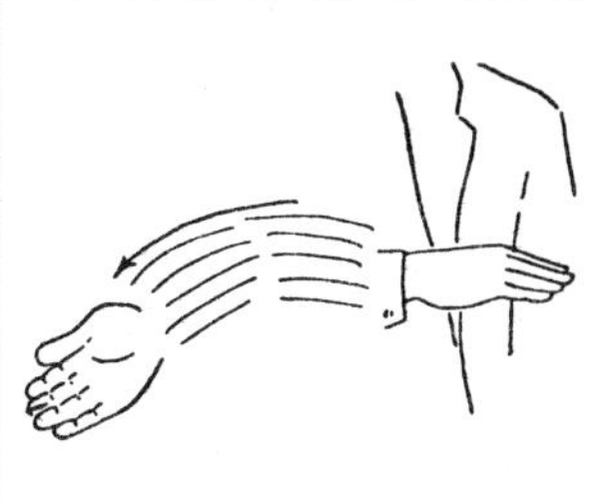
Fall (to)

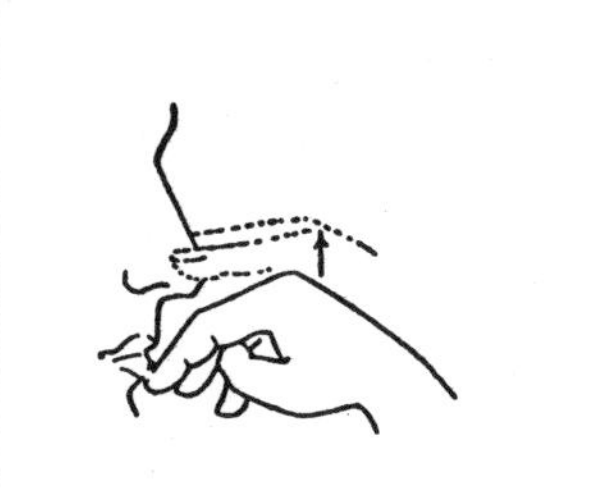
Fragrant

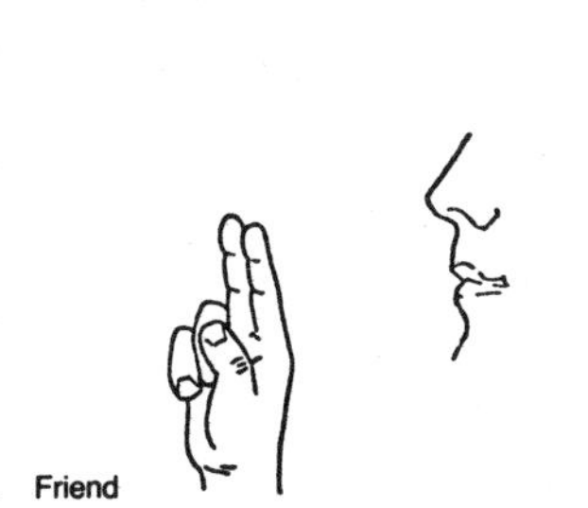
Friend

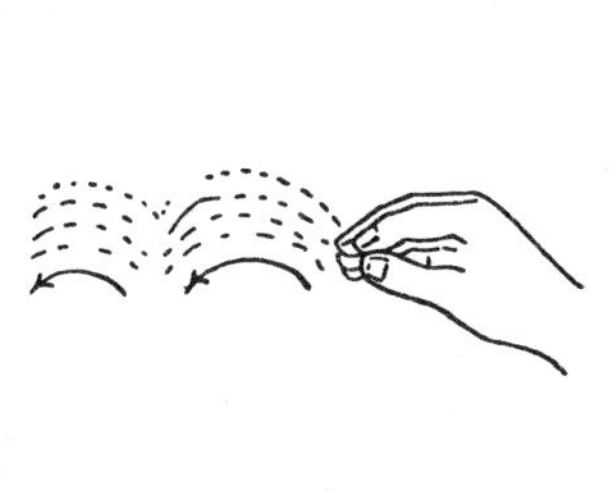
Frog

Future

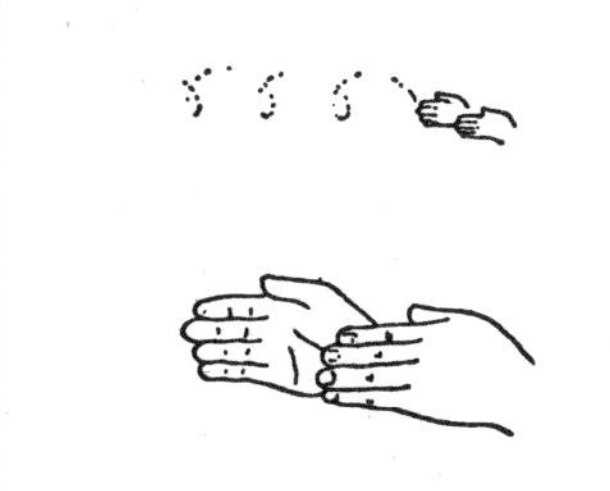
Gallop

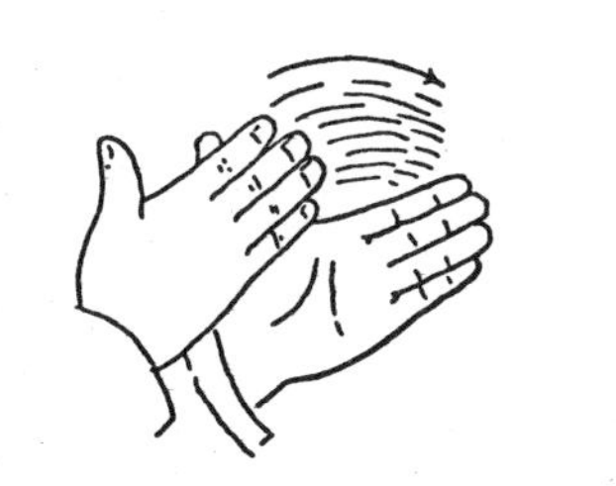
Gap

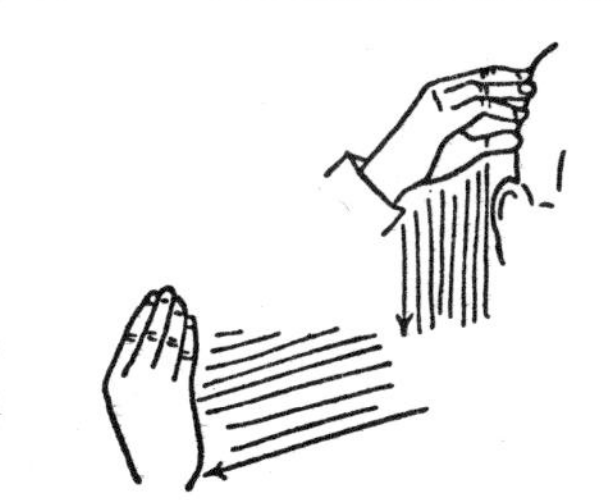
Girl

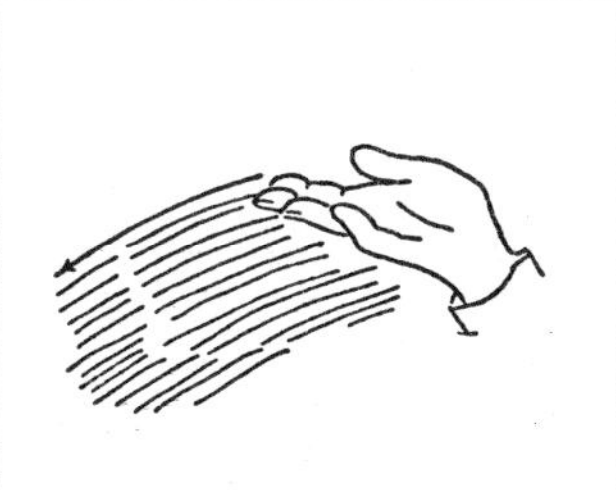
Give

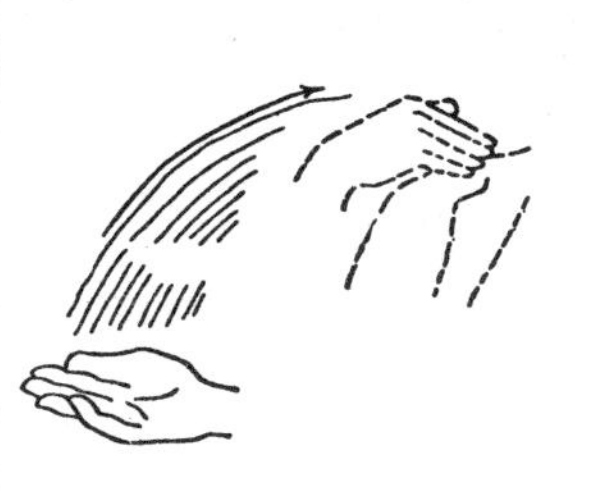
Give Me

Gloomy

Glove

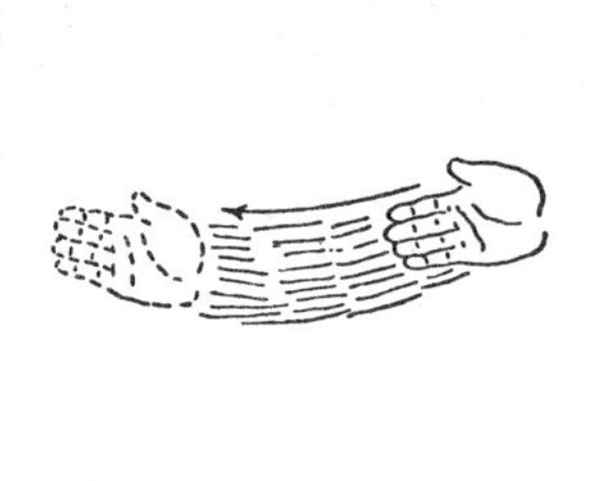
Go

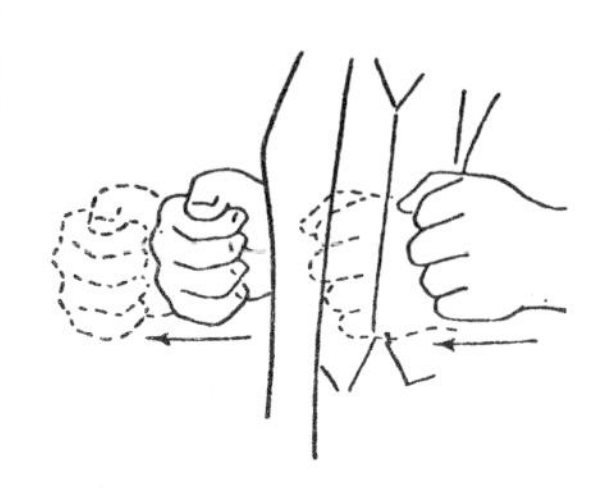
Go Ahead

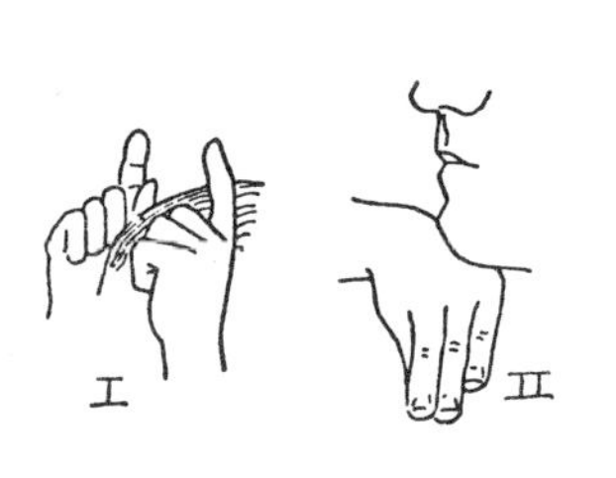
Goat

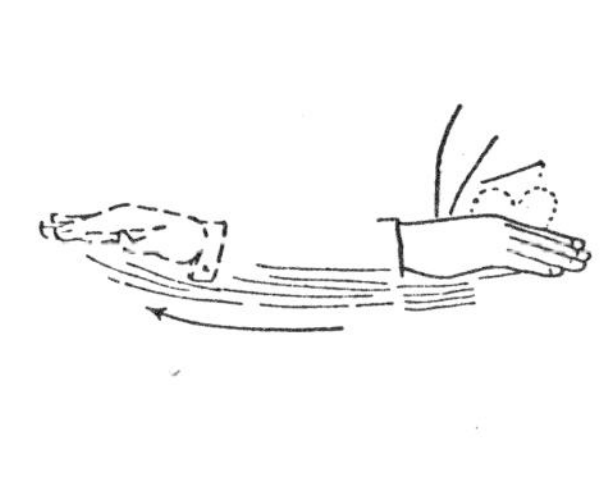
Good

Often

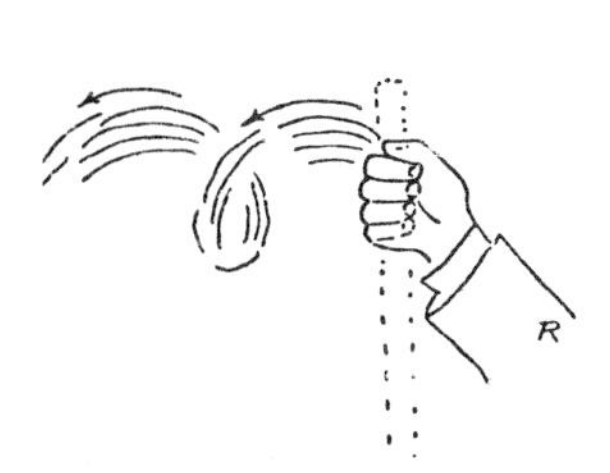
Old

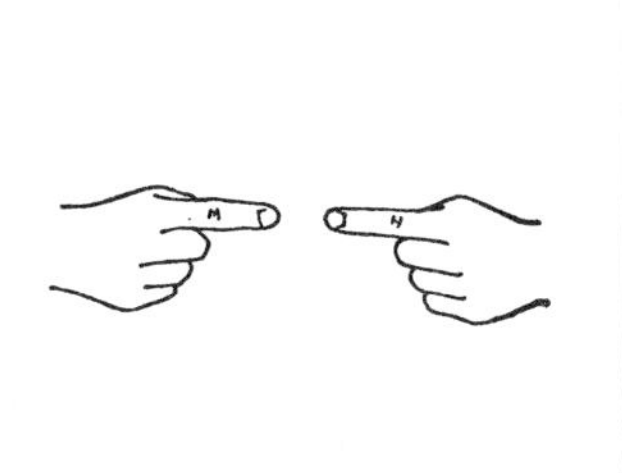
Oppose

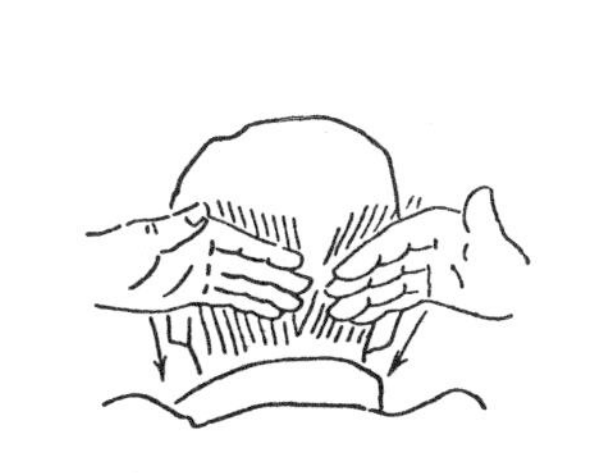
Osage

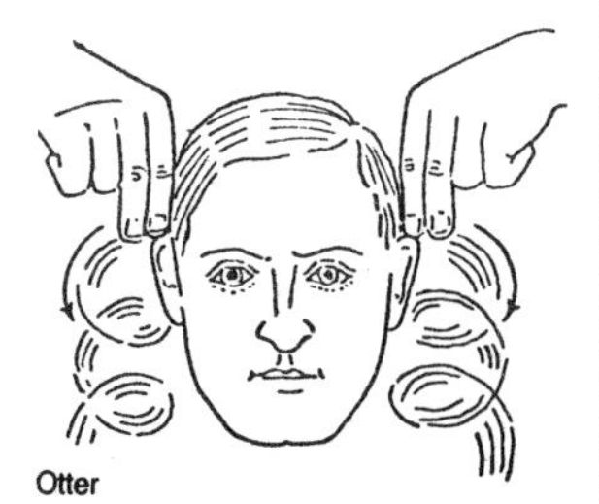
Otter

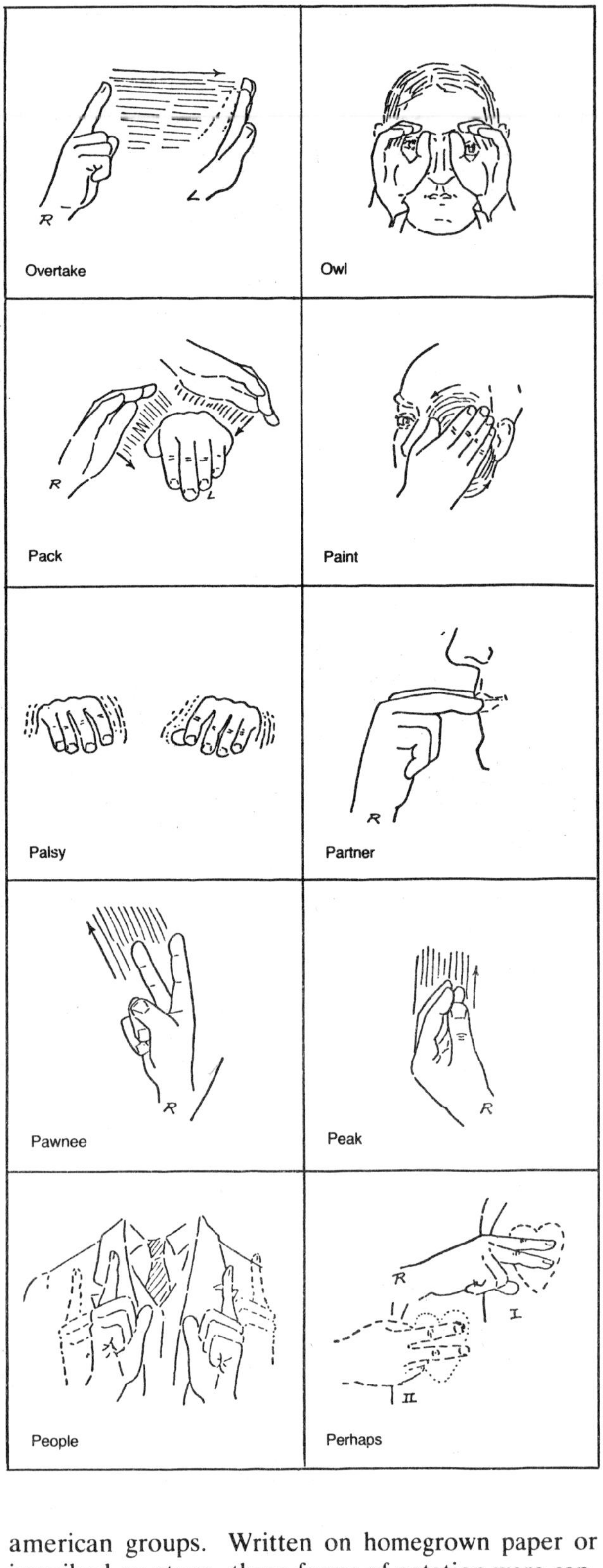

american groups. Written on homegrown paper or inscribed on stone, these forms of notation were capable of recording numbers, dates, and pictographic representations of names. Since they represented such a restrictive vehicle for expression, these forms of notation can not properly be called writing.

A similar form of notation may have existed in South America at the time of European contact. In the Andes of Bolivia and Peru, a notational system consisting primarily of pictographs was used as a memory aid in recitation of extended religious texts in Quechua. Among the Cuna of Colombia another form of notation was developed for similar mnemonic purposes—to assist in the recitation of spells in curing rituals.

Similar in form and function though probably of less antiquity are some North American forms of notation. These include the calendar sticks of the Pima and Papago and the calendar history of such Plains groups as the Kiowa and Sioux. The calendar sticks were wooden sticks in which marks had been inscribed to serve as a symbolic reminder of some significant event. They served to aid native historians in the recitation of chronological accounts. The calendar histories of the Plains Indians groups were pictographic symbols painted on skins which, like the Papago calendar sticks, served a similar mnemonic function for the native historian.

Though, with the exceptions of Mayan, no indigenous writing system existed in Native America, many have developed in response to European contact. One of the most famous North American examples of these is the system which was developed by Sequoyah for his native language, Cherokee, in the early nineteenth century. Though the writing system represents pronunciation, it is a syllabic form of writing rather than an alphabetic one. In other words, each written symbol represents the pronunciation of a syllable rather than that of smaller units of sound (as in the alphabetic system of a language like English). Sequoyah's system promoted a brief flourishing of literacy among the Cherokee before much of his tribe was forcibly removed from the Southeastern United States and relocated in what is today eastern Oklahoma.

Elsewhere in North America, syllabic forms of writing were developed for languages such as Cree, Ojibwa, Fox, Kickapoo, and Slave (Northern Athapascan) by missionaries. For other languages—including Choctaw, Chickasaw, Creek, Dakota, Tewa, Navajo, and several Northern Athapascan—alphabetic systems were developed by missionaries, educators, and linguists. Most of these languages employ a writing system which consists of the conventional symbols of the Roman alphabet and the addition of minor language-specific modifications to indicate such phenomena as tone, nasal vowels, glottalized consonants, etc.

In Mesoamerica, alphabetic writing systems have a

On the opposite page are examples of pictography and ideography used by the North American Indians.

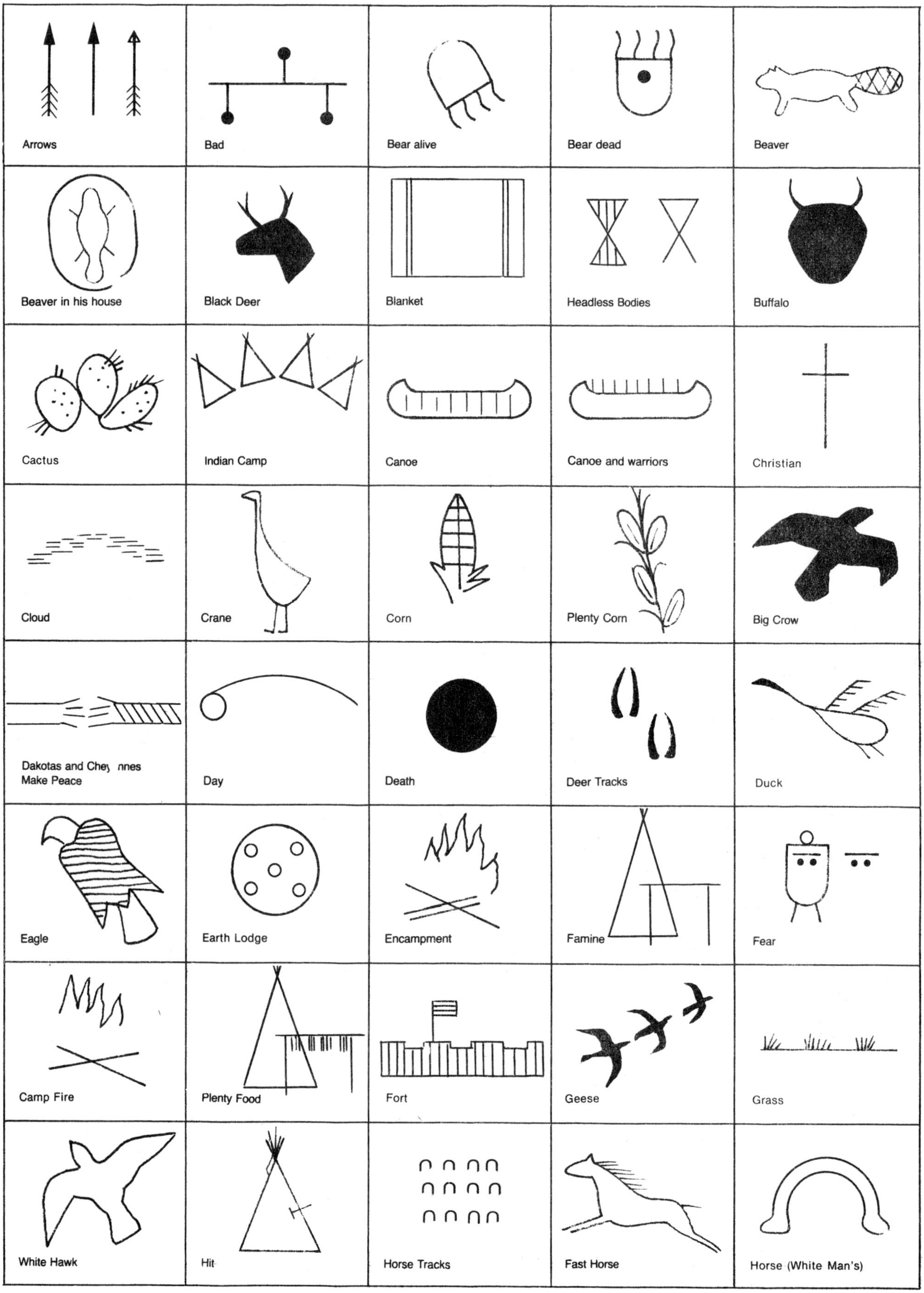
Arrows
Bad
Bear alive
Bear dead
Beaver
Beaver in his house
Black Deer
Blanket
Headless Bodies
Buffalo
Cactus
Indian Camp
Canoe
Canoe and warriors
Christian
Cloud
Crane
Corn
Plenty Corn
Big Crow
Dakotas and Chey nnes Make Peace
Day
Death
Deer Tracks
Duck
Eagle
Earth Lodge
Encampment
Famine
Fear
Camp Fire
Plenty Food
Fort
Geese
Grass
White Hawk
Hit
Horse Tracks
Fast Horse
Horse (White Man's)

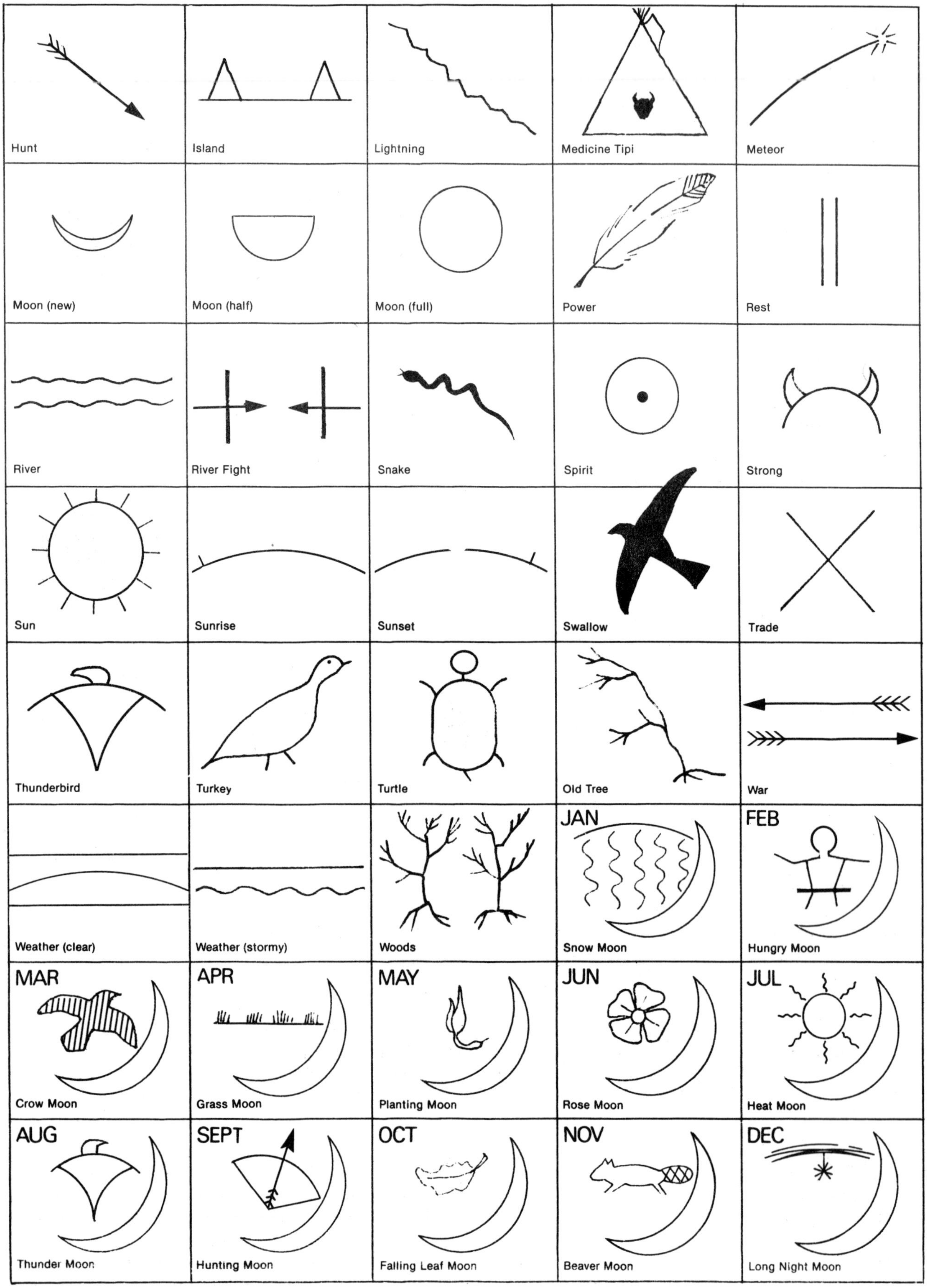
Hunt
Island
Lightning
Medicine Tipi
Meteor
Moon (new)
Moon (half)
Moon (full)
Power
Rest
River
River Fight
Snake
Spirit
Strong
Sun
Sunrise
Sunset
Swallow
Trade
Thunderbird
Turkey
Turtle
Old Tree
War
Weather (clear)
Weather (stormy)
Woods
JAN
Snow Moon
FEB
Hungry Moon
MAR
Crow Moon
APR
Grass Moon
MAY
Planting Moon
JUN
Rose Moon
JUL
Heat Moon
AUG
Thunder Moon
SEPT
Hunting Moon
OCT
Falling Leaf Moon
NOV
Beaver Moon
DEC
Long Night Moon

longer history. In the sixteenth and seventeenth centuries Spanish priests encouraged some Aztec and Mayan Indians to write their native languages in a Latin-based alphabet. Within this century the Mexican government has developed programs designed to foster the cooperation of speech communities, linguists, and missionaries in order to promote native literacy.

Two languages in South America—Guarani and Quechua—have also had alphabetic orthographies developed for them by Spanish missionaries in the seventeenth century. Today, native literacy in South America continues to be primarily in the hands of missionary-linguists. Most notable in this regard has been the Summer Institute of Linguistics (SIL.) Members of this organization have prepared literacy materials in more than 100 Meso and South American Indian languages.

Though missionary influence has endowed some Meso and South American Indian languages with longer traditions of writing and has continued to be an important source of linguistic activity in the present, this influence has also exercised some negative effects. With few exceptions the record of texts produced under missionary influence deals with the religion these missionaries wanted to import, not with Native Americans and their cultures. As such it reveals little of native customs and beliefs. The situation contrasts markedly with that of North American Indian languages which have been studied primarily by anthropologists and linguists. Here a significant portion of a rich oral tradition has been recorded in the form of texts which preserve the language and provide an important source of knowledge concerning Native American cultures and their verbal arts.

The present situation

The importance of this preservation is magnified by the many extinctions of American Indian languages and the moribund states of so many more. As the table indicates, many languages in North, Meso, and South America have become extinct. This list includes such languages as Mattole, Tunica, Mohegan, Yana, and Karankawa in North America, Chiapanec, Subtiaba, and Lenca in Mesoamerica, and Taino, Taruma, and Camacán in South America. Many other languages are on the verge of extinction since they are only spoken by members of the oldest generation. Included among these are Wappo, Abnaki, Delaware, Tubatulabal, and Pomo in North America, Seri, Chilinga, and Chicomuceltec in Mesoamerica, and several Tupi-Guarani languages in South America.

Many factors can be advanced as causes of the demise and near-demise of many American Indian languages. In the early stages of contact with Europeans, Indians fell victim to diseases against which they had no natural immunities. This and the competition with Europeans and Euro-Americans for land and other resources—a competition which often resulted in warfare and/or forced migration—greatly depleted aboriginal populations and severely disrupted many American Indian societies. While these factors continue to threaten the existence of some Native American groups—especially those in more remote regions of South America, other forces are now responsible for the gradual depletion of native speakers in many areas. Many young people on Indian reservations in the United States, for example, are removed from their native communities in order to attend urban-based boarding schools during their formative years. This removal has, in many cases, interrupted the transmission of cultural knowledge from generation to generation—an interruption which threatens the existence of many American Indian languages.

Though the prospects for American Indian languages—in general—are not good, some individual languages continue to thrive. In North America Navajo boasts more than 100,000 native speakers and continues to grow. Other languages in North America with large numbers of speakers include Ojibwa (40,000), Cree (30,000), Dakota (15,000), and Cherokee (15,000). In Mesoamerica, Aztec (over 1,000,000), the Mayan languages (including Yucatec, Quiche, Mam, Kekchi—about 3,000,000), and the Oto-Manguean languages such as Otomi, Mixtec, and Zapotec (approximate total—1,500,000) represent the most populous languages. South America possesses perhaps the most prolific American Indian language in Quechua with its approximately 5 million speakers. Other well-represented languages in South America include Aymara (1,000,000) and Guarani (about 700,000). The latter of these, Guarani, is an official language of Paraguay. In addition to the number of native speakers should be added almost one million non-native speakers.

Within the last decade or so some rather important developments have occurred which may help rescue many American Indian languages—particularly those of North America—from a probable demise. One of the most important of these is the growing awareness, on the part of some American Indian communities, of the need to preserve their linguistic and cultural heritage and insure its availability to future generations. This expression of deep concern for their native tongues has promoted a fruitful cooperation between speech communities and professional linguists that has resulted in the production of classroom materials and techniques of instruction designed to foster the knowledge of these languages within their communities. Among the groups currently involved in such projects are the Hualapai, Iroquois, and many Pueblo groups. Another relatively new development is the increasing number of native speakers of American Indian languages who have sought linguistic training and become professional linguists. Collectively such trends provide brighter prospects for many American Indian communities and their associated languages than their former circumstances would have permitted.

PAUL V. KROSKRITY

COMOGRE (Cuna; fl. 16th century), chief of a tribe of Cuna Indians who lived in the region of Punta Mosquito on the Atlantic coast of southern Panama, invited the explorer Balboa to his territory in 1513. Comogre, who occupied a large and magnificent palace, ruled about 10,000 Indians. The old chief accepted baptism as Don Carlos. It was his eldest son, Panquiaco, who told Balboa of a gold-rich region to the east, and guided Balboa on his discovery of the Pacific Ocean. When Balboa returned east in December, Comogre had died.

COMOX is a tribe located on Vancouver Island in the Pacific Northwest with a similar history as the Cowichan.

They were part of the Salishan linguistic family. The Comox tribe was the most abberant of the Salishan tribes. Culturally the Comox resembled the Kwakiutl.

Their houses were different from Salishan houses, being long, planked houses, with a sloping roof, the high side facing toward water. Inside there were fully enclosed family quarters. Their doors were carved to look like animals' heads. Their food, largely fish and other seafood, ws roasted in spits, baked in earthen ovens, or stone boiled in wooden vessels. One thing they did that was traditionally Salishan was salt their seaweed cakes.

Their social structure was based on status. Nobles were highest and commoners lowest, but all considered themselves free men. Nobles treated commoners with courtesy and encouragement, for commoners could advance up the social system. Only lazy people were truly despised.

Primogeniture was the rule, but females could inherit property. Inheritance didn't necessarily go to the oldest son; it was allocated according to a parents' favorite children.

The marriage ceremonies of the Comox were some of the most elaborate of any tribe. Taking up to weeks at a time, weddings were also extremely expensive, for gifts had to be exchanged with each of the guests and participants. Marriages were usually contracted between equals. But aristocrats ocasionally went through a farce of marriage with no bride simply to gain property. For this reason marriages were often unstable.

The Comox's history was virtually the same as the Cowichan except they were first met by whites (1592) later than when Juan de Fuca met the Cowichan. At one time they were moved from their home at Cape Mudge by the *Lekwiltok* to Vancouver Island. Comox became an important group in trading with the whites, and for that reason they were never moved from Vancouver Island. Today there are several hundred still there.

COMPADRAZGO. The *compadrazgo* (godparenthood) system is a form of ritual kinship first brought to Latin America by the Spaniards. It is still present in Latin culture and has been adopted by Indian society, where it performs a vital integrative function. Two relationships are created by this system, one involving the children and his godfather (*padrino*) and godmother (*madrina*), and the other consisting of the godparents and the parents, who address each other as *compadre* (cofather) and *comadre* (comother). The whole complex is formally begun at the baptismal ceremony, but may be reinforced or actually initiated at confirmation. It may also be initiated as part of an effort to effect a cure if the child is seriously ill.

Parents choose a couple whom they consider responsible, well-off, or lucky, who can offer their child protection and assistance. If the couple agrees to accept the position, they take the child to the baptismal ceremony, providing his clothes and then holding a party in his honor. From that time on, a special relationship exists between the two families, theoretically providing a second set of parents for the child and a close set of friends for the natural parents.

In this culture the position of godparent is primarily honorary, and many of the social and economic motives have been lost; however, the system establishes a set of intimate friends who will provide assistance or loyalty if needed and who often perform the role of a surrogate family. In short, it is an extension of the kinship circle and performs the same functions. Latins may act as godparents to Indians, but never the reverse.

In the Indian culture ritual kinship performs a more vital and influential role. The form which it takes varies from one township to another, but it is almost always present. The most important set of godparents are those who are chosen at the baptismal ceremony. The relationship which this establishes is characterized by a set of patterned activities and reciprocal duties involving all members.

In some townships the godparents are expected to provide moral and religious guidance to their godchildren, initiating them into many cultural activities. They are the only persons outside of the nuclear family who are allowed to discipline or reward the children. They also assume the expenses of the burial, if the child dies, and will usually provide part of the cost of his wedding.

For his part the child is expected to demonstrate complete obedience and respect for his godparents, bowing his head when meeting them. He generally takes them gifts at specified times and goes to them for advice and guidance. He considers their children his sisters and brothers, on the same level as his own natural siblings. The bond between them is so strong that often the child will request that his same godparents serve at his confirmation, marriage, and the birth of his first child.

The relationship between the two sets of parents (*compadres*) is equally important and provides a means of extending the kinship circle. In many townships it is more influential than the kin relationships, involving extensive reciprocal duties. Parents always consult the godparents in major decisions regarding the child and on private and public matters involving financial, religious, and political problems. In addition, the godparents are supposed to act as mediators in arguments between the father and the mother of the child. Both sets of adults turn to each other for mutual aid, and a man prefers to borrow money from his *compadre* than from kindred. They greet one another with formality, removing their hats and bowing. The tone of the relationship is one of quiet reserve, stressing the quality of respect.

In choosing godparents, the father and mother generally ask people outside the kinship circle. Occasionally, however, the parents may choose relatives, and some believe that one will only meet parents in the afterlife if they have served as godparents to their grandchildren. Usually, the choice of godparents is made among people with whom one has amicable but distant relations. In many towns the closets friends are excluded, since the existing intimate and informal bond would have to be replaced with a relationship of respect.

Indians sometimes seek Latins or Spaniards to act as godparents to their children because this enables the Indian family to establish a special bond with at least one Latin in the community. This means that their child can expect small favors, and if the parents die he will be cared for. More importantly, however, the family itself now has access to a Latin household and will usually receive financial assistance in case of need, protection from the law, or even preferential treatment in the renting of land. Thus, a bridge is formed between the two cultures and, even though the equality between both sets of parents is missing, the advantages are numerous enough to maintain the bond.

CONCHAS, from Spanish "shells," is a name for a shell midden deposit at the site, a Middle Formative ceramic site near the Pacific Coast at La Victoria, in the Department of Retalhuleu, Guatemala. Archeologists have been able to distinguish two distinct periods: Concha I (800-500 BC), and Conchas II (500-300 BC), growing out of an earlier Formative era. This is an Olmecoid culture marked by the early use of obsidian, extremely hard-fired pottery vessels and figurines, and seems to be a continuum from the preceding Ocós-Cuadros phases in Mesoamerican pre-history.

CONCHEROS. Central Mexico is the home of several dances that clearly evoke an image of the ancient warlike inhabitants of this region. And all of these dances conserve elements of the socio-religious organization of pre-Hispanic times. There are the Dance of the Apaches, the Indians, the Chichimecas, the Wild Indians, the Archers, etc.; but the most important and popular Indian dance is the Dance of the Concheros, also known as the Shell Dance.

The name "concheros" derives from the accompanying instrument which is a guitar made of an armadillo shell. The armadillo is an earth symbol.

Nowadays executants are members of three great troupes: that of Great Tenochtitlan covering the Federal District, of the Bajio which includes the states of Guanajuato, Queretaro and Hidalgo, and that of Tlaxcala. Each troupe is controlled by a military type organization which confers graded ranks. Unlike most dance groups, they admit women. A statute governs all members of these organizations and still calls for corporal punishment for violators.

This ritual and ceremonial dance is obviously of pre-Hispanic origin. for discernible in it are the following ancestral symbolic elements: the presence of the two old sorcerers, Oxomoco and Cipactonal; the cult of the Suchil with a mirror at its center and which is revered with incense blown to the four cardinal points; invocations, also directed at the four winds, to the souls of the "concheros"; placing bunches of fennel in the four corners of the temple and paying homage to each by weeping and dancing. Another such sign, permission to enter the temple is sought from the four

Indian in ceremonial costume playing a conchero.

borders—Villa de Guadalupe, north, Chalma, south, Los Remedios, west, and Amecameca, east, which is followed by dancing. A further symbol is the holding of festivals on dates coinciding with seasonal changes.

It is believed that these dances originated in 1522 during the conquest of Queretaro, when the Spaniards and their Otomi allies defeated the Chichimecas and imposed Christianity on them.

The costume has undergone several changes and even includes an imitation of the attire of the Aztec noblemen, but the traditional dress is made up of a leather headdress trimmed with spangles, tinfoil beads, mirrors, etc., and topped with long, bright-tinted feathers; and a knee-length spangled tunic or skirt, stockings and sandals. All dancers dress alike, except for one who takes the part of the devil. He wears a mask and red trousers and jacket. His role serves to clear space for the dancers—a task he accomplishes by wielding a whip among obstructing spectators.

CONCHO were the inhabitants of Concho Bay, on the east coast of lower California, on which Loreto Mission was established in 1697. The people spoke the Cochimi dialect.

CONDOR of South America, *Vultur gryphus*, is the largest surviving bird, with a 10-foot wingspread. Although a scavenger, it also occasionally has been known to carry off small llamas and other mammals, and has been charged with taking small children, although this is rare. It is black-bodied, with white patches on the wings and neck. Due to the condor's ability to fly at great heights, it was revered as a messenger to the gods, and was a major figure in prehistoric Andean religion. The Inca held a Condor Dance in its honor, in which the flight of the bird was simulated by the performers. The feathers of the condor were treasured, and it is frequently depicted in pottery and textile arts. In California, the *Gymnogyps californianus* species has a slightly smaller wingspread—approximately 9 feet—with an orange instead of red head coloring. It is far less common than the Andean bird, having become an endangered species in recent years. Condor feathers and ceremonies were also observed by California tribes.

CONDORHUASI ("house [home] of the condor") is an early prehistoric culture in the Villaserrana region of Tucuán, occupying the Hualfin Valley as far west as Belén, Catamarca. From its beginnings *circa* 200 BC it developed into a major complex notable for pottery and remarkable stone sculpture unique in the ancient Argentina area. The Condorhuasi people merged into the Aguada complex, about AD 700, and both became extinct by AD 1000.

CONESTOGA . *See* SUSQUEHANNA.

CONFEDERATION is a more or less formal league of independent nations formed to pursue certain common ends. Most confederations of North American Indians were fragile, and often resembled temporary alliances more than firm political confederations. The primary reason for the formation of a confederation was frequently threats from white settlers, and, consequently, the only area in which these confederations had any political authority at all was in matters of mutual defense.

According to tradition, the League of the Five Nations was founded in 1570, inspired by a dream of an Iroquoian prophet that was promoted from village to village by his councilor, the Mohawk Hiawatha. A more likely possibility, however, is that early contacts with the French provided an immediate need for a mutual defense pact. The league was expanded to six nations in 1722 with the admission of the Tuscarora. Other Iroquoian tribes that were not part of the confederation included the Huron, Erie, and the Susquehanna. Concerned solely with matters related to self-defense, the league could not levy taxes nor enforce any of its decisions, and it had no authority in matters internal to an individual tribe. Real unity was lacking in the league, as is amply testified by the voluntary basis of participation in warfare, both for tribes and for individual warriors, and by the participation of the Oneida and a portion of the Tuscarora on the side of the colonists during the Revolutionary War while the remainder of the confederation sided with the British. The league was headed by a council of chiefs whose power was mainly advisory.

The Powhatan Confederation, named after its principal tribe, was one of the most important confederations among the North American Indians. It included thirty tribes, all but six of which were brought into the confederation by the famous Powhatan warrior chief, Wahunsonacock, more usually known as Powhatan from the name of one of his frequent places of residence. In 1607, when the English settled in Virginia, the Powhatan numbered some 200 villages with a population of about 9,000. During much of the seventeenth century they were embattled both with whites and with other Indians, and by the end of the century they numbered no more than 2,000.

The roughly fifty Creek tribes never formed more than a loose confederation, even under pressure from the whites. Confederation meetings were held only irregularly and were most successful in settling intertribal disputes. The confederation failed miserably in presenting a united front to the whites, never once managing to draw representatives from all member villages for a battle.

In southeastern North America the Manahoac formed a confederation of at least eight tribes, and the Monacan had one of about five tribes. After first contact with the whites and a depletion of their numbers in war, these confederations joined with other peoples, including the Tutelo and Saponi Indians, and relocated to New York where they were eventually adopted by the Iroquois confederation.

The Assiniboines were a Siouan tribe that separated from their fellow Sioux some time during the sixteenth or early seventeenth century over a now obscure dispute. After the split, they sought and obtained an alliance with the Cree—one example of a confederation formed for reasons unrelated to the arrival of the whites. The two peoples then embarked on a career of military expansion that saw their influence spread over wide areas of North America, from the Rocky Mountains in the West to the Churchill River in the North.

Related to the idea of confederation is the idea of nationalism, the attempt by Indians to emphasizing their distinctiveness and independence in relation to the dominant white culture. Terms such as Indian nationalism, supra-tribalism, pan-Indianism, and tribal federalism have been used to describe the phenemenon. Most of these terms, including Indian nationalism, can be interpreted to refer to basically pan-tribal identity set against the surrounding white culture. But there are also distinctive tribal nationalisms—ideals taht maintain not only Indian culture in general, but also tribal distinctiveness in particular—in relation to other tribes as well as to white society. Indeed, this emphasis on the character and traditions of individual tribes is often a part of pan-tribal movements; in such cases, the tactical necessity of unit among all Indians in their dealings with white governments is accepted, although no effort is made to overlook the distinctiveness or independence of particular tribes.

Among the North American Indians throughout traditional and recorded historical periods, tribalism has been the rule, confederation the exception. When confederation occurred, the bonds uniting separate tribes were weak. The tendency among Indian tribes toward autonomy is one of the most distinctive traits of their political development. The arrival of whites in North America did encourage further efforts to confederate, usually, as stated, as a defensive measure against the colonists. As the Europeans consolidated their hold on the continent, pan-tribal movements increasingly developed as a response to the threat. One such early movement was led by the famous Shawnee chief, Tecumseh, who traveled across the continent telling Indians of all nations that they were all of one family, all children of the Great Spirit. His movement, however, died with him when he was slain during the War of 1812.

Tecumseh's movement was largely secular in orientation, though it included some important religious themes. Other nineteenth-century Indian nationalist movements were more purely religious in nature, including the Ghost Dance movement of the 1880s and 1890s, which was based on visions of the Prophet Wovoka which appeared to him during a severe illness. The movement was popular for essentially the same reasons as earlier and later movements, reflecting as it did the crisis of Indians in the face of an unceasingly expansionist white society. In the Ghost Dance, however, spiritual forces rather than political ones were called on to turn the tide in the favor of the Indians.

In the nineteenth century, pan-tribal movements were encouraged by the concentration of Indians on reservations, which facilitated communications among them. Also important were improvements in roads and the mails. Similarly, some Indians acquired literacy in English, providing a lingua franca to overcome the diversity of Indian languages.

Today, the same forces facilitate the growth of nationalistic movements among the Indians. The movement of Indians to the cities, for example, is a modern parallel of the earlier concentration of Indians on reservations, bringing Indians together and easing the problem of communication. Similarly, the continued expansion of white culture, as seen in the growth of cities and in the spread of industry, presents another severe challenge to the continued existence of traditional Indian culture. Especially for Indians living in cities, the contrast between what is purely Indian and what is not may be emphasized anew, providing an immediate reason for seeking a movement that would preserve their heritage.

CONFESSION is a limited phenomena among Indians. It has been reported for the *Inca* of Peru, the *Ica* and *Cágaba* of Colombia, and *Tupinamba* of the Brazilian coast. As a rule, confession to a priest or shaman served as a means of preventing or allaying private and public disasters which were the consequences of the violation of taboos; sometimes it served as a purification rite before the celebration of a feast.

In Peru confession was obligatory in times of illness and also in anticipation of certain feasts (e.g., the *oncoy mitta*, which was celebrated in June in honor of the Pleiades). When excessive frost endangered the plantations, twins and all others who had had an abnormal birth (e.g., those born feet first, with a harelip, etc.) were subjected to special treatment and had to confess their sins.

The confessors, who were recruited from among the diviners (huacuc) and who were called *ichuri* or *aucachic* (Cajatambo and Huaylas), heard all the members of their own ayllu including their wives and children. At one time confession seems not to have been secret, but it became so later; certain hideous crimes were reported to the supreme priest (*huillac umac*) or his assistant (*hatun huillac*).

The confession took place near a stream. After the person had enumerated his faults, the confessor gave him maize and shell powders to blow away, struck his head with a small stone, and ordered him to wash in water mixed with maize. Sometimes the penitent bathed in the stream. The confessor consulted auguries to discover whether the sinner had lied or withheld a fault. He also meted out penances which took the form of temporary observance of chastity, fasting, or abstaining from certain foods (e.g., salt and pepper), or a period of isolation on a mountain top. Wealthy persons made offerings to the gods.

In very exceptional circumstances, the *Inca* emperor confessed to the Sun and the Great Priest to Viracocha; neither one confessed to a person on any occasion. When they performed the rite they held in one hand a bunch of straw or grass on which they spat before throwing it into a stream or fire.

One of the most important functions of the *Cágaba* and *Ica* mamas (priest-shamans) was to hear confessions. A man would confide his "sins" to a priest under the following circumstances: When he was ill, before starting the treatment; when he feared he might become ill; before a feast in which prophylactic rites were celebrated; and after an eclipse or an earthquake. Most so called sins were sexual (e.g., intercourse with a relative of forbidden degree or with the servant of a mama, adultery with an unpurified widow, etc.). Planting coca without the priest's permission and stealing (*Cágaba*) also were considered offenses against the gods. The mama imposed a penance, but its form is not specified.

The *Tupinamba* attached great importantance to confession. When a great shaman (*pagi*) visited the villages he ordered everyone, but especially women and young girls, to confess to him. If they refused to comply, he threatened them, saying that his spirits would punish them for not declaring their offenses. Afterward he gave them absolution.

HARRY WALDMAN

CONNECTICUT. Early in the seventeenth century there were probably about 6,000 Indians living within the present state of Connecticut. The northwest portion of the state was virtually unoccupied. In the southwest dwelt a number of small clans, of which the largest was apparently the Paugusetts (Wepawaugs), who occupied 15-18 miles of shoreline and the lower Housatonic Valley. Near New Haven were the Quinnipiacs, and the Hammonasetts lived west of the Connecticut River. The Connecticut Valley was occupied by the Podunks and a number of smaller groups, and south of them the Wangunks. In the northeast were the Nipmucks and in the southeast the Western Nehantics and the Pequots (Mohegans), the largest and most powerful tribe in the state. Straddling the Rhode Island border were the Eastern Nehantics and the Narragansets.

The massive reduction of the Indian population began with the "Pequot War" of 1637 and was accelerated by the defeat of the Wampanoags of Massachusetts in King Philip's War in 1675. By 1774, there were only some 1,300 left. They continued to dwindle until 1910, when the federal census reported 152. Since then, the number has increased and in 1976 a statewide Indian census listed 4,014. Most are living in urban areas, with the largest numbers in Bridgeport, New Haven, Hartford, Waterbury, Bristol, Meriden, Norwich and Groton.

Brief history

The origin of the Connecticut Indians is unknown. All of them except the Pequots may have been only fragments of one large tribe or confederacy of tribes. The Pequots apparently split off from the main body of the Mohegans along the Hudson River, arriving in Connecticut early in the 17th century.

At first, they were primarily hunters. The sea and rivers provided such an abundance of finfish and shellfish that eventually the people concentrated where they could fish easily. The forested hills were used primarily for hunting. By the time the English and Dutch arrived early in the 17th century, however, they were cultivating maize, beans, squash and pumpkins, tended by the women and children, and tobacco, raised only by the men. For fishing and transport they used both birchbark and dugout canoes.

Most Indians lived in houses of varying size made of poles placed in the ground, bent over and tied at the top. The framework was then covered with thatch, sometimes with bark. They had frame beds but no other furniture. All tools and implements were quite simple except for large woven baskets and water-tight bark pails. The houses were closely grouped into villages sometimes protected by palisades. Most groups had summer homes on the shore and winter homes in the forests.

The chief of each group was a hereditary sachem; beneath him were lesser chieftains called sagamores, who served as councillors. Religions varied considerably, but they shared belief in a great invisible deity who was little concerned with men in this life; in a spirit of evil, who was greatly venerated; and in a group of lesser deities or spirits called *manittos*, each with a specific character, responsibility and name. There were healers, called *Powwows*, and a variety of methods, primarily sweating, for treating illnesses. The dead were buried with considerable ceremony.

Warfare was almost incessant, but seldom was there much bloodshed. In the largest recorded battle, that between Uncas of the Pequots and the Narragansett Sachem Miantinomo in 1640, only thirty men died. Generally there were small raids resulting in some losses of property and scalps. Battles were also fought at sea, in fleets of large canoes. The Pequots were the most warlike group, but they were challenged by the Narragansetts. Iroquois war parties frequently raided the western part of the state and exacted tribute from some of the tribes and clans there. The smaller groups welcomed English and Dutch protection and even helped them fight the larger ones.

In 1633, the Dutch established the first European trading post in the state, where Hartford is now. The Pequots resented this, attacked some Indians there, beginning a desultory war with the Dutch, and invited the English of Massachusetts Bay to settle in Connecticut. They were generally welcomed as they established a number of settlements during the next few years, but several incidents touched off the "Pequot War" in 1637. This massacre of over 600 Pequots at Mystic broke their power and the tribe was dispersed by the English as far as Barbados. The Dutch and English thereafter fought several Connecticut Indians, joined the war against Philip and his Narragansett allies. After his defeat, there were only a few more skirmishes among the Connecticut Indians and with the Mohawks.

Meanwhile, the sale of Indian lands to whites continued. As their land dwindled they were furnished with small reservations around the colony. Throughout the 18th century the Connecticut Indians were unsettled, many emigrating, forming and disolving tribes. As their numbers diminished they gradually settled down, lost their distinctive culture and nearly disappeared.

Current status

There are no federally recognized Indian tribes in Connecticut today, and only five recognized by the state. Four of them have reservations. They are the Schaghticoke in Kent (400 acres); Mashantucker or Western Pequot in Ledyar (213 acres, five resident families), Eastern Pequot in North Stonington (225 acres, ten resident families), and Golden Hill-Paugussett in Trumbull (one house on one lot, one resident family). A number of Mohegan families still live on former reservation land in Montville. Those living on reservations are governed in part by the General Statutes of Connecticut, which provide for an Indian Affairs Council in the Department of Environmental Protection and contain rules on such things as reservation land, services and programs, hunting and fishing, housing and tribal trust funds.

Of the 4,014 Indians in Connecticut in 1976, only 28% are members of indigenous Connecticut tribes, though 54% of the total were born in Connecticut. More than 60 other tribes are represented, and 8.4% were born in Canada. While their educational level is higher than the national average for Indians, it is well below that of the general Connecticut population. For example, 20% of all Connecticut Indians have completed eight or fewer years of school while 18% have completed one or more years beyond high school. About 18% of the adult Indians are unemployed. Of those working, nearly one-third are craftsmen, and only 22% are in managerial, professional and technical occupations. Income figures also reveal the poor economic condition of Indians: 41.5% earn $4,000 per year or less and only 17.5% earn over $10,000.

There is a new awareness now among the Connecticut Indians of the need to preserve what remains of their culture, and the state is beginningto help them do that.

MARTIN GLASSNER

CONQUISTADORS. *See* EXPLORERS AND CONQUISTADORS.

CONTAINERS used by Indians of the Americas varied greatly in form, function, method of manufacture, and level of craftsmanship. The most commonly used materials in container manufacture were hide, bark, wood, baked clay, and woven plant materials. These natural materials were fashioned into a wide array of storage and transport receptacles, dishes and other household utensils and vessels for hot-stone or direct-fire boiling and cooking. The form and ornamentation of containers often served symbolic functions as they still do, for example, in Hopi basketry.

Animal hide was made into a variety of bags, pouches, cases, quivers, and other receptacles, especially by the Eskimos and Plains Indians whose heavy reliance on hunting provided a large supply of hides. In the Subarctic and Plains areas the hide as well as other parts of the animals such as the belly, thorax, and intestines were sometimes used for boiling or baking food. Plains and Rocky Mountain tribes made a number of box-like rawhide cases, or parfleches, which were frequently painted with geometric designs and fringed.

Bark, especially birch bark, was the primary material used for containers throughout the Subarctic. It was cut, bent, and sewn with root or other fibers to form the desired shape. Sewn-bark containers were

Embassy of Venezuela.

Piapocas Indian water vessel from the Rio Negro, Amazon territory.

faster to make than woven basketry but generally not as long lasting, and bark was sometimes broken down into fibrous material for use in basket making.

Wood containers were the primary type used on the Northwest Coast in Canada and Alaska where woodwork was most highly developed. There were two primary types of wood container construction. One was the carving out of an appropriate piece of wood to form dugout storage vessels, dishes, and utensils. The other method was the cutting and sewing together of boards, which were shaped by steaming if necessary, to form boxes and chests which served many purposes and were often carved in relief and painted.

Basketry of woven plant materials was the most important type of container in the Eastern Woodlands, Plateau, Northwest Coast of the United States, and in California and parts of the Great Basin, Southwest, and Prairies. In the more western of these areas, baskets sealed with pitch or woven tightly enough to be watertight were widely used for carrying water and cooking. Baskets and bags were woven primarily by women. Carrying nets manufactured by a method known as knotless netting were used throughout North America.

Baked clay containers were used primarily by tribes who had sedentary and agricultural lifestyles and were little used by more nomadic tribes, who favored lighter and less breakable containers. Pottery north of Mexico was almost exclusively made by women. Pottery-making was done to a limited extent in many areas of North America and became a considerably advanced craft in the Pueblo region of the Southwest and the great mound province of the Mississippi Valley and the Gulf States.

Jars as containers are used widely by Indians of the Americas for holding and serving food and drink, carrying and storing food, medicinal agents, and other materials, and for ornamental and ceremonial purposes. Jars were used primarily by more sedentary tribes. Their weight and bulk, and especially the fragility of clay jars, discouraged their use among more nomadic tribes who preferred lighter, more resilient containers. Jars were of special value for the vital function of the protection and storage of food, especially seed and other plant foods, for winter or other periods of food scarcity.

In areas where bark or basketry containers were commonly used, these were sometimes made in semi-rigid watertight forms which approximated jars. Gourds, where they were cultivated in the Southwest, Prairies, Eastern Woodlands and Southeast, were frequently used to make jars. Specimens carved from soapstone have been found in some of the many areas north of Mexico where this material was used.

Throughout much of the United States, southern Canada, and Alaska where clay utensils were in general use, baked clay jars were the common type and were often decorated with incising or engraving. The fashioning of jars was most advanced and their use most prevalent where pottery was highly developed in parts of the Southwest and in the mound provinces of the Mississippi Valley and Gulf States. In these areas jars were made from a wide range of colored clays and were sometimes shaped and decorated for exclusively ornamental and ceremonial purposes.

COOK, JOHN A. (St. Regis Mohawk; April 22, 1922-), is a tribal chief who has also served as director of the Economic Opportunity Council of Franklin County, New York. Cook, who served in the U.S. Air Force during World War II, is an iron welder by trade.

COOK, LEON F. (Chippewa; July 30, 1939-), is a noted social worker and government official who has directed several social service programs for Native Americans in Minnesota and Arizona. He has also been a leading figure in the National Congress of American Indians (NCAI).

Born at Redlake, Minnesota, he worked his way through college, despite financial hardships. He became acutely aware of the serious economic and social problems of many Indians while working as a volunteer at Waite House in Minneapolis. Serving as consultant to the director of the Office for Economic Opportunity (OEO) in Minneapolis, he did the preliminary work that led to the establishment of the Minneapolis Indian Center. In the mid-970s he was a senior official of the Economic Development Administration of the U.S. Department of Commerce.

Cook, Leon F.

COOK, SOLOMON (Mohawk; Jan. 8, 1920-), is a noted teacher of agriculture in New York State. Born at Hogansburg, New York, on the St. Regis Mohawk Reservation, he worked his way through school, eventually receiving his doctorate from Cornell University. After military service in World War II, Cook taught horticulture at South Dakota State College, before returning to New York. He is also manager of his own dairy farm and has served as a guidance counselor.

COOLIDGE, SHERMAN (Arapaho; ?-*c.* 1933), was a minister who served as a missionary in Wyoming and was a canon of the Protestant Episcopal Cathedral in Denver, Colorado, at the time of his death. As a child he was found on a battlefield by a U.S. Army officer, was adopted, and was educated for church service.

COOPER, JAMES FENIMORE (September 15, 1789-September 14, 1851). The American Indian was the most popular subject in early American literature. During the 18th century, the oratorical skills of Indians were appreciated and recorded during treaty-making and the texts printed for general circulation. When the whites started to desire to acquire the Indians' land in the eastern United States, the Red Man was looked on as a foe; but as the frontier drifted westward in the first half of the 19th century, the image of the Indian began to be viewed as a romantic figure, thanks especially to the popularity of Cooper's historical novels of romance and adventure dealing with the native American scene, best represented by the *Leatherstocking Tales.* (He was the first to achieve substantial fame outside the United States.) He was born in Burlington, New Jersey; his father later became a judge and a member of the New York State legislature. When James was barely a year old, his family settled in what was then wilderness of Otsego Lake, New York, cultivating large land holdings which developed into the little town of Cooperstown. James' childhood was influenced by the surrounding woods and by his contacts with the Indians who later were featured in his most famous novels. In 1802 he enrolled in Yale from where he was expelled after 2 years for some boyish prank but was allowed to graduate. He returned to Cooperstown for two years. Then his father decided to have James join the U.S. Navy. His career as a sailor and a naval officer lasted five years. Then two events changed his life completely. After his father's death at the hands of a political enemy, the family's large estate was soon dissipated by his brothers. Secondly, on January 1, 1811, at the age of 21, he married Susan De Lancy, only 18 years of age; she induced him to resign from the Navy in May, and saw to it that they settled down on her farm at Scarsdale, N.Y., where four daughters and two sons were born. A trifling incident made him an author instead of a country squire and part owner of a whaling

Photo by Clifton Adams

"The Indian Hunter" marks the site near Otsego Hall, Cooperstown, New York, where James Fenimore Cooper lived and wrote his immortal tales of redskins.

Cooper, James Fenimore

boat to Patagonia. In 1819, when reading aloud to his wife from a new English novel, he remarked "I could write you a better book myself." Since he had resented even writing letters, his wife laughed at him. Out of obstinacy, he published in 1820, anonymously, *Precaution*, a half humorous imitation of the more lady-like English novel of the period. It was a poor novel but not unsuccessful, and this induced Cooper to publish a year later what Henry Walcott Boynton calls "The first living American novel," *The Spy,* Cooper's first success which started a whole succession of novels on the Revolution, but none of them matching the original. But Cooper's fame as a novelist rests on the five works of the *Leatherstocking Tales*, not written in the order of the story which gives a broad and noble picture of the woodsman Natty Bumppo and the Indian. First of the series was *The Pioneers* (1823); though Leatherstocking and Chingachgood fail to have the breath they later attain, and though there is too much conversation, there is featured one of Cooper's better heroines; old Leatherstocking is arrested for shooting out of season, but saves people from a panther and a forest fire. *The Last of the Mohicans* (1826) has the best executed plot of the series; it deals with noble Indians in Uncas and Chingachgood. It is a fine chase story, with good minor characters in Cora, Adam, and Heyward. The feeling for nature and the excitement of the action are remarkable, but less so than the nostalgia of the Indians who have to leave their homes. *The Prairie* (1827) ennobles the aged Hawkey who had gone to the upper Missouri to flee civilization, and rescues a bride from some kidnapping squatters. (His death as he stands up facing the setting sun and calling "Here!" was imitated by Thackeray in *The Newcomes*). *The Pathfinder* (1840) is partly a water story; Natty, in love with Mabel Dunham, wisely gives her up for his real love, the forest. (Here Cooper anticipated Howell in breaking the romantic clichés). *The Deerslayer* (1841) is probably the best in this series. It shows conscious art in rounding out the character of Natty Bumppo, who acquires the name Deerslayer, is made ill when he shoots his first man, and refuses the advances of Judith Hutter, because of his self-respect. (Hetty Hutter, a subnormal girl, is also well done). Cooper also authored a historical novel, *Wyandotté* (1843); it describes an Indian attack on the Wyoming Valley, and shows both the virtues and vices of the Indians affected by whites.

Cooper also authored four sea stories and four historical novels. His literary productivity has been highly praised as well as severely criticized. Suggested merits feature Cooper's ability to maintain suspense through the use of the chase in his plots, being at his best, a master of rapid action; his descriptions often give feelings of the expanse of the wilderness, with a large variety of vigorous characters from all races and classes, featuring especially comic and low characters, with courageous and active heroines. Natty is especially one great character. Cooper's rapid narrative style improved with his writing experiences. His critics have pointed out that he kept reusing the same literary devices to the point of monotony, with often improbable action. His descriptions were often excessibly lengthy and dull. His heroines were clinging and fainting and his comic creations are boring. His dialogues were atrociously styled, his style crude, with the 18th century formality.

His novels sold fairly well for a time; at one period he had an income of about $20,000 per year—a figure almost unprecedented for the early 19th century. But he had a heavy burden of debt, left by his extravagant elder brothers; and he himself lived in grand style. Thus he was hard pressed for money and wrote literally for his bread and butter. The day before his 62nd birthday, he died of sclerosis of the liver. His heritage was the romantic story of American wilderness (and the sea), with immortal characters, Natty Bumppo and Uncas.

JOSEPH S. ROUCEK

COOS, now nearly extinct, lived in Oregon.

The name is an adaptation from the Kusan family. They spoke a Penutian-based language.

The Coos lived along the central coast of Oregon, along Alsea, the Siuslaw, and the Umpqua, all of which are nearly extinct.

Scholars know virtually nothing about these tribes' social organization. What they do know comes from the few survivors who were moved from their traditional home in the 1850s.

It is known that their cultural and economic life was probably a cross between the Salish and Chinookian cultures, probably closer to the Salish.

If this is so, then the Coos probably lived in wooden lodges and depended on seafood and fishing as their major economic activity. Their government may have consisted of a male chief.

It is known that the Coos did not have clans, and allowed natural relationships to develop in the confined areas of the villages. We also know they did not practice head deformation.

Living along the coast in an area around the Coos River the tribe probably extended much further down the river originally but was pushed into the more constrained area by their Athapascan neighbors.

When they were visited by Lewis and Clark in 1805, it was estimated there were some 1,500 Coos. In the 1850s they were moved to the Siletz Reservation in Oregon. Today there are possibly no pure-bloods left.

COOSA, now extinct, were at one time a small but important Muskhogean people related in all probability to the Creeks, and living in South Carolina. At one time or another they were called "Couexi" (1562), "Cocao" (1569), "Kussoes" (1707), and lastly "Coosah" in 1743, after which there is no record of them. They opposed the colonists in the 17th century, but in 1675 ceded land to the English. By the middle of the 18th century they appear to have been incorporated into the Catawba tribe, and some others may have joined the Creeks. They have also been referred to as the Cusabo. (*See* CUSABO).

COPAL (Náhuatl, *copalli*, "resin"; Maya, *pom*) is the resinous substance obtained from several trees throughout the world, but known most commonly by its American name. It occurs in colors ranging from transparent to deep yellow, and is used today in manufacturing paints, varnishes, and printing inks. The ancient Maya regarded copal as sacred, and gathered it to burn as an offering in large urns, braziers, and clay *incensarios*. It was a basic ingredient in Mayan religious ceremonies, as well as a tremendously valuable ritual sacrifice. The Spanish priests realized the close parallel between the use of copal and the Christian "frankincense and myrrh," and incorporated this successfully into their efforts to convert the Indians. Today, an interesting custom can be seen in Guatemala, where contemporary Mayans enter the Catholic church at Chichicastenango to worship and burn candles at the altar, and then retire to pray and burn copal at their own ceremonies. Copal can occasionally be found in Indian markets throughout the Maya area, offered for sale, put up in small leaf-wrapped packets.

FREDERICK DOCKSTADER

COPÁN, from Mayan *Copantli*, is the name of the ancient capital; a political *Departamento* in northwestern Honduras; and the locale of a major Classic Maya site overlooking the Copán River in the Motagua Valley. Although construction of the center apparently started *circa* AD 300, the primary period of its expansion from AD 500-800; the earliest glyphic date is 485. Copán is famous for its magnificent ball court, one of the most impressive Mayan constructions for that game built anywhere, and testifying to the ceremonial nature of *pok-ta-pok*, as it was called. The core of the city was built on a raised area, or Acropolis, and features a Great Plaza, which holds some of the world's sculptural triumphs; among these are some 38 esthetically superb monolithic stela, measuring between 9 and 12 feet in height, carved in elaborate designs from light green trachyte in the forms of humans—priests or nobles—dressed in ornate costumes and heavily laden with jade jewelry. The oldest of these is relatively simple, indicating the introduction of a new art form; but they become increasingly detailed, and the latest are astonishingly intricate. Another architectural feature is the 63-step Hieroglyphic Stairway, 33 feet in width, whose 2500+ individual carved designs constitute the largest single glyph inscription yet discovered. Copán was a major scientific center of the Mayan people, and specialized in astronomy; it was presumably here that the Great Calendar was perfected, which proved more accurate than any other chronological system until the development of modern calculating techniques. The last stela bears the date May 26, AD 800, after which Copán apparently plunged into a precipitous decline for unknown reasons, and was

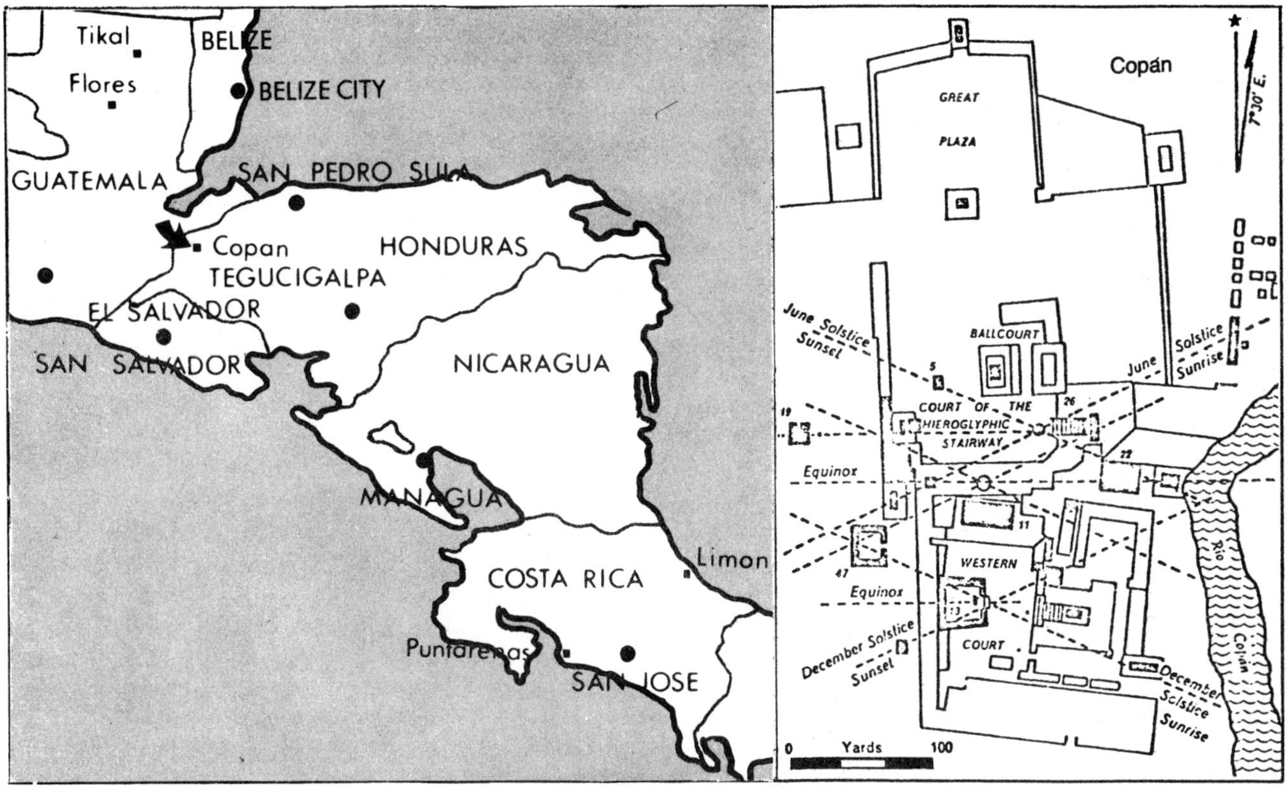

Copán, Copán Honduras.

The back of this stela is wedge-shaped, the personage is facing west, with a coiffeur similar to a jaguar's mask on top of which is two more elongated faces. In its rich ornaments are a chest-shield with a face framed by two hands; the sling has another face, cacao fruits and other designs. In its dome, various offerings were found. It dates from the year AD 622, Copán, Honduras.

Stela, Copán, Honduras.

This altar is one of the biggest and most recent found in the City of Copán, Honduras and dates from the year AD 800.

This stela was erected AD 735 near Monticulo 2, in the northern part of the main courtyard or amphitheatre, Copán, Honduras.

abandoned within a short time. In 1839 John Lloyd Stephens purchased the entire site for $50, to save it from further destruction by local people seeking building material. Today the area is occupied by the Chorti, who are thought by most scholars to be the descendants of the original occupants of Copán.

FREDERICK DOCKSTADER

COPEHAN. *See* WINTUN.

COPILCO, Náhuatl, meaning "on the peak," is a Middle Preclassic site in Villa Obregón, Mexico City, Mexico; dating *circa* 1800-1300 BC. It was covered by lava during the eruption of Xictli volcano, similar to Cuicuilco, *q.v.*, and as at Pompeii, Italy, many ruins can be seen *in situ* in the lava crust.

"COPPER." The primary manifestation of wealth among the Northwest Coast Indians included several objects among which dentalium shells, trade beads and woven textiles were most prominent. But by far the best known was the sheet copper *tinneh*, hammered and cut into a form resembling a large shield. These were made in various sizes ranging from some six feet in length to small miniatures two or three inches long; the average size was probably about 30 x 44 inches. The upper section usually had a totemic design painted or incised on the surface, with a large T-shaped embossed design below. Early *tinneh* may have been made from native copper lumps obtained in trade from the Athapascan people in the Copper River region, but most were created from ingots or sheets of commercial copper. One of the main sources was the copper sheeting obtained from wrecked ship hulls. At a potlatch, it was a frequent custom to cut up a portion of a *tinneh* and cast it away—usually into the sea, as a gesture of disdain for wealth. Their value was tremendous, even in early days, some being reckoned as worth eight or ten slaves, and a man wealthy enough to own one became famous for that fact alone. Legendary names were attached to well-known *tinneh*; they were carved as symbols of prestige on totem poles; and their ownership was an important economic fact. It gave a man, in effect, a bank account upon which he could draw when the occasion demanded; since the ownership was widely known, it was not possible to falsify one's wealth by a fraudulent claim.

FREDERICK DOCKSTADER

COPPER INUIT are so named for their extensive use of copper. Copper was used for both weapons and tools. In addition, the Copper Inuit also had a huge storage of soapstone, a valuable commodity. Some Eskimo tribes were known to travel hundreds of miles to mine soapstone. The Copper Inuit also traveled south to harvest wood, which was scarce in the north.

The general location of the Copper Inuit seems to vary, but they are most associated with the Coppermine River in Canada.

They were the last tribe of Eskimos to have contact with whites; hence there is still much material regarding their life patterns which is unknown.

It is known their chief deity is female. She is the Mother of Sea Mammals, called the "terrible one down there below." Legend says sea mammals were created when the joints of her fingers were cut off and fell into the sea. She ensures the food supply, and provides protection while gathering food. She has rules concerning unclean women, products of sea and land and dietary rituals. Curiously, rituals of the dead do not seem to involve her.

As legends indicate, sea mammals were an essential part of their diet although they also hunted caribou and moose inland, particularly on their wood gathering expeditions. During those expeditions they were sometimes forced to fight inland Indians for rights to hunt. Their dwellings were portable huts of wood and skin.

It is believed they would trade with other Eskimos as far east as Baffinland for such valuable commodities as soapstone and wood.

COPWAY, GEORGE (Ojibwa; 1818-1863), was a noted minister and author who challenged government misdealings with the Indians.

Born to a medicine man and chief of the Rice Lake

Chippewa (Ojibwa) near the mouth of the Trent River, Ontario, he was converted to Christianity in 1830 and became a Methodist minister in 1834. He collaborated with the Rev. Sherman Hall on Chippewa translations of *The Gospel of St. Luke* (1837) and *Acts of the Apostles* (1838). Copway, whose Indian name was Kah-ge-ga-gah-bowh, was also a strong proponent of the Indian heritage, producing works such as *The Life, History, and Travels of Kah-ge-ga-gah-bowh* (1847); *The Ojibway Conquest: A Tale of the Northwest* (1850); *Recollections of a Forest Life* (1851); and *Indian Life and Indian History* (1858).

Copway traveled and lectured extensively in Europe and the U.S. In England in 1851 he denounced the British land deals for Ojibwa ancestral lands as "robberies." In the U.S. Copway spoke out vigorously against treaty violations by the federal government and urged passage of a bill to create a permanent Indian territory on the land east of the Missouri River in what is now South Dakota. He died at Pontiac, Michigan.

COQUO (or Cocuo) was the name of a chief reportedly of the Gulf of Urabá, where Panama meets Colombia. After the Spanish conquistador Diego de Almagro undertook in 1524 the exploration of South America (leading to Pizarro's conquest of Peru), the Indians of the Gulf of San Miguel told him of Coquo's rich gold holdings. It is thought that the Chocó Indians were named for Coquo.

CORA exist as a large, diversified series of groups in the highlands of eastern Nayarit, Mexico; in the deep mountain canyons (especially of the Rio Jesús Maria and Rio San Pedro, with some in the Rio Grande de Santiago Canyon); and in the foothills and coastal zones of the Pacific lateral of Nayarit.

The Cora (pronounced kóra) have been known as the "Chora," "Chora Nayalita," and the "Nayarita." "Nayar" is a toponym of a central mesa of population and ceremonial importance. The term "Nayarita," though, was also used to refer to the Huichol, Tequal, and Tepecano. As in the past, most Cora identify themselves by their community of residence.

About half the Cora today live in titled grants of land from the Spanish Crown (*comunidades*). The other half live in mixed, at times dispersed, communities of peasant farmers or as day-wage workers on the coastal plantations. Aboriginally, there were probably a dozen territorially and culturally distinct groups that merged to form what today is "Cora." Boundaries were fluid.

Confusion exists as to which group should or could be classified as "Cora" at any one time. If "Cora" means the composite mountain-canyon dwellers of eastern Nayarit, then their territory today is less than half what it was at Spanish contact. In addition, fluctuations occurred as the Cora invaded (folk and military) other canyons and the coastal area. Today, Cora territories are receding quickly.

The Cora language belongs to the Huicholan subdivision (*i.e.* closely related to Huichol, Tequal, Guaynamota, and probably Totorame) of the generalized western Uto-Aztecan branch. Cora and Huichol dialects are mutually intelligible. Dialectation is pronounced among the Cora. This reflects territorial considerations as well as acculturation. East (canyon), west (mesa and foothill), north, and south dialects can be easily recognized, in addition to those from specific *comunidades*.

As in the past, the Cora today are predominently subsistence agriculturalists. Maize, beans, and squash are the most important crops. Hunting is unimportant, but gathering of wild crops is still an important supplement. Cattle raising is regionally important, but there are difficulties with quality and access to market. Meat is infrequently consumed.

The settlement pattern varies from region to region. In the most traditional areas, farmsteads are dispersed but located within a day's walking distance from a ceremonial center. Many Cora also live permanently in pueblos. The pueblos serve as focal points for most religious and governmental activity. Family social organization is loosely patrilineal. Lineages, however, are no longer very important.

Weaving and bead working are the two best developed crafts. Cora weaving is quite distinctive and very attractive. Regional styles are still preserved. Craft work for the tourist market has become an important income supplement for many Cora.

The Cora are a diversified group both in their culture and social organization. They are not tribal, but rather *comunidad* oriented peasants, living a colonial rather than strictly indigenous past. Cora diversification is

Cora

best seen in their religiious symbolism. Contemporary religion, in general, is a result of the syncretism of Catholic and native beliefs. The native cycle stressed nature gods and ancestors. Many of these gods now have semi-Catholic characters. For example, *Tayaó* (the sun god) is identified with God, *Gualu Tetéwa* (spirit of the underworld) with the Virgin of Guadalupe, and so on. Shamanism is still very important, especially for the agricultural cycle and curing Most religious activity, whether syncretized or native, is oriented toward agriculture and health. Extremely colorful ceremonies with masked dancers and animal sacrifices used to mark the important events of the yearly cycle. Many of these rites are quickly being modified, changed, and even discontinued.

The *comunidad* is governed by a large council of church majordomos and civil officers headed by a *Tatuán* (governor). Each majordomo is in charge of a saint and its yearly festival. The civil officers are responsible for the juridical and fiscal management of the *comunidad*. The offices are rotated among the qualified members of the *comunidad*, though the rotation is closely supervised by the elders and ex-officers. Government activities are concentrated at the *Casa Fuerte* (government house). Small churches exist in the pueblos and serve as the second focal point of civil-religious activity.

Cora mythology is rich in symbolism and historical content. The entire universe and all its phenomena are explained in detail in the many legends and myths. Only a few men each generation are able to master all this knowledge. They are called *baúsi* and are given very special treatment.

Very little archaeology has been accomplished in the Cora zone. Surveys have indicated that there is little complex architecture in the area. This most likely means that the pre-Hispanic Cora were very marginal to the Mesoamerican civilization. Contact with the Spanish began in the late 1520s. Many of the first contacts were violent and, after the Guzmán expedition, thousands of neighboring Indians, many in organized groups, took refuge among the Cora. Most of these refugees were from the civilized Totorame area of coastal Nayarit. A long period of merging of refugee and mountain cultural traits began. The Cora became a composite society dedicated to resisting the Spanish and raiding them whenever possible. Their violent raids were accompanied by livestock rustling and kidnappings. Their area continued to function as a refugee area for other Indians and slaves who were disgusted with Spanish rule. The Spanish finally decided to conquer the Nayaritas, but it was not until 1722 that a successful expedition was launched. The zone was at that time theocratically organized around two temples, *Thuacamota* and *Tauta*, each with a priesthood and soldiers. The area after conquest was reorganized into the Nuevo Reino de Toledo, and it included the Huichol. Jesuits were introduced to missionize the Cora. The zone remained marginal and unstable—a hot-bed for regional revolution and renegade activities. The most widespread revolt in which the Cora participated was that of Lozada's. Lozada was part Cora and understood their problems. He joined the French invaders during the 1860s to fight against the liberal government of Juarez because the French promised to preserve the *comunidad* land tenure system. He even attempted to capture Guadalajara with an Indian army after the French left Mexico.

During and after this period, Cora society developed a defensive stance which was accompanied by cultural conservatism. Relations with outsiders were difficult. This encapsulization lasted through the Mexican Revolution (1910-19) and the Cristero Revolt (1927-29), which continued as vendettas until the 1940s. Recent government activities have stressed economic development rather than military submission, and relations with outsiders have improved. The area is still regarded as volatile, however.

The Cora are currently undergoing an enormous cultural and social transition. As incorporation into the national economy becomes more complete, traditional lifestyles are quickly eroding. Cultural change is at times less obvious than social change among the Cora. Some Coras have become astute regional politicians and are encouraging economic integration into the national network. Various governmental and development bank programs for economic change and education are active within the zone. Many of these programs have been well received. Points of integration into the national economy are cattle raising, contract labor, and craft sales.

Estimates for the pre-Hispanic Cora populations are sheer guesses, but the figure 8-9,000 does not seem too high. By the time of the chartering of the *comunidades* in the late 1700s, the population was *c.* 2-4,000. Today, there are around 14-16,000 Cora including many thousand that live in the cities and coastal areas.

The Cora are a composite series of diversified societies. They survived as an independent refugee for 200 years after the Spanish had conquered most of the neighboring areas. Today, they live more a colonial lifestyle than a purely Indian one. Their traditions are quickly changing.

PHIL C. WEIGAND

CORBITANT (Wampanoag; fl. 17th century) was a minor sachem who unsuccessfully attempted to undermine the friendship between the settlers of the Plymouth Colony and Massasoit (*q.v.*), the principal chief of the Wampanoag. Corbitant conspired with the Narraganset to upset both Massasoit and the English simultaneously. In August 1621, while the Narraganset were moving against Massasoit, Corbitant kidnapped Squanto (*q.v.*) and two other Wampanoag Indians who were living at Plymouth. Intimidated by an English show of force, Corbitant released his captives and then on September 13 he made peace with the colonists, although he was never completely trusted by them.

CORICANCHA, also Curicancha, is "The Golden Enclosure," or the major Inca ceremonial center at Cuzco, Peru. Believed to have been constructed by the Emperor Viracocha as the Great Sun Center for purposes of unifying the people around a religious core, it was perhaps the largest single prehistoric center of the ancient Inca empire, covering over 1,200 square feet, housing between 3,000-4,000 inhabitants, and was certainly the most sacred enclave of the Inca world. The layout consisted of some six buildings constructed around a large patio, each dedicated to a different deity, whose manifestation was housed within the structure. The entire Coricancha was surrounded by a stone wall, with a single opening to guard against intrusion by outsiders. It was administered by the high priest, Huillac Umu, and a group of *mamaconas* whose lives were dedicated to the various deities, and who served the needs of the enclosure for life. Other inhabitants were a large number of *aklyaconas*—young girls selected for their physical beauty and noble birth, who were given to the Inca as concubines, as gifts to important nobles, or sacrificed to the Sun on major ceremonial occasions; and the hundreds of children who were ultimately sacrificed, or sometimes adopted into noble families. In one corner of the great enclosure was the *nina villca*, an ever-burning fire which ignited the sacrificial flames on religious occasions. The rich contents of the Coricancha, consisting of decorative gold sheet panels for the walls, gold offerings to the Sun, mummies of the ancestral dead (also covered with silver and gold ornaments), and magnificent textiles, provided much of the ransom paid by Atahuallpa in his ill-fated efforts to gain his freedom from Pizarro. In one section of the patio was the famous Inti Pampa (Field of the Sun) in which life-size golden replicas of corn, squash, beans, amid a field of solid gold straw, attended by llamas, alpacas and shepherds were erected in simulation of an agricultural garden, for the purpose of doing honor to the Great Sun. This magnificence was totally destroyed when the Dominicans built the Monastery of Santo Domingo in the 16th century, although the foundation walls can still be seen. Beyond the records of the golden loot taken from the Coricancha and the accounts made by the Spaniards at the time of the Conquest, we know little of the extent of this fabulous center.

FREDERICK DOCKSTADER

CORN. *See* MAIZE.

CORN DANCES. Corn was the premier plant food produced by Indian farmers and therefore had a major relation to their lifestyle and their economy. As such it entered deeply also into their religion, becoming a subject of ceremonies and dances. Corn or maize was probably developed as a domestic food crop somewhere in Central America or Mexico, most likely in Guatemala, at least by 2000 BC and probably much earlier. By the time of the coming of Columbus it had been bred and re-bred into many varieties to be growable in many climates and habitats from dry deserts to wet jungles, from cold coniferous forests to hot tropical savannahs, and also high up on the mountains.

General characteristics

Corn dances were found almost wherever corn was grown, from the plains of Patagonia, and the forests of southern Chile north through much of South America and most of Central America to the southwestern United States and then east and north to the Dakotas and to the St. Lawrence River in Quebec. The dances were almost completely religious in nature, as the successful growing of the corn crop was vital to the life of the Indian farmers, and times of drought or otherwise bad conditions for the corn were traumatic periods of near-starvation. Many of the dances were likely derived from such bad times and came to symbolize the efforts of each tribe to propitiate higher powers and make sure such disasters did not occur again. Thus a legend of the Delaware actually stated that during such a period the elders of the tribe counselled together to devise a dance ceremony to protect their people from such catastrophes. In many such dances the waving of the corn in the wind, its graceful symmetry and marvelous growth, were emphasized in the dance steps or other movements of the arms and body, while the deep beat of the drums symbolized the thunder and the tintinabulation of the rattles or gongs spoke of the good rain coming.

When a hunting and gathering tribe partially gave up its nomadic life for the more settled life of farming, symbolically the male element of the chase and war, identified among many American Indians with the eagle, became gradually tamed by the female element of growing things, symbolized by the corn maidens or corn goddesses. In another mythic meaning, gentle Mother Earth began to civilize Father Sky of the sun's blazing heat, the lightning's fiery spears, the wind's roaring and the rain's pelting in torrents. We can think of Mother Earth reaching up with her waving plants to meet the rain and sunlight of Father Sky, and the two joining together to fertilize the land and produce growth. But growth without fruition, corn without corn cobs, brought disaster to the Indian farmers, as sometimes happened because of disease, insect pests or other dangers. To the Indian this often meant that he had done something wrong, either through bad thoughts and actions or through imperfect performance of the ceremonies and dances. In some legends of North America this is put quite poetically in stories of the shy young corn maidens having to run away because of bad thoughts and actions on the part of the people so that they never become fertilized nor come to fruition in the form of the corn cobs, whose symbolic partner is the mature woman, the bearer of children.

All these ideas and others similar are often expressed in the dances. The corn dances are given at different times of the year, sometimes in the spring as encouragers to the corn to grow, other times, as at the winter solstice, to call the corn back to life from the death of winter, and, most joyously of all, as festive celebrations in the fall when the crop has been good and food is plentiful.

Regional variations

North America. North of the Rio Grande the warlike or Father Sky-like nature of the men's way of dancing is probably more emphasized. Like the jagged lightening, the men step up and down much higher and more vigorously than the women, who usually dance demurely with their feet scarcely rising above Mother Earth, as if they can only have strength by closeness to Her, yet both men and women dance in harmony. The violence of the men seems to beckon down the rain, while the sucking-like motion of the bare feet of the women appears like it is trying to pull the plants up out of the earth.

In the southwest, at such pueblos as the Zuñi and San Domingo, the male-female combination grows in strength hour after hour so that the watchers feel as if the very air is charged with power. They are not surprised when often after such a performance the desired rain falls.

Among the southwest Pueblos Koshare dancers put both ghostly and humorous elements into the Corn Dances. These men are usually painted all over white with black spots, but often with other colors on an arm or leg, and act as both clowns and warners while supposedly being spirits of past ancestors who are invisible to those present. The other dancers act as if they do not exist. The Koshare dancing is often made up of such leaps and gyrations as at times to appear unbelievable. As warners they not only poke awake sleepers, warn those who break rules, and pick up objects dropped by the regular dancers, but also act as rescuers of small lost or hurt children. The humorous tricks they pull are actually meant to emphasize by contrast the deadly seriousness of the other dancers.

The so called Busk or Green Corn Dances of the southeastern tribes, such as the Natchez, the Creeks, Cherokees, and Choctaws, generally happened at the time of the first harvest of the corn in lkate August. Besides being harvest dances, they also were thought of as a time for purifying, in which useless things were thrown away or burned, the whole village cleaned up, old fires put out and, after three days or so of fasting, new fires were started, and both men and women were purified by taking a special drink that caused vomiting and other internal cleansing. Then followed several days of dancing, with different dances, such as the turkey dance of the women, a tadpole dance to symbolize "new life," and so on. Besides a march down to the river where the men dived in to each retrieve four sacred stones, the Busk was finally finished by a Mad Dance, which symbolized the last chance the people had to act wantonly, for after that they must act with decorum and purity. During the Busk all bad feelings were supposed to be ended, old debts forgiven, and a new era of peace and goodwill started.

The Bread Dance of the Shawnee of the Ohio Valley was given at the time of first planting, in mid-May. The Shawnees usually used slow and dignified steps, the men and women dancing either intermingled or in separate lines, the changing lines and circles beautifully managed and designed. Later the women danced with a peculiar twisting motion of both feet. Between dances there was often fun and repartee as both men and women would claim to have done the best dancing and so won the competition.

At most North American Corn Dances old chiefs or medicine men often gave speeches, warning the people and their children to be good and honorable and to help each other and the tribe.

Mesoamerica. Probably the main Corn Dance of the Aztecs of Mexico involved a woman who was dressed up beautifully in embroidered clothes and red sandals, with a turquoise disk necklace, and a brilliant headdress of green and crimson quetzal plumes. The Sacred Quetzal Bird's long beautifully emerald tail feathers represented the growing corn all through Mexico and Central America. The woman herself symbolized the goddess of corn, *Xilonen*. In her hand she carried a magic rattle and a shield. In the dawn, after a sleepless night, the men formed lines, all holding aloft stalks of corn called *totopantli*, to represent the harvest. The women followed *Xilonen* and everybody began to dance and sing, the symbolic goddess shaking her rattle, as she led the way to the Temple of Tineopan, where the priests blew on their horns and conches and the priestesses banged the two-toned gongs to create a terrific din. As usual with the Aztecs, such ceremonies had to end with a human sacrifice and the representation of the Goddess *Xilonen* lost her head to the swish of a gold-handled knife, symbolizing the corn losing its heads before being eaten.

The ancient Maya of Yucatan and Guatemala were generally not so bloodthirsty with their dances. Perhaps their most unusual corn dance came in certain years when there was a scarcity of water and a great abundance of corn sprouts, when the Mayan priests turned to a god called *Yax Cocay Mut*, "the green firefly pheasant," and called on the old women of the tribe to perform a spectacular dance done on stilts, three feet or more high, after which they offered to the god dogs made of pottery with food placed on their backs. This was supposed to help the corn produce.

In western Panama the Guaymi tribe of the mountain country had an even more spectacular dance at the time of the planting of the corn, called the Balseria by the Spanish, in which two lines of men took turns whirling six foot long sticks and then throwing them at each others' legs, which made the opposite side dance to escape them. The dance, if done properly, they said, would help the corn grow and give a good crop.

South America. The great Quechua and Aymara tribes of western South America, the back-bones of the

Inca Empire, probably put on the most spectacular corn dances of their continent. The first was given in the month of Capac Raymi (December) and was part of the major religious ceremony of the whole year, in honor of Pachacamana—the Earth Mother. Everybody in the Inca Empire, including the Incá himself, always preceded by a contingent of Sacred Sun Virgins, took part in the dances in the streets, and in the temples.

In the month of Aryihua (April), the "Month of the Corn Ears of a Thousand Colors," there was another great harvest festival at which a Sacred White Llama was dressed in bright red cloth, hung with Big Ear ornaments, surrounded by royal attendants, and given coca and chicha (a corn drink). Fifteen ordinary llamas were sacrificed to give honor to it, and then the dancing began. This usually consisted of men playing on drums and horn pipes while the women danced in circles, first in one direction and then in the other, but sometimes the men, blowing their panpipes, also danced in circles. The tunes were very haunting and beautiful.

Contemporary situation

Where agricultural tribes are still clinging to their ancient culture and religion or some elements of it the Corn Dances are still yearly events. This is particularly true of the Pueblo tribes of Arizona and New Mexico and the Quechua and Aymara of South America. Usually the dances and ceremonies are somewhat simplified over what they used to be, or changes have been made. For example, the Aymara in South America now kill the Sacred White Llama at the time of the dance instead of letting it live and die of old age as was done in the ancient times. Other dances have been corrupted because of too much alcoholic drinking. Thus the Balseria or Stick Game Dance of the Guaymi of Panama was so ruined by liquor that it often turned into a drunken brawl.

In the modern pluralistic Indian societies, particularly in North America, where there are so many people of mixed blood from different tribes, corn dances have not been as popular as war, hoop and round dances, etc., because the corn dances are directly associated with unified tribal efforts to produce a successful corn crop.

VINSON BROWN

CORNPLANTER (Seneca; *c.* 1732-Feb. 18, 1836) was a chief who fought against the Americans during the U.S. War of Independence, but who later concluded treaties that ceded substantial tracts of Indian land to the U.S. Born at Conewaugus, New York, Cornplanter was of mixed parentage. He derived his exalted position among the Seneca from his mother, descendant of the tribe's ruling family. Cornplanter's father was a white trader of either English or Dutch ancestry named John O'Bail or O'Beal who lived in Albany, New York. Cornplanter was also known as John O'Bail; his Indian name was Gayentwahga. Little is known of his early life, although it is generally believed that he was present at the defeat of Gen. Edward Braddock near Fort Duquesne (present-day Pittsburgh, Pennsylvania) in 1775. Also as a young man he visited his father in Albany.

Although he was reluctant to join the other tribes of the Iroquois League on the British side during the American Revolution, Cornplanter finally went along with the tribes in the confederacy who pledged allegiance to the crown. He was one of the two Iroquois war chiefs named by the British. Throughout the hostilities, Cornplanter participated in raiding parties that terrorized white settlements throughout New York and Pennsylvania. When Gen. John Sullivan invaded Seneca country in 1779, Cornplanter fought valiantly; but his hated rival—another Seneca chief named Red Jacket—fled upon catching sight of Sullivan's troops at Lake Canandaigua. Sullivan defeated the Seneca, inflicting heavy losses, burning the villages and destroying the crops.

Nevertheless, the Seneca—as well as the other Iroquois tribes—never felt that they had been conquered by the Americans. Therefore, when Cornplanter participated in the treaties of 1784, 1789, 1797, and 1802—all of which ceded substantial Indian territory in western New York to the U.S.—his stature among the Seneca went into eclipse. Meanwhile, Red Jacket

Cornplanter

seized upon the tribe's sense of humiliation at this time to promote his own power and popularity; he protested the land cessions to which Cornplanter signed his name. In fact, Cornplanter became so despised that for a time his life was in danger of being taken by members of his own tribe. Cornplanter, however, an eloquent orator, continued to work to assure that the U.S. government would live up to the provisions of the treaties. In 1790 he sent a message to Pres. George Washington in Philadelphia, laying before him the grievances of the Seneca.

The white inhabitants of New York and Pennsylvania began to look upon Cornplanter in a different light. Far from the terrifying enemy he had been during the Revolution, Cornplanter was later considered to be a "good Indian." On March 16, 1796, therefore, the State of Pennsylvania granted the Seneca chief a 640-acre tract of land "for his many valuable services to the whites." By 1816 Cornplanter owned 1,300 acres along the banks of the Allegheny River, and he received a pension of $250 annually from the U.S. government.

About 1820 Cornplanter experienced a series of visions which he claimed were confrontations with the Great Spirit. Instructed by the Great Spirit to sever all ties with white people, Cornplanter suddenly renounced Christianity and then burned all the mementos (flag, medals, belt, hat, sword, etc.) of his warrior days. Moreover, his favorite son, Henry O'Bail, who had been carefully educated, became a drunkard, thus adding to the trials of Cornplanter's later years. He was still an impressive figure at the time of his death in 1836. A monument was erected to his honor by the State of Pennsylvania at the site where he was buried on his land near the Allegheny.

CORNPLANTER, JESSE (Seneca; ?-*c.* 1961), was a tribal leader who was an author, a carver of ceremonial False Face masks, a painter, and a singer for tribal ceremonies. The last living descendant of Chief Cornplanter (*c.* 1732-1836), he was born at Cattaraugus Reservation, New York. Much of his work, including *Legends of the Longhouse* (1938), was an attempt to present and interpret the myths and legends which form the basis of the Longhouse religion (or the religion of Handsome Lake).

Cornplanter, Jesse

CORNPLANTER INDIAN RESERVATION is a tract of land given to the Indians of Pennsylvania by the state in honor of the Seneca chief Cornplanter "for his many valuable services to the whites." The land was given to Cornplanter on March 16, 1796, and was 640 acres in size in northwest Pennsylvania on the banks of the Allegheny River. By the early 1970s there were no Indians on the reservaton because of the construction of the Kinzua Dam on the Allegheny River.

CORNSTALK (Shawnee; *c.* 1720-1777) was a chief, known to both Indians and whites as a skillful general and an impressive orator, who resisted the encroachment of settlers on Indian lands along the Ohio-Virginia frontier.

Cornstalk (properly Keightughqua) was the leader of the Shawnee living on the Scioto River, Ohio. He led raids against the British colonists in the French and Indian War (1763-64). During 1764-74 he participated in minor outbreaks along the Ohio-Virginia frontier, but he was most often a mediating influence and at times provided escorts for white traders. Cornstalk's hostility was directed toward settlers who were moving onto Indian lands.

When his brother Silver Heels was shot in 1774, Cornstalk approached Lord Dunmore, governor of Virginia, to help end frontier hostilities. Dunmore's response was to organize a force of 1,100 colonial volunteers against the Indians. On October 10, 1774—in what is known as Lord Dunmore's War—Cornstalk led 1,000 warriors against Dunmore at Point Pleasant, at the mouth of the Kanawha River in present-day West Virginia. Cornstalk lost the bloody battle, but his strategy and tactics gained him the respect of the whites. Driven back to the Scioto River, Cornstalk signed a peace treaty in November near present-day Chillicothe, Ohio.

Despite opposition from his people and increased pressure from white settlers Cornstalk persuaded the

Shawnee to honor the treaty. In 1777 Cornstalk returned to Point Pleasant to warn of possible renewed hostilities. He and then his son were taken hostage, and soon after they were murdered in retaliation for the death of a white settler by a group of Mingo Indians. This triggered an uprising of the Shawnee who were not quelled until 1794.

COROADO are closely related linguistically and culturally to the Puri and *Coropó*. Over a hundred years ago the Coroado were a single tribe with the Puri, who later, as the result of a feud between two families, became their enemies.

At the beginning of the 19th century, the Coroado occupied the plain bounded in the east by the Serra de São Geraldo (São Joze) and in the west by the Serra da Onza in eastern Brazil. They lived mainly along the Xipotó Novo River (Rio dos Coroados). The Coroado were originally divided into three main subgroups: the Maritong, the Cobanipaque, and a third (the name of which had been lost).

During the 17th century, the Coroado were raided by the Paulistas and, as a result they remained bitter enemies of the whites until 1763, when they were induced to make peace. In 1767 they were placed under the authority of special government agents. They were harshly treated by the colonists who exploited them.

In 1813, the Coroado were scattered in 150 settlements, each consisting of one or two families. The total population was about 1,900.

In recent years, some Coroado still remained in the Aldea da Pedra on the upper Parahyba River. The population is probably several hundred.

Culture

Subsistence activities. Originally typical forest nomads, the Coroado subsisted by hunting and collecting fruits and roots, especially the fruits of palm shoots, caratinga, cava, and many other tubers. During the dry season, the Coroado gathered larvae of *bixo da taquara*, which they kept in bamboo receptables, using the fat mainly for preparing corn cakes. Like most forest nomads, they were constantly on the lookout for honey.

The Coroado learned to grow crops and, at the beginning of the 19th century, cultivated maize, gourds, bananas, cará and beans. They were poor farmers, however, and continued to subsist, in large measure, on the produce of the bush.

The Coroado were skillful stalkers and expert trackers. They lured birds by perfectly imitating calls. Little is known of their other hunting methods except that they caught animals in pitfalls and traps. Birds were captured by means of a noose fixed to the end of a long pole.

The Coroado, who raised some crops, had elaborate cooking techniques and utensils, such as basketry sifters and various earthenware vessels. They prepared mush with maize pounded in cylindrical wooden mortars, boiled game, roasted it on a spit, or smoked it on a babracot.

Domesticated animals. The Coroado had dogs and fowl which they had acquired from the whites.

Dwellings. The hut of the Coroado was obviously derived from the primitive Puri lean-to. It had the form of a thatched gabled roof resting directly on the ground. Larger huts with wattle-and-daub walls were imitations of the mestizo house.

The main piece of Coroado furniture was the cotton hammock. The Coroado hut contained a platform for storing food and small articles, a wooden mortar, gourds, and various pieces of pottery.

Dress. The aboriginal Puri, Coroado and Coropó went naked; but the men, when first described had already adopted European clothes, while Coroado women wore homemade skirts.

Feather headdresses and feather bracelets were worn by both Puri and Coroado men. Both Puri and Coroado hung around their necks or slung across their chests necklaces composed of animal teeth and of various seeds. Young women wrapped bark strips around their wrists and arond their legs, under the knees and around the ankles. These bindings, which served to make the joints slender, were removed after marriage.

All body hair was removed. Both Puri and Coroado painted dots and linear motifs in red (urucú or red clay) and black (genipa) on their persons.

Among the Coroado, both sexes were tattooed by a method not reported elsewhere in South America except for the Tehuelche.

Transportation. No craft of any kind was used by the Coroado.

Women carried their goods in large baskets. Children were suspended on the hip with a bark sling or carried on their mother's back, supported by a tumpline or hanging in a net.

Social and political organization. The Coroado tribe was split into small groups or bands, each of which comprised one or two extended families totaling some 40 people. Each group lived apart, uniting with others only for defense against enemies or to wage war. Such a group was under the authority of a chief, generally the oldest man of the community.

Within this group there existed a great amount of cooperation. They cultivated their fields in common, hunted together, and enjoyed "commonly the produce of their work." Young people submitted willingly to the authority of older persons and of valiant hunters and warriors. Leaders were distinguished by beautiful feather diadems.

Rites. When two parties met, one would make a speech and then both would burst into laments for the dead.

Warfare and cannibalism. The Coroado have been accused of cannibalism, without evidence.

Childbirth. The Coroado woman when pregnant observed chastity. She and her husband refrained from eating the flesh of certain animals and lived chiefly on fish and fruits. Delivery took place in the forest in a spot protected from moonlight, which was considered harmful to a newborn baby. Soon after the birth, the mother washed herself and resumed her normal activities. A few days later, both she and the baby were fumigated with tobacco smoke by a shaman, an occasion which was celebrated by hearty drinking. Children were nursed until they were 4 to 5 years old.

Marriage. Men married at the age of 18, girls when they were about 12. The marriage ceremony consisted of the presentation of game and fruit to the bride's parents. Acceptance of the gift sealed the marriage. The new couple settled with the family of either spouse. Monogamy seems to have prevailed, though chiefs or good hunters had two or more wives. Marital ties were brittle and easily dissolved. Women were often blamed for the separation because of their misconduct.

Death observances. The Coroado placed their dead in large jars, if these were available, after they had broken the limbs of the corpse, lest the ghost return to haunt the living. A person was buried in his hut, his possessions were deposited over the grave, and the house was burned or abandoned. If the deceased had been a chief, the whole settlement was deserted. Relatives cut their hair, and the women painted their bodies black. They uttered funeral laments at dawn, in the evening, and whenever they passed a grave.

Ghosts (which often appeared in the guise of lizards, caimans, jaguars, deer or deer-footed men) were the souls of wicked persons or of people who had not been buried according to prescribed rites.

Shamans. Shamans consulted the souls of the dead about the outcome of important events, such as a war party or an expedition to collect *ipecacuanha*. They also summoned spirits to inquire where abundant game could be found or to ascertain whether they were threatened by a war party. When the Coroado feared an attack by their traditional enemy, the Puri, their shamans conjured up the souls of a dead Puri and asked him the whereabouts of his fellow tribesmen. If the answers were alarming, the shamans advised the people to take defensive measures and to build a fence around the camp.

The Coroado shaman conjured spirits at night while blowing clouds of smoke from his pipe. Spectators could hear the steps of the approaching spirits and their whistled answers to the questions of the shaman. The spirits departed crying "like macuco birds."

The Coroado lived in great fear of sorcerers. If witchcraft were suspected to be the cause of a death, some flesh or skin was cut from the victim's head and countermagic was practiced on it.

Medicine. Sick people were treated by shamans, who sucked them, fumigated them with tobacco smoke, and rubbed them with saliva or with certain herbs.

The Coroado practiced bloodletting with a small bow and an arrow headed with a piece of crystal. This operation was also performed at intervals on healthy persons, especially women. The Coroado incised the skin around a sore spot with a sharp stone or a piece of bamboo. Some men, to improve their marksmanship, cut themselves slightly across the upper arm.

Shamans used various herbs in their massages and put different leaves and grasses on wounds and infections. Most of their drugs were for external use, and like the Chaco, the Coroado showed a strong reluctance to taking internal medicine.

COROBICI are named after a chieftain encountered by Gil González Davila during the conquest of Central America by the Spaniards. During the Conquest Period, the Corobici were located along the southern shores of Lake Nicaragua between the Rio Frio and the Cordillera Volcánica. It has been claimed that they inhabited the Solentiname Islands in the lake, as well as the territory extending westward across the Cordillera de Tilleran and through the valley of the Rio Tenorio to the north shore of the Gulf of Nicoya. Spanish intrusion into the area forced the Corobici to retreat to the plains near San Carlos. Later, known as the Guatuso, they were located in the inaccessible region at the headwaters of the Rio Frio and in the valleys of the Rios Zapote, Guacalito and the Cucaracha to the west. Separate groups of these people, either indigenous or fugitive groups, were found in the region between Bagaces and Esparata. In the 18th century they raided the countryside until they were eventually driven back north across the mountains. By the 1860s they were relatively isolated occupying areas in the upper Rio Frio Valley. Recent exploration and conquest of the valley has resulted in the decimation of the Guatuso leaving only remnants of these people in the upper sections of the Rio Frio Valley.

The locations of the Corobici or the Guatuso and their relationship to other known tribes in the area is a controversial issue. The tribe may have been originally Guetar people but as a result of their social relationships with their neighbors, the Chontal and the Chorotega, had become a heterogeneous population and culture. It has also been suggested that the Corobici and the Guatuso are different peoples. The Guatuso, located in the Rio Frio area, may be part of the Rama Indian tribes. The Corobici may have occupied the Nicoya Peninsula proper as well as the lands on the northern side of the bay. Two factors are significant: 1) the tribes in the Central Costa Rican area, including the Corobici, were undergoing considerable intermixing of populations and culture; and 2) the tribes existing in the pre-Hispanic period, as a result of high population densities and consequent warfare, were forced to migrate out of their territories into regions quite different from their original place of habitation. The delimitation of the habitat of the prehistoric, the contact period, and present-day Corobici depends upon the discovery on the coast as well as in the highland areas of social forms and material culture which may be assigned to the Corobici peoples.

The Corobici are classified with the Talamanaca division of cultures of Central America. These were quickly overrun by the Spaniards and a majority of the cultures have long been extinct. Practically all of the people that have survived the Spanish Conquest, as well as subsequent intrusions by black slaves from the Caribbean islands, have been dislocated from their aboriginal habitats.

The archaeological record and the reports of the early chroniclers in comparison to the modern social structure of the Corobici (and other tribes in the area) show drastic changes in the organization of the society. Among modern populations intensive horticulture, dense populations, large villages, class-structured society, the mounds, temples, idols and priests, warfare, cannibalism and human trophies, the elaborate death rites and the technological and esthetic sophistication in metallurgy, weaving, ceramics and stone sculpture are absent. The modern tribes live in small villages, weave simple cloths, make only plain pots. The societies are unstratified and the religious cults are attenuated.

Early chroniclers reported agricultural activities to have been more extensive in the past than in the present. Slash-and-burn agriculture is universally employed. Men clear the fields with their male relatives or friends and simple ceremonies are practiced at this time. Aboriginal foods (maize, beans, yucca, gourds, camote, cacao and others) remain the basis of the diet except where rice, plantains and pigeon peas are grown in large quantities. Game is hunted with the bow and arrow or with the gun. Wild honey and larvae from the hives are collected from the forest and considered a delicacy. Nets, fiishhooks, spears and bows and single or multiple-pointed arrows are used to fish. In small cases small fish are caught by hand. There are early references to the presence of domesticated animals including the dog. In modern times people keep dogs, cattle, poultry, tamed parrots and small native mammals. Most food is prepared by boiling. Meat is smoked or salted if it is not immediately consumed. Maize is boiled and later ground on the metate. It is either eaten fresh or allowed to ferment. It is also formed into cakes, wrapped in husks and steamed.

Early chroniclers report that dwellings were either large or organized in small clusters and were usually fortified by means of a stockade. Unfortified hamlets of several houses were also reported. In modern times the houses are grouped in small communities. Most families live in single structures but larger families have two buildings, the second serving as a kitchen and the home of older people. The modern house lasts about five years; is seldom repaired and the new house is built on an unoccupied site. Round, rectangular or square houses are built, none of which have a specialized function. House sites are usually inherited through the male line. The Guatuso (Corobici?) had houses scattered over a considerable area. The houses were low, pitched-roofed buildings, open at the ends and sides under the eaves.

The aboriginal man's clothing consisted of a breechclout, a narrow strip of bark cloth about two meters long which was passed between the legs and wrapped around the waist. Usually it was held up by a belt. The woman's clothing consisted of the breechclout and a knee-length, wrap-around skirt. Both sexes frequently were bare-breasted but a short jacket was also worn by both males and females. The Guatuso (Corobici?) were reported to have decorated themselves with paint.

The economy depends on agricultural production but a system of trade for additional items is also carried on. European goods such as cattle, clothing, machetes, fishhooks, and sugar have forced the people to adopt a system of money exchange which is apparently foreign to their traditional trading patterns.

The whole social structure of the Corobici, as well as other tribal groups in the Central Costa Rican area, is now being modified. At the time of the Conquest, the Guetar (Corobici?) were divided into three classes: nobles, commoners, and slaves, the last being women and boys captured in war. Captive men were sacrificed. The modern tribes are less stratified. The basic social unit is the family, a man, his wife or wives, and their children. Land, cattle and other property is held in the names of the men and the boys although women own some land, cattle and all of the household goods. Evidence from the early colonial documents and from more recent sources indicates that the tribes were organized as feudal states. During the wars with the Spaniards, each Indian polity was welded into a strong unit. When these were broken up after the Conquest, realignments were attempted but in modern times the heads of small localized groups hold political power. All of the tribes in the area, including the Corobici, are more or less warlike. The early chroniclers emphasize the fact that the wars were waged for the purpose of acquiring captives for sacrifice but economic, political and territorial competition for control over lands and people also were contributing factors to the incidence of warfare. Early accounts of religious activities are confined to remarks noting that the priests were sacred and secular officials. Only the more important of the many ceremonies reported during the past centuries are still celebrated. Ceremonies from the pre-Conquest period had a religious background and in the modern day involve varying degrees of drunkenness and brawling.

Ellen R. Kintz

COROBICI (Corobici; fl. 16th century), (spelled variously Caribici, Corevisi, *etc.*) was chief of a populous tribe of Costa Rica, living along the southern shores of Lake Nicaragua at the time of their discovery by the Spanish explorer Gil González Dávila in 1522. Corobici's tribe allegedly had migrated before this encounter, and later were to flee to the north. The

Spanish named the tribe after its chief, though it was later called the Guatuso.

CORTINA RANCHERIA, in Colusa County, California, is a federal reservation of 640 acres. It is home to members of the Wintun tribe. By the early 1970s there were very few residents upon the land. Tribal members live off the reservation.

The land for the rancheria was purchased by the Secretary of the Interior in 1907. While few members live on the rancheria, it is still used to bury the dead. There are no services on the rancheria; and the relations between Indians and whites in the area have been strained in recent years. Whites let their cattle graze on the Indian land, and the Wintun, feeling estranged from the white men, do not object. In recent years, the Wintun have been attempting to terminate their ownership of the rancheria.

COSMOLOGY. The basic characteristic of the Indian socio-religious system appears to have been an excessive interest in the movements of the heavenly bodies, in particular Venus, and a catastrophic cosmology involving the destruction of previous world orders. Such religious rituals as human sacrifice and the sacred ball game (*tlachtli*) were closely tied to cosmic events. The *Popol Vuh* and other native texts clearly express a relationship between a dread of recurring disasters and propitiatory human sacrifice, including the decapitation of the ball game losers. The legendary ball game in which Hunter and Jaguar Deer win out over the Lords of Hell can be interepreted as referring to the advent of the present Sun and Moon, stated to be the successors of those of earlier, catastrophically destroyed world orders. Many of these disaster-constructs clearly held an almost equally important place among the peoples of North and South America from whom there are no written records and less systematic information with regard to cosmic myths.

Regional variations

Such strong similarities of cosmology and of astronomical practice as are evident in different areas of the Americas suggest a common point of origin. They may represent, however, an attempt by various peoples to record traumatic experiences commonly suffered over the entire continuum and to keep a close check on celestial events. It may be argued that roughly similar astronomical observatories and observations might result from the objective astronomical facts that are on display nightly. Longitude, latitude, and time, however, strongly affect the events that could have been observed. Moreover though the objective astronomical facts may have been roughly the same as similar latitudes and dates, the subjective interpretation of these events and the mental constructs built on them—such as zodiac and solar and lunar calendars—should not be the same unless contact between the peoples had taken place. In fact, similar architectural practices and a similar use of astronomy for the timing of agricultural and other rituals extend over a wide range of latitude as do various of the subjective constructs.

The early development of Native American astronomy cannot as yet be closely pinpointed as to time or place, but it is significant that, in general, the regional variations in architectural traditions, cosmologies, and subjective astronomical constructs are more a matter of degree than of kind. A continuum exists between the intense astronomical concern evident in the Mesoamerican high cultures and the practices that can be detected in the North American Southwest and in the Mound Builders areas of the Midwest. The remarkable beauty and variety of Mayan and Mexican architectural structures, as well as the enigma of the abandonment of the sacred centers, has long intrigued archeologists and astronomers.

Cataclysms on Earth. Mesoamerican archeoastronomy and ethnoastronomy may help solve a question upon which scientists are divided—*i.e.*, whether the Earth has in reality undergone catastrophic events within historical times. A large-scale comparison of Mesoamerican site destructions between 1500 and 600 BC and a systematic study of Mesoamerican astronomical records of early planetary movements, should be of use.

One especially notable feature of Mesoamerican ceremonial centers, the ball court, has long been thought to have been associated with a solar cult, but may instead show a significant association with Venus. Evidence has been produced to demonstrate an association with Venus by comparing iconography on the four walls of the ball court at Tajin (dated AD 1000) with a legend in which the planet-god comes down to earth, indulges in a sinful love affair, suffers, dies, and is transformed. The Caracol at Chichén Itzá also appears to have had significant alignments with regard to Venus.

The sacred ball game may have commemorated a cosmic catastrophe in which, as the epics specifically state, a former world age ended and the present one began, the successful ball game players (Hunter and Jaguar Deer) becoming the present Moon and Sun. It is not uncommon for the heroes of an astronomical myth to end up as celestial bodies, but rarely is the process terminating a world age as explicitly described as in the Mesoamerican epics and legends. The Mesoamerican cosmology of world ages ended by cosmic destruction parallels the sequence of events outlined in a hypothesis of the history of Venus. In that hypothesis, Venus entered the solar system as a comet, and the Earth passed through the tail of this comet in 1400 BC, after which Venus reapproached at dreaded 52-year intervals until in 700 BC it came into collison with Mars, and was propelled to its present, safe orbit. Whatever the explanation, clearly the catastrophic legendary materials and the anomalies of the Olmec site destruction must be explained. Although the objective reality of the cosmic disturbances described in Mesoamerican epics is not yet scientifically studied, mathematical analysis of possible orbital changes, based on findings from space exploration and on astrophysical hypothesis, indicates that such a celestial dislocation as is described in the *Popol Vuh* and in the *Ipuwer* papyrus is by no means impossible. Studies of Venus observations made by ancient Mesopotamian observers also suggest that the early behavior of Venus was erratic. Ancient descriptions and iconographic representations of Venus suggest that the planet had a much greater size and brilliance than at present. Clearly the Mesoamerican, Mesopotamian, and Egyptian observations and cosmologies, as well as the *Ipuwer* documents, should be made the subject of a comparative study. The "errors" reported may lie not with the observations of the ancient astronomers but in the assumption that present planetary orbits may be taken as models for those of earlier periods.

The destruction of early American ceremonial centers, similarly, should be compared with that of Bronze Age site destructions elsewhere, and equated with geological and other evidence of tectonic and volcanic events. One scholar's suggestion that Mesoamerican cultural discontinuities may be attributed to the collapse of a theocracy that had shown itself unable to control destructive celestial events is worth consideration. It must be noted, however, that Olmec construction dates are suspect, due to the possibility of contamination during large-scale combustion attributable in a hypothesis of cosmic disaster. *Trez Zapotes*, for example, yields a quite improbable date of 9000 BC; its early levels are sealed with volcanic ash. Also, asphalt lumps have been noted at San Lorenzo. Clearly the Olmec site destructions are of importance with regard to Bronze Age site destructions elsewhere.

The classic Mesoamerican cultures flowered so late that textual references and astronomical notations may well contain information with regard to the actual and objective events that were the basis for Mesoamerican and other legendary and epic accounts of the destruction that ended the last world age and brought about the present orbits of Sun and Moon, Venus and Mars. It may not be coincidental that the events described in American accounts are strikingly similar to those described by *Ipuwer*, half a world away. In short, Mesoamerican and other ancient historians may have been romancing or they may have been recounting ancestral stories and eyewitness accounts of events that did indeed happen in the "real world out there."

COSTANOAN Indians were a comparatively simple people found mainly along the coast of California from the Golden Gate and Susuin and San Pablo bays on the north to the Big Sur River south of Monterey on the south, and extending inland to the crest of the main Coast Range from just north of Mount Diablo in the north to about Santa Rita Peak in the south. The name Costanoan is derived from the Spanish word "Costaños," meaning "Coast Peoples," and has become, by steady usage, the only name generally accepted for this group of small tribes with a similar language.

Social and cultural boundaries and subdivisions

The Costanoans were a part of the Central California Culture Area, which included the Coast Miwok, Pomo, Wintun and Maidu to the north, the Bay, Valley and Hill Miwok, and the Yokuts of the San Joaquin Valley to the east. The Esselen and Salinan peoples to the immediate south had a similar sparce culture, but were more strongly influenced by the culturally complex and creative Chumash and Gabrielino of southern California.

The Costanoans themselves were divided into two main subdivisions, those who dwelt around San Francisco Bay and south to Santa Cruz on the coast, and then inland to the drainage of the Coyote River that empties into the south end of the bay; and those who dwelt farther south in the drainage systems of the lower part of the Salinas River, and all of the river basins of the Carmel and San Benito rivers.

Language

The Penutian Language Family, to which the Costanoans belonged, is a very large family, covering many tribes along the Pacific Coast. Other Penutian-speaking tribes in California besides the Costanoan included the Miwok, Wintun, and Maidu to the north and northeast of the Costanoans, and the widespread and numerous Yokut peoples in the San Joaquin Valley to the east and southeast. The Costanoans themselves had at least seven separate dialects, of which the two most widely different, were the Soledad to the far south, and the Saklan to the far northeast by Susuin Bay, which, by some linguists, is considered more closely related to the Wintun.

Summary of tribal culture

Subsistence and economy. Deer was hunted in the usual Pacific coastal way of using a deer head and skin to disguise the hunter when he crept up on the game with bow and arrow. Rabbits were shot with arrows, but also driven in a communal drive aided by fire to a central place where they were killed with clubs. Deadfall traps included one with a heavy board, propped up to fall on mice, rats, etc., and a twig cage with one end propped up to trap quail. A kind of bola, unique for central California, of two bones on a string, was whirled and thrown to catch birds. Large wood rat nests were burned to drive out their occupants for killing with clubs. Dogs were used for hunting, deer, raccoons, etc., something unique on the central coast. A feather fan was used to blow smoke into ground squirrel holes, forcing them out. Bows were either simple self-bows, or very well made and strong sinew-backed bows. Fish spears and nets were used to catch fish, and night fishing, with a bonfire to attract the fish, was unique on the central coast. Soaproot was mashed up and thrown in pools to poison fish.

An important food was acorns, knocked down mainly from live oak trees and later leached with water to take out the poison, either in a sand basin, through fern leaves, or in an open-work basket. Acorns were ground up to a fine meal and often cooked into a very thick mush in water-tight baskets with the help of red-hot stones. Ground seeds were cooked this way, but also by parching them when tossed in a basket over hot coals, so skillfully the basket did not catch fire. Yellow jacket larvae were eaten raw, but grasshoppers were caught and roasted in pits. Seaweed was dried and eaten to provide salt, but salt was also taken after evaporation in ocean rock pools. Roots and bulbs were dug up with digging sticks, while mussels and clams were the main sea food, especially relied upon in winter.

Technology and arts. The domed and circular or conical dwellings were usually small, meant only for one family, and covered with either tule mats or brush over a willow framework. The old was burnt down and a new home was built whenever fleas inside got too numerous. Skins were used for bedding and placed over tule mats on the floor. An earth oven was used for baking acorn or other seed bread. A small conical sweat house was built, not in a pit as was usual elsewhere, and here men sweated by a hot fire, or held men-only meetings, or otherwise relaxed.

The balsa, or tule raft boat, made of bound-together tules, lashed together in bunches and shaped with a prow was quite expertly navigated with double-bladed paddles on the bay or large rivers. Stone mortars, some in bedrock, others portable, were hollowed out and stone pestles used to grind grain or nuts in them. Special small ones were used to make paint, medicine and tobacco. There were also wooden mortars hollowed out of logs. Household implements included brushes made of soaproot or hair, a paddle-shaped food-stirrer, spoons made usually of mussel shell, and bark platters for eating meat. Skin scrapers were made of rib-bone or split cobbles.

Hair was worn long or short, often in two braids, but women alone had bangs over the forehead. Beards were plucked with bone tweezers; hair was sometimes doubled back on a woman's head. Men used nose stick ornaments, while both men and women tattooed their face, but women alone on forehead and arms. Men finger-painted their bodies with red and white stripes, while women were likely to wear shell necklaces or ear pendants. Yellow hammer quill bands were used by men on their heads for dances; also bunches of magpie feathers were tied into the hair. Robes and capes of otter skin were used by the well-to-do, while woven rabbitskins were worn by the poor. Women wore a network of plant fibers in front, and a tanned skin behind to make a double dress, but men mostly went naked. The red paint they used came from mercury ore and caused many deaths by poisoning.

Social and political organization. Each tribe was ruled by a hereditary chief and orator. Sometimes the chief uniquely acted as a war leader. Wars were mainly minor skirmishes between tribes.

Traditions, folklore, religion and tribal medicine. Very little of this is preserved. Coyote was the great folk hero, who was a hero when he created life, or taught men to hunt or to use acorns, but was a villain when he chased after women or tried to fool the people or other animals and birds. The religion was mainly influenced by shamans who used their powers to make or stop rain, heal the sick, propitiate evil spirits or prevent poisoning or magic by other shamans. There were some women shamans, unique for this part of California. Shamans healed mainly by sucking out supposed evil objects from their patients or by using certain herbs, such as yerba buena. There was a partial introduction of the elaborate Kuksu Cult healing and initiation ceremonies from the more sophisticated tribes to the north. A bit of quiet humor shines through when we hear that part of the people's astronomical knowledge was calling the Pleiades "the bunch of little ones shaking!"

Games, such as shinny and kick ball, and gambling games, using marked sticks to hide and guess about, were the greatest occupiers of leisure time. Rattles, split-stick clappers, whistles, flutes and the musical bow were the main musical instruments, with the split-stick used for the dances.

Life cycle. At birth the baby was usually helped come by a midwife, and both baby and mother were kept warm on leafy branches placed over an oven. At the onset of menstruation the girl was secluded in one corner of the hut for about 3-5 days. Presents were exchanged at the time of marriage, which was more likely to be successful if both parents and the young couple were in favor of it. Chiefs had more than one wife, and some other men in the north married sisters. The dead of the poor were usually buried the same day of death; the better class people usually had cremation.

Summary of tribal history, population and contemporary condition. History began with the coming of the Spaniards in 1774. The missions wre established soon after this and at first there was friendliness on both sides, but unfortunately the Padres felt it necessary to use in time the whip, and soldiers to discipline the Indian converts; and disease and inadequate sanitation caused a great many deaths. The Indians, unused to these conditions, became sullen or in despair, so that later visitors to the missions called them spiritless and devoid of intelligence, without understanding the traumatic experiences they had suffered.

The original population of the Costanoans has been estimated by Drs. A. L. Kroeber and Robert Heizer as between 7,000 and 10,000 people. By the mid 20th century it had dropped to zero. Contact with these people was lost too quickly and too tragically to have a very true picture of them and their culture today.

VINSON BROWN

COSTA RICA is one of the most unique Latin American countries. This 19,600 square mile country stretches from the Pacific to the Caribbean coast of the Central American isthmus and is bordered on the north by Nicaragua and by Panama to the south. The terrain is varied and rugged. Even today travel to and within Costa Rica is relatively limited. It has developed in isolation since the first successful Spanish settlements of the 1560s. Costa Rica's population of nearly two million is one of the most homogeneous in Hispanic America. White Spanish Americans and mestizos (of European and Amerindian ancestry) comprise 97% of the population. Afro-Americans from the British West Indies number over 30,000. Amerindians account for 5,000 to 8,000 individuals or less than 1% of its total population. Most people live in a highland valley, Meseta Central, which has a temperate climate. Limón Province on the Caribbean Sea serves as home for almost all of the Afro-Americans. The few remaining Indians who maintain much of their cultural heritage live in an isolated tropical rain forest on the Caribbean coast. Access is only by horse or foot.

Costa Rica has a compulsory free elementary school system, an elective secondary school system, and a university which is located in the capital city of San José. The literacy rate in Spanish is 85%; the highest in Central America. Although Spanish is the official language, English is rapidly becoming a second language due to commerce with the United States and the presence of resident British West Indians.

The pre-Colombian indigenous Indian population lived in villages and raided one another. When the Spanish came in the 16th century, they found the Indians formidable adversaries and never actually succeeded in subjugating them. The Indians eventually retreated to isolated refuge areas. Many died in the fighting and even more died from European diseases such as measles, from which the native population had not developed immunities. An estimated 27,000 Indians populated Costa Rica in the 1500s. They were divided into five major groups: Corobicis, Borucas, Chorotegas, Caribs, and Pipils. The Corobicis lived in the northern valleys and were the oldest local group. Very little is known about them other than only 900 were present at the time of contact. Most probably they suffered large losses during years of raiding by other Costa Rican Indians.

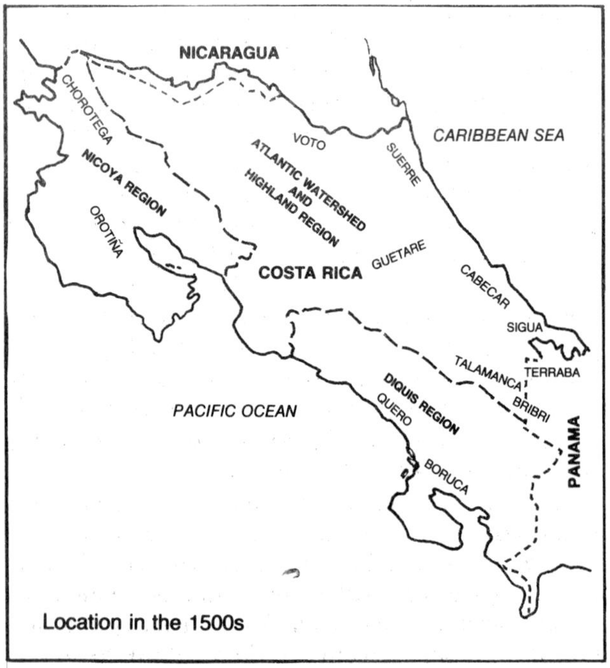

Costa Rica regional areas and Indian tribes.

During AD 1000, the Boruca migrated to southern Costa Rica from Columbia. They lived in small permanent fortified villages of approximately 400 people. Women cultivated maize (corn), cacao, fruit, and cotton. Fields and ceremonial plazas were often found within village walls. The Boruca were warlike and women supposedly sometimes joined the men in raids. Male captives were sacrificed, while women and children were enslaved. Upon the death of village headmen, women and children would be sacrificed and buried with the individual as retainers. Elderly men wore elaborate garments. Gold was taken from local rivers and made into varied treasured ornaments.

Upon the arrival of the Spanish, some 13,000 Chorotegas lived in unfortified villages on the Nicoya Peninsula. Each village had a market place and ritual center. The Chorotegas came from Chiapas, Mexico during the 15th century. Women cultivated large fields of maize, beans, cacao, fruits and cotton. The Chorotegas were hostile, too, and reportedly practiced human sacrifice and ritual cannibalism. A hieroglyphic writing system on deerskin parchment was in use. This probably came from Nicaraguan Indians. Pottery and woven cloth were of high quality. Gold and silver ornaments were omnipresent.

Carib Indians from Venezuela and the Caribbean arrived on the Caribbean coast in the 1400s. About 12,000 were present at contact. They lived in temporary villages of several hundred people. The women grew maize, beans, and yucca; hunting, gathering, and fishing were also important subsistence activities. The Carib Indians who arrived had few material artifacts, but were very warlike.

Two colonies of Nahua speaking Indians from the Mexican highlands were present when the Spanish arrived. These were warrior-traders who probably came to the area only 50 to 100 years prior to the Europeans. Such colonies of highland Mexican Indians are known as Pipils. These two settlements came to establish trade with the Aztec Empire of Mexico. One colony was situated in Coaza Valley to the southeast, while the other was in the northern Guanacaste Province. Coastal sea travel and fishing were important. Cultivated crops and techniques practiced were similar to those of local Costa Rican Indians. These Nahua speakers may have managed the tribute the Caribs paid to the Aztecs; and it possibly was the news of the Spanish conquest of the Aztec Empire which encouraged these Indians to remain in Costa Rica.

Columbus stopped at Costa Rica in 1502. He named the area "rich coast" as the Indians he met and traded with, had many gold and silver ornaments. This misnomer began a long-term Spanish belief in the precious metal riches of the country. Numerous Spaniards attempted to establish settlements in Costa Rica from which they could further explore and seek out the supposed golden caches of the Indians. The passionate quest for gold caused as much fighting between competing conquistadors as with the intractable Indians. The lowland jungle also deterred settlement with its rough topography, hurricanes, floods, and yellow fever. In 1519 Gil González Dávila began a successful expedition and returned to Panama with a fortune in gold ornaments, but a devastated contingent. Juan de Cavallón established the first successful colonial outpost in 1561. Memories of González Dávila's treasure pursued Cavillón and others before and after; but none returned with such wealth. A few years later Juan Visquez de Coronado moved the original settlement and renamed it Cartago, which remains one of Costa Rica's important cities. Peace was made with some surrounding Indians, while many others retreated ultimately to dense lowland areas.

Throughout the colonial period of 1505-1821 Costa Rica continued to be one of the most isolated, smallest and poorest of the New World Spanish Empire. The colony was included as part of the Captaincy General of Guatemala. Unlike most other Latin American countries, the descendants of the original Spanish settlers from Andalucia, Estremadura and Galicia in Spain did not heavily miscegenate with the local Indians. The development of a mestizo population segment was extremely slow and small. The continual retreat and hostility of the already small indigenous populations, together with the inbreeding marriage patterns among the Spanish settlers, maintained the situation. During the 1700s Costa Rica's population grew to less than 20,000. Unable to rely on local Indian labor, the colonists had to see to their own subsistence needs. Although cultivation and herding of cattle, sheep and goats supplied enough food, manufactured goods from Europe were very scarce. This encouraged illegal trade with French, English and Dutch ships.

The Indians retreated into the Talamancan region and frequently raided Spanish settlements. Mosquito Indians from Nicaragua posed such a threat that from 1779 to 1841 the Costa Rican government agreed to pay these Indians tribute to stop the raiding. Indian raids were often supported by the English who sought to harass the Spanish and weaken Spanish control in Central America. From 1600 to the late 1700s pirate attacks of ships and towns also proved extremely crippling to Costa Rica. Both the British and French often encouraged these raids, as well as those of the Indians. Eventually external trade was virtually stopped, as a defense measure. Roads were deliberately undeveloped to discourage attacks and, hence, internal trading was minimal. Costa Rica remained an isolate. Only sporadic commerce with Panama and Nicaragua continued. Despite these impediments the local population persisted and grew. New towns were established, especially in the thickly populated Meseta Central Valley. The San José district, site of Costa Rica's capital since 1838, developed into a thriving area in the mid-eighteenth century. Cacao, sugar and tobacco plantations provided the main exports.

Costa Rica's independence from Spain was declared in 1821 and assured by the civil war of 1822. From 1823 to 1838 Costa Rica participated as an independent member in the loose federation of the United Provinces of Central America. A republican government has persisted (in form) since 1823. In comparison with the rest of Latin America, Costa Rica has had very few military dictatorships.

Coffee plantations began operations in the Meseta Central region during 1825 and became Costa Rica's largest export from 1829 until the 1970s. In 1875 the country's railway system was under construction and several banana plantations were started. Costa Rica quickly became the world's largest banana exporter until 1913 when a disease destroyed many banana trees of the Caribbean lowland plantations. Since the 1940s the banana industry has again grown until in the 1970s the export of bananas surpassed that of coffee.

During the construction of the railroad in the 1870s-1890s, 30,000 British West Indians of Afro-American descent were brought to work laying tracks. Most of these people were Jamaican and remained in the Caribbean province of Limón. They became subsistence cultivators and worked in the banana estates concentrated in Limón. These immigrants have remained and comprise the country's largest minority group. Although the younger generation is bilinguel in English and Spanish and consider themselves as Costa Rican, much cultural continuity is maintained with their British West Indian heritage. They are further distinguished from the predominant Hispanic population by their Protestantism and locally developed cultural differences.

The contemporary Indian population varies from those who are biologically and culturally mestizo to others, mostly remnant refuge groups living in isolated lowland areas. The Central highland Indians were essentially all destroyed. Chorotegas of the Nicoya Peninsula are part of the large mestizo population in Guanacaste Province. The Borucas, a few Chorotegas, and the Talamancas are the major cultural Indian groups remaining. Despite limited contact, they have also undergone social and cultural changes resulting from the development of Costa Rica as a Latin American nation.

There are approximately 4,000 Talamancas living an almost traditional lifestyle in the Caribbean lowlands. Only in this century have the colonization efforts of

Costa Ricans been more than minimally successful in this area. Talamancas are composed of various Indian populations who migrated to escape the white settlers. They practice slash and burn agriculture, gather wild foods, hunt and fish. They are matrilineally organized and the mother's brothers serve as important kinsmen. Upon agreement to marry, the groom resides near his wife's family and contributes to their subsistence. Shamanism is practicéd in divination, curing and religious ceremonies.

The Borucas number about 1500. They also are slash and burn agriculturalists. Some grow small crops of banana, cacao and tobacco for sale to white exporters. Their cultivation has been influenced more by Hispanic methods. Borucas are the only group who still weave cloth. This is a woman's occupation and some of the products are being sold in Costa Rica's small tourist trade. Monogamous marriages are the most numerous among both the Talamancas and Borucas, but polygamy still occurs. Healing and magic are the domain of Boruca women. When an illness does not respond to local curers, Borucas will hire Talamanca shamans. Unlike the Talamanca, the Borucas are nominal Catholics; but their traditional culture continually frustrates priests who visit the area several times a year.

Although these contemporary Indians will continue much of their traditional culture for some time to come, increased contact with the dominant Hispanic Costa Rican population will effect many changes. Yet the Indians have displayed a 400 year cultural conservatism and will not be Latinized without a creative syncretism of Hispanic and Indian culture.

John H. Phalan

COSTO, RUPERT (Cahuilla; 20th century), is a writer and the founder of the American Indian Historical Society in San Francisco. He has organized and directed convocations of Indian scholars at Princeton, New Jersey, and at Aspen, Colorado. Costo is the author of *Contributions and Achievements of the American Indian* (1973).

COTTER, LEONARD N. (Wyandotte; July 3, 1906-), has served thre terms as chief of the Wyandotte Tribe of Oklahoma after having previously been second chief. He wrote the *Constitution and By-laws* and the *Corporate Charter* of his tribe in 1937. He has also worked as a diesel mechanic.

COTTON. Native American cultivation of cotton extended from the *Hopi* and the Rio Grande pueblos of New Mexico to Central Chile, Tucumán, and Paraguay. In North America, the limits of its cultivation fell significantly short of the areas climatically suited. Cotton was not cultivated by the tribes of the south, notwithstanding the favorable soil and climate. (The cotton blankets seen by De Soto's troops on the lower Mississippi were said to have been brought from the West, possibly from the far-off pueblo country of New Mexico and Arizona.) Although New Mexico and Arizona seem less favorable to its cultivation, cotton has been raised to a considerable extent by the Pueblos, especially the Hopi, from time immemorial, and cloth, cord, thread, and seed are commonly found in ancient deposits in caves, cliff-dwellings and ruined pueblos throughout that region.

The Hopi are now the only cultivators and weavers of cotton, their product consisting chiefly of ceremonial robes, kilts and scarfs, finding their way through trade to many other tribes who, like the Hopi, employ them in their religious performances. In the time of Coronado (1540-42) and of Espejo (1583), Acoma and the Rio Grande villages in New Mexico, and the Pima of southern Arizona also raised the plant, until about 1850; but the introduction of cheap fabrics by traders has practically brought the industry to an end everywhere among the Indians, the Hopi alone adhering to the old custom of cultivating and weaving it, and that chiefly for ceremonial garments. In ancient Hopi and Zuñi mortuary rites, raw cotton was placed over the face of the dead, and cotton seed was often deposited with food vessels and other accompaniments in the grave.

In South America, the Andean populations were supplied with cotton in quantity from both flanks of the

Distribution of cotton during the Inca period.

Andes. In the arid coastal lowlands much cotton was grown by irrigation. In both *Inca* and pre-*Inca* coastal sites there is found, in addition to the cotton textiles, a good deal of cotton in the seed (both the large naked and tufted seeds, probably *barbadense* at Ocucaje, for instance). On the eastern flank the Yungas of the Antisuyo were noted producers, as were, farther north, the Chachapoyas-Moyobamba and Quijos-Canela regions.

In aboriginal Venezuela the district of Tocuyo produced coarse cotton piece goods, from which the name "tocuyo" passed into wide Spanish usage for coarse cotton cloth. Very fine thread is found in Peruvian textiles; at the other extreme twine and cordage were made from cotton; especially in areas lacking the coarser fibers of cabuya and maguey. The natural fiber colors, white, tawny brown, red, and green are known. Seeds were not generally used for food, but had medicinal uses.

Both in the New and the Old World the cottons grown before the industrial revolution were mainly perennials, annual forms making their appearance where seasons did not admit perennial habit. In higher latitudes, with long summer days, an annual, more herbaceous form tended to replace the perennial form. Where winter cold was encountered, only the annual forms, it appears, could exist. In the polar parts of the range, therefore, annual forms should have prevailed, and it is from such margins probably that the sea island and upland cottons were selected. Early historical references to annual cottons in the New World are lacking.

Handbook of South American Indians.

Wapisiana woman spinning cotton.

Geographically, there are two large species of New World cultivated cottons: *Gossypium barbadense*, and *G. hirsutum.* (Genetically, there is a third, *G. tomentosum*, endemic to Hawaii, which is "generally further removed from *G. hirsutum* than *G. hirsutum* is from *G. barbadense*").

With regard to *barbadense* the situation is well clarified. Here belong Peruvian and some woody Brazilian cottons. Its aboriginal range included the West Indies, the Caribbean mainland, coastal Peru, and the Brazilian lowlands. In its most ordinary form, that of a vigorously branching shrub, *barbadense* is restricted to low latitudes (short-day habit).

Prehistorically, the *barbadense* complex appears to have been almost wholly South American, meeting the North American *hirsutum* complex only in lower Central America and in the West Indies.

G. hirsutum in the large sense extended aboriginally from the Colorado Plateau in the north (archeologically), southward along the Pacific coast to the Tumbes area of Peru (Boza), across the West Indies and along the northern shores of South America into northeast Brazil. Its major area was Middle America, both mainland and island, and its South American penetration appears to have been principally from the northern shores southward, and along the coast.

COTUBANAMA (Arawak; ?-1506), was in 1502 chief of an Arawak Indian village of Higüey, in the modern Dominican Republic section of Hispaniola island. The Spanish captain Juan de Esquivel, under the colonial governor Nicolás de Ovando, subdued an Indian rebellion that year, but Cotubanama revolted again in 1506. Cotubanama was then captured and executed.

COTZUMULHUAPA (also COTZMULGUAPA; COTZUMOLHOAPA, etc.) from Mayan *cuzamatl* + *lo* + *pan*, "in the waters [lake] of the weasels," is a site and culture in Classic Mayan times, located in the Department of Escuintla, on the Pacific Coast of Guatemala. Known to archeologists as Santa Lucia Cotzumalhuapa, it is famous for remarkable stone sculptures which have been found in several areas of the region, notably at El Baúl, Bilbao, and Santa Lucia Cotzumalhuapa, some of which depict human sacrifice and decapitation—motifs unusual in Mayan art. A series of unique hieroglyphs have also been discovered at the site, which are believed to reflect the influence of

Maya-Pipil cultural intermix; nothing like them has been found elsewhere. Scholars are not in complete agreement as to the dating of this cultural expression; while most believe it flourished as a Late Classic site, *circa* AD 650-925, one important body of opinion holds that it is an early period, perhaps about AD 300-650. Strong Mexican influences seem to be apparent in much of the architecture and art styles of the region, which has produced some of the most remarkable stone sculpture of the Classic period of Middle America. One of the several unsolved mysteries of early American archeology, this small region, less than 74 miles in length, developed a distinctive cultural style which includes nine ceremonial "temples" or structures which suggest relationships with such widely-spread Mexican elements including Teotihuacán, Toltec, Maya, and Tajin and Pipil qualities, yet has left little indication of how this remarkable intermingling came about.

FREDERICK DOCKSTADER

COUGAR MOUNTAIN CAVE is the site that has produced evidence of Desert culture in southeast Oregon. There is a collection of notched points, milling stones, and basketry, dated about 7000 BC, that has led scholars to speculate on a common ancestry of the Desert and Cordilleran traditions.

COUNCIL is a group of leading members of a society having jurisdiction over various aspects of community life. Among the North American Indians, every tribal unit, including bands, clans, villages, tribes, and confederations had the right to hold a council. Sometimes, as among the Omaha, the council acted as a court, passing judgment in cases brought before it and having the power to inflict penalties. The Omaha council even sat in cases of murder, keeping a poisoned staff ready in case death was decreed.

The three Hidatsa villages on the Knife River each had its own council, but after a smallpox epidemic reduced their population they established a tribal council to promote cooperation between the villages. Formed of about ten notable warriors from each village, the council lasted from the end of the eighteenth century until the three villages were united in 1845. The council was concerned only with warfare and mutual assistance, and not with the internal affairs of the individual villages.

The council of the Cheyenne was active only at special tribal gatherings, such as during preparations for war or during the annual summer hunt. It was composed of forty-four chiefs assisted by the leaders of the warrior societies. The chiefs served for a period of ten years; at the end of their terms they selected forty chiefs to succeed themselves, and chose four of their own number to remain on the council as head chiefs.

The Cherokee held their most important village councils at the same time each year, the date being set to coincide with the ceremonial renewal of tribal unity. The councils reflected the drive for tribal unity, since they could reach no decision without unanimous consent—often a tedious procedure, especially when different clans had conflicting interests, as in the case of warfare. The Cherokees created a tribal council during the first half of the eighteenth century to meet threats from the colony of South Carolina.

The Pueblo council at Zia could be called by any one

An Iroquois council meeting, 18th century.

of three officials, including the war chief, the governor, and the fiscal mayor (the head of the Roman Catholic Church in the pueblo). It dealt with a variety of problems arising within the pueblo itself. In the past, unanimity was required before council decisions could be reached, but this is no longer necessary.

In many places, councils are now replacing older forms of tribal leadership. Chiefs were formerly the leaders of Kwakiutl clans, for example, but now their chiefly status is widely seen as irrelevant to the situation of the Indians. By the 1950s all but two of the twelve Kwakiutl clans had adopted a council form of government.

Until 1923 the Navajo were led by chiefs whose authority was based on the fluctuating qualities of personal leadership. With the discovery of oil on Navajo lands in that year, a more stable political system was sought, by the Indians as well as by the American government, in order to facilitate relations between the two parties. Although the first council was an ineffectual agency that poorly represented the interests of the tribe, later modifications have improved its effectiveness.

Eskimos and other native groups of Alaska have recently begun to form village and regional councils to study native land rights and to ensure that the natives receive their fair share of the profits from the exploitation of Alaska's natural resources by whites. Complementary organizations—native corporations—have also been formed to invest the profits from such operations to the benefit of the native population.

COUNTING. *See* NUMBERS and NUMERICAL SYSTEMS.

COUP designated the formal token or signal of victory in battle by North American Plains Indians. Coups were usually "counted," as it was termed—that is, credit of victory was taken, for three brave deeds, killing an enemy, scalping an enemy, or being first to strike an enemy either alive or dead. Each one of these entitled a man to rank as a warrior and to recount the exploit in public; but to be first to touch the enemy was regarded as the bravest deed of all, as it implied close approach during battle.

Among the Cheyenne it was even a point of bravado for a single warrior to rush in among the enemy and strike one with a quirt or gun before attempting to fire, thus doubly risking his own life. Three different coups might thus have to be counted by as many different persons upon the body of the same enemy, and in a few tribes four were allowed. The stealing of a horse from a

Smithsonian Institution, Bureau of American Ethnology.

International Indian Council at Tahlequah, Oklahoma, June 1843. Photo of an original painting in the U.S. National Museum, by John Mix Standley.

Smithsonian Institution, Bureau of American Ethnology.

Two young braves returning with their first scalps; their faces, with the exception of their noses, which are painted white, are blackened, to indicate the making of a "coup."

hostile camp also carried the right to count coup. The stroke (coup) might be made with whatever was most convenient, even with the naked hand, a simple touch scoring the victory. In ceremonial parades and functions an ornamented quirt or rod was sometimes carried and used as a coup stick. The warrior who could strike a tipi of the enemy in a charge upon a home camp thus counted coup upon it and was entitled to reproduce its particular design upon the next new tipi which he made for his own use, and to perpetuate the pattern in his family. In this way, he was said to "capture" the tipi. Warriors who had made coups of distinguished bravery, such as striking an enemy within his own tipi or behind a breastwork, were selected to preside over the dedication of a new tipi. The noted Sioux Chief Red Cloud stated in 1891 that he counted coup 80 times.

COURCHENE, DAVID (Ojibwa; 1926-), helped revive the Manitoba Indian Brotherhood in 1967 and served as its president from 1968 to 1974. Born at Fort Alexander, Manitoba, Courchene worked as a foreman at an all-Indian lumber corporation until illness forced him to retire in 1964. While at the mill, he served as councellor for his band at the Fort Alexander Reserve. Through his efforts, the band elected an Indian School Committee (a first of its kind in Manitoba) over which he presided from 1959 to 1966.

Courchene was elected chief of the reserve in 1966 and immediately began to make changes. Under the new chief Anglican and Roman Catholic schools were replaced by nondenominational schools, a new townsite with water and sewage was built, and a recreational program was begun.

By 1967 Courchene was convinced that the original treaties between the Indians and the whites were signed by "natives who unknowingly surrendered all their rights for a handful of beads." He and others began reviving the Manitoba Indian Brotherhood, which became the active and dynamic voice of Manitoba Indians. In 1970 he told Queen Elizabeth II of England when she visited Manitoba: "It is with sorrow we note that the promises of peace and harmony, of social advancement and equality of opportunity, have not been realized by Indian people."

Courchene has been an advocate of a training program to develop native leadership and administrative skills, and he is a promoter of a pilot project in Manitoba that helps Indians manage and guide their financial affairs and social welfare planning.

In 1970 Courchene, a high school dropout, was awarded an honorary doctor of laws degree from the University of Manitoba. Retired from the Manitoba Indian Brotherhood in 1974, Courchene became head of a private development agency which assists Indian people in economic development.

COURTSHIP CUSTOMS. Basically there is only one generalization that should be made about the customs and cultures of Native Americans in precontact or aboriginal and early historic times, and that is that they were characterized by much linguistic and cultural diversity. This is also true of customs of courtship and marriage, where the primary generalization that can be made is that for most tribes marriage was a normal, expected, and often mandatory state of affairs where it was expected that every person would marry. In some societies adult status was dependent upon marriage and parenthood. The actual forms of courtship and marriage ranged from informal and casual practices, like those of the Eskimo, to formal and structured patterns, like those of the Natchez in the Southeast and of the Northwest Coast tribes. This discussion will be limited to customs of the North American continent, although similar practices may be found among the native populations of Middle and South America.

To illustrate the range of marriage customs found in North America, a brief description of Eskimo and Northwest Coast practices will be given. For the Eskimo, marriage was a cooperative relationship between males and females that was built up over a time of cohabitation during which children were born and ties of economic interdependence and cooperation developed with both sets of kindred. Courtship was casual; a young couple from groups with no existing relationships of mutual aid began having sexual relations, and if they were compatible, they would remain together. There was no formal ceremony. Permanence and stability in the relationship came with the birth of children. Polygynous marriages were permissible if the male was capable of supporting more than one wife. While the economic balance and division of labor made marriage necessary, this same economic balance of property rights helped make marriages last. However, marriages were brittle, ending through disagreements, strife, and involvement with other men. Most marriages were dissolved due to sexual rivalries; indeed, most male rivalries were over women and sexual adjustment and dominance predominated in interpersonal relations.

Northwest Coast tribes could be regarded as falling toward the other end of a continuum of formality and structure in marriage customs. Here virginity appears to have been valued, as virginal brides were dowered and constantly chaperoned. A girl was considered marriageable after her puberty ritual, and the most desired quality in a bride was industriousness. Marriage arrangements were made by the groom and the bride's family. The suitor brought gifts to her family; he might sit at the door of her house for a period of days while he was insulted and sent on errands by her family. Following the successful bargaining over bride price, which might include skins, canoes, fish, and oil, the wedding was celebrated with a feast and a potlatch. When the bride went to her husband's canoe, she walked on a carpet of skins that were part of her dowry. Sororal polygyny was practiced, with bride price paid for each bride. In a society oriented toward the accumulation of wealth and social status, the more wives a man had, the more wealth he could accumulate. Marriages were not easily dissolved; divorce was rare, especially in families of chiefs.

Criteria for selecting a bride

Certain criteria in selection of a bride seem to have been fairly common in North America. In societies where there were girls' puberty rituals, the girl had to have gone through the ritual before she could be considered marriageable.

One universal criterion in spouse selection was blood relationship; all Native American societies practiced some form of kin group exogamy, although this ranged from nuclear family (Eskimo) to class (Natchez), with clan, lineage, and moiety exogamy found most commonly. The Natchez system probably was the most unique. There were two exogamous social classes, the nobility, divided into Suns, Nobles, and Honored Men, and the commoners, called the "Stinkards" by the French. The nobility were required to marry Stinkards; the children of women of the nobility had the status of their mothers in this matrilineal society, while the children of fathers of nobility and commoner mothers moved down one step in the social scale: Suns became Nobles, Nobles became Honored Men, and Honored Men became Stinkards. Kinship criteria also included cross-cousin marriage as a preferred form of marriage in some societies. In matrilineal systems, patrilateral cross-cousins often were preferred marriage partners.

Among the Navajo, Algonquins, and tribes of the Southeast and Northwest Coast industriousness and competence were also valued traits in a bride. Other traits with more limited distribution included health, social position, age, observation of menstrual taboos (Southeast), and beauty and chastity (Plains). Among the Plains tribes, it was not the young men who were expected to do the heavy work of tanning and preparing hides and making tipi covers, but older married women. Hence beauty was more important among Plains tribes in selection of a bride than was industriousness. Chastity in a bride was also not commonly a critical factor in choosing a bride. It was found primarily among the Plains tribes and in the Northwest Coast; among the latter, it was usually found in conjunction with the factor of social class. Among most tribes, premarital sexual freedom was accepted and expected behavior. The Catawba had a class of "prostitutes," attractive young women who offered their sexual favors for a fee, which was then turned over to the chief. There was no social stigma attached to this "occupation"; after several years of prostitution, the women married, had families, led normal lives, and were not looked down upon.

Actual courtship among Native Americans, in which young men wooed young women, was relatively rare. It was found among the central Algonquins and some Plains tribes, where during the summer young men wooed young women with flutes, love songs, and gestures. Generally, however, marriages were arranged by the families, particularly if bride price was involved. For example, in the Southeast, the young couple had no choice in the selection of their marriage partners. Once a boy had received his adult name, after he had performed an act of bravery, he was ready for marriage. His bride was selected by the female members of his clan and his maternal uncles, and they made the arrangements with the bride's clan. Among the Plains tribes, where chastity was honored and girls chaperoned, men married only after they had achieved some degree of social position through war exploits of counting coups and stealing horses. The horses were necessary for the gift made to the bride's brother, who made the arrangements for the marriage.

In the Southeast, Northwest, and northern California, where bride price was found, it was necessary to legitimate the marriage and often for purposes of social status as well. It was usually found in conjunction with bride service for those who could not pay the bride price, although bride service without bride price occurred among the northern Algonquins like the Slave, Dogrib and Yellowknife. In some societies the groom's family gave gifts to the bride's family. Among the Navajo, horses or livestock were given; on the Plains, horses were given to the girl's brother; among Great Lake Algonquins, meat was the gift; and among the eastern Algonquins, the gift was wampum. Gift exchanges were found in California (among the Pomo they were pledges of good will between the two families) and on the Plains. Dowries were uncommon, found primarily among Northwest Coast tribes in conjunction with status and virginity.

Spouses could also be acquired through inheritance, through the practices of the levirate and the sororate, which usually occurred together. These practices were found in the Southeast, California, and among some of the Plains tribes.

Marriage rituals

Some tribes had little or no ritual accompanying marriage. Among the Zuñi, where marriage arrangements were made by the groom and the bride's father, if the girl agreed to the marriage, the couple would go to bed and then the bride washed the groom's hair. Four days later, she took a basket of corn to her mother-in-law, and they were considered married. Among many California tribes, like the Mohave and the Luiseño, there was no bride price, gift exchange, or ceremony. Marriage simply involved cohabitation.

Among most tribes, however, there was usually some form of ritual to mark the transition in status in the life cycle, usually involving a feast. Among the Southeastern tribes this was a secular and economic event that was also necessary to seal the union. It involved breaking an ear of corn in two and planting two reeds and then a trial period for the marriage until the next Busk (Green Corn ceremony). The Navajo ceremony was held in the hogan of the bride's parents after they had received the gift of livestock. The ceremony involved a ritual meal of corn mush eaten from a new wedding basket (colloquially called "dipping the corn") with the bridal couple symbolically feeding each other and then passing the basket to the guests. An older man, usually a singer, exhorted them on the responsibilities and spiritual aspects of marriage, and then the guests shared a feast of mutton and coffee.

Elopement was an alternative escape to arranged marriages, common in societies where there was little choice to the individuals involved.

Marriage forms and practices

While the actual form of marriage was usually monogamy (serial monogamy in the case of some Puebloans), polygyny, generally sororal polygyny, was frequently the preferred form of marriage. It was found among the Athapascans, the Northwest Coast tribes (where it was related to social status and wealth), the Iroquois, the Algonquins, Plains tribes, Eskimo, Basin-Plateau tribes, and in the Southeast. Polyandry is reported to have occurred among some of the northern Athapascans (Slave, Dogrib, Yellowknife) and in the Basin.

Post-marital residence practices were frequently related to the kinship system. Matrilocal residence practices were frequently related to the kinship system. Matrilocal residence usually was found with matrilineal descent systems (southern Athapascans, Southeast, Iroquois, and Pueblo) and was also usually associated with mother-in-law avoidance. Virilocality was found among the tribes of California, the Northwest Coast, and the Algonquins.

While premarital sexual freedom was generally the rule among Native Americans, post-marital chastity was universally required, except in cases where wife-lending or wife-hospitality occurred (among the Natchez and the Eskimo, and here it was permitted only when the husband offered the sexual favors of his wife to persons he selected). Adulterous women often were physically punished, by having the tips of their ears or noses cut off, for instance. Among the Algonquins they were disowned by their husbands; among some Plains tribes they were subjected to rape by all men of the band or tribe, and divorce was frequently the result. Sometimes the male partner might be killed as well.

Dissolution of marriages

While death was the one universal way of ending marriages, attitudes towards divorce varied. Divorce was easy and common in the Southwest, California, and the Plains, although steps would be taken to prevent it. Among the Southwestern tribes it was often the women who instituted divorce proceedings by placing the husband's possessions outside the hogan or pueblo, an indication that the marriage was over. It terminated when he took his possessions to his home. In the Southeast, Northwest Coast, Plateau, and among the Iroquois, however, divorce was both rare and difficult.

Grounds for divorce were varied; adultery or infidelity was the most common, followed by childlessness or barrenness. Other reasons included inability to resolve differences, laziness, nagging, and incompatibility.

RACHEL A. BONNEY

COURTS, TRIBAL, are the judicial branch of Indian legal or political affairs, aimed at establishing guilt and innocence or at settling disputes. Although many of the court systems of North American Indians were highly informal, at least according to contemporary standards, the differences between Indian and modern courts is more apparent than real. The Yurok court system, for example, has seeming parallels in the modern practices of personal negotiation and arbitration; but the well-defined and universally accepted rules by which these procedures were pursued indicates their status as a true court system. Parties to a conflict contracted with unrelated members of the community, who served as "crossers." The disputants themselves did not usually negotiate directly. This task was left to the crossers, who negotiated with each other and reached a settlement that had to be accepted by the parties to the conflict. The crossers were compensated with a piece of shell money.

Another example of a court that members of modern societies would likely have difficulty recognizing is found among the Eskimos. Here, a person who has murdered on more than one occasion was usually thought of as an enemy of the whole community. When this happened, someone could take the responsibility of speaking with each adult male in the community,

"Delaware Court." Gouache illustration (1971) by Donald Secondine (Cherokee/Delaware).

one at a time, to obtain their consent for the execution of the offender. If unanimous consent was received, the man could perform the execution without fear of revenge from the victim's family and with full approval of the community.

In the eastern Subarctic, shamans often acted as judges. Complaints were delivered to the shaman who then investigated the case. If he decided that the complaint was justified, he warned the offender to rectify his misdeed, and if this was not done he could punish him, usually through witchcraft.

Other tribes possessed court systems that more closely resemble the modern institution. For example, a council of chiefs served as a court for the Omaha Indians. They heard cases and rendered decisions, having the power to inflict whatever punishment was appropriate. A poisoned staff was kept available in case they decreed the death penalty. Among the Cheyenne, only three crimes were recognized—murder, repeated horse thievery, and misconduct during the tribal buffalo hunt. Members of the military societies were chosen to carry out the decisions of the court. If the murder occurred at a time when the tribe was scattered in winter camps, messengers notified the chiefs who then gathered to hear the case.

COUSHATTA was a large branch of the Alabama people. They were a Muskhogean speaking people, who also, originally, were called *Soasati*. They adopted Coushatta some time around the 19th century. Their language was such that men and women had differences in their speech patterns.

From 1500 to 1600 they lived along the Tennessee River. Later they moved below the junction of the Coosa and Tallapoosa Rivers.

Like other Muskhogean tribes they relied heavily on hunting, some fishing and agriculture. The Coushattas also made fine baskets and wove cloth, industries the women continue today on the reservations.

They were, in addition, noted for nose decorations.

De Soto was the first white to establish contact with them. In his chronicles he called them *Coste, Acosre, Cotche,* and *Acosta.* In 1561 they were ready to join with the Creeks and other tribes to prevent Pardo, whose expedition had taken cruel advantage of the Indians, from progressing any further inland. It is not recorded whether they actually fought the Spaniards. Not long after this they began their move to the Coosa and Tallapoosa rivers, where they had their greatest contact with the French. The French found them industrious and impeccably honest in all their dealings.

They remained here until the French ceded their power east of the Mississippi in 1763. A large number then went to Tombigee River. They later returned. In 1795 another section crossed the Mississippi to the Red River. Later those in Texas joined the Alabama. Those who stayed moved to Oklahoma, where many lived with the Creeks.

Today there are several hundred (there were more than 500 in 1850), in Texas, Louisiana and Nebraska.

COUVADE. In South America, the term *couvade* is applied to the observance of a series of taboos by the father before, during, and after a child's birth. South America may be considered to be the classic land of the couvade. Since the custom in one form or another is almost universal on the continent, one may surmise that wherever it has not been recorded, as among the *Araucanians,* it existed formerly but died before it was observed.

In most tropical tribes, both parents refrain from eating certain foods, generally animal flesh, an avoidance usually based on the belief that some unfavorable characteristic of the animal or plant could be sympathetically transmitted to the infant. A great many activities that might endanger the child's life (e.g., hunting, swimming, or the handling of cutting implements) likewise are tabooed for a time after its birth.

The fact that the father takes to his hammock at childbirth need not be viewed as a symbolic lying-in; in most tribes where the couvade has been observed the woman herself is not especially confined and resumes her normal activities a day, or even a few hours, after giving birth. (The hypothesis that the husband reclines in his hammock principally because there are no activities in which he is permitted to take part, cannot be dismissed as a mere vagary). In all the literature about the South American couvade there are only two references that definitely suggested that the custom actually is an imitation of childbirth. Dutertre (1661-71, vol. 2) writes, "The father begins to complain and takes to his hammock," and Yves d'Evreux describes the event:

> He (the husband) lies-in instead of his wife who works as usual; then all the women of the village come to see and visit him lying in his bed, consoling him for the trouble and pain he had in producing this child; he is treated as if he were sick and very tired without leaving his bed as women here keep their beds after childbirth when they are visited and taken care of.
> (Yves d'Evreux, 1864, p. 89).

It is not unlikely that the two writers have given an interpretation rather than an exact description of the custom.

Characteristically, the South American couvade is based on the belief that a powerful bond exists between the father and the child which prevents the former from doing anything that might harm the infant until it is strong enough to stand the strain or avoid the danger.

Prenatal taboos

Among a considerable number of tribes the series of taboos that constitute the couvade begin during the women's pregnancy. Both parents avoid eating or even touching plants and animals with characteristics that, if transmitted to the unborn child, might impair its appearance or temperament. Other taboos serve to prevent a difficult delivery. For example, among the *Pilagá*, a prospective father abstained from eating armadillo meat to prevent breech presentation, tripe lest the infant be strangled by its navel cord, stomach lest it be born wrapped in the matrice, legs lest it be born with deformed legs, and brains so that it will not be born with an open skull. In addition, the father could not carry on certain normal activities, such as saddling or riding a horse, playing hockey, cleaning a pipe, handling a weapon or cutting implement; nor could he use new pots lest the child remain glued to the mother's womb. Some of these restrictions continued after birth, generally until the child's navel cord dropped off.

Postnatal taboos

The observance of postnatal taboos by the father probably is universal in South America; the most common one is abstinence from some foods.

Both *Yahgan* parents observed certain food and other taboos for some time before and after a child's birth. Sometimes, especially in the case of the firstborn, the father remained quietly in the tent, abstaining from most work, while relatives and friends supplied the family with necessities. Under the same circumstances, *Alacaluf* parents only drank water for two days. Among the *Ona*, the father merely kept a light diet. There is no information about the couvade among the *Tehuelche* and *Araucanians*.

An *Abipón* father at first fasted and lay in bed covered with mats and skins and then for some time refrained from shaving his eyebrows, snuffing tobacco, eating capybara flesh, riding horseback until he perspired, tasting honey taken from places in the earth that had been stepped on, and swimming across rivers.

The father's confinement has not been reported among any modern Chaco tribe except the *Tereno.* In all tribes, however, the father refrained from eating foods deemed harmful to the infant, and resumed his normal life only after the child had "hardened," that is to say, after four weeks.

A *Tupinamba* father shunned game, fish, and salt for 3 days and did no work until the infant's navel cord had fallen off. Infringement of these rules was believed to cause the mother and child to suffer from diarrhea. The father also placed the baby's carrying sling in a miniature trap as if it were game, shot at it with a small bow and arrow, and threw a fish net over it in an endeavor to make his son a good hunter and fisherman. In the same tribe the father of a newborn child lay in his hammock carefully wrapped up so that he would not catch cold and so impair the child's health; during this time he was visited by friends who brought him gifts. As soon as the navel cord had dropped off he could walk about again, though he still had to avoid violent exertions, like felling trees.

The couvade was probably customary among all the *Tupi-Guarani* tribes. After the birth of a child, *Guarani* fathers idled in their hammocks until the navel cord fell off. During this time they loosened their bows and gave up setting traps, hunting, and the making of tools and weapons. Modern *Cainguá* and *Chiriguano* fathers merely fasted on the occasion of a child's birth; formerly, *Chiriguano* took to their beds. Only in some *Cainguá* tribes of Brazil is the couvade in the strict sense still in vigor. In this respect, the *Guarayú* remained quite conservative; there the new father slashed his skin with an agouti tooth, stained his feet and articulations with arucú, and and fasted in his hammock for three days.

Bororo parents observed food and tobacco restrictions for 10 days or so; during this period they were not permitted to touch their hair with their hands lest it turn white. *Carajá* fathers stayed at home for six days; they were not permitted to eat fish or manioc and were obliged to clean their stomach by vomiting every day.

The *Apinayé* fathers stayed in bed and abstained from all labor until the navel cord dropped off.

Both parents speak as little as possible, even with each other, and keep a strict diet on manioc flat-cakes baked according to ancient usage on a hot stone slab.

Immediately after the delivery, *Sherente* parents partook only of white manioc flat-cakes and the milky juice of the babassu palm kernels. The father could not touch an ax for three days.

In the Xingú region, the father dieted on cassava diluted with water and avoided all foods that, if eaten by the child, might have harmed it. *Paressi* parents remained at home for five days; the father ate only cassava moistened with water. The *Ipuriná* father ended his fast only when the mother returned from her confinement. *Culino* men were not permitted to eat paca or tapir flesh for three days after the birth of a child. Meat was also taboo to *Paumari* fathers. *Miranha* fathers lay in their hammocks for three weeks keeping a diet of manioc flour, certain birds, and fish. *Araua* men avoided certain fish, male turtles, and turtle eggs during their wives' pregnancy and after childbirth.

Among the *Guaques* of Popayán, the parturient was confined to a special hut for three months. During that time the husband fasted and carried on no activities. At the end of the period the parents smeared themselves with ashes and genipa.

The *Catawishi* stopped all heavy work and ate neither game flesh nor large fish for a month.

An Awishiri couple rested for two weeks in their hammocks, avoided work, and abstained from several foods (e.g., meat); whatever they could eat was prepared by other people. Among the *Ssimaku* (*Urarina*) the father shared his wife's diet and shunned every kind of heavy work for a week. The same type of couvade is reported for the *Yameo*. Among the *Mayoruna*, the father reclined in his hammock in a compartment of the hut from the moment his wife felt the onset of birth pains; he remained confined with her and observed a strict diet for 20 days. The couvade of the *Muinane*, Bora, Cashibo and *Campa* consisted only of some food taboos. Among the *Candoshi*, the father remained in his hut fasting and singing; his wife meanwhile went to her parents' home. Among the *Pioje* and *Nocaman*, the couvade lasted only for one day.

In the Guianas both parents remained in their hammocks until the navel cord had dropped off. Among the *Mucushi* they were separated by a mat wall. They ate only cassava cakes and manioc soup and for three or four months they could not work. Since a man could not use any sharp instrument, he had to give up hunting, fishing, felling trees, carving wood and similar activities. Among the ancient *Galibi*, the new father subjected himself to flagellation and to the bite of venomous ants. Moreover, in several Guiana tribes he was not permitted to scratch himself with his fingernails, but used for this purpose a splinter, especially provided, form the midrib of a cockerite palm. The *Palicur* father was not permitted to cut cipo or drink its sap, cut tauary, or allow game to rot; besides he had to be careful not to fall from a tree lest the child would get a big belly. The father remained with the woman for 10 days, during which time he could eat only a little tapir and piranha fish. The mother stayed at home for two months and ate only uéua fish.

A *Conibo* father was confined to his hammock; he was forced to refrain from cutting "any creeping vegetation or touching chambita yarn other than his hammock. He was not allowed to sing or to play the panpipes or drums for a period of 10 days." Until the child could walk, neither parent could eat fish or other river game.

Until his child could walk, a *Jivaro* father avoided animal and plant foods containing tsarutama (magic stuff) for, "such foods had power over the spirit of the child and could wreak harm upon it."

Among the *Siusi*, the parents lived in isolation for five days without working or washing themselves and ate only manioc wafers and pepper. On the fifth day the maternal grandfather recited a charm and enumerated the foods which could then be eaten.

At the conclusion of the couvade period among the *Cubeo*, the headman of the sib or some other old man charmed all the fish and game so that they could cause no harm to the child; he said, for example, to a spiny fish, "Let no spines lodge in the throat of our little one."

Among the *Island Carib*, the father of a first-born child was confined in a small hut. During the first 10 days he ate only dry cassava and water; later he added some ouican or manioc beer. He ate only the center of the wafers and saved the rest for the feast which ended his fast. He could leave his hut only at night; no one who had partaken of fish or beer could visit him. After three months, two shamans took him to the plaza, where he was made to stand on two cassava wafers while they incised his skin with aguti teeth and washed the wound with a concoction of urucú, red pepper and tobacco. The baby's face was rubbed with the blood to make it courageous. Then the father sat down on a red-painted bench and was offered food as if he were a small child; he could taste only some fish and drink while his neck was supported like an infant's. The shamans distributed the cassava rinds to the crowd, and the father ate the wafers on which he had stood. After this ceremony, the father rested for several days. For six months more he refrained from eating turtles lest the child become deaf, parrots lest it have a long nose, crabs lest it get long legs, and many other meats for similar reasons. After the birth of subsequent children, the father only kept a diet for five days.

The observance of "couvance" restrictions often have been interpreted by the Indians themselves as an expression of the close bond between the father and the infant's clinging soul. An *Itonama* father never bathed in deep water lest the baby's soul drown; to prevent the soul from following him, the women tied the baby's legs. When a *Palicur* father went to the bush he carried a miniature bow and arrows for his child's soul; if he had to travel in the forest at night, he always hund a cord from his left shoulder for the soul.

The reason why a *Carib* father in Guiana remained at home for a week without working was that the child's body might ache.

The second week he will go out to the woods, but not too far for otherwise the child gets too tired. If the path divides itself, he will cover up one path in order that the soul of the child will not take the wrong path and lose its way. Near a creek he will not come at all, least *okoyumo,* the water spirit, should take his child, and yet during the first two weeks the baby is with its mother in a little room especially built for the occasion. She is not allowed to take it out. The father himself has not yet seen it.

The *Betoya* seriously believed that if the father were to walk, he would step on the child's head; if he were to split wood, he would cleave its head; if he shot birds, the arrows would pierce its body.

The identity of father and child is expressed in the name given the infant by the *Bacairi:* "little father."

This mystic bond between the bodies of parents and children does not cease entirely with the completion of the couvade rites. Among the *Sherente*, for example, married persons of either sex refrained from sexual intercourse when their parents were seriously sick, for they were convinced that it had an unfavorable effect upon the patient.

COWICHAN is the principle dialectic tribe of the coastal Salishan family.

The Cowichan live, as they have for years, on the Southeast corner of Vancouver Island in British Columbia, Canada.

The Cowichan closely resemble the Comox in customs. For example, their elaborate wedding ceremonies which involved many people, took several days and were quite expensive. Every groom went through the ritual refusal by his bride, the arguments his friends and family made on his behalf, the acceptance, the ceremony, the celebration. And to each individual involved, gifts, such as blankets or other valuable items, were exchanged. Unlike the Comox however, the Cowichan never went through the act of a marriage without the bride simply to gain property.

Like other Salishan tribes the Cowichan had ranks with nobles and commoners. The nobles took an active part in government.

Their religion was essentially an individual search for contact with the great spirit. Their main religious festival was the winter dance which anyone could join once they had had the dream contact with supernatural powers.

The Cowichan lived in long, planked dwellings covered with carvings. Salmon was their staple food, along with sturgeon and sockeye. To capture fish they used nets and harpoons and occasionally went to Luther Island to fish.

Juan de Fuca may have visited the Cowichan as early as 1592. Between his visit and the 19th century they were visited by other explorers and traders.

Their large involvement with whites did not come until the Hudson Bay Company came into the area in the early 1800s. The Cowichan then became involved with trade. In 1843 Victoria was founded and the Cowichan lived continuously and harmoniously with whites. For this primary reason they have never been moved from their land. Today some 1,500 to 2,000 live there.

COWLITZ were a small tribe of the Salishan linguistic family who at one time were an important power in the Northwest. Over the years they mingled with the Chehalis, and today are inseparable from them. The Cowlitz were located in southwest Washington, and by 1887 were removed to Puyallup Reservation.

COXCATLAN, from Náhuatl *cozcatl*, "precious stone necklace," + *an*, "place," a confusing reference to "an abundance of precious stones [or] gemstone necklaces," is a cave in southern Puebla near the Oaxaca border in Mexico, where the earliest evidences of corn cultivation in the New World have been found, *circa* 5000 BC, marking the beginnings of agriculture and a subsequent sedentary lifestyle.

COXCOX (Toltec; fl. 14th century), also spelled Coxcoxtli, ruler of Toltec descendants at Culhuacán on the southeastern shore of Lake Texcoco around 1300, whose vassals were the Mexica (later, Aztecs), is remembered for being involved in a series of memorable though perhaps fictional, episodes with the Mexica whom he used as mercenaries.

Once he sent them into battle against Xochimilco

and derided them as cowards when they returned to Culhuacán without prisoners. The Mexica then dumped baskets of ears they had severed from their sacrificed prisoners over Coxcox's feet.

On another occasion, the daughter Coxcox gave the Mexica chief as a bride was flayed and a priest wearing her skin appeared before Coxcox who had come to visit.

COYOTES have been known by many names throughout history, from complimentary names, such as: God's dog, First Worker, God of the Plains, prairie wolf, and Slim-trotter; to the more derogatory names like: the trickster, mischief-maker, roamer, fool, and back-biter. This duality of roles is common within numerous cultures, who regard the coyote as both a creator and a devious trickster.

The common name, coyote, is derived from the Nahuatl word "coyotl." The word was apparently adopted by the Spanish from the Aztecs in the sixteenth century; and from there its usage spread.

Natural history

The family Canidae, which is represented today in North America by the wolves, coyotes, foxes, and dogs, probably originated during the close of the Eocene epoch, circa 40 million years ago. The genus *Canis* did not appear until the early or middle Pliocene circa 15 to 5 million years ago. The modern species of coyote, *Canis lantrans* say, has been identified in the late Pleistocene deposits at Rancho La Brea.

Today, coyotes are strictly a new world species. Their distribution currently extends from the northern tip of Alaska, across most of Canada and the United States, south to western Costa Rica, excluding Yucatan. The modern range, however, includes several extensions of the coyote's original habitat.

In Mexico, the coyotes are most numerous in the plains and semiarid valleys. Their range excludes the dense tropical forests. With the arrival of the Spanish in the sixteenth century, the forests were cleared and livestock was introduced. These two factors enabled the coyote to move into new areas as far south as Costa Rica and to increase in number. Large herds of Spanish sheep and goats were frequently allowed to roam unattended. In addition to predation upon live domesticates, coyotes benefitted from the increased carrion as weaker members of the herds succumbed to various casualties.

A similar extension of the northern boundary of the coyote's range occurred within the past century because of deforestation of the Yukon and Alaska. In the 1880s, the coyotes were reported to have moved north following the trail of dead horses as men pursued the gold rush.

Deforestation is a prime factor in the expansion of the coyote's range, because it meant the eradication of the wolf, the greatest barrier to the coyote. The coyote could not compete with or defeat either the gray wolf, *Canis lupus*, or the mountain lion, *Felis concolor*. When the red wolf, *Canis rufus*, was nearly exterminated in the southeastern United States, the coyote moved in to replace it.

Although the eastern boundary of the coyote's range

"Coyotes." From a painting by Frederic Remington.

was the Mississippi River in historic times, specimens from the Pleistocene deposits in Florida and Pennsylvania indicate that the early range was much larger. In modern times the coyote has relocated in these areas, proving that it is highly adaptable to a wide range of altitudes, latitudes, and ecozones.

Cultural significance

Coyotes are in the extraordinary position of being closely related to, similar in appearance to, and yet very different behaviorly from a ubiquitous domestic animal, the dog. Because of their similarities, much of the evidence for the importance of coyotes to prehistoric people is inseparable from that of dogs. Postcranial skeletal remains are virtually indistinguishable, except where historic breeds of dogs differ greatly in size and proportion from the coyote. To complicate the matter, coyote puppies have frequently been raised and tamed by people. Reports of coyote/dog hybrids are also numerous. Representations of canids in the form of paintings and effigies are often difficult to classify as dogs (*Canis familiaris*), coyotes, or wolves. Therefore, with the exception of cranial fragments from coyotes found in many prehistoric sites in Northern America, we are virtually limited to ethnohistorical and modern accounts to reconstruct the role of the coyote in the Indians' lives. Folklore and religion are the two most fruitful areas of research to learn of the native Americans' relationship with this creature.

Archaeological data on coyotes are difficult to synthesize. Reliable faunal analysis has only very recently become a regular part of published reports. Numerous authors discuss the distinguishing characteristics of the skulls of coyotes and domestic dogs but postcranial elements are generally unreliable for separating the two species. There is a nearly complete coyote skeleton from Grasshopper Pueblo, in east-central Arizona, dating between AD 1275 and 1400, which may or may not be an intentional burial. The historic Hopi village of Awatovi, in northeastern Arizona contained several coyote skeletons. Such isolated reports are not uncommon in the western United States and Mexico, but little is known of the temporal or spatial distribution and significance of coyote remains in an archaeological context.

One of the earliest known artistic renderings of a probable coyote was found at Tequixquiac, a late Pleistocene site in Mexico. The sacrum of an extinct camelid was carved to resemble the head of a coyote.

The best evidence for the importance of the coyote to native Americans exists in their religion and folk tales. In Indian mythology and folklore, the coyote has assumed a dual personality. Among many North American tribes, particularly in the Plains, it is esteemed as the creator of the sun, moon and stars. According to some beliefs, the coyote bestowed man with fire, but also introduced death. Most frequently it is renowned as the creator of animals and the one who allows man to hunt or denies him prey. This is the sacred side of the coyote.

The coyote's most mischievous side is portrayed in a multitude of folk tales. The majority of these could be classified as stories with a moral, meant to teach children not to be foolish and greedy. The coyote is generally trying to trick another animal because it covets the other's possessions or its favorable attributes. The stories usually end with the trick being turned on the coyote, and it is either seriously injured or killed.

The Aztec, Pima, Papago, Navajo, Apache, Zuñi, Pauite, Hidatsa, Arapaho, and Crow Indians, as well as many others, have extensive folklore about the coyote. All of these tribes regard the coyote as a trickster, a bungler, a coward, one who is envious, greedy, and easily duped. These same tribes also view the coyote as a poweful spiritual entity.

Among certain tribes the coyote is closely linked to illness and witchcraft. The Pima Indians of Arizona believe the strength of the coyote is a causal agent for particular kinds of sickness. Such maladies differ from those carried by germs, and are usually treated by a shaman rather than a physician. Behavior such as eating a melon into which a coyote has bitten, or killing a coyote may cause illness. The cures often consist of waving a coyote tail over the ailing person and singing special songs. The same method of treatment is employed by the neighboring Papago Indians.

The Navajo associate the coyote, as well as many other animals, with illness. The traditional belief is that if a hunter breaks the rules of the hunt, a coyote may entrap the man in its skin, that is, transform him into a coyote. A ceremony must be performed to rid the person of the animal's appearance and the related malady. At one time there was a "Coyoteway healing ceremony" for curing insanity and symptoms of witchcraft. Through the years coyote came to be regarded more and more as a trickster who dabbled in witchcraft. As a result, the strong association of coyotes with witchcraft has led to a decline in the practice of the Coyoteway healing ceremony.

There are countless other religious beliefs closely linked to the coyote. For example, the Cheyenne rarely killed coyotes or wolves. Instead, they prayed to coyotes for guidance, leadership, and warnings. The howls of wolves and coyotes were interpreted by some men as forewarnings of approaching enemies. Medicine arrows were always wrapped in coyote skins and women were forbidden to touch them.

To the Zuñi of New Mexico, the coyote is the god of the West. Six coyote fetishes are carved for the four cardinal directions and the upper and lower regions. The Coyote of the West is the master of the coyotes of the other five directions.

The Papago tribe is divided into the Coyote and Buzzard moieties. The coyote also plays an important role in their creation myth.

The Aztecs worshipped the deity known as

clothing, furniture, tools, and implements used in cooking. The Chilkat blankets of the Tlingit incorporated into weaving the patterns common to carving and painting.

Chilkat blanket, a unique form of blanket woven by the Tlingit, is perhaps the most significant craft of these people of the Northwest Coast.

The Chilkat blanket is woven form mountain goat wool or dog hair on a crudely designed loom, where the single warp beam is cedar. The blankets are five-sided, and have a pointed base and straight top edge. Since weaving is traditionally the work of women in the Northwest Coast area, Chilkat blankets are woven by women. They are, however, designed by men who are also the carvers and painters of the more dramatic Northwest Coast crafts. The decorative scheme is therefore quite consistent with the decoration of less static craft forms, such as carving and painting.

The blankets are highly decorated in the traditional Northwest Coast manner, which is made up of a stylized complex flat pattern. The major design elements of this culture are carefully architected into the blanket forms: all available space is covered, an animal or human figure is shown as though split into two symmetrical halves, and the use of x-ray views and eye joints (the repetition of circles) is included. The blankets share the same mysterious ambiguity of content with other Northwest Coast crafts. Anthropomorphic and zoomorphic forms are divided by lines which show the figure simultaneously frontally and in profile. The figures are made confusing to the observer by the addition of "filler" material: circles and geometric shapes which have questionable symbolic implications. Scholars speculate that their full meanings are known only to the weaver and original owner of the blanket.

The blankets are brightly colored. The older blankets were woven in natural colors: yellow, black, and blue; yarns dyed with European pigments found their way into Chilkat blankets only as trade and interaction with the non-Indian peoples grew.

In the north, the naturalistic treatment of form was translated into a more abstracted stylistic treatment wherein animals were distinguishable from one another through the inclusion of certain key identifying features. The central tribes were more naturalistic, and, as in dancers' masks and costumes, were created to convey an impression of the infusion of the supernatural force into the physical object.

The objects created by Plains artisans were equally as functional; however as their lives revolved around buffalo hunting, buffalo hide was the most commonly utilized material. It was sewn into containers, especially parfleches; clothing; tipis; drums; and shields, and was decorated either by polychromy painting or with embroidery. Objects were embroidered with porcupine quills and later, with glass beads obtained by trading with Europeans; painting was, however, the more extensively used form of decoration. Some wooden and stone objects used in ceremonies were also painted and decorated with beads, feathers, and quills. Both geometric and naturalistic styles were common in painting and embroidery, and were often invested with symbolic significance, as was the choice of colors used.

Pueblo Indians of the area now known as the Southwestern United States were quite diversified. Basketry, jewelry, pottery, carved figures, mural painting, sand painting, and blankets were all created, since the area was not limited by one material. Most decoration—whether painted, woven, or carved—was traditionally geometric, and frequently was religiously symbolic; however much of the decoration was abstracted from naturalistic forms. There are as many varieties of pottery and basketry as there are tribes in the Southwest. Navajo rugs and blankets are also found in a diversity of styles. Hopi, Zuñi, and Navajo jewelry all utilize the same materials—silver, coral, turquoise, and sometimes shell—but have quite readily distinguishable characteristics. Sand painting and mural painting were both based in ceremonial traditions; sand paintings, which are made by using many colors of dry materials in forming symbolic figures of humans, animals, plants, and celestial bodies to appeal to spiritual forces, rarely survive after their ritual use is completed.

Crafts of tribes of the East were quite varied; few examples still exist, however. Body ornamentation, including painting and tattooing, was prevalent and was widely utilized for ceremonial purposes. Other ornamental objects were made of wood, shell, copper, and even stone. Clothing was decorated with animal skins, feathers, and hair. Utilitarian objects were carved from wood and painted in bright colors: human and animal figures (often larger than life-sized) in decorated villages. Small stone figures were also carved. Baskets, woven in colored materials, were decorated with geometric designs. Pottery was often decorated with figures of living things.

The current interest in Indian culture and crafts has led to a greater appreciation by non-Indians of these objects, and to a deeper understanding of the philosophies of the people who created them. This increased popularity brings with it a tendency toward creating crafts solely for sale to the tourist or collector trade, rather than for use as a part of everyday life. It has, more encouragingly, also led toward the recognition of Indians as individual craftspeople, and has opened up new areas in art to Indians, such as pottery.

Pottery

Pottery, which has been developed to an incomparable level of sophistication among some Indian tribes, occupies an especially prominent place in the study of Indian crafts. Pottery making was not common to all Indians. Since it was impractical for nomadic people to transport breakable clay pots and jars as they travelled and desert and coastal dwelling peoples had other materials (wood and plants) from which to carve and weave containers. Areas in which pottery was significant were those regions in which a sedentary agriculturally dependent culture survived. For the areas in which pottery making was prominent, most particularly the pueblo Southwestern United States and the Mississippi Valley and Gulf region, its development from prehistoric times (*c.* 300 BC) through the present has resulted in spectacular craftsmanship.

Potters have traditionally been women, since the craft is considered a sedentary one. It has only been in the past twenty-five years, with the recognition of individual potters and artisans, that a few notable men have become potters. Pottery containers were used extensively in cooking and eating, and as vessels for carrying and storing waters and foods. The variety of elements that comprise the making of pottery—the clay, temper (material which is added to the clay to prevent its cracking in the drying and firing stages), size and shape of the pot, its decoration and ultimate use—insure the uniqueness of each piece of pottery. It is interesting, however, that very strong stylistic features have evolved which make pots of each tribe (and often of individual potters) easily distinguishable from one another. Most pottery was created for functional everyday purposes, but some tribes did create pottery solely for ceremonial usage or for commercial trade.

The three methods of pottery making were coiling, modeling, and molding the clay. Coiling has been the predominant method, especially as American Indian potters traditionally have not used a potter's wheel or a kiln. In making a coiled pot, the potter formed the base and then added coils made from rolled out balls of clay, connecting the coils by rubbing or pinching their ends together. This method was the most popular in the southern half of North America, the area in which most Indian pottery was produced. Modeling a pot consisted of building the rectangular sides of the pot onto the base, pinching them together at the edges of contact. In molding, a pot was constructed around another pot or basket or even a hole in the ground whose form was being followed by the shape of the new pot. Except for the pottery of one Eskimo region, the earliest pottery in the northern half of the continent was modeled or molded, but the coiling technique of the southern half soon became a prominent method of pottery construction in this area too. Often, paddles and anvils were used both in smoothing and shaping the pots, and in applying decorative stamps or designs to the exteriors. Other decoration was made by incising the clay with geometric and often symbolic designs of living organisms. Coloration of pottery was frequently employed.

The potter dug the clay out of the ground. Her tempering materials included sand, crushed stone, and shells. The pot was hand-built from the mixture of clay, temper, and water; once it was shaped, the pot was left in the shade to dry. It was then scraped and smoothed with a stone (although the Navajo potters used corncobs as a smoothing tool) and moistened with slip. If the pot was to be painted, pigments originally ground from minerals (with the exceptions of a black color sometimes used in the Southwest which came from a weed, and the poster paints used by the Tesuque and neighboring Santa Domingo Indians) were applied with a brush made by chewing the end of a yucca stem until it was malleable. The basic colors, using the mineral-based pigments, were black, white, tan, off-white, yellow, red, and orange. Only rarely were glazes employed, and when used they never covered the entire pot. In fact, the base of an Indian pot is always left unpainted and unglazed. The pots were then baked in clay ovens heated to temperatures of 1200-1500°F, or in open or covered fires.

The pottery of the Southwestern United States, particularly that of the Pueblo Indians, is considered to be the most revealing recording of the life and artistic behavior of the inhabitants of that area. Pottery has been produced in this region for an impressive amount of time (*c.* 300 BC to the present). The forms and decorative aspects show the variety of uses of pottery by the people of the Southwest throughout this span of time. The adherence to traditional shapes and decorative elements is a profound expression of the Indians' belief in the continuity of life and their respect for tradition. Pottery is one of the few crafts in which the influence of non-Indian cultures has not caused tremendously reckless changes in the quality or conception of the crafts.

The three major traditions in pueblo pottery were the Mogollan, Hohokam, and Anasazi. The Mogollan bowls and round narrow-necked jars were quite simple in form. The earliest Mogollan pottery was molded, but the coiling technique was used. First the potters scraped the coiled exterior surface until it became smooth, but later the coils around the neck of the jars were left unscraped. In this early stage of Mogollan pottery the usual red or brown color was supplanted by the use of reduction firing, a process in which the amount of oxygen is reduced in firing, thus causing a blackening of the pottery. Although the inclusion of geometric patterns was not unknown, undecorated simple pottery was the hallmark of this stage. Hohokam pottery, uniquely lacking in protuberances, was made in a multitude of shapes. The "Gila-shouldered" jars are the largest pots ever made in the Southwest. The famous Mimbres paddled coiled bowls and pitchers were covered with black ornamentation painted on a white background. The majority of these were decorated with complex geometric patterns, but later some were painted with stylized life forms: figures of people, fish, toads, lizards, birds, dogs, insects, and other animals. Other Hohokam vessels were tan, gray, or red, or a combination of these colors. The first polychrome painting on pottery was introduced in Hohokam pots with the use of yellow pigment. The Anasazi pottery tradition was by far the most diverse, the pottery of different regions showed many variations of form and decoration. Following the Mogollan tradition, the early Modified Basketmaker vessels were coiled and scraped; and in the same tradition, some potters even left the neck coils unscraped. Early pottery had black designs on gray, or white or red or orange. The ornamentation was simple geometric line patterns. In the Developmental Pueblo stage which followed this early period, coiled pots were made in which thc coils were not smoothed over, as well as the plain gray pottery. Most of the decoration was black painted on white or red, and utilized innovative geometrical variations incorporating not only simple linear designs but also step motifs, spirals, meanders, triangles, dots, scrolls, and complex interwoven patterns. There was some geometrical treatment of life forms. The great regional variety in pottery was a characteristic of all stages of Anasazi pottery making. Modern pottery for the most part, has adhered to the forms and decorative elements of the three traditions, particularly the dominant Anasazi.

Hopi pottery, the most outstanding of all pueblo pottery, is still created for utilitarian purposes in almost every village of the three Mesas. Like their ancestors, the contemporary Hopi use the bowls for cooking and serving and the jars (*ollas*) for storing food and water. Many of these vessels are undecorated and are brown or gray or a variegated orange.

The decorated pottery, made in First Mesa, is famous for its complex treatment of space and form. The low wide bowls and short bulging jars are covered with curvilinear patterns reminiscent of earlier pottery yet increasingly innovative. The potters' control of line can be seen in the geometric shapes and abstracted (often beyond recognition) representations of animals or parts of animals, lightning, rain clouds, and kachina figures. Bowls are decorated on the inside, sometimes with additional repeating geometric patterns appearing in a band on the exterior of the rim. Interior decoration can be either symmetrical or asymmetrical, commonly employing a variety of linear curves and stylized birds. Bcause of their shape, the jars are decorated on the outside. Banding begins just below the area at the top of the jar. The geometric pattern on the band can be repeated across the jar, or the band can be divided in several ways: into two symmetrically ornamented halves; into anywhere from four to six parts either of equal or unequal size, and decorated wtih repeating parts of equal size which are filled with one of three design patterns. The colors are usually black on tan; red, black and white on red; or black and red on tan. Very often the clay used by Hopi potters does not require a temper. The bowls and jars are commonly quite thin and smoothed.

The clay of the Zuñi has always been heavy, by contrast, although the surface of Zuñi pots appears smooth. In addition to the bowls and ollas, for about 100 years the Zuñi have made pottery owls. Bowls are no longer made and jars are not produced in any quantity today, although the owls are commercially successful. The owls are painted with black over a white base; the feathers and wings and round open eyes are painted in a conventionalized manner. The jars are divided vertically between the neck and body by a

Dover Archives.

Zuñi pottery and jar designs.

horizontal band, referred to as a "life line." Based on a legendary belief that the potter's spirit should not be trapped inside her pot, the life line is broken at one point on each jar to insure that the spirit will have a way to escape so the pottery will not die. The painted decoration was much less refined in Zuñi pottery than in Hopi. Zuñi jar decoration is made up of geometric elements: simple squares, diamonds, hooks, scrolls, step patterns, and rosettes; as well as representations of birds and deer. The painting on modern jars has degenerated considerably in both quality of work and treatment of space. Zuñi bowls were decorated, like their Hopi counterparts, with an internal geometric elaboration of lines and a band around the external rim containing a simple repeating unit of geometrical forms. The interiors of the bowls were designed so that a complicated band covering the deepest part of the bowl was beneath a more simply designed thinner band. The more complex larger band utilized a combination of the same geometric elements seen in jar decoration.

The pottery of the Rio Grande pueblos has gained great notoriety in the 20th century, for it was in San Ildefonso where Maria Martinez and her husband Julian developed the matte-polished pottery, which is the single most important innovation in modern Indian pottery. Through the 19th century the pottery of this area had been made for everyday use in cooking and storing food and water. Geometric decoration was black (sometimes with red) painted on white or off-white, or black on red, and a monochromatic pottery of all-red or all-black was also produced. In the early 1920s, Maria and Julian Martinez arrived at a process by which a stylized matte design on a highly polished background was created. Best known in its all-black form, it has also been adapted for monochromatic pottery in red, light blue or gray, rose, tan, or combinations of white matte on polished tan or red backgrounds. Carved pottery was also developed at San Ildefonso and has been incorporated into the matte-polished ware. Potters in the nearby Santa Clara and San Juan pueblos have followed Maria Martinez' technique and have enjoyed similar commercial rewards. Often, the matte-polished pottery of Santa Clara is indistinguishable from that of San Ildefonso. There are two shapes, however, which are distinctly Santa Claran: the dual-necked "wedding" jar and the jar with a singularly high neck and wide mouth. In addition, small animals and some vases with handles were made in Santa Clara. Santa Clara pottery frequently features ornamentation made by depressing dull objects into the clay, rather than painting on the surface of the clay. San Juan pottery incorporates incising into monochromatic pottery. Santa Domingo pots both in bichrome and polychrome have large geometric curvilinear designs. Zia pottery combines stylized birds and deer with leaves on a field of swirls and pointed shapes. The Acoma pottery, perhaps the most refined of all Rio Grande area pottery, has also the thinnest walls of all Southwestern pottery. No Acoma bowls have been made other than for comercial use in the past century. Acoma pottery decoration, black painted on orange tones, has two styles: naturalistic and geometric. The naturalistic style shows large birds separated by plant-like swirls, eating flowers or berries. The geometric style consists of a pattern of angular linear shapes (with the frequent addition of scallops and curves) which covers the jar. Recently an emphasis on linear hatched squares and diamonds has been popular. Cochiti jars and bowls are crudely shaped and painted in a relatively simplistic way, leaving large areas of pastel yellow or pink background between the large black figures of animals and humans. The unpainted pottery of Taos and Picuris are difficult to distinguish from one another. Potters from both pueblos use a clay containing mica, so that the resulting jars and bowls (and in Taos, bean pots) are shiny. The only ornamentation is the occasional indentation around the rim of these brown or gray pots. Their appearance is much closer to Navajo and non-pueblo pottery. For the two centuries before they became familiar with poster paints in the early 1920s, Tesuque and Jemez potters created lovely pots with simple shapes and flowing linear designs. Since the first quarter of this century, however, this pottery has degenerated into a glaring example of the effecct of commercialism on art. Not only do the potters of these pueblos now make jars and bowls in miniature (useless for utilitarian purposes), but they also break another tradition by painting them with brightly clashing commercial paints in blocky solid shapes. The pots continue to be commercially successful, either due to or in spite of their garishness.

Of the non-pueblo pottery, the most outstanding has come from the Mohave, Maricopa, Pima, and Papago. Most other non-pueblo Indians produced only crudely formed and decorated cooking pots. Mohave jars and bowls are simply shaped and decorated with angular patterns of lines with solid shapes filled in. Some jars are topped with human heads modeled onto the jar. Mohave modeled toads, made of thick clay and covered with red spots, are also popular. Maricopa pottery, the most sophisticated non-pueblo pottery, is usually red or red with black geometric ornamentation and has been highly polished. Pima and Papago tribes, excellent basketmakers, are no longer prolific potters. Traditional pottery of these tribes were red or black wide-mouthed ollas decorated with linear and solid shapes, used for storing water. Contemporary Papago and Pima pottery consists of small jars, square or rectangle boxes, bowls, and ashtrays, all created and decorated with curvilinear lines and forms and sometimes even flower patterns, for commercial use.

None of the non-pueblo pottery comes close to matching the sophistication and elegant vitality of Hopi pottery, in form or decoration.

The Mississippi Valley and Gulf area of the United States was the second productive pottery-making region. Again, pots were used for cooking and storing food and water. Often, pottery was unpainted and decoration of these modeled jars and bowls took the form of incising or stamping the clay before firing, or engraving the hard clay walls after removing the pot from the oven. Sometimes holes were poked into the clay or roughly textured fabrics were pressed against the soft clay to form an impression from the weave. In addition, effigy figures of humans, animals, and plants were common decorative elements modeled onto the utilitarian vessels and pipes. Vases were quite colorful. Not infrequently, effigy figures themselves were modeled. If painted, southeastern pottery was usually red, or red decoration was painted on pots of white or tan. There were also some monochromatic black or brown pots, and some white based pots with black decoration. Thse painted designs, like their stamped, incised, or engraved counterparts, were both abstracted naturalistic forms or, more frequently, geometric. Southeastern pottery employs a more curvilinear treatment of design than does the pottery of the Southwest. The shapes of the pots, from the Mississippi to Florida, such as the three-legged ones, were influenced by trade with Europeans and West Indians.

The only other area in which pottery was mildly

The *"Artesanias"* pavillion (Peru) displaying handwoven baskets, *"retablos"* from Ayacucho, ceramic bulls from Pucará, figurines from Cuzco, carved gourds and handwoven alpaca rugs.

significant was in Alaska. There, fired pottery with designs made by stamping curvilinear patterns or impressing cord into the soft clay have been found ranging in age from 1000 BC to AD 900. There was a lack of pottery in the Pacific states and Northwest Coast. What little pottery came from southern California was most likely influenced by that of th nearest Southwestern Indians. The Iroquois of the mid-Atlantic region made some simple cooking vessels and pipes.

The influence of non-Indians and commercialization on the pottery of the Indians has had a variety of effects. Most obvious is the degeneration of traditional styles and decorative forms, as seen in the popularity of miniature bowls and jars in the Southwest and the use of poster paints by the Tesuque and Jemez. With the advent of the railroad and through increased trade, non-Indians also encouraged Indian potters to model clay to resemble animals (the Zuni owls and Mohave toads) because they were easily salable. For the same reason, new forms such as ashtrays, candlesticks, square boxes, and individual plates and saucers were created. The increase in travel and trade made it easier for Indians of one tribe to become familiar with the forms and designs of potters of other tribes, and the distinctions between tribal styles began to fade as they were copied and modified. The most encouraging effect of 20th century commercialization upon Southwestern potters has been the recognition of individual potters' contributions to the development of modern pottery. By valuing a pot with the potter's signature on the bottom more than an unsigned pot, white traders and collectors have introduced the element of financial success into the potter's feeling of pride in her careful artistry. At times, this recognition has influenced potters to attain levels of fine craftsmanship.

Latin America

When the Spaniards first landed on Mexican soil, one of their greatest sources of amazement, among the many marvels of the New World, were the beautiful pieces of craftsmanship which the Indians used in their religious ceremonies, daily wear and personal ornaments. The praise rendered toward these objects by many of the chroniclers is proof that this art deeply impressed the Spaniards and its influence was a determining factor in the formation of the new American culture.

The samples of native craft which Cortés sent to Europe brought forth phrases of admiration from many of the well-known figures of the Old World, such as this one of Durer's: "...I also saw the things that were brought to the King from the new land of gold: a sun, six-feet wide, made of pure gold, and also a moon, of the same size, in silver; further, several curious weapons and missiles; many strange garments, beds and all types of articles for human use, all of this more beautiful to behold than miracles. So precious were these objects that they were valued at one hundred thousand florins. And as for myself, I have never, in all the days of my life, seen things that so delighted my heart. For I saw among them wonderful works of art and was astonished at the subtle ingenuity of the men in those distant lands. I cannot say enough about the things which were before my eyes."

U.S. Department of Agriculture.

Replica of an Inca statue is painted by Tulio Alvarez, Bogota, Colombia (1965).

Although future artisans were obliged to adopt new aesthetic and ideological concepts in their work, the spirit of those ancient artists has endured up to our times. Thus the arts that the Spaniards introduced from Renaissance Europe acquired, in this new land, new life, new outlines, new essence. Sculptors and builders, both Indian and mestizo, created architectural forms of the most extraordinary baroque art, all impregnated with the spirit of their ancestral deities.

Potters, members of one of the most traditional and important of craft groups, ceased making ceremonial earthenware (at least in the eyes of the church and its spies) and soon adopted European and Chinese techniques. They thus succeeded in creating the new hand-varied ceramic work which is seen today. The great mass of Mixtec silver and goldsmith was absorbed almost in its entirety by the church for the fashioning of religious objects of gold and silver; only a small number of silversmiths remained who were dedicated to the making of feminine ornaments and jewelry, and relics which the people offered to their patron saints in gratitude for some favor. The gold and silver crafts went into decline when the influence of the church was limited by the Reform laws, and it was not until this century that they regained importance with the flourishing of new silver centers.

One of the handicrafts which underwent almost no change in style was that of textiles—the costumes of today are almost identical with those worn before the Conquest. However, new industries were established, such as that of the rebozo, possibly Oriental in its origin, and the sarape, derived from the Spanish shawl of the Jemez region.

Textiles and ceramics are the two most widespread crafts in Latin America.

There are several large pottery centers in various regions whose wares have an ample distribution. Such is the case of the pottery made in Tonalá and Tlaquepaque, Jalisco; the so called "talavera" or mayolica whose origin is undoubtedly Chinese and which is made in Puebla, Dolores Hidalgo, Guanajuato and Aguascalientes; the glazed earthenware from Oaxaca; the earthen pans and jars for cooking from Puebla, Texcoco, Tecomatepec and Metepec in the State of Mexico. Other ceramic centers sell their products within a certain limited area near the production center, such as Patamban, Purépero, Huantzito, Tzintzuntzan, Capula and Sta. Fe de la Laguna, in the State of Michoacán; Encarnación and Atemajac, in Jalisco; Tolimán and Amayaltepec, in Guerrero; Actlán, Huaquechula, San Mateo Acteopan and San Martin Texmelucan, in Puebla; Ocotlán in Tlaxcala; Huatusco in Veracruz; Ocotlán, Tehuantepec, Coyotepec and Atzompa in Oaxaca; Amatenango, in Chiapas; Tepakan in Campeche, and Ticul in Yucatán.

Ceramic products are fundamentally domestic in their purpose: cooking bowls, jugs and jars to carry or drink liquids, plates, etc. Used for ceremonial purpose are candlesticks, urns, and incense holders. There is, however, an interest in aspect of ceramics which is of great importance to the people: toys. These are made mainly in Tonalá, Jal., Metepec, Méx., Huaquechula and Acatlán, Pue., Huatusco, Ver., Amayaltepec and Talimán, Gro., Coyotepec, Atzompa, Juchitán and Tehuantepec, Oax., and in Ticul, Yuc. In spite of the fact that the mestizo population regards toys as such, for the indigenous population these have a deep ritualistic significance. They are made for such occasions as the Day of the Dead, Corpus Christi, Holy Week and Christmas.

These "toys" are very similar to the clay figurines whose significance is still not clear, which were made in Mexico more than three thousand years ago. Although they served a religious purpose, they did not always represent gods. Thus, the present "tangu-yu" of Juchitán and Tehuantepec, brightly colored clay dolls and horsemen on strange mounts, are placed on the altars on New Year's Eve, side by side with the patron saints. The toys from Metepec for the most part represent religious personages such as the Three Kings, St. James, Archangels, the Virgin Mary, Adam and Eve, etc. But the most popular and deeply-rooted toy in Mexico is that relating to the Day of the Dead (All Souls Day). Imagination runs wild in such objects as skulls whose lower jaws move by pulling a thread, skeletons which, by pulling another string, emerge from tombs, or whose joints move by springs, or "dance" at the slightest movement. All these toys of the dead, plus a variety of other ceremonial objects made of clay, paper, palm leaf, flowers, wood, sugar and bread constitute the most important elements in the Mexican cult of the dead.

Lacquer work is another craft which goes back to ancient pre-Hispanic times when it was used not only on gourds, but also on ceramics and onyx. The basic method is to apply many coats of color mixed with a resin extracted from a certain insect and a drying oil. Techniques differ according to the region. In Uruapan, Michoacán, the inlaid technique is used, i.e., carving out the design on the lacquer and then filling in with the chosen colors. This is the original method as can be seen on archaeological objects painted in "cloisonné." In other parts, a black, red or white lacquer base is applied and the design drawn on top with a brush. The main lacquer centers today are Uruapan and Pátzcuaro, in the State of Michoacán; Olinalá in Guerrero and Chiapa de Corzo in Chiapas.

Blown glass is another important handicraft which was introduced from Europe. Large factories exist in Mexico City, Guadalajara, Puebla and Texcoco.

Basketry, even earlier in origin than ceramics, is another significant craft. The principal production centers of baskets, cordage and hats are found among the various Otomi groups in the State of Hidalgo, the Chochopopolocas in southern Puebla, in the central region of Guerrero, south the Balsas River, and among the Mayas on the Yucatán peninsula where the famous "Panamá" or jipi japa hats are made.

Leatherwork, another industry of note, is best exemplified by the huarache or sandal, and the saddle. The largest production centers are Guadalajara, León, Puebla, Mexico City, Oaxaca and Mérida. The saddles made in Puebla are veritable works of art for their richness in decoration.

Amozoc, in the State of Puebla, excels in the making of objects of forged iron such as spurs with a blui tint, buckles, iron work for saddles and other charro accessories, machetes and cutlery.

Jalisco, Guerrero and Oaxaca are also famous for their machetes, those of Oaxaca being particularly beautiful for their engravings and inscriptions such as "if this snake bites you, there is no remedy at the drugstore," or "don't expose me without reason or put me away without honor," etc. In Santa Clara del Cobre, near the famous pre-Colombian copper mines of Hinguarán, Michoacán, the "beating" method is used on this metal: hammering the pieces of copper and shaping them into pots, jars, flower holders, fruit bowls, plates, etc., of lovely and elegant lines. In Puebla, Mexico City, Cuernavaca, Toluca, Guanajuato, Guadalajara and Taxco, tin is shaped into lanterns, candle-holders, mirror frames and other decorative objects.

Although Mexico is a country that produces an infinite variety of precious woods, these are employed to a comparatively small degree in the popular arts and crafts. Such objects as inlaid boxes for keeping rooster blades are made in Jalostotilán, Jalisco; jewel cases and chocolate beaters in Campeche and Yucatán; in Teocaltiche, Jalisco, and Uruapan, Michoacán, the wood is worked by turning and the use of bone applications is common. Furniture for popular use is made in Parcho, Mich., Puebla, Tehuantepec, Oax., and other places in southeastern Mexico. Dance masks and carved religious figures are made in Jalisco, Michoacán, Guerrero, Querétaro, Guanajuato, Chiapas and the State of Mexico.

In recent years, the artisans of Taxco have combined silver with precious woods such as rosewood, ebony and mahogany in the making of salad bowls, jewel cases and a variety of lovely brooches and bracelets. Colonial furniture of pine or white cedar is also mass-produced in Taxco.

And so, whether it be in the clothes he wears or the candy he eats, in the festive toys or the solemnity of his religious festivals, the Indian is always surrounded by beauty. For this reason, almost ten percent of the rural indigenous population is made up of artisans. Among the rural population, craftwork is as much a basic activity as agriculture. The latter insures the daily sustenance, while the former is the only means of obtaining a cash income without having to sell or transfer the crop. Thus, the Indian, in this productive pastime, lovingly and with no thought of praise, surrounds himself and his society with the beauty his spirit requires.

CRAIG is an Indian village located on Prince of Wales Island, Southeastern District, Alaska. It is incorporated as a town in Alaska, and has a population of 220 Tlingit Indians.

Sometimes the term "Indian Reservation" has been used to describe Craig. By the 1926 Alaska Native Townsite Act, Craig was established, and is now held in trust by the federal government. The Tlingit who live in Craig were formerly one of North America's more powerful tribes. They crossed the Canadian Rockies to seek the coast. In 1741, Russian explorers found them on Prince of Wales Island, and established rule over them. Today, no longer subjugated, they participate actively in Alaska's political affairs.

Craig lies in an area where the Pacific currents provide a mild and moist current year 'round. Rainfall is plentiful, and temperatures are moderate. The major industries in the town, which center on trout and salmon fishing, and bear and deer hunting, are all owned by non-Indians. Services in the town include water, sewer, and electricity. The nearest medical care is in Ketchikan, 80 miles away. Commercial transportation is available by air, bus, and truck.

The Tlingit Indians today still make use of their traditional crafts, and are considered excellent boat and canoe builders. Their goat wool and cedar bark ceremonial blanket are still in great demand as a trade item. Totem poles remain important decorative records of outstanding events of the past.

CRAZY HORSE (Oglala Sioux; 1842?-Sept. 5, 1887) was one of the most brilliant tacticians and determined warriors in the resistance of the Sioux (Dakota) to the movement of the white man into the northern Great Plains.

Crazy Horse—whose Indian name was Tashunke, or Ta-Sunko, Witko—grew up with the Brulé Sioux, his mother's people, but then went to live with his father's people, the Oglala Sioux. Known as Curley in childhood, he has exhibited such great bravery in battle by the time he was 17 that his father, one of the Oglala holy men, gave him his own name. In time the younger Crazy Horse was also referred to as the Strange Man of the Oglala because of his quiet, unassuming nature and his visionary powers.

It is believed that Crazy Horse was active in the Sioux wars as early as 1865, taking part in the joint Cheyenne-Sioux attack on the Julesburg stockade in Colorado Territory on January 7 in revenge for the savage attack on the Cheyenne camp at Sand Creek by Col. John M. Chivington. He rose to full power as a brilliant warrior at the time of the massacre of Capt. William J. Fetterman and his men near Fort Phil Kearny, Wyoming Territory, on December 21, 1866, and at the Wagon Box fight on August 2, 1867, near the same fort. Crazy Horse refused to honor the terms of the Second Treaty of Fort Laramie (1868). As "hostiles," he and his followers moved to unceded buffalo country, where they continued to hunt and to fight both their enemy Indian tribes and the white man.

Throughout 1873 Crazy Horse is said to have participated in attacks on railroad survey parties escorted by military forces under the command of Col. David S. Stanley. Lieut. Col. George A. Custer was in command of the Seventh Calvalry under Stanley. The following year Colonel Custer led his Seventh Calvalry back into Indian territory for field training, further antagonizing the Indians. In that same summer (1874), gold was discovered in the Black Hills—the Indians' sacred hunting ground. Unable to halt the rush of gold seekers, the U.S. government attempted to buy the Sioux lands, but the price offered by the commissioners was far from acceptable to the Indian chiefs. Alarmed government officials decided to abrogate the treaty clause which permitted the Indians to roam in the unceded territory, and they demanded that all hostiles be confined to reservations by January 31, 1876.

It is doubtful whether this order, issued in December 1875, even reached Crazy Horse at his winter encampments on the Tongue and Powder rivers. Brig. Gen. George Crook, commanding the Department of the Platte, immediately undertook to force the hostiles to come to the agencies. On March 17, 1876, General

Crook's advance column under Col. Joseph J. Reynolds made a surprise attack on an Indian camp on the Powder River about ten miles north of the Wyoming line. It was mistakenly reported that this was Crazy Horse's camp; in fact, the Indians were Northern Cheyenne together with a few Oglala Sioux. The survivors of this encounter then joined Crazy Horse and his Oglala Sioux, and both groups eventually joined with Sitting Bull and his Hunkpapa Sioux.

On June 17, 1876, a group of Indians, supposedly under the command of Crazy Horse made a surprise attack on General Crook's superior column in the valley of the Rosebud, Montana Territory, forcing the soldiers to withdraw. On June 25, Colonel Custer and his Seventh Calvalry attacked the great combined camp, which was then encamped on the Little Big Horn River. Crazy Horse played a leading role, along with Gall and other noted chiefs, in the counterattack that succeeded in wiping out Custer's immediate command.

After the Battle of the Little Big Horn, the hostile tribes went their separate ways. Crazy Horse and his followers resumed their nomadic way of life. But times were not the same. Col. Nelson A. Miles was determined to force all Indians to surrender at the agencies. Many families wanted to desert Crazy Horse for reservation life. Game was diminishing; they wanted peace, and the government promised food and clothing for those who would come in voluntarily.

On January 8, 1877, Colonel Miles caught up with Crazy Horse at Battle Butte in the Wolf Mountains, a spur of the Bighorn Mountains. While a group of warriors held off the soldiers, the main band escaped, helped by a snow storm which turned into a blizzard by the early afternoon. Crazy Horse held out until May 5, when he surrendered to General Crook at the Red Cloud Agency at Fort Robinson.

There are various accounts of the events that led to the death of Crazy Horse a few months later. Some say that he rode out from Fort Robinson to place his ailing wife under the care of a physician at the Spotted Tail Reservation; others that he received permission to hunt buffalo a few miles from the fort. His lack of cooperation on the reservation had given rise to rumors that he was planning to kill General Crook, then to collect his own followers and flee northward. In any event, he was arrested at the Spotted Tail Agency and returned to Fort Robinson on September 5. At the guardhouse door he bolted. In the confusion that followed, he was mortally wounded. When the Oglala left the Red Cloud Agency later that fall, Crazy Horse's remains went with them to the Pine Ridge Agency. Allegedly they were later moved to Manderson, South Dakota, and buried in the shadow of Crazy Horse Butte.

No photograph has ever certainly been identified as that of Crazy Horse. This fact is a source of pride to Indians who see it as a sign that the white man never had complete control of the great chief.

Capt. John G. Bourke, one of the last white men to know Crazy Horse, said of him: "All Indians gave him a high reputation for courage and generosity....He was one of the great soldiers of his day and generation."

CRAZY SNAKE is the translation of the Creek name of *CHITTO HARJO*, also known as Wilson Jones, a leader of the Crazy Snake Uprising in Oklahoma in 1901. He was born in 1846 in Creek Territory (near Boley, Oklahoma). Following considerable dissatisfaction with the manner in which the government carried out the terms of the Treaty of 1866, many full-blood Indians separated from the main Creek group and refused to enroll. Finally, facing the threat of the loss of their treaty land, Chitto Harjo became their representative in negotiations with the federal authorities, and established his "Snake Government" in 1897 at Hickory Hill, I. T. A short-lived uprising took place in January-February of 1901, which attracted some 5,000 followers. This soon collapsed after some desultory skirmishing, and after a brief trial, Chitto Harjo and his immediate group were found guilty, but released by a sympathetic judge, who understood their grievances, and realized that there had been no serious menace in their actions. This adventure was followed by continuing political unrest,

Crazy Snake

and in 1911, Chitto Harjo became involved in the famous Smoked Meat Rebellion, from which he emerged with a bullet wound which is thought to have caused his death on April 11, 1912 near Smithville, Oklahoma.

FREDERICK DOCKSTADER

CREE was a huge, diverse tribe of hunters who occupied a large part of Canada. Their lands went as north from the coast of the East Main River nearly to the Churchill River; towards the East they extended to Lakes Mistassini and Nichiheu. Towards the west their boundaries were less certain; in the early 1500s they probably wandered over country west of Lake Winnepeg, and possibly between the Red and Saskatchewan rivers. Once they obtained firearms, however, they made great movements both west and north. By the mid 18th century they controlled northern Manitoba and Saskatchewan as far as the Churchill River, all of northern Alberta, the valley of the Slave River and parts of the land surrounding the Great Slave Lake.

Their name comes from a contraction of *Kristineaux*, which is a French form for the name of a Cree branch. The meaning of *Kristineaux* is unknown. The Cree's linguistic stock was Algonquian.

Although a huge tribe numerically, estimates in the 18th century listed 15,000 Crees, there was never any central government. The Crees lived in bands. Like other Athapascan nations Crees took on some characteristics of tribes they contacted. Generally the Cree bands were divided into two types: the plains Cree, living on the Canadian plains, and the woodland or Swampy Cree living in the woodlands.

Some aspects of band life differed from one band to another. For example, dwellings varied. The Southern woodland Cree constructed bark and wooden wigwams. Toward the north, the Cree constructed skin tipis. However, most basic aspects of life, such as hunting and tool construction, were alike. Deer, caribou, and moose were the main source of meat; and rabbits were extensively used both for food and skin blankets. Though the Crees despised fishing, they took it up when other food was scarce. To catch fish they used hooks of sturgeon bones. Other animal bones were used, such as awls made of moose bnes. In the north, Crees used an oddly curved knife probably borrowed from the Inuit. Other bands to the south and west used a chiseled sharp tool similar to other Plains tribes. Flints were used for arrowheads, spear points, and hatchets. Cooking vessels and pottery were made of stone. As contact with whites increased these tools were replaced with European items.

Physically the Cree were copper colored, of medium height and proportion. MacKenzie thought Cree women were the most beautiful of any Indians he had seen. Chastity was not considered a virtue but a wife's infidelity was often severely punished. Polygamy was common and a widower was expected to marry his wife's sister, if she had one.

Tattooing was common until it was prohibited because of white displeasure. Women wre content to have simply two lines drawn from the corners of their mouths to their jaws. But many men had lines and patterns drawn all over their bodies.

Government usually consisted of just one chief for each band.

Their religious customs were similar to the Ojibwa's. The major religious group was a secret society which both men and women could join. There were four levels of membership to which one could advance. But few reached the highest levels, for each succeeding level involved heavy payments. Those that were at the highest level were medicine men, and in a position of great power. The Crees believed the great spirits had endowed everything with a soul, so medicine men were those who could appeal to those souls to help cure a sick individual. But Crees also believed that many evil spirits existed, and a medicine man could use these spirits to harm people. There was a great fear of witchcraft. On hunting trips the men would carry little bags of herbs for protection.

Burial places for the dead were covered with stones to protect the bodies from animals. Some items owned by the deceased were placed on the grave.

The tribe always had good relations with the French and the English, who allowed the Crees freedom to pursue their lifestyle. But Crees had difficulty with other tribes. In 1786 a smallpox epidemic struck, reducing the Crees to half their numbers. Other tribes particularly the Blackfeet, had acquired firearms, and used these against the Cree. Then alcohol was introduced into the tribe; and its effects were ruinous. By the 1830s another epidemic struck and the population fell to under 3,000. Today, however, there are more than 20,000 Cree living mostly on reservations in Manitoba.

CREEK are an important Muskhogean tribe, who, along with the Cherokees, Chickasaws, Choctaws and Seminoles, were one of the "Five Civilized Tribes," so named because they adopted white culture more rapidly than others.

A Muskhogean speaking tribe, they were part of the great Muskhogean confederacy. Interestingly only about half of the tribes forming this confederacy spoke Muskhogean. The Creeks lived in Alabama and Georgia. Like the Chickasaws and Choctaws they migrated there from the north.

As their village life changed, Creeks lived in small wooden houses that were clustered together according to clans. Agriculture and hunting provided the basic staples. Corn was prepared 42 different ways, according to one observer. They ate a variety of fruits and meats and brewed a mildly alcoholic drink called "Hickory Milk." The women spun superb cloth on looms.

As to the social organization, the Creeks, like so many other tribes, were organized into clans. Marriage was only permitted outside the clan. Girls were trained and educated by their oldest maternal aunt; while men handled the young boys.

Adulterous or misbehaving wives could have their ears and noses clipped. Many of these women became prostitutes. Women could start divorce proceedings against husbands, however, by tossing their possessions out of the house. Such men had then to return to their mother's house.

The Creeks were generally a forgiving people. One of the most outstanding characteristics of their religion is that at the annual Green Corn Dance, the most important of Creek ceremonies, every sin or violation, short of murder, was forgiven. The Creeks' religious structure was a combination of priests and shamans. Priests had verbatum religious prayers and the individual sought direct contact with the Gods through dreams. Medicine men were trained in schools, and there were three classes of medicine men.

There were the "knowers," people who had psychic power; the medicine men who could control weather and other phenomena; and witches, who were full of lizards and caused murder. If a doctor's patient died he was suspected of witchcraft and was often killed by the deceased's family.

The dead were usually buried in the bed they occupied in their house. Mothers also buried their dead children in their house to ease their mourning.

One ritual commonly practiced by men before going to war, playing ball, having council meetings, or any auspicious event was the drinking of *Asi*, the Black Drink. This was a mild narcotic which caused nausea. It was taken for spiritual and physical purification.

Every Creek town had its own chief and was autonomous in local government. The chief and his vice-chief were approved by a council. Though the position was not hereditary one clan usually furnished the chief.

The Creeks had no war chiefs; all chiefs were called *Peace Chiefs*. There were three classifications of warriors, each with a certain degree of authority. One went up the ranks according to one's valor in war.

Certain Creek towns called *White Towns*, were designated only for peace ceremonies, and certain others, called *Red Towns*, were designated only for war ceremonies.

The Creeks were first met by De Soto in 1540. In 1559 Tristan de Lunia visited them but all that can be said of the visit is he left the tribe in a deplorable condition. Sometime between then and the alliance with the English the Muskhogean confederacy was formed between the Creeks and other smaller tribes.

The Creeks came into prominence as English allies in the Apalachee War of 1703-08. They remained friendly to British while hostile to the Spanish in Florida.

Following the American Revolution, certain bands became anti-American while others allied with the Americans. Creek warriors helped Jackson defeat other Creeks at the Battle of Horseshoe Bend in 1812.

Soon after there developed a major split in Creek-American relations, and this resulted in the Creek Wars of 1813-14. This time they fought Jackson, and the bloody war ended with their total defeat and the loss of many of their lands. Between 1835-43 was the Seminole War, a torturous affair which finally secured peace between the Creeks and southern tribes, and ended with most of the Creeks removed to Oklahoma.

In Oklahoma they established a nation based on the U.S. Constitution, with a single executive, a House of Kings—similar to the Senate—and a House of Warriors—similar to the House of Representatives.

The first estimates of Creek population were in the 18th century when they had between 11,000 and 20,000. Today several thousand live on the reservation.

See map page 285.

CREEK CONFEDERACY was a loose union of southeastern tribes formed in 18th century Alabama and southern Georgia.

The confederacy was an amalgam of Muskhogean-speaking people whose territory was first penetrated by white men in 1538 when the Spanish explorer Hernando de Soto brought an expedition north from Florida. There were about 50 Creek towns with a population of from 20,000 to 30,000 in two main divisions. The dominant Upper Creeks or Muskogee lived along the Ocmulgee Rvier and were called Indians of the Creek by early English traders, thus bringing the confederacy its name. The Lower Creeks, the Hitchiti and Alabama, spoke a slightly different language. The Apalachicola of the Lower Creeks were an important force in the organization of the confederacy early in the 18th century.

Creek women farmed the flatlands of Alabama and Georgia and the men were hunters as well as warriors. Community life was organized around a town square used for festivals. There were two major kinds of towns. In the white towns the square was used for joyful peace or harvest festivals. The red towns were used for war ceremonials.

The Creeks were never a truly unified people. About six different languages were spoken within the confederacy which, in addition to its dominant members, also incorporated small alien nations and the remaining members of earlier Indian powers. Politically, the Creeks frequently allied themselves to the British in battles against tribes such as the Apalachee people of Florida and the Spanish. On the other hand, there were sizeable pro-Spanish groups in the Lower Creek towns. The Seminoles of Florida were an offshoot of the Creeks.

Unity particularly dissipated after Tecumseh's visit in 1811. The Shawnee Pan-Indian leader urged a united Indian front against further white encroachments on Indian lands. Varying reaction to his emotional plea soon split the Creek union into rival factions engaged in civil war. During the Creek War (1813-1814), state militias and pro-Americans Creeks vanquished the anti-American 'Red Sticks' faction.

After a series of land-ceding treaties at Fort Jackson (1814) and Indian Springs (1814 and 1825), the Creeks agreed to an 1832 treaty and moved to Indian Territory (now Oklahoma). They became one of the Five Civilized Tribes along with the Chickasaw, Seminole, Choctaw, and Cherokee.

In Oklahoma, factionalism continued and increased because of the actions of William MacIntosh, the principal pro-American leader. The Lower Creeks were centered on the Arkansas River while the Upper Creeks settled on the Canadian River. By 1839 the tribe had entered a shaky union and differences slowly eased until, in 1867, a constitutional government was adopted.

CREEK WARS were a series of conflicts between the United States and the Creek Confederacy of Alabama and southern Georgia. One was the Creek War from 1813-14. The defeated Creeks were forced to cede their homelands and move west of the Mississippi. Inequities in the removal process triggered another "war" in 1836-37.

The Creek nation, a union of disparate farming and hunting peoples, was beginning to feel the pressure of approaching white civilization at the turn of the 19th century. In 1811 they were visited by Tecumseh, the charismatic Pan-Indian leader, who urged all Indians to unite in holding off further white takeover of Indian homelands. Tecumseh's plea split the Creeks into pro- and anti-American factions and a civil war began in 1812.

Tensions increased with the War of 1812 between the United States and England. The anti-American faction, numbering about 25% of the Creek nation, was led by William Weatherford (Chief Red Eagle) and Menawa, "Great Warrior." Menawa was the leader of the Creek Okfuskee towns on the Tallapoosa River. Their warriors painted their war clubs red and were known as "Red Sticks."

Chief Red Eagle, of mixed Creek and Scot ancestry, attacked Fort Mims on August 30, 1813. The fort, about 40 miles north of Mobile, was a refuge to white settlers from the surrounding war-torn countryside. Less than 100 militiamen defended the fort as the large war party arrived. Most of the 350 white and black occupants were massacred.

The prominent pro-American Creek leader, William MacIntosh, retaliated for the Fort Mims Massacre. His force killed some 200 "Red Stick" warriors. An outraged American populace demanded that the rebels be put down completely. Surrounding states dispatched militias under five volunteer generals to hunt the "Red Sticks." One of these volunteers, Tennessee's Andrew Jackson (later seventh President of the United States), was especially effective. He achieved minor successes in fighting the Creeks at Talladega on November 9; Emuckfau on January 22, 1814; and at Enotochopco on January 24.

Jackson's biggest victory was the decisive engagement of the Creek War, the Battle of Horseshoe Bend (Tohopeka, Alabama) on May 27, 1814. Chief Menawa had gathered almost the entire remaining Creek opposition, nearly 1,000 warriors, on a peninsula of the Tallapoosa River. The peninsula was protected by a log fortification at its narrow neck on the river bank. The "Red Stick" women and children encamped in a nearby village.

The opposition force numbered 2,000. Jackson's Tennessee militiamen were augmented by Creek, Yuchi, and Cherokee warriors. Chief Junaluska commanded 600 Cherokee warriors and scouts. With the Cherokees was young Sam Houston who had been living with them in Tennessee. The several hundred Creeks and Yuchis who fought with Jackson were led by William MacIntosh and Yuchi Chief Timpoochee Barnard.

A two-hour cannon barrage opened the attack on the peninsula on May 27, 1814. Jackson's Indian auxiliaries then attacked from both river banks and the main militia followed. Several hours later, Creek opposition to U.S. expansion had been destroyed. The "Red Stick" village was captured and the women and children were taken as prisoners. Only 70 opposition warriors, including Menawa, survived the battle.

Horseshoe Bend had made Jackson a national hero and a major-general in the U.S. Army. He had built Fort Jackson at the confluence of the Coosa and Tallapoosa rivers and there, on August 9, 1814, a treaty with the Creeks was concluded. The Creeks ceded 23,000,000 acres of land in Alabama and southern Georgia. Jackson's Indian allies found that some of their lands were included in the cession.

The Creek War was followed by 15 years of pressure to move the southeastern tribes to lands west of the Mississippi. The Creeks and others were forced into further land-ceding treaties and, finally, emigration with the passage of the Indian Removal Bill of 1830.

A Creek war in 1836 was precipitated by groups of white men who were defrauding the Indians in the sale of their possessions prior to the move west. The land companies triggered rebellion to stall an ongoing government investigation of the fraudulent deals. In February 1836, 2,500 destitute Creeks wandered among the Cherokee and were attacked by Georgia militia. They then took refuge with the Cherokee in Alabama. In May groups of Lower Creeks attacked white property owners between Tuskegee and Columbus. General Thomas Jesup arrived with a force to end the war and ship the Creeks westward. More than 11,000 U.S. troops were used in the following year and this force included nearly 2,000 Creeks under Opothleyaholo.

Some of the Creeks found refuge in Florida with the Seminoles. Eneah Emathla, leader of the uprising, was captured and many of his people then surrendered. By

July 1836, most of the insurgents had been captured, handcuffed, and prepared for the subsequent removal west to Indian territory (now Oklahoma). Nearly 15,000 Creeks were removed from their homelands in 1836.

CRIME AND DELINQUENCY, the violation of principles of social control defined by the rulers, is one of the most difficult subjects in the study of Indians in the Americas. Official crime and delinquency figures cannot be accepted as an accurate index of the actual level of criminal activity for the general population, much less for any one area or the members of any particular group comprising a small proportion of the national population. Some categories of crime, usually the less serious from the rulers' point of view, are inevitably underrepresented in official records and are sometimes dramatically affected by changing standards of law enforcement. Other behavior which a subject group may consider criminal, such as witchcraft, is missing altogether from official records. In addition to these standard pitfalls in the study of crime, criminal records for Indians may also be biased by the way in which justice is administered to this group in comparison to other groups, and broad generalizations about Indian crime are likely to be of limited value because of the differences from one tribe to another and between reservation and non-reservation Indians of the same tribe.

Perhaps because of these serious problems with sources, few aspects of Indian crime have been studied in a thorough and convincing way. The few general treatments of Indian crime based on official statistics such as those published in the *Uniform Crime Reports* suggest higher crime and deliquency rates for North American Indians than for the general population, especially after 1967; on the order of three times the rate for black Americans and ten times the rate for white Americans. Most Indian crimes were misdemeanors and other petty offenses, but Indian crimes against persons (e.g. homicide) and alcohol-related crimes also were substantially higher than for the general population, up to twenty times higher on some reservations. Indians have had the highest rate of arrest of any racial group in the U.S. for alcohol-related crimes and urban crimes. Simple drukenness has been a far more common cause of arrest among Indians than among other racial groups, this may be partly the result of bias in the administration of justice, although most studies find that Indians have a high rate of alcoholism and cirrhosis of the liver, and that alcohol is an important factor in other criminal offenses including homicide and suicide. The generally high Indian arrest rate also should be tempered by the fact that black Americans have higher arrest rates for the serious crimes of homicide, rape, assault, burglary, larceny, and robbery; and some Indian tribes and reservations have reported crime rates at or below the national average. (Since Latin American crime statistics usually do not identify Indians specifically, no comparisons can be made on these points.)

Crimes against property seem to be proportionately less important for Indians than for other groups. Summary figures suggest that Indians commit about twice as many crimes against persons as against property; the proportion is reversed for the general U.S. population. This pattern of Indian crimes against persons over crimes against property is repeated for the few communities of Mesoamerica that have been studied, and seems to be a pattern with considerable historical depth in the highland Indian regions of Latin America.

For North American Indians, homicide, suicide, and juvenile delinquency have received the most attention. They provide the basis for some tentative observations about Indian criminality and comparisons to the few studies of Indian crime in Latin America.

Homicide is perhaps the only social act almost universally regarded as a crime by rulers and subjects throughout the Americas since the arrival of Europeans. It is, therefore, the only category of crime for which the written documentation can be accepted with some confidence. Homicide has been studied for a number of reservations and rates have been compiled for a group of twenty-four reservations states, mostly west of the Mississippi River. Several characteristics of Indian homicides are shared with the general population. Roughly three-fourths of all homicides were committed by men, and the high points in age of offenders are the young to middle adult years. In the rate of homicide, however, Indians depart from the general population. Crude homicide rates for Indians in these studies prior to 1967 generally have been about three times as high as rates for the general population; age-adjusted rates have been three and one-half to four times as high (the Indian age-adjusted rate between 1959 and 1967 varied from 19.6 to 26.6 per 100,000 per year). Following 1967, the rates of Indian homicide jumped substantially and homicide is now the eighth leading cause of Indian death, following accidents, heart disease, cancer, influenza and pneumonia, diseases of early infancy, stroke, and cirrhosis of the liver. The apparent incidence of homicide before 1967 may not be especially high compared to earlier periods. Recourse to homicide, commonly an end result of feuding and retaliation, is documented for various tribes before the establishment of reservations.

Homicide cannot readily be studied for Indians as a group in Latin America, but a few community studies suggest that, while some villages are anti-homicidal and record only occasional violence, homicide rates are generally high (ranging up to 251/100,000 per year) and that political homicide is the main reason for high homicide rates in Indian areas of Mexico, Guatemala, Peru, and Bolivia. For Indian communities of Mexico that have been studied, people kill over blood revenge, factionalism within their communities, and jealousy over the suspected adultery of wives. These patterns seem to be fewer and clearer than the circumstances surrounding homicides among North American Indians in the twentieth century.

Historical studies of the patterns of homicide in Indian regions of Mexico based on numerous trial records are beginning to suggest relationships between Indian violence and peasant values and the conditions of life in the countryside. In these exceptional circumstances of personal and political violence, features of the society that are taken for granted in everyday life, such as social values, sometimes rise to the surface of consciousness. Social patterns of homicide have been studied for two regions of eighteenth-century Mexico: the Mixteca Alta region of Oaxaca in southern Mexico along the trade route from Mexico City and Puebla to Guatemala; and central Mexico, the hinterland of the colonial metropolis at Mexico City.

In looking closely at the setting and personal relationships in homicides, central Mexico and the Mixteca Alta traced somewhat different patterns. In most ways, the central Mexico homicides reveal a richer and less predictable variety of patterns. They spanned more evenly all levels of social relationships from husbands and wives to neighbors to officials to outsiders. The motives ascribed in the offenders' declarations in central Mexico often amounted to vague statements about passions and uncontrollable forces without clear reference to rules of social relationships among members of the community which were typical of the offenders' declarations in the Mixteca Alta cases. The central Mexico killings more often involved alcohol (although alcohol was present in less than half of all homicides for both regions) and the setting was more often a tavern. Disputes that led to violent deaths in central Mexico more often involved economic conflicts such as disputes over stolen property, unpaid debts, and damage to cropland or livestock.

Two features of central Mexico killings are especially distinctive. One is the "fighting words"—the insults exchanged before a lethal attack. Virtually every insult imaginable is documented as a prelude to at least one central Mexico killing. Many of these insults have in common a strong macho tone, pungent with the intent to defame and humble through verbal combat. Rather than being literal accusations, they were figurative insults of the grossest kind. The other special feature of peasant homicides in central Mexico is the weapons used. They were often deadly by design—especially firearms and long knives. Mixteca Alta villagers, on the other hand, tended to use whatever was at hand at the time of attack (rocks and knives) and their fighting words wre literal accusations rather than figurative insults.

These regional contrasts between central Mexico and the Mixteca Alta suggest some important differences in the social characteristics of the Indian villages and the differing effects of subordination within the colonial system. Patriarchy and male dominance were, at least in the formal sense, common to Indian villages in both regions, as they were to most Indian groups in the Americas, but the homicide evidence suggests that self-assertive and less sociable forms of manliness so characteristic of lower-class life in modern societies were diluting community-oriented values in central Mexico in the late eighteenth century. Accompanying this mixture of individual responsibility to the community and self-expression and self-interest were two other developments: a modern form of *caciquismo* or local boss rule and the beginnings of the modern pattern of political homicide.

Suicides by North American Indians are said to be numerous compared to the general population although inter-tribal rates vary from a relatively low figure of 8/100,000 per year to the extremely high figure of 120/100,000. On the average, modern Indian suicides are roughly one and one-half times the national age-adjusted rate and, like homicides, the rate has increased since 1967. Suicides are notoriously underreported, especially automobile "accidents" that are really suicides, and these comparative figures may be exaggerated. Suicides occurred before European contact but apparently were rare and usually associated with the shame of a wife's adultery. In the 1920s, after the establishment of many reservations, the rate of Indian suicide in North America was 10.2/100,000, roughly comparable to the national figure. While hard figures are lacking for Indian groups in Latin America, the contrast to North America seems substantial. Very few Indian suicides are recorded for Latin American groups; this is especially true of the areas of former highland civilizations such as Mexico, Guatemala, and Peru.

The important characteristics of North American Indian suicides, in addition to their apparently high incidence, are: 1) in general, and for most reservations that have been studied individually, far more males than females commit suicide (83% of the Indian suicides from 1959-66 compared to 74% for the general population); 2) there is a fairly strong pattern of teenagers and young adult men who have problems with alcohol committing suicide; 3) many of the suicides occurred in jail or at home shortly after release from jail for drunkenness; 4) hangings and self-inflicted gunshot wounds were the usual means of death, although in the 1960s there was a growing pattern of self-immolation; 5) suicide attempts seem to occur in clusters within extended families and high-risk groups such as boarding school students; and 6) suicides seem to be completed more often by Indians who moved to cities compared to members of the same tribe living on reservations.

With delinquency, also, North American Indians seem to have relatively high and rising rates in recent years compared to the general population, although the difference is exaggerated by the small groups of reservation Indians who have been studied. For the Wind River Reservation in Wyoming, the official delinquency rate has been 12 court appearances per 100 youth per year compared to 2.5 for the general population. Like the figures for Indian crime in general, the delinquency mostly involves minor offenses such as curfew violations, malicious mischief, disturbing the peace, minor in possession of alcohol, and drunkenness; and many of the charges have been for alcohol-related offenses. Indian girls perhaps have been more involved than their Anglo counterparts in running away from home and offenses against school property.

Explanations for these apparently higher rates of homicide, suicide, alcohol-related crimes, and delinquency among North American Indian men often center on the Indian as a "marginal man" who is caught in a cross-cultural conflict—not totally committed to or accepted by his tribesmen or the world outside the tribe. Conditions of poverty, poor education, unemployment and family disruption have led to feelings of aimlessness, frustration, and alienation not unlike the situation that produced the aggressive and often self-destructive Pachuco Gangs of East Los Angeles after World War II.

While these conditions and behavior seem to be common to lower-class life in general—part of a reaction of dominated peoples against the process of domination—Indian history has seen the play of some peculiar factors—particularly the reservation system—which account for some variation in the patterns of Indian crime compared to other groups. Not all of Indian crime can be directly attributed to white domination and culture contact. Some types of crime mentioned here occurred in pre-reservation times as well as afterwards, such as homicide and suicide, and some patterns of crime such as the prevalence of crimes against the person over crimes against property are consistent with aboriginal values. However, the semi-nomadic life of most North American groups in aboriginal times made the reservation a particularly disruptive change which has affected social behavior in important ways, and there seems to be good reason to believe that crime rates have increased among Indians since contact with and subordination to Europeans. The reservation setting and missionary activity contributed to new uncertainties, geographic isolation, chronic seasonal unemployment, and social disorganization as well as a kind of legal protectorate for tribal groups. Division of tribal lands into family plots at the end of the nineteenth century discouraged patrilocality which, in the case of the Nez Perce Indians of Idaho, has been part of a process of declining aboriginal communal discipline and marital instability. The nuclear family, a weak cultural institution in these Indian societies, has not effectively replaced the declining community in controlling drunkenness, interpersonal violence and other unlawful behavior. In sedentary Indian societies of Spanish America, by contrast, reservations were not instituted and, in spite of great changes imposed from outside, communities often have not lost the practice of communal discipline nor experienced the high rates of suicide, alcoholism, and delinquency of their North American counterparts. Despite the resort to homicide in these Indian communities, especially for political reasons, local hostilities have been slower to accumulate in ways that weaken community bonds, although in one Tzotzil community in southern Mexico the growing number of homicides seems to be closely related to a breakdown in the traditional system of social control.

WILLIAM B. TAYLOR

CROATAN are a group of mixed-blood survivors from various eastern tribes, living in Robeson County, North Carolina, of very uncertain ancestry. Originally they seem to have inhabited the island of that name north of Cape Hatteras, today known as Cape Lookout, in North Carolina. Said by some to represent the remnants of the famous "Lost Colony" of Sir Walter Raleigh, they have an almost mythical history. When Raleigh sent his exploring party to "Virginia" in 1585-86, he authorized a party to colonize Roanoke Island. The effort failed, and Sir Richard Greenville assigned 15 men to stay behind to preserve the English claim to the land. In 1587 a second group of 117 persons was sent over, under John White, who had been instructed to avoid Roanoke due to the earlier failure. Instead, he landed there, found no trace of the 15 occupants, but nevertheless decided to settle. In August of that year, with supplies running low, he returned to England; unfortunately the War with Spain intervened, forcing him to stay until August of 1590, when he returned with the needed provisions, but the colony had vanished. The only indication of their occupancy was the word *Croatoan* carved on a tree; no indication was to be seen of hasty flight or hostile action. Because of the inscription, White felt that the colonists had gone to Croatan Island, or to nearby Hatteras; but their fate has never been accurately determined. This has given rise to the commonly-argued theory that their descendants are the present-day "Croatan Indians" of the region. Certainly the Indian population of Robeson County is a greatly mixed-blood people; some appear obviously Indian, others are apparently half-Indian and half-white, while others demonstrate considerable Negro blood. Of greater interest is their retention of many Shakespearean locutions and 16th century English speech habits, many of English family names, and similar Old World customs. The problem was made even more complicated during the Civil War period, when many Negro slaves escaped from nearby plantations and sought refuge among the Indian population. Although the latter refused intermarriage insofar as was possible, inevitable liaisons occurred to increase the problem of ancestral clarity. To defend their sociological position, the Croatan refused to attend Negro schools; since they were not accepted into white schools, they established their own educational system; eventually a state system of three separate-but-equal schools prevailed in North Carolina. On February 10, 1885, under political pressures, the General Assembly of the state designated the Indians of Robeson County as "Croatan Indians," and this status was observed for many years. However, in time this became a label of derision and discrimination, and the Indians sought another term; also, many Indian people themselves opposed the name. Finally, to try to end the quarreling, the term "Cherokee Indians of Robeson County" was applied to them by statute on March 11, 1913. Although even less satisfactory, this held until 1953; but dissident Indians sought other appellations, among them "Siouan Indians of the Lumber River." Meanwhile, one major division had become more active in the effort towards individual definition for social, political and economic reasons, realizing that their state of limbo was a threat to any complete success in American life. In June 7, 1956, they were able to obtain a third legal definition, this time as the "Lumbee Indians of North Carolina"—by which they are known today. The present population numbers some 15,000 persons living in Robeson County and adjacent areas.

FREDERICK DOCKSTADER

CROSS, a common symbolic and decorative element in Indian art, must be understood in relation to the Indians' philosophical ordering of the universe. The four directions—north, south, east and west—were of primary importance to cultures which depended on natural phenomena such as wind, rain, and sun for the production of crops. These directions were so important that a system of symbolism with colors representing each direction was developed by Indians in the Southwestern United States. The four seasons, whose influence was equally strong, can be symbolized by the four-pointed figure.

Navajo sand paintings invariably incorporate the cross into their design as well as the ritual sequence involved in their creation. The cross is also found as an abstract decorative part of the design scheme of Navajo blankets. Although these blankets were woven after the Christian missionary influence in the Southwest, it is doubtful that the significance of the cross had any religious relevance to Christianity, as the cross is common to all peoples' decorative schemes throughout the world.

Crosses may be preliterate abstractions of human figures, but more often are a successful decorative attempt to fill space in an aesthetically pleasing manner and a way of incorporating symmetry and the division of space into an overall design structure.

CROW lived in the northern Great Plains in the neighborhood of the Bighorn Mountains and part of the Yellowstone River Basin of what is now Montana and northern Wyoming. They are a big people, the men often over six feet. As first seen by explorers and mountain men they were said to be friendly as a whole, but often haughty and warlike in demeanor. They had to be brave and good fighters, surrounded as they were by such powerful and warlike tribes as the Dakota to the east, the Cheyenne to the southeast and the Blackfoot to the northeast. They called themselves the *Absaroka,* translated also as the *Apsaruke.*

Social and cultural boundaries and subdivisions

The Plains tribes were so mobile that it is often hard to define their boundaries. The Crow had two main divisions, the River Crow (Minisepere), along the Yellowstone River down to its meeting with the Missouri; and the Mountain Crow (Acaraho) of the Big Horn and Little Big Horn rivers and nearby mountains. But another at least partial division was formed by the people called Kicked-in-Their-Bellies (Erarapio), who joined the Mountain Crow in the spring, but spent the winter in the Wind River Region of the Shoshones in what is now Wyoming at some wonderful hot springs. Though united in language these three divisions generally operated as separate tribes, each under a head-chief. However, the basic social and political unit was more often the extended family or clan, and these did not obey very well any head chief except in especially large hunts or in great danger, such as war.

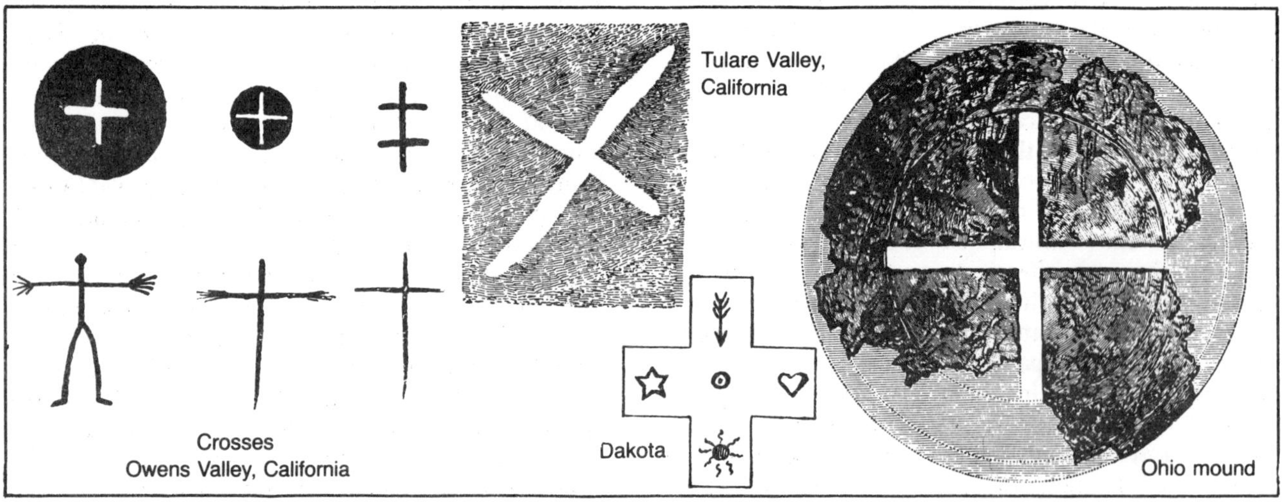

Museum of the American Indian.

Ration day on the Crow Reservation, Montana.

Language

The Crow belonged to the very large Hokan-Siouan language family, which included their greatest enemies the Dakota (Sioux) on their east, their close relatives, the Hidatsa on the North Dakota Missouri, various southeastern tribes such as the Creek and Choctaw, and tribes as far west as California, such as the Pomo and the Chumash.

Summary of tribal culture

Subsistence and economy. Perhaps five hundred years or so ago the Crow broke off as a tribe from their close relatives, the Hidatsa, who had developed the cultivation of corn, beans and squash along the Missouri River, and struck out into the Great Plains to become nomadic buffalo hunters. They were noted for their very strong and beautiful bows made from elk and mountain sheep horns, cut and shaped symmetrically by much scraping, bound together with rawhide and sinew-backed. But in the days before they had the horse, death from starvation due to the difficulties in catching the swiftly-running buffalo, elk and antelope, or attacks by grizzly bears or Indian enemies, must have often been near. With the horse, which probably reached them through the Shoshone to their southwest about 1750, their striking ability and speed greatly increased, and life became easier. However, for some time they still used the ancient method of driving game over a cliff or into stockaded surrounds where the wounded and dying were killed and butchered.

Hunting on horseback was a great adventure, but it had to follow definite rules or game could be lost. Only when the military society that had been given the duty of policemen decided that the hunters were close enough and correctly arranged for attacking a herd of buffalo was the word given to charge. Then silently the hunters raced their horses over a ridge and down upon the herd, each man trying to get up as close as he could to the left shoulder of his victim where he could drive a lance, arrow or bullet into the heart. Buffalo, unlike a modern cow, could turn on a dime and spear a man

Painting by George Catlin.

Crow lodge of twenty-five buffalo skins.

with its needle-sharp horns in the next second. After flencing off the skin with knives, gutting the carcass and cutting up the meat, pack horses brought up by boys would be loaded with the meat and hides to carry back to the camp. Cooking was done either by roasting or by boiling the meat and wild vegetables in a hide cooking pot, the water heated by red-hot stones. Boys sometimes prankishly dashed up to where the women guarded the meat that was hanging in ranks over the cooking fires and tried to run off with pieces without being caught.

Women and children gathered berries, roots and other wild plant food as the neighborhood allowed, sometimes guarded by men if enemies were thought to be near or grizzly bears were ad. Boys hunted rabbits, prairie dogs and other small game nearby with bows and arrows, so preparing for manhood. When the best hunters came into camp with game, they usually shared their meat with the sick, the disabled and the old. There was also much trading off or giving away of food at the times of ceremonies, which helped see that everybody had enough to eat.

Technology and arts. The Crow tipi was noted for its very long poles, usually made of cottonwood or pine saplings, and giving an hourglass effect, sometimes 25 feet in height. It was usually erected by women, one holding up the main pole until others could be tied to it, then the sewn skins pulled around it. Before the horse, tipis were much smaller, having to be carried on the top of dog travois of long poles with crossbars. Such a tipi was probably not much more than ten feet high, and made of only 8 to 10 buffalo hides, compared to the 12 to 18 hides of the horse days. Logs for poles had to be stripped of bark and scraped down in the thickness to make them manageable. Tipis were decorated usually rather plainly, but skin screens might be covered with drawings depicting war or hunting exploits. There were no bedsteads, only piles of skins for beds, but backrests of willow strung together with sinew were used.

Clothing and blankets were made of skins, which had usually been kept for several days in water, then scraped of hair and flesh, brains spread on them to soften, and then scraped again with an adz-shaped shoulder blade or other large bone before finally being smoked to tan. Such skins when well-done stayed soft and flexible whether wet or dry. Skins were sewn together to make clothing, which included shirts, hip-high leggings, single-piece moccasins, often decorated with porcupine quills in the old days, later with beads. Also decorated with such quills or later with colored beads were bags, particularly parfleches and the long fringed pipe bags. The Crow used lots of triangles and diamond shapes in their designs, often with a central cross.

Social and religious culture. Crow society was essentially democratic, chiefs leading clans or tribes by virtue of forceful character and kindness and thoughtfulness towards their followers, being soon elected out of office if they proved otherwise. There were several unusual features to Crow society. They had to prove their courage by such acts as standing in place without flinching in the face of an enemy attack, but the Crow had certain clubs that engaged in wife stealing. For example, the Foxes and the Lumpwoods would raid each other's families for wives. The man usually had no recourse but to let his wife go, and once gone never take her back. Consequently a husband who really loved his wife often went to extraordinary lengths to hide so she would not be stolen.

Though the Crow were noted among Plains tribes for their loose moral standards, there were three unusual features about this. One was that they continued to treat sexually promiscuous men or women with respect so that their lives were not made hard and bitter as in some tribes. A second was that despite the general looseness of sexual relations, the men and women who were most held in respect and given great honors and even riches were the truly virtuous ones. A third was the intense emotional linkage between parents and their children, so strong that when families broke up there were many heartbreaking scenes. Possibly very high standards were once general in this tribe, but became corrupted among the majority in recent centuries.

Vision seeking and colorful dances preceded the sending out of war parties by the military societies, but the societies also often acted as peacemakers when feuds erupted between clans. They tried to stop them by claiming the whole tribe would be weakened by such fights and so made more vulnerable to enemy attack. In war it was more an honor to strike an enemy and get away than actually kill him (called "counting a coup") and, among the Crow, horse stealing from enemies ranked so high that they became probably the most adept and clever of all horse thieves.

Religious life. Religion was closely tied to warfare, as the warrior usually sought a vision before going on a war party to make sure of his success and also to give him courage. Visions by both men and women often determined many actions of life and helped decide whether a man would be a success or a failure. Cutting off a finger joint as a sacrifice to induce a good vision was very common. Visions could also be tied in with a religious society, such as the Tobacco Society, determining how the tobacco would be handled or planted. The Tobacco Society had ceremonies using tobacco that could be called the development of sympathetic magic to help the different members of their lives.

Unlike their neighbors, the Crow did not make extensive use of the Sacred Pipe and did not form a society around it. A pipe owner might adopt a "son" or "daughter" to pass on the power of the pipe, and at such a time a dance was held and presents exchanged. It could also be used as a peace pipe when travelling, preventing conflict.

The Sun Dance of the Crow was different in several

ways from other tribes. It was usually held much less frequently, mainly because of the difficulty of finding a man to sponsor it who would go through the rigorous fasting and other tests required by the tribe. Nevertheless it was a great occasion every few years and people would come from far to watch its dances and ceremonies. Though ostensibly dedicated to the Sun, it was bound tightly to vengeance and war. The pledger of a Sun Dance was called the *Whistler,* and he chose as *Father* a medicine man who essentially acted as master of ceremonies. The medicine man had to be specifically the *Owner* of a Sacred Sun Dance Doll, which he then used, along with severe fasting and some torture to bring the Whistler into a state of ecstacy that would lead to a vision showing the death of an enemy warrior. Other dancers also went through torture, usually with skewers through the flesh and tied to buffalo skulls, to aid in the revenge against the enemy. There was a feast also when hundreds of cooked buffalo tongues were given out to all present along with other meat, so all was not grim in the Sun Dance.

Brief history and present condition

The Crow, influenced by leaders such as Plenty Coups and Bell-Rock, felt that the Dakota (Sioux) were a greater menace to their small tribe than the white men, and so cast their lots with the whites, serving as scouts for the U.S. Army (1855-1880). For this loyalty they were given the present large and well-watered and forested Crow Reservation in south central Montana.Their estimated 1830 population of about 3,500 dropped to a low by 1910, but has since come back today to more than equal this 1839 figure. In modern times the old enmity for the Dakota has died out and these and other tribes are invited to the great Crow Fair which is held every summer and brings many Indians together for dance and drum and other contests. Even the Sun Dance has been revived, though it no longer has the war emphasis it once had. Today the Crow are developing businesses and ranches on their reservations.

VINSON BROWN

CROW, JOHN ORIEN (Cherokee; Sept. 7, 1912-), was a career official of the U.S. Bureau of Indian Affairs (BIA). Born on a farm in Salem, Missouri, Crow was one-quarter Cherokee. He grew up in Commerce, Oklahoma, and went to Haskell Institute in Lawrence, Kansas. After graduation in 1933, he briefly played professional football and then began his career with the BIA. After a series of local and federal appointments, he became Deputy Commissioner (1961-66). For the next five years Crow was Assistant Director of the Bureau of Land Management in the Department of the Interior before returning to the BIA, once again as Deputy Commissioner, in 1971.

Crow was considered by some to be an assimilationist because he had pushed through the termination of the Ute tribe while he was their agency superintendent in the 1950s. Indian militants accused him of being placed in the BIA to block the reforms begun by Commissioner Louis Bruce (*q.v.*), also an Indian. In November 1972, Indian militants occupied the BIA building in Washington, D.C., and they included his removal among their demands. On December 6, 1972, both Bruce and Crow were dismissed from office.

CROW CREEK RESERVATION, in Buffalo, Hyde, and Hughes Counties, South Dakota, is the home to about 1,150 Wiciyela Dakota (Sioux) Indians. The reservation is 123,531 acres in size.

The Wiciyela (or middle) Dakota Division, who speak the Nakota dialect, were first met by whites in north central Minnesota about the end of the 17th century. They then moved west, and opposed the white man to protect their dwindling supply of buffalo. Under the Treaty of 1868, all the land held by the Dakota Indians east of the Mississippi, with the exception of Crow Creek, Yanton, and Sisseton Reservations, were ceded to the United States. When the buffalo disappeared by the late 1870s, the Indians accepted reservation life.

The culture of the Wiciyela has changed over the years. As they moved westward, they warred with semi-sedentary tribes, and adopted characteristics as earthlodges, bullboats, agriculture, and ceremonial dress. Today, the tribe, unlike other tribes, is not organized under the Indian Reorganization Act of 1934. The six member tribal council, operating under bylaws passed in 1949, is elected by the entire tribe. The chairman is the administrative head of the tribe. The reservation affords the Indians an excellent hunting and fishing area. Services include water, gas, and health care. The area is dry and, at times, windy.

CROW DOG (Brulé Sioux; 1832-after 1890) was a leader of one faction of the Brulé Sioux in the 1880s who became notorious as the assassin of the famed Brulé chief Spotted Tail (Sinte Gleska).

Born at Horse Stealing Creek, Montana Territory, Crow Dog (Sunka Kangi) was a member of a family of noted warriors and, before coming to the reservation, he had established himelf as a warrior. In September 1977, when Crazy Horse was taken as prisoner from Spotted Tail Agency to Fort Robinson in northwestern Nebraska, Crow Dog was one of the agency warriors who escorted the great Oglala chief. He helped to maintain order when Crazy Horse was wounded shortly after their arrival at the stockade.

Cicero Newel, the agent at Rosebud during the later 1870s admired Crow Dog for his poise and leadership ability, so he selected him as chief of the Indian police force. As chief of police, Crow Dog determined that Spotted Tail was collecting grazing money from white ranchers and putting the money in his pocket. He then decided to champion the cause of the common people and raised additional issues concerning Spotted Tail's honesty and integrity—namely, that he sold Dakota (Sioux) land to the railroads, that he was operating the

Portrait by Nancie Anne Gille. Crow Dog

Indian police to suit himself, that he was a nonprogressive, and that he had a huge mansion built for himself as a reward for helping whites steal from the Dakota.

On July 11-12, 1880, the White Horse Group, of which Crow Dog was a leading member, called for a general council concerning Spotted Tail. In a speech before the council, Spotted Tail exonerated himself of all complaints, and the council voted to retain him as head chief. Following this vote the White Horse Group dwindled in size. Crow Dog, however, remained convinced of Spotted Tail's dishonesty, and on August 5, 1881, as Spotted Tail was returning home from a council meeting, he shot and killed the head chief.

According to tribal custom, Crow Dog paid blood money for murdering Spotted Tail—$600 cash, several horses, and many blankets—but officials in Washington demanded further action. He was arrested by Indian police, sent to Fort Niobrara, and then moved to Deadwood in the Black Hills where he stood trail. A jury convicted him of murder and sentenced him to be hanged, but the U.S. Supreme Court ruled that the federal court in Deadwood had no jurisdiction over a case of one Indian killing another on a reservation. In 1883 Crow Dog was released and returned home to Rosebud.

In his later life, Crow Dog took part in the Ghost Dance Movement and was one of the leaders of the band that fled from Rosebud to the South Dakota Badlands and defied the soldiers under Gen. J. A. Brooke. He eventually led his followers back to the agency toward the close of December 1890, and the rest of his life was passed in relative obscurity on the Rosebud Reservation.

CROWE, AMANDA M. (Cherokee; July 16, 1928-), is an internationally known wood sculptor who teaches her craft on the Cherokee Reservation. Born at Murphy, North Carolina, she was orphaned and grew up in Chicago where she attended DePaul University and the Chicago Art Institute.

CROWFOOT (Siksika Blackfoot; *c.* 1830-1890), Indian name Sahpo-Muxiko, was a famous warrior and chief who was a strong advocate of peace with the whites in western Canada.

Born at Blackfoot Crossing (near present-day Calgary, Alberta), Crowfoot, known in his youth as Bear Ghost, was only 13 when he participated in the first of 19 battles credited to his warrior role, sustaining injuries in 6 of those battles. But it was his rescue of the Roman Catholic priest Albert Lacombe from hostile Cree Indians that brought him to the attention of white settlers in 1866. They made him head chief of the Blackfoot at the signing of Treaty Seven in 1877, the same year that England's Queen Victoria commended him for refusing to join Sioux chief Sitting Bull, who had escaped to Canada following the Battle of the Little Big Horn (popularly known as Custer's Last Stand) and proceeded to instigate hostilities against Canadian whites.

Though the Blackfoot were dependent on the vanishing buffalo for food, clothing, and shelter, Crowfoot counseled peace when railroad survey parties crossed his lands in 1883. Eventually the tribe was forced to sell its horses to survive, but Crowfoot was rewarded with a pension by the Canadian Pacific Railroad.

Not entirely without guile, Crowfoot capitalized on the fears of the whites as he accepted their tribute in the hope that they would help fight his traditional enemies, the Cree. Although highly pressured by his tribe and by his adopted son, Poundmaker, he refused to engage his people in the Riel Rebellion of 1885. To this day he is popular with historians and Indian image-makers.

CROW RESERVATION, in Big Horn and Yellowstone Counties, Montana, is home to nearly 4,000 crow Indians. The reservation, about 25% tribally owned, is about 1,500,000 acres in size.

The Crow, known to other Indians as the Absarokee (Children of the Large-Beaked Bird) were once a northeastern tribe. Colonial policies of the white man forced them west, where they became nomadic. They sided with the white man in wars on the Plains, and in a treaty of 1851 were given 38.5 million acres of land in Montana. By 1888, they were confined to their present reservation. It is the site of the Battle of the Little Big Horn.

Today, the Crow are governed by a general council composed of all male members of the tribe 21 or over, and all females 18 and above. The executive committee has 17 members. The council has worked on such areas as industrial development, water and utilities, and recreation. Indians on the reservation are involved in land purchases, housing development, and the ownership of private establishments.

CRUMBO, WOODROW WILSON (Potawatomi; Jan. 31, 1912-), is a major Indian artist and art teacher who has endeavored to raise the standard of Indian arts and crafts to a high level. Although he works in a variety of media, he always adheres to traditional Indian subjects.

Born at Lexington, Oklahoma, Crumbo received broad academic training. Between 1934 and 1938, with study as Wichita University under the noted watercolorist Clayton Henri Staples and at Oklahoma University under O. B. Jacobson, Crumbo developed his own art style and techniques. He worked tirelessly, acquainting himself with various Indian tribes in order to depict them in an authentic manner. In 1938 he became director of art at Bacone College, Oklahoma, where his influence was felt by many aspiring Indian artists.

At different periods in his career, Crumbo has executed murals, taught silver-smithing, designed stained glass windows, mastered the silk-screen process, sculpted in bronze, directed a group of Indian dancers for the U.S. government, and taught and performed Indian dancing. He served as artist-in-residence at Gilcrease Foundation in Tulsa (1946-49) and held the position of curator and acting director of the El Paso Art Museum for eight years.

CUAUHTÉMOC (Aztec; *c.* 1495-1525) "descending eagle," symbolic of the setting sun, was last lord of Tenochtitlan (1521), son of Ahuitzotl (1486-1502) and of his niece Tiacapantzin, whose father Moquihuix—last "king" of Tlatelolco (1467-1483)—died when that city was conquered by Axayácatl. Cortés and Codex Ramirez both state that Cuauhtémoc was 18 years old in 1520 when he repudiated Moteczuma II (1502-1520), which would place his birth in 1501 or 1502. For Bernal Diaz, when Cuauhtémoc was enthroned, (February 1521, according to the Mexicáyotl Chronicle) he was 25 years old, and "some 26" when he was captured (August 13, 1521); his birth in this case would have been in 1495. Toscano situates it in 1496 and Caso in 1500, but as Caso mentions that "Cuauhtémoc was approximately 26 years oild when he died in 1525" and that in 1515 when he was named "king" of Tlatelolco (where he governed until 1520) "he must not have been more than 15 or 16," then 1499 or even 1498 would be admissible, since he asks: "Why, on electing their first king, would they choose a 16 or 17 year old adolescent?" Torquemada writes that the same year Nezahualpilli died (1516) he had sent his troops, together with those of Tenochtitlan and Tlacopan, against Quetzaltepec and Iztactlalocan, and that "heroic exploits were performed in this war by Ihuitltemoc and Quauhtemoctzin (Cuauhtémoc), who was the ruling Lord Tlatelulcatl when the Spaniards took possession of this City of Mexico." The conquest referred to occurred no later than 1515 (Codex Telleriano-Remensis and Annals of Tlatelolco), and even the Annals of Cuauhtitlan place the event in 1515. If this date is correct—and it is hard to believe that Cuauhtémoc could have been younger than 15 or 16 (although Ixtlilxóchitl II of Tetzcoco did wage war at 14)—then his birth date would be in 1499 or 1500. In the latter year Ahuitzotl carried out his last campaign (Xaltepec, in the Isthmus), but since 1499 he had been quite ill from

CUATEMOC—The last ruler of Mexico who died a martyr's death at the hands of Spanish invaders

Cuauhtémoc

a blow on the head received during a flood caused by the aqueduct Acuecuéxatl, and before that, since 1497, he had been absent for long periods fighting in Tehuantepec and Soconusco. It is plausible that Cuauhtémoc at 15 or 16 years of ago should be named Lord of Tlatelolco (inasmuch as Chimalpopoca was named to that position in Tenochtitlan at 12), but not that he should be made high priest when still an adolescent (and performed in that capacity, according to Torquemada), seeing that he entered the Calmecac at 15 (Codex Mendocino); and it is not credible that with less than three years of study he could act as a priest, less yet as pontiff. If he became this in 1515, he must have been born at least 18 years earlier (1497), if not 20 (1495). This then is the earliest admissible date, since no one accords him more that 26 years in 1521, and it is certain that when he died in 1525 he was no older than 30, even though the Mexicáyotl Chronicle refers to him as though he were the first-born of Ahuitzotl's 20 children (with more than one wife).

Thus it was between 1495 and 1497—Toscano strikes the average of 1496—that the life of the hero, began. We have little knowledge about him before he opposed Moctezuma in 1520 when this ruler was haranguing his people in favor of the Spaniards. Cuauhtémoc allegedly cried out (Codex Ramirez): "What is he saying, this rascal Moctezuma, this Spaniards' woman as he can be called, since with womanly spirit he surrendered to them from sheer fright...We do not want to obey him because he is no longer our king!" And Cuauhtémoc dared to shoot arrows at him. A short time later the tlacatecuhtli died and was succeeded by Cuitláhuac, who reigned only 80 days since he died of smallpox. Cuauhtémoc was enthroned and—according to Torquemada—"he understood the needs of his city and people, and thereupon...continued with all the precepts of his predecessor...He assembled a vast supply of arms; he introduced many people into the city; he expelled a large portion of the useless ones, sending them to the mountains; he stored in the city all the provisions of food to be found in the region; he ordered the people drilled in the use of arms; he offered rewards to those who excelled at this; he took great care to observe what his enemies were doing and...harangued them, exhorting them to the defense of the region, the fatherland, and the lives of men, women, and children...and they promised him to die in that defense."

The details of the heroic resistance of Tenochtitlan are well known and how after a long siege, during which hunger and countless hardships were suffered, Cuauhtémoc was captured and brought before Cortés, to whom he declared, according to Bernal Diaz: "Señor Malinche, I have carried through my obligations in the defense of my city and my vassals. I can do no more..Take that dagger thou have and kill me here and now." A short time later the Spaniards, eager to find treasure, burned the feet of Cuauhtémoc and other caciques, without the consent of Cortés.

In 1525 the conqueror went to Hibureras (Honduras) and took Cuauhtémoc with him, and—alleging that he plotted a revolt—ordered that he be hanged from a tree, after having him baptized. Before he died Cuauhtémoc exclaimed: "Oh Malinche, for many days I have understood that you would put me to death in this fashion and have known your false words, for you kill me unjustly! May God send the same to you, for I did not kill myself when I surrendered to you in my city of Mexico." The execution took place in Acallan or Izancanak, Campeche, on Shrove Tuesday of 1525.

According to the same source Cuauhtémoc "was handsome both in body and features, his face somewhat long and cheerful, with eyes that reflected an earnest expression," and Aguilar described him as astute, courageous, and perceptive. He married a daughter of Moctezuma—apparently the beautiful Doña Isabel Tecuichpoch with whom Cortés later produced a daughter—and he fathered only one child, a girl whose fate we ignore.

A symbol of Mexico in its frequent struggles against adverse destiny, Cuauhtémoc has been immortalized by the sculptor Miguel Noreña in the statue on Paseo de la Reforma (in Mexico City) erected in 1887, and painted by such outstanding masters as Leandro Izaguirre and David Alfaro Siqueiros. The clash of the Conquest and fusion of cultures has been beautifully presented by the painter Jorge González Camarena. Poets from Ignacio Rodriguez Galván to Ramón López Bermúdez—have sung the praises of this hero worthy of Homer. No critical biography exists but historic-literary accounts by Hector Pérez Martinez and Salvador Toscano are of value.

The discovery of Cuauhtémoc's alleged remains in Echcateopan, Guerrero, on September 26, 1949 by Professor Eulalia Guzmán, greeted with general delight, turned out not be authentic according to the opinion reached that same year by a commission of experts from the National Institute of Anthropology and History. On the motion of the Mexican government another commission was appointed, composed of representatives of more competent cultural institutions, and it arrived at the same conclusions in February 1951, contrary to the opinion of Professor Guzmán and her followers who proclaimed the authenticity of her find.

CUAUHTITLAN, also CUAUTITLAN was a pre-Conquest Chichimec site located on the northwestern shore of Lake Texcoco. There are two conflicting interpretations of the name: the more common derives the term from Náhuatl *cuahitl,* "tree," + *titlan,* "among," meaning "among the trees" or "in the forest." Another, perhaps correct but less widely accepted, is from *"cuauhtli,"* "eagle," + *tlan*, a place, meaning "place of the eagle." The history of the city is to be found in the *Annals of Cuauhtitlan*, also known as the *Codex Chimalpopoca*, and is an important source for information concerning this region.

CUBA. The name of the island of Cuba is aboriginal; its etymology is not known. Archaeological and historical research has shown that the inhabitants, sometimes called *Cubeño*, fall into three culturally distinct groups. The western tip of the island and certain isolated places elsewhere were occupied by *Ciboney*. On the eastern tip were *Taino*, who are said to have migrated from Hispaniola only 50 years before the Spanish conquest. The remainder of the island was inhabited by *Sub-Taino*, who are also believed to have come into Cuba from Hispaniola, after the *Ciboney* but before the *Taino*. The population of all three groups, taken together, has been variously estimated from 16,000 to 600,000; this would indicate that the island was more sparsely settled than either Hispaniola or Puerto Rico.

Culture

The difference in culture between the two *Arawak*-speaking groups (*Taino* and *Sub-Taino*) are difficult to determine. From the standpoint of archaeology, however, the *Taino* had essentially the same culture as their namesakes in Hispaniola, and therefore most of the features in which the culture differed from Hispaniola apply to the *Sub-Taino*.

The *Arawak* of Cuba used the suckerfish (*Remora*) to catch turtles and other fish, attaching its tail to a line and float. They snared parrots with nooses fastened to the ends of rods. More improvident than the *Taino* of Hispaniola, they are said to have had at any one time only enough food to last 4 to 8 days. Cotton was particularly common, but gold was rare. The villages were located in high areas along the coast and inland.

The *Arawak* of Cuba were most peaceful. They had neither the bow nor the arrow. Their chieftainships, although numerous, were smaller than in Hispaniola and were apparently not divided into districts ruled by subchiefs. There is some indication, too, that the power of the chief was not so great as in Hispaniola.

Some archaeological data from the *Sub-Taino* sites may help to fill out this ethographic picture. The *Sub-Taino* had a preference for locating their villages on hilltops. They built no ball courts, nor did they carve petroglyphs, as did the *Taino*. They were particularly fond of shell ornaments and made a simpler pottery than is found in the *Taino* sites. Three-pointed stones, collars, and many other typically *Taino* representations of zemis are absent from their territory, but they did construct many idols of clay, bone, shell and stone, most of them simpler in conception that the *Taino* zemis.

CUCH, IRENE C. (Uintah Ute; 1938-), was the administrative officer of the Ute Indian Tribe in the mid-1970s and a member of numerous local, state and national boards and organizations. Born and educated on the Uintah and Ouray Reservation, Utah, she attended Utah State University (1957-59). She is married and the mother of five children. She was the second woman elected to the Business Council, the governing body of the Ute tribe (1969-73), and she has been particularly active in programs for the aged.

CUECA is one of the most popular folk dances in both Chile and Bolivia. In a strict sense, the dance is Chilean of origin, and has diffused to neighboring Bolivia. However the cueca is derived from a black African slave substrate, originally termed the "zamacueca." It is very similar to the "zamba" and "marinera" of Peru and more northern Andean countries, and in a general sense the cueca is the Bolivian and Chilean variant of the zamba and marinera.

The dance began as a rather bawdy confrontation, originally found in only the lowest of cantinas and dives. It gained popularity throughout the nineteenth century among the "mestizo" or "criollo" portions of the population. By the middle of the twentieth century, it had become one of the most popular dances in Chile,

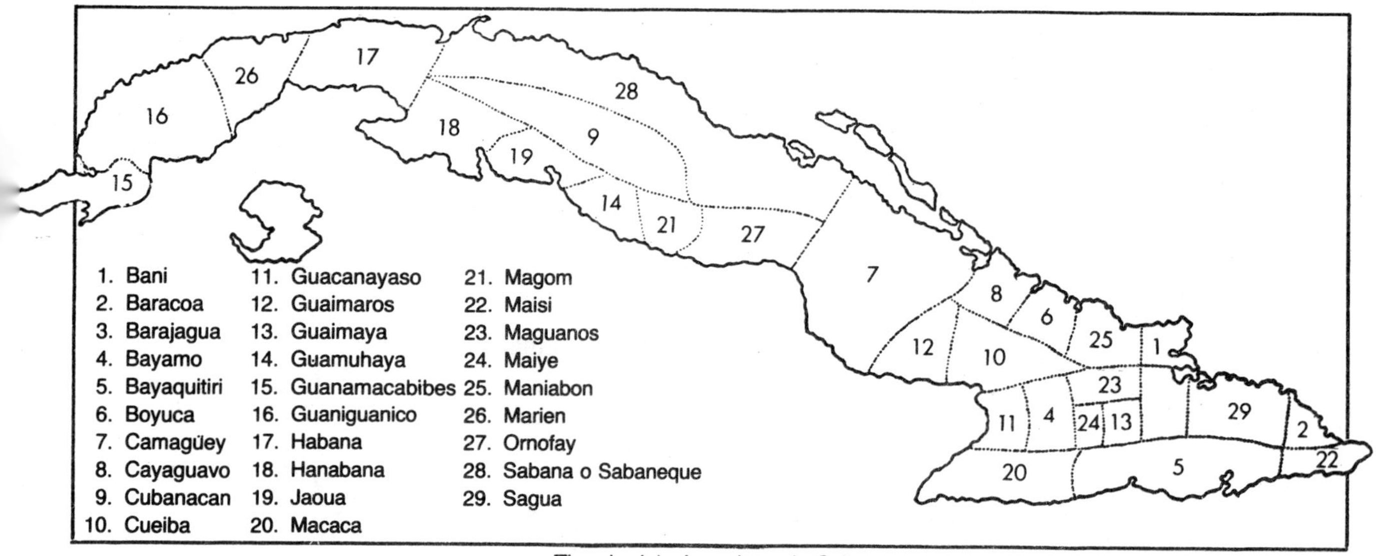

The aboriginal provinces in Cuba.

danced from the Presidential Palace to the waterfront saloons. In recent years it has spread from the cities in Bolivia to the countryside, an important new addition to the inventory of Indian dances. For much of the altiplano, the cueca has become as popular as the "huayno" in the Peruvian sierra, and is now danced at all important fiestas.

The cueca changes tones, style and emphasis from region to region. Common to all variations is the general theme, a flirtation aimed at seduction. The dance begins with a mild flirtation, with handkerchiefs waved provocatively in the hand. The female partner uses all her wiles and appeals to arouse the male interest, with seductive hand and body motions. The man is supposedly initially indifferent, but as the couple advances and retreats, the dance quickens in coquetry and intensification. In the classic forms, the end of the dance is exciting and passionate, with the successful seduction of the female partner by the male.

DAVID L. BROWMAN

CUERNO VERDE (Comanche; ?-1779) was a celebrated warrior who raided Spanish settlements in New Mexico until a large force of Spanish and Indians was assembled to pursue and kill him. So successful were Cuerno Verde's raids along the Rio Grande that in 1779 Juan de Anza, the Spanish colonial governor of New Mexico, was compelled to organize a force of nearly 650 soldiers and Ute Indians to eradicate the daring Indian outlaw. The government force tracked Cuerno Verde to a point near present-day Pueblo, Colorado, where they annihilated not only the celebrated Comanche but also his son and many of his followers.

CUEVA. *See* CUNA.

CUICUILCO, perhaps from Náhuatl *cui*, "temple," + *cuilco*, "place of dancing, or singing," is a Late Preclassic site in the *pedregal* near the University of Mexico, in the State of Mexico, dating *c.* 900 BC. It was later covered by the eruption of Xictli volcano. The 75-foot circular stone pyramid may be the earliest known pyramidal structure in Mexico. Cuicuilco was a leading city of the Ticomán culture.

CUITLAHUAC (Aztec; fl. 16th century), also spelled Cuitlahuatzin and Cuitlahua, was the valiant and tragic tenth *huey tlatoani* (chief speaker) of the Aztecs who reigned for only 80 days in 1520 but expelled the Spanish from his capital, Tenochtitlán (Mexico City).

Cuitláhuac was Moctezuma Xocoyotzin's brother and unsuccessfully urged him to fight the Spanish from the moment they landed in Mexico (1519). Later, when Moctezuma became a Spanish prisoner in the capital, Cuitláhuac worked with Cacama, ruler of Texcoco, and others to organize the resistance their kinsman refused to sanction. At Cortés' bidding, Moctezuma had the plotters delivered to Cortés who put them in chains.

After the Spanish garrison massacred hundreds of Aztecs at a religious ceremony while Cortés was out of the city, Cortés allowed Cuitláhuac's release to restore order and provide the Spanish with food. Instead, he summoned the Aztec electoral council, they deposed the priestly Moctezuma, and Cuitláhuac, a trained warrior, was chosen to succeed him.

With a warrior as leader, the formerly hesitant Aztecs became ferocious. Moctezuma was killed trying to talk to them and the Spanish tried to sneak out of Tenochtitlán on a rainy night (June 30, 1520). They were caught on a causeway linking the island city to the mainland, and nearly wiped out. Cuitláhuac pursued them as they tried to return to Tlaxcala, the city of a Spanish ally, and a major battle was fought in the maize fields at Otumba, northeast of Tenochtitlán. Spanish calvalry, never seen by the Aztecs in open-field combat, won the battle and the Aztecs had to return to Tenochtitlán.

Cuitláhuac died of smallpox, a disease the Spanish brought, before Cortés could put together sufficient forces to return for the conquest.

CULHUACÁN is Náhuatl for "place of the Colhua." It is a major city-state of the Colhua refugees from Tula, located in the southwestern section of present-day Mexico City. Founded in AD 1064, Culhuacán was conquered in the mid-15th century by the neighboring city of Atzcapotzalco. According to tradition, the Colhua were intermixed with the Toltec and later infused with Chichimec blood, thereby providing a link between the Toltec dynastic sequence—which was important to the Aztec. The first Mexican sovereign, Acamapichtli, was chosen from the Colhua nobility. Culhuacán is not to be confused with Culiacán, in Sinaloa.

CULTURE AREAS are geographical regions in which most of the inhabitants have developed common types of industry, methods of food-getting, and a style of life that is influenced by the regional climate, topography, and available natural resources.

Indians of the Americas have been classified into a number of major culture areas. Each of these areas included many different tribes, often speaking different languages. Not all tribes of an area conformed to the predominant living pattern, and among those who did, there were substantial variations in custom and belief. But the following geographical groupings provide convenient units for the study of Indian culture.

North America

Northwest Coast. One of the most dynamic and spectacular cultures of North America was developed by the Indians who lived on the islands and mainland along the Pacific coast from southeastern Alaska to northern California. An assured supply of salmon and other fish gave them leisure to cultivate arts and to develop a complex social organization that included hereditary chiefs, nobles, commoners, and slaves. They lived in permanent wooden houses made of cedar or redwood from the surrounding forests. They were master woodworkers and decorative carvers, famed for their totem poles and dugout canoes. Unlike most Indians they owned and accumulated private property that they distributed in lavish giveaway ceremonies called potlatches.

California. An area heavily populated by numerous small tribes who spoke different languages but lived sedentary, harmonious lives in close contact with one another. Except for the Yuma and Mohave tribes along the Colorado River, the Californians practiced no agriculture. Their simple, rather primitive culture underwent little development over centuries. Their principal diet was a flour made by grinding and leaching acorns; it was supplemented by fish, game, and gathered plants. Their major art was basketry. The Yurok, Karok, and Hupa tribes of northern California reflected a modest version of the Northwest Coast culture.

Plateau. A high, bleak, rugged land of steep canyons, mountains, forests, and grassland that lies between the Rocky mountains and the coastal ranges. Extending over parts of the present states of Washington, Oregon, Idaho, and Montana in the U.S., and the provinces of British Columbia and Alberta in Canada, it was the home of several tribes who wintered in villages along the banks of the Columbia and Fraser rivers or their tributaries, and depended on salmon and trout for food. In the summer many villages camped together in the camas meadows to gather the bulb of the camas lily. Many of the tribes adopted the horse at an early date and with it, to some extent, the Plains culture. The Shoshoni became noted horse traders and the Nez Perce became breeders and stock raisers.

Eastern Woodlands. The area stretching across the northern part of the U.S. and southern Canada from the Atlantic seaboard past the Great Lakes. It was sparsely populated by many warlike Iroquois and Algonquian tribes. These were the Indians known to the early French and English settlers in colonial times. They lived in villages in dome-shaped wigwams or long houses and cultivated crops, but they were primarily woodsmen, oriented to the forests, which they knew intimately. They used the resources of the woodlands for medicines, maple sugar, food, and to make distinctive artifacts such as their graceful birchbark canoes.

Great Basin. An arid and extremely inhospitable environment extending across the present states of Nevada and Utah. It was inhabited by many different branches of Shoshoni and Ute Indians. These nomadic desert dwellers, who were considered the poorest and most primitive of North American Indians, were scornfully called Diggers because of their tireless probing of the ground with digging sticks in search of food. They lived in family units and migrated vertically to seek seasonal foods that were always insufficient. They ate seeds, grasshoppers, crickets, and rodents, had few possessions, and took shelter in primitive brush wickiups or windbreakers. As some of these tribes acquired horses and became buffalo hunters on the Plains, their standard of living was vastly improved.

Southwest. The area that embraces Arizona and New Mexico and parts of bordering states was inhabited from ancient times by highly civilized agriculturists, the Pueblo Indians, who lived in communal abode and stone buildings. They raised cotton and mined turquoise and are famous for their pottery, woven cloth, jewelry, and religious ceremonials. Latecomers to the area were the nomadic Navajo and Apache tribes. In time the Navajo learned agriculture and other crafts from the Puebloes and surpassed their teachers as woolen weavers and silversmiths.

Southeast. The Southern part of the U.S. from the Atlantic seaboard to the Mississippi was inhabited by settled agriculturalists, who grew corn, melons, pumpkins, and tobacco. They were organized socially into towns that usually had a central temple or public building. Their general high level of civilization and survival in some tribes like the Natchez of Mississippi of a divine monarch and a complex hierarchical class system suggests that these people were the descendants of the ancient builders of temple mounds.

Plains. The area between the Mississippi and the Rockies extending from Alberta and Saskatchewan in the north to Texas in the south was the territory of the nomadic Plains Indians, hunters of buffalo and other big game. The buffalo provided their food; its skin was used for clothing and artifacts and for the conical tipis in which they lived. The introduction of the horse added a decided flair to their way of life in which brave deeds such as sudden raids on enemies were accorded the highest honor. Many tribes from the Woodlands, the Plateau, and the Basin, pressed by white settlers, adopted the Plains culture to an extent that it came to be regarded by the whites as the typical Indian culture. For Indians the historic battles against whites on the Plains constitute a heroic age.

Subarctic. A vast, sparsely populated area extending from interior Alaska across northern Canada and Labrador. While arctic coastal areas were the province of Eskimos, small bands of Indians lived in family groups in the subarctic forests or on lakes and rivers as hunters and fishermen. They traveled in toboggans or canoes or by snowshoe. The fur trade revolutionized their culture. Most of them now live as trappers.

Arctic. Perhaps eighty-five thousand Inuit and Aleut, the native peoples of the Aleutian archipelago, are spread from south Alaska along the coasts of the Arctic Ocean to Greenland. Subsistence is based mainly on seal mammals, the seal, the walrus, in the west whales, and on the tundra (i.e. the vast treeless plains of the arctic regions) caribou. The Inuit inventions have enabled them to exist effectively in their environment. Tailored skin and fur clothing, harpoons, the stone lamp, and effective boats and sleds attest to the interest of these cultures in the material.

The Inuit house is only rarely of snow blocks. In the western Arctic, sod houses are used, coursed-stone in Greenland. Small settlements or encampments in general are the rule. Lacking political organization as such, the Inuit stress family and kinship as a means of holding a community together. In other words, a group is often one of demonstrably related people. Marriage is always across group lines, and serves to expand the horizons of all-important kinship cooperation. Inuit religion is not out of keeping with a hunting culture where relations to animals are primary. The feeling is that animals allow themselves to be captured by magic, and each hunter has rituals to perform for effective hunting. A second element in religion is shamanism—the presence of a curer to treat the illnesses resulting from having given offense to the world of animal spirits. Inuits have an elaborate mythology. Remarkably similar in both language and culture across the wide expanses of the Arctic, Inuit lack tribes as such: instead, various local designations are employed.

Mexico

South of the Rio Grande and southward to Central America is a great range of cultures of the Mexico culture area, from the high civilizations of the Mayas, Toltec, Olmec, and Aztec to the gatherers of the deserts of the north. A rich history, populations in excess of millions, although varying from time to time through the long prehistoric periods, and numerous inventions, especially of agriculture, makes Mexico the high point of any survey of the New World cultures. The Mexican civilizations, along with those in South America, such as the Inca of Peru, are comparable to those of the Old World. It seems clear that north of the Rio Grande only tribal existed; Mexico and South America represent the pinnacle of New World development.

Antillean culture area

The Caribbean people occupy the islands of their sea world, as well as the Orinoco delta of Colombia, the littoral (coastal region) of Venezuela, and part of the Guyanas. Like their neighbors, they, too, had a Paleo-Indian tradition which has come to light in western Venezuela, and part of the Guyanas and like their neighbors, they, too, had a tradition which has come to light in western Venezuela, called the *Joboid Series.* After 5000 BC this developed into a meso-Indian hunting culture, as the people took to hunting those animals which survived the Ice Age. Those who lived on the shores of their sea gleaned their food from the water and, in time, set their roving eyes upon the islands of the Lesser Antilles and the West Indies. Later, when pottery was made and some of the people began to plant manioc and maize, there developed a Neo-Indian culture which advanced to a level of petty chiefdoms which, at the time of European intrusion, were strongly militaristic. Within a terrifying short period after the meeting of the Old and New Worlds the natives were all but obliterated, and their place was taken by thousands of black slaves.

Amazon culture area

The Amazon Culture Area is the region of South America drained by the Amazon River and its tributaries, which, as a whole, forms the largest river system in the world. It has a flow five times greater than that of the Congo River and 12 times greater than that of the Mississippi River. Nearly one-fifth of the fresh water received by the oceans comes from the area. Its source is the Marañón River, which emerges from Peru. Plunging down steep ravines, it collects fertile sediments that are ultimately deposited on the flood-plain or carried out to sea.

At the time of the European arrival in the 16th century, the inhabitants hunted, fished, and farmed when the water was low and stored a surplus for use when the river rose. Population density on the terra firma region was less.

Aboriginal man adjusted to the limitations of the environment, as did the plants and animals. His small garden clearings were abandoned after two or three years and were swallowed up by the forest which slowly restored the limited fertility of the soil. His villages were sufficiently small, seldom exceeding a few hundred inhabitants, and frequently moved to prevent irreversible depletion of the wild plant and animal resources that provided much of the food supply. His mythology and religion emphasized his kinship with other components of the ecosystem.

The first European explorers commented on the healthiness of the Amazon area and the small amount of effort required to obtain abundant food. The food-plain is now devoted to the cultivation of sugar cane, jute, rice, and other crops, and to the breeding of cattle. The introduction of smallpox, malaria, yellow fever, measles, and other Old World diseases exterminated much of the indigenous population and made the region unsuitable for European settlement until the application of DDT and other control measurers during and since World War II. In 1950, the population in the Brazilian portion of Amazonia was about 2,400,000; by 1960, it had increased to nearly 3,600,000.

Andean culture area

The Andean culture area, or Central Andes, encompasses the coast and highlands of Peru and the adjacent sector of highland Bolivia. When the Spanish conquistadores entered the Central Andes in 1532, the area was the seat of the Inca Empire, the largest political unit ever formed in native America.

Until the beginning of the 20th century, it was generally believed that Inca civilization was the only high culture of Andean prehistory. The steady accumulation of archaeological data during the 20th century has radically altered this view. Today, the Inca Empire appears not as a sudden, rootless phenomenon but rather as the culmination of a cultural tradition that originated at least 6,500 years before the Spanish Conquest.

The Andean culture area is one of marked environmental contrasts. A latitudinal cross section of the area spans only a few hundred miles, yet it transects two widely different environmental zones— the coast and the highlands.

The Central Andean coast is a long, narrow shelf of desert along the western foot of the Andes. Desert conditions are caused by the Peru Coastal, or Humboldt, Current, which parallels the coast. The cold waters of this current chill winds approaching the coast from the Pacific Ocean, producing fog and clouds. Upon reaching land, the winds are warmed, and their capacity for retaining moisture increases. As a result, the fog and clouds seldom turn to rain.

Despite its dryness, the coastal zone provides people with a variety of valuable natural resources. First, the offshore waters are one of the world's richest fishing grounds. Second, the desert strip is interrupted by some 40 small river valleys that descend from the western slopes of the Andes to the sea. The valley soils are deep and fertile; when watered, they become prime agricultural lands. Accordingly, these oasis valleys have been, and continue to be, the primary centers of human occupation on the coast.

The Central Andean highlands have an average elevation of over 10,000 feet. Scattered peaks rise 15,000 and 20,000 feet, and one mountain, Huascarán, reaches 22,205 feet. In the north the mountains form three distinct ranges separated by intermontane valleys; in the south there are two ranges, separated by the high grasslands known as the *puna*, or *altiplano*.

The Intermontane valleys and the *puna* have traditionally been the centers of human occupation in the highlands. They have fertile soils and receive adequate water from agriculture during the local rainy season, which normally occurs between December and March. In addition, they are natural transportation routes that have facilitated the spread of cultural currents through the region.

The presence of these separate but interconnected environmental zones was a major factor in the growth of the Andean civilization. Successful adaptation to relatively small but resource-rich habitats— the coastal and highland valleys— resulted in population growth and the development of complex social and political organization. In turn, the circulation of resources and ideas from one zone to another provided the Central Andean peoples with bases for cultural innovations and promoted further increases in social and political complexity.

Chibcha culture area

The *Chibcha* culture area is one of the most famous in South America. The *Chibcha* represent one of the culminations of native civilization of the Americas, equal to, or only just behind, that of the *Aztec, Maya* and *Inca*. But the *Chibcha* left no historic impress, no persisting influence on the modern life in their former area. They have also left surprisingly few physical monuments; their archaeology is meager. Their speech died out in the 18th century. It is clear that they achieved much less of a cultural construct in their day than Mexicans or Peruvians. Yet they do stand out.

They were in a fair way to attaining to political structures of type similar at least to that of the *Aztec*, if not the *Inca*. Considerable masses of men had come under the control of individuals, to that they moved, in peace and at war, with direction and at any rate with the possibility of consecutive development. That there were several such states and that these were still contending, does not reduce the situation materially below the level of conditions in the *Aztec* area: not by more than a generation or two. The *Chibcha* had definitely passed out of the amorphous, endlessly reshifting status of mere tribal life, which seems to us so essentially less historical in its potentialities. It is true that they possessed very little history, as yet, when the Spaniards broke them by 1541. (But the same might be said, with only relative qualification, of the Peruvians.)

To what this poltical development was due, which in Colombia was so highly localized among the *Chibcha*, is not wholly clear. The most nearly satisfying explanation, probably, is in terms of a population of superior density, due in turn to a favorable terrain: an altitude sufficient to temper the climate of the Tropics, a series of good-sized valleys with much level land, a fertile soil, and a grass savannah interspersed with enough larger vegetation to take it out of the type of mere semiarid plains. Not that these geographical conditions will of themselves produce political organization, but a natural environment more or less favorable to concentration of numbers does seem a necessary requisite for political development to spring up spontaneously, without import. The peoples of the culture area today include the *Chibcha,* the *Paez,* and the *Cuna.*

Araucanian culture area

The Araucanian culture area of South America includes different sub-ethnic groups, some of which are now extinct. Once a relatively large population spread extensively over the southern region of South America, in the mid-1970s they wre reduced to several ethnic groups— the Mapuche of southern Chile, the neighboring Argentinian Araucanians of southwestern Neuquén province, Argentina, the Atacama, and Diaquita.

It is difficult to define traditional culture because so many changes have taken place in the last 500 years. Prehistoric and pre-Inca culture can be classified as that of a simple slash-and-burn agricultural tribal society, based on large and mostly patrilineal families (there were also matrilineal-extended families) with very little political cohesion and in the tribe. There was lineage or tribal ownership of land and possibly of llama herds as well. The traditional culture of the area that is best known is that of the Mapuche-Huilliche from the historical period of Spanish colonial and Chilean independent times.

Chaco culture area

Chaco, which is derived from *Quechua* meaning "hunting ground," is applied to the vast plain which lies in the center of the South American continent between the fringe of the Matto Grosso Plateau and the Argentine Pampa.

Geographically, the Chaco is a depressed area, bordered on the west by the first ranges of the sub-Andean mountains, and on the north by the low hills and summits detached from the central Brazilian massif and from the Sierras de San José and San Carlos, south of Chiquitos. On the east the Chaco is bounded by the Paraguay and Paraná rivers and by the widely scattered rocky hills which rise along the Paraguay River. To the south it ends at the foot of the Sierras de Córdoba and Guayasán. Between these mountains and the Paraná River there is a wide gap where the Chaco merges without marked transition into the Pampa.

The boundaries of the Chaco as a culture area do not coincide with those of the Chaco as a geographical entity. The sub-Andean range of hills (Western Cordillera) lying north and south of the Pilcomayo river falls within the habitat of the *Chiriguano* and *Chané*, two tribes, for example, that culturally and linguistically have little or nothing in common with the Chaco peoples. For purely cultural reasons, the Parapiti River and the marshes of Izozog mark the northwestern limits of the Chaco. On the east, however, there was a close correspondence between natural and cultural boundaries until the end of the 17th century, when the *Mbayá* invasions into the regions east of the Paraguay River annexed to the Chaco culture area the *Guarani* lands situated between the Apa and the Miranda rivers.

The impact of white civilization during the past 300 years has also modified Chaco culture in many respects. Changes were brought about by the horse, and most of the tribes have received sheep, goats, cattle and dogs. Wealth in sheep favored the development of weaving, which became one of the main industries. Woolen garments replaced the former skin clothing. The Chaco Indians also received the following: tinder boxes for flint and steel, clarinets of cow horn, knitting with needles, certain folk-tale motifs, decorative patterns (on *Caduveo* pottery). They have also adopted plants, such as caña de Castilla (*Arundo donax*), watermelons, sugar cane, and others.

The Chaco Indians share several culture traits with the tribes of Patagonia culture area: skin mats, bow strings of leather, bows without notches at the ends, cloaks of several skins sewn together, skin skirts, leather girdles, hairbrushes, bags made of ostrich (rhea) necks, bags made of the whole skin of a small animal, hockey, and twisting of skin thongs. However, it is rather by their general type of life that the Chaco Indians resemble the southern tribes, and the analogies with them grow as one goes from the northern Chaco to the south. It is, for instance, difficult to distinguish the *Mocovi* from the *Charrua*.

In some remote past before they came in touch with the people of the Andes or with the *Arawak* and *Guarani* tribes to the north and east, the Chaco Indians were nomadic collectors, fishermen, and hunters. They dressed in painted skin cloaks and lived in flimsy communal houses. They had neither basketry nor weaving, but excelled in making netted bags. They were grouped in small bands formed by a few extended families; their religious practices consisted mainly of magic rites which aimed at expelling or controlling evil spirits. Their shamans derived their power from familiar spirits after a voluntary quest. They celebrated puberty rites for girls and in some, if not all the tribes, initiation ceremonies for boys.

The Eastern Brazilian Highlands culture area

In eastern and southern Brazil (and part of northern Paraguay), were Indians, most of whom speak Gé, who resemble the tropical forest, village type Indians yet differ from them in several ways. Formerly nomadic hunters and gatherers, they are now landsmen. While their villages are independent units, each is divided into a number of kinship divisions, moieties, age grades, associations, etc., unequaled in other areas of South America.

These attributes are most evident in the Gé-speaking people of the highlands of eastern Brazil.

These peoples are: the Northwestern Gé, who in turn include the Timbira (Canella and Apinayé), Cayapó, and Suyá; the almost identical Shavante, Sherente, and the now-extinct Shacriaba; and several groups known as the Acroa, who form the Central Gé.

Caingang refers to a number of peoples who make up the southern branch of the Gê-language family—the Guayaná, Coroado, and others. Sharing many cultural characteristics that may be described as a unit, they live in the plains and forests of southeastern Brazil. Since contact with whites, their numbers have been greatly reduced.

The Bororo, speaking an isolated language, live along the upper reaches of the Paraguay River and its affluents, north of the Guarani. Consisting of a western and an eastern division, the Bororo have seen several villages become extinct and their population dwindle in recent times.

Much of the northern portion of the Gé area in eastern Brazil was once occupied by non Gé-speakers. These peoples seem to have migrated from the southern *sertão* into the northern regions and then dominated the area.

This Eastern Brazilian culture area remains little known even today. Only partially settled by Brazilians, the area is home to Indians who are openly hostile to whites. Some knowledge of these Gé people comes from several monographs by the late German ethnologist, Kurt Nimuendajú, who lived among, and studied, the Indians of the Amazon and eastern Brazil from 1906 until his death in 1946.

In the early part of the nineteenth century, the Apinayé, Shavante, and Sherente are believed to have numbered 12,000 speakers. Warfare with Indian and white groups, combined with European diseases, however, seriously reduced their population. Recent estimates provide for lower population figures.

Patagonia culture area

Patagonia culture area is the region of South America that now comprises part of Argentina. It has been inhabited for at least 12,000 years. Mystery still surrounds the first arrival of native peoples into the area, and their early history is little known. Since the arrival of the Spanish in the 16th century, the native population has been gradually disappearing in the face of the white settlement. The Indians have been forced from their original territory and now occupy only isolated areas. These peoples are the Huarpe, Puelche, and Tehuelche.

In the mid-1960s there were an estimated several thousand Indians in this area. Although some groups practiced agriculture similar to that of native Andean peoples, most engaged in a subsistence economy of hunting, gathering, and fishing. In order to enter the money economy of the Argentine Republic, some Indians worked as salaried, seasonal laborers on cotton or sugar plantations and cattle ranches, or worked as tenant farmers or miners.

Southern culture area

The Southern culture area was home to the Chono, Alacaluf, Ona and Yahgan Indians, who occupied the whole Chilean archipelago from the Guaitecas Islands to Cape Horn. An inhospitable area, it is rugged, windswept, cold, and mountainous, with hundreds of islands, fiords, and channels. With an annual rainfall that reaches from 80 inches in the north to 120 inches in the south, and an average temperature of 32°F in winter and 50°F in summer, the country is covered by a dense, almost impenetrable rain forest. These conditions, a formidable deterrent to travel and farming, have made canoe transport vital to subsistence. The people of this region have been accurately described as "canoe nomads."

Despite the topography, anthropologists, ethnologists and other travelers have been interested in the cultures of the Yahgan, Ona, and the Alacaluf. (Less is known of the Chono, the northernmost people, who became extinct in the nineteenth century). Almost extinct today, the Alacaluf and Yahgan have a combined population of only several hundred speakers. Even in past times, they probably numbered no more than several thousand, and the Chono considerably less. Today, the surviving Ona Alacaluf and Yahgan are acculturated into the dominant white society.

CULTURE HEROES. The tradition of a creator or culture hero is general throughout South America. Because of the contrast between the loftiness of the figure and the significance of his active part in religion, which has many times been pointed out, there is a tendency to consider him to be no more than a mythical character. Nevertheless, even though the Creator or Cutlure Hero usually keeps aloof from human affairs, his remoteness is less absolute than our imperfect knowledge of the Indian religious systems may lead us to suppose. Among certain tribes like the *Tupinamba* and *Guarayú* there are traces of a cult dedicated to the Creator, and a closer examination of the ceremonies of other tribes may well show that the Indians sometimes turn to him in their prayers and expect his assistance. The Great Ancestor generally is the ruler of the Land of the Dead and in this capacity is associated with funerary practices and beliefs about the afterworld (*Tembé, Guarayú,* etc.). The Creator often is described as a Transformer and, as a rule, he is the lawgiver and instructor of the young humanity. After he has accomplished his tasks, he wanders westward to the end of the world, where he rules over the shadows.

An originator and civilizer of this kind could easily become a Supreme Being or a High God; this change seems actdually to have taken place in ancient Peru. The fragmentary myths about the God Viracocha—whose full name, Con-Ticci-Viracocha-Pachayachachic, means something like "the ancient foundation, the lord and instructor of the world"— represent him with all the typical characteristics of a Creator-Transformer-Civilizer. According to the myths, he made the earth, the sky, the stars, and mankind: destroyed the first people by a flood and created new men; wandered across Peru establishing the social and moral order and instructing mankind in many arts; and gave men their staple food plants and taught them the secrets of cultivation. In addition, he was a great transformer who changed mountains into plains and valleys into mountains and turned men into stones. We may well surmise that these are the deeds of the original Culture Hero of the *Quechua* or some other Andean people who, in the course of time and through the speculations of priests, was elevated to the position of a Supreme Deity, greater than all the other gods, even the powerful Sun God. Viracocha was worshipped in special temples by sacrifice and prayer and was represented in anthropomorphic images. Because of his exalted position and the comparatively recent emergence of his cult, he was less popular with the multitude than were the Sun deity and other lesser gods, but his worship was well established in the 16th century, and there can be no doubt but that he was a functioning god.

Con or Coniraya, who was worshiped by the coastal people of Peru, has been associated or compared with Viracocha. This deity, about whom few traditions have survived, was a solar god and had many attributes of a Creator, a Transformer, and a Culture Hero.

Pachacamac, the god of the famous temple, may have belonged to the same category of supernaturals.

Modern *Araucanians* celebrated the cult of a Supreme Being whom they addressed as "Master of men," "Master of the land," "Father," "King Father," or "Blue (sky) King Father." He not only was the creator, the giver of life and fecundity to men, animals and plants, but also was directly concerned with the welfare of mankind. Unfortunately, it is impossible to decide whether this conception of a High God was pre-European or came of the *Araucanians'* long contact with white people. Our knowledge about this Supreme God's cult does not go back further than 150 years. The many close analogies between *Araucanian* beliefs and customs and those of the people of Peru suggest the early existence of a figure of a Creator and Culture Hero who, in the course of years, was refashioned into a Supreme Being, probably under Christian influence.

Belief in a High God seems to have been one of the most fundamental concepts of the religion of the *Ona, Yahgan*, and *Alacaluf*, who are considered to be the most primitive tribes in South America. The evidence about the Fuegian Supreme Being was gathered from 1920 to 1926 by Father Gusinde and Father Koppers, both disciples of Father Wilhelm Schmidt, so that most of our information about the religion of these Indians was obtained when they had long been subject to white influence and when both the *Yahgan* and *Ona* were on the verge of extinction. Gusinde and Koppers undoubtedly are right in insisting that the Fuegian belief in a High God was independent of any Christian religious teaching, but many details and traditions concerning him may have been lost and the data gleaned at the last moment perhaps give us the illusion of a more philosophical and abstract deity than he actually was.

(The High God of the Fuegian tribes cannot be regarded as a deified Creator and Culture Hero, for he has few of the attributes of these mythical characters; in his nature he is closer to the Christian god than to Viracocha and other wandering Transformers and Teachers.)

The *Ona, Yahgan,* and *Alacaluf* believed that the Supreme Being was an invisible spirit without material needs, omniscient and all powerful, who lived in the sky beyond the stars. The *Ona* called him Temáukl'; the *Yahgan*, "The Old One"; and the *Alacaluf*, Xél'ás, "The Star." The *Ona* avoided the use of his name, preferring to call him "The one who lives in the sky." When praying, the *Yahgan* said, "My father" or called him "The Good One," "The Strong One," or "The Highest One"; when they were angry they spoke of him as "The Murderer in the Sky."

The *Ona* and *Alacaluf* believed that the Supreme God was the creator of the Universe; the *Yahgan* did not specifically regard him as such, though they considered him to be the master and owner of the world and provider of food. He was endowed with a highly moral nature, and, since he introduced the norms of conduct, he was the custodian of morality and the dispenser of justice. Disease and death were manifestations of his wrath—hence, the real or apparent resentment expressed against him when a person died. His good will was gained by living in accordance with the moral code of the tribe. The *Alacaluf* are said to have refrained from any worship because the very perfection of the High God rendered vain every attempt to change his will. The *Yahgan* prayed to him for food and health and thanked him for his favors. The *Ona* offered him morsels of food in a symbolic gesture.

The *Yahgan* High God was more alive and closer to man than was the *Ona* deity, who was somewhat pushed away in a distant and cloudy world.

The distinction between a Creator who is worshiped and, therefore, is part of the religious system and a Creator who is purely a mythological figure is more theoretical than practical. The *Guarayú* prayed to Tamoi, their Great Ancestor, and performed ceremonies in his honor. Although Nanderuvuçú, whose name means "Our Great Father" or "Our Great Grandfather," was typically an idle deity, his existence was not a matter of indifference to the *Apapocuva*, for they believed that one day, as once before, he would destroy the world. They conceived of his abode as a paradise and during the last century made several attempts to go there and live under his law.

The Noma—"Father"—of the *Witoto* is certainly a more abstract figure, who almost appears to be the product of a single brilliant and metaphysical mind. According to the *Witoto* creation myth, he was originated by the "word"; that is to say, by magico-religion formulae and by myths impregnated with magic power. He was the personification of this "word," which he is turn passed on to the first men. As a Culture Hero, he introduced all the religious ceremonies and also cannibalism. His relationship to the *Witoto* religion was not expressed in any form of direct worship, yet he was more than a theological concept, for without him the chants and ceremonies would have been without power. Unless Preuss (1921-23) has overstressed the metaphysical character of this God, he also must be regarded as an embodiment of vegetation.

Among the matrilineal *Cágaba,* the Supreme Being was a goddess whose titles are indicative of her exalted position. She was believed to be the "Mother of all human races, of the world, of animals, fruits, trees, rivers, thunders, the Milky Way, songs, dances, sacred objects, and sanctuaries." Her four sons were the ancestors of mankind. Because she was the source of all things, all ceremonies were performed for her to see. The *Cágaba* asked her to send rain and to grant them abundant harvests.

Less information is available about Eschetewuarha, the goddess of the *Chamacoco*, and for this reason her position within the *Chamacoco* religion is more difficult to ascertain. She was believed to be married to a Great Spirit whom she controlled as she did everything else in the world. The Indians prayed to her for water, for she was the mother of the Osasero birds (the clouds).

Kumana, the great goddess of the *Yaruro*, may have been a deity of the same type as the *Cágaba* "Mother of all things," but because of the fragmentary and contradictory nature of our sources, this cannot be positively ascertained. One informant said, "Everything sprang from Kuma, and everything that the *Yaruro* do was established by her" and "the other gods and culture heroes act according to her law."

The number of High Gods in South America was certainly larger than this summary indicates, but in most cases our information is either scanty or unreliable. Both the nature and the functions of these High Gods require more detailed investigation.

Inca religion with its array of gods, its numerous priesthood, and complex ritualism differs vastly from the diffuse and often amorphous animism of the tropical tribes as well as from the simple theism of Tierra del Fuego. The constant is, however, not so profound as it may appear. On the one hand, only strong animistic beliefs can explain the cults of the countless huacas or minor deities and fetishes of ancient Peru; on the other hand, some of the nature gods of the *Inca* pantheon crop up here and there among the tribes of the forests.

Throughout South America natural objects and phenomena are personified or are believed to be the abodes or manifestations of supernatural beings. There is, nevertheless, considerable variation in the degree of individualization of these spirits, in their functions, and in the nature of their relationship with people.

In Peru the heavenly bodies, the natural phenomena, and the elements as well as the earth and the sea were conspicuous deities that were worshiped in temples and served by priests. In most of the primitive tribes the same natural objects were either mythological figures without religious significance or were animated by spirits with little individuality. The personification of nature sometimes brings about situations which are difficult to define in terms of our usual notions about religion. For example, among the *Mataco*, Sun was a mythological figure but not a functioning deity, for no prayers were addressed to him and no ceremonies were performed in his honor; yet shamans "visited" him to take advantage of his great knowledge in solving their problems.

Outside of Peru, where Sun was the ancestor and the principal god of the *Inca* dynasty, Sun and Moon were potent deities only in three small *Gê* tribes of Eastern Brazil: the *Apinayé*, the *Sherente*, and the *Canella*. There were also traces of a solar cult among the ancient *Guarani* and their modern descendants, the *Apapocuva*, but its importance probably was slight.

Although from Tierra del Fuego go the Guiana stars and constellations were visualized as Culture Heroes or mythical animals that had migrated to the sky, the phenomena were deified only in Peru and among the *Sherente*, to whom they appeared in visions as deputies of Sun and Moon. It is possible that the Pleiades were worshiped by the *Guaicuruan* tribes of the Chaco, but we have no details.

The sky never has been personified in South American, but human will and feelings were attributed to it in Chaco mythology when, for instance, the sky changed place with the earth so as not to be soiled by it.

The Thunder God ranked very high in the *Inca* pantheon and survived to modern times under the name Santiago. In the Chaco and in the Tropical Forest, thunder was attributed either to birds or to spirits. The Thunder Spirit of the ancient *Tupi-Guarani* of the Brazilian coast underwent a strange metamorphosis after the Discovery. The missionaries, in their search for the notion of a Supreme Being, heard the Indians refer to this sky demon, and raised him to the dignity of a High God. Today Tupan is the name of the Christian God among all the people of Brazil and Paraguay who speak a *Guarani* dialect; Tupan also has taken on the meaning of "sacred."

The Earth-mother is a typical Andean deity whose cult was perhaps more important in the popular religion than that of the Sun or other *Inca* major gods, for it remained almost intact from Ecuador to the Argentine long after most of the gods of the *Inca* pantheon had been forgotten. The cult of the Earth Goddess has been reported among the *Jivaro*, but there she was probably a simple vegetation demon, for only female plants were under her protection.

In Peru the term huaca was applied to everything sacred; in the chronicles it designates the gods, demons, and spirits worshiped by the people of the Empire. Some of these huaca were nature gods adored in the several provinces, but the majority were no more than local spirits or demons that haunted the hills, lakes, rivers, and caves or that animated the countless fetishes worshiped by the lineages and families of the Empire. Without any doubt, these spirits were similar to those that filled the world of the forest Indians, but many assumed the character of gods by becoming protectors of a large social group that developed a cult around them. The accumulated myths and traditions gave them individuality and increased their prestige. Other spirits, such as the mallcu and samiri of modern *Aymara*, remained simple fetishes—cones or earth and stones that were the custodians of an ayllu and were only dimly conceived of as the receptacles of spirits.

The Guiana Indians regarded rapids, waterfalls, conspicuous mountains, strangely grown trees, and other natural oddities as the abodes of special spirits that bore a distinctive name and incarnated themselves in animals (e.g., water serpents, hawks, caimans, etc.). These localized spirits differ from the Peruvian huaca only in the absence of a regular cult, yet in some cases simple rites were performed in their behalf. For example, before crossing a rapid haunted by a spirit, Indian crews sometimes rubbed red pepper in their eyes to ward off danger.

The Peruvian Indians gave a very secondary place to such vegetation deities as Mother Maize or Mother Potato, for in Peru the fertility of the soil was under the protection of the Sun and especially of the Earthmother. Nevertheless, plant spirits had a cult and were symbolized by unusually large and oddly shaped ears of corn or tubers. In tropical South America, the Spirit of the Cassava or the Maize, though no more important than other spirits and like them subject to the will of the shamans, nevertheless assumed some of the characteristics of a vegetation god. The *Cashinawa* performed dances to propitiate the Maize Spirit. The Barama *Carib* asked their shamans to consult with the Cassava Spirit about crop prospects; during the interview, the spirit was given manioc beer, a gesture of courtesy that might perhaps be interpreted as an offering.

Among the spirits that tend toward a greater individualization are the supernatural protectors of the animal species usually called the "Father or Mother of such-and-such kind of game or fish." In the myths these spirits are represented as particularly large specimens of the species, and, as a rule, they may take on human form at will. To this category belong Rato, an aquatic monster who, the *Taulipáng* said, was the father of all fish and water animals, as well as the *Toba* Indians' Soinidi, who was both a water spirit and the protector of the fish. These custodians of the species freely permit the use of their protégées as food, but they do not tolerate their wanton destruction by man, and they punish severely hunters who kill more than they actually need to survive.

CUMANA comprise several tribes who live along the northeast coast of Venezuela. Carib-speaking, they are agrarian. Their numbers are not known, but the population is probably several hundred.

Culture

Women do all the work, as the men only clear the land for cultivation. They raise manioc, maize, and fruits. A man, after he marries, works for his wife's family for one year. Chiefs are permitted to have more than one wife. Social classes range from slaves to powerful chiefs. Trading takes place among the Cumana tribes for goods, and with other tribes for gold.

CUNA of eastern Panama are a people of romantic history noted for their warlike character. Their territory edged on what is now the Panama Canal Zone, and extended eastward and south in both high mountains and valleys to the northern tributaries of the large Tuira River of Darien. Smaller in stature than most neighboring tribes, they made up for this by fierce energy and national pride. The name Cuna means "the people," but those who live on the San Blas Islands off the northeast coast of Panama came to be called the San Blas.

Social and cultural boundaries and subdivisions

The two major divisions of this people are the Island Cuna or San Blas and the mainland Cuna. The Island Cuna had their culture influenced early and changed by their contacts and wars with the Spanish conquistadors, as well as by their collaboration with Dutch, British and French pirates. The mainland Cuna, protected by high mountains and jungles, maintained a purer original culture, though, but in the last half of the nineteenth century, they too were changing. The Cuna were also vertically stratified in the old days into the social subdivisions of chiefs, nobles, commoners and slaves. Today there seem to be only two divisions, the rich and poor. To the west of the Cuna were the equally warlike Guaymi, while to the east and south were their near and possibly ancestral relatives the Cueva, plus the more primitive Choco and Catio tribes.

Language

The Cuna belong to the Chibchan-Paezan language family, which includes all their neighbors to their west, east and southeast, as outlined above, plus the more highly-civilized Chibcha, who once dwelt in walled city-states in what is now the country of Colombia in South America.

Summary of tribal culture

Subsistence and economy. By the time of the arrival of the Spaniards the Cuna had become mainly an agricultural people, using the slash-and-burn technique to clear jungle land for the planting of crops. Corn, beans and squash were the primary vegetable foods, but bananas, plantain, rice, yams, sweet manioc, sugar cane, sweet potatoes, pineapples and tobacco were added later. Other fruits include oranges, limes, mangos, papaya, avocado, coconut palms (especially on the islands) and coffee. Planting in the old days was done by the dibble, a sharp pointed stick, probably tipped with stone and later with iron, to punch holes in the soil in which seeds could be dropped. This tool was also used for weeding.

Hunting was once quite important, most of the men of a village often going on expeditions into jungle areas where game was plentiful, usually taking along some women to do the cooking. Peccaries or wild pigs were hunted individually or by the surround method, while the large elephant-like tapirs were most often trapped in deep pits, covered with screens of branches and dirt. Other animals commonly hunted included deer, squirrels, agoutis (large rodents), spider and howler monkeys, and the large lizards called iguanas, whose flesh is delicious. Crested Guans, related to the wild turkey, quail-like tinamou, and other birds were shot. Hunting was done mainly with bow and arrows, but also with spears and, recently, with blowguns with poison darts (imported from the Choco). Fishing in the rivers and seas was done with spears, later with harpoons borrowed from Bush Negroes, bows and three-pronged arrows, brush and stick dams or weirs, and by nets. Turtle-like decoys were used for trapping sea turtles in stationary nets.

Domesticated animals were dogs, cats, pigs and chickens, though wild pets such as toucans, parrots and monkeys, were often kept. Food preparation was simple, with many items boiled singly or in groups to make a kind of mush such as of bananas, plantains and fish. Bananas, plantains and tubers were often baked, while meat was either roasted or smoked, as was fish. A popular unfermented drink was made of roasted corn meal, sugar cane juice, cocoa and water.

Technology and the arts. The Mainland Cuna live in small villages strung along river banks, while the San Blas or Island Cuna have towns made up of regular rows of houses along one or more streets. The rectangular houses are built on the ground except along large rivers to the east where they are often raised on poles to escape floods. A cook house is either attached to the main house or is separate. Hammocks hang from poles for sleeping, while attractively carved and shaped low wooden stools form seats. Women may be seen busily weaving cotton cloth or hammocks on vertical looms while other women twine bast fibers together with cotton to make rope. Beautiful, geometrically-designed, and overlapped with many colors are the applique display bouses for women, a high art of the Cuna.

Clothing at the time of white invasion was a simple penis cover for the men of shell, gold or reeds, while women wore cotton skirts reaching to the ankles, the blouses probably being added later. Feather-decorated aprons were once common, but today only feather-decorated crowns, with four upright feathers, denoting rank, are worn.

Many large ornaments of gold were once worn, but white greed for these items led the Cuna to change, so today's women wear only necklaces of glass beads or cheap coins including constricting anklets, armlets and necklets of beads.

Originally the Cuna constructed narrow dugouts with platform ends, still used on the mainland rivers, but the sea Cuna now have oceangoing dugouts each with a jib and a triangular mainsail. Crutch-handled paddles or poles propelled them.

Social and religious culture. Marriage is now monogamous, but in the old days chiefs and nobles often had two or more wives. Marriage residence is with the wife's family, with the oldest man in a multiple household usually acting as head of the males; his wife heading the females. No payment is required in marriage and no penalties levied on divorces, yet stable family life is the rule. In the old days the position of family head was ordinarily passed by direct inheritance to the oldest son, but today both chiefs and sub-chiefs are usually democratically elected. The head chief of a village generally chants a moralizing sermon every few days to all his people, based on legends and standards

Cuna Indian women and children, Colombia, 1969.

Cuna village, San Blas Islands.

of conduct passed down from past spiritual leaders. On the island villages there are usually two political parties, each headed by a high chief, elected from village chiefs.

Near to one percent of the Cuna are albinos, who are believed to have special powers, but are limited in their skills because of poor eyesight. Though boys have no puberty ceremonies, girls have two, the second one a formal debut in which it is announced the girl is ready for marriage. Peculiar to this ceremony is the smoking of cigars with the lighted ends held in the mouths and the smoke blown over the faces of various leaders to sanctify them, while one leader sings long chants giving life advice.

The Cuna were often successful in war with the Spaniards, using fortified villages with loopholes in the wals, alliances with French and English pirates, and the luring of invading armies into ambuscades in the jungles.

Musical instruments once included large hollow long drums, skin-headed drums, and bamboo drums, but these were given up in recent years, though calabash rattles, panpipes and flutes, some fantastically shaped, are still used. A fermented corn drink called *chicha* was used in some ceremonies and dances, and husbands might be seen afterward in hammocks, with their wives splashing them with water to sober them up!

In religion the union of the Great Spirit and his wife was the source of all things. Other lesser gods or spirits had crept into the religion, as had some fetiches, possibly adopted from the Bush Negroes. Three kinds of shamans, each more powerful than the other, cured people with chants and herbal medicines, the most important being able to prophesy the future. Mnemonic picture writing on boards was used and still is used by chiefs and shamans to help them memorize chants and other ceremonial observances.

Brief history and present condition

The Cuna migrated west and north into Panama from Colombia many centuries ago. After the coming of their great Culture Hero or Prophet some 900 years ago, they were led by his disciples and then by ten great shamans. Some of these heroes led the San Blas Cuna into the islands, and others helped them in the wars against the Spaniards, who never completely conquered them. Today the Cuna, especially on the islands, attract numbers of tourists who buy their finely woven and decorated cotton garments and other artifacts.There seems to be a revival now of many cultural motifs and a return of the high standards of conduct taught to them by their culture heroes.

VINSON BROWN

CUPISNIQUE culture of Peru can be placed in the North Coast sequence as antecedent to Salinar, which was in turn followed by Mochica (Proto- or Early Chimu). Sculpture, ceramics, and the carving of small objects in stone and bone were advanced in development. The sculptural art is of particular merit. Metals were unknown, and the presence of small plates or disks of gold in some of the Saninar-Cupisnicoid tombs can probably be attributed to Salinar influence. Settlements at this time were small groups of houses which may represent some sort of joint family arrangements. The Cupisnique culture contributes strongly in culture elements to the formation of the Mochica culture.

Culture

There is no evidence concerning actual agricultural practices or techniques, but several domesticated food plants were known at this early period. Ceramic representations of plants, as well as the original foodstuffs, have been found buried with the dead. These include peanuts, yuca, a cultivated species of caigua, and gourds. It is surprising that maize, potatoes, and other products common to the region in later archaeological periods have not been discovered.

In addition to horticultural product the Cupisnique people added llama and deer meat to their diet. The remains of shellfish and edible land snails testify to the importance of these as a food. Fish were, undoubtedly, another important food item.

It seems reasonable to believe that they domesticated the llama and the dog, as skeletons of both of these animals have been recovered from human graves.

Architecture

The few known ruins in the vicinity of Cupisnique and elsewhere in the Valley of Chicama show three types of construction: (1) those of stone; (2) those of conical adobes that pertain to a probable later period; (3) a subtype of combined stone and adobe.

The sole pottery vessel of Cupisnique style depicting a house probably corresponds to the stone-adobe subtype. This vessel shows a house of simple rectangular plan with a gabled roof. The rectilinear figure seen on one side seems to be a doorway.

On the Pampa de los Fósiles and at Hacienda Sausal (Barbacoa and Palenque) there are remains of walls constructed of fairly large, irregular stones set in mud and fitted with stone spalls.

Adobe structures of the period are built up of conical or odontiform adobes. Walls of adobe were built up by placing rows of conical adobes point to point and then by filling the angles and interstices with clay mortar. In the construction of walls of great thickness, a double row of adobes was laid point to point. On these another layer of adobes was alined in reverse in such a manner that their pointed ends touched the bases of the lower row, and likewise fitted base to base with each other. The conical adobes always had their flat bases toward the outside, in order to form a flat surface for the wall.

Handbook of South American Indians.

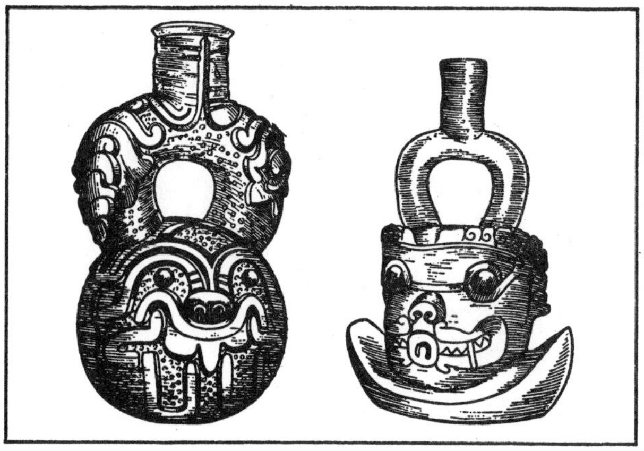

Cupisnique pottery.

The adobes were laid on a slight incline, so that a transverse cut shows the rows as a series of undulating faces. The walls were given a uniform surface by coating them with clay plaster. Both solid circular and pyramidal constructions were initiated in this cultural period.

Clothing and ornaments

The Cupisnique people wore a simple loincloth, leaving most of the body uncovered. The headdress consisted of a cap with an attached covering for the back of the neck. The bone ear ornaments mentioned below, necklaces of stone and bone beads, and bone rings were common adornment. Necklaces of beads usually had a central piece with magnificent engravings. Some of the dead were found with rings on two, three and even five fingers.

CUPSTONES are the most plentiful of small decorative objects that have been found. They are found everywhere—even where no other evidence of habitation has been found.

The stones are plain blocks with cavities in them, some made from rough pecking and others smooth, semicircular shapes approximately two inches in diameter. On irregular blocks there are up to twenty additional pits made by gouging with flint. These are on one side only, on less than half of the surface. On smoother stones they are on both sides. They have been called nutstones in the unlikely belief that the pits were used for nut-cracking.

CURARE, from *woorari, urari, cuarari*, all meaning "poison," is the name of a liana, *Strychnos toxifera*, from which a deadly alkaloid poison is manufactured by several South American tribes for use on blowgun darts. There are several types, used in pot, calabash, or tube containers which are carried by the hunter; since the substance loses its power fairly quickly, it is usually smeared on the hand and then the small dart is coated for immediate use. The blowgun, which was a late introduction into the Amazon region, was only made practical by the effective power of curare to kill small game, and to incapacitate larger animals. The advantages of the weapon are numerous, of course: it is noiseless, allowing the hunter to approach close to the prey; it is light in weight and easily transported; and with curare, is extremely effective in a short time on small game. Although dangerous to humans, curare is less effective on them, and was almost never used in warfare, but was restricted for hunting. The poison was made and used mainly by the Nambicuara, Makú, Macushi, Paressi and Tucuna; the latter seem to have produced the most effective product. Curare has become widely adopted in contemporary physiological medicine due to its muscle relaxant properties.

CURAZABA was an Encabellado Indian of the Brazilian highlands who in January of 1744 led an

Indian uprising against the Spanish Jesuit missionaries of the San Miguel de Ciecoya settlement. Convincing his tribesmen that the Jesuits were planning to sell the Encabellado children as slaves, Curazaba plotted the murders of Father Francisco Real and his two assistants, the Spaniard Domingo and the mestizo (possibly Indian) Juanico Ibarra. In the uprising eight of the 13 Encabellado pueblos were deserted. Curazaba and his followers fled to the hills.

CURLEY (Crow; 1859-*c.* 1935) was a scout with Col. George A. Custer at the Battle of the Little Big Horn, Montana Territory, June 25, 1876, who, like the battle itself, became a subject of controversy. He was only 17 at the time, and as long as he lived he was subjected to the examination and cross-examination. As he openly stated, Curley was not in the fight. Supposedly he obeyed the command or suggestion of a superior to join the wagon train, or to watch from a ridge, but he has been accused of leaving the battle scene too soon. Apparently he made no effort to help the beleaguered Maj. Marcus Reno or Capt. Frederick W. Benteen. Nor did he attempt to inform Gen. Alfred Terry, en route with reinforcements. According to Curley, he just went "home," although some say that on June 27 he reached the mouth of the Little Big Horn, where he boarded the "Far West" and told Capt. Grant Marsh the story of Custer's fate.

Curley

Many writers have contributed to the Curley myth to satisfy the insatiable appetite of the reading public for every scrap of sensationalism surrounding the tragic battle. The "standard" Curley account first appeared in the *Helena Herald* on July 15, 1876. His final interview was given three years before he died.

CURLY HEAD (Chippewa; ?-1825) was a chief who challenged the Dakota (Sioux) near the upper Mississippi River, making the region safe for Chippewa (Ojibwa) settlement. After a particularly devastating Dakota raid that weakened the Chippewa, Curly Head settled his tribe on the edge of Dakota territory, near Gull Lake, Minnesota, and collected an especially fierce band of warriors. He then raided the Dakota so successfully as to drive them permanently from the area.

Curly Head was also a noted civil chief, beloved by his people for his generosity, and was principally responsible for keeping the peace between the Chippewa and whites at that time. He received a medal and a flag from Lieut. Zebulon M. Pike who wintered near his village in 1805-06. Curly Head signed the Treaty of Prairie due Chien on August 19, 1825, as Babaseekeendase. He died returning from this conference.

CURRIE, WALTER (Ojibwa; 1922-), was chairman of the Native Studies Department at Trent University in Peterborough, Ontario, and a leader of the Canadian Association in Support of the Native People in the mid-1970s.

Born in Chatham, Ontario, he received his B.A. degree from the University of Western Ontario in London. After teacher training at London Normal School, Currie taught elementary school in Kitchener (1953-58). He became principal of an elementary school in the Toronto area in 1963.

As an executive member of the Indian-Eskimo Association (now the Canadian Association in Support of the Native People), Currie chaired a national conference on "Indians and the City" in 1966. In 1969 he became chairman of the Indian Hall of Fame at the Canadian National Exhibition in Toronto, and he is also acting chairman of the Ontario Human Rights Commission. He took his position at Trent University in 1971.

Currie is an advocate of programs to upgrade education for Indians, and he has worked to have textbooks for Indians that reflect their background of hunting, fishing, and trapping. He has suggested that grade school textbooks be written in the Indian languages and that they be taught by teachers who speak the language.

CURRY, REGINALD ORAN (Uncompahgre Ute; Oct. 20, 1915-April 28, 1973), was a leading official of the Ute tribe on the Uintah and Ouray Reservation,

Utah. He was known as an advocate of Indian water rights and a protector of Indian natural resources.

CURTIS ACT of June 28, 1898, forced allotment upon the Five Civilized Tribes of the Indian Territory.

The five nations (Cherokee, Chickasaw, Creek, Choctaw, and Seminole) held communal title to their lands and had been exempted from the Dawes Act of 1887 which authorized the breakup of tribal lands into individual 160-acre homesteads. When the Dawes Commission (established in 1893) failed to negotiate an allotment agreement, the U.S. Congress passed the Curtis Act.

Sponsored by Representative Charles Curtis of Kansas, the Curtis Act called for the restructuring of Indian Territory (now Oklahoma) into individual homesteads. Tribal funds were likewise ended by payments to individual members. It consolidated previous congressional actions which undermined tribal autonomy and abolished all tribal governments as of March 4, 1906. The Department of the Interior took over the Five Nations' school systems.

The Curtis Act was implemented by the Dawes Commission. After allotment, remaining lands were sold to white settlers. In 1907 the territory was merged with the adjacent Oklahoma Territory and admitted to statehood.

CURTIS, CHARLES (Kansas/Osage; Jan. 25, 1860-Feb. 8, 1936), was the first person of Indian descent elected to a major U.S. government office. He was born on Indian land later included in North Topeka, Kansas. Through his mother, Helen Pappan, he was descended from White Plume, a Kansa (Kaw) chief, and Pawhuska, an Osage chief. His father, Orren A. Curtis, the descendant of early New England settlers, was an abolitionist and a Union calvalry officer in the U.S. Civil War.

After his mother died when he was three years old, Curtis was raised on the Kaw Reservation and in Topeka, Kansas. For several years he rode as a professional jockey and worked at odd jobs. Befriended by a Topeka lawyer, A. H. Case, Curtis worked as a law clerk and in 1881 was admitted to the bar.

Curtis was elected as a Republican to the office of county prosecuting attorney in 1884 and 1886, and he was elected to the U.S. House of Representatives in 1892. As a congressman, he sponsored an 1898 law permitting Indians to incorporate their own towns and to elected municipal officials, and he opposed the removal of restrictions on federal supervision of Indian affairs.

In 1907, when the Kansas legislature elected him to the U.S. Senate to fill an unexpired term, Curtis became the first U.S. senator of Indian ancestry. Although defeated in 1912, he was returned to the Senate in 1914, when U.S. senators were first elected by popular vote. He was reelected in 1920 and 1926.

Curtis supported U.S. involvement in World War I but opposed U.S. entry into the League of Nations. He worked for national prohibition, was an early supporter of women's suffrage, and favored farm-relief laws. He served as Republican party whip (1915-24) and majority leader (1924-29). In 1924, as chairman of the Senate Committee on Indian Affairs, he sponsored the Indian Citizenship (Curtis) Act, which declared Indians to be U.S. citizens but protected their tribal property rights.

In 1928 Curtis was nominated and elected vice president on the Republican ticket headed by Herbert Hoover (even though he had opposed Hoover's nomination). Along with Hoover he was defeated for reelection in 1932. After leaving office, he headed the short-lived National Republican League. He resumed the practice of law in Washington, D.C., and became president of a gold mining company in New Mexico. Curtis died of heart disease in 1936.

CUSABO, now extinct, was a conglomeration of tribes living in Southeast United States.

The word *Cusabo* may mean "*Coosawhatchie* River People." The name is used collectively for the Cornbahee, Coosa, Edisto, Etiwaw, Kiawaw, St. Helena, Stono, and Wapou Indian bands that lived together between Charleston, South Carolina and the Savannah River. Most of these tribes were Muskhogean.

They lived in permanent villages pursuing their basic economy of fishing and hunting.

One of the tribes may have been mound builders, or they may have inherited them when they took the territory to live. Like the Guale who were also located in the Southeast, they used a pentagonal shaped mound structure for important meetings, government and religious ceremonies. Another circular structure was used for burials.

Very little is known about their governmental organization but apparently there was a male chief.

Their first white contact was De Allyon's visit in 1521. The Cusabo graciously welcomed De Allyon. The Spaniard returned the courtesy by kidnapping 70 Indians and selling them as slaves. Many more slave raids were made against the Cusabo.

Their history is full of various relations between the Spanish, French, and English colonists, besides neighboring Indian tribes. The French, as they did with most tribes, allowed the Cusabo to live peacefully. Many English made continual raids against the Indians. The Spanish continued slaving raids, selling the Indians to Spanish colonists in Florida and the Caribbean.

In January, 1715, there were estimated to be 295 Cusabos living in four villages. But that year the Yamasee War began. It is assumed that all Cusabos were exterminated, for none were ever found again.

CUSI TITU (Quechua; fl. 16th century), was the instigator of a violent messianic uprising among the Quechua tribes of the Vilcabamba region of Peru, beginning in 1565. Cusi Titu is believed to have sent out Indian representatives into neighboring provinces, where they turned other, more pacifistic Indians against the Spanish overlords. The rebellion ended in 1572 when the Spanish disbanded Cusi Titu's separatist government and killed the Inca ruler Tupac Amaru I.

CUYAPAIPE RESERVATION, in San Diego County, California, is a reservation of 4,100 acres for the Cuyapaipe Band of Mission Indians. In the early 1970s there was one Indian living on the land.

The reservation was established in 1893, under authority of the Act of 1891. Much of the area around the reservation today is settled by the U.S. Park Service. The climate is generally mild and cool in the area, and temperatures are moderate. The only service on the reservation is water. There is no gas, electricity, or sewer system. The nearest medical services are in Alpine, 13 miles away. San Diego is 75 miles from the reservation.

CUZCO was the political and religious capital of the Inca Empire—a native American state that stretched for more than 3,000 miles through the mountains and along the coast of western South America and had more than 15,000,000 subjects at the time of the Spanish invasions in the 1530s. It is located at the upper end of an 11,000 foot high mountain valley in southern Peru. Cuzco was a small village until about the middle of the fifteenth century, when the Incas began to conquer other ethnic groups in the Andes and incorporate them into their state. Pachakuti, the Inca emperor at that time, had laborers rebuild Cuzco in a manner that would reflect its newly acquired status as a seat of power. This construction project lasted more than five years and involved the entire upper portion of the valley where the new capital was situated. Rivers were straightened and channeled; the valley floor was leveled; and the hillsides were terraced to expand the area under cultivation. Cuzco itself was laid out in the shape of a giant puma with a fortress called Sacsahuaman forming its head and great square surrounded by temples, the palace-mausoleums of past and current rulers, and a few government buildings forming the body.

Braniff International

The fortress of Sacsayhuaman in Cuzco.

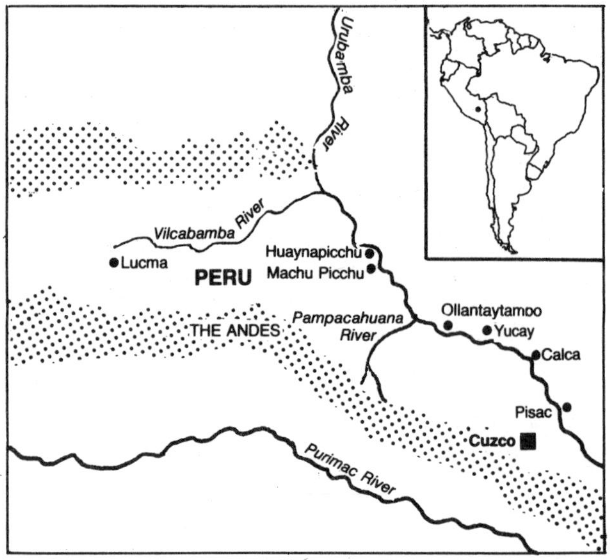

Cuzco

The population of the capital was relatively small—members of the royal families, priests, and a few government officials. An early historical account indicates that no poor people lived in the city, which suggests that no individuals, except servants who did not belong to the nobility, resided there. The non-nobles, the farmers, the craftsmen and specialists working for the state, important nobility from the provinces, and others resided in a series of residential settlements around the capital and utilized the state-controlled storehouses and other public facilities that were available in the city and its environs. In other words, the majority of the population lived outside of the capital but in close proximity to the public facilities that were available in the valley.

The internal structure of Cuzco differed dramatically from cities located in other parts of the world. There was a major distinction between the city proper and the residential settlements surrounding it; there was little duplication of public facilities—like shrines or markets—that was so characteristic of Western cities; and each part of the city was organized to serve a particular function. Cuzco was clearly the product of distinctly Andean social institutions, and its internal structure and layout reflects them.

THOMAS C. PATTERSON

Luis E. Valcárcel

Foundations of the Torreón of Muyumarca at Sacsahuaman in Cuzco.

A habitation at Sacsahuaman in Cuzco.

Section of wall.

Looking along the fortifications.

Smithsonian Institution, National Anthropological Archives.

DAGANETT, CHARLES A. (Peoria; *c.* 1872-?), was a career government official in the Indian Bureau. He was born in Indian Territory (present Oklahoma), where his grandfather had been agent of the Miami-Peoria Reservation. Daganett attended Carlisle Indian School (1887-91), learned the trade of printer, and became editor of the *Red Man*, the school newspaper. He later attended Dickinson College and eventually graduated from Eastman College in Poughkeepsie, New York.

Daganett edited a newspaper in Miami, Oklahoma, for a time and joined the Indian Service in 1894. He worked his way up through the ranks, being successively teachere, disciplinarian, and clerk before his appointment as supervisor of employment about 1907. He was one of the leaders of the Society of American Indians.

DAGGER, a knife-like weapon designed for stabbing, was used by the American Indian aborigines primarily for war and ceremonial purposes and to a limited extent in hunting. The prevalence of this weapon in prehistoric times is unclear. Stone weapons designed to be used primarily as daggers were relatively rare and often were edge sharpened, making such artifacts difficult to distinguish from knives. As with knives, they are often not easily distinguished from lance-head and projectile-point artifacts unless the handle is still attached or was formed in a single piece with the point or blade. Daggers were often made from antler, ivory, and animal long bones, and these are more easily identifiable. Copper daggers, including a double-pointed form, were used in the Great Lakes area. A specialized dagger-like implement called a fish needle was used by the Eskimos to kill fish by piercing the brain after they were caught.

The introduction of iron and steel was followed by the employment of a greater number and variety of daggers by the North American Indians. Among tribes of the Northwest Coast, the manufacture of broad-bladed daggers of copper, iron, or steel, patterned after European and Asiatic forms, became economically important.

Smithsonian Institution. National Anthropological Archives.
Drawing of Tlingit warrior wearing visored wooden helmet, slat armor and daggers of a type collected in 1860s.

DAKOTA or Sioux (or Dakota Sioux) designates the western Sioux, or Lakota. It has been used so long that it has become established in our minds probably too deeply to be changed to the more correct name of *Lakota.* A fuller name for them is the *Teton Lakota,* or again, as the white man makes it, the *Teton Sioux.* Teton means "the dwellers of the prairie." Strangely the name *Dakota* actually applies to the Santee Sioux, who remained in what is now Minnesota as a forest people. The Yankton Sioux, calling themselves the *Nakota*, were in between the two larger groups. The Lakota or Teton Dakota (Teton Sioux) will be discussed here. The word *Sioux* itself probably comes from the old Chippewa (Ojibwa) name for enemies to the wes, whom they called *Nadowe-is-iw*. Early French traders or trappers evidently garbled the last part of this name into "Sioux".

The Dakota are to most white people the epitome or classic example of Plains Indian warriors. More than any other tribe in the 1800s they were thought of as an ominous threat to western expansion of trappers, settlers and miners. Their great power to create fear is remarkable when you consider that they were originally a shy forest people driven eastward and into the Plains by the Chippewa or Ojibwa, who obtained guns from the traders before the Dakota and used these to defeat them in battle.

But the Dakota, by obtaining horses in the late 1800s (probably from the Kiowa to the west), with guns from the traders soon following, and sweeping grandly across the spaceless plains, became in a comparatively short time mighty warriors: bold, brave, fierce and clever, driving other tribes before them. The Pawnees, Cheyennes, Kiowa and Crow reeled before their attacks, the Cheyennes later becoming their allies, while the whites learned to treat them with respect due to mastery of military tactics and war.

In this article the Dakota's ways which made them a special people or those ways in which they were pacesetters for the other Plains tribes, will be described more fully. The economy of the way they lived, their food gathering and preparation, their making of clothing and tents and weapons, and so forth, were so much like those of the other Plains tribes, such as the Crow and Cheyenne, that you can turn to articles on these people to understand such matters as they were with the Dakota.

Social and cultural boundaries and subdivisions

The Teton Sioux or Lakota, included seven divisions or Seven Council Fires, the most populous being the

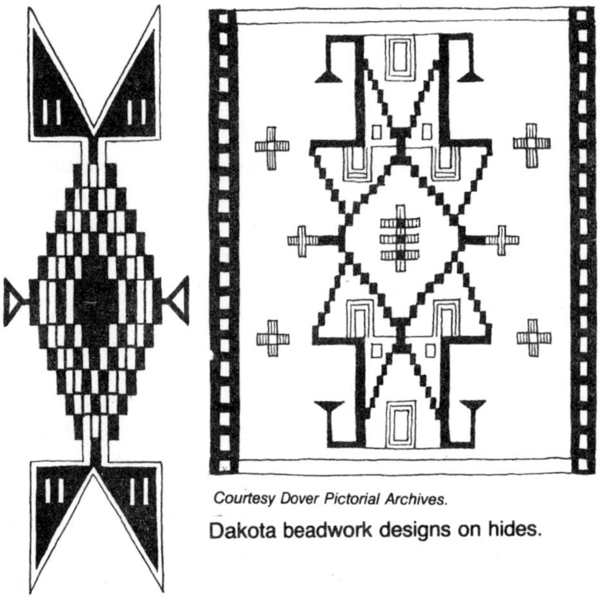

Courtesy Dover Pictorial Archives.

Dakota beadwork designs on hides.

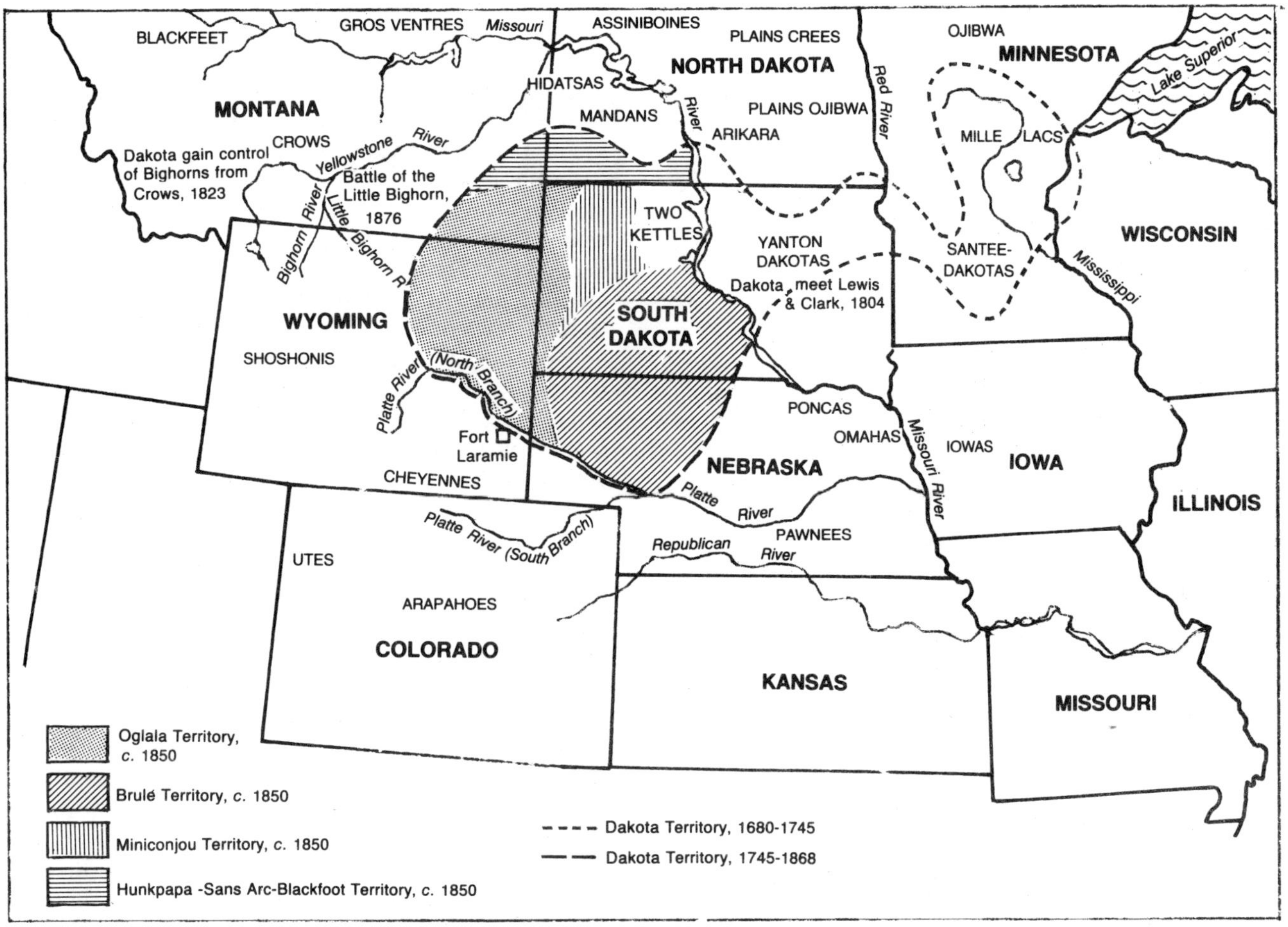

Dakota territory, middle 17th century-mid 20th century.

Oglalas ("Scatters Ones Own") on the southwest, the main cutting edge of the westward-moving tribe, who drove the Kiowas out of the Black Hills in 1765. Second were the Brules, also called the Sichangus (Burnt Thighs), to the southeast, possibly the strongest in war power. Third, on the middle of the eastern side were the Miniconjous ("Those Who Plant by the Streams," probably referring to these people planting corn long ago). To the north were, fourth, the Hunkpapas ("Those who Camp at the Entrance"), whom Sitting Bull made famous at the Battle of the Little Bighorn. Also in the north and, fifth, were the Sihasapas (the Black Feet Sioux, probably called this after they had walked through a burnt grass area). Sixth, again in the north, were the Itazipchos or Sans Arcs (as the French called them, meaning "without bows"). Seventh, and probably smallest of all, were the Oohenonpas ("the Two Kettles"), who lived to the east, in between the Miniconjous and the Brules.

Language

The Dakota Sioux belonged to the immense Hokan-Siouian language family, which included their enemy peoples, the Crow to the west by the Teton Mountains, the Hidatsa to the northeast on the Missouri River, and the closely related Assiniboine to the north. But many other great tribes of this language family included the Pomo in California, the Iroquois to the northeast, the Cherokee, Choctaw and Creek in the southeast, and the Osage in what is now Arkansas.

The cycle of life

This cycle was very similar, with minor local variations, in all the Plains tribes. To begin with the pregnant woman was treated with great respect and consideration as the coming mother of new life, or as one

Dover Pictorial Archive.

Dakota shield cover.

Dover Pictorial Archive.

Dakota beaded pipe bags.

"growing strong" with such life. Two usually wooden "sand lizards" were carved or shaped at this time, one of which would later hold the umbilical cord, while the other would act as a kind of decoy, drawing off evil forces from the new child. Also before birth one of the father's sisters would lovingly, and as a symbol of respect, make a handsome cradle for the new baby.

As the birth came close, the pregnant one and her mother would be alone in the tipi where the mother would prepare such things as a clean square of soft deerskin and a stout stake, driven securely into the ground, plus braided sweet grass, soaked in warm water, a bowl of buffalo grease, a large puff ball with a hole cut into it, and a strong strip of soft deerskin. As labor started, the young woman squatted in front of the stake and held her knees against it, then knelt on the ground when the pains grew strong, holding the stake with her hands and straining to help the baby emerge.

As the baby came out, the grandmother would place it on the square of deerskin, and cut the umbilical cord three inches out from the body. The freed navel cord was then throughly dusted with fungus powder as it was pulled through the hole in the puff ball. Twisting the navel cord around, she fitted it into the puffball. Then the strip of deerskin was tied around the baby's stomach to hold the remaining navel firmly in place. Cleaning the child with warm water and sweet grass, she wiped it all over with buffalo grease, then wrapped it in blankets and placed it beside the mother. Mother's milk was given to the baby for at least two years and sometimes much longer. After about two months the baby was put in a baby bundle in which it was securely wrapped and then attached to a carrying cradle. Cattail down in summer and pulverized buffalo chips in winter were used as absorbents for urine and bowel movements. Carried about in the cradle the baby had a wonderful view.

Young children were raised with a great deal of love and fondling by the mothers, sisters, aunts and grandmothers, with very little discipline. Yet, as they grew old enough to understand, the constant telling of stories about the great heroes and heroines of the tribe, as well as the teachings of the gods and the culture heroine, plus stories about children who became lost or destroyed because they were foolish or evil, all combined to teach the child how to behave as it grew up.

While girls and boys played together up to the age of eleven, copying all the activities of their elders, including hunting and making complete mock villages, the games of the girls put more emphasis on cleverness and dexterity, while those of the boys, including rough war games, put emphasis on strength, endurance and courage. After eleven the girls were separated from the boys and began to be carefully guarded by their mothers and other female relatives, as chastity and modesty in girls were high ideals among the Dakota Sioux. At this age Dakota fathers and uncles began more assiduously to teach the boys all the tricks and ceremonies that dealt with hunting, telling also many stories about war parties and battles. Almost every boy became eager to go to war.

There was no adolescent ceremony of any kind for boys, but the first initiation to coming manhood happened when a boy went on a war party. Even boys as young as eleven went on such war parties, though usually protected at first from actual combat. Called "water boys," they had to endure the hardships of the trip, and were constantly worked hard by the men at different camp tasks. Some boys could not take all this hazing and turned toward mystical experiences instead, becoming medicine men or shamans or priests, while a small proportion became homosexual female impersonators.

One of the greatest bits of training for the boy came when he was given his first horse, which he had to care for himself. The boy and the horse often became like one animal, a glory to see when the two were off for an adventure on the plain, the boy's hair streaming behind him as he rode like the wind. Rough games on horseback acted as training for war, including trying to pull opposing players off their horses. By fourteen or fifteen a boy often sought or was asked to join one of the *Akicita* or soldier societies after he had a few war party experiences.

The girls, on the other hand, developed more and more excellence at such jobs as cooking, taking care of children, but particularly at the sewing of clothes, the tanning of skins and learning to do beautiful quill or beaded designs on dresses, robes carrying bags and tipis. Unlike the boys who became more and more aggressive and boasted about their deeds, the girls learned to be retiring and shy, especially in the presence of men and older women. Yet she needed to be industrious in her work, loving and generous to other people, learning to be a true Dakota woman.

At her first sign of womenhood, the first menses, the girl of good family usually had a *puberty ceremony*. One of three such ceremonies was the Ball-throwing Ceremony. A man called the Buffalo Dreamer, who had a vision of a buffalo and represented the fecundity of the Buffalo, was hired by the father to direct this

Painting by George Catlin. Sioux Indians pursuing a stag in their canoes on St. Peter's (Minnesota) River.

ceremony. The girl was taken to a small tipi, such as all women retired to during their periodic illness, and there spent four days doing quill work or making moccasins. Later the Buffalo Dreamer talked to the girl about how to develop all the feminine virtues and painted a red streak over her cheeks and nose. Then either she or the Dreamer tossed a red ball out among the people. Whoever caught it received a gift. The ball was thrown out again and again until all the gifts were exhausted, giving prestige to the family.

Courtship of a girl for marriage was usually done under the watchful eye of a mother or some aunt. To be sure during this period that the girl was not seduced, she might be obliged to wear a chastity belt or, when sleeping at night, have her legs tied together. However, well-brought up girls of strong willpower and spiritual strength were trusted by their mothers and usually had little trouble avoiding the wrong kind of advances.

It was allowed for a young man to draw the girl who interested him into the shelter of his buffalo robe when both were standing under the watchful eye of a female relative. In this blanket or robe, however, the two were hidden enough to talk together privately in whispers.

Powerful families usually tried to make sure the daughter married a man they approved, the brothers being very watchful of her, but sometimes young couples eloped. If the man was fair to the girl in such a case, he usually had his relatives bring horses and other gifts to the family, which if accepted, consecrated the elopement and *marriage.* Usually, however, a young man would have his family approach the girl's family and ask them for her hand. If acceptable, then horses and other gifts were brought. Marriage took different forms, but one common one was for the brothers of the girl to bring her over on a horse to a feast being given by the family of the young man where she would be formally given to him as his wife. They soon had their own tipi to avoid the man breaking the taboo of talking to his mother-in-law, or the girl to her father-in-law, but the son-in-law was supposed to bring meat for his in-laws.

Cause of divorce was usually either because of laziness or infidelity. If a man had a lazy wife, he would usually go to the lodge of his Akicita society and beat a drum announcing the divorce. If she were unfaithful he would make her take their tipi down and get out. Then he would take his clothes and weapons and go back to his parents. Women could leave their husbands for the same or similar reasons. Yet, in the old days, divorce was not too common. One thing that helped was that successful marriages gave great prestige to such couples. Fidelity was considered a supreme virtue!

At time same time, as with most warriors more than one wife was permitted. A husband usually selected as a second wife a sister of his first wife, as the two women could be expected to work together amicably.

In the family, as with most Plains tribes, there was great closeness and assistance between brothers and sisters. In any crisis the family drew all its forces together to meet the trouble.

The final end of the cycle of life, *death,* was a time when the usually stoical and poker-faced Dakota men and women fully let loose their emotions. A funeral was often an extravaganza of weeping and of self-torture. The women made knife cuts on their legs and arms to let the blood flow, and might even cut off a little finger to honor the dead one. The members of the Akicita, to whom the dead man belonged, would usually join the family in mourning, helping to put up a framework on which his important belongings were hung. Each man present usually had sharp pegs inserted between the muscles in their thighs, calves and knees as a sacrifice by self torture. If the man had died in battle, many horses might have been given away and usually his favorite horse was killed out at the scaffold erected high on sticks on the Plains where the body was finally taken. Poor people usually buried their dead in a grave with rocks over it to keep out scavengers.

Society and religion

Society. Cohesion in the Teton Lakota was brought about not only by organization, but by the intense feeling they had of being a special people. The generosity of well-to-do families in giving away quantities of gifts at ceremonies, including horses, to the poor helped with the feeling of unity.

The soldier societies or Akicitas were not only connected with war but even more so with the peaceful discipline of the tribe. Each such society usually took a turn acting as policemen to the camps or on hunts, keeping the people in order and preventing and punishing anti-social acts. Thus the Kit Fox Society might treat a proved liar or thief by beating him severely and even destroying his tipi and all its contents. Joining such societies could lead a young man in time into more and more responsible leadership. Becoming a chief of his society or his band, a fine war leader, or a wise and powerful shaman, might lead eventually to his being invited to join the Naca Ominicia, or chief's society, which acted as a supreme legislative council. This body met at the Red Council Lodge to determine tribal hunts, rules of conduct, feuds in the tribe, war and peace, etc. Usually they acted in unison after deliberations. They also appointed the executive officers of the tribe, such as the ten Wicasa Itacans of the Brules or the seven of the Oglalas. The Wicasa Itacans in turn appointed still another executive group called the "Shirt Wearers." The Shirt Wearers were considered to be supreme councillors to whom all the people turned in time of trouble, so they had to be not only fine leaders but very wise. Crazy Horse was one until he tried to take away another man's wife.

The Sioux probably never equalled the fine tribal organization of the Cheyennes, nor their excellent method of justice and law, but they made up for it by their tremendous energy and their ability to understand the psychology of other tribal peoples. For example, some of their successful war leaders were able to disguise themselves in enemy clothing and enter other tribes' villages, acting so much like the enemy that they were not detected, and then come back with all the knowledge necessary to make a successful raid. Probably only the Crow were better horse thieves than the Dakota!

The Dakota were not as successful as the Cheyenne about stopping murders. Unlike the Cheyenne, the Teton Dakota felt murder should be punished by death, but the punishment was generally left up to the victim's family. This unfortunately led to family feuds, something the Cheyenne largely avoided. It also allowed more of the dominance of powerful bullies. Bull Bear, chief of a band of the Oglala, was such a man, who not only killed other men with impunity because of his great war record, but also stole several men's wives. Finally he had too many enemies and another chief cleverly planned the end of him in revenge for a humiliation.

Women among the Dakota were less liable to fight for their rights or to take part in war than among the Cheyenne, mainly because of the pressure on them to act meekly and patiently, but they did undoubtedly influence their husbands in private conversation. A Dakota woman repaid with love and loyalty a man who treated her kindly and listened to her advice, but took this away from a man who treated her badly. Unfortunately, in Dakota society, men who had a great war record were considered the best catches for girls, even though their other qualities might be less than desirable.

As the overwhelming need for a man in Dakota society was to be successful in war and hunting and to show fortitude and bravery at all times, this put a tremendous psychological pressure on the men that helped later make the defeat of the Sioux by the whites so catastrophic to them. It is very probable that their refusal to inwardly accept a peaceful existence under white dominance made them easy marks for alcoholism and all its attendant evils, including wife beating and the desertion of families.

Religion. Though the Dakota worshipped many gods, most of them being manifestations of various natural phenomena such as the sun, moon, earth, the rocks, the sky, the winds and the thunder, the more sophisticated among them, particularly the ones called holy men, or Wicasa Wakan, spoke of all these deities as being only the representatives of the Great Spirit, Wakan Tanka. These men were few, as they had to show in their daily lives such purity of thought, such as humbleness, such wisdom in settling disputes and such kindness that they could be thought of as living saints. To most Dakota males the four great virtues were bravery, fortitude, generosity and wisdom. But the Wikasa Wakan were among the very few who showed real wisdom, and they probably insisted that purity was a part of that wisdom, exemplified as it was by the Sacred Pipe and the White Buffalo Maiden.

The strongest direct expression of the Great Spirit that the Sioux had was White Buffalo Calf Maiden, who came to them some ten generations before the coming of the white men. She was a sacred woman, thought sometimes to be the daughter of the sun and the moon, who brought to the Dakota the Sacred Pipe in a special form and taught them ceremonies they could use with it as well as speaking to them of the highest qualities of life, with kindness and purity emphasized most, saying as long as they followed these teachings they would be a great people, but if they lost them they would be in despair.

The Sun Dance was in the old days the most sacred dance and ceremony of the Dakota, and its ceremony and meaning spread to many other tribes of the Great Plains; however, at present we cannot be sure whether the Dakotas were the originators of this dance. It was definitely a part of the vision quest, because sun dancers deliberately sought visions while they danced, and it probably originated from a vision. In its most common form, the vision quest had a young man (sometimes a young woman) get the help of a holy man by bringing his pipe to him so it and he could be purified and he instructed. He would then climb a lonely butte or hill where he fasted for usually four days and nights without food or water, while crying (praying) for a vision in a ritualized way, circling to the sacred directions with his pipe. People who received visions usually had spiritual powers given to them, such as foreseeing the future, healing certain ailments, finding lost articles and people, and so forth. They were called Dreamers and had considerable prestige, some later becoming holy men or shamans.

The Sun Dance was usually held once a year in the summer (July—Moon of the Red Cherries), and just before the great unified buffalo hunt. Though the Sun Dance was often started by one man who was the instigator, he quickly combined with a priest or shaman who acted as actual director of the dance, in fact as spiritual and practical leader of the entire tribe during the ceremony. Many other men contributed to the dance by dancing, sacrificing and torturing themselves in it. This was done sometimes to obtain spiritual powers, sometimes to give it to others, but most often to fulfill a vow made when they were saved from danger or sickness. Others took part in the dance and the self-sacrifice to prepare themselves to become priests or shamans. But all felt it was a unifying group enterprise of sacred nature and of great value in renewing the spirit of the tribe.

The ceremony was held for twelve days. The first four were a combination of festival and preparation, and many groups came together who had not seen each other for a year and renewed acquaintances. Men of ability and honor were selected by the shamans to act as assistants, as were virtuous women, needed to chop down the Sacred Cottonwood Tree. The second four days saw the candidates for dancing learn their special instructions. The last four days were the Holy Days when the ceremonial camp was set up, including a large circular construction of poles and leafy boughs, all facing a Sacred Lodge where the dancers received their final instructions. During the first Holy Day the Buffalo Dance was held to attract the buffalo, supervised by a Buffalo Dreamer. The second and third day included the capture of the "enemy" or cottonwood tree, cut down by chaste young women, and brought to the camp in four successive stages to be the central pole for the main dance.

Hung on the pole, among other things, were images of the two evil gods, Iya and Shaske, who allowed for a brief time sexual license in talk, but were then shot down by the warriors. This and the piercing of the ears of children lasted through the third day. Before dawn of the Fourth Holy Day, the instigator of the Sun Dance and the shamans and priests went to the top of a hill to pray for goodness for the people as the sun rose. Then the dancers were painted, dressed and decorated, each wearing a wreath of sacred sage around his head and a long red kilt or dress. Many other formalities led to the final dancing, just before which the skin and often the muscles of back or front or face of the dancers were pierced by bone skewers thrust through skin and flesh, during which they were expected to sing songs of defiance. Some of these skewers were attached to heavy thongs which led to the Sun Dance Pole or to such things as buffalo skulls that they dragged about to prove their fortitude, devotion and sacrifice. This lasted for many hours during the fourth day, most dancers blowing eagle bone whistles and some staring at the sun. As the drum beats, singing and other music increased, the dancers tried to tear themselves loose from the skewers by pulling strongly on the cords. Symbolically, all the dancers gave themselves up to torture to gain not only the true way of life, but to assist the spirit and fortunes of all the tribe during the year. Some who received visions during the Sun Dance were given special powers; others sought the help of shamans afterward to become shamans themselves.

Brief history and present condition

While the Battle of the Little Bighorn in 1876 against Custer and his soldiers was a great victory for the Dakota and their allies, it was followed very soon by the defeat of the Plains tribes and their being placed on reservations. The Ghost Dance of 1890, an attempt through spirit search and sacred dancing to overcome the whites, plus the Battles or Massacre of Wounded Knee the same year, was the last gasp in this bitter struggle, for in 1890, the Dakota finally realized the end of the old days had come.

Wounded Knee has been looked at from two prejudiced extremes, that of the whites who felt they needed to frighten and control those they called savages in order to civilize them, and that of the Dakota who felt almost everything the whites did was to deliberately hurt and destroy them. The truth almost certainly lies in between because even good men act with violence and injustice in wartimes, and great misunderstandings and prejudices on both sides caused men to act badly when wisdom and understanding could have prevented this.

During reservation days weak Indian agents allowed chiefs like Red Cloud and Spotted Tail to have their own way, as they did at Pine Ridge and Rosebud. The strong agents, such as Mcgillicuddy at Pine Ridge and James McLaughlin at Standing Rock, were better for the Dakota in that they helped them move more steadily in directions they had to go anyway, but even these men and those behind them made serious mistakes, such as trying to stop all ceremonies and treating the Dakota like children; and this led to such tragedies as Wounded Knee and the unneeded death of Sitting Bull in 1890.

McLaughlin had the wisdom to let some of the Hunkpapas try cattle ranching with considerable success, since they were much more naturally suited for this than for farming, but others tried unsuccessfully to make them into farmers, which led many Dakota in time to simply give up and live off welfare, a direction demoralizing for everybody concerned.

In recent years new schools and more freedom have allowed the training and self-discipline to gradually develop to create new enterprises, but the continued prevalance of alcoholism and drug use, plus unemployment, has still held the Sioux far below their potential.

VINSON BROWN

DANCE can be said to mark the entire trail of life, from cradle to grave, of the Indians of the Americas. A number of anthropologists in recent years have remarked that they now realize a more thorough study of the dances in earlier times would have been most helpful toward an understanding of the various cultures because they were so involved in the overall pattern on Indian life.

To many people Indian dancing means a group of contorted, bent-over figures, feet moving awkwardly up and down, a silly whooping punctuated by tapping the mouth with the hand, accompanied by weird and monotonous chanting undeserving of the title of music.

Indians have usually been presented to the public as a type of side-show attraction. The effort has been to make them savage or romantic, and the presentations have usually been cheap and gaudy. It started before the Revolutionary War and has been continued to the present day.

"Real Indian" showmen have sometimes been the worst offenders in giving a bad portrayal of their people. They have done either what they were told to do by some non-Indian producer or have played up to the popular notions in an effort to please their audiences. Sometimes they have been handicapped by a personal lack of knowledge of the former life and customs of their people.

The average American places Indian dancing in one

of three categories: he takes it for granted, as something still going on just as it always has been and which he can see at any time he chooses to visit and Indian reservation; or he considers it a little boy interest, now outgrown; or he thinks of it as Wild West or Hollywood hoopla dreamed up for motion picture and television shows. In any case, he cannot believe that real, honest, authentic Indian dancing is of itself worthy of consideration as an art.

Dancing played a very important role in the lives of the Indians of most tribes. The Indians themselves probably never thought of it as art for they knew nothing of art as a subject in itself. It was, however, an important part of their lives and dancing was art in the truest sense for it was interwoven in their daily lives, part of almost everything that they did. In some ways the dance was the highest expression of all their artistic endeavors for it combined all other art forms—it embodied not only music and motion, but color, line, form, pattern, legend, poetry, and ritual.

Dancing was such an integral part of Indian life that it is difficult for the average non-Indian to understand its significance. And yet, perhaps many people in positions of power and influence did realize something of the importance of dance in Indian society, for government representatives and missionaries did everything possible to suppresss it as being the epitome of savagery, hence to be arbitrarily destroyed in order to "civilize" the Indians. Indian dancing was frowned upon from earliest reservation days and much of it completely prohibited. Bans were issued against the Sun Dance in the 1880s which were enforced at the point of arms. In 1904 the *Regulations of the Indian Office* established a Court of Indian Offenses which included bans on all dances as well as on almost all Indian customs and practices. These bans remained official until 1934 and unofficial on many reservations until the 1950s. Although removed by the Indian Office in Washington many of them were still enforced by employees in the field who had no understanding of Indian people or their rights and were intent on making white men out of Indians.

During the period of enforcement permission was granted to Indians over forty years of age to participate in Wild West and other type of shows—also to dance at home on such holidays as Fourth of July (Independence Day), Flag Day, Labor Day, Christmas, New Year, and so on. Anyone over forty years of age was considered hopeless as a candidate for civilization. Once the enforced bans were removed and dances once more could be held at any time, small boys sometimes turned out to learn from the few old-timers but when school was in session the teachers scolded them and sometimes even punished them for daring to attend a dance. It took another twenty years for Indians to become interested enough in theor own culture to turn out in any great numbers for a dance and to bring the so-called "powwow dancing" to its present popularity. Much of this change of attitude was due to the rebellion of the blacks against their position of inequality and servitude and a similar movement quickly developed among young Indians.

Now there are "powwow" circuits throughout the Indian country and dancers from various tribes follow these circuits in the hope of winning prizes for "fancy" and "traditional" dancing. So far the dancing is mainly of the "war dance" type and little effort has been made to revive other dances which might be even more important from an artistic or aesthetic standpoint. However, there has been quite a revival of the Sun

Smithsonian Institution, Bureau of American Ethnology.

Arapaho Sun dancers (1893)

Dance among western tribes but this is a religious ceremony and not a secular dance. Nevertheless, even secular dancing has an importance to Indians that would hardly be ascribed to it by non-Indians. Indians do not go to a dance entirely for a good time. Even though most dancing today is of a social nature and much of the old significance has been lost, a dance is still an opportunity for a social, political, and religious meeting all in one. The dance often opens with a prayer by some old man or woman, and during intermissions there are usually speeches on matters of tribal importance.

In their hearts Indians remained Indians. It was impossible to entirely destroy their inherent love of beauty and their desire to express themselves in some artistic way. Interest in dancing seems to be growing all the time and even this social dancing is outstanding—often brilliant and expressive. There are certain "Indianisms" noticeable even in this modern dancing which go back directly to old days and which show definite age-old tradition that could not be destroyed, even though many young Indians today know little of the traditions involved.

Although there is no such person as a typical Indian, there were certain customs and characteristics common to most of the Indians of North America and even to some extent in South America. Consequently there are phases of Indian dancing that can be described in general terms. From observations among Indians of Woodlands and Plains, as well as some in the Southwest, it can be said that all these have a similar way of handling their bodies and feet in dancing. In other words, all have a similar manner of execution. The characteristic position is with knees slightly bent and backs straight, quite different from anything to be found in either classical or ballroom dancing. There is a great freedom of movement, almost a loose-jointedness, and except in a few dances, or for accent, the dancers seems to be relaxed.

In most dances the arms are used little or not at all. Formerly in many dances the hands were placed on the hips, fingers extended, making a straight line from fingertips to elbows— not palms on the hips and wrists bent, as we sometimes see today. Or one might hold a fan or other article in one hand and place the other on the hip. Hands often hang at the sides or are held with belt elbows, but they never appear to be dangling or "flopping" and are not thrown wildly about, as in American black or African dancing. In fact, even the most active dancing is generally dignified and controlled. There may have been some exceptions to this, as among tribes of the Northwest Coast, and in some medicine men's performances, but by and large these statements hold. This may sound as if the dancing is stilted, and we know that many early observers felt it to be, but actually a good Indian dancer uses every muscle of his body. When imitating birds and animals he shakes his head and shoulders, moves his back muscles, and sometimes brings his arms, hands, and fingers into play.

The Indian has a duplicate or a substitute for almost every known dance step. The very simplicity with which some of these steps seem to be executed is a compliment to the grace and skill of the performers. The Indian, wearing a flat-soled moccasin and walking on the natural surface of the ground, often used a toe-first motion of the foot. One of the fundamental steps, from which many more complicated ones

Smithsonian Institution Museum of Natural History. *"Dance to the Berdash"* by George Catlin (1836).

evolved, is merely an exaggeration of the Indian's walk, combined with the bent knee feature. Most steps were double-beat steps, done to two beats on the drum.

There is a subtlety of motion that is usually completely lost to the casual observer but is one of the most interesting aspects of Indian dancing. Even when it is noted it is difficult to acquire. But it makes the difference between a genuine and a false interpretation.

Sudden but subtle shifts in weight and rhythms add to the difficulties of trying to imitate Indian dancing. For these reasons many observers, especially show producers, tend to discount authentic Indian dance as show material. They want exaggerated movement, spectacular leaps and jumps, great masses of performers, uniformity, and girls with little on but their figures. Indian dancing is generally the opposite of these demands.

Many people think of Indian dancers as being always in a crouched position. The only continuous "crouch," if it may be called that, would be the slightly bent knees. On occasion dancers get down into such a squat as to be nearly resting on their heels, but this cannot be considered a typical position. It is used mainly in contests, to test endurance and agility. In the old days the squat position was also used in part of the Scalp, or Victory dances and in the Eagle Dance. Even in such a position, the back is straight and the head up. The back is seldom hunched, unless in imitation of buffalo or in order to aid in telling the story. Occasionally we do see young Indians today who let their shoulders sag and their heads hang as they dance but this is not an old-time Indian dance attitude.

The well-known anthropologist, Clark Wissler, spent much time with Indians in the early 1900s. He remarked that he used to enjoy watching the important old men walk, for it would put the slouching gait of the white man to shame. But even then the young men were taking on the awkwardness of the whites. The beautiful posture of the old-time Indians made an impression on most people who saw them, whether standing erect, walking as if their moccasins barely touched the earth, or dancing with head and shoulders up and backs straight.

In some dances only men took part, others were danced only by women, while in social dances, men, women, and children all danced together. Men and women did not dance arm in arm, as white people do, in the old dances. As in the animal kingdom the male is outstanding in appearance, so among Indians the men wore the most striking costumes and did most of the dancing.

An Indian child learned to dance almost before it could walk. A baby, unable to stand alone, might be held erect, supported by his father's hands, and his little feet taught to stamp in rhythm to the drums and chants. He early imitated the steps of his father in the ceremonial dances.

One might almost say that every step and every

Smithsonian Institution, Bureau of American Ethnology.
"Arapaho Ghost Dance: Praying. Oklahoma Territory, 1893.

motion had a meaning and practically every article of finery and decoration worn was symbolic and told its particular story. A dancer could not wear a costume just because he liked its appearance. He had to have the right to wear it.

Religious dances, of course, were ritualistic and sometimes had their own peculiar steps, used for no other dance. Often there was little that non-Indians would call dancing in these rituals. There was movement, to be sure, but sometimes only a swaying of the body, or flexing of the knees, or raising on the heels, but Indians often called these rituals "dances," which shows the importance given to dancing.

Indian dances ran the gamut of emotional experience and covered practically every phase of life: birth dances, children's dances, puberty dances, dances to celebrate weddings, medicine dances of magic and healing, dances for games and for pleasure, honorous dances, dances to welcome strangers, to cement alliances, of mourning, and to honor the dead; dances to assure good hunting and to celebrate the resulting success. There were dances of planting and harvesting, of preparation for war, and of victory and peace. When a chief was "raised" there were dances to honor him. There were dances of sacrifice, of appeal for future blessings, of thanksgiving, dances to portray dream experiences.

Women did not dance the active, vivacious dances of the men. Specially privileged women, who had been to war and distinguished themselves as warriors did, could dance with the men in men's dances. In recent years, coinciding with the women's "liberation" movements everywhere, there has been a movement among Indian women to dress in men's costumes and dance like men. Old Sioux Indians, and perhaps oldsters of other tribes, were horrified at this change in traditional women's roles and were sure that some great calamity would be the result.

Originally most men's dances were done with a minimum of clothing, breechclout and moccasins being the most important articles, along with proper personal headdress, face and body paint. Every limb was free to respond to the dancer's moods and emotions. But beginning in the late 1800s and continuing until recently, government authorities and missionaries demands that such nudity be curtailed and Indian dancers, when permitted to dance at all, were no longer able to paint their bodies and dance in the old way. So they wore suits of long, dyed underwear—red, blue, yellow, green, black, or even one half one color, the other half a contrasting color. For a time, fine dance ornaments, such as bustles, arm wheels, porcupine hair broaches, and beautiful war bonnets nearly disappeared among the Sioux, Cheyenne, and Arapaho, who were perhaps the most persecuted of any Indians because of their outstanding record of defiance toward the troops sent against them, and of government regulations, once they were settled on the reservations.

In some areas, notably Oklahoma, almost the opposite effect took place. "Show Indians" produced gaudier and more spectacular costumes, with great circles of feathers for bustles and neck ornaments and huge feather crests, sometimes referred to by more conservative Indians as "Zulu hats." Fortunately, at the time of this writing, both extremes are now moderating. There is a strong movement toward "old-time" and "traditional" costumes and some interesting developments are the result.

During the period while dancing was so restricted a new type of social dance developed which in many cases was encouraged by white officials, or at least not prohibited, because it was copied directly from white styles of dancing. Such dances as the Rabbit Dance, which for a time became popular among tribes as far away as the Seneca in New York State, were influenced by the Fox Trot and the Waltz. To the present time other such dances are still popular on many reservations, such as Indian Two Step, or the Arapaho Slug Dance. In these dances men and women do dance arm in arm, or holding hands with arms around each other's waists. The songs used are usually funny, or silly, but the dancers are not supposed to laugh during the dance he or she is pummeled, in fun, by the other dancer.

A little later on, real white dances became quite popular among the young people. Indians were encouraged to go to these white dances in another effort to get them to give up everything Indian. In actuality, the Indian dances were much more dignified and decorous than the white dances, where drinking usually took place and fighting sometimes broke out.

The white man's dances were usually done in "white man's" clothes although Rabbit Dance and another later dance, the Forty-Niner (nothing to do with the Gold Rush of 1849) were often done at Indian dances and those in "War Dance" costume also took part.

In former times even social dances were involved with religious beliefs and since religion played such an important role in Indian life it is logical to realize that all dances had religious significance at one time. The dancing of people here on earth portrayed the actions of spirits in the after-world. When the spirits were unconcerned for man's welfare the people danced to revive their interest.

Early observers claimed that the Plains Indians were the finest dancers, with the Sioux at the head of them all. But Plains Indian culture was dependent mainly upon the buffalo hunt and with the disappearance of that great animal much of the culture disappeared with him. the Indian saw no further use for most of his dances and ceremonies in those empty days. Only a few aged warriors remembered, and so today, the younger Indians, who are now interested in reviving their own customs and dances, are working under a great handicap. The fact that they are interested at all, after the many years of persecution and opposition, is remarkable.

Different culture groups had different methods and manners of dancing. The Plains people were hunters and warriors. Many of their dances were naturally quite different in spirit and in character from those of their more settled agricultural neighbors to the east and southwest or from those of other tribes whose ways of life were different. War exploits and experiences played an important part in their dances but "the War Dance," especially as related to Plains Indians and to

"War Dancer" by James Auchiah (Kiowa) 1938.

"Shield Dance" by Spencer Asah (Kiowa), date unknown.

Indian dancing today, is largely an invention of the white man. Indians of the woodlands did have a real war dance, a dance of preparation for war, but with the Plains tribes there was no honor in going to war. It was expected of every young man. The celebration came with a successful homecoming—bringing horses, honors, scalps, without the loss of a man. Then the Victory, or Scalp dances were held and these have often been called "War Dance" by the whites. Scalp dances were usually performed by the women, who sometimes wore their husbands' war clothes and bonnets as a special honor to them and insult to the enemy. On the Plains these Scalp dances usually led in a circle to the right, whereas most of their other dances move to the left, in a Sun Circle.

The typical Plains tribes, of course, had no planting or harvest dances except for some tobacco ceremonies. But in addition to their most important religious ceremony, the Sun Dance (also known as Medicine Dance, Medicine Lodge, Thirsting Dance, Sacrifice Dance, New Life Dance) they had other minor religious ceremonies, buffalo and hunting dances, bird and animal dances, warrior society dances, dances of various women's societies, elaborate adoption ceremonies, puberty dances and ceremonies, dances known as beggars' dances which solicited aid for "the poor," dances belonging to various cults, such as Bear, Wolf, Elk, Thunder Dreamers, and so on. The Sioux alone had a list of thirty-five different dances and other Plains tribes probably had as many, but few of these are given today.

The most popular dance today all throughout the Indian country is the so-called War Dance, which ought rather to be called Warriors' Dance. It is the social part of the old Grass or Omaha Society Dance. Originally, only warriors with good records could take part but it has become a dance for everyone, and as mentioned earlier, even some women take part, as "warriors," nowadays. The Fancy War dancers use all the fancy steps they can think of and each contestant tries to outdo the others. It has become largely a contest dance.

There is good evidence that the Grass Dance originated among the Pawnee but the Sioux learned it from the Omaha, added to it, developed it, and passed it to other tribes, so that it has become known as Omaha Dance because the Sioux credited the Omaha for it. The Omaha wore braided grass tails on their belts, signifying scalps taken in battle. The Sioux did not understand this symbolism, so called it Grass Dance also, and so these names are still popular among many tribes, although most now speak of it as War Dance, following the misinterpretation of the whites. It is performed in variations of Fast, Slow, and Fancy War Dance.

Originally, there were only two wearers of the feather dance bustles, men especially chosen for outstanding bravery. Gradually other dancers were permitted to wear them and today almost every dancer considers a bustle as part of his necessary costume. The bustles have changed considerably over the years, the modern "swing bustles" and "neck bustles," being far larger and more elaborate than the simpler and more dignified original types.

At first, a "bustle dancer" wore, in addition to clout and moccasins, only the porcupine hair and deer-tail crest, or roach, which originated in the east and eventually made its way to the prairie tribes. Gradually other ornaments were added, such as bone bead or otter fur breastplates, quilled or beaded armbands and garters, fur anklets and strings of sleight bells. The bells became popular about the time of the Civil War and arc still an essential part of the dancer's outfit, although originally each bell was worn to symbolize a wound. Before the bells, rattles of hoofs and turtle shells were worn around ankles and knees.

In some districts an older form of dance, called Straight Dance, has once more become popular. The dancers wear "traditional" costumes, which imply shirts, leggings, clouts, and moccasins, with long hair and often fur turbans, with very dignified danging—no fancy footwork. The Sioux call such dancing Straight-Up and it was performed by chiefs and other dignitaries, many wearing full eagle feather war bonnets. The true war bonnet was found only on the Plains but its origin may trace back to Mexico, or even to Central America, for representations of similar headdresses are found on ancient carvings and paintings of those regions. Some woodland tribes had headdresses of eagle or of turkey feathers but they did not have the elegance of the war bonnet, which came into its full development with the arrival of the horse. The eastern headdresses were usually "straight-up" bonnets without the grace, charm, or spread of their western counterparts.

During the late 1950s there was also a revival among the Kiowa of Oklahoma, of a former warrior society dance known as the Gourd Clan Dance. Many Indians, when speaking English, use the term "clan" to mean society or club. The dancers wear full costume, which includes a blanket, and carry rattles which they shake in time to the songs and jump hard on both feet, as in most of the old warrior society dances. This dance spread all over Oklahoma and then to many reservations in other states and is still very popular at this writing.

A number of representative Plains tribes moved out onto the prairies from the woodlands within the past 200 years. The Village tribes, like Mandan, Arikara, Hidatsa, Pawnee, and a few others, did have planting and harvest dances but the nomadic tribes, depending almost entirely upon the buffalo, gave them up. Nevertheless, there are still many similarities between some Plains and Woodland dances. Calumet, or Pipe dances, were known to both areas and in some tribes Eagle dances, which were related in purpose and also in execution, were also given. Both dances were used to great strangers, to create ceremonial friendships and relationships, to bring success in hunting and war, to bring good luck or overcome back luck and to make peace between warring tribes.

The Calumet Dance was performed with two feather decorated wands, or pipestems, but motions of the eagle were incorporated in the movements. Eagle dances of these two areas was highly conventionalized, and although using eagle movements, little or no effort was made to portray eagles realistically through costuming. The Iroquois still have such an Eagle Dance, each dancer using a feathered fan in one hand and rattle in the other. In early times the dance was used as stated above, but today it celebrates existing friendships and is used to cure disease, to bring rain, to hearten the unhappy and depressed, for thanksgiving, and has until recently been given to obtain success in hunting. One of the old Iroquois war dances is also used today to bring rain, showing how the original function of a dance can be changed to meet existing conditions. It is remarkable that, after more than 400 years of contact with non-Indians, the Iroquois still hold many of their old dances and ceremonies.

Tribes of the Southwestern Pueblos and also of the Northwest Coast did have naturalistic eagle dances and yet there is strong evidence that the Southwestern

Smithsonian Institution, National Anthropological Archives.

"Scalp Dance," drawn by an Assiniboine in Fort Union (1853).

eagle dances originated on the Plains, or at least were greatly influenced by them. But today it is the other way around and some plains tribes, notably in Oklahoma, are now doing eagle dances very similar to those of the Pueblos. There is so much visiting back and forth by Indians of various tribes today that a number of dances have become Pan-Indian rather than strictly tribal.

Scalp and Victory dances were common to tribes, not only across the United States and Canada but also to some tribes of Mexico and South America.

At present-day Indian shows and gatherings one of the most popular dances is the Hoop Dance. Good dancers of many tribes now perform it. Its present popularity began with Indians of Taos, perhaps fifty years ago. The dance probably originated among Indians around the Great Lakes, for a dance with one hoop was known to Menomini, Chippewa, and Ottawa, and the latter had a dance with two hoops. From this region the dance could easily have been picked up by Eastern Plains tribes. The Taos Indians have long been associated with southern Plains tribes and so, in some such fashion, they obtained the dance and called it to the attention of the tourists. At first the Taos dancers used only two hoops, but gradually more hoops were added. For a time four hoops were considered more or less standard and four is a sacred number to most Indians. Then they used six, still a sacred number, but today some dancers use a dozen or more. The Lake Indians used very small hoops, which of course increased the difficulties of the dance. The Ottawa permitted hoops in size only from the ground to the dancer's knees, but today the hoops used by most dancers are much larger. A hoop, being a circle, carried the symbolism of the circle—tribal unity, complete and perfect life, the return of the seasons, and so on. Some of the old symbolism remains and dancing in and out of the hoops symbolizes the difficulties encountered in life. With all the additional hoops the dance has become mainly a showpiece and contest dance, however. It remains a solo dance and each dancer has his own routine and series of tricks he performs, so no two hoop dances are ever alike.

Each area of the country had dances typical of the culture and activities of the region. As we travel across North America we find that at one time practically every activity of life was represented in dance. In the east there were special strawberry festivals when the wild strawberries were ripe. In the north there were dances portraying the excursions by canoe during seasons of open weather and snowshoe dances celebrated the arrival of winter and its enveloping blanket of white. In the south there were alligator dances. On the Plains there were many buffalo dances and horse dances. In the thick, dark forests of the northwest where a gloomy religion full of powrful, often dreaded spirits had developed, there was even an echo dance, intended to confuse malevolent spirits and keep them away from the villages. In the southwest almost every dance had the bringing of rain as its primary purpose.

The Indian, wherever he was found, was a product of his environment and his culture was built around it. Indians of all the heavily wooded regions had religions was gloomy concepts. The people of the open plains and prairies seem to have been happier. but, regardless of tribe or cultural development, all seemed to be content with their lot. Each tribe believed itself to be "the People," and the only personal desire was to be worthy and recognized among one's own. (Enemy tribes were usually designated as "snakes," or "adders."

The Indian culture of the Southwest remains strong but factions have recently developed between the "conservatives" and the "progressives," the latter intent upon following the white man's road. The culture of the Plains, Woodlands, California, and the Northwest Coast have suffered greatly through their contacts with modern civilization. The culture of the Woodlands was built upon war, farming, and hunting; that of the Plains on war, the horse, and the buffalo. The village tribes of the Plains, also being farmers, suggests that in this area there was an overlapping of Woodland and Plains features. With the exception of planting and harvest dances, however, we find both Woodlands and Plains can be roughly grouped together for dance styles, although Plains dances ordinarily move to the left, or clockwise, "following the sun," whereas Woodland people, both north and south, usually moved to the right, "with their hearts toward the fire." Both areas featured many solo dances but footwork seems to have been more elaborate on the Plains.

It is interesting to note that most Pueblo dances also move to the right, or counter clockwise. Does the fact that they are also farming people have anything to do with it? But Navajo also farm, and among them we find dances moving in clockwise circles again, with some dances in opposing lines. To add to the confusion, we now occasionally find Plains Indians dancing to the right.

Perhaps the most popular ceremony for the tourists in the southwest is the Hopi Snake Dance. Each Hopi village gives the Snake Dance every other year, alternating with the Flute Ceremony, also given to bring rain. So a Snake Dance is given every year but in different villages. The Snake Dance doubtless traces back to the snake cults of Mexico and Central America and it is certain that other Pueblo tribes had similar dances at one time.

The Hopi are also famous for their Kachina dances, which portray the activities of the gods, or spirits, of the Spirit World, but the most famous of the Pueblo dances of this type is the Shalako of the Zuñi. Many of the Pueblo have dances of lesser importance, such as Braiding of the Belt, eagle dances, buffalo or animal dances, in addition to planting and harvest dances, all of which involve a great deal of symbolism and have religious aspects.

The Navajo also had quite a variety of dances, some

of which are still given today, but few of them have been seen by outsiders. The ones we most often hear about are the Squaw Dance, a white man's term for part of a ritual known as the Enemy Way, which today is given to cure sickness, the "enemy" being the disease; the Mountain Chant, and the Yeibichai, or Night Chant. Navajo are among the few Indians who designate a gathering as a "sing," or "chant," rather than as a dance, but in their original forms there was a great deal of dancing in these rituals.

Not too much has been reported for the desert tribes of southern Arizona and California but even in these regions there were some dances, held to assure a supply of food and also for recreation.

On the Northwest Coast and among the Eskimo, the dances are largely solo, but with much audience participation. there is also what we might call a cult of frenzy, with much exaggerated movements, not too much footwork, but swinging of arms, jerking of the head, spasmodic moving of the muscles, and a preoccupation with the fantastic and horrible. They used some of the most elaborate and spectacular masks found anywhere in the world.

In California we find dancing in lines again, with beautiful and detailed accoutrements, some jumping and leaping, but not the virtuosic footwork we find on the plains.

Indian dancing has sometimes been criticized because it lacks great jumps and leaps, but accounts by early observers give considerable prominence to jumping and leaping and the present writers witnessed surprising leaps by a Cheyenne dancer some years ago. The leaps he made were definitely Indian, showing no outside influence whatever.

Regardless of area, we always find some circle dancing for it is the most logical formation for group dancing. With the exception of something like the Sioux Elk Mystery, which progressed literally for miles, dancing is generally limited to a small space, either surrounded by an audience or with an audience on one to three sides. A dancer must dance in place, move in a circle left or right, or dance forward and backward. The same

Smithsonian Institution, National Anthropological Archives.

Kachina dancers at Hopi village of Shongopovi *c.* 1900. Attempts to force white culture on the Indians were not always successful.

University of Alaska Archives, Charles Ekim Collection.
A Tsimshian native in full potlatch-dancing costume.

applies to a group, with the additional features of forming lines that move forward or backward, face each other, or sashay through each other. Or a group can also move in a spiral, which we find in stomp dances of the Southwest.

In some regions costumes have changed as much, or more, than the dances. From the beginning of white contact Indians admired the goods the strangers brought to trade. Cloth was early substituted for buckskin, commercial dyes for native colors, beads for porcupine knives for flint. Ribbons and mirrors, ostrich and peacock feathers, were added to personal adornment. The overall change was gradual and of the Indian's own choosing and Indian costume was often enhanced by the addition and substitution of new things. For awhile there was a trend to go too far but now there is much interest in going back to "traditional" costume.

No Indian would evern think of dancing without the proper song to accompany him. It would be impossible to separate song from dance and it would be difficult to answer the old question as to which came first, music or dance. Even today Indians are continually composing new songs for dances established long ago.

Singing is one Indian art that is not dying out, although on the Plains some of the old manner of singing is gone, as are many of the old songs. In some of the former ceremonies, such as the Cherokee Green Corn Dance (or Busk), at least one new song was required for each annual presentation. Plains and some Woodlands singers sing in a high, sometimes falsetto voice, with a quaver, or tremolo which white people think is bad but which the Indian likes and strives to cultivate. These people think it almost sacreligious to sing in a normal speaking voice, for all songs have a certain religious aspect and the high, quavering voice is used to approach the mysterious world of the spirit. Navajo, too, have songs in their Yeibichai that are unbelievably high in pitch. On the other hand, Iroquois, Pueblo and some desert tribes, as well as California and Northwest Coast people, generally sing in a more natural voice.

Older Indians often sang in a manner that sounded off-key to whites and this way of singing is no longer heard, but that it was deliberate and according to certain standards of earlier days cannot be doubted for the songs were repeated by different singers the same way each time.

Most Indian songs are short and repeated as many times as necessary for the occasion. Most have few, or no words, the tune being the important thing, meaningless vocables being used. There were special types of songs for differing dances and ceremonies. Indians did not need words to tell them what kind of a song was being sung for they could tell by its structure and its melodic progressions. When words were used, however, they were often very important, one word sometimes symbolizing a thought which would require an entire sentence in English for its translation.

Drums of various kinds were the usual accompaniment to the songs and dances, although there were some tribes which used no drums. The drum governed the bodily movements of the dancers; the song voiced the emotion, the appeal of the dance itself. Life was a great dance; dancing was life. All drums were regarded as having sacred, mysterious power so not just anyone could own or even play a drum. The sound of the drum represented all of the life forces and its rhythm was symbolic of the rhythm of the entire universe: the heartthrob of all creation.

There were some dances accompanied only by songs and rattles. Rattles were not children's toys but had great ceremonial value, being able to drive away evil, and sometimes to bring rain. There were many kinds and types of rattles, just as there were drums.

A foot drum was known to California, basket drums were used on the desert, water drums were common in the east, and some tribes, such as the Ute in their Bear Dance, used a morache, or raspidor—the notched stick. Hopi, Havajo, Apache, and perhaps a few other tribes use the bull-roarer, or buzzer, in some ceremonies, which has an association with the thunder.

From early Spanish records it is almost certain that dancing played as important a role in the lives of the Indians of Meso and South America. Very little of the original Indian dancing of Mexico and Central America has come down to us today because of the persecution of the conquistadores and the missionaries. There are remnants of ancient Mexican dances to be found in the highlands and other isolated areas of Mexico, and groups of Aztec dancers have been taking part in the Indian ceremonials held in Gallup, New Mexico, in recent years. Their striking headdresses are patterned after those of quetzal and rhea feathers shown in the old records. The Ballet Folklorico has won international acclaim for its outstanding performances but it presents little of the original Indian dancing. The late Miguel Covarrubias, noted artist and Director of the Museo Nacional of Mexico, who helped organize the Ballet Folklorico, stated to these writers following their portrayal of early Indian dances at the American Museum of Natural History in New York that there is much more indigenous material left in the United States than anywhere in Mexico. Nearly everything in the way of native material to be found in Mexico today shows a great deal of Spanish influence. The same might be said for the countries of Central America, where there is very little original dance material to be found, although the people are predominantly Indian by blood.

People are amazed to learn that there are still approximately two hundred different Indian languages and dialects spoken north of Mexico. But when we realize that before the Spanish Conquest there were about 1800 languages spoken in Meso and South America, representing literally hundreds of tribes, we know it would be practically impossible to have reports on all the dances. Today there are about half of these tribes still in existence, which is still a formidable number. In isolated regions of South America it would probably be possible to find some aboriginal dancing. Recent, as well as historical reports indicate that in many tribes there were dances for all of the most important occasions of life and the yearly tribal activities, just as there were for North America. At the southern

Chicago Historical Society.

Mexican dances.

tip of the continent, however, the dances seem to have been entirely of a social nature and no war or hunting dances have been reported.

In the Chaco area, on the contrary, there were Scalp dances similar to those of North America, with the women taking the lead, but with more running than actual dancing. A few tribes actually took scalps but others used heads or skulls as battle trophies. Such trophies were hung on a post in the center of the dance ground and one account states that an old woman began the dance in front of these trophies. Warriors had a triumphal victory call of tapping the mouth with the hand, as was also done by many North American tribes, but only in the heat of battle or following a victory.

The people of the Chaco had recreational dances during seasons of abundant food and favorable weather. They also had many dances of a ceremonial nature; dances to ripen fruit, to ward off jaguar attacks, for girls coming of age, to bring quantities of fish, to ward off and to cure diseases. Their drum was like some water drums of North America—a cooking pot containing water and covered with a rawhide head, struck with a single stick.

The Araucanians of middle Chile on the west coast were said to dance to a rather slow tempo, the dancers' feet hardly being lifted from the ground. In modern dancing there is considerable clowning and also use of masks.

Arawakan people north of the Chaco also used masks in some ceremonies. Masked men impersonated spirits and terrified the women, levying tributes of food and drink, but sometimes the women resisted the attack, apparently as part of the pantomime. One man, painted in red and black, with feathers on his head, entered the dance arena and amused the audience with his antics.

In one ceremony the men built a temporary house which was taboo to the women, then disguised with paint and feathers, danced for hours around it. In the case of an initiation ceremony some men ran around a central tree while others danced and shouted for joy. The wild running was carried out for three or four successive nights, then was followed by a feast of armadillo.

The Mochica of northern Peru had masquerades representing animals and strange beings. Some were dances, others dramatic scenes, more sophisticated than the performances of the most primitive tribes.

Before the Conquest the Inca had many dances with elaborate costumes, masks, animal skins, and special garments cut like everyday clothing. Costumes and dances varied widely from province to province. The dancers were principally men, and in some dances there was a great deal of jumping. A Warrior's Dance was performed only on solemn occasions, both men and women taking part, the men dressed for war. It was done in a circle, holding hands. The Emperor's family had a special dance, accompanied by a great drum which was carried on the back of a person of low birth and beat by a woman. Men and women again joined hands, this time forming long lines, sometimes with sexes mxed, at other times the men in one line, women in another. Two hundred to three hundred people took part. The dance was slow and dignified, with one step back and two forward, progressing across the Great Square to the place where the Emperor sat.

In another Inca dance, which seemed to please the Spanish priest who reported it, a man with a noble lady by each hand, twisted and untwisted without letting go. The priest probably liked this dance because it was similar to European dances with which he was familiar. At the same time, some masked dancers took the part of buffoons. The steps were very simple. The dancers were accompanied by drummers, sometimes using a single drum stick. In some dances each dancer carried his own drum, like the tambourine, or hand drum of North America. Dancers wore copper or silver bells and sometimes rattles of snail shells around their ankles.

Drums were scarce or non-existent in Brazil. In the eastern part they used bamboo trumpets, rattles, whistled, and a stamping tube made of bamboo about forty inches long. Dancing was so important that a new village site was chosen with relation to a good dance ground. During the dry season men and women danced three times a day, but many dances, including masquerades, were entirely recreational. It was usual for a singer with a rattle to stand in the center while the women circled about him and the men formed another circle outside of the women. Some male dancers also carried rattles.

In the Brazilian interior there were also periods when dances were performed three times a day, the first one as early as 3:00 or 4:00 in the morning, another a little before sunset, and an evening performance began about 7:00 p.m., lasting two hours or longer. Boys and girls, as well as adults, took part. The women lined up, a young woman, serving as their leader, took her place in the center of the line. The women never left their positions but bent their knees and swung their bent arms back and forth while the Dance Leader shook his rattle and danced in front of them. He pointed his rattle at some girl, stamped his feet, belt low, then jumped as high as possible with legs outstretched, apparently to make an impression on the girl. The young men, usually armed with some weapon or a staff, gathered in a body and began dancing on the second or third song. A few blew bamboo trumpets and all stretched their legs apart while rocking their knees as they advanced on the women's line, the Dance Leader in front. When he turned to make a semi-circle they turned and leaped back to the place where they first gathered. Similar dances were given to promote the growth of crops and to bring success in hunting.

The Indians of coastal Brazil had dances in two straight lines, the men in front with bows and arrows, the women behind. In yet another tribe of this region there were circle dances to dramatize hunting, while others were done in a line to represent a "road to the sky."

Indians of the Pampas took to the horse as readily as did our own Plains Indians but did not develop a new culture of their own, as the Plains Indians did. Instead they copied the Spaniards in every way—riding techniques, and gear—except for the use of the bolas, which was their own and carried on to this day. Although Indian blood is still in evidence, the Indians of this region, as a people, are extinct. The Mexicans also adopted Spanish riding but used the lariat instead of the bolas.

Indians in the Amazonian forests made marvelous headdresses, necklaces, and many decorations of macaw, parrot, and other exotic feathers of tropical birds.

The Kamarakoto, living in the northern forest, had a Great Serpent Dance to cure snake bites and ulcers and also dances to aid in taking game and fish, as well as dances to prevent illness and trouble which they say were revealed to them in the very spirits which could cause them.

The Aymara, formerly a very warlike tribe living in Bolivia, now have dances they present for church fiestas, weddings, funerals, to dedicate a new house, for harvesting, phases of sheep raising, but all show Spanish influence and all are recreational except those for a fertility ceremonial following the harvest and to bring rain. Dancers sometimes had small, spherical copper rattles sewn to their costumes. They were accompanied by panpipes, a snare drum with laced heads, sometimes a cane raspidor, but singing for the dances here seems to have been unimportant.

Costumes today also show Spanish or mestizo influence and the masks used are of Spanish origin. Some are said to represent spirits but women and children are now allowed to look at them, which they formerly were not permitted to do. Parrot feathers, obtained from the jungle, are used but seem to have no ritual significance.

Three demons in the Devil's Dance, Oruro, Bolivia.

Dance groups, which formerly had specific functions, such as war, hunting, and rain making, no longer have them. In one dance, held by unmarried people, the girls ask the boys to dance, which is also a custom among some Plains Indians.

There were many types of dances, some for men only, who trotted slowly in a circle, swaying their shoulders and playing panpipes. In a fertility ceremony, said by some to imitate mountain spirits, (which is the case with the Apache), a line of women do a posture dance, the men circling around them playing end-flutes.

In another dance, representing jungle Indians, men and women form lines and dance in unison, wearing feather headdresses and carrying bows and arrows. Circle dances of Spanish origin are performed by both sexes. Dance groups progress around the plaza, halting at each corner and occasionally at each side to perform. Some dancers imitate birds, other burlesque the Spaniards. There was also a dance in which the Inca Emperor was impersonated and a mock battle with slings took place.

Musical instruments are played only by men, usually in troupes, or what we might call orchestras, but a women's chorus sings songs of hunting, important to the fertility ceremony, and both men and women sing together in rain making ceremonies.

In Colombia, also, dancing was once very important in making war, in religious ceremonies, for weddings, and initiations.

In summary we might say that in North, Meso, and South America dancing is still very important in some areas. Whether on a reservation or in the Indian communities of large cities in the United States dancing is the one sure way of getting Indians together. Some of the old intertribal jealousies and animosities persist, but Indian from diverse tribes will show up for a dance and these dances are now tending to ameliorate the old feelings and bring about understanding. Indians are beginning to recognize themselves as an entity, rather than as small reservation or tribal groups. On the reservations, however, the dancing is instrumental in retaining both tribal identity and cultural preservation.

The repertoire at present-day "powwow" (a misnomer, as the word really means a shaman, or medicine man), in addition to the ever popular Fast and Slow War dances, usually includes the following:

Round Dance, an old-time social dance, executed in a circle moving to the left.
Indian Two Step, a modern social dance of couples.
Forty-niner, a north modern circle dance, with fast limp step.
Contest Dances, known variously as Ruffle, Get Down, Braided Tail dances. Also Humming Bird and Hoop dances.
Buffalo Dance, known sometimes as Grass Buffalo because of its association with the Grass (War) Dance. This is not one of the old Buffalo dances. No buffalo costume or headdress is used. It is done in "War Dance" costume.
Shield and Spear Dance, by two young men.
Eagle Dance, usually a duet, by two male dancers.
Mountain Spirit Dance, Apache, associated with young woman's puberty ceremonies, occasionally given, but seldom in the day time.
Gourd Clan Dance, now popular in the Plains area.
Straight Dance, called by Sioux Straight-Up Dance, a dignified full costume dance, formerly by chiefs and dignitaries.

Until recently a "giveaway" was an important part of almost every Indian gathering across North America, although no reference was made to it in reports of South American Indian dances. In former times bravery and generosity were practically synonymous and persons, groups, or societies "proved" their bravery by publicly giving away various presents: blankets, horses, beadwork; more recently: blankets, quilts, groceries, money, to tribal members and visitors. Although the custom is still carried on in many communities, it is no longer as prevalent as it formerly was and in some regions seems to have been discontinued.

With interest in Indian cultures now growing among non-Indians the time may come when the public at large recognizes Indian dance as a significant art form, part of the heritage of all Americans. The Indians may yet make great contributions to the world of dance, as they have in so many other fields.

REGINALD AND GLADYS LAUBIN

DANCING RABBIT CREEK, TREATY OF

was an 1830 agreement in which the Chocktaw nation of Alabama and Mississippi ceded their homelands and agreed to move west of the Mississippi River.

Although numerous solemn treaties and the Indian Trade and Intercourse Act oif 1802 had declared the inviolability of Indian lands, the states of Georgia, Alabama, and Mississippi extended their jurisdiction to Indian property. In 1830 Mississippi officially abolished Choctaw government. After the passage of the Indian Removal Act on May 28, 1830 and President Andrew Jackson's decision not to interfere with state's rights, the Indians of the southeast were informed that they would have to move.

The Choctaw people met with U.S. agents on their councilgrounds at Dancing Rabbit Creek to negotiate a treaty. On September 28, 1830 they ceded 10,000,000 acres and agreed to move to Oklahoma where it was promised that their lands would again be inviolable. Chiefs Greenwood, LeFlore, Mosholatubbee, and Nitakechi (nephew of the great chief, Pushmataha) led their people to the new territory from 1830 to 1833.

Choctaw family heads who preferred to stay were promised an allotment of land and citizenship; however, those who remained (more than ⅓ of the nation) were soon outcast and deprived of their farms by white settlers. Most of them eventually moved west to Oklahoma.

DANGER CAVE, located in the Great Basin in northwest Utah, is the earliest known center of the Desert Tradition in the West.

Zone I, 8500-9000 BC, is marked by fires on the beach sands left by the lake and may be pre-Desert culture. Zone II, dating from 8000 to 7000 BC, is marked by slab milling stones, twined basketry and bone awls. Zone III has coiled as well as twined basketry, cordage, and many wooden implements. In Zone IV there are many chipped-stone points and core tools. Zone V, marked by the innovation of a triangular point for the bow and arrow, dates from as late as the Christian era.

DANZANTES are a series of flat stone slabs at Monte Albán, in Oaxaca, Mexico, with outline designs of human figures carved in very low relief. The name was attached in early days from a suggested similarity in appearance to figures which were apparently dancing (*danzante*, from Spanish "dancer"). All of the examples depict nude males of various ages in different poses. Their significance is completely unknown, but the depiction of humans, in distorted poses with open mouths and closed eyes, some with mutilated sex organs, and one with a severed head, suggests that these were corpses—either victims of warfare, execution, or (more likely) represent ceremonial sacrifice. They were first reported by Capt. Guillermo Dupaix in 1806 during his exploration of the Oaxaca region, but did not receive major attention until the early 20th century. Located in and around the *Tonapohualli* (Temple of the Dancers), to date some 42 major slabs have been discovered, plus approximately 270 minor examples; they form the largest corpus of carved monuments known in Mesoamerica. The dating of these is early Zapotec, to which culture they are most closely related; they were made during the Monte Albán I era with some carved in Monte Albán II; the period covers *ca.* 700 BC-AD 200; most are usually dated 700-400 BC. Some writers refer to them as "Olmec," but while they do show some Olmecoid resemblances, they are not truly related to that culture other than the historic carry-over of the early Olmec civilization into the later cultures of central Mexico. An interesting features is the presence on many of the sculptures of carved hieroglyphic texts, often erroneously called "Mayan glyphs." These are actually writings in the Zapotec writing system, which is yet to be fully deciphered; most students suspect they may refer to historical individuals, or possibly labels dating or commenting upon the event.

FREDERICK DOCKSTADER

DART is properly applied to two kinds of projectiles: the short, arrow-like shaft breath-expelled from a blowgun, and the spear cast by the atlatl, also called the spear thrower.

The blowgun is a hollow tube, sometimes simply a length of cane, reed or bamboo, sometimes a double tube-within-a-tube, sometimes two half tubes joined together. Two kinds of ammunition were used: clay pellets, in Mexico, which made the Mexican blowgun the prototype of the school boy's pea shooter; and wooden darts, in South America and Eastern North America.

With few exceptions (the Jivaro of the upper Amazon jungles and some other South American jungle tribes) the blowgun, whether the projectile was pellets or darts, was a hunting weapon only, used on small game such as birds. Tipping the dart with the curare or other poison made it effective against peccary and tapir but the amount of poison a dart could implant was not ordinarily fatal to larger game, nor to man, despite exaggerated tales to the contrary.

The blowgun dart is a sharply pointed sliver of well-dried, light wood about 6 inc. long, to which is attached, at the proximal end, a wad of wild cotton or similar compressible material. It is against this wad that the force of expelled breath acts to impel the dart. The hunter carried a supply of wadding material with him, along with curare, if that was being used, and "armed" the dart with wadding and curare only when he was in position to shoot. When poison was used the hunter notched the dart just behind the poisoned tip so that it would break off in the flesh of the prey, like a nettle, if the prey succeeded in dislodging the shaft. Darts were carried in quivers with a capacity of from 100 to 200.

Eastern North American, Mexican and Middle American blowgun hunters did not poison their darts. In Eastern North America where, in late prehistoric times (for which the use of the blowgun is documented) the principal weapon for hunting and warfare was the bow; the blowgun was a boy's or a sportive weapon.

The atlatl and dart in America, recent evidence seems to indicate, dates to about 12,000 years ago among the Paleo-hunters of big game such as the mammoth and now extinct species of bison. It was the army weapon of the Aztecs, Incas and Chibchas in their wars of conquest and against the European invaders of their territories and the Eskimo, though they used the bow and arrow for land hunting, did not give up the atlatl for the modern rifle until well into the 20th century for sea hunting. The bow and arrow, replacing the atlatl and dart, did not appear among the tribes of the Southwest of the present United States, according to archaeological record, until AD 1 and in the Northeast not until AD 1000. Over the span of American prehistory many more times the tonnage of game was taken by the dart than by the arrow.

The atlatl (an Aztec word) or spear thrower is a length of stick, rounded or narrowly lath-like, from 15 to 30 in. (with 24 in. probably the optimum) in length, with a spur or hook carved or inserted into the after end. The spur has a convexly rounded tip so that the butt of the dart, concavely rounded, will fit against it in a ball joint. Near the forward end are finger holes or loops with which the atlatl is held for casting. At the beginning of the cast the atlatl and the dart, with the

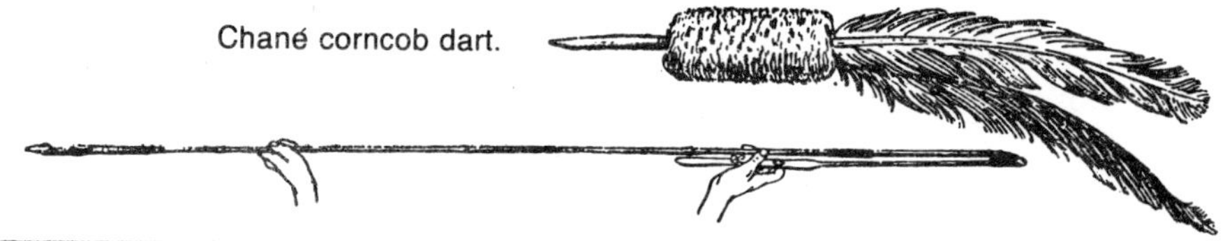

Handbook of South American Indians.

butt engaged with the spur, are held parallel, horizontal and at about ear height. The cast is made with an overhand motion, like a pitcher throwing a baseball. Because it adds, in effect, length to the arm, the atlatl and dart is much more effective than the javelin cast out of hand. This effectiveness was enhanced as early as 6,000 years ago in America by the addition of a weight (4 to 5 oz.) usually stone and generally called a bannerstone, to the atlatl. Some modern experimenters place this weight at the after end of the atlatl, near the spur; others place it near the hand grip. Both schools claim equally significant results: an increase of about 10 per cent in the range of the dart.

Atlatl darts were of three kinds: the simple shaft, the fletched (feathered) shaft and the compound shaft. Elemental in design, the simple shaft, a length of reed, cane or arboreal shoot about 6 ft. long, had to be made to close tolerance specifications, with the whole, including stone projectile point, balancing on a knife edge at 31 per cent of the distance between the tip and the butt or nock end. The material of the shaft had to be slender for maximum carry and to have "spine" or stiffness; faulty shafts will shatter or veer erractically in flight. The simple shaft dart had a range of about 250 ft., although this range was probably not a particularly sought capability. Aboriginal hunting methods emphasized stalking, to as near point blank range as possible. The simple shaft took stone projectile points up to 2¼ in. long and ¾ oz. in weight.

Because the feathering kept the shaft on a true axis of flight the fletched shaft was not so exacting to make. It took smaller projectile points, was 4 to 5 ft. in length, was inherently more accurate at short ranges and its range was less than that of the simple shaft. On the evidence of the size of most American pre-bow projectile points, modern experimenters believe that fletched and compound darts were much more widely used than simple shafts.

The compound dart consists of two parts: a short (9 to 15 in.) slender, arrow-like foreshaft to which the projectile point is attached; and a back shaft, 4 to 5 ft. long, into the fore end of which the foreshaft is plugged or dowelled. When prey, or target, was struck by the dart the foreshaft lodged in the flesh, with the back shaft falling away. It could then be recovered and rearmed by the insertion of another foreshaft. Thus the hunter was relieved of the encumberance of an armful of long-shaft darts and could go forth armed with one of two back shafts and a quiverful of foreshafts. The short-handled foreshaft was also handy as a knife or dagger.

The likelihood that the compound dart was being used, almost certainly with the atlatl, as early as 11,000 years ago derives from the discovery of several probable foreshafts cut from mammoth long bones discovered with Clovis (Paleo-hunter) projectile points at the Anzic Cave site, near Marshall, Montana. Such bone foreshafts seem to have been in vogue only among the Paleo-hunters.

Projectile point size-weight is a clue to what kind of shaft a point was attached to, though by no means a certain clue, since the weight of the point was a significant factor in the ballistic equation. Very large points were probably used on hand held thrusting spears, which might occasionally be used for casting; points in the ⅝ to ⅞ oz. range were probably used on javelins and simple shaft darts; the average weight of fletched and compound shaft darts was probably about ½ oz.

L. A. BRENNAN

DATING TECHNIQUES. The ability to date material found at sites obviously is very important. The two ways to establish dates, relative and absolute, have been refined greatly in this century.

Excavation is a first step in locating evidence. The archaeologist establishes the sequence of communities at a site represented in successive layers of material. If he can determine an absolute date for one part of a sequence, he can date other artifacts at the site in relation to it. An accurate relative chronology can be established in this way, and, in turn, the entire sequence of a region can be pieced together.

The most frequently method for long-range dating is the geological method. The key to this method is the concept of stratigraphies and the correlation of local stratigraphies with regional or worldwide geological or paleontological sequences. Geological dating also can be based on varves, laminated clay deposits of glacial melt water runoff. Each band of varve represents an annual deposit, and counting the bands gives an almost absolute dating.

Radiocarbon dating, using carbon 14, the most revolutionary advance in dating, was developed in 1951. It is based on the assumption that cosmic ray flux in the upper atmosphere by cosmic rays converts nitrogen 14 into radioactive carbon, which combines with oxygen to form radioactive carbon dioxide throughout the biosphere. It is distributed through the food chain up to man. Thus all organic matter will have a portion of radioactive carbon comparable to the biosphere. Knowledge of the half-life of modern organic material has made it possible to date any specimen by its present radiation.

Flourine-testing is the most important chemical dating method. All bones in a stratem will contain flourine ions, the older bones containing more than the younger ones. This provides an accurate relative date.

Dendochronology (tree-ring dating) is one of the most precise techniques. In areas of limited rainfall certain plants, for instance, the yellow pine, grow in direct proportion to rainfall. By comparing the wide and narrow rings which indicate the tree's growth with other trees, a very accurate chronology of a region can be obtained.

Although finds of cultural remains of early man in the New World are now relatively common, discoveries of actual physical remains of pleistocene man are still exceedingly rare. In June, 1953, an amateur archaeologist, Keith Glasscock, while exploring a field of active sand dunes near Midland, Texas, came upon fragments of fossilized human skeletal material, folsom points, and other artifacts partially exposed in an eroding blow-out. A careful archaeological and geological investigation of the dunes, called the Scharbauer site after the owner of the property, was made by Professors Fred Wendorf, Alex D. Krieger, and Claude Albritton.

At five different localities excavated at the site bones and cultural materials were found. The human skeletal remains consisted of a nearly complete calvarium plus some teeth and facial parts, two rib fragments, and three metacarpals, together with remains of extinct horse, bison, and four-horned antelope, all heavily fossilized and embedded in a gray sand deposit of late Pleistocene age.

The calcarium, restored by Dr. T. Dale Stewart of the Smithsonian Institution from more than sixty fragments, was found to be small, long, and narrow, probably representing an individual about 30 years of age at time of death. Like the Minnesota Man, "Midland Man," upon careful scrutiny, turned out to be a woman.

In addition to the Folsom points another distinctive projectile point was found. It can be best described, briefly, as a non-fluted Folsom, and the type is now named Midland. Although at the Scharbauer site the Midland points were found stratigraphically below the Folsoms, in other sites they subsequently have been found in close association with Folsoms and Dr. Henry Irwin reports at least one occurrence, in Wyoming, where the Midland types were found above Folsoms. So, the discoverers date the Midland remains, conservatively, at approximately the time of the makers of the better known Folsom points, some ten to eleven thousand years ago, prior to the last advance of the Wisconsin glaciation.

The Midland discovery is notable not only for producing one of the very few early North Americans with convincing stratigraphic validity, but it also was the first time in this country that micro-chemical techniques were used to establish that the human skeletal material was indeed contemporaneous with the gray sand deposits in which it occurred and with the extinct animal remains found with it.

DAVIDS, DOROTHY W. (Stockbridge-Munsee; May 2, 1923-), is a noted educator who has done considerable work developing programs in the area of human relations. Born at Gresham, Wisconsin, she taught in public schools for several years (1945-62), before receiving her master's degree in 1963. After working with inority groups in Chicago, she took a position at the University of Wisconsin-Madison where, since 1972, she has worked with the Center for Community Leadership Development. She is also active in the National Congress of American Indians, serving as treasurer in 1970.

DAVIS, GLORIA ANN (Navajo-Choctaw; Sept. 5, 1933-), is a Roman Catholic nun who has served as a teacher and guidance counselor for elementary school children, mostly from minority groups, in Louisiana, Pennsylvania, and Arizona. Born at Fort Defiance, Arizona, she entered the Order of the Blessed Sacrament in 1952, the first Native American in the congregation. While teaching in a mission school at Houck, Arizona, she broadcast a radio program in the Navajo language (1957-63). In 1968 she began working among the Navajo at St. Michaels, Arizona.

DAVIS, JOHN (Creek; ?-*c.* 1840), was a interpreter and translator for white missionaries in Indian Territory (present Oklahoma). Captured as a boy during the War of 1812, he was reared by a white family in Alabama. In 1829 he emigrated west and was educated at the Union Mission after reaching Indian Territory. He worked for the missionaries as an interpreter and speaker in public meetings. Davis was a joint author with J. Lykens of a translation into Creek of the Gospel according to St. John. He also collaborated with R. M. Loughridge, D. Winslett, and W. S. Robertson in the translation into Creek of two volumes of hymns.

DAVIS, RUSSELL G., a Narraganset Indian, is the author of several books and a professor in the School of Public Health at Harvard University. He was born in Boston, Massachusetts on October 29, 1922 and received his Ed.D from Harvard i 1955. Among his books are *The Lion's Whiskers* (1959), *The Choctaw Code* (1961, and *Strangers in Africa* (1963).

DAWES COMMISSION was an official presidential commission whose purpose was to extend allotment to the Five Civilized Tribes.

The Five Civilized Tribes (Cherokee, Chickasaw, Creek, Chocktaw, and Seminole) owned and governed the eastern half of Indian Territory (now Oklahoma).

They had been exempted from the Dawes General Allotment Act of 1877 which authorized the breakup of all communally-owned land and the allotment of 160-acre homesteads to individual tribal members.

As white intruders advanced on the eastern territory, special interests lobbied for the extension of the Dawes Act to the Five Tribes. The white residents hoped for eventual statehood through union with the newly formed (1890) Oklahoma Territory to the west.

In 1893 the Indian Appropriation Act authorized negotiation through a commission. Its first chairman was Henry L. Dawes and the commission lasted for 12 years. It filed annual reports on the state of both Indians and whites in the region. In addition to negotiating the end of tribal land titles, the commission was to ready the rolls for individual allotment. The remaining lands were to be sold to whites.

Power of tribal government abolished

Strong Indian resistance to allotment was finally worn down as the five nations found their power eroding through acts of Congress. In 1897 Congress repudiated their sovereign councils by demanding presidential approval of every council move. The Curtis Act of 1898 authorized allotment of all tribal properties. The Dawes Commission implemented the Curtis Act which abolished tribal governments as of 1906.

DAWES GENERAL ALLOTMENT ACT or Dawes Act of February 8, 1887 had a profound effect on the course of Indian history by destroying the tradition of communal land ownership. It provided for the compulsory allotment of tribally-owned lands to individual tribal members.

Also known as the Dawes Severalty Act, it was engineered by Senator Henry Dawes of Massachusetts who felt that individual ownership would develop Indian initiative. Removed from the closeness of tribal society, it was hoped that the Indian would become an independent farmer.

Land was parceled out in 160-acre tracts for family heads 80-acre tracts for single adults, and 40-acre tracts for children. An amendment of 1891 reduced allotments. Surplus lands were made available for white settlement. The surplus eventually totaled ⅔ of the Indians' original holdings which had been guaranteed them by solemn treaty. From 1887 to 1934, when the allotment policy ended, lands under Indian control decreased from 140 million acres to less than 55 million.

While beneficial to westward expansion of white society, the Dawes Act was a disaster to Indian social stability. No lands were held in reserve for future generations and some Indians soon lost their land titles to scheming land speculators. The allotees were to become citizens and their lands were to be held in nontaxable trust for 25 years but the citizenship provisions were delayed by amendment in 1906. The Five Civilized Tribes and a few other tribes were exempted from the Dawes Act but, beginning in 1893, the Dawes Commission attempted to negotiate allotment. The Curtis Act (1898) eventually forced allotment upon these people.

In 1928 the Dawes Act was criticized in the Meriam Report. It was suspended in 1934 by the passage of the Wheeler-Howard Act.

DAY, FRANK (Maidu; *c.* 1905-), was the historian of his tribe in the mid-1970s and an artist whose painting deals solely with Maidu mythology and history. Day, who did not begin to paint until late in life, has a unique style and technique. His later works are distinguished by a surrealistic feeling, and by the boldness of their color and lines.

DEER, ADA (Menomini; 20th century), is a prominent Indian activist who was a leader in the struggle to reaffirm her tribe's treaty rights and to restore its federal status, which was accomplished in 1973 when the U.S. Congress repealed the termination of the Menominee Tribe of Wisconsin. Holder of a master's degree in social welfare from Columbia University, she was named the Outstanding Young Woman of America in 1966 for her work in helping Native Americans recapture and retain their heritage.

Portrait by Nancie Anne Gille. Deer, Ada.

DEERFIELD RAID was an attack on an English frontier village by French-Canadians and Indians in 1704 during Queen Anne's War.

The European War of the Spanish Succession (1701-14) was felt in America as an English-French contest along New England frontier and seaboard settlements. Its American segment is known as Queen Anne's War and both European powers used their Indian allies in the contests.

The village of Deerfield, the western frontier of the Massachusetts Bay Colony, was located near the Connecticut River and comprised a large stockade with more than 40 houses and about 300 English settlers. On February 29, 1704, 50 Canadians and 200 Indian allies launched a surprise attack on the settlement. Before a relief force arrived, one-half the homes were burned, 50 Englishmen were killed, and 100 people were taken as prisoners.

The raiders marched their captives on a grueling journey up the Connecticut Valley to the White River and northwest across the Green Mountains to the Winooski River headwaters. Some of the prisoners died during the rigorous winter march. The survivors arrived at Lake Champlain near the present site of Burlington. Many of the survivors eventually returned to their people and others remained in Canada. Eunice Williams, daughter of the minister at Deerfield, married an Indian.

The Deerfield Raid was regarded with horror and cries for revenge echoed through Massachusetts Bay. Deerfield had existed for nearly a generation and had survived previous attacks during King Phillip's War (1675-1676). In retaliation Benjamin Church led an expedition of 700 colonists and Massachusetts Indians to the east where they burned villages and flooded the Minas Basin in French Acadia.

DEITIES. *See* GODS AND GODDESSES.

DEKANAWIDA (Huron; fl. 16th century) was a prophet, statesman, and lawgiver who set out to unite the entire human race into a confederation based upon the principles of equity and righteousness, and succeeded in laying the moral and political foundation for the Iroquois Confederacy. A mystical being during his lifetime, Dekanawida has been shrouded in mystery ever since. No doubt a real person, he ranks as a demigod in Iroquois legend. In fact, stories about him often confuse Christina theology with Iroquois tradition.

According to tradition, Dekanawida was born in the vicinity of present-day Kingston, Ontario, the son of a virgin. After the baby's birth, however, the mother and grandmother attempted to murder Dekanawida, fearing that the child possessed an evil destiny. The grandmother learned in a dream that the child would indirectly cause the destruction of the Huron people; as a matter of fact, the Iroquois Confederacy which Dekanawida helped establish did destroy the Huron Confederacy. Mother and grandmother tried three times to kill the newborn infant, pushing him through a hole in the ice of a frozen stream; but in each instance the baby was found alive and unharmed in its mother's arms when she awoke the following morning.

Dekanawida grew up as an outcaset, shunned by the Huron. No doubt his alienation from the tribe contributed greatly to his inability to speak without stammering. Nonetheless, he was convinced that he had a divine mission, a conviction reinforced by his vision of all mankind united, living in peace and brotherhood. Three sets of double principles formed the constitutional framework for his unification of all tribes throughout the world: 1) Equity and justice; and righteousness in conduct, thought, and speech. 2) Physical strength and civil authority; and inner spiritual power. 3) Sanity of mind and physical health; and peace among individuals and groups. Dekanawida, sure of his destiny, set out from the land of the Huron to go to Iroquois territory; there he would win converts to what would come to be called "The Great Peace."

The exact circumstances are buried deep in mystery and obscure legend, but in some way Dekanawida joined forces with Hiawatha (*q.v.*) who had been trying to unite the Iroquois. Although well-intentioned, Hiawatha had lacked the specific principles upon which to construct a lasting confederation. Dekanawida converted Hiawatha to his code for the unification of all people under the three sets of double principles,and the two embarked upon winning over the main stumbling block to the Iroquois Confederation—the Onondaga chief Wathatotarho (*q.v.*). Dekanawida was the prophet; Hiawatha was the spokesman. Together they succeeded both in converting Wathatotarho and in aligning the five Iroquois nations (Onondaga, Mohawk, Cayuga, Seneca, and Oneida) into a powerful league that would last for more than two centuries.

The league was ruled by a council of 50 peace chiefs, known as sachems, who were chosen from specific clans. Since he was not an Iroquois by birth, Dekanawida became a chief on the basis of merit, and he forbade the appointment of a successor to his office.

Believing that this great triumph was merely the beginning of the realization of his divine mission, Dekanawida departed from the Iroquois to take his message of universal peace and brotherhood to the ends of the earth. As legend has it, he paddled out of Lake Onondaga in a canoe made from brilliant white stone and disappeared into the sunset.

DEKANISORA (Onondaga; ?-*c.* 1730) was an Iroquois chief, a noted orator who tried to maintain peace with both the French and the English.

The first historical reference to Dekanisora (Teganessorens) mentions him as a leader of an Iroquois peace embassy to Montreal in 1682. In 1688 he was one of the deputies captured and then released by Adario (*q.v.*) in his successful effort to reopen hostilities between the French and the Iroquois.

In 1694 Dekanisora arranged a truce with the French at Quebec. But he insisted that his English allies be included in the peace negotiations. At Albany, Dekanisora found the English opposed to any reconciliation between the Iroquois and the French. He reaffirmed his loyalty to the English but asserted the Iroquois right to act independently of them. Nevertheless, the Iroquois could not come to terms with the French, and a general peace failed to obtain at this time. But in 1701 Dekanisora represented the Indians at the conclusion of a lasting peace treaty with the French.

In 1726 Dekanisora was again an ambassador to Albany, where he helped to execute an agreement that placed Iroquois hunting grounds under the protection of the king of England. He died about 1780 at an advanced age.

Because of his reputation as a speaker among the Iroquois, Dekanisora took part in most of their negotiations with the French and the English. He was described by his contemporary Cadwallader Colden as having "a great fluency in speaking and a graceful elocution, that would have pleased in any part of the world." He may have been a Christian convert. Dekanisora helped to preserve, so far as was possible, the independence of the Five Nations from both European powers.

DEKAURY, CHOUKELEA (Winnebago; 1730-1816), also called Choukeka, was a chief known for his constant friendship to white settlers in Wisconsin. He was the son of Sabrevoir de Carrie, who had been an officer in the French army, and Hopokaw, daughter of a principal Winnebago chief. He was known to the whites as "Spoon" Dekaury.

After he became chief, Dekaury led his warriors in joint expeditions with the Dakota (Sioux) against the Ojibwa (Chippewa), but he maintained friendly relations with the whites. Most of the Winnebago chiefs distrusted all whites, and they refused to send representatives to a peace council held at Portage des Sioux, Wisconsin, in July 1815. Largely through Dekaury's influence, however, they signed a treaty with the U.S. on June 3, 1816, at St. Louis, Missouri. By its terms, the Winnebago recognized all territorial boundaries of lands ceded to the U.S. by Great Britain, France, and Spain, and they agreed not to give aid to tribes that had not yet concluded peace agreements. Later in 1816, Dekaury died at Portage.

Dekaury's wife was a daughter of Nawkaw (*q.v.*), an important Winnebago chief. They had six sons and five daughters.

DEKAURY, KONOKA (Winnebago; 1747-April 20, 1836), was the eldest son of, and successor as chief to, Choukelea Dekaury (*q.v.*). During the War of 1812, Dekaury (also known as Schachipkaka) joined a band of Winnebago who, on August 2, 1813, took part in the attack by the British under Gen. Henry Procter on Fort Stephenson on the Lower Sandusky River, Ohio. Under Tecumseh's leadership, Dekaury also participated in the Battle of the Thames, Canada, on September 28, 1813.

After succeeding his father as chief in 1816, he signed the treaty of Prairie du Chien (August 19, 1825)which established peace between the U.S. and the Indian nations of the Great Lakes area. Although not a participant in the 1827 Winnebago outbreak, Dekaury was held briefly at Prairie du Chien as a willing hostage for the delivery of Red Bird (*q.v.*).

Dekaury was described by J. A. Kinzie as "the most noble, dignified, and venerable of his own or indeed of any other tribe," having a fine Roman countenance, his head bald except for a solitary tuft of long, silvery hair neatly tied and falling back on his shoulders.

DELAWARE are an Algonquian-speaking group whose ancestors inhabited the lower Hudson River valley and the entire Delaware River drainage when the Europeans first came to North America. With an aboriginal population variously estimated from between 10,000 to 40,000 persons, the traditional Delawaran homeland extended throughout the Middle Atlantic coastal plain and adjacent highland interior of southwestern Connecticut, southeastern New York,

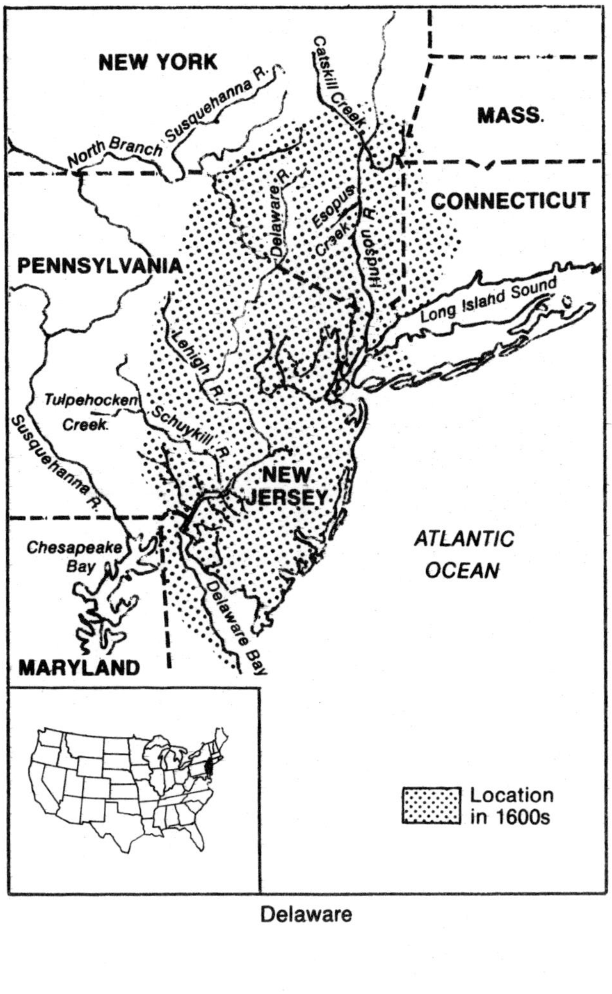

Delaware

western Long Island, all of New Jersey, southeastern Pennsylvania, and the State of Delaware.

The Delaware knew themselves as the *Lenni Lenape*, "common, original, or real people." The English named them after the Delaware River, which in turn had been named in honor of Sir Thomas West, Lord de la Warr, the first colonial governor of Virginia. Known among their Eastern Algonquin brethren as "grandfathers," their Iroquoian-speaking neighbors to the north and west called the Delaware "nephews." The Algonquin and Siouan peoples who shared their long westward exile knew them as *Wapanachki*, "easterners, or people of the dawn." The Delawarans on their part knew the European colonists that streamed upon their lands as *Swannekens*, "salt water, or bitter people." Long years of struggle led the Delaware to name the American successors to the Europeans *Kwun-nah-she-kun*, "long knives."

Never politically united, the Delawarans did share a common tongue. The Algonquian linguist Ives Goddard has identified two closely related Delaware languages, *Munsee* and *Unami*. Goddard has stated that Munsee was spoken by the lower Hudson and upper Delaware River valley groups while Unami was used by the Delawarans of the lower Delaware River watershed. Each language was further divided into a presently unknown number of dialects. Most closely related to *Mahican* and the *Southern New England Algonquian* languages to the north and *Nanticoke* to the south, the relationship between Delaware and other Algonquian languages is poorly understood.

The Dutch merchant-explorers that first visited the Delawaran homeland during the seventeenth century came upon a neolithic farming, fishing, hunting, and gathering people whose settlements thickly lined the watercourses, lagoons, and beaches of their territories. Those who lived near the coast drew their lives from the sea. They hooked, speared, netted, and trapped cod, salmon, herring, sturgeon, and many other kinds of fish. Hard clams, oysters, mussels, crabs, lobsters, and other forms of shellfish were also very important parts of the coastal Delaware diet. Sharp fishbones were used as needles and awls while the cracked shells of molluscs provided keen cutting edges. The shells of hard clams and periwinkles were ground into tubular white and purple beads. These became a species of currency known as *sewan* or *wampum*. The flesh and eggs of seabirds, a galaxy of berries, many forms of seaweed, and the meat and oil from seals and stranded whales were other major coastal Delawaran food sources. Wetlands supported luxuriant stands of tall grasses that provided the raw material for the mats that served as floor, wal, and roof for the coastal Delaware roundhouses and longhouses. Grasses were also woven into the bags and baskets that served as the furniture for their dwellings and the luggage for their journeys. Rimless conical pottery, bark and skin containers, and hollowed logs further furnished their homes and lined their cooking fires. Low sleek dugout canoes expertly plied the waterways of their territories, bringing people and resources together. White tailed deer, bear, and smaller mammals were hunted and trapped for their flesh and fur. Corn, beans, and squash were cultivated in small garden plots. These crops, however, made only a modest contribution to coastal Delawaran subsistence.

The coastal Delawarans made their homes in large villages located in sheltered bays and sounds during the blustery winter months. These settlements broke up during the spring, and the villagers moved to small fishing, shellfishing, and hunting camps during the warmer months. Large numbers of coastal people periodically joined their relations in the interior at this time. Many inland people were hosted in their turn by their coastal relatives from the late spring through the fall.

The Delaware of the highland interior made their livelihood from the upland fields, forests, and streams. Large gardens yielded abundant harvests of corn, beans, squash, sunflowers, and other crops. Spawning anadramous fish like shad, salmon, and herring added to the substantial catch of pike, bass, pickeral, catfish, carp, and other lake and river fish. Individual and group hunts brought in an abundance of meat and skins from white tailed deer, elk, black and brown bear, forest bison, beaver, and many other forest animals. Extensive rock outcrops of argillite, jasper, and quartz furnished the raw materials for a wide range of cutting and piercing tools. An extensive selection of tubers, greens, fruits, and berries were available during the warmer months. The flesh, feathers, and eggs of passenger pigeons, ducks, geese, turkey, and other birds rounded out the interior Delawaran diet. The bark of elm, hickory, and birch trees provided building materials for longhouses, cooking utensils and containers, and the skins of frame canoes. The deep forests of oak, hickory, maple, pine, and other trees furnished fuel, house frames, tool handles, and a multitude of other necessary utensils. Clays gathered from riverbeds and lakebottoms were transformed by Delawaran craftswomen into globular pots with high elaborately decorated castelated rims.

The interior Delawaran groups inhabited small scattered hunting camps located in sheltered upland valleys during the winter months. The families gathered by the falls and rapids of the rivers and their major tributaries to harvest the massive anadramous fish runs of the early spring. The matriclan segments then moved into the large agricultural villages located along the fertile river bottoms during the late spring and early summer. Lower Delawaran villages were strung out along sections of large river valleys. Upper Delawaran agricultural villages were far more concentrated, with many of the larger settlements fortified with timber palisade walls during periods of hostility.

Inland and coastal Delaware people exchanged visits to each others' settlements following the spring planting and fishing harvests. Summer was the time for trading and raiding, and the able bodied accordingly roved widely throughout the region while the very young and very old tended the fields and gathered wild plants.

The people rejoined their families in the agricultural villages for the fall harvest and its attendent festival. They then returned into their forests for the annual communal hunt. Parties numbering from several score to several hundred individuals surrounded a section of woodland, set it afire, and then drove whatever game contained within the circle of flame and people into an enclosure located at the section's center. The game slaughtered in this trap was preserved and used during the coming winter months. The families then returned to their hunting camps until the spring.

Little is known about aboriginal Delawaran religion. Early European observers noted that the Delawaran groups followed an extensive round of religious dances and feasts. Guardian spirits obtained through dreams and visions played an important part in Delawaran life. Medicine people of both sexes were active in Delaware society.

Delaware men and women were lightly clad during the warmer months. Men generally only wore skin breechclothes, while the women dressed in skin kilts. Both sexes wore mocassins made from tanned deer hide. The people normally applied clarified bear grease mixed with onion grass to protect their bodies from the sun and insects. Both sexes adorned themselves with paint, ear and nose ornaments, and tattoos. Successful warriors and gifted medicine persons sported particularly elaborate tattoos located all over their bodies. Men and women usually wore their hair long in a wide variety of styles. Warriors shaved their heads and wore a small scalp lock decorated with feathers, wampum, and fur. Both sexes wore leggings, loosely fitted shirts, and bearskin robes during the colder months.

The longhouse was the predominant Delawaran housetype. Ranging in length from thirty to sixty feet and from ten to fifteen feet wide, the longhouse was constructed of thick saplings joined together to form a series of arches. these arches were connected by supporting branches, and the frame was covered with grass mats or bark. Fireplaces were located along the central corridor, and families occupied cubicles on their side of the hearths. The center portion of the roof was left open to let the smoke from the fires out, and access to and from the structure was made possible by doors located at either end of the long central corridor. Goods were stored in baskets below the family sleeping compartments, and matrilineage possessions were kept in storage rooms located at the ends of the longhouse. Dried foodstuffs and other perishables were either hung from the ceiling, kept in caches above ground, or buried in pits near the settlements.

Each Delawaran house sheltered a matrilineal-matrilocal kinship group. The Delawarans reckoned descent through their women. Groups of related women and their male kinsmen made up a matriclan segment. These segments were parts of a larger matriclan whose members resided at various locations throughout the Delaware homeland. Later sources suggested the existence of three Delaware matriclans, the wolf, the turtle, and the turkey. Such a division of lineages has not been confirmed in the seventeenth century record, and aboriginal Delaware society was probably organized into a larger number matriclans.

The Delaware practiced matriclan exogamy, which required people to select marriage partners from other lineages. The rule of matrilocal residence saw to it that Delaware husbands moved into their wive's households. Important or wealthy men were permitted more than one wife, but these were usually from the same matriclan. When wives were of different lineages, the man either lived with the senior wife, a favorite, or divided his time among the households of his various spouses.

The matriclans owned all rights to land and resources. Land was held in usufruct, and lineage members were free to use any matriclan lands not used by other relatives. The cooperative efforts of women living in the same household on the land assured continued control over the lineage territorial holdings. The marriage of men into other matriclan groups further insured the benefits of foreign resources and out-group assistance.

The seventeenth century Delaware never acted as a distinct political entity. Though they shared significant linguistic, kinship, and ethnic ties, locality was always the single most compelling aspect of Delawaran political life. Family ties claimed the strongest allegiance in aboriginal Delaware society. Organization above the clan level was flexible and largely voluntaristic.

Four levels of socio-political integration beyond the matriclan have been identified in the Delawaran documentation. The village consisted of one or more dwellings, each housing a matriclan segment. Villages contained a population that varied from a few dozen individuals to several hundred persons. The village was the most important international agent of seventeenth century Delaware society.

Districts were a flexible combination of villages and separate matriclan organizations in a relatively limited territory. The district area permitted a number of loosely affiliated social groups to cooperatively exploit the resources of a given area.

The Delawaran tribes were a fluid combination of matriclan, village, and district organizations that generally held jurisdiction over a portion of a river drainage and its hinterland. The tribal level of socio-political integration was only convened during periods of international stress.

Confederacies were the shortest-lived and highest level response to the socio-political problems of the Delaware. The confederacy usually consisted of a group of tribes, and was generally only invoked during major wars. Confederacies were usually disbanded immediately following the end of the conflict. The Esopus of the mid-Hudson River valley, however, appear to have been organized as a confederacy both before and after the bloody Esopus Wars and Iroquoian Five Nations. The threat of sustained hostility with these groups may have caused the Esopus to confederate to an extent unparalleled by other Delawaran societies. It should be noted that the Delaware never united into a single confederacy at any time in their history.

Each level of Delawaran socio-political organization was led by a civil chief, known as a *sachem* or *sagamore* during peacetime and a war captain in times of war. Both chiefs were further supported by their respective councils. The office of civil chief was transmitted hereditarily and descended through the matriclan. War captains achieved their rank through battlefield successes. Councils were constituted of chiefs of the same approximate rank, and council leaders were very much "first among equals." War captains could compel absolute obedience during military operations. Sachems, however, were not permitted to arbitrarily order any action. All civil decisions were made by consensus, and a leader's authority depended upon diplomatic ability rather than coercive power.

Just as Delaware settlement-subsistence patterns could be understood in terms of interior and coastal types, the socio-political life was organized into the Munsee-speaking Upper Delawaran and Unami-speaking Lower Delawaran culture provinces. The major Upper Delawaran groups included the Wappinger, Nochpeem, Kichtawanck, Sint Sinck, Wiechquaesgeck, Manhattan, Canarsee, Nayack, Rockaway, Massapequa, and Matinecock of western Long Island; the five confederated Esopus tribes, the Haverstraw, Tappan, Hackensack, Raritan, and Neversink to the west of the Hudson River; and the Minisink and Forks of the Delaware groups of the north reaches of the Delaware River. The major Lower Delawaran peoples were the Sanhican of the Trenton, New Jersey area, the Atsayonck of Crosswicks Creek, the Remkokes, Armewamex, Mantaes, Naraticonck, Little Siconese, and Sewapois of the eastern shores of the tidewater Delaware River and the Quineomessinque, Minguannan, and Big Siconese of the western banks of Delaware Bay.

The coastal Delawaran groups were first contacted by Europeans during a series of exploratory voyages during the 1500s. The first sustained contacts occurred during the Dutch and English expeditions of the opening decades of the seventeenth century. The Dutch West India Company established their colony of New Netherland in the heart of the Delawaran homeland during the 1620s, and major Dutch trading posts were built at the mouths of the Hudson and Delaware Rivers and 160 miles up the Hudson River near modern Albany, New York by the early 1630s. The Dutch post on the Delaware was destroyed by the Lower Delawarans shortly after it was built, and the upriver post, known as Fort Orange, exclusively catered to the Mahican and Mohawk trade. The Dutch desired furs, and paid for them with iron tools, kettles, textiles, alcohol, and firearms. These trade goods were strongly desired by the native groups, and competition over the trade soon followed the first contacts. The Delawarans quickly exhausted their local fur resources, and were denied access to interior sources by the powerful Susquehannock to the south and the Five Nations and Mahican to the north. These inland groups repeatedly attacked their Delawaran competitiors during the early years of the trade, and Dutch refusal to trade muskets to the Delawarans put them at a serious disadvantage. The Delaware did manage to secure firearms from clandestine Dutch traders and from the Swedish trade forts along the lower Delaware River established during the 1640s. Massive smallpox and measles epidemics combined with warfare against the Dutch, the interior groups, and each other killed over 90% of the Delawaran people. Exhausted by their losses, the Delawarans eagerly allied themselves with the English following the fall of New Netherland to a British fleet in 1664. The Delaware groups pursued a policy of peaceful trade with the English, and paid for their alliance by both providing small parties of warriors and guides for the wars between the English and the French and by the gradual sale of their land holdings at low prices. The Delawaran groups slowly withdrew into the upper reaches of their river valley domains as the English acquired the more desirable lowland tracts. Population losses coupled with land sales caused most of the Delawaran groups to merge in their upriver retreats scattered throughout the traditional Delaware homeland during the last decades of the seventeenth century.

By 1700 the bulk of the Delawaran groups were concentrated in the Esopus country, the Minisinks, the Forks of the Delaware, the Falls of the Delaware, and at the Schuylkil and Brandywine River valleys. Smaller concentrations were located in the lower Berkshire Mountains, Rockaway, Long Island, the upper reaches of the Passaic and Raritan valleys, the interior of southern New Jersey, and the eastern branch of the Susquehanna River. Parties of Delawarans moved among the Miami in the Ohio country and others settled along the Allegheny River in western Pennsylvania at this time. The eighteenth century Delawarans had undergone profound changes during the preceding century. They had fully adapted to an interior woodland settlement-subsistence pattern and had further been fully incorporated into the European economy. They lived in large permanent villages, and their menfolk were absent throughout the winter tending their traplines. Furs and military service provided the European trade goods that the Delawaran groups had become dependent upon. Relocation onto heavily forested lands favored hunting and trapping and discouraged farming. Agriculture had furnished the greater part of the traditional Delawaran diet, and the deemphasis on cultivation forced them to increasingly depend upon white foodstuffs. Socio-political power was fast moving from the matriclans into the hands of powerful chiefs.

The steady centralization of Delawaran society further saw the rising importance of confederacies throughout their territories.

Extensive land sales, including the notorious fraudulent "Walking Purchase" of 1737 that alienated most of the upper Delaware River valley forced most of the Delawaran people to relocate in the Susquehanna and Allegheny valleys under the sponsorship of the Five Nations during the 1730s and 1740s. These groups swiftly affiliated with and absorbed elements of the Mahican, Nanticoke, Conoy, and other Algonquin refugees settling under Iroquoian auspices. These communities, located at Shamokin, Wyoming, Otsiningo, Chugnut, and Kanestio in Pennsylvania, were governed by representatives of the Five Nations, who gradually sold these lands from under them, forcing them to move into the upper Ohio River valley by the 1750s.

Many Coastal Algonquins who remained in their traditional Middle Atlantic homeland came under the influence of missionaries during the 1730s and 1740s. Mission communities at Stockbridge, Schagticoke, Shekomeko, Cranberry, Crosswicks, and the Forks of the Delaware attracted large numbers of Delaware people. Most of these mission stations collapsed during the 1750s, but the Moravian Brethren at the Forks of the Delaware persisted. The Moravian settlements contained contained a high percentage of Delawaran converts, and both the communities and their missionaries shared the gradual Delaware westward exile into the lower Great Lakes during the next half century.

Embittered and directly threatened by the consequences of a complete English victory, the Susquehanna Delawarans sided with the French during the opening years of the Seven Years War (1755-1762). Both sides suffered heavy losses during the conflict, and most of the Delawaran groups signed a separate peace with the English at Easton, Pennsylvania in 1758. The bulk of the Delaware groups relocated in the upper Ohio drainage after the war, and many of these people fought against the English during the Pontiac War of 1762-1764.

An uneasy peace followed the end of the Pontiac War, and the Delaware prepared for future conflicts by establishing strong ties with their Miami, Shawnee, Chippewa, Ottawa, and Wyandot neighbors. The Delawaran groups largely attempted neutrality when the War of Independence against England broke out in 1775. By 1778 the Delaware were promised entry into the Union as a separate Indian State in return for their continued non-involvement in the conflict. The Delaware were strongly divided by the struggle, however, and the pro-English faction finally won the support of the Delawaran villages following the American massacre of the Delaware-Mahican mission community of Gnadenhutten in 1782.

Most Delawarans withdrew deeper into Ohio after the end of the War of Independence. Other Delaware groups settled the upper White River valley of Indiana during the 1780s. The Delawarans fought in the resistance against the American armies during the 1780s and 1790s, and large Delaware contingents were present during the defeats of the armies of Generals Harmar and St. Clair in the Indiana country. The defeat of the Native Coalition at Fallen Timbers in 1794 finally forced them to abandon the Ohio, and most of the Delawarans withdrew into Indiana. The English continued to support the Delawarans and their allies against the Americans during the next decades, and many Delaware followed Tecumseh and his brother, the Shawnee Prophet during the first decade of the eighteenth century. Defeat during the War of 1812 caused many Delaware to remove to Ontario, Canada, where their descendents continue to reside at Muinceytown, Newfairfield, and Grand River.

Those Delawarans that had remained in Connecticut, New York, and New Jersey removed among the Oneida and Seneca of upstate New York by 1810. Most of these groups followed the Oneida west to their reservation near Green Bay, Wisconsin between 1821 and 1825. Others assimilated into the Seneca, and either remaining on the Allegheny reservation in New York or joined the Seneca reservation in Oklahoma. The descendents of the Delawarans that joined the Oneida today reside on the Stockbridge-Munsee reservation in Wisconsin.

The main body of the Delaware gradually removed from the Indiana country to southern Missouri in 1815. Continual pressure for their lands forced them to move to a reservation in eastern Kansas in 1829. This reservation was liquidated by 1854, and the bulk of the Delaware Nation settled among the Cherokee and Creek in northeastern Oklahoma, where their descendents live to the present day.

The long century of westward exile worked profound changes upon Delawaran society. Repeated removals and continual military reversals at the hands of the white armies and hostile Native groups impoverished the Delawaran people. The termination of the fur trade and the end of their utility as allies for the contending European forces forced them to depend upon the annuity payments they received in payment for their lands by the Federal government. Prophets rose among them, and the rise of the Big House religion allowed the Delaware to continue their traditional cultural life while making drastic adjustments to changing economic conditions. The men gradually turned to farming, ranching, and wage labor for the whites. The clans lost their importance, and the Delaware languages began to disappear. Participation in the white economy devalued women, and the shift to patrilineal-neolocal kinship organization was virtually completed by the end of the nineteenth century. Most Delaware were sent to white schools, at least nominally adopted white religion, wore white dress, and spoke English. The last Big House ceremonies were "brought in" during the 1920s.

The modern Delawarans have largely assimilated

into white culture. Only a few very old people still speak the language or follow the old ways. Most Delawarans in the United States and Canada still live on the reservations, however. The Oklahoma Delaware have been the recipients of the $12,000,000 from the Indian Lands Claims Commission for lands taken from them during their westward exile. The economic success of the Stockbridge-Munsee and the relative success of the Ontario Delawarans clearly demonstrate that the Delaware show every sign of continuing their four century old tradition of cultural persistence in the face of the most damaging attempts to eradicate them as a cultural entity.

ROBERT STEVEN GRUMET

DELAWARE. The major inhabitants of what is now Delaware were the Unilachtigo subtribe of the Delaware (Lenni Lenape) Indians. Unilachtigo means "People who live near the sea." Their totem was the wild turkey. In the migration legends of the Delawares they are sometimes referred to as *Nantego*, and are apparently identical with the Nanticoke tribe, from which a few mixed bloods presently living in Sussex County claim descent. Other Indians who hunted or traded in Delaware were those called *Minquas* by the Dutch—actually Susquehanna (Conestoga) people.

The first white settlement in Delaware was Swanendael (present Lewes), founded in 1631 by Dutch patrons on land purchased from the Minquas. The colony was massacred by Minquas within a year. Peace was reestablished by that remarkable friend of the Indians, David Pieterzoon de Vries, who ascertained that the quarrel with the settlers had grown out of an Indian's trivial theft. Subsequent settlers, such as the Swedes who founded Fort Christina (Wilmington) in 1638, lived on good terms with the Indians and peace prevailed under the proprietorship of William Penn. After Penn's death, the Delawares were cheated out of their Pennsylvania lands by the Walking Purchase of 1737, and moved gradually west.

A Nanticoke Indian Association was formed in 1922 by a small remnant of people of mixed white, Negro, and Indian ancestry, who consider themselves Nanticokes although they have not preserved their language or traditions.

DELCE, ALPARIS (Mosquito-Carib; fl. 18th century), ruled the Pearl Lagoon region of eastern Nicaragua in the late 18th century. He signed the 1778 treaty of friendship with the Spanish negotiated by Jeremiah Terry. In 1780, however, Delce sided with the English, aiding them in attacking the Spanish Fort Inmaculada. In 1789, Delce rose against the Spanish, leading to the assassination of his Spanish-allied uncle, chief Colville Breton. Delce and the Sambo-Mosquito king George II shared power in a general state of anarchy.

DELGADITO (Navajo; fl. 1860s) was a headman who at first resisted the U.S. Army effort to round up the Navajo at Bosque Redondo, New Mexico, but eventually turned himself in and subsequently tried to persuade others to do the same.

With his brother Barboncito, he took part in several meetings in 1861-63 with the army leaders—first Col. Edward R. S. Canby and later Gen. James Carleton—in New Mexico, attempting to halt the fighting between the whites and the Navajo. But the Indians remained steadfast in their refusal to leave their traditional lands for the Bosque Redondo Reservation on the Pecos River at Fort Sumner.

In November 1863, as army scout Kit Carson's "scorched earth" program began to take its toll and his people were suffering from cold and starvation, Deladito surrendered. General Carleton told him that he and his family could return to Fort Wingate, in his homeland, if he would persuade the other Navajo leaders to go to Bosque Redondo. By Janaury 1864 Delgadito had persuaded 680 Navajo to surrender. Along with Barboncito, Manuelito, and the other Navajo leaders, he signed the treaty of June 1, 1868, and went to live at the new Navajo Reservation.

DELINQUENCY. *See* CRIME AND DELINQUENCY.

DELORIA, ELLA CARA (Standing Rock Sioux; ?-1971), was a noted anthropologist, linguist and

Portrait by Nancie Anne Gille. Deloria, Ella

author. She was appointed to the faculty of Columbia University in 1929 and worked as a specialist in the department of anthropology. Among her publications were *Dakota Texts* (1932), a bilingual collection of tales from several Dakota (Sioux) reservations, and *Speaking of Indians* (1944), an examination of Dakota life before white settlement.

DELORIA, P.. SAM (Standing Rock Sioux; 20th century), is a noted administrator of povery and legal aid programs for Native Americans. The younger brother of Vine Deloria, Jr. (*q.v.*), he worked with the Office of South Dakota Opportunity at the University of South Dakota before becoming director of the University of New Mexico Indian Law Center at Albuquerque.

DELORIA, VINE, JR. (Standing Rock Sioux; March 26, 1933- , is a noted author and one of the most prominent spokesmen for Indian rights in contemporary U.S. society.

Born at Martin, South Dakota, he is the son of a distinguished Episcopal Church minister, who was himself the son of a Yankton Sioux chief and minister. After serving in the U.S. Marine Corps (1954-56), Deloria received his bachelor of science degree from Iowa State University in 1958. He then studied for the ministry at the Lutheran School of Theology, receiving

Portrait by Nancie Anne Gille. Deloria, Vine Jr.

his bachelor of divinity degree in 1963. He was not, however, ordained a minister because he was disillusioned with the white man's religion. According to Deloria, religion for the white man is something to talk about, something to study; for the Indian religion is something in his heart, something he feels, something he lives.

Deloria became a staff associate for the United Scholarship Fund of Delver, Colorado, and developed a program that placed more than 40 Indian students in independent prep schools in New England. The young Indians in this program found that they could become productive members of the general society and still "retain their Indianness." For Deloria acculturation means adopting those things that the general society has to offer that the Indians consider to be of value and to their best interests.

From 1964 to 1967 Deloria served as executive director of the National Congress of American Indians (CAI), the largest U.S. tribal federation. He resigned from his NCAI position to enroll in the University of Colorado law school, receivign his law degree in 1970. He taught for a year at Western Washington State College in the ethnic studies program. In the mid-1970s he was chairman of the Institute for the Development of Indian Law in Washington, D.C. Working out of both his office in Washington and his home in the Denver area, he has been deeply involved in the social, economic, political, and legal problems confronting the Indian peoples.

Deloria has written several books, articles, and other pubications. In 1969 he achieved national prominence with the publication of *Custer Died for Your Sins: An Indian Manifesto,* a best-selling account of American Indians in contemporary U.S. society. In it he discusses the roles of treaties, government policies and agencies, the white man's law, missionaries, and anthropologists in contemporary Indian affairs. *We Talk, You Listen: New Tribes, New Turf* (1970) is a series of essays treating the meaning and consequences of the differences in world view between Indians (tribal) and whites (individualistic). Deloria says that the white society must adopt a tribal-communal way of life if it is to survive in humanistic form. In *God Is Red* (1973) he analyzes the religious crisis in contemporary U.S. life and argues that Christianithy has failed both in its theology and in its application to social issues. He calls for a complete change in the social and theological outlook of white society and a return to the religious concepts of Native Americans.

DELSHAY (Tonto Apache; between 1835 and 1840-1874), an Apache leader in the early 1870s and one of Gen. George Crook's most wanted renegades, is remembered best for having lost two heads.

In 1868 the military in Arizona Territory was operating in utter confusion; civilian agencies wrangled with the military or among themselves; local contractors leaped at the chance to make huge profits in league with Indian agents. The advent of more miners and settlers compelled the Indians to inhabit the most unproductive regions. Wild game was vanishing. Forced to starve or steal, many bands chose the warpath.

While Gen. T. C. Devin, commanding the Prescott District, had no authority to make a treaty with the Indians, he did arrange a meeting with Delshay during which he offered the Tonto refuge in an area bounded by the Salt and Verde rivers and the Black Mesa. Of Delshay's reaction there is no record, but a few months later he and many of his people came to Fort Reno, where they accepted rations and employment. Other bands were similarly induced to establish villages near military establishments. But in view of continued chaos, these measures were not effective. Moreover, many Indians who surrendered themselves were mistreated. Delshay himself was shot in the back by an army officer for no apparent reason, and from that time he stayed clear of the military posts.

Delshay was only one of many who continued to terrorize the region, but his band was one of the strongest. Capt. George M. Randall almost got him near Bad Rock Mountain; 25 Indians were kiled, but Delshay escaped. In 1873 hostiles were reported to be gathering at his rancheria a few miles from Camp Verede. By the time Gen. George Crook, then in command of the Department of Arizona, could send men to arrest Delshay, he had vanished.

Early in 1874 Crook set into motion a new program. His troops were ordered to take no prisoners; in essence, the Indians were to be killed on sight. But cruel winter temperatures forced some of the renegades to return to San Carlos, where they pleaded for forgiveness. At first Crook refused, but finally a compromise was reached. The Indians could stay if they would bring in the heads of their ringleaders. Proof of the Indians' sincerity of purpose was evidenced two days later when some of them presented him with a grain sack, out of which they dumped seven Indian heads. Just whose bodies the heads belonged to was never certain, but Crook was convinced that the same proposition might work if it was offered to some peace-seeking Tonto. The price of peace was Delshay's head.

Recounting this experience, Crook said, "When I visited the Verde Reservation they would convince me that had brought in his head; when I went to San Carlos they would convince me they had brought in his head. Being satisfied that both parties were earnest in their belief, and the bringing of the extra head was not amiss, I paid both parties."

Actually, the head brought to San Carlos was Delshay's, according to scouts who knew him well. The warriors who killed him were led by the well-known Apache leader Des-a-lin.

DEMMERT, ARCHIE W. (Tlingit; May 17, 1909-), is an educator in the Alaska school system, noted for his skill in inspiring students with the desire to learn. The son of a salmon fisherman, Demmert was born on a boat at sea north of Prince of Wales Island in the Northwest Territories, Canada. His family lived at Klawock, Alaska, where in 1930 Demmert began teaching after attending Western Washington College. Since then he has taught in schools all across Alaska, devoting much of his effort to Native Americans. After World War II service he completed his college education at the University of Wisconsin (1946-49) and eventually received a master's degree at the Univrsity of Alaska (1964). In 1969, while a sixth-grade teacher in Sitka, Alaska, Demmert was named to the National Teacher of the Year honor role.

DEMMERT, WILLIAM G., JR. (Tlingit-Dakota; March 9, 1934-), is a noted educator who has been a U.S. government official in programs for Indian education. After graduating from Seattle Pacific College, he taught at Forks, Washington (1960-64), and Fairbanks, Alaska, his birthplace, as chief administrator of the public schools (1968-70). In 1969 he attended the First Convocation of American Indian Scholars at Princeton University organized by the American Indian Historical Society. As an outgrowth of that meeting, he was one of the founders and original directors of the National Indian Education Association.

While attending Harvard University (1970-73), where he received his doctorate in education, Demmert became a consultant to the U.S. Senate for the development of the Indian Education Act of 1972 (Title IV, P.L. 92-318). In 1972 he joined the U.S. Department of Education as an official in the area of Indian education.

DEMOGRAPHY. A large literature exists pertaining to the numbers of Indians living at the point in time of the arrival of Europeans. Much less is known about Indian population densities for the various pre-Columbian periods and phases, although archaeological research with the goal of learning more about such matters has become more frequent and sophisticated within the last 20 years. Still, many problems remain. Surface survey of archaeological sites is the only methodology currently suitable for the collection of such data, but in many areas, for example the heavily forested and farmed eastern woodlands of the United States, sites, especially small villages and camps, are difficult to find. In spite of this, some progress is being made: (i.e., estimate of a population of 30,000 for Cahokia, a site near St. Louis, for the period about AD 1,000). The bulk of systematic research designed to elucidate ancient population trends, for American Indians, has been done in highland Mesoamerica, although similar work has been done also along the coast of Peru, and in the American Southwest. Most of the work done in Mesoamerica has been done in the Valley of Mexico, the Tehuacan Valley, and the Valley of Oaxaca. The data accumulated in these surveys is vast and complex. The basic patterning is as follows: from the end of the pleistocene some 10,000 years ago up to the point in time when the first villages formed (roughly 1500 to 2000 BC), the human populations were highly mobile, and existed at extremely low densities (possibly as low as 1 person per 50 miles). The early period of village life, up to about 400 or 500 BC was a period of growth of the human population, but our estimates of carrying capacities (the numbers of people who could have been supported) indicates a significant underuse of resources. The pace of population growth increased during the final centuries BC, culminating in the growth of densely populated empires centered on large cities during the Classic Period (*c.* AD 200-700). By far the largest of these cities was Teotihuacan, in the Valley of Mexico, with a population estimated to have been nearly 200,000 at its peak. Local fluctuations in population sizes occurred after the collapse of the Classic Period empires, but, toward the end of the pre-Hispanic sequence there was a significant increase in numbers almost everywhere, in some cases to levels higher than any prior period, especially in the Valley of Mexico, which was the center of the expansive Aztec empire. This pattern in population dynamics for highland Mesoamerica should be no means be considered to be representative of all the New World. Each sub-area will undoubtedly prove to have had its own pattern of periods of growth and decline; even within Mesoamerica there was apparently much variability by subregion. For example, in the Peten region of Guatemala, the "core" area of Maya civilization, the period of maximum population growth, from *c.* AD 700 to 900, followed the collapse of the highland empires. This was followed by a precipitous decline in population to very low levels, where it has remained to this day.

It is not until after the time Europeans arrived that one can finally begin to put together a picture of varying population densities of the American Indians in all parts of the New World. The data come primarily from estimates made by soldiers, priests, traders, explorers, and, in some cases, state censuses. A bewildering quantity of such sources exist, many still untapped.

One of the major problems facing anyone attempting to estimate the aboriginal population of the American Indians for the time of the European discovery and conquest is the fact that the sounder estimates, especially state or missionary censuses, were in all cases done years after the initial contact. Probably in all cases the intervening period was one of rapid population decline due to the introduction of diseases new to the Indians, especially smallpox, typhus, and measles, exacerbated by warfare, disruption of social, political, and economic institutions, and the mistreatment of Indians used as slave labor. For example, in pre-Hispanic Central Mexico, especially in the Valley of Mexico, much exchange of foodstuffs as well as non-food items flowed through a complex marketing system. The Spanish presence disrupted this system, leaving many Indians without access to needed resources. A method for accounting for these declines is to derive a hemispheric value for the declines, then multiply this value by the nadir population for each region (which is usually fairly securely known). Overall, the nadir populations for all regions were roughly 1/20 to 1/25 the original numbers.

Table 1
Estimated Aboriginal Population

Area	Nadir Population	Date of Nadir	Projections x 20	Projections x 25
North America	490,000	1930+	9,800,000	12,250,000
Mexican Civilization	1,500,000	1650	30,000,000	37,500,000
Central America	540,000	1650	10,800,000	13,500,000
Caribbean Islands	22,150	1570	443,000	553,750
Andean Civilization	1,500,000	1650+	30,000,000	37,500,000
Marginal South America	450,000	?	9,000,000	11,250,000
Western Hemisphere			90,043,000	112,553,750

From Dobyns (1966)

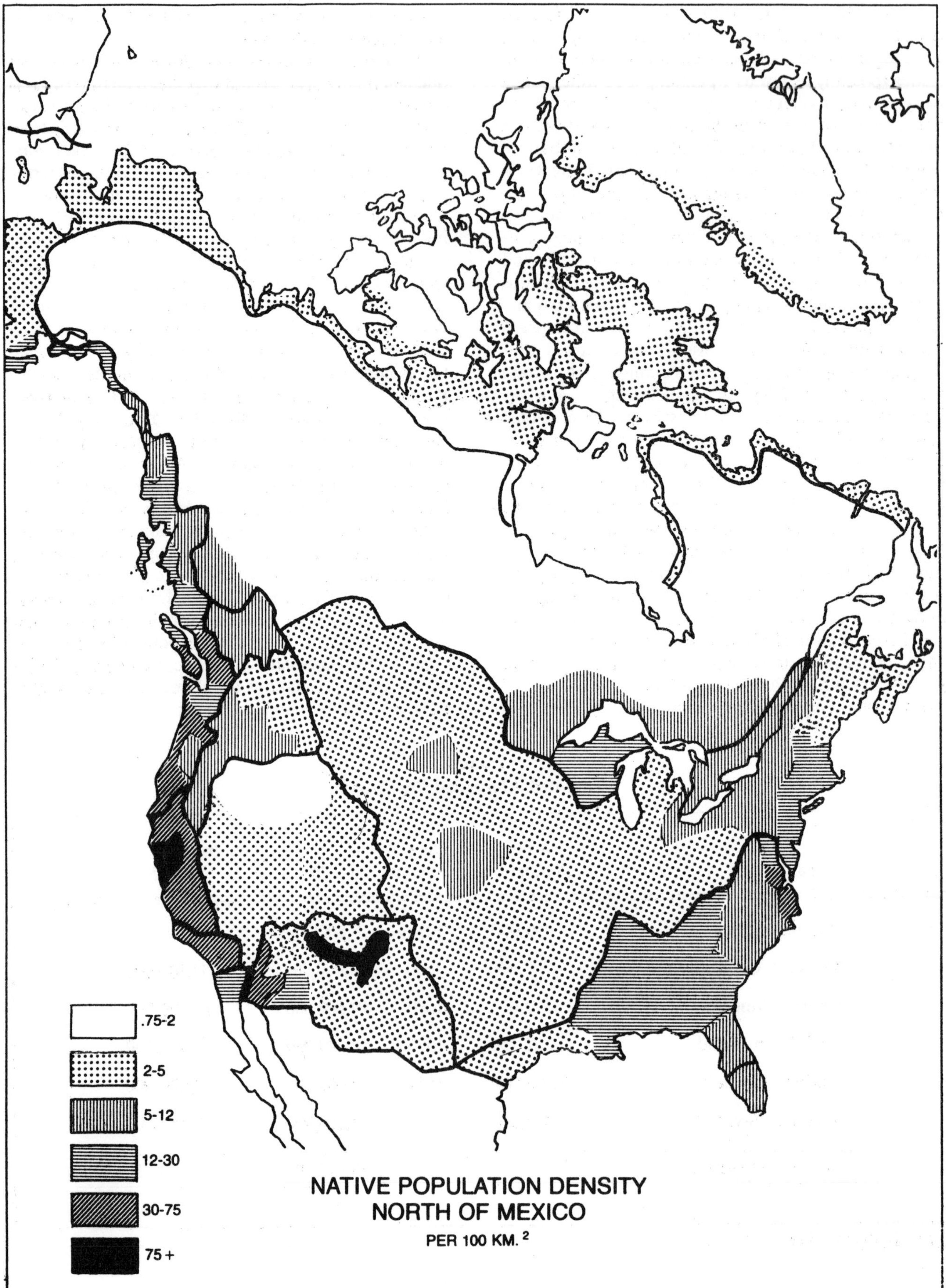
.75-2
2-5
5-12
12-30
30-75
75+
NATIVE POPULATION DENSITY
NORTH OF MEXICO
PER 100 KM. 2

Although the sub-area and hemispheric estimates still need much refinement, the relative densities of populations in the various New World areas have been reasonably well established. Two published maps, showing native densities in persons per 100 km have been published (Stewart, 1949: Map 16, and Kroeber, 1939: Map 18); see map illustrations. Recall that the absolute densities indicated in these two maps may not be correct (Kroeber, in particular, had a tendency to underestimate native densities)—of value in these two maps is the information they convey about relative population densities by area. Several patterns are apparent. The lowest densities occurred in areas populated by highly mobile hunters and gatherers, especially in the Arctic, sub-Arctic, and Argentinian Plain. Intermediate densities were fond in tribal areas including the Southern Andes, the Amazon Basin and related areas, and over much of what is now the United States and northern Mexico. Interestingly, the settled hunters of the California coast and coastal groups to the north along the same coast had population densities as high or higher than the tribal agriculturalists of the Eastern Woodlands. By and large the highest densities were in the "core" areas of the New World civilizations, the Central Andes and Mesoamerica. The latter of these, unfortunately, does not appear on Kroeber's map-densities there; however, we know they were comparable to those of the Central Andes.

Modern trends

A map showing the population densities of Indians in recent times would look something like the illustrations included with this article, insofar as the highest densities continue to be in what were the core areas of the New World civilizations. Indians are, by and large, relatively fewer in numbers elsewhere. Only two areas outside Mesoamerica and the Central Andes, in fact, have relatively high densities of Indians today (and these densities are much lower than those in Mesoamerica and the Central Andes)—the innaccessible portions of the Amazon Basin and adjacent areas, and the American Southwest (along with the state of Oklahoma, which was designated "Indian Territory" by the United States Congress, where Indians removed from other parts of the country were placed). For Latin America it can be argued the variability in the nature of Indian-white relations determined the nature of contemporary Indian distribution. Thus, the Spanish, who were interested primarily in labor, not land, protected the peasant populations they encountered in the Central Andes and Mesoamerica, where the aboriginal populations were both dense and relatively easy to tax and control (the Spanish could easily take over existing political and economic institutions which had generated tribute and labor in aboriginal times). Today, then, these are both areas where there is much Indianness, both in genetic and behavioral senses. Actually more people in these areas are wholly or partially Indian in a genetic sense, but have become "mestizoized" by giving up the Indian features of their behavior and adopting European traits. In the 17th century in Mexico there were 250,000 persons classified as white or mestizo, and 1,270,000 Indians. By the end of the 18th century there were 5,200,000 Indians, but the mestizo group had grown to 2,270,000, and today the mestizos outnumber the Indians.

Spanish influence

Tribal societies and band-organized hunters and gatherers felt the impact of the Spanish (and Portuguese) much more than the "civilized" peasants. In these areas, no overarching political or economic institutions existed aboriginally which could be utilized by the conquerors to achieve their ends. Instead, more often, tribes were eliminated (some to be replaced by slaves imported from Africa), or conquered and exploited in a more direct, personal manner, resulting in much more Europeanization. In Latin America outside Mesoamerica and the Central Andes, there are few people who are considered to be, or who consider themselves to be, Indians.

Population decline

This relative paucity of Indians today is similar in North America north of Mexico, but for different reasons. While some aboriginal groups have been, relatively speaking, spared from the decimation of European conquest (especially those in the economically marginal Southwest United States and the Arctic), most Indian populations north of Mexico experienced rapid declines due to a combination of warfare, disease, loss of land and other resources, and removal. The British, French, and Dutch were more interested in land than labor, and thus had little reason to protect the Indians. Instead, Indian survivors were placed on reservations. Today more than 800,000 Indians and Eskimos live in the United States, roughly half of these on reservations. This is less than ½ of one percent of the total United States population (see list of Indians by state).

Although the American Indians and Eskimos north of Mexico were seriously affected by the invasion of Europeans, they are by no means on the road to total disappearance today. In fact, they are now experiencing a period of rapid growth and cultural renascence. The growth rate of Indians in the United States is now much higher than the general population, increasing from 551,669 in 1960 to 827,108 in 1970. This is due in part to the higher fertility of Indians compared with the general population. (In 1959 the Indian birth rate was 41.4 live births per thousand, while that for the general population was only 24.1 per thousand.) Too, the mortality rates of Indians and Eskimos in the United States is declining, nearly approaching that of the general United States population.

RICHARD BLANTON
GARY FEINMAN

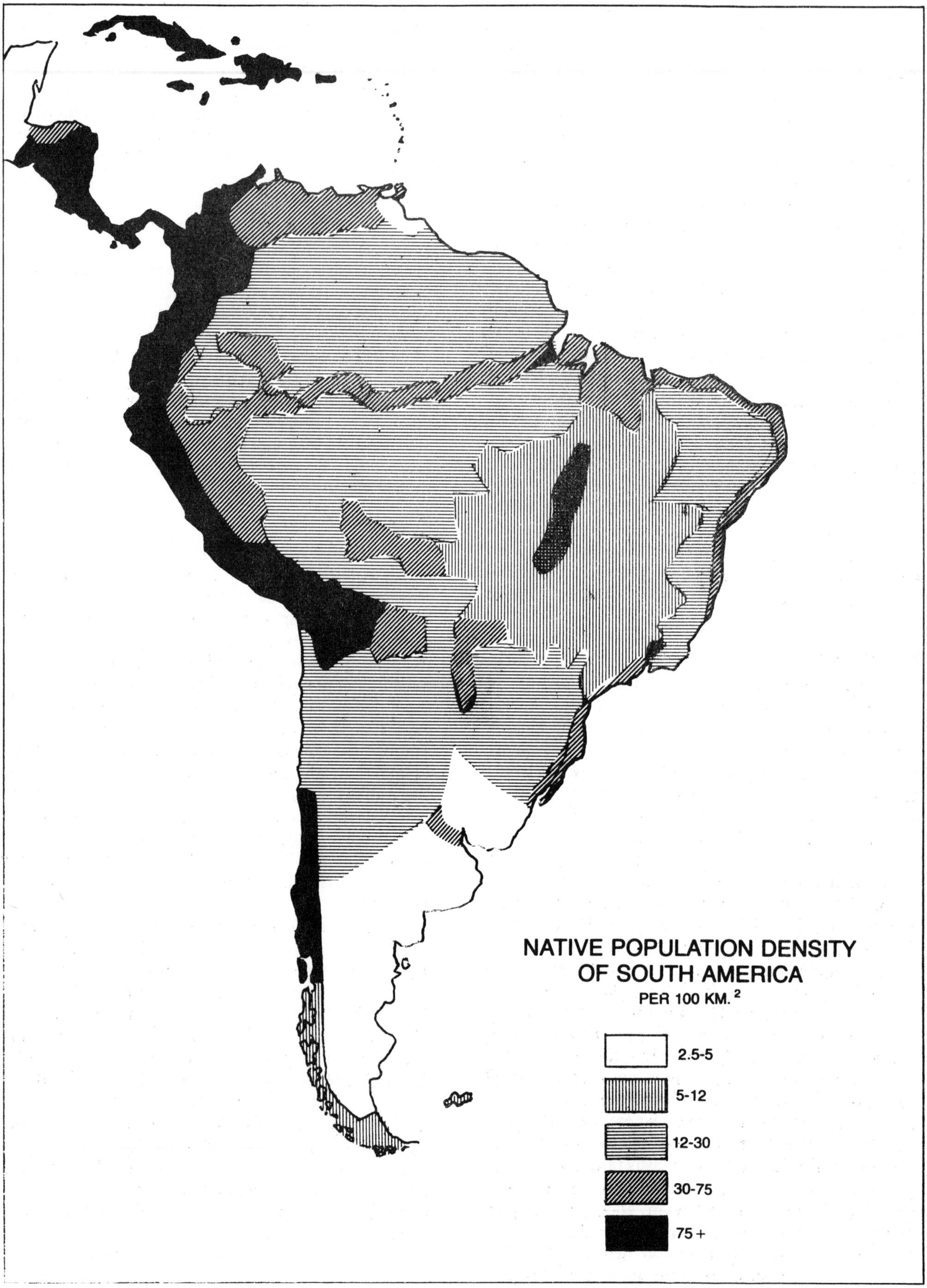
NATIVE POPULATION DENSITY
OF SOUTH AMERICA
PER 100 KM.^{2}
2.5-5
5-12
12-30
30-75
75 +

Table 2. Indians and Alaskan Natives by State, United States, 1970

Alabama	2,443	Missouri	5,405
Alaska	50,654	Montana	27,130
Arizona	95,812	Nebraska	6,624
Arkansas	2,014	Nevada	7,933
California	91,018	New Hampshire	361
Colorado	8,836	New Jersey	4,706
Connecticut	2,222	New Mexico	72,788
Delaware	656	New York	28,355
District of Columbia	956	North Carolina	44,406
		North Dakota	14,369
Florida	6,677	Ohio	6,654
Georgia	2,347	Oklahoma	98,468
Hawaii	1,126	Oregon	13,510
Idaho	6,687	Pennsylvania	5,533
Illinois	11,413	Rhode Island	1,390
Indiana	3,887	South Carolina	2,241
Iowa	2,992	South Dakota	32,365
Kansas	8,672	Tennessee	2,276
Kentucky	1,531	Texas	17,957
Louisiana	5,294	Utah	11,273
Maine	2,195	Vermont	229
Maryland	4,239	Virginia	4,853
Massachusetts	4,475	Washington	33,386
Michigan	16,854	West Virginia	751
Minnesota	23,128	Wisconsin	18,924
Mississippi	4,113	Wyoming	4,980
		United States	827,108

From Bureau of Indian Affairs Statistics Division, Census Report, July, 1972.

DE MONTIGNY, LIONEL H. (Turtle Mountain Chippewa; Oct. 17, 1935-), is an physician and an official with the U.S. Public Health Service (PHS). Born at Belcourt, North Dakota, he joined the PHS in 1962 as field medical officer. He was the first appointee to the preventive medicine program of the University of Oklahoma's school of medicine. In 1965 he was appointed deputy director of the PHS Portland (Oregon) Area Office and has been instrumental in starting tribally operated health programs.

DENBIGH FLINT CULTURE, located on Norton Sound, is an especially important site because it provides a sound reference point for establishing a continuum between pre-Eskimo and Eskimo cultures in the. Arctic.

Radiocarbon dated to 3000 BC, is unique among complexes found in the Arctic in North America. The assemblage of flint artifacts includes some long blades similar to Eden points, harpoon blades, one or two fluted points, crescentic-sided blades or points, keeled and flaked scrapers and a variety of burins, some of which are small prismatic flakes and others which are large and irregular.

The use of the primatic flake and the possession of the burin point to a closer affiliation with the Mesolithic Eurasiatic complexes of Lake Baikal. Also, Denbigh is considerably different from later Eskimo cultures. On the other hand, some residues of the Denbign Flint Culture are evident in later Eskimo traditions, for instance at Dorset. The exact relationship is unclear because there is no evidence of the type of house or other important matters that could shed light on this question. However, the origin of Eskimo culture is generally believed to have been Asian. Thus Denbigh can best be seen as one important kind—though only one—in the chain that connects Eskimo culture to its Asian origins.

DEPTFORD CULTURE, in southeast Georgia, is known as a transition in the development of Woodland pottery technique. It is part of the Cavdy Creek phase of the Burial Mound I period of Woodland Culture in the Southeast.

Three variations of stamping decorations with carved wooden paddles on vessels were developed. They were the check, linear, and complicated. Deptford pottery was a precursor of the complicated style of stamping curvilinear and rectilinear designs; it is apparent that more sophisticated experimentation with the checked and linear began in Deptford.

The same sense of transition is evident in burial sites. The large burial mounds at Deptford were constructed after the Cavdy Creek phase, but there are indications that small sand or earth burial mounds were built during Deptford.

DESCENT. *See* KINSHIP.

DESERT CULTURE is one of the stages of Archaic cultures that existed in the arid western United States. Covering a period from approximately 8,000 to 10,000 BC to AD 1850, the Desert Culture was rooted generally in the Archaic tradition of concern with total exploitation of subsistence resources and a gradual expansion of skills in using the food resources available, both animal and vegetable, and the culture is rooted specifically in the Archaic in its means of adapting to the ecosystem of the arid West.

The Great Basin had a semi-arid climate from 8,000 to 10,000 BC, when there was an extinction of big game. Thus, the culture is contemporary to the Lithic stage. The culture was quite stable, and, aside from a few regional differences, there is a basic complex of artifacts and cultural behavior that identify Desert Culture. The typical Desert inhabitants wore fur clothing, woven sandals and used a wide variety of instruments made from flint, bone, and vegetable fibers.

Some of the more prominent artifacts that have been found include the atlatl, small projectile points and knives, most often made by percussion chipped flaking, and flat and basin-shaped milling stones. They used special flint tools called pulpers, choppers and crude types of scrapers, wooden clubs, blunt points, tubular pipes or sucking tubes, vegetable quids, and shells.

They used caches for storing valuables and generally lived in caves. They practiced an intensive but unrestricted exploitation of their environment by hunting and gathering small seeds. Food was eaten in the form of mush and gruel.

There are three important variants of the Desert Culture. The best-documented is the Cochise Culture in southeast Arizona. The earliest sites were open by streams and the only evidence being the milling stone, which was used for milling seeds, hand-husked fruits and insects. Most important has been the discovery of modern fauna—the horse, camel and dire wolf—with Desert artifacts. The Mogollon (ancestral Pueblo) probably developed from this cultural base. Cochise apparently developed out of the Nevada-California complex, which developed specialties associated with its lake and marsh environment, although it took advantage of the full range of subsistence resources. The oldest of the variants seems to be the Oregon-Utah variant. Similar artifacts have been found at these sites, except that a wide range of footgear, including sandals woven from plant fiber as well as moccasins, have been found.

DESJARLAIT, ROBERT PATRICK (Chippewa; March 1, 1921-), is a commercial film artist known both for the original animations used to advertise Hamm's Beer and for serious paintings of the life of his people at Red Lake Reservations, Minnesota, done in fine-point tempera. Born at Red Lake,

Smithsonian Institution, National Anthropological Archives.

Hopi stone corrals at Oraibi, Arizona.

Desjarlait (also known as Nagawbo) has received several awards and has had numerous exhibitions and one-man shows.

DE WOLF, PERCY (Blackfoot; Dec. 15, 1904-), is a state senator of Montana (1959-) who chaired the Banking and Insurance and the Bills committees in the mid-1970s. born at Browning, Montana, De Wolf, who is a cattle rancher, previously served two terms as a member of the Montana House of Representatives.

DIAGUITA peoples, whose linguistic affiliation with other South American Indians is imperfectly known, have been extinct since the eighteenth century. At one time, the so-called "Diaguita world" occupied the largest portion of northwest Argentina and an extensive area in what is now Chile. The Chilean Diaguita seemed to have entered their region from the east across the Andes with an already developed culture and social organization. They are known solely through their archaeological remains. The Argentine Diaguita are known both through extensive archaeological investigations and a fairly good body of Spanish chronicles which makes it possible to reconstructd some of their social organization, especially their governmental and military practices.

Diaguita is a generic designation for a large number of societies, the best known of which is that of the Calchaqui, others being the Colalao, Tolombon, Quilme, Paccioca, Pular, Cayapan. These societies were all ruled by chiefs and made occasional alliances among themselves in time of war, especially against the Spanish invaders, but were not held together by a centralized government and were separated by certain cultural differences as well. Nevertheless, all these people shared an attenuated Central Andean culture, as did the Atacama immediately to the north of them. Their culture was markedly different from that of the peoples of the Gran Chaco to their east.

We know from architectural remains that there was a tripartite division of unfortified agricultural villages, fortified agricultural villages, and structures built in strategic places solely for purposes of military defense. The peaceful villages were built whenever possible along streams which provided the main source of water. The Diaguita seemed not to depend upon irrigation agriculture, even though the region was extremely dry. They had a characteristic Andean inventory of crops which were planted at the time of annual rains. Throughout the rest of the year, water was very scarce.

The villages were made up of a large number of individual houses which were made of *pirca*, a dry-masonry construction with pole and thatch roofs, again in the Andean tradition. The fortified sedentary villages, those with defensive works, were much larger than the unfortified villages and had granaries which

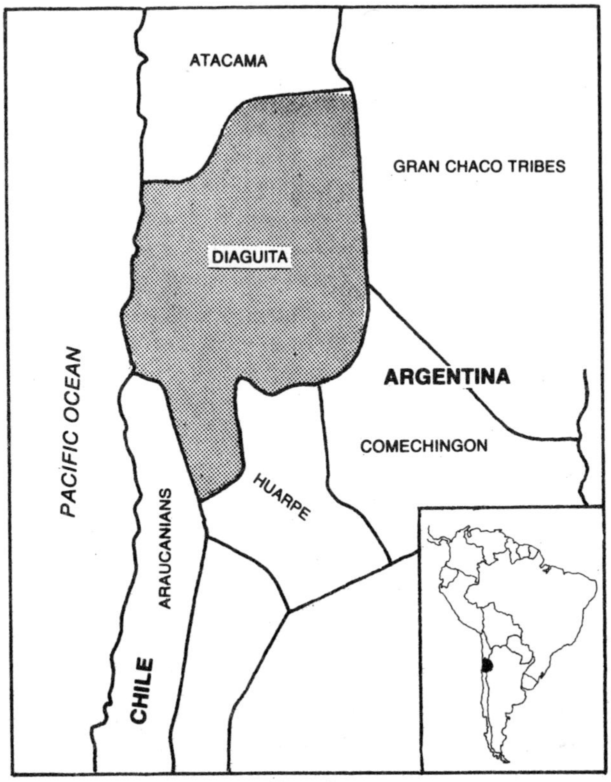

Diaguita

Handbook of South American Indians.

Diaguita designed pottery.

might have been built to provide emergency rations for the population when under military siege. Agricultural terraces were built to level the tillable land and for the purpose of holding rainwater. The third type of architectural remains, the fortifications, or *pucaras*, were located in strategically defensible places and had no agricultural lands around them, being temporary retreats during times of attack.

Very little information about the non-military social organization has come down to us through Spanish records, since the chroniclers paid most attention to warfare. Given the small size of Diaguita houses, the widespread existence of large extended-family groupings living under a single roof is most unlikely. Early Spanish census material indicates that family size was between four to five persons, but this was at a time when the overall population was declining rapidly under the ravages of the *encomienda* system.

There are a number of indications which support the probability that the Diaguita were patrilineally organized. Chieftainship was inherited along patrilineal lines from a man to his brother or to his son. Certain statements about marriage rules would also indicate patrilineal organization; for example; "a man must marry his dead brother's widow or widows." The descriptions of polygynous marriages and sororal polygyny might also indicate alliances between patrilineal descent groups.

Certain statements in the chronicle materials indicate the existence of ideas about age-grades among the Diaguita. One of these refers to the fact that men did not marry until relatively late in life, suggesting that there might have been a military age-set who were forbidden to marry until military service had been fulfilled and it had been replaced by another age-set. Another such statement has to do with circumcision rites which were celebrated on a societal level by a tribal shaman when young men reached puberty and changed age-group status, becoming warriors.

Some of the best information we have from the sources is about political organization. All sources agree that the Diaguita were essentially warlike and that they lacked any permanent governments but were divided up into many groups, each with its own leader.

Handbook of South American Indians.

Petroglyphs (reinforced with chalk) from the Diaguita region. (*Top*) Anthropomorphic figure from the Mesada Agüero. (*Bottom*) Anthropomorphs, serpents and animal tracks.

Handbook of South American Indians.

Diaguita plain pottery.

These small societies were completely independent of each other and chronically engaged in inter-tribal hostilities. After the arrival of the Spaniards, Diaguita resistence encouraged the development of federations of these small groups under the leadership of a single military leader. A similar but very special development took place when a Spanish adventurer, Pedro de Bohorquez, effected an alliance of 117 chiefs and their people, who posed the most serious rebellion against Spanish control of the area. Thus, the arrival of the Spaniards engendered the formation of large tribal alliances throughout Diaguita territory. Bohorquez is alleged to have taught the Indians how to use firearms and eventually horses. The Calchaqui, especially, became very skilled cavalrymen and used their horses in warfare against the Spaniards.

These Indian rebellions took on the aspect of total warfare against the Spaniards. Both sides attempted to destroy the economic resources of the other, especially the food supplies, burning wheatfields and maize crops and destroying settlements whenever possible. To defend themselves, the Diaguita usually retreated to their hilltop fortifications. To help break the power of the united Diaguita forces, the Spaniards resorted to the distant places, some to the Peruvian highlands and others as far away as Buenos Aires.

The Spaniards finally attained victory after a number of years and after having destroyed the basic agricultural economy of the Diaguita peoples, incorporating them first into the system of *repartimiento-encomienda* as a labor and tribute-paying force and later as workers on the *haciendas* and *estancias*. Nothing remains of Diaguita social, political, economic, or military organization, which was effectively destroyed by the early part of the eighteenth century. Even their traditional manufacturing techniques, such as "Calchaqui bronze" and magnificent pottery, their esthetic and recreational activities, ideas about sickness, death, and burial, their religious beliefs, and their organization of priests and shamans did not survive.

L. C. AND S. R. FARON

DICTIONARIES may be classified according to their intended uses. Native speakers, language learners, linguists, and others may have rather different needs. We find no dictionary of any American Indian language which meets the needs of all potential users at the same time.

The ideal bilingual dictionary will attempt to meet everyone's needs while being relatively comprehensive and usable. All users require an adequate and accurate orthography; native speakers and language learners will benefit from a practical rather than technical linguistic orthography. They also fare better when whole words are cited; entries of stems or roots may presuppose skills in segmenting meaningful pieces of words that natives and language learners lack. In all cases, the good dictionary will explain how it is to be used, including a description of those aspects of grammar which the user needs to understand in order to control references to conjugation classes, derivations, identification of stems, and idiosyncracies of whatever sort. The dictionary would do well to explain any of its own limitations, how the lexical material was collected, where the language is spoken, how it is related to other languages, and other such things.

Lexical material for the production of a dictionary of an American Indian language may and should be obtained in a number of ways. It can be elicited from universally and locally relevant word-lists. Vocabulary may be extracted from texts. All previous word-lists and dictionaries should be considered. Culturally salient semantic domains should be probed. Finally, phonological patterns of roots may be exploited. For example, Mayan languages tend to have monosyllabic roots of the form Consonant-Vowel-Consonant (CVC); a potential meaning can be sought for all the limited combinations of consonants and vowels in possible CVC forms.

Finally, the ideal dictionary will present instructive sample sentences illustrating the use of the word in context.

Various kinds of dictionaries have been produced for different American Indian languages. The earliest dictionaries were prepared by missionaries. Notable North American examples are Baragas 1853 for Ojibwa, Bruyas 1667 for Mohawk, Cotton 1830 of Massachusetts (Natick), Cuoq 1882 of Mohawk, LaCombe 1874 of Cree, Rasles 1833 of Abnaki, Riggs 1852 of Dakota, Sagard 1632 of Huron, Zeisberger 1887 of Onondaga and Delaware, etc. The earliest dictionaries prepared by Spanish priests of Latin American Indian languages were often excellent, later ones being frequently of much less value. Some of these very early dictionaries remain the best available for the particular languages. Some better known examples in Middle America are Alvarado 1593 of Mixtec, Ara *c.* 1550 of Tzeltal, Córdova 1578 of Zapotec, Cuidad Real *c.* 1590 of Yucatec, Gilberti 1559 of Tarascan, Molina of Nahuatl 1571, Vico *c.* 1550 of Cakchiquel, Tapia Centeno 1767 of Huastec, Zúñiga *c.* 1608 of Pokomchi, etc. Notable examples from South America are Bertonio 1612 for Aymara, Montoya 1639 for Guarani, Santo Tomas 1560 of Quechua, Gonzalez Holguin 1607 of Quechua, etc.

The simplist "dictionaries" are mere word-lists with glosses (see for a modern example Kuipers 1975 of Shuswap [Salish]). In many cases such word-lists are all that is known of varous extinct languages. Some very important early examples are Campanius 1696 of Susquehanna (Iroquoian), Cartier 1534 of Laurentian (Iroquoian), Thomas Jefferson 1836 of Unquachog (Connecticut) (Algonquian), Roger Williams 1643 of Narragansett (Algonquian), etc. The number of such lists for other extinct languages of the Americas is large.

"Vocabularies" are one-way bilingual dictionaries of restricted coverage. There are very few true dictionaries of native languages of the Americas, most fall under the "vocabulary" class. Vocabularies have been prepared, for example, by members of the Summer Institute of Linguistics (Wycliffe Bible Translators) for some fifty American Indian languages, largely in Middle and South America, but with several in North America as well. Two good examples of these are Schoenhals and Schoenhals 1965 for Mixe (353 pp.) (Mexico), and Reid and Bishop 1974 for Totonac (418 pp.) (Mexico).

Semantic-domain dictionaries organize entries by meaning categories relevant to the culture of the speakers of the language. An excellent early example is Pantaleón de Guzmán's (1704) for Cakchiquel (Mayan) (336 pp.). There are very few domain dictionaries for Indian languages. The best known examples are Austin 1972 for Navajo, the Franciscan Fathers 1910 also for Navajo, and Voegelin and Voegelin 1957 for Hopi.

True etymological dictionaries, concerned with the origin and history of words within a language or family of related languages, exist for no American Indian language or language family. There are, however, lists of cognate sets and of reconstructded lexical items which stand as good beginnings. Some examples are Miller 1967 for Uto-Aztecan, Kuipers 1970 for Salish, Kaufman 1964, 1969 for Mayan, Rensch 1976 for Otomanguean (Mexico), McLendon 1973 for Pomo (California), Girard 1971 Takanan (South America), etc.

Modern bilingual dictionaries of many American Indian languages exist in several guises. One kind is found as part of a more comprehensive linguistic description, including grammar, texts, and other relevant material, as well as the dictionary component. A model of this kind of treatment is Bright's (1957) description of Karok (California). Some others are Teeter 1964 for Wiyot (California), Chafe 1967 for Seneca (Iroquoian), Kuipers 1969 of Squamish (Salish), etc.

Some of the most comprehensive bilingual dictionaries of American Indian languages are rather technical in nature, using linguistic symbols, arranged according to roots, and so on. By far the most complete for any American Indian language is Laughlin's (1975) of Tzotzil (Mayan) with over 30,000 entries. Other notable examples are Hiojer 1974 for Navajo (over 10,000 entries), Sapir's and Swadesh's (1960) dictionary of Yana (California), Lira 1944 for Quechua (1,201 pp.), etc.

The following is a list of other reasonably well-known and representative dictionaries of North American Indian languages: Alford and Wayne 1976 Cheyenne, Barker 1963 Klamath, (Oregon), Berthelsen et al 1977 Greenlandic Eskimo (14,000 entries), Bloomfield 1975 Menominee, Bright 1967 Luiseño (Uto-Aztecan, California), Dorsey and Swanton 1912 Bilox and Ofo (extinct Siouan languages of the Southeast), Feeling 1975 Cherokee, Freeland and Broadbent 1960 Miwok (California), Haas 1953 Tunica (Louisiana), Krauss 1970 Eyak (Alaska), Michelson 1973 Mohawk, Newman 1958 Zuni, Powell and Woodruff 1976 Quileute, Sapir and Swadesh 1939 Nootka (Vancouver Island), Saxton and Saxton 1969 Papago and Pima (Arizona), Staff of the White Mountain Apache Culture Center 1972 Apache.

BIBLIOGRAPHY

Alford, Dan K. and Wayne E. Leman
1976 *English-Cheyenne Student Dictionary.* Lame Deer, Montana: The language research department of the Northern Cheyenne Title VII ESEA bilingual education program.

Alvarado, Francisco de
1593 *Vocabulario en Lengua Misteca.* Mexico.

Ara, Domingo de
c. 1500 Vocabulario en Lengua Tzeldal. Mexico.

Austin, Martha
1972 *Saad Ahaa Sinil.* Rough Rock, Arizona: Navajo Curriculum Center.

Baraga, Frederic
1853 *A Dictionary of the Otchipwe Language.* Cincinnati.

Barker, M.A.R.
1963 *Klamath Dictionary.* University of California Publications in Linguistics 31. Berkeley: Berkeley: University of California Press.

Berthelsen, C., I. Kleivan, F. Nielsen, R. Petersen, and J. Rischel
1977 *Ordbogi.* Copenhagen: Ministeriet for Gronland.

Bertonio, Ludovico
1612 *Vocabulario de la Lengua a y Mara.* (Reprint, facsimile edition, Julius Platzmann, Leipzig 1879.)

Bloomfield, Leonard
1975 *Menominee Lexicon.* Edited by Charles F. Hockett. Milwaukee Public Museum Publications in Anthropology and History, 3.

Bright, William
1957 *The Karok Language.* University of California Publications in Linguistics, 13. Berkeley: University of California Press.

Bright, William
1968 *Luiseño Dictionary.* University of California Publications in Linguistics, 51. University of California Press.

Bruyas, Rev. Jaques
1667 *Radices Verborum Iroquaeorum.* (Radical works of the Mohawk language). Edited by John Gilmary Shea. N.Y.: Cramoisy Press (1862).

Campanius, Johan
1696 *Vocabula Mahakuassica.* Ofwersatt pa American-Virginiske Spraket. Stockholm.

Cartier, Jacques
1534 *Laurentien Vocabulary* published in H.P. Biggar (1924), *The Voyages of Jacques Cartier.* Publications of the Public Archives of Canada, 11. Ottawa.

Chafe, Wallace
1967 *Seneca Morphology and Dictionary.* Smithsonian contributions to anthropology 4. Washington.

Ciudad Real, Fray Antonio de (Supposed author).
c. 1590 *Diccionario de Motul, Maya-Español.* Republished, edited by Juan Martinez Hernández, Mérida: Talleres de la Compania Tipográfica Yucateca (1929).

Córdova, Juan de
1578 *Vocabulario en Lengua Zapoteca.* Mexico.

Cotton, Josiah
1830 *Vocabulary of the Massachusetts (or Natick) Indian Language.* Collections of the Massachusetts Historical Society, series 3, 2.147-257. Cambridge, Mass.

Cuoq, Jean-André
1882 *Lexique de la Langue Iroquoise.* Montreal: J. Chapleau.

Dorsey, James Owen and John R. Swanton
1912 *A Dictionary of the Biloxi and Ofo Languages.* Bulletin of the Bureau of American Ethnology 47.

Feeling, Durwin
1975 *Cherokee-English Dictionary.* Edited by William Pulte. Tahlequah, Oklahoma: Cherokee Nation of Oklahoma.

Franciscan Fathers
1910 *Ethnologic Dictionary of the Navaho Language.* St. Michels, Arizona.

Freeland, L.S. and S.M. Broadbent
1960 *Central Sierra Miwok Dictionary.* University of California Publications in Linguistics, 23. Berkeley: University of California Press.

Gilberti, Maturino
1559 *Vocabulario en Lengua de Mechuacán.* Mexico. [Tarascan].

Girard, Victor
1971 *Proto-Takanan Phonology.* University of California Publications in Linguistics 70. Berkeley: University of California Press.

Gonzalez Holguin, Diego
1607 *Vocabulario de la Lengua General de todo el Perú Llamada Lengua Qquichua o del Inca.* Reprinted by Instituto de Historia, Universidad Nacional de San Marcos. Peru.

Guzmán, Pantaleón de
1704 *Compendio de Nombres en Lengua Cakchiquel.* Guatemala. Manuscript in Bibliothèque Nationale, Paris.

Haas, Mary R.
1953 *Tunica Dictionary.* University of California Publications in Linguistics 6.175-332. Berkeley: University of California Press.

Hoijer, Harry
1974 *Navajo Lexicon.* University of California Publications in Linguistics, 78. Berkeley: University of California Press.

Jefferson, Thomas
1836 *Vocabulary of Unquachog Recorded in 1791.* Published in Albert Gallatin, A synopsis of the Indian tribes. Transactions of the American Antiquarian Society 2.305-67 (1836). Manuscript in American Philosophical Society Library, Philadelphia.

Kaufman, Terrence S.
1964 *Materiales Lingüísticos para el Estudio de las Relaciones Internas y Externas de la Familia de Idiomas Mayanos.* Desarrollo cultural de los Mayas, ed. by Evon Vogt, 81-136. Special publication of the Seminario de Cultura Maya. Mexico.
1969 *Teco—A New Mayan Language.* International Journal of American Linguistics 35.154-74.

Krauss, Michael E.
1970 *Eyak Dictionary.* Cambridge: MIT, Department of Linguistics.

Kuipers, Aert H.
1967 *The Squamish Language: Grammar, Texts, Dictionary.* The Hague: Mouton.
1970 *Towards a Salish Etymological Dictionary.* Lingua 26.46-72.
1975 *A Classified English-Shuswap Word-List.* Peter de Ritter publications on Salish languages, 3. Lisse: Peter de Ritter Press. [1,800 items].

La Combe, Albert
1874 *Dictionnaire et Grammaire de la Langue des Cris.* Montreal [Cree].

Laughlin, Robert
1975 *The Great Tzotzil Dictionary of San Lorenzo Zinacantan.* Smithsonian Contributions to Anthropology, 19. Washington.

Lira, Jorge A.
1944 *Diccionario Kkechuwa-Español.* Tucuman, Argentina: Universidad Nacional de Tucuman [1,201 pp].

McLendon, Sally
1973 *Proto Pomo.* University of California Publications in Linguistics, 71. Berkeley: University of California Press.

Michelson, Gunther
1973 *Thousand Words of Mohawk.* National Museum of Man, Mercury Series, 5. Ottawa.

Miller, Wick R.
1967 *Uto-Aztecan Cognate Sets.* University of California Publications in Linguistics, 48. Berkeley: University of California Press.

Molina, Alonso de
1571 *Vocabulario en Lengua Castellana y Mexicana y Mexicana y Castellana.* Republished by Porrua (1970). Mexico.

Montoya, Antonio Ruiz de
1639 *Resoro de la Lengua Guarani.* Republished, Paris: Maisonneuve (1876).

Newman, Stanley
1958 *Zuñi Dictionary.* Publications of the Research Center of Anthropology, Folklore, and Linguistics, 6. Indiana University.

Powell, J.V. and Fred Woodruff
1976 *Quileute Dictionary.* Memoir 3, Northwest Anthropological Research Notes.

Rasles, Sebastian
1833 *A Dictionary of the Abnaki Language in North America.* Edited by John Pickering. Memoirs of the American Academy for the Advancement of Science 1.375-565. Cambridge, Mass.

Reid, Aileen A. and Ruth G. Bishop
1974 *Diccionario Totonaco de Xicotepec de Juárez, Puebla.* Serie de Vocabularios y diccionarios indigenas, 17. Mexico: Summer Institute of Linguistics.

Rensch, Calvin R.
1976 *Comparative Otomanguean Phonology.* Language Science Monographs, 14. Indiana University Press.

Riggs, Stephen R.
1852 *Grammar and Dictionary of the Dakota Language.* Smithsonian Contributions to Knowledge, 4. Washington. [Dictionary reprinted, ed. by James Owen Dorsey, in Contributions to North American Ethnology (1890). Washington.]

Sagard, Gabriel
1632 *Dictionnaire de la Langua Huronne.* Paris: Denys Moreau. Republished in Gabriel Sagard-Theodat, 1866, *Histoire du Canada*, 4. Paris: Librairie Tross.

Santo Tomas, Domingo de
1560 *Lexicón o Vocabulario de la Lengua General del Perú.* Peru.

Sapir, Edward and Morris Swadesh
1939 *Nootka Texts: Tales and Ethnological Narratives, with Grammatical and Lexical Materials.* Philadelphia: Linguistic Society of America.
1960 *Yana Dictionary.* Edited by Mary Haas. University of California Publications in Linguistics, 22. Berkeley: University of California Press.

Saxton, Dean and Lucielle Saxton
1969 *Dictionary, Papago and Pima to English. English to Papago and Pima.* Tucson: University of Arizona Press.

Schoenhals, Alvin and Louise C. Schoenhals
1965 *Vocabulario Mixe de Totontepec.* Vocabularios indigenas, 14. Mexico: Summer Institute of Linguistics.

Staff of the White Mountain Apache Culture Center
1972 *Western Apache Dictionary.* Fort Apache, Arizona: White Mountain Apache Culture Center. [2,600 entries].

Tapia Centeno, Carolos de
1767 *Noticia de la Lengua Huasteca.* Mexico: Imprenta de la Biblioteca Mexicana.

Teeter, Karl V.
1964 *The Wiyot Language.* University of California Publications in Linguistics, 37. Berkeley: University of California Press.

Vico, Domingo de
c. 1550 *Vocabulario de la Lengua Cakchiquel y Kiché.* Manuscript in the Bibliothèque Nationale, Paris.

Voegelin, C.F., and F.M. Voegelin
1957 *Hopi Domains: A Lexical Approach to the Problem of Selection.* Indiana University Publications in Anthropology, Folklore, and Linguistics, 14. Bloomington: Indiana University Press.

Williams, Roger
1643 *A Key into the Language of America.* London.

Zeisberger, Rev. David
1887 *Indian Dictionary.* Cambridge: John Wilson and Son. [Onondaga and Delaware].

Zúñiga, Dionysio
c. 1608 *Diccionario en Pochomchi.*

LYLE CAMPBELL

DIEGUENO were a coastal, hill and desert people found mainly in what is now San Diego County, California, and the northwestern corner of Baja California, from the Pacific Ocean inland over the Cuyamaca Mountains and out into the Colorado Desert. There is considerable confusion about the name *Kamia*, which is a native name that has also been applied to them, as some anthropologists gave the name *Kamia* to the people inhabiting the desert. The name *Diegueño* come to them from their association with the San Diego Mission. Their northern neighbors, the Cupeño and Luiseño, called them the *Kichamkuchum*, while their relatives, the Mohave, on the Colorado River, called them the "Kamia-shewe," which means the "Far-away Kamia."

Social and cultural boundaries and subdivisions

The Diegueño were a part of the Southern California Culture Area, which included the Shoshonean-speaking peoples to their north, such as the nearby Luiseño and Cahuilla, under whose descriptions it is more completely described than here. The Diegueño were divided mainly into the Northwestern Diegueño (Ipai) of northwestern San Diego County (from Del Mar north to Oceanside), the Southeastern Diegueño (Tipai), who lived around San Diego Bay and in the mountains and deserts to the east, and a division in the adjacent areas of northern Baja California (Metipai). There were no tribes as such and the principal political unit was the lineal family of rarely more than one hundred individuals.

Language

The Diegueño belonged to what was probably the most ancient language family in California, the Hokan, which included (among others) the Pomo and Karok in the north, the Chumash in the Santa Barbara area, and the Yuma and Mohave along the Colorado River to the east. The Diegueño were divided into at least five dialects, but with no great difference between them, of which the main two were the Ipai and Tipai.

Summary of tribal culture

Subsistence and economy. The Diegueño included some inland and desert peoples, but a denser population was found along the ocean and bay shores where their main subsistence consisted of fish, shellfish and seaweeds. Fish were captured with crude nets or with hooks made of ground pieces of shell; shellfish were pried with a stick tool from the tide pool rocks or dug from the mud flats with sticks. Seaweed was dried on rocks and wrapped in bunches to be stored in homes. Boats were used for fishing, principally the balsa rafts made of bound hollow reeds in bay waters (see POMO for a description of these boats), but fire-hollowed dugouts were used in the ocean as well as some of the Chumash-type board canoes (see CHUMASH), though not for the adventurous Chumash voyages out to sea.

Everywhere except in the desert areas acorns were a major portion of the diet, the cañon and live oaks being the main trees used (see POMO for common methods of leaching acorns to make them edible). They were

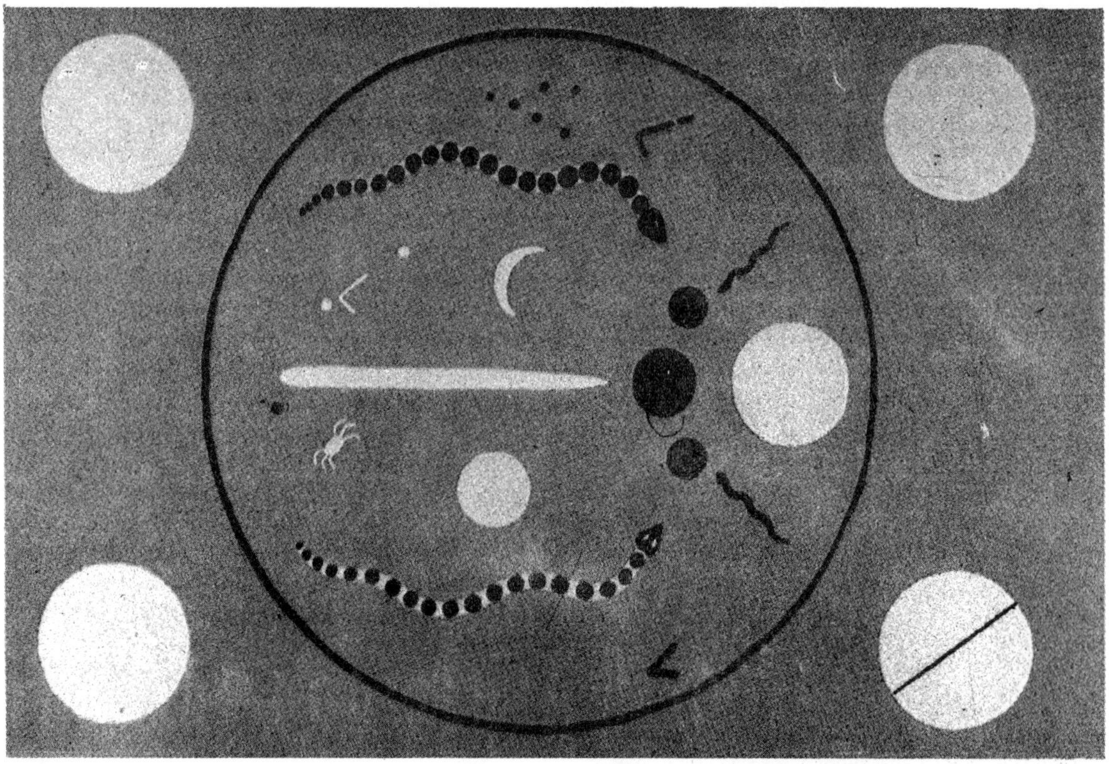

"The Coming of Age Initiation" for Diegueño boys. From a sand painting by David Villaseñor.

ground in hollows in the rocks or in stone mortars and boiled into mush or baked into bread in earth ovens. There were at least forty varieties of plants used by the Diegueño for food, of which seeds were the most common, eaten raw or parched and then ground up into flour for mush or bread. The long-sustaining chia seeds were popular in the hills, while the beans and seeds of the honey and screw mosquitos were major foods in desert areas. The striking-looking desert agave or mescal provides a wonderful example of the complete Indian use of plant foods. The huge heads or clusters of flower buds were extracted with a long sharp stick or bevel while the long sharp-spined leaves were cut off and used for needles. Seeds were ground into flour, while the blossoms of mature plants were parboiled, but preparing the ends and leaves was long and arduous, including baking in hot rock-lined pits for several days, after which they were cut into small portions and preserved as a rich food source for years. Like most Indian food-gathering times, it was a most joyous occasion, with the work interspersed by games, songs, stories and wild animal hunts in the neighborhood.

Hunting was done by using a rather poor bow made of mesquite or willow and the reed arrows were rarely, if at all, tipped with bone or stone. Hunting methods were so similar to those of the neighboring Cahuilla and Luiseño that accounts of these can be read under these tribes' names.

Technology. Houses were rather steep-roofed, the ridge pole held up by three posts and long branches or poles leaned against it through which brush are woven thickly until it could hold the weight of dirt or clay thrown upon it and patted down. the sweat house was differently shaped by four posts being placed in a square over which was set the steep roof. As usual in California, sweating was induced by fire alone, not by steam. This is the farthest south and east of the typical California sweat houses, the Yuma and Mohave along the Colorado River having none.

Pottery was made from reddish clay mixed with fine-crushed rocks, and was shaped with a stone or a wooden paddle as it was coiled and then fired to make the usual water jars and cooking pots. Basketry was mainly coiled and was used for bowls and plates, instead of their being made of pottery, also for carrying and storage baskets. But the most truly unique art of the Diegueño was the making of beautifully woven and decorated hand bags, usually of red and white milkweed strings.

Social and religious culture. Politically the Diegueño were based mostly on the extended family, though occasionally families united into what might be called a sib or clan and occupying together a large village, sometimes with subsidiary hamlets. Heads of families might join together to elect a village headman or chief. There are no moieties or marriage-relating divisions of the tribe, but marriages were made outside of the family.

The Northwestern and Southwestern Diegueño were distinguished from each other religiously by the Northwestern accepting considerable parts of the Chungichnich religion of the Shoshone-speaking Luiseños to the north, including the use of toloache or jimson-weed for producing visions and of initiations for boys using sand paintings, while the southwestern division was more influenced by the religion of the Colorado tribes such as the Yuma and Mohave with their emphasis on non-drug-induced dreams and the songs that stemmed from them. The Diegueño girls' puberty ceremony was apparently a more ancient rite, leaving out the tobacco-swallowing ordeal and the sand paintings of the northern peoples and using a warm, large crescent-shaped stone placed between the legs, evidently to prepare girls for easy childbirth. Diegueño sand paintings (see illustration) were much more realistic than the very symbolic sand paintings done to the north, demonstrating the more practical attitude toward life of the Diegueño.

The northern Diegueño had accepted the eagle feather dance and the fire dance (see LUISEÑO) from the northern peoples, but also used a distinctive dance of their own called the *Hortloi* (sometimes called a war dance), in which male dancers, arm-locked together in two rows, danced counter-clockwise in large circles, jumping and stamping alternately.

Brief history and present conditions. The Diegueño or Kamia were more stubbornly resistant to white conquest than most California tribes. The San Diego Mission was twice furiously attacked and once burned to the ground (in the 18th century). Passive non-violent resistance and non-cooperation followed in later years. Though much land was taken from the Indians, about nine small reservations in the mountains to the east and northeast of San Diego remain as protective areas in which some remnants of their culture and oral history has been kept.

VINSON BROWN

DIFFUSION, CULTURAL. No cultural pattern was ever created from scratch. Each is a patchwork of ideas old and new, ideas invented at home and borrowed from abroad. The present culture of the United States has elaborated and built on borrowed ideas, many from Native American sources. And Native Americans themselves, those First Americans, have from their earliest appearance in this hemisphere borrowed from one another and introduced to one another ideas brought from an Asiatic homeland. Pathways of diffused ideas and techniques can be traced sometimes in the ethnographic record—in the studies of living people, their habits and beliefs. Sometimes diffusion can be traced only through material objects used, discarded, buried in the earth, and retrieved from it.

From Old World to New—technology

Archaeologist Richard MacNeish reads in the changing styles of Paleo-Indian tool kits the results of three waves of diffusion from Asia and one from an

American center of invention. In archaeological terms, the Paleo-Indian Period is a time span stretching from some 70,000 years ago to about 9000. During these years, hunters pursued big game—mammoth, mastodon, giant sloth, giant buffalo, native horses, native camels, and others. First hunters made and used choppers and scrapers shaped roughly from nodules of glassy stone. Dr. MacNeish compares these to tool forms manufactured in the Far East at somewhat earlier times. Dates of arrival of this ancient tool kit and its diffusion through the Americas become firmer each year as new materials are excavated and new techniques for telling the time of antiquity devised.

About 40,000 years ago in North America, so Dr. MacNeish believes, sharp-edged implements, struck whole from pre-shaped stone cores, came into use. Called *flake tools*, they resemble others manufactured years ago in Asia. The technique itself appears to have been pioneered 100,000 years or so ago in Africa and Europe. After yet another time lag, flake tools made their way into South America.

By 20,000 years ago, First Americans had received the technique for producing elegant leaf-shaped points, pressure flaked on both faces. They were also making many objects carved of bone, including needles. Ideas were now diffusing more swiftly. The time lag between appearances in Old World and New, in North and South America was shorter.

Thirteen thousand years or so ago a new sort of projectile point came into general use. Invented in the New World, it was unique in displaying long flutes, concavities, on each face. The indentations may have been intended as anchors for bone splints used in hafting point to spear body.

Spear itself was soon given speed and thrust by means of a technique diffused from the Old World. The spear thrower, with a source of original invention in Upper Paleolithic Europe, probably arrived in the New World during Paleo-Indian times. The spear thrower was long to be the primary missile launcher for First Americans. Darts propelled by Aztec spear throwers, called *atlatl*, are said to have pierced Spanish armor. Everywhere except among Tarascan Indians of Mexico, the spear thrower gave way gradually to the bow and arrow, which may have been brought to this hemisphere by Nadene-speaking people some 3,000 years ago.

From Old World to New—ideas

Hunters the world over have watched night skies, traced constellations, and followed the cycles of the moon. As long ago as twenty thousand years, men of Europe were recording lunations on plaques of bone. Experimental archaeologist Alexander Marshak has so interpreted artifacts which, in other years, were called "hunting tallies."

In North America over the Plains from Canada to Texas are to be found more than a million circles of stone, some of them as large as 200 feet in diameter. They have been called "tipi circles" for want of a better explanation. Astronomer John A. Eddy believes they were celestial observatories designed to plot solstices or the risings of certain stars. From the most famous of these circles, the Bighorn Medicine Wheel of Wyoming, one radiocarbon date of AD 1750 has been obtained. Whether the wheel was built earlier is not certain. The pattern of its alignments, however, and those of similar Canadian wheels suggests to Dr. Eddy an antiquity of at least a thousand years. Artifacts found in association with other wheels suggest for them an initial construction four or five thousand years ago.

Did the ideas of celestial observation and recording diffuse from Europe through Asia? Possibly. Almost certainly it was from the skyward orientation of Paleo-Indian hunters, borne by them ever southward, that the astronomical and calendric genius of the Maya would develop in later times.

The hunter may lift his soul to a sky peopled with beings powerful and bright, beings whose benevolence must be celebrated at the proper astral cue. On earth he confronts still other powers, beings whom he hunts and by whom he is himself hunted. How can he relate himself to these beings, to animals he does not think of as "lower" but simply as "other?" How can he reconcile the competing claims of fear, need, and respect? Through ritual, as often as not. We see this in the caves of European Neanderthals where shrines enclosing cave bear skulls were built to celebrate the beast who was at once food and force.

Respect for the bear can be found all around the Arctic Circle among people who, to this day, call him Grandfather, Shaman, and Lord. For them he is a being who is never to be dishonored, never to be hunted with iron weapons, always to be celebrated in death by special ritual.(Indeed,the Chukchi of Eastern Siberia decline to whisper ill of the bear lest he hear and punish.)

The First Americans brought to this hemisphere that same reverence for the bear. It can be found today among hunters or among those who honor the hunter's memory. To Eskimo, the bear is "Great Lonely Roamer" or the "Great One Who Walks"—often as shaman in bear's skin. The width of a continent lies between the Ojibwa of the Great Lake region and the Salish of the Northwest Coast. Yet both have in earlier times paid equal honor to the bear. The hunter tendered apologies to the great shaman in disguise. Dead, he was carried home on the hunter's back, never dragged over the grond. His eyes were pried from their sockets and replaced with tobacco. And his remains were buried with honor and prayer.

Far to the south, the Navajo equate the killing of a bear with the killing of a man: both acts constitute murder, for both ceremonial purification must be undertaken. Among the Hopi, anciently in the Southwest, the Bear Clan was accorded most prestige, owned the important winter solstice rite, most often provided village leadership. The Zuñi in New Mexico have long delegated curing ritual to a special association, one whose members dress and dance as beasts and whose chief priest is privileged to wear the paws of the bear.

At this southern boundary, the power of the bear to stir wonder and imagination seems to wane, to give way to other animal themes at least two of which appear to have originated in Mexico and South America.

Within these shores—animal themes

The great Mexican artist, Miguel Covarrubias, long ago noted the importance of eagle, jaguar, and serpent as themes in religion and in art. Throughout the Americas Thunderbird, symbolized in eagle, condor, hawk, bore lightning, storm, and rain. The serpent—earth being, bringer of corn, culture hero—appeared as widely. In southern lands, however, it was jaguar who attracted the greatest number of attributes and carried the most compelling force. Aztecs associated him the rumbling earthquake, the starry sky, and Tezcatlipoca, the god of war and night. He signified both ceremony and rule. One of the few Maya writings to be transcribed in Roman letters is the *Chilam Balam,* the Book of the Jaguar Priest.

Like the northern bear, Jaguar was also the shaman's beast and even the shaman himself, for man and beast were one. Among rainforest tribes of South America, the belief is still widespread. The jungle is often said to harbor the shaman's jaguar double, or shaman becomes jaguar by donning the spotted pelt. Cubeo of the Northwest Amazon, so we are told by anthropologist Irving Goldman, believe that their supreme shamans consort with jaguars, kill as jaguars, and keep the great cat as ordinary folk might keep a dog. We hear less frequently of the jaguar under the mask of humanity. Yet this was a belief held by the Mexican Olmec, as anthropologist Peter Furst demonstrates in rare Olmec figurines.

Olmec is an Aztec name for people who live in the Veracruz region. Scholars have applied the same term to the mother civilization of Mesoamerica, which can be traced back to sometime before 1200 BC. One hesitates to call this an origin, for, as archaeologist Michael D. Coe points out, the oldest archaeological site in Veracruz reveals an Olmec phase already complex in structure and in skills. The god of the Olmec was part human, part jaguar, and very much baby. The baby aspect may symbolize, somehow, the connection between tears and rain, a connection the Aztecs were to make millenia later when babies (hopefully in tears) were sacrificed to Tlaloc, the rain god. The jaguar itself is an animal associated with water so that the combined themes may represent a welding of the hunter's reverence for the power beast to the farmer's natural anxiety about rain.

The appearance in rain-drenched Veracruz of a ritual complex focused on water may represent yet another example of diffusion. Corn is a plant domesticated in the dry highlands. The rain-wooing devotions and symbols which there attached to its cultivation must have traveled intact to find both acceptance and elaboration in lands where everything was wet.

The god as cat with fang and claw appears as well in the Chavin Cult of Peru with an estimated date of origin at 1000 BC. Whether he marks the trail of influences traveling southward or whether he is yet another transposition of the hunter's power beast cannot be told. We can, however, trace the continuity of the jaguar theme in Peru: from Chavin to the coastal cities and temple centers of 200 BC to the mountain empires of Huari and Tiahuanaco (AD 600-1000).

Within these shores—mound and temple building

Eagle, jaguar, and serpent can be seen most clearly where art served ritual directed toward community concerns. One would expect to find in the tall, pyramid-studded temple centers of Mesoamerica and Peru the animal themes sacred to the Americas. One finds them as well in the Mississippi Valley of North America in that vast complex of mound building which marks the Adena and Hopewell Burial Cults (1000 BC-AD 700).

Even though North American monumental construction differed in purpose from that in Mesoamerica, specialists have long traced impetus and origin to this source. Mound building now appears to have begun among northern Archaic folk who interred their dead in shell mounds or under even larger rock cairns until there developed in the Ohio region and points north a full-fledged cult of the dead. This cult required quite complicated treatment of the deceased, communal burials, and grave treasure of exquisite beauty and workmanship: ceramic figurines and pipes, beaten copper effigies, mica plaques, and quantities of river pearls. The avenues, circles, walls and ways of earth associated with burial mounds suggest ritual processions led by priests. Some scholars believe these rites were not entirely lost with the demise of the Hopewell folk but persisted, much modified, in the mourning and investiture rites of the historic Iroquois who built no mounds at all.

Sometime after AD 700, earthen structures of quite another sort began to appear in the Mississippi Valley. Temple mounds, these were, quite like those which mark the great centers of Mesoamerica. With them came art forms which do indeed bespeak the diffusion of themes both religious and political from Mexico. Perhaps they were brought by the long-distance traders already important in the Olmec Culture. Perhaps the ideas accompanied corn in its travels northward.

Within these shores—domesticated plants

Corn appears to have had a single source of domestication: in the dry highlands of Mexico (5000 BC). Dr. MacNeish has traced in the caves of Tehuacan Valley its evolution from a tiny, wild pod to the familiar ear. Beans and squash, on the other hand, may have been domesticated several times and in widely scattered locations. In the Andes, Dr. MacNeish has found domesticated beans dated to 5600 BC. The potatoes, both sweet and white, were ealy cultivated in the highlands and never traveled far afield. Manioc, that starchy and sometimes poisonous root, remained within these shores, a rainforest favorite. But tobacco, like potato and manioc, a South American cultigen, diffused throughout the hemisphere.

Its popularity may owe as much to religious meanings as to sensory stimulation. Among all peoples, the fragrant smoke, rising to the heavens, put a smoker in touch with the infinite. But even where tobacco was chewed or eaten or, mixed with liquids, drunk, it carried similar meanings: peach, reconciliation, purification, curing, sacredness. Nearly everywhere its use, and often its cultivation as well, was confined to men. North American pipe stems, as anthropologist Robert L. Hall points out, were often designed to resemble the *atlatl* and later the arrow. By joining symbolic weapon to tobacco and its use, a suspension of hostilities could be doubly reinforced.

Within these shores—metallurgy

First Americans early discovered that copper and gold nuggets could be beaten cold into desired shape. True metal smelting was invented in South America sometime before the beginning of the Christian Era. The exact place and date are as yet unknown. By AD 1, however, there had developed in Central America the skill to produce exquisite art works in metal by use of the use of the lost wax technique. By AD 800, metallurgy was known in Mexico.

Across the Pacific

The knowledge of ceramics represents an earlier technology. It is one thought by archaeologists Betty Meggers and Clifford Evans to be a gift from across the Pacific, one which was to be diffused throughout this hemisphere. The New World's oldest pot, found in a shell mound on the coast of Ecuador, has been dated by means of associated charcoal to more than 3000 BC. In form and style, the pot resembles those made at the time by fisher folk them living in the Japanese Islands. Could a boatload of such people, blown out to sea by typhoon and borne east by prevailing current, end their inadvertent journey in Ecuador? Dr. Meggers and Dr. Evans believe this to have been possible.

Other specialists disagree. Pottery very nearly as old and quite different in form and temper has been found by archaeologist Geraro Reichel-Dolmatoff in a shell mound on the Caribbean coast of Colombia. Colombian style ceramics appear to have been carried to Florida where they turn up in sites dated to 2500 BC or thereabouts. The line of march turned northward. In Virginia advancing pottery encountered a brisk trade in soap-stone vessels and effected a replacement. By 1000 BC ceramics were in use in the northeast. Here is or appears to be diffusion at its most obvious. Continued excavation may yet give evidence of many separate inventions of pottery—in addition to the Asiatic gift.

Dr. Meggers believes that a good deal more than pottery has been carried across the Pacific. She sees specific similarities in Olmec themes and art styles to themes and styles characteristic of China's oldest civilization—that of the Shag Dynasty, *c.* 1500 BC. The importance of the feline theme is perhaps the most striking similarity in Old World and New. Other Mesoamericanists are quick to note that Shang Civilization was riverine but not marine and that, since Olmec came to flower at much the same time as Shang, it is unlikely to be derivative.

Contacts in later times, however, have often been suggested. Boat forms and "totem poles" along the northwest coast of North America have been compared to similar phenomena in Oceania. In South America, the habit of chewing narcotic cocoa leaves with lime has been compared to betel nut and lime chewing among Pacific Islanders and in Southwest Asia. The source of Mesoamerican bark cloth and blowgun, feather cloaks and decor, pan pipes and accordion-shaped, bark cloth books all have been sought in Southeast Asia.

With the Europeans

Whatever the number and nature of contacts from across the Pacific—or over the Atlantic, for that matter—only those after 1492 were to bring permanent change to Native American cultures. Change came, not only through dominion and duress, but also by way of introduced artifacts and ideas diffused from tribe to tribe. Two items of Western Culture, introduced at much the same time in the grasslands of the two Americas, were to transform the life ways of nomadic hunters there. Horse and gun in the North American Great Plains and the South American Gran Chaco and Patagonia were to enhance native mobility, emphasize individuality in hunting, and make of warfare an elaborate game. This late-flowering lifeway was to become for many New Americans the very essence and image of the "Indian."

American culture and Native Americans

Ideas never travel down a one-way street. Whatever Native Americans borrowed in the way of ideas and technology, they repaid many times over. Mention the huge roster of plants domesticated in this hemisphere, mention rubber ball games invented in the home of rubber, and mention drugs long known to native healers, and the surface of contribution has barely been scratched. It is with Indian names that we identify the rivers, lakes, mountains, cities, and states of our childhood, the places we call home. There is yet more.

In those portions of North America where English colonists and strong tribal groups remained for long in a kind of balance, something of the perceived character of Native Americans was added to the New Americans' image of themselves. Something of the persistent sense of personal equality in Indian tribal law left its imprint in the laws meant to define and govern a great nation. Whatever is unique in the collective Amerian personality and way of life owes much to diffusion from the forerunners, the earliest pioneers, the First Americans.

OLIVIA VLAHOS

DIGGING STICKS were used primarily by agricultural tribes for cultivation operations such as clearing land, loosening soil, planting, weeding, irrigation, and building up the soil around growing corn and other crops.

The simplest tool consisted of a hardwood staff with a flattened and edged end and was used in the northeastern United States, southeastern Canada, and parts of the Southwest. In the northeastern regions implements of this type were provided with a footrest on one side.

Hoes and spades, digging tools with a flat-edged blade, were used commonly throughout the Eastern Woodlands, Southeast, Prairies, and to some extent in parts of the Southwest. The blades frequently were made from bone, particularly the shoulder blade of buffalo or deer. Some blades were of wood, especially where large shoulder blades were scarce. Stone, shell, and fishbone blades were also used.

Numerous chipped flint and some ground stone blades have been found in the Mississippi and Ohio valleys. These are roughly elliptical-, fan-, or rectangular-shaped, and the tops of many are stemmed, notched, or provided with side points for attaching the handle. The larger blades, some as long as one foot, are often classified as spades and the smaller or notched blades, as hoes. Most, however, could have been helved in either way.

DIGHTON ROCK. For approximately 300 years, the ancient, probably prehistoric, inscription on Dighton Rock, a large, silicious rock on the shore of the Taunton River in Bristol County, Massachusetts, has intrigued scholars. It is 11½ feet long, 5 feet high and is covered with irregular lines and outlines of figures, some resembling rivers.

The rock is probably one of the most copied of all artifacts. Damforth transcribed it in 1680, as did Cotton Mather in 1690; they were followed by a host of others. The number of theories of the origin of its inscription is almost as numerous as transcriptions. It has been described as Punic, Siberian, Roman

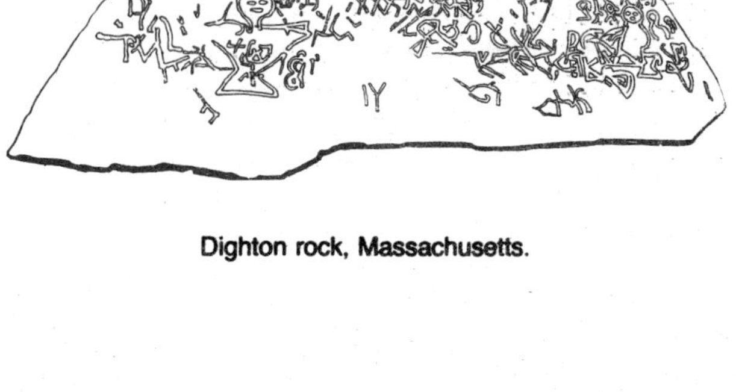

Dighton rock, Massachusetts.

Catholic ciphers, and as Indian ("translated" by an Algonquin chief who claimed it was the story of a battle between two tribes). It probably is from the ancestors of a tribe from the west Pennsylvania area.

DIRIAGEN. A powerful Indian chief of Central America at the time of the Spanish conquest, Diriagen (or Diriangen) led a tribe named after him, the Dirianes. They were probably related to the numerous Chorotegan peoples of Nicaragua. Diriagen's name is preserved in the modern town of Diriamba.

Early in the sixteenth century, Diriagen assembled a large army and acquired a substantial treasure of gold ornaments. He made his stronghold in the hilly regions around Diriamba on the Pacific coast, south of the modern Nicaraguan capital of Managua, in the Carazo area. (Diriamba in the Chorutegan language means "big hill"). Diriagen thus dominated the triangle formed by the Pacific and the two large lakes Nicaragua and Managua. So, when the Spanish explorer Gil González Dávila entered Nicaragua from the Pacific side in April of 1522, he was met by the rich and wily Indian leader.

Diriagen nearly outwitted the Spanish. He greeted them with a large retinue laden with foods and gifts. González Dávila received Diriagen affably, accepted the gold, and immediately offered the tribe baptism into the Catholic faith. Diriagen asked for three days' time to ponder the situation. Feeling himself master of the situation, the Spaniard allowed the Indians to withdraw to discuss their conversion.

In fact, Diriagen and his soldiers plotted a bold sneak attack by night on the invaders. But one of Diriagen's men opportunistically revealed the plot to González Dávila, who was consequently prepared for action. Though the Indians fought tenaciously in the face of their obviously ruined strategy, the Spanish were able to beat them back and take control of the area.

It is uncertain whether Diriagen died or fled to the hills, but no one thereafter could organize any opposition to the Spanish in the fertile Carazo highland. In their first intrusion in the Pacific regions of Nicaragua, the Spanish had, by a narrow escape, been triumphant.

DISCOIDAL STONES are circular-shaped objects whose great variety has made it especially difficult to pinpoint their use.

Their shape can vary greatly. Their perimeter is circular, the diameter can vary from 1 to 8 inches, and their thickness can vary from ¼ to 6 inches. Some are convex on only one side and flat on the other, while concave stones are concave on both sides. They can have the slope of a double convex or double concave lens. The latter often have a depression in the center, which sometimes is so large that the stone is a ring.

The first name given to these stones was chunky stones, from the name of a game played with them by Indians in the Southwest. Three types have been identified: (1) perforated (least common), (2) symmetrical unperforated, (3) assymetrical unperforated. The gradation from one kind to the next is almost imperceptible. The smooth, polished chunky stones gradually become pestles, mortars, banners, and polishing and grinding stones and then ornaments.

They were probably used in all of these stages, and although they cannot be universally classified, they can be distinguished within particular geographic areas.

DISEASE among Indians in prehistoric America is difficult to determine. Historic accounts by Indians and early white observers as well as examination of aboriginal artifacts and skeletal remains indicate that the Indians north of Mexico at the time of initial European contact had relatively good health in comparison to their European contemporaries. Indians were by no means free of ailments aboriginally, but were comparatively well nourished, physically well conditioned, free from deformity, and free of many contagious diseases present in other societies. From the time of the first colonial settlements to the end of the 19th century, the Indians' general state of health radically deteriorated. The trend was at least reversed for most tribes during the twentieth century, but as of the 1970s Indian health conditions remained markedly poorer than those of the general population of the Americas.

Aboriginal health and disease were strongly influenced by the high level of physical activity and close relationship to the natural environment of the Indian way of life. Periodic food scarcity, severe climatic conditions, and injury while hunting and fishing or during combat were significant dangers. Infant mortality was high, and there was a tendency toward types of illnesses associated with a physically stressful life-style. Among individuals who survived to adulthood, hereditary and congenital deformities and infirmities were relatively rare. Endurance and other factors of physical conditioning were comparatively high. Minor injuries were probably common, but healing of wounds was rapid, resistance to infection high, and bone fractures were relatively rare. Foot problems such as fallen arches were rare. Accounts of early observers mention longevity among healthy individuals as being not uncommon, with several reports of individuals close to or over 100 years old. Older persons who became sick or unable to care for themselves were generally cared for by sedentary tribes, but in severe environments, as in many northern areas, they frequently could not be kept alive.

The chief diseases afflicting aboriginal Indians appear to have included: dysentery and other digestive disorders, eye disorders, ear infections, pneumonia and other respiratory ailments, pleurisy, arthritis, and rheumatism. Patterns of disease varied with locality and means of subsistance. Several diseases which appear to have been present but relatively rare include neurological disordres, heart disease, arteriosclerosis, and cancer. Dental disorders were rare, being most frequent among farming tribes who ate a great deal of maize. Diseases of the skin and psychological disorders found in more advanced societies were comparatively rare.

USDA—Foreign Agriculture Relations.

Holding a little boy, who is hospitalized for malnourishment, is American-trained Medical Director, Dr. Juan Antonio Gomez of Lorencita Villegas de Santos Children's Hospital in Bogota, Colombia (1965). The hospital, which specialized in cases of undernutrition and malnutrition, received U.S. foods from CCC stocks of the Department of Agriculture.

Most recent authorities agree that scarlet fever, typhoid, cholera, diphtheria, smallpox, measles, malaria, and yellow fever were absent north of Mexico. There is no well authenticated evidence of gonorrhea and syphilis. As white settlements spread throughout the continent, the Indians' lack of immunity to and treatments for these introduced diseases resulted in many epidemics causing great suffering and high mortality in the three centuries after the first European settlements. Tuberculosis was apparently absent or rare among aboriginese, but after continuous contact with whites it became common and reached epidemic proportions among many tribes. Alcoholic beverages were introduced widely through trade with Europeans. Alcohol had been used aboriginally, generally sparingly, in parts of the Southwest and Southeast. After its introduction elsewhere, its overuse became a major and persistent health problem for many Indians.

Aboriginal diets, though frugal, were generally better balanced than those of European contemporaries. The primary nutritional problem was food scarcity, which in some areas such as the Great Basin and parts of the farth north was a constant threat, but which for most tribes was seasonal or otherwise periodic. Analysis of the probable diets for various parts of aboriginal North America indicates that tribes who depended nearly totally on hunting and fishing were generally well nourished except during periods of scarcity, as were tribes who depended predominantly on meat but supplemented it substantially with vegetable foods. Tribes who depended almost entirely on gathering wild plant foods or on farming apparently suffered some degree of protein deficiency. Vitamin and mineral deficiencies were uncommon and localized. Generally, micronutrient deficiencies seem to have been somewhat more likely to occur among tribes who depended a great deal on farming.

Nutrition underwent sharp changes after European contact. The major initial pattern was a lowering of protein and micronutrients in the diet due to depletion of game animals. Reinforced by forced migrations from native territories, malnutrition and starvation became common. Overcrowding and dietary deficiencies present after settlement on reservations further reinforced the frequency and seriousness of nutritional disorders as well as of native and introduced infectious disease. During the 20th century, improved medical and nutritional care and the migration of some Indians off reservations has somewhat alleviated these conditions.

USDA—Foreign Agriculture Relations.
A medical clinic in Bolivia, 1940s.

Estimates of the aboriginal population north of Mexico at the time of the arrival of Columbus vary enormously. The estimate of one recent authority, which lies between extremes of earlier estimates, of the population of the area now constituting Canada, Greenland, and the continental United States including Alaska is roughly 3,500,000. The Indian population at that time was probably increasing slowly in most areas. According to the same estimate, by the end of the 19th century, famine, disease, and war had reduced the total Indian population to roughly 450,000. During the 20th century, with stabilization of white settlement and some improvement of medical and nutritional conditions among Indians, population declines for most groups were reversed. Among some tribes population increase has become rapid enough to significantly add to the difficulty of alleviating nutritional disease problems.

As of 1980, infant mortality was much higher and life expectancy lower among Indians than in the general population. Death from cancer, heart disease, and stroke was relatively less frequent. Diseases such as typhoid, cholera, diphtheria, and smallpox had been largely eliminated among Indians along with the general population through immunization programs and improved sanitation, although the latter measure was still seriously inadequate on many reservations. Most common contagious diseases, including eye and ear infections, measles, veneral disease, and hepatitis were several times more prevalent among Indians. Death resulting from diseases such as tuberculosis, intestinal infections, influenza, and pneumonia occurred with significantly greater frequency. Protein and micronutrient deficiencies serious enough to impair mental and physical activity and resistance to disease were still common.

DISMAL RIVER CULTURE existed in western Nebraska, Kansas and eastern Colorado. It is particularly important because it provides an insight into Athapascan Apache tribes that had moved into the area from the west and north and later moved south.

Evidence at sites in Nebraska is clearly Apache, dating from AD 1600. However, additional evidence indicates a settlement existed as early as AD 500, well before Athapascans lived there. The Dismal River inhabitants were probably descendants of an older culture. They practiced some corn agriculture in addition to their primary buffalo-hunting activity. The Apaches who lived here later moved into the Southwest and displaced Pueblo tribes. It has been posited that Apache agriculture was influenced by this culture rather than by the Puebloes. Although this issue has not been resolved fully, the Dismal River Culture undoubtedly exercised some influence on the Athapascans.

DIVORCE, the dissolution of the bonds of marriage, was generally easily accessible to Indians. Among the

Eskimos, the slightest excuse sufficed for either partner to pursue divorce. Children usually remained with their mother and remarriage was not prohibited. Divorce on the Northwest coast was also easy to come by, but the man had to return his wife's dowry if he could not show sufficient cause for his action; if he did show good cause he might demand the return of the wedding gifts he had given to his wife. In southern California the procedures were much the same. In this region, the man could keep the children, in which case he could demand only half of what he originally had paid for his wife.

The Hidatsa, among whom divorce was common early in a marriage, experienced divorce less frequently the longer a marriage lasted. A Hidatsa woman could simply tell her husband to leave her lodge, and this would constitute a divorce. If the couple lived in the husband's lodge, however, the man might be reluctant to tell his wife to leave unless he had not paid a price for her; otherwise a divorce would simply constitute a financial loss for him. Children commonly stayed with their mother, although in some cases the father kept them. Among the Kiowa-Apache, older children had the right to choose with which parent they would stay.

DOCKSTADER, FREDERICK J. (Oneida-Navajo; Feb. 3, 1919-), is a distinguished anthropologist, author, and expert on Indian arts. He was born at Los Angeles, California, and spent much of his early life on the Navajo and Hopi reservations in Arizona.

After an early teaching career, Dockstader became a staff ethnologist at the Cranbrook Institute of Sciences (1950), and he later became the curator of anthropology at Dartmouth College (1952). He joined the staff of the Museum of the American Indian, Heye Foundation, in New York city as assistant director (1955) and became director in 1960. Dockstader, a practicing silversmith, was named the commissioner of the Indian Arts and crafts Board of the U.S. Department of the Interior in 1955. His publicatons include *Indian Art in America* (1961), *Indian Art in Middle America* (1964), *Indian Art in South America* (1967), and *Pre-Columbian Art and Later Indian Tribal Arts* (1968).

DODGE, ATLEE A. (Menomini; April 10, 1934-), is a tribal and civic leader. A founding member and registered agent and secretary of the Menominee Indian Tribe of Wisconsin, Inc., he managed and supervised the tribe's assets in the mid-1970s. Dodge served as a salesman for lakefront property belonging to the tribal development company. He worked to gain hunting and fishing rights for the Menomini, and was of assistance when the reservation acquired legal status as a Wisconsin county, no longer under federal supervision, in 1961.

Dockstader, Frederick J.

DODGE, HENRY CHEE (Navajo; fl. early 20th century), was the first chairman of the Navajo Tribal Council. He was one of the three members of the Navajo "Business Council" established in 1922 to negotiate oil leases with refining companies. On July 27, 1923, the Navajo Tribal Council was formed and Dodge was chosen as the chairman. In 1933 he worked with John Collier, the U.S. Commissioner of Indian Affairs, in a program to reduce the number of livestock on the reservation. Although the program was opposed by many Navajo, it is credited by many with having saved the natural resources of the Navajo from complete destruction.

DOG. Since human beings entered the Western Hemisphere via the Bering Strait from Siberia some 25-30,000 years ago, the domestic dog (*Canis familiaris*) has played an important role in the lives of the native peoples of the Americas.

Due to the extreme difficulty of determining the domestic status of canids on the basis of skeletal remains, few specific details are known of the early relationship between dogs and humans in the Western Hemisphere. We can assume that in the case of the earliest examples, such as the dog recovered from Jaguar Cave in the Birch Creek Valley of Idaho, the animal may have served as a companion in the hunt, or possibly as an item of consumption itself. Dating to approximately 8,400 BC, the Jaguar Cave dog is the earliest clearly documented domestic dog recovered to date in the Western Hemisphere.

As most of the original domestic dogs in North America are probably derived from the northern wolf (*Canis lupus*), it is not surprising that a number of early sites in the Arctic and Subarctic have produced remains of canids provisionally assigned domestic status.

From an overview of the data, it seems apparent no evidence exists for the use of domestic dogs as traction animals for hauling sleds until comparatively recent times. While this lack of evidence may be a function of poor preservation in the archaeological record, it is apparent that once established, the tradition became a very widespread phenomenon.

Table 1: Early Domestic Dogs from the Arctic and Subarctic Regions of North America

SITE/REGION.	PHASE OR CULTURAL AFFILIATION	TIME RANGE	PROBABLE USE
Namu, British Columbia	Paleoarctic Tradition	7000-6000 BC	Aid in Hunting
Glenrose Cannery, British Columbia	Paleo-plateau Tradition	c. 5000 BC	Aid in Hunting
Iglulik Region, N. Canada	Pre-Dorset Culture	2000-1000 BC	Aid in Hunting
Belcher Islands, Hudson Bay	Dorset Culture	1000 BC-AD 500	Aid in Hunting
Numerous Alaskan Sites	Thule Tradition	AD 100-1800	Hunting and beasts of burden

The southwestern portion of the United States has produced not only the largest quantity of early domestic dog remains in the Western Hemisphere, but has also generated the greatest amount of research on the subject. An environment favorable to the preservation of organic remains has been largely responsible for this abundance. Research has yielded evidence for a variety of breeds of domestic dogs in the American Southwest by at least the beginning of the Christian Era, and probably much earlier.

Possibly the earliest domestic dog in the Southwest was recovered in levels 7 and 8 of the Upper Member at Ventana Cave, Arizona. Dating perhaps as early as 2500 BC this domestic dog has been designated as such on the basis of firm osteometric evidence.

There remains considerable doubt as to the domestic status of these canids.

Two well-preserved mummies from White Dog Cave, near Kayenta, Arizona, are among the earliest examples of vastly different breeds of dogs in the Western Hemisphere. Dating between AD 1 and AD 450, these Basketmaker II culture dogs may have been kept as pets in addition to serving as aids in hunting game.

Archaeological sites associated with later cultures often produce remains of numerous domestic canids.

Table 2: Selected Early Domestic Dogs from the Western United States

SITE/REGION	PHASE OR CULTURAL AFFILIATION	TIME RANGE	PROBABLE USE
Jaguar Cave, Idaho	Paleo-Indian	c. 8400 BC	Aid in hunting
Ventana Cave, Arizona	Cochise Culture	c. 2500 BC	Aid in hunting
White Dog Cave, Arizona	Basketmaker II Culture	AD 1-450	pet and aid in hunting
Mancos Canyon, Colorado	Pueblo I to Pueblo III Cultures	AD 800 1150	pet and aid in hunting
Black Mesa, Arizona	Pueblo II to Pueblo III Cultures	AD 1000-1200	pet and aid in hunting
Pueblo Bonito, New Mexico	Pueblo II Culture	c. AD 1050	pet and aid in hunting
Grasshopper Pueblo, Arizona	Late Mogollon Culture	c. AD 1275-1400	pet and aid in hunting
*Awatovi, Arizona	Historic Hopi Culture	AD 1629-1701	pet and aid in hunting

*Represents an early introduction of European (Spanish) domestic dogs into the traditional Amerindian lifeway.

Domestic dogs from White Dog Cave, Marsh Pass near Kayenta, Arizona. Basketmaker II Culture (AD 1-450

By Pueblo times (beginning about AD 700) the American Southwest was undoubtedly characterized by diverse breeds of dogs that fulfilled a variety of functions ranging from hunting companion to beast of burden (sleds and travios) to domestic pet.

Early domestic dogs are known from the eastern United States as well. Domestic dog remains were recovered from post-glacial deposits in Coles County, Illinois (see Table 2). Found in questionable association with the skeleton of an American Mastodon (*Mammut americanum*), these finds, if proven to be those of a *domestic* animal, may represent one of the oldest domestic dogs in North America (perhaps 10-12,000 years old).

A 7500 year-old domestic dog has been recovered from the Archaic Rodgers Shelter in Benton Couunty, Missouri, and at the famous Middle Archaic Koster Site in Greene County, Illinois, remains of a domestic dog 7,000 years old have been uncovered. The Koster dog was subjected to ritual interment—an interesting occurrence if it is true, for by 5000 BC, the practice of ritual dog burials had been established in the Midwest.

On the Eastern Seaboard, the recovery of domestic dogs has been made from New York state and from Martha's Vineyard. During the Frontenac Phase (*c.* 2500-1800 BC) of the Late Archaic in New York, dogs were commonly buried with people attesting to their symbolic significance. During the Frontenac Phase dogs were placed in male burials.

Table 3: Selected Early Domestic Dogs from the Eastern United States

SITE/REGION	PHASE OR CULTURAL AFFILIATION	TIME RANGE	PROBABLE USE
Polecat Creek, Illinois	Paleo-Indian	*c.* 12,000-10,000 BC	aid in hunting?
Rodgers Shelter, Missouri	Early Archaic Culture	*c.* 5500 BC	ceremonial, hunting aid
Koster Site, Illinois	Middle Archaic Culture	*c.* 5000 BC	ceremonial, hunting aid, pet
Various New York Sites	Late Archaic, Frontenac Phase	*c.* 2500-1800 BC	ceremonial, hunting aid, pet
White's Mound, Georgia	Deptford Culture	*c.* 500 BC	ceremonial, hunting aid, pet
Various Ohio Sites	Hopewell Culture	*c.* AD 1-200	ceremonial, hunting aid, pet

The presence of domestic dogs in nearly all U.S. sites that are Archaic or later in age attests to the importance of these animals in the variety of Amerindian cultures manifest by that time.

Early domestic canids from the southeastern United States are fewer in number although specimens exist from Kentucky and Alabama as well as from Georgia.

Early domestic dogs from Mexico and Central America

As in the case of South America, to be discussed below, very little is known of canid domestication in Mexico and Central America prior to about 3500 BC.

The earliest domestic canids in Mesoamerica, at present, are associated with the Abejas Phase (3500-2300 BC) of the Tehuácan Valley sequence from southeastern Puebla, Mexico. Not much can be said about these dogs other than they were probably consumed regularly.

Some of the earliest unquestionable domestic dogs from Mexico have been recovered from sites of the Olmec culture, such as the one at San Lorenzo, Veracruz (1500-700 BC). The discovery of juvenile dog remains at San Lorenzo that are unquestionably the refuse of consumption has been reported. Here, at San Lorenzo, we have definite proof that the dog was being bred as a source of protein as early as 1500 BC—a tradition in Mexico carried on by later peoples, such as the Aztec to be discussed below.

About 8000 BC, during the Middle Formative Period of Mexican prehistory, dogs are represented in collections of ceramic figurines recovered from the archaeological context. Among other subjects, these artifacts depict dogs being carried affectionately by women, clearly indicative of their role as a domestic pet. Undoubtedly, dogs were also consumed during the Middle Formative Period.

With the rise of the Aztec or Mexica civilization about AD 1200, the region of central Mexico witnessed a great cultural fluorescence.

Sites associated with this period, termed the Late Postclassic (AD 1200-1520) have produced remains of a wide variety of domestic dogs including a hairless breed known as *xoloizcuintle* by the Aztecs. The xoloizcuintle, whose name means in Nahuatl, "he who snatches his food with teeth as sharp as obsidian and who represents the god Xolotl," was a very important animal to the Aztecs for economic as well as ceremonial reasons. In addition to being eaten, the hairless breed was valued as a living hot-water bottle for the treatment of arthritis, and a xoloizcuintle was usually placed with a corpse upon burial to serve as a guardian on the trip to a place of eternal rest.

With the arrival of the Spanish in the early 16th century AD, new forms of European dogs, previously unknown to the Amerindians, were introduced. Accustomed to much smaller breeds, a typical Aztec description of a Spanish canine is, "And their dogs were very large. They have fiery eyes—blazing eyes; they had yellow eyes—fiery yellow eyes. They were very tall." Many early Spanish accounts describe the use of large dogs in Mexico and Florida to subdue the indigenous populations of these regions.

In southern Mexico and Central America, the presence of the dog is not well documented before the Middle Preclassic (900-300 BC). The recovery of domestic dogs from a Maya site at Siebal in Guatemala has been reported. Here, by about 600 BC, at least two beeds of dogs were known, strongly suggesting a much earlier ancestry for domestic dogs in the area.

Dogs are also depicted in the written records of the Mixtec, Aztec, and Maya, where they often conveyed negative connotations such as "worthless rains" or a skin infection. Thus, we may see that the domestic pervaded many aspects of life in Mexico and Mesoamerica and served a variety of purposes in so doing.

Domestic canid remains recovered in South America

Less is known of the history and dynamics of canid domestication in South America than in regions to the north.

The evidence for what may represent the earliest domestic canid in South America suggests the Falkland Island Wolf (*Dusicyon australis*). Historic records exist that indicate members of the genus *Dusicyon* were tamed if not domesticated for use as hunting companions by the Amerindian inhabitants of the Falkland Islands (Islas Malvinas), off the southern coast of Argentina. Although there is no archaeological evidence as yet to support such a position the possibility exists that South America may be viewed as a separate hearth of dog domestication utilizing *Dusicyon* as a basal ancestral stock in contrast to the wolf (*Canis lupus*) of Central and North America.

What may be the earliest domestic from the South American continent has been recovered from early Holocene Paleo-Indian sites such as Chobshi Cave, Ecuador; Hacienda los Toldos, Patagonia, Argentina; and Tagua-Tagua, Chile. These remains have yet to be established as domestic animals, however. Their early date (around 10,000 BC) however, and the fact they are associated with human material culture and remains of animals frequently hunted with dogs today, makes these finds especially interesting.

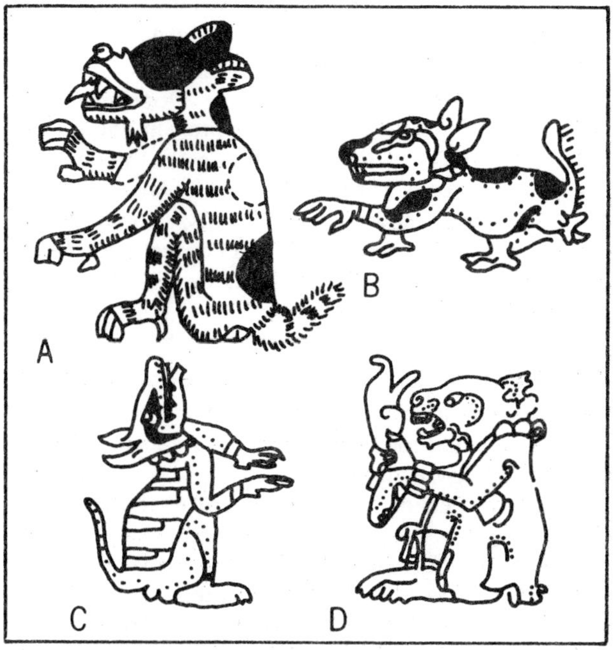

Representations of the domestic dog in Mixtec and Maya codices dating prior to the Spanish Conquest in the 16th century AD. A. Dog from Codex Nuttall (Mixtec, pre-Conquest). B. Dog from Codex Tro-Cortesianus (Maya, pre-Conquest). C. Dog from Codex Tro-Cortesianus (Maya, pre-Conquest). D. Dog from Codex Dresden (Maya, pre-Conquest).

Table 4: Selected Early Domestic Dogs from Mexico, Central, and South America

SITE/REGION	PHASE OR CULTURAL AFFILIATION	TIME RANGE	PROBABLE USE
Tehuacán Valley, Puebla, Mexico	Abejas Phase	3500-2300 BC	food and hunting companion
San Lorenzo, Vera Cruz, Mexico	Olmec Culture	1500-700 BC	food and hunting companion, pet
Tlatilco, Valley of Mexico	Middle Formative Period	food and c. 800 BC	hunting companion, pet
Chupicuaro, Guanajuato, Mexico	Preclassic Period	400 BC-AD 1	ceremonial
Various Aztec Sites, Mexico	Mexica Culture	AD 1200-1521	ceremonial, food, pet
Seibal, Guatemala	Middle Preclassic Maya Culture	600-300 BC	ceremonial, food, pet
Lighthouse Site, Puerto de Supe, Peru	Cupisnique (Chavin) Culture	c. 1400-700 BC	ceremonial, food, pet
Ancon, Peru	Chancay Culture	AD 900-700 BC	ceremonial, food, pet
Macchu Picchu, Peru	Inca Culture	c. AD 1500	ceremonial, pet

There exists a substantial hiatus in our knowledge of South American dog domestication between the appearance of dogs in Paleo-Indian contexts at the close of the Pleistocene (*c.* 12,000 years ago) and late prehistoric times (*c.* 2,000 years ago) when the record becomes more complete.

Perhaps the earliest examples of domestic dogs in South America are found in Peru in sites of the Cupisnique or Chavin culture dating to about 1400-700 BC. One such site, excavated at Supe, produced the mummified remains of a small brown dog which may indicate ceremonial interment. Domestic dogs have been reported from sites in the region of Ancon that date to *c.* AD 900-1476. These mummified remains have been recovered from extensive cemeteries indicating they may have been placed there as a result of ritual activities.

Among the oldest clearly domestic dogs from Peru are those associated with sites of the Salinar Culture dating to *c.* 300 BC-AD 200). Human burials located in Salinar cemeteries are often accompanied by a dog burial placed at the feet, again attesting to a significance greater than merely that of hunting companion.

From these finds, it is evident that domestic canines were well established in South America by 1500 BC and probably a great deal earlier. Dogs appear to have had ceremonial significance from a very early date in South America by 1500 BC and probably a great deal earlier. Dogs appear to have had ceremonial significance from a very early date in South America, and this trend is further reinforced in later examples. The Inca Empire (AD 1438-1532) was characterized by a dependence upon a small number of domestic animals. In spite of this reliance on so few domesticates, the dog appears to have been kept only as a pet and was never consumed. Inca utilization of the dog in ritual sacrifices is also well established and many fine examples of Inca dogs have been recovered from Late Horizon sites. For example, finds have reported at the Inca city of Macchu Picchu, near Cuzco in Peru. All evidence from these late sites indicates that the peoples of Late Horizon Peru were familiar with many varieties of dogs, including "hairless" and "toy" breeds.

The history of the domestication of canids in South America is as yet not fully understood, owing in large part to a lack of intensive archaeological investigation in many crucial areas (such as the Amazon Basin). It is hoped that as such archaeological studies are initiated, we may begin to fill in the gaps in our knowledge and learn to what extent South America may be viewed as a separate hearth for the domestication of canids.

In conclusion, it is probable the domestic dog accompanied the first inhabitants of the Western Hemisphere across the Bering Strait from Siberia perhaps 25-30,000 years ago. An important question yet to be answered is whether or not areas of the New World (South America in particular) should be considered independent centers of dog domestication. Archaeological evidence indicates the dog has served the Amerindian as a beast of burden, a hunting companion, and item of consumption as well as an inspiration for myriad folktales and mythology.

Many works exist on the relationship of living Native Americans and domestic dogs, but all serve to illustrate the continuity between the archaeological and contemporary examples. The domestic dog plays as vital a role in the Amerindian lifeway today as it has throughout most of the history of human occupation in the Western Hemisphere.

JOHN W. OLSEN

DOGRIB is an Athapascan tribe living in Northwest Canada.

The name Dogrib was given them by white traders who mocked their belief that they originally stemmed from dogs. Their own name is *Thlingchadine*, the meaning of which is unknown.

Little is known about their governmental or religious life. They were between 1,500 and 2,000 nomadic hunters and fishermen. They lived in double lean-tos which were easily constructed. They travelled in a variety of ways. During the summer they used their feather-light and superbly crafted canoes. During the winter they travelled largely by toboggan and snowshoe. There was some use of dogsled but it was not widespread until the time of white contact.

For food they relied largely on caribou, which were trapped in enclosures. Smaller game was trapped in snares. Tools and weapons were made of stone and copper. The Dogribs did not make pottery.

The Dogribs would tattoo their faces; a tattoo usually consisted of 3 or 4 parallel lines. Women do not seem to have played an important role in government and were probably relegated to lower social strata. Women were often taken as prizes in war.

These people seemed to have been quite warlike with other Indians; but were painfully shy and fearful of white men. MacKenzie recorded that when he first saw one of their tribes the Indians all ran from him in terror. Eventually he gained their confidence.

Though the Dogribs became an important trading nation they originally did not seem to have any interest in the business. They got into it almost by accident. Sometime around the mid-1700s other Indians spent some time with the Dogribs. These Indians had tools of European manufacture and the Dogribs instantly sensed these tools were superior to their own. The others wanted skins so the Dogribs made their original trade. By the 1760s they were trading with Canadians.

Their later history was tied intimately to the development of the Hudson Bay Company. At one point, the Ojibwa had denied them access to regular trading posts so the Dogribs were forced to trade on an independent basis, getting poorer prices for their goods. Eventually, though, trade was reestablished on a regular basis with the great forts and outposts.

Before contact with whites, the Dogribs were a naturally friendly people, shy of whites though warlike with other Indian nations. After contact they became supposedly greedy and petty and gave whites difficulty in establishing new trading terms. Some bands, however, which have had limited contact with whites seem not to have changed their nature to any significant degree.

DOHASAN (Kiowa; ?-1866) was the greatest of a hereditary line of chiefs of the Kiowa tribe, noted for his courage and for his defiance of threats from agents of the U.S. government.

Dohasan became chief in 1833 after the Osage Indians massacred the Kiowa and captured their sun dance gods. At that time his predecessor, Dohate ("Bluff"), who was the first member of the line of whom there is record, was deposed. Originally also known as Dohate, his name was changed to Dohasan ("Little Bluff") to distinguish between the two chiefs. George Catlin called him Teh-toot-saw when he painted his portrait in 1834.

Dohasan's career as a great chief almost came to an

end in 1837 when he went with nine other Kiowa, led by Guadalonte, on a raid into the Southwest. On the verge of turning back north, the expedition was cornered by Mexican dragoons and forced to spend six days in a cave without food or water. Only Dohasan's great strength and courage helped the survivors to arrive home safely.

Although Dohasan signed a number of treaties, including the Fort Atkinson treaty on July 27, 1853, and the Little Arkansas River treaty on October 18, 1865, it cannot be said that he had any love for the white man or any intention of abiding by treaty covenants. To him, fighting was a man's business, and he never understood why the Indian was denied the right to fight for what he wanted, while the whites fought both among themselves and against the Indians. In fact, he identified with and respected the Mexicans, who thought and fought very much as he did.

His speech in 1862, when the Indians gathered on the Arkansas River to receive their annuities, is evidence of his defiance of the U.S. whites. The agent had threatened punishment if the Indians did not stop raiding. Pointing to the hundreds of tipis spread in the vicinity, Dohasan said: "The Spanish chief and myself are men. We do bad toward each other sometimes—stealing horses and taking scalps—but we do not get mad and act the fool. The white chief is a child, and, like a child, gets mad quick. When my young men, to keep their women and children from starving, take from the white man passing through our country, killing and driving away our buffalo, a cup of sugar or coffee, the white chief is angry and threatens to send his soldiers. I have looked for them a long time, but they have not come. He is a coward. His heart is a woman's. I have spoken. Tell the great chief what I have said."

Upon Dohasan's death at the hands of a Dakota (Sioux), his name was borne by his son, also a distinguished warrior, who died in 1894, and a nephew, author of the Scott calendar, who died in 1892. The name disappeared after 1894.

DOLLS and other miniature figures of human beings have been produced by American Indians throughout their history. They have been as varied as the cultures they represent, and the materials from which they were made were as diverse as the regions from which they sprang. Those figures produced as children's toys or as collector's items are *dolls*. Non-toys such as *effigies* are representations of specific beings. *Figurines* are carved or molded statuettes. *Religious miniatures* have supernatural connotations. Some figures may be classified as all four. Sometimes making the distinction between toy dolls and other figures is difficult or impossible, especially concerning archaeological finds where there may be no historical documentation concerning the use of the object.

Dolls, sometimes looking like miniature members of the family, were often used as toys by American Indian children. They were made of a variety of materials including stone, animal hair, animal hide, wood, shell, seaweed, grass, cornhusk, ivory, bone, clay, trade goods, and other substances.

Little girls mimiced their mothers' child-caring activities by playing with dolls. They learned household skills that they would need as adults. Boys were less likely to play with "baby" dolls and more often played games with dolls such as "going hunting," and "going to war," in imitation of their fathers. In these ways, playing with dolls helped to enculturate Indian children.

The costumes of American Indian dolls reflect cultural affiliation, climate, hair and clothing styles, as well as other aspects of culture such as art, war, social class, religion, and wealth. The materials from which the dolls were constructed also indicate the availability of naturally occurring materials and trade goods.

American Indian dolls have been sold as souvenirs since white contact. Some of those dolls were used as toys; others joined collections as new exotic specimens; and others were sent home to show how the Indians dressed. Doll collecting was in full swing as a hobby by 1900, which greatly increased the demand for Indian dolls made by craft workers. Many of those dolls are preserved in museum and private collections. Buying Indian dolls is still a popular activity among tourists, and many tribes make and offer dolls for sale. The best are usually found in remote areas.

Miniature figures of human beings have played a role in the religions of American Indians for centuries.

W. H. Over Museum, University of South Dakota, Vermillion.

Female Dakota doll from South Dakota is dressed in blue wool tradecloth dress cut in the old buckskin dress style (note the side gussets). Seedbeads on the dress represent elk incisors or cowrie shells used on full-size dresses. The doll dates about 1870-1900, when these dresses first became popular in the Plains.

W. H. Over Museum, University of South Dakota, Vermillion.

Male Teton Dakota doll is dressed in buckskin and beads. Dates about 1880, Lower Brule Reservation, Dakota Territory. At this time the dress of the Dakota was elaborately decorated with glass beads available through traders. Note the tobacco pouch, pipebag, and knife sheath attached at the waist.

Joanita Kant Collection.

Female Teton Dakota doll from South Dakota in traditional buckskin dress, leggings, and moccasins. Porcupine quills make up the earrings and decorate the toes of the moccasins. A baby doll on a cradleboard is attached at the waist. Dates 1970. Dolls of this quality are rare, today.

They were often the embodiment of the spirit of a person, place, or thing which was dealt with by a shaman or priest. Religious figurines were treated with great respect and were often feared for their power. Whereas toy dolls were most often dressed with attached clothing, religious figures were more often carved or molded.

North America

Eskimo toy dolls were often made of animal skins stuffed with reindeer hair or fur. Others were made of bone, ivory, wood, or mammoth teeth. They were often dressed in a parka and mukluks. Eskimos occasionally hung carved bone figures of human beings in their kayaks to protect them from capsizing. Ivory shaman figures have been recorded as early as 1850. As early as 1900 the Salish Indians of the Pacific Northwest Coast made carved cedar baby dolls in cradles covered with cotton quilt swaddling and lacing. The Tlingit Indians used carved wooden shaman figures which have been found in gravehouses.

Many of the Plains and peripheral Plains tribes, including the Blackfoot, Cheyenne, Dakota, Apache, Crow, Winnebego, and others, produced buckskin dolls stuffed with wool, vegetable fibers, clay, or animal hair. Their traditional clothing was decorated with seedbeads or porcupine quills. European clothing became popular after about 1870, but buckskin shirts and dresses were still in vogue. A rawhide cutout of a man was traditionally used in the religious Sun Dance of the Dakota. The eastern Dakota used a little carved wooden human figure, a "tree dweller," in a hollow log housing, in an eastern variant of the Grand Medicine Lodge Ceremony at least prior to 1908. The Ojibwa also used a little carved wooden human figure in the rites of the Grand Medicine Society. In about 1860 the Menomini Indians used wooden figures with cotton cloth costumes decorated with shells and beads. By 1919 they still used carved wooden figures to perform magic tricks.

The most popular religious miniatures in the Southwest are the Katchinas of the Hopi, Zuñi, and Pomo tribes. They are representations, in human form, of spirits of persons, animals, places, or things. Katchinas are made of carved cottonwood or cactus root, painted and decorated with bits of feathers, cloth, shell, and other materials. They are given to children at annual ceremonies, but they are not toys. They are religious objects for children to study. Among the Navajo Indians, simplistic carved wooden sacrificial figurines in human form are made by medicine men and placed near ruins to atone for violated taboos. Modern Navajo make and sell tourist dolls which are sometimes weaving rugs, that skill for which the Navajo are so famous. Stone fetishes in the human shape may be found among the Indians at Zia Pueblo. The Keres Indians of Laguna use stick figures of human beings in offerings during religious ceremonies. The Mohave Indians of Arizona made tattooed terra-cotta dolls. Some were infants; others were standing or sitting figures, sometimes on platforms. They were dressed in real skirts or breechcloths, beaded collars and earrings.

Cornhusk toy dolls, dressed in traditional clothing of cloth and buckskin with feathers and beads, were made by the Seneca in New York in the late 1800s. By about 1850 the Deleware still used spirit figures which protected them in return for a dance held in their honor and a new set of clothing each year. Those figures were often dressed in cotton cloth wrappings, leather moccasins, and many seedbead necklaces, silver discs, shells, and beads. The Iroquois made little wood carvings of snake dancers as late as 1935.

Mesoamerica

Effigies, figurines, and religious miniatures in the form of human beings are often found among Aztec and Maya ruins. They are sometimes found in grave sites and are usually considered religious in function. One cannot be certain that any of them were used as toy dolls. Some were household idols that may later have been used as dolls. Figures in the form of ball players, weapon-bearing warriors, female fertility

Mrs. Allen Millar Collection.

Female Winnebago doll from Nebraska, about 1890. Doll wears European influenced cotton clothing with ribbonwork and embroidery, similar to their full-size counterparts at that date.

Mrs. Allen Millar Collection.

Male Winnebago doll from Nebraska dates about 1890. The doll is dressed in buckskin shirt, leggings, and moccasins.

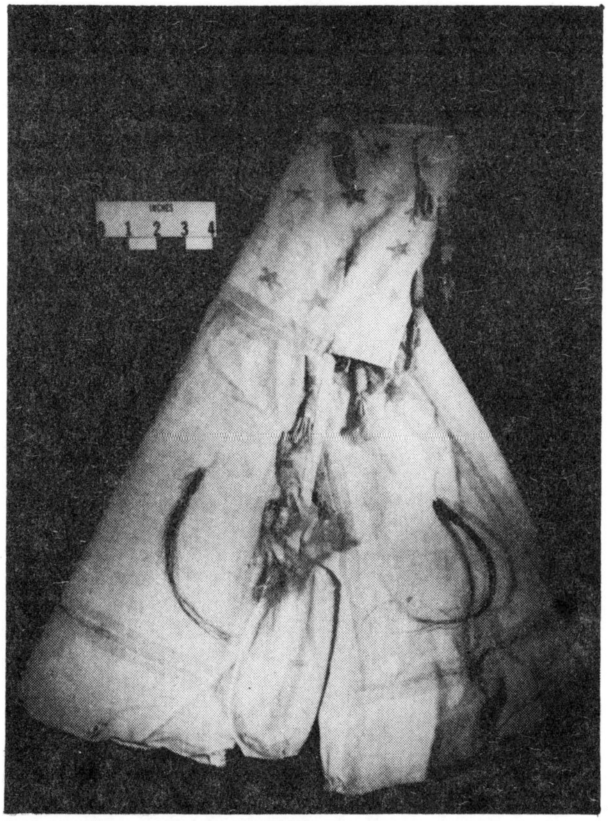

W. H. Over Museum, University of South Dakota, Vermillion.

Plains Indian miniature tipi from South Dakota, about 1900, was probably used as a dollhouse by children at play.

forms, shamen, dancers, acrobats, and others have been found. They are made of terra-cotta or pottery (either hand-formed or mold-produced), jade, serpentine, and other stone. The figures depicted indicate a preoccupation with war, fertility, and religion. Some are stiff and stylized. Others are ironic caricatures. Some are complicated and elaborate, while others are simple suggestions of the human form. They may be serene or active in appearance. Much is known about Aztec and Maya dress from their effigies, figurines, and religious miniatures.

The Seri Indians of Sonora in northwest Mexico, recently, make simple little carved wooden dolls barely suggesting the human shape, wrapped in cloth and bound with yarn.

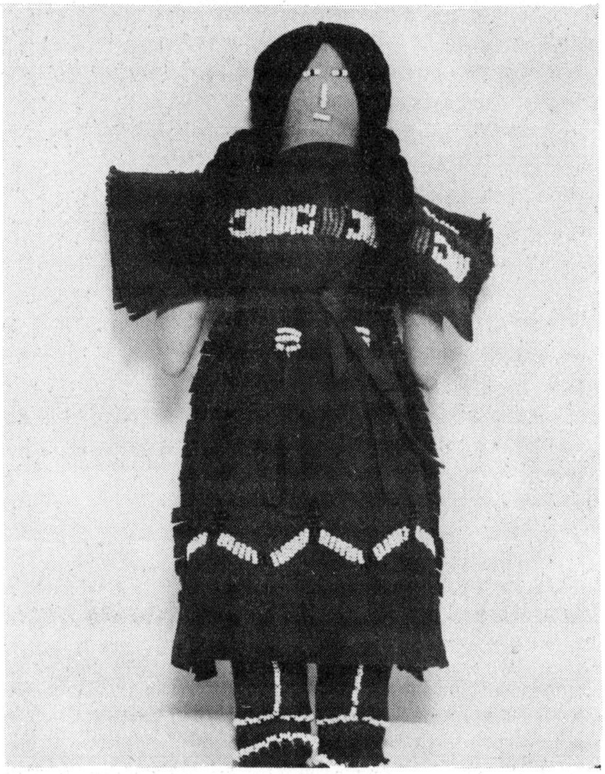

Joanita Kant Collection.

Female Cheyenne doll from the North American Plains wears a red leather dress decorated with bands of seed beads. Dates about 1930. This type of doll was produced as a toy or collector's item.

Joanita Kant Collection.

Female Navajo doll from Arizona in a velvet shirt and cotton skirt. The doll is weaving a wool rug, that skill for which the Navajo are famous. This type of doll was produced as a tourist item.

South America

The most famous figurines from South America are those produced by the Incas. They are not as abundant as Mesoamerican figurines. Beautiful figurines of solid gold casting and of pottery have been recovered. A solid gold casting molded figurine from Columbia has been found which is at least 500 years old. It is a mace-carrying figure with rounded contours, shining surface, and false filigree in some parts.

Knitted dolls made of wool are still produced in Peru among the Quechua Indians, descendants of the Incas. They also produce dolls of clay, wood, and gourd. Modern dolls include masked dancers dressed in traditional clothing.

The Araucanian Indians of Chile produce dolls made of animal hide dressed in cotton clothing. Some are mounted on toy horses with loads of wool blankets. Dolls from Chile and Brazil are sometimes little cork- or wooden-headed figures with bodies of yarn-wrapped wire.

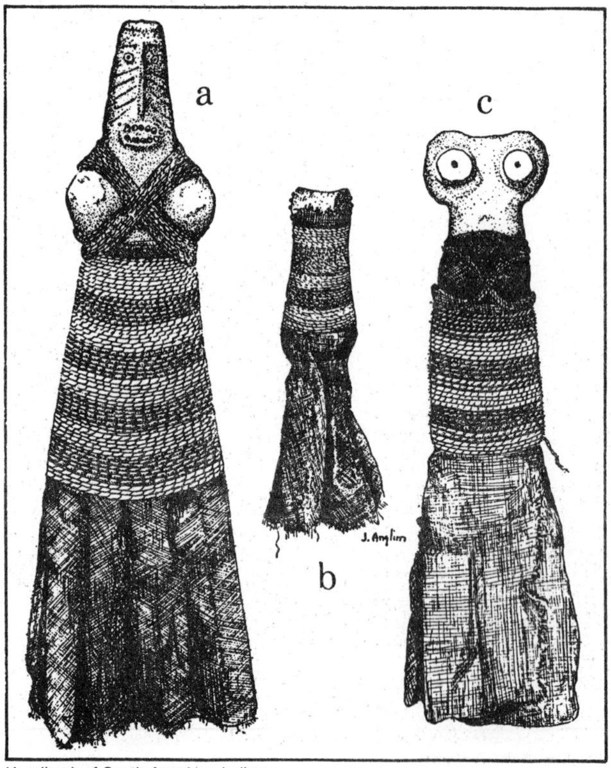

Handbook of South American Indians.

(A, C) Mataco and Pilagá clay dolls; (B) Pilagá doll made from a cow knuckle.

DOMESTICATED PLANTS AND ANIMALS. Little wonder that plants and religion were intricately linked by primitive man, for most of his food, shelter, narcotics, stimulants and medicine were derived from plants. Moreover, early man believed that the plants were inhabited by spirits and that it was necessary to propitiate these spirits. Thus among the agricultural Indians there were almost always special rituals connected with planting and harvesting, as well as sacrifices to the rain gods whose help was essential in producing good plant growth. In many groups of people plants are prominent in their creation myths.

Until nearly 7000 years ago all of the peoples of the Americas were hunters and gatherers, and they made use of an extensive number of plant species in their daily lives. Virtually all of the plants that could furnish edible roots, stems, leaves, fruits or seeds were discovered by trial and error, as were also those plants that could serve other purposes. In some regions a particular plant resource became a staple, such as the oak in the western United States. Twenty-seven different species of North American oaks provided acorns that could be used for food. In order to make the acorns suitable for human consumption it was necessary in most cases to remove the tannins by leaching with water. In many regions grasses became the wild food staple: for example, wild rice in the western Great Lakes region. Other wild food staples included camass in the northwestern United States, pinon in the Great Basin, mesquite in the Southwest and Mexico, potatoes in the Andes, and many palm fruits in tropical America.

Although many groups of Indians still had a hunting-gathering economy at the time of the Spanish conquest, probably the majority were farmers. This farming is perhaps best designated as horticulture, for true agriculture involves the use of draft animals which were not available until introduced by the Spanish. More than 100 species of plants were domesticated in the Americas, and the great majority, as might be expected, were food plants.

Cereals. Maize was domesticated in Middle America some 6000 years ago, and no plant was more important to the Indians. It was grown almost everywhere that horticuture was practiced, from sea level to over 11,000 feet in the Andes, extending from southern Canada

Arawak dance to the earth goddess. Reproduction from BAE Annual Report no. 25 by Fewkes, Jesse Walter.

to the Island of Chiloe. Swamps were drained, woodlands were cleared, deserts were irrigated, and terraces were built in mountain sides in order that the plant could be grown. In art, religion and everyday life most of man's activities were centered around this plant. For food it was prepared in a great variety of ways: popping and parching were probably the most primitive ways; hominy and meal were made from it; and by chewing or germinating the grain an alcoholic beverage could be prepared. In Mexico and some other areas the traditional method of preparing the grain for food was to soak the grain in alkali-water made from lime, wood ashes, lye or shells. Maize is now one of man's most nutritious foods, and recently it has been shown that the alkali cooking technique actually enhances its nutritive value.

Legumes. Only slightly less important to the Indians than maize, and frequently grown with it, were a number of different kinds of beans (*Phaseolus*). Maize and beans together supply a fairly adequate diet for man, for the protein content of beans is quite high and their amino acid composition largely complements that of maize. Beans appear at the earliest levels of horticulture in both Peru and Mexico. Domesticated forms of both the common bean (*P. Vulgaris*) and the lima bean (*P. lunatus*) have been found in deposits in highland Peru over 7000 years old, and the common bean appeared in Mexico more than 6000 years ago. The lima bean was to become known in Mexico at a much later date. The tepary bean and the scarlet runner bean appear fairly early in Mexico and were both to become important food plants.

The peanut (*Arachis hypogaea*), which apparently was domesticated in Bolivia, is found in coastal Peruvian deposits in the second millenium BC and is reported from Tehuacan, Mexico at the beginning of the Christian era. Different species of jack bean (*Canavalia*) were also grown in Mexico and Peru, and the chocho (*Lupinus mutabilis*) was cultivated in the Andes for its seeds.

Cucurbits. All the squashes and pumpkins had their origins in the Americas; five different species were domesticated. *Cucurbita pepo, C. mixta,* and *C. moschata* were domesticated in Middle America, and *C. maxima* in South America. Where the fifth species, *C. ficifolia,* a squash adapted to highland conditions, was domesticated is still uncertain. It has been suggested that these cucurbits may have been first grown for their edible seeds and that the thick flesh of the fruit, for which they are largely cultivated today, was a later development.

Other members of the cucurbit family were also cultivated for their fruits, including the chayote (*Sechium edule*) in Middle America and achocha (*Cyclanthera pedata*) in the Andean region. The bottle gourd (see below) may also have served for food at times.

Roots and tubers. The underground parts of a number of plants are important sources of carbohydrates. A far greater number of these plants became domesticated in tropical South America and in the Andes than in other parts of the Americas. Three of these plants, manioc, the Irish or white potato, and the sweet potato became important staples.

Manioc (*Manihot esculenta*), also known as cassava and yuca, was widely cultivated in tropical areas, and in some parts, particularly the Amazon region, was more important than maize. Manioc comprises both sweet and bitter varieties; the bitter varieties, which require special preparation to remove the poisonous cyanogenetic glucosides to make them safe to eat, were apparently more widely grown than the sweet kinds. The implements presumably used in their preparation are rather common in the archaeological record but the actual remains of the plant are seldom encountered. There is some disagreement as to whether the original type was bitter or sweet, but most authorities think that the sweet forms arose from the bitter.

Wild potatoes are common in the Andes, and in time one or more of them, probably in the area of Lake Titicaca, became domesticated. The Irish potato (*Solanum tuberosum*) is a highland crop and grows well at 15,000 feet, which is beyond the range of maize and most other cultivated plants. In the high Andes special methods of dehydrating the potato by repeated freezing and stamping on the thawing tubers produced a food, known as chuno, that could be stored for long

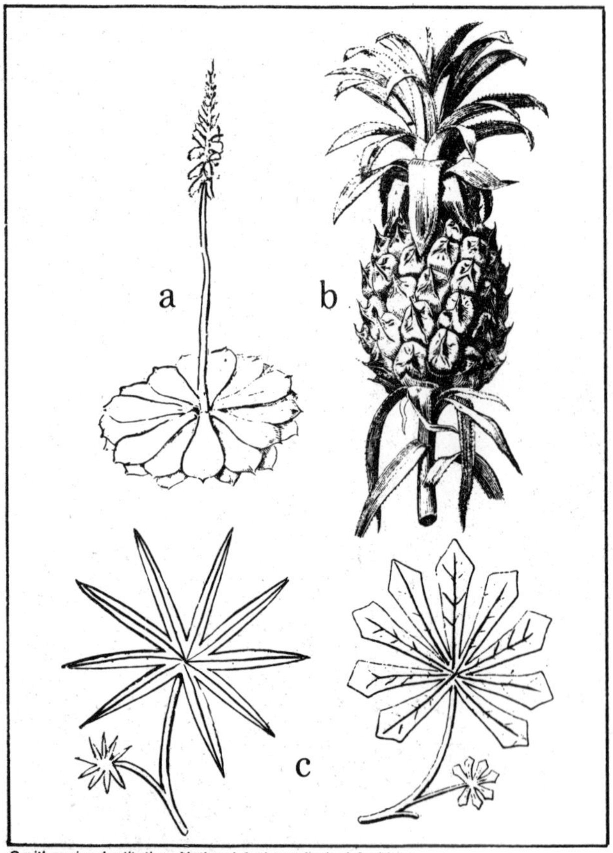

Smithsonian Institution, National Anthropological Archives.

Hispaniola plants; (a) the maguey, used by the Taino to make cordage; (b) the pineapple; (c) leaves of the bitter manioc.

periods of time. The Irish potato was unknown in Middle and North America until post-Conquest times.

The sweet potato (*Ipomaea batatas*) was cultivated in Middle America, the West Indies, and northern South America in prehistoric times. The exact place of origin is as yet unknown, but some evidence suggests northern South America. There is fairly general agreement that the sweet potato had also reached some of the islands of the Pacific in pre-Columbian times. Although it seems probable that its introduction there was by the agency of man, a natural means of dispersal cannot yet be entirely ruled out.

Among other underground crops are oca (*Oxalis tuberosa*), ulluco (*Ullucus tuberosus*), and anu (*Tropaeolum tuberosum*), all confined to the high Andes. At lower elevations, species of yam (*Dioscorea*), yautia (*Xanthosoma*), and achira (*Canna edulis*) were cultivated in various parts. The yam bean (*Pachyrrhizus erosus*) was one of the few root crops, in addition to manioc and the sweet potato, known for Middle America; a related species (*Pachyrrhizus tuberosa*) was utilized in Peru.

Fruits. The term "fruit" botanically refers to the ripened ovary or ovaries of a flower, and thus both grains and pumpkins are fruits. The tomato, the husk-tomato, and the avocado are among the important fruits utilized as vegetables. Whether the origin of the cultivated tomato (*Lycopersicon esculentum*) was in Mexico, or in Western South America where its wild relatives occur, is still uncertain, but it seems clear that the fruit was more important in Mexico than in South America in pre-contact times. A husk tomato (*Physalis philadelphica*) was an important vegetable in Mexico, and may have been domesticated earlier than the tomato. The tree tomato (*Cyphomandra crassifolia*), another member of the nightshade family, was cultivated for its fruits in western South America. The avocado, a food rich in oils, was fairly widely grown. It apparently was domesticated independently in Middle America, the West Indies, and Peru.

Fruits that appealed to man because of their sweetness were rather numerous, and both Middle America and South America contributed many kinds. A large number of species of *Anona* — ilama, cherimoya, guanabanana, sweetsop, soursop, and anona — were domesticated. Other important cultivated fruits were pineapple (*Ananas comosus*), a cherry (*Prunus serotina*), the papaya (*Carica papuya*), sapodilla (*Achras zapota*), the guava (*Psidium guajava*), the hog plum (*Spondias mombin*), sapote (*Calocarpum viride* and other genera), cactus or prickly pear (*Opuntia*) and many more. The cashew (*Anacardium occidentale*) was valued more as a fruit than as a nut.

The coconut (*Cocos nucifera*), another fruit that eventually became an important food source in the Americas, apparently had an exceedingly limited dis-

Smithsonian Institution, National Anthropological Archives.

Panoramic view of terraced gardens, irrigated by a spring north of Walpi, Arizona. Also called *"Weepo (cattail-water) Gardens".*

tribution in Middle America at the time of the conquest. The coconut was at one time considered to be a native to the Americas, but it is now known to be indigenous to southeastern Asia. Whether its arrival in America was by floating or through the agency of man is still somewhat controversial.

Condiments and flavorings. The major condiment in the Americas was chili or red pepper of the genus *Capsicum.* Wild species, which are found from the southern United States to southern South America, are used in many present day dishes. Four species became domesticated: the chili (*C. annum*) in Middle America, two kinds of ajis (*C. baccatum* and *C. frutescens*) and the rocoto (*C. pubescens*) in South America. The last named species was adapted to the high Andes. The pepper became almost indispensable in the diet of the Indians and received almost the same reverence as did the staple crops. Red peppers are, of course, food as well as condiment, and supply both vitamins and minerals.

The vanilla orchid (*Vanilla planifolia*) became a cultivated plant in Mexico and was used by the Aztecs as a flavoring.

Alcoholic beverages and stimulants. Apparently primitive man discovered that beers or wines could be made from a large number of plants. In the Americas a chicha or beer made from maize had a very wide distribution. Manioc was also frequently employed for the manufacture of a beer. The root was chewed and then spat into containers. The mastication changed the starch into sugar, thus producing a suitable substrate for microorganisms that would convert some of the sugar into alcohol. Among other basic food plants, both quinoa and sweet potatoes were sometimes used to make beers. A large number of fruits were used to make wines, and since they naturally contained sugar no special processing was necessary to initiate fermentation. Among the cultivated plants, pineapples were often used, and among wild plants, palms and algarroba (*Prosopis chilensis*) were particularly important in South America. Several kinds of maguey (*Agave*) were used for making pulque in Middle America. In the eastern United States wild persimmons were used to make a beer.

The two most important caffeine-containing plants were cacao or the chocolate bean and various kinds of *Ilex.* Wild cacao (*Theobroma cacao*) had a wide distribution from Mexico to central South America, but only in Middle America did it become a domesticated plant, prized both as a food and drink. In time the beans or seeds became used as currency. Leaves of varius species of *Ilex* were used in South America to prepare a stimulating beverage, and one, *Ilex paraguariensis,* eventually became domesticated, and today is the course of yerba mate or Paraquayan tea. Apparently its use was rather local until the arrival of the Spanish, who were responsible for much of the improvement in the plant and its wider distribution. *Ilex vomitoria* was used for the "black drink" of the Indians of eastern North America.

Leaves of coca (*Erthroxylum coca*), the source of cocaine, usually with the addition of lime, were chewed

U.S. Department of Agriculture Office of Information.

Airview of topography of the Pacific Coastal Plain with grazing lands, fields of sugar cane and citronella grass. Esquintila, Guatamala, (1947).

in the Andean region and in a few other places. It served to allay thirst and hunger and to enable one to carry out physical exertion for prolonged periods of time.

Narcotics and hallucinogens. In no other part of the world did plants become more widely used as narcotics and hallucinogens than in tropical America. Like many of the food plants, and perhaps even earlier, they often became a direct object of worship. They were most often taken by shamans for magic, divination and the curing of disease but were also employed in boy's initiation ceremonies and in other ways. Although the Spanish tried to stamp out these "heathen" practices, they were only partially successful, and the use of many of these plants flourishes to this day. The majority of the plants used for these purposes have various alkaloids as their active ingredients.

Of these plants, tobacco had the widest distribution in the Americas and was the only one eventually to become widely used throughout the world. Tobacco was chewed, snuffed, smoked, licked or drunk, and its use was mostly religious or ceremonial in contrast to a secular use which largely came after the Conquest. Two species, both South American in origin, were domesticated — *Nicotiana tabacum* became the chief tobacco of South America and the West Indies (and eventually the rest of the world) whereas *N. rustica,* the stronger of the two species, was the tobacco of Mexico and eastern North America. Various wild species of tobacco, sometimes apparently deliberately cultivated, were utilized in western North America.

Mushrooms and flowering plants from several different families furnished the hallucinogens, most widely used in Middle America and western South America. In Mexico and Guatemala, teonanacatl, or the "flesh of the gods," (*Psilocybe mexicana*), as well as several other kinds of mushroom were of great significance. The genus *Datura* of the nightshade family furnished the greatest number of species used as hallucinogens. In eastern North America, the jimson weed, *D. stramonium,* was employed, in southwestern North America and Mexico, the angel's trumpet, *D. inoxia,* was used, and in northwestern South America, the tree Daturas, particularly *D. sanguinea* in the highlands and *D. suaveolens* in the lowlands, was prominent. Peyote, from the cactus, *Lophophora williamsii,* became the basis of a cult in Mexico in prehistoric times. Its use spread to the United States in the eighteenth century where it is now incorporated in the ceremonies of the Native American Church. A few other kinds of cactus were also found to have hallucinogenic properties. Ololiuqui, long a source of confusion as to its identity, has been determined to be seeds of morning glories (*Ipomoea violacea* and *Rivea corymbosa*). Several legumes have been used, particularly yopo snuff from *Anadenathera peregrina* of northern South America and the West Indies, and the mescal or red bean, *Sophora secundiflora* of the American Southwest and Mexico. Among the other important hallucinogens are caapi or ahuahuaso from *Banisteriopsis caapi,* a tree of northern South America and a snuff prepared from various species of *Virola*

A Honduran tapper using a ladder to reach the upper parts of a Castilla rubber tree.

USDA—Foreign Agriculture Relations.

USDA photo.

Topography of the community of Tabio, Colombia (1944). The fields of this agriculture district are carried as far up the mountain slopes as possible.

used in the north western Amazon and only recently known to science. Much of the information on the nature and uses of these plants derives from the studies of the Harvard botanist, Richard E. Shultes.

Fibers. Two species of cotton, distinct from the species of the Old World, were domesticated in the Americas. The archaeological record reveals that *Gossypium hirsutum* was the species of ancient Mexico whereas the textiles found in Peruvian graves were made from *G. barbadense.* Both of the American species of cotton are polyploids that arose from hybridization of two species followed by chromosome doubling. At one time it was postulated that one of the ancestral species had been carried to the New World from the Old by man, but more recent investigations do not substantiate this view.

The other important domesticated fiber plants include various members of the family Agavaceae. Henequen, maguey and sisal belong to various species of *Agave* and were cultivated in Middle America, while various kinds of cabuya, species of *Fucraea,* were grown in South America.

A number of wild plants, particularly palms and bromeliads, also furnished fibers used by the Indians, and bark cloth was made from some trees.

Gourds. Two plants produced fruits that were widely employed for vessels as well as in a number of other ways. Before the invention of pottery these plants must have been particularly valuable to man, and their use continued after the arrival of pottery, as it does today in many parts of the Americas. The fruits of both plants have been called both gourds and calabashes and sometimes the distinction between them is not made. However, the plants producing them are very different. One, usually called the bottle gourd, comes from a cucurbit (*Lagenaria siceraria*) whereas the other, the tree gourd, comes from a bignoniaceous plant (*Crescentia cujete*). The latter is a small tree, widespread in the American tropics, whereas the former is a large vine, also widespread in the tropics but whose cultivation extended into the temperate zone as well. It is generally agreed that the bottle gourd is native to Africa, but it is found in Mexico at 7000 BC and nearly as early in Peru. Thus it appears to be one of the oldest domesticated plants in the Americas, and how it arrived here has been the subject of much discussion. Some have held that it must have been carried by man, whereas others believe that the fruits must have floated across the Atlantic. Since the fruit has been shown to float for long periods in salt water without losing seed viability, the latter view is quite plausible.

Other plant uses. Among the plants used for dyes, two with wide distributions in tropical America merit special notice. Achiote, a red pigment, which was obtained from *Bixa orellana,* was used as a body or hair paint in South America as well as in other ways. Indigo or anil was obtained from *Indigofera suffruticosa.* Plants such as the cochineal cactus were cultivated as hosts for cochineal insects, which were used for a dye.

A large number of plant species were employed in medicine. Many of these were wild plants, but some plants cultivated primarily for other purposes, as, for example, the sunflower, also had medicinal use. Some of the drug plants, such as ipecac, have found their way into modern medicine. Rather surprisingly perhaps, the bark of the *Cinchona* tree, which yields quinine, was apparently not utilized by the Indians.

An extremely large number of plants were also employed as fish poisons. Over 100 different species have been reported with such use in South America. The legumes, barbasco (*Tephrosia*) and cube (*Lonchocarpus*) were particularly prominent in this regard. Although most of the plants used were wild, some apparently were intentionally cultivated for use as pesticides. The usual method of using them was to mascerate the stem or leaves in the water which caused the fish to be stupified so that they could be easily collected. The fish could then be eaten with no harm to man.

Arrow poisons, including curare, were also made from several plants. Latex from several plants was used to make rubber, the primary purpose of which seems to have been to make balls. Some plants furnished material for shampoos or soaps. A number of plants were deliberately grown as living fences, and other plants, such as marigolds and dahlias, were cultivated for their beauty as ornamentals, particularly in Mexico.

There was an early practice of horticulture in both Mexico and Peru. At present it is impossible to say where it was earlier and whether the developments were entirely separate or whether there was the diffusion of the idea of planting from one region to the other. The common bean is found quite early in both centers, and although the possibility exists that it may have been carried from one area to the other, it is also quite possible that it had independent origins as a domesticated plant in the two centers. Several other plants, such as chili pepper and squash, were also early known in both Mexico and Peru, but they usually involve different species of a genus, which appear to have been domesticated from species native to the respective areas. Thus there was not necessarily any early transfer by man of plants from one area to the other. The appearance of maize in South America, however, almost certainly involves an introduction by man from Middle America. According to our present knowledge, however, maize appeared in South America after horticulture was already established.

While a large number of species were domesticated in both Middle and South America, very few cultivated plants were developed in North America. The four most important horticultural plants in North America, maize, beans, squash, and tobacco, all apparently came by way of Mexico. The sunflower (*Helianthus annus*), however, is one plant that seems clearly to have been domesticated north of Mexico, and it is still not clear whether its domestication occurred before or after the North American Indians had acquired these other plants from Mexico. The Jerusalem artichoke (*Helianthus tuberosus*) also became at least a semi-domesticated plant in eastern North America. The marsh-elder or sump weed (*Iva annua*) appears to have been domesticated in central North America, although

USDA—Foreign Agriculture Relations.

Rubber (*Hevea brasiliensis*) trees less than 5 months old growing at the Estacion Experimental Agricola del Ecuador, Pichilingue (1943).

Rice (*Fortuna*) being hand harvested in San Andres, El Salvador.

USDA—Foreign Agriculture Relations.

Lettuce in a school garden which is directed by the Extension Department of the Cooperative Agricultural Station. These grade school students do the planting, watering, cultivating and harvest the crops which are sold to the residents of the village. Tingo Maria, Peru (1947).

USDA photo.

Wheat is threshed by a steam-driven threshing machine that moves from farm to farm in adjoining communities in Tabio, Colombia (1944).

it had become extinct as a cultivated plant before the arrival of the Europeans.

Columbus introduced some of the Old World domesticated plants and animals to the Americas in his later voyages and in the 16th century a large number of Old World plants appeared in the Americas. The new plants had great impact on the Indian's diet in some areas and little or none in other areas. To this day, for example, in parts of the Amazon the Indians are still cultivating their traditional plants. Some of the newly introduced plants, for example, bananas and plantains, were so eagerly adopted that they became widespread in a short space of time and were sometimes regarded as indigenous to the Americas by the later Spanish.

At the same time that the Americas were receiving many plants from the Old World, they were furnishing many to the Old World, such as maize, potatoes, and peanuts, which were to become widely appreciated. The Indians' tobacco also soon spread around the world. It was perhaps, as someone has said, the Indians' revenge for their conquest by the European.

ANIMALS

Animal domestication is a phenomenon which is difficult to explain or define accurately. Rather than limit the definition to any single condition, it seems best to consider several conditions and several classes or degrees of domestication.

A distinction must be made between "domesticated" and tamed "wild" animals. The latter generally are isolated individuals which are caught wild (usually when young) and tamed as pets. All tamed wild animals are utilized, at least as pets in an esthetic sense, so the fact of utilization should not enter into the definition of either a domesticated or a tamed animal — all animals taken purposely by man into his company are utilized in some way.

Domestication should apply to an animal species which meets the following conditions: That it (1) is integrated into human culture; (2) is kept forcibly under human control for a purpose; (3) is dependent upon man, either voluntarily or involuntarily, for survival under this prior condition; (4) generally breeds under the artificial conditions of human control; and (5) generally is modified into breeds (or strains) through selective breeding by man.

This definition gives several degrees of domestication: (1) ordinary, or highly domesticated animals — those which answer all conditions (generally widespread geographically, also); (2) semidomesticated animals — those which answer at least the first three conditions. Some semidomesticated animals, e.g., pearl oysters, silkworms, honey bees, etc., have been called "cultivated."

The reasons that some animals have been

Santa Fe Collection. *"Navajo Ponies"* by Gerard C. Delano. Horses captured from herds brought to America by the Spanish completely revolutionized Indian life and warfare.

domesticated to any degree whatsoever are also difficult to state. However, they certainly involve cultural as well as zoological factors, and some of the following may be important: (1) cultural stimulus (either religious, economic, or esthetic), which gives and sustains a purpose and value to the act and the animals, and which in most cases probably originates in concentrated settled populations of peoples who have already had the knowledge and background of cultivated plants; (2) calm and docile disposition of the animal, which results in easy adaptation to confinement and generally involves no difficulty in breeding; (3) play instinct well developed (in mammals); (4) chance (meeting of the animal and the culture); (5) perhaps a symbiotic tendency of behavior in the animal, which manifests itself (a) in some sort of stratified social organization in nature and docile subjection to man in captivity, and/or (b) in some degree of attraction to other organisms, especially under stresses of nature, (famine, drought, cold, flood, extinction, etc.), because, generally, physically subnormal or exhausted animals are more easily tamed than robust healthy ones, and/or (c) in some "domestic" attachment to man which later turns into a domesticated symbiotic relationship.

It would seem that there exist many wild animals which are potentially domesticable, and perhaps chance has so far prevented their domestication; but, on the other hand, nearly all truly domesticated animals have an ancient history, and few new ones have been added recently. Hence, there may exist very good zoological reasons, or lack of certain factors, zoological as well as cultural, which have prevented and will prevent domestication of such forms. A study of seemingly domesticable animals, from the cultural and biological viewpoint, may clarify the positive factors favorable or necessary for domestication of others.

Fear is a strong factor in the behavior (and in the domesticability) of an animal. Young animals of these species are easier to tame than older members. However, some animals can be tamed in the adult as well as in the immature states (falcon, otter, etc.). There is obviously much to be learned about domestication, but also enough variability to preclude facile generalizations.

The establishment of special breeds of domesticated animals is an interesting phenomenon. The general idea of the mechanics of reproduction, and of heredity, must have been known to Indians, especially to those with cultivated plants and domesticated animals, but it seems that the conscious establishment of a breed is generally a function of a culture which gives a special stimulus to the production and preservation of the breed. Without some cultural stimulus, the perpetuation of domesticated stock appears to proceed haphazardly as far as selective breeding is concerned. However, with a stimulus from religious (producing breeds of black llamas, white llamas, white alpacas, and perhaps 5-toed llamas), or from economic pressure, or from war, hunting, or sheer amusement, special breeds will be perpetuated and perhaps consciously developed by merely isolating and breeding desired like-with-like and segregating the results. Special craftmanship, secret or public, with special hereditary groups of animal husbandrists, will subsequently develop, and this will accelerate the process of breed development and improvement. In addition, breeds or strains can be developed naturally and unconsciously by natural selection, when the domesticated animal in question is continually forced to live in more extreme conditions of climate or to perform more arduous conditions of work. In these cases, only those individuals with the inherent ability to survive and breed can perpetuate the species, with a consequent fixation of the naturally selected combinations of characters in the newly developing breed.

The Indians of the Americas learned a great deal from, and were helped by animals in their wild state. The period of domestication began when he held them in captivity for the gratification of his desires or they became attached to him for mutual benefit. In this process there are the following gradations:

1. "Commensalism" begins when food is left for serviceable animals to devour, so that these may give notice of danger or advantage. The coyote is said to reveal the presence of the mountain lion. Small animals are tolerated for their skins and flesh. Plants would be sown to attract such creatures as bees, and tame animals would be regularly fed at later stages.

2. Confinement is represented by such activities as keeping fish and other aquatic animals in ponds; caging birds and carrying off their young, gallinaceous fowl last; tying up dogs or muzzling them; corralling ruminants, and bobbling or tethering wild horses so as to have them near, keep them away from their enemies, or fatten them for eating. The Indians had no difficulty in breeding some animals in confinement, but few wild birds will thus propogate, and the Indians could obtain those to tame only by robbing nests.

3. Keeping animals for their service or produce, as dogs for retrieving game or catching fish, hawks for killing birds; various creatures for their fleece, hides, feathers, flesh, milk, etc., and taming them for amusement and for ceremonial or other purposes, were a later development.

4. Actually breaking them to work, training dogs, horses, and cattle for packing, sledding, hauling travois, and, later, for riding, constitutes complete domestication.

In pre-Columbian times the dog was the most perfectly subdued animal of North America, as much so as the llama in South America. But other species of mammals, as well as birds, were in different degrees rendered tractable. After the coming of the whites, the methods of domesticating animals were perfected, and their uses multiplied. Moreover, horses, sheep, cattle, donkeys, hogs, and poultry were added to the list, and these profoundly modified the manners and customs of many Indian tribes.

Domestication of animals increased the food supply, furnished pets for old and young, helped him to go about, multiplied his wants, furnished a standard of property and a medium of exchange, took the load from the back of women, and provided more abundant material for economic, artistic, and ceremonial purposes.

Domestication had a different development in each culture area. In the Arctic region the dog was preeminent; it was reared with unremitting care, and all its life it was trained to the sled. As the dogs were never perfectly tamed, it was no easy task to drive a team of them; yet by the aid of dogs and sleds, in combination with umiaks, the whole polar area of America was exploited by the **Inuit**, who found these an excellent means of rapid transit from Asia to the Atlantic. The Mackenzie-Yukon area is a canoe country, and domestication of the dog was not vigorously prosecuted until the Hudson's Bay Company gave the stimulus. But southward, among the Algonquian and Siouan tribes of the Great Lakes and the Plains, this animal attained its best as a hunter and a beast of burden and traction. It was also reared for food and for ceremonial purposes. Not more than 50 pounds could be borne by one dog, but twice that amount could be moved on a travois. The coming of the horse (*q.v.*) to the Great Plains was a boon to the Indian tribes, all of which at once adopted the new instrument of travel and transportation. The horse was apotheosized; it became a standard of value: and fostered a greater diversity of occupations. But the more primitive methods of domestication were still practiced throughout the middle region. In the north Pacific area dogs were trained to hunt; but here and elsewhere this use of the dog was doubtless learned.

In the California-Oregon area birds of gray plumage were caged, plucked, and then set free. On Santa Catalina island, birds called large crows by the Spaniards were kept and worshipped. In the Southwest, the desert area, the whole development of domestication is seen. The coyote was allowed to feed about the camps. The Querecho (Vaquero Apache) of Coronado in 1541 had a great number of large dogs which they obliged to carry their baggage when they moved from place to place. Some of the Pueblo tribes practiced also the caging of eagles, the rearing of turkeys, and, since the coming of the Spaniards, the herding of sheep, goats, burros and horses.

Middle and South America. South America, Central America, and the Antilles are noted for rich fauna, composed of a great number of unique or endemic forms, and invaders (some now distinct) from North America since earliest times.

At present there are many diverse species, but time has seen the extinction of many others, particularly

USDA photo.
Plowing with oxen and a wooden plow near San Salvador, El Salvador (1949).

large forms. Man perhaps hastened the extinction of some. This extinction, for one reason or another, reduced the Plains faunas particularly, though less so in the southern temperate areas than in the central and northern tropical parts.

Middle and South America are divisible into four subregions: (1) Guyana-Brazilia, (2) Central America, (3) Antilles, and (4) Patagonia-Chile. The first three constitute at least 75 percent of the whole region, and are tropical. The rich ethnozoology of these tropical subregions may be separated further into continental-tropical, and Antillea tropical on the basis of the different faunas. Patagonia-Chile is south temperate, and is characterized by the very large number of its primary endemic forms, which include the guanaco-llama-alpaca-vicuna fauna of the plains and mountains. This fauna, with and without domestication, was thoroughly utilized in many special ways by Indians.

The domesticated llama probably was derived from similar wild guanacos. The alpaca probably was domesticated from a now extinct wild ancestor. Domestication of the llama and alpaca undoubtedly was accomplished in Peru, Bolivia, Chile, or Argentina.

The other domesticated mammal of South America is the cavy (guinea pig); it probably was domesticated in the Central Andean region also, from the wild stock which exists there today.

The remaining domesticated animal, a bird, the Muscovy duck, was domesticated, in the Central Andean region.

SOUTH AMERICA

Domesticated animals. Llama (*Lama glama glama*, or *L. glama*): Transport of burdens; meat, wool, hide, medicine, ceremony, sinew, pets.

Alpaca (*Lama pacos*): Wool, meat, ceremony, medicine, hide, sinew, pets.

Cavy, or guinea pig (*Cavia porcellus*, or *C. p. porcellus*): Meat, ceremony, medicine, pets.

Muscovy duck (*Cairina moschata*): Meat (with eggs), pets.

(The dog, *Canis familiaris*, and the turkey, *Meleagris gallopavo*, were not endemic, though they were found in South America in aboriginal times as cultural elements diffused from North America.)

Semidomesticated animals. Hunting huron (*Galictis furax*): Pets, hunting chinchillas.

Otter (*Lutra* sp.): Pets, fishing.

Extinct abrocoma (*Abrocoma oblativa*): Ceremony, food (?).

Extinct paca (*Cuniculus thomasi*): Ceremony, food (?).

Rhea (*Rhea americana* and *Pterocnemia pennata*): Food, feathers, pets.

Tree ducks (*Dendrocygna viduata* and *D. bicolor*): Food, pets.

Steamer duck (*Tachyeres pteneres*): Food, pets.

Trumpeter (*Psophia*): Pets, sentinels.

Chachalacas (*Penelope, Ortalis*): Food, pets.

Curassows (family Cracidae, several genera): Food, sentinels, pets.

Stone-plover (*Oedicnemus dominicensis*): Pets, sentinels.

Parrots (family Psittacidae, especially genus *Amazonia*): Pets, feathers.

Suckerfish (*Echeneis naucrates*): Capture of turtles, manatee, and fish.

DONACONA (Huron; ?-*c.* 1536) was the chief of the town of Stadacona on the St. Lawrence River, west of present-day Quebec City, whom Jacques Cartier took with him to France in 1536. The Indian chief died there soo after. He had apparently first met Cartier in 1534 in the Bay of Gaspé and allowed two of his sons to accompany the French explorer on a trading expedition as guides. Cartier returned with them a year later. wintered in Stadacona in 1535, and then either persuaded or lured Donacona on board his ship for the trip to France.

DONA INEZ (Inca; fl. 16th century) Ines Huayllas Yupanqui originally named Quispe Cusi, was an Inca princess who was the sister of the ruler, Atahuallpa, and the mistress of his conqueror, Francisco Pizarro.

Born about 1519, Inez was the daughter of Inca Huayna Capac and sister or half-sister of the Inca rulers Manco Inca, Huascar, Paullu, and Tupac Huallpu.

At age 15, Inez bore Pizarro a daughter, Francisca, one year after the Spanish executed her brother. She also bore him a son, Gonzalo, the following year.

Pizarro married her to one of his servants, Francisco de Ampuero, in 1538 and her descendents by Ampuero are still an important Peruvian family.

Busts of Inez, Pizarro and their children look down from the walls of the palace built by Hernando Pizarro at the Pizarro birthplace, Trujillo de Extremadura, in 1561.

DOONKEEN, EULAMAE NARCOMEY (Seminole; Dec. 12, 1931-), is an artist, a teacher, a tribal official, and an active participant in social action programs. Also known as Hay Gay Kee Hooduh Lee ("Crying Wind"), she was the vice chief of the Seminole Nation of Oklahoma in the mid-1970s, and an active leader in the National Congress of American Indians and in Oklahomans for Indian Opportunity.

DORRIS, MICHAEL A. (Modoc; Jan. 30, 1945-), is an anthropologist and chairman of the Native American Studies program at Dartmouth College (1972-). He previously taught at the University of Redlands and Franconia College. Besides numerous articles and papers, his publications include *Native Americans Now* (1976).

DORSET SUBTRADITION was a part of the Arctic tradition located in the eastern areas of the Canadian Northwest Territories, including Southampton Island, the Melville Peninsula, Baffin Island, the eastern Hudson Bay region, Labrador, Newfoundland, and Greenland. It dates from materials on Southampton Island and the Melville Peninsula at 800 to 600 BC and continued until it was replaced by the Northern Maritime Thule culture around AD 1000-1200.

Probable origin

Like other branches of the Eskimo Tradition, it had its origins in the Arctic Small Tool Tradition. Beyond this, its origins are unknown, though the area in the triangle between the Great Lakes, James Bay, and Newfoundland has been cited as the probable source of the distinct elements of Dorset. Dorset houses were fairly large, rectangular, partially below the ground, and had side benches. Many earlier types of blades were used with slight variations in shape, but they were usually made of slate rather than flint and were larger than their predecessors. Innovations in the Dorset tradition included multibarbed bone fish spears, ula-like knives of bone, snow knives, and bone sledge shoes.

Port-aux-Choix-2 in western Newfoundland is an example of a Dorset community. It is approximately three acres and has 35 to 40 houses. Floor levels are several feet below ground level, and while five pits were lined with rocks, the walls and roofs were only skin-covered. There was a large amount of seal meat, whale, fish, caribou and other mammals. It has been speculated that this was a seasonal camp, used as a temporary station for hunting.

DOUBLEHEAD (Cherokee; ?-1807) was a chief who is remembered for his traitorous dealings in ceding Cherokee lands to the U.S. government. In 1793 he led a party of Indians that murdered and mutilated two white men in retaliation for attacks on the Cherokee villages by whites. In 1796 he became speaker of the nation and served as spokesman for the Cherokee in talks with the U.S. government. He was prominent in negotiations in 1798, 1804, and 1805 in which lands were ceded to the U.S. Doublehead probably received bribes in all these negotiatons. In 1806, after being promised two tracts of land for himself, he illegally ceded further lands to the federal government. For these manipulations, and also for his brutal treatment of his wife, he was assassinated by a group of Cherokee in 1807.

DOWNING, TODD (Choctaw; fl. 1930s), is an author noted for a series of detective-mystery novels set in Mexico and the U.S. Southwest. The series, which was written in the late 1930s, included *The Case of the Unconquered Sisters* and *The Cat Screams.* He also wrote *The Mexican Earth* (1940), a depiction of Mexico from personal experience.

DOZIER, EDWARD P. (Santa Clara Pueblo; April 23, 1916-May 2, 1971), was a leading anthropologist and outspoken advocate of Indian rights. Born on the Santa Clara Pueblo, New Mexico, he grew up within the Pueblo culture and tradition and got his schooling at a reservation school. He first became interested in anthropology as a profession while serving as an officer in the U.S. Army Air Force in World War II. He graduated from the University of New Mexico in 1947 and received his doctorate in anthropology from the University of California at Los Angeles in 1952.

Dozier taught anthropology at the University of Oregon (1951-52), did research work for the Wenner-Gren Foundation (1952-53), and was an associate professor of anthropology at Northwestern University (1953-58). As a research fellow at Stanford Univrsity (1958-59) he studied American Indian life in the cities. He later conducted research for the National Science Foundation in the Philippines (1959-60). For many years he was a professor of anthropology and linguistics at the University of Arizona. dozier was on the steering committee for the First Convocation of American Indian Scholars at Princeton University in March 1970. From 1969 until his death, he was a professor of anthropology and chairman of the Indian Studies department at the University of Minnesota.

Dozier's many publications include *Hano: A Pueblo Community in Arizona* (1966) and *Pueblo Indians of the Southwest* (1970).

DRAGGING CANOE (Cherokee; ?-1792) was a chief remembered for his fierce opposition to Americans during the Revolution. His Indian name was Tsujungunsini; he was also called Chincohacina and Cheucunsene or Kunnesse.

Dragging Canoe's hatred of Americans arose from the cession of Cherokee lands in the 1775 treaty negotiated by his well-known father, Attakullaculla (*q.v.*). By July 1776 Dragging Canoe had established the Chickamauga towns on Chickamauga Creek (near present-day Chattanooga, Tennessee), away from the main Cherokee settlement. From there, he and his warriors—who were kept wel-supplied by the British agent Henry Stuart—raided white settlements until the Chickamauga towns were destroyed in 1782 by an expedition under the leadership of John Sevier. Dragging Canoe, however, moved down the Tennessee River and continued to fight the encroachment of white settlers until his death. In 1788 he led an army of 3,000 warriors, including many Creek, against the invading forces of Gen. Joseph Martin and succeeded in repulsing the whites.

DRAMA. Native American ritual was carried out because of the power possessed by the music and dances to heal illness, to win battles, to grow crops. The drama inherent in the rites was to some extent the manifestation of that power. Awe-inspiring occurrences that crossed and re-crossed the lines between real and unreal, physical and metaphysical were tangible expressions of the supernatural, enabled and taught by the spirits themselves. Drama as a conscious, independent form was not present. Still, it was invariably present in the ceremonies as historical events were portrayed, as clowns poked fun at themselves and everyone else, and as shamans became supernatural spirits.

Animals influence on music and dance

Dances, songs, and instrumental music were seldom created or used for entertainment, though some evolved into this as the magical symbolism and need faded. An example of this evolution can be seen in Cherokee dances that portray animals and their hunters. Since the turn of the century, these have served as informal entertainment, imitating the actions of animals and people. But earlier, when animals were crucial to the society, the same dances had been used in an attempt to control the mutual behavior of persons and beasts.

Rain ceremonies

In ceremonies seeking certain blessings, the thing sought was often acted out or symbolized. The Anasazi of about AD 700, ancestors of the southwestern Pueblo people, turned nearly all their religious power toward bringing rain. They used fringe on ceremonial garments, gourd rattles, and spruce boughs to imitate the streaming rain, its sound, and its fertile result. Lines of many dancers in modern Pueblo rites are another dramatic portrayal of flowing, falling rain.

The whole Pueblo community became involved when the Kachinas arrived from their homes in the mountains to spend six months living and dancing among the people. "Kachina" has three meanings: a spirit or natural force; a dancer in whom the spirit temporarily resides; and a Kachina doll, carefully carved by cult members for Pueblo children. The Kachina dancers wore elaborate costumes of many kinds — some with animal heads covered with fur, others carved and painted in geometric designs. Feathers, brilliant paint, hides and cloth decorated their bodies. On certain days, the Kachinas danced in the village streets, distributing food to each house and dolls to the children. Kachina ogres threaten to steal bad children, who were ransomed by their mothers. The night dances took place inside the kiva, a sacred house partly underground. Women, children, and elders were gathered when loud footsteps on the roof told them the Kachinas were there. The Kachinas came down the ladder, one after another, into the room filled with firelight, drumbeats, and sacred music. The dancers were the spirits of ancestors — not only to the uninitiated children, but also to the priests themselves whose bodies had been taken over for this time and purpose.

Clowns were present at some dances, and, like European court jesters, they often were able to speak more freely about serious things than ordinary people bound by ordinary etiquette. A Tewa Pueblo clown, the *kossa,* had special power to protect the Pueblo and increase fertility. When their pantomime and jokes became obscene, which was often, they pretended to be invisible. The Yaqui tribe of Arizona (U.S.) and Sonora (Mexico) had a one-man-band clown who played a flute and drum at the same time.

Another dance that masked serious, even frightening, reality with obscene hilarity was the Booger Dance of the Cherokee in the southeastern U.S. In this dance, several men took the parts of Europeans (the Boogers) who had come to visit the tribe. The picture thus presented of the white man is telling, for he was acted out as a wild, uncouth, noisy, pushy creature who only wanted to steal women or fight. When they finally agreed to dance, it became a mockery and exploitation of the Cherokee women (who remained serene), and, hence, the whole tribe. The name, "Booger" or "Ghost," (boogey-man) referred to any horrifying thing. This ceremonial impersonation of the invaders was believed by the Cherokee to have been given them by spirits before the arrival of whites as a protection against the coming foreigners.

A *potlatch* was a great feast and dance given by northwest coast families. The central action was extravagant gift-giving by the host. Each gift was preceded by a speech of praise for the donor. A potlatch was occasioned by a birth, marriage, or inheritance, and validated the status and hereditary rights of the participants, especially the host. If two people claimed the same inheritance, they gave opposing potlatches until the guests declared one supreme or until one gave away all he had and had to stop, thus being the loser.

Eskimo men frequently carried out a dramatic resolution of conflict. Instead of physically fighting, they had a duel in song, each ridiculing the other in excess with the audience sitting as judge and jury.

Eskimo shamans, like Siberian shamans, were possessed by spirits that could transport them to the living-places of the gods or to far-away regions to bring back animals to hunt. During such a "spirit-flight," the people would sit in a totally dark room with drum pounding. The shaman, usually bound and behind a curtain, would cry out, telling the people where he was, what he was seeing, and what supernatural beings he was encountering. At other ceremonies, the shaman danced around the fire in the great dance house while his personal song was sung and a drum pounded. He imitated animals and birds. Finally he shrieked — the signal that a spirit had entered his body and he would prophesy. More informal Eskimo dances included improvised pantomime.

Aztec ceremonials in ancient Mexico involved orchestras, choirs, and thousands of dancers in costumes of gold, feathers, and flowers.

This Indian tradition that includes comedy and tragedy acted out with pantomime, narrative, dance, and song with careful costuming and staging, had in the early 1970s manifested itself in a modern drama company, the Native American Theater Ensemble. Based in New York and having roots deep in Indian country. The players are all Indian and from many different tribes. They have created and produced works from and about their past, such as *Na Haaz Zan,* Navajo creation myth, as well as stark presentations of frustrating, disintegrating, contemporary Indian life. These dramatists viewed traditional Indian ritual as pure and functional drama. They have taken a 20th century mode to capture and increase it, trying to engender and continue a shared cultural experience for Native Americans.

DREAMS AND VISIONS were sought at specific times by most tribes across the Americas under various circumstances and through strenuous effort, usually for the purpose of gaining the aid of a supernatural being. Dreams came unbidden but visions usually were sought through the performance of rites involving personal deprivation. Few tribes believed that the dream sought the individual, coming to him before and after birth and during mature life. Visions occurred usually during the time of fasting and among the hunter-gatherers. Parents prepared their children for vision seeking by making them go without food for a day or two. Algonquins and Salish believed that girls and boys were both eligible for these preparatory visions as a sign of favor from the spirits, but at puberty girls usually stopped the vision quest. A youth or man who desired a vision must stay away from women, since male and female powers were considered incompatible. The vision was commonly a major part of the puberty rites, and though a spirit might appear beforehand in a dream it was a chance occurrence, and a boy had to think constantly of the sort of power needed if he was to be sure of a spirit coming with aid and the promise of ability in hunting, war, gambling, or as a medicine man. Occasionally a vision brought an undesirable spirit such as a Water Monster, and the youth was advised to refuse the offered power.

The puberty vision followed a standard form usually for which a youth was prepared in advance. An animal disguised as a human would appear and take him to the forest, the sea, or other secluded spot and give instruction that might consist of a song to bring power and the giving of a fetish. If a reported vision did not take the proper form the older men of the group would say that it was a false spirit who had come and the vision should be tried again. Throughout the Great Lakes area, in the Mississippi Valley, and in other scattered groups the vision was a necessary part of a youth's growing up. If the quest for a vision was not successful a boy might cut off a finger to induce the Supernatural to take pity on him.

West of the Rocky Mountains the vision quest was not as important, and often only medicine men and shamans sought visions to gain help in curing disease, exorcising evil spirits, bringing rain, et cetera. Where visions were not an integral part of the Indians' life they were scarcely distinguishable from dreams. In certain areas such as in southern California a vision was made a certainty through the giving of a narcotic drink. In British Columbia and on the Plateau the visionary would plunge himself into a pool, rub himself with thorny branches until he bled, fast, and refrain from sexual intercourse with his wife until a vision came. Among the Kwakiutl, spirits would only come in visions to rich chiefs and when their sons were psychologically unsuited to the vision experience they would be secretly coached to simulate a vision experience.

Dreams or visions often were used as a means of relieving frustration, such as among the Eskimo when confined to cramped quarters because of bad weather. Visions then were interpreted as soul flights. This explains somewhat the vision of the shaman too. When called upon to predict or control weather, to supply game animals, to cure disease, to bring fertility to barren women the shaman was under pressure to get results through his visions. The subjective experiences of the hallucination were interpreted as real and the spirit that came might be a human being, a common ghost, a *Tornait,* or an animal spirit. Supernatural sanction through visions of the shaman often were necessary before major undertakings in various tribes. In the Prairies and the east the smallest raid would not be carried out until the shaman had told of the spirits' recommendations through his vision.

Many of the ceremonies observed by tribes were believed to have been established around visions. Actual performances of rites followed to the detail the prefiguration of a vision. Shrines and sacred objects were seen in visions or dreams first. The time of the performance of certain rites often was dictated by visions or dreams. Most Indians believed that the images seen in visions were not fanciful projections but the real glimpsing of the unseen world. Anything that was to take place in the world was already determined and prefigured and was available in a vision.

The Iroquois had a yearly feast called the Dream Feast when the problems and troubles of the year were expressed in dreams and purged by the telling of the dream to another person. If a man dreamed he was caught by enemies and burned alive he would tell his dream and villagers would enact a mock execution of burning him alive to purge the dream. Among the Osage, warriors were directed to try for visions and spirits came in the visions such as Canoe People, Property Woman, and War Spirit. The vision seeker usually was taken ill with an undiagnosed disease and mumbled a song taught in the vision. Then the medicine man and helpers would continue the song and address questions to the spirit regarding the visionary. Among the Blackfoot it was believed that the songs were cherished property and could be sold if the transfer were made physical through sexual intercourse. On the Prairie, the peace journey or *Hako* was an occasion in which visions did not come to individuals through their own efforts but were brought to everyone through way of a communal ceremony and the bidding of the *Tirawa.* In the Native American Church visions were common and expected through the eating of peyote. In these visions spirits or departed loved ones would appear, aid would be given in the solving of personal problems, and warnings would be made to abandon evil thoughts or deeds.

Visions were regarded most highly in areas that lacked organized religions such as the Plateau and Plains. An Indian's success in life seldom was due to his own efforts, but through the sanction of the supernatural through dreams, visions, or hallucinations. Dreams came naturally during sleep and visions through strenuous ecstasy, and both served as the vehicles for spiritual guidance in all areas of Indian life.

DRESS. *See* CLOTHING.

DRESSLERVILLE COLONY, in Douglas County, Nevada, is a federal reservation of 40 acres. It is home to 150 members of the Washoe tribe.

In 1917 the United States purchased, for $10 in gold, the 40 acres of land for the Washoe Indians. The seller of the land was named W.F. Dressler. The Washoe, who for many years had lived in Nevada and California, had a once simple existence. Crafts were designed for practical purposes such as seed-gathering, and survival was the call of the people. Today, very few of the members speak an Indian language, and traditional customs and arts are no longer practiced, on or off the reservation.

The Dresslerville Community Council governs the reservation. It is a sub-council of the Washoe Tribal Council. The Washoe own and operate a ranch, where they grow and harvest hay. It provides the annual income of several hundred dollars. Services on the reservation include water and sewer. There is no gas. Health care is provided in Schurz or Gardnerville, several miles from the land. The few tribal ceremonies take place in quonset huts.

DREW, ROBERT E. (Creek; Junw 12, 1922-), is a public health official. Born in Eufaula, Oklahoma, he worked as a teacher for the Bureau of Indian Affairs in several communities in South Dakota (1947-57) before joining the Division of Indian Health, U.S. Public Health Service in 1957. In 1966 he became acting chief of the Office of Tribal Affairs for the division.

DRILLS AND DRILLING were used from earliest times by Indians for starting fire and for making holes in the construction of utensils, tools, weapons, pottery, and many other objects. Some of the earliest drills were simple awls or awl-like instruments. Also of great antiquity was the hand drill, consisting of a wooden shaft with a sharpened end or a point of stone, shell, bone, ivory, or copper. It was operated by rotating the shaft between the palms of the hands. The hand drill with a blunt wooden tip, rotated against a stationary wooden hearth to produce heat through friction, was one of the earliest and most widely used methods of fire-making.

The points of perforating drills were of two types: the common solid point of wood, bone, stone, ivory, or rarely, copper; a hollow point of reed or tubular copper, which was used in a few areas. With wooden points particularly, wet or dry sand was sometimes used as an abrading material to aid in drilling.

Hand drills were used by a majority of Indian tribes. In parts of the Arctic, western Subarctic, and upper Northwest Coast, more elaborate strap and bow drills were also used for both perforating and making fire. The strap drill consisted of a pointed wooden shaft which was rotated by means of a cord wound one or more times around it. The cord ends, sometimes supplied with bone, ivory, or wooden handles, were held in each hand and pulled alternately to each side. The drill was held in position by a socket held in the mouth or by another person. The bow drill operated on the same principle, but the cord was strung on a wood, bone, or ivory bow so that it could be operated with one hand and the socket held in the other. Both the strap and bow drills allowed faster drilling than the hand drill. Two other types of drills, the pump drill and the disk drill, utilizing a cord wound around the shaft were used by some Indians in post-Columbian times, but there is no adequate evidence of their use aboriginally in the Americas.

DRUM, a percussion instrument, played an integral part in ceremonies and religious rites in many parts of the Americas. Drums were almost always played with dancing and singing. The drum beat often differed from the rhythm of the song, with the dancers' steps following the drum. The beat varied from steady pulsation to elaborate rhythmic compositions.

Drums were decorated with carving, feathers, fur, or paint. Often the decorations were symbolic or expressed the ceremonial purpose of the instrument, as a picture painted on a drumhead of the thunderbird breaking through the sky, releasing rain.

Hide drums were usually like a tambourine with skin stretched over only one side of a hoop; these were present in the Arctic, the Plains, and eastern U.S., and spread to other areas in the 19th century. Double-headed drums are probably modern. Foot-drums were planks over a hole in the ground or floor; slit-drums were a hollowed-out log or a canoe turned upside down. Baskets, boxes, and folded rawhide were beaten and scraped. On the Northwest Coast, men reached up with long poles and beat on the ceilings of the wooden dance houses, turning the whole building into a drum. In the 20th century, the pottery kettledrum, half-filled with water and covered with animal skin, spread from the southwest with the Peyote religion (now Native American Church).

Eskimo shamans used a drum like the Siberian shamans, a large, thin tambourine, perhaps four feet across and six inches wide. It was held upright and swung in a revolving motion back and forth so that first one side, then the other hit a thick drumstick held stationary in the other hand. Helping spirits came to the shaman through his drum.

During the Sun Dance of the Northern Arapaho (Wyoming), each singer brought his drumstick down on a big drum with terrific unison beats. When recruiting volunteers for war, the eight war captains of the Osage **(Prairies)** danced around the village twice daily, stopping to drum and sing.

The Aztec of Mexico had a wooden slit-drum called a *teponaztli* with separate tongues, each tuned to a different pitch. Elaborate melodic compositions were performed when these drums were played together.

DRYPAINTING has reached its highest form with the Navajos who adapted and expanded it from the Pueblo Indians. Although drypainting is used by most Southwest tribes it is best known as part of Navajo healing ceremonies. Each of these ceremonies or chants is concerned with a specific illness and has its own songs, prayers, medicines, and sandpaintings. Between 500 and 1,000 different sandpaintings have been recognized.

A drypainting is a symbolic picture usually made on the floor inside the hogan where the healing ceremony is held. A dozen or more medicine men and assistants may work on the painting. Women may not observe sandpaintings while they are being made. After the painting is completed, ceremonies are performed in which a medicine man or singer invokes help from gods. The patient sits on the painting and parts of it which relate to his illness are placed on him. When the treatment is over, the patient leaves the hogan and the painting is destroyed in the same order in which it was made. The evil which caused the sickness is believed to be absorbed by the sand so the sand must be disposed of. Navajo sandpaintings are destroyed by sundown of the day they are made.

Drypainting is called sandpainting because it is often made with materials such as sand. Vegetable material, such as pollen and corn meal, minerals, and charcoal

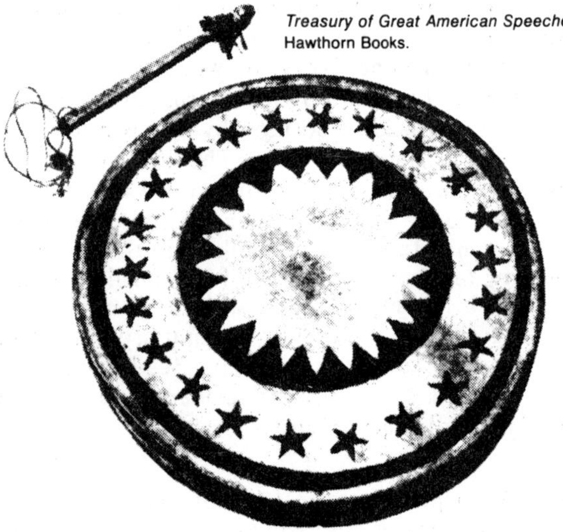

Treasury of Great American Speeches, Hawthorn Books.

Tsimshian drum.

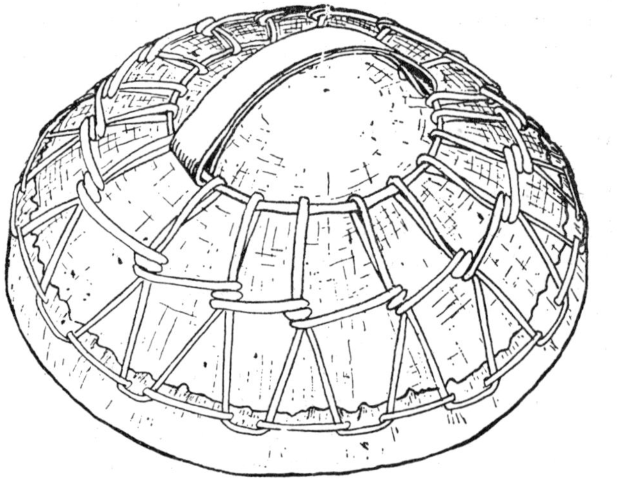

Smithsonian Institution, National Anthropological Archives.

Machi drum.

Courtesy Dover Pictorial Archives.

Wooden drum, Maya.

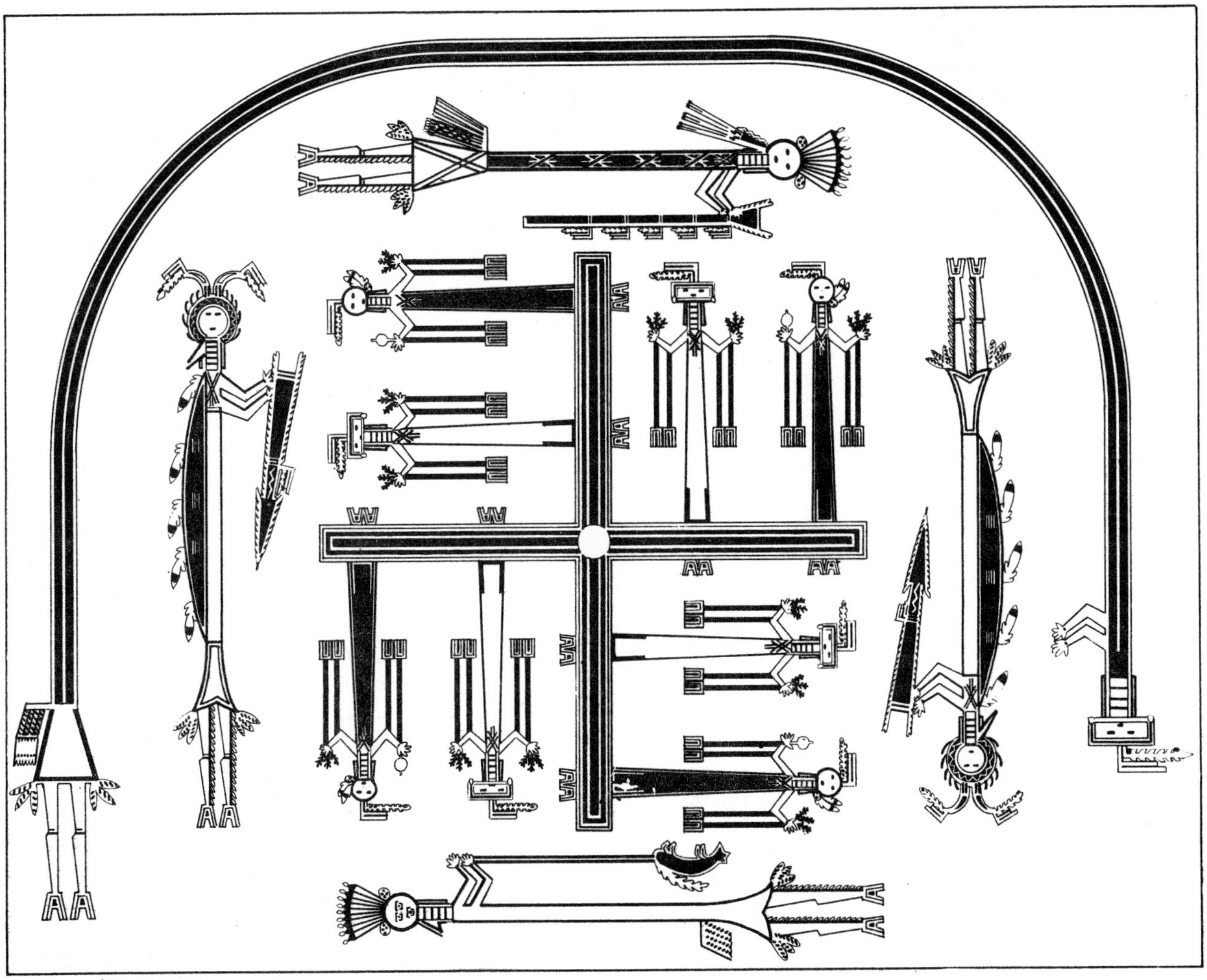

Courtesy Dover Pictorial Archives.

Navaho sand painting. Black cross-bars denote pine logs; the circle represents water. Figures of gods with their wives (goddesses) sit upon the logs. Round heads denote male; rectangular heads, female. Rattles and sprigs bring male and female rains which bring forth vegetation. Arching over all is the rainbow goddess upon which the gods travel. (After Stevenson)

(from a tree struck by lightning) are used. After they are crushed into powder they are sometimes mixed with sand and dirt. The artist holds a small amount of this colored powder in his hand and sprinkles it on the surface. The surface is usually a flat layer of clean sand but sandpaintings have been made on buckskin.

Sandpaintings depict gods from legends and myths, animals, and plants. The earth is represented as a female, the sun as a male. The six cardinal points in Navajo mythology, north, south, east, west, up, and down, are represented by symbolic colors, usually including black, white, yellow, blue, and red. Sandpaintings range in size from one foot to twenty feet in diameter.

Drypaintings were made from memory with designs handed down from one medicine man to another. In 1919 a medicine man named Hosteen Klah broke the taboo against reproducing sandpaintings when he wove a rug which copied a sandpainting. Klah made colored drawings of sandpaintings which are studied by some medicine men who visit the Museum of Navajo Ceremonial Art in Santa Fe. Today sandpaintings are reproduced in paintings, photographs, rugs, and in sand.

DU BRAY, ALFRED WILLIAM (Rosebud Sioux; April 1, 1913-), is a career official with the Bureau of Indian Affairs (BIA). Born in Tripp County, South Dakota, he joined the BIA in 1938. He became superintendent of the Winnebago Agency, Nebraska, in 1963.

DUCKENEAUX, FRANK DOUGLAS (Cheyenne River Sioux; Feb. 28, 1903-), is a charter member of the Cheyenne River Sioux Tribal Council and chairman since 1972. He was born on the reservation at Promise Community, South Dakota, and became a member of the council in 1935. A rancher, he has been active in numerous organizations and commissions, including the South Dakota State Indian Commission, primarily concerned with seeking legal aid and economic and social betterment for Native Americans.

DUCK VALLEY RESERVATION, in Elko County, Nevada and Owyhee County, Idaho, is home to nearly 1,000 Shoshone and Paiute Indians. The reservation is 290,000 acres, split evenly between Nevada and Idaho, and is totally tribally owned.

The Duck Valley Reservation was established by executive order in 1877 for the Western Shoshone. In 1826, a group of Paiute settled on the north side of the reservation by government order. The Indian Reorganization Act of 1938 organized the groups into one tribe. However, there is no grouping according to culture, but only according to standards of the community. Indian culture on the reservation is disappearing through mixed marriages, the school system, and other non-traditions.

The organizational structure on the reservation is governed by the bylaws and constitution approved in 1936. The governing body is the business council, composed of seven members elected to three year terms. The tribe belongs to several associations and cooperatives. Services on the land include water, sewer and electricity. Medical care is available in Owyhee, several miles away.

DUCKWATER RESERVATION, in Nye County, Nevada, is home to 63 members of the Shoshone tribe. The reservation is 3,785 acres.

Duckwater reservation was established in the period 1940-1944, when lands were purchased for the Shoshone Indians in the area. All the land is tribally-owned. The original settlement of Duckwater Valley came in 1868, when white settlers homesteaded the land, which Shoshone claimed was theirs. As they had lived here long before the coming of Columbus, their claim was valid, but nonetheless went unheeded. The Shoshone lived in the Great Basin area, which barely provided a subsistance level. They ate nuts, roots, berries, and wild game. They had little social organization, and usually travelled in extended-family bands. Beyond speaking their language, the Indians of the reservation today retain little of their traditions.

Organized under the Indian Act of 1934, the tribe is governed by a council of five members. The tribe has no income, and the reservation has little in the way of natural resources. Most of the Indians are unemployed or underemployed. The reservation provides water and waste disposal, and little else. Other services are available in Ely, 40 miles away.

DUCOIGNE, JEAN BAPTISTE (Kaskaskia; ?-*c.* 1832), was a chief in Illinois who developed a friendship toward whites and a loyalty to the U.S. that earned him the hatred of most of the surrounding chiefs. He almost slavishly copied white ways of living, and he maintained that none of his tribe had ever attacked or injured a white man. In August 1803 he signed the treaties arranged at Vincennes and was granted a house and 100 acres of land. Ducoigne probably died shortly before October 1832 because in the treaty of Castor Hill, Missouri, of that date the Kaskaskia ceded to the U.S. all of their land east of the Mississippi River except a single tract reserved to Ellen Ducoigne, "the daughter of their late chief."

DUGOUT, a canoe-like boat made from a tree trunk, was used by North American Indians throughout most of the Eastern Woodlands, Great Lakes region, Northwest Coast, and parts of Alaska, the California coast, and the Plateau. It was made by alternately charring and adzing out the interior of the trunk, a process which took several weeks. The dugout was more durable but heavier in portage and more time consuming to make than the bark canoe. After the introduction of steel tools, the time needed for its construction was greatly shortened, and it was adopted in some areas where the bark canoe had previously been used exclusively.

Most dugouts were paddled with single-bladed paddles. The largest dugouts reported by early observers were built by the Haida after acquisition of steel tools. Some of these were sixty or seventy feet long and capable of sea voyages of eight hundred miles down the coast to trade with or attack Puget Sound tribes. In the Puget Sound and Georgia Straits region, boats made from two dugouts joined by a platform were reportedly used for freighting purposes.

DUKES, JOSEPH (Choctaw; 1811-1861), was a noted interpreter and translator of the Bible into Choctaw. Born in Choctaw country in the present state of Mississippi, he attended a mission school at Mayhew, where he often acted as interpreter for the Rev. Cyrus Kingsbury, the pioneer missionary. Dukes remained in Mississippi for sometime after the Choctaw had ceded their lands to the U.S. During this period he helped the Rev. Cyrus Byington prepare a Choctaw grammar and dictionary.

In Indian Territory (present Oklahoma) in 1851-52 Dukes preached under the direction of the Rev. Allen Wright, with whom he translated the Old Testament. When Wright was succeeded by the Rev. John Edwards in 1853, Dukes taught him Choctaw and worked with him on further translation of the Bible.

DULL KNIFE (Northern Cheyenne; *c.* 1828-Jan. 9, 1879, or 1883), was a prominent chief who resisted the encroachments of white settlers onto Indian hunting grounds in the northern Great Plains, and whose attempt to lead his people from Indian Territory (present Oklahoma) back north in 1878 rivals Chief Joseph and the flight of the Nez Percé for sheer courage and determination.

From early manhood, Dull Knife had led his band in intertribal warfare and attack on whites. He was closely allied with Red Cloud (*q.v.*) and the Oglala Sioux, as well as other Sioux (Dakota) leaders. Dull Knife was his Sioux name; the Cheyenne called him Morning Star.

Portrait by Nancie Anne Gille. Dull Knife

His name crops up in most of the fights that bloodied the northern Plains from 1865, when he was involved in the fight at Platte Bridge Station. During that same summer he fought against the Powder River Expedition under the command of Brig. Gen. Patrick E. Connor. In the spring of 1866 he was present at the treaty negotiations at Fort Laramie which ended abruptly when the Indians learned of the arrival of Col. Henry B. Carrington and his 700 officers and men who were en route to the Powder River country for the purpoise of establishing a series of military forts for the protection of a road along the Bozeman Trail through Indian country. Dull Knife remained at Fort Laramie and signed the paper giving the soldiers permission to build the forts, although he insisted that he had done so only to get the presents of ammunition and blankets. He was soon with the other Indian leaders engaged in guerrilla warfare along the Bozeman road. He participated in the Fetterman Fight near Fort Phil Kearney on December 21, 1866, and in the Hayfield Fight near Fort C. F. Smith on August 1, 1867. In May 1868 he signed the treaty made by the Northern Cheyenne and the Northern Arapaho with the U.S. In June 1876 Dull Knife was one of the Cheyenne leaders at the Battle of the Little Big Horn.

After that last tragic event, Dull Knife moved his village in the Bighorn Mountains, along the Powder River, where troops under Col. Ronald S. Mackenzie succeeded in a surprise attack at dawn on November 25, 1876. The Indians suffered heavy loss of life; 173 lodges were destroyed and 500 ponies captured. With no food, deprived of cooking utensils and clothing, the Indians made their way to Crazy Horse's retreat, but they surrendered in the spring of 1877.

On May 1, 1877, Dull Knife was one of some 900 Northern Cheyenne sent Fort Reno in Indian Territory, where their bodies succumbed to malnutrition and disease, and their hearts yearned for their homeland.

Dull Knife and Little Wolf told agent John D. Miles of their intention to go north, asking only that the agency grounds not be desecrated by post-departure fighting. They struck their lodges on September 9, 1878—89 men, 112 women, and 134 children, alternately traveling and fighting pursuing soldiers. Beyond the North Platte River, the bands separated, Little Wolf moving toward the Powder River, Dull Knife and 148 followers toward what had been the Red Cloud Agency. In the Sand Hills they were surrounded by the Third Cavalry under Capt. J. B. Johnson. Disarmed, the captives were taken to Fort Robinson.

In January the Cheyenne were told that they were being hereded back to Indian Territory. When the chiefs refused to budge, the officers tried to starve them into submission, even withholding drinking water. Preferring death to Fort Reno, the captives broke out on the night of January 9 and were shot like rabbits in the snow. Dull Knife and his wife are reported by some historians as escaping to the Pine Ridge Agency, where he died in 1883; others say he was killed at Fort Robinson that dreadful night. His son Bull Hump declined to succeed his father as chief of the band, saying that chiefs were no longer needed among the defeated Indians.

DURANT, WILLIAM A. (Choctaw; *c.* 1886-Aug. 1, 1948), a member of a prominent Choctaw family, was a state legislator and principal chief of the Choctaw Nation. Born in Indian Territory, he was a sergeant-at-arms at the Oklahoma Constitutional Convention (1907). He was a member of the Oklahoma House of Representatives (1907-12), serving as Speaker of the House during his last two years of office. He was chosen principal chief of the Choctaw Nation at the tribal reorganization in 1934.

DUSCHANE, HOWARD (Shawnee; July 10, 1911-), is an official with the U.S. Bureau of Indian Affairs (BIA). Born at Seneca, Missouri, he joined the BIA in 1934. He served at Truxton Canyon Agency, California (1934-50); Hoopa, California (1950-55); Portland, Oregon (1955-57); Fort Belknap Agency, Montana (1957-60); and Cheyenne Agency, South Dakota (1960-66), before becoming area credit officer of the Albuquerque Area Office in 1966.

DUTCH POLICY governing the relationships between the Dutch and Indians in the New World were a direct result of competition between the Dutch and other European nations interested in the Americas, especially Spain. Spanish hegemony in the New World began to be challenged by 1600, at which time the Dutch were their major opponents. At that time the Netherlands were called the Low Countries and were governed by Spain. In 1579 the Dutch formed a rebellious state, the United Provinces, and waged an eighty year war for independence, 1568-1648. Dutch ships would trade with the Indians and Spanish colonists in the Caribbean, Mexico, Central America, Venezuela, Colombia, the Guianas, and with Portuguese Brazil. Spain did not maintain a regular supply of European goods with its American colonies and the Dutch took full advantage of the resident Spanish-Americans' willingness to engage in what the Spanish Crown considered an illegal trade, the *rescate.* The United Provinces also licensed privateer ships, who would attack and ransack Spanish shipping and sometimes Spanish settlements. The most precious prize desired was the capture of one of Spain's silver fleets which sailed annually in convoy back to Europe. A Dutch Admiral by the name of Piet Heyn, succeeded in doing this in 1628 off Matanzas Bay, Cuba.

Although the English colonies of North America were also dealt with by the Dutch beginning in the 1600s, interest was only peripheral, as anti-Spanish activities took precedence. The Dutch did create trading relationships for furs with the Indians living in the northeastern United States, however. Such trading was carried on by the United Provinces through the auspices of the original Dutch West India Company.

The Dutch West India Company (1621-1674) was a semi-public organization supported by private investors and a large government subsidy. The States General (*Staten*) Central Government chartered the West India Company and proclaimed all of the territories of West Africa, the Americas, and the Caribbean as subject to its administration. In actuality, very little of this area could be effectively controlled or even claimed by the Company. From its inception the Company wanted monopolistic control of all legal and illicit commerce and privateering; but it realized that individual sponsors would have to be licensed to trade and raid in some of these regions. Those areas not involved in the Company's avowed major purpose of crippling Spanish control via privateering and harassment were the regions with the greatest amount of individual activity, in particular North America. Conflicts of interest between monopoly and individual trade, commerce and colonization, and eventually war and peace with Spain, emerged early in the Company's existence. The major political advantage of using such companies as agents of war by the Dutch, English, and French was that outside of Europe and European waters, these organizations could wage undeclared warfare. The states were therefore not legally involved in an open recognition of the extent of the hostilities. This legal fiction is generally expressed by the phrase, "no peace beyond the line."

The West India Company was divided into five chambers: West Frisian Towns; Maas; Groningan and Friesland Provinces; and the two most important ones of Zeeland and Amsterdam. An executive board of directors (the *Heren* XIX) consisted of 19 officials: 1 representative of the States General; 2 from each of the less important chambers; 4 from Zeeland and 8 from the dominant Amsterdam chamber. A rivalry between the Amsterdam and Zeeland chambers arose and persisted upon formation of the Company. Zeeland was interested in colonization and the development of a plantation economy (sugar and tobacco) in New Walcheren (Dutch Tobago, 1628-1678), New Netherland, New Holland, and on the Wild Coast (The Guianas, especially Surinam). Maintaining a company monopoly was also of major concern. Amsterdam was interested primarily in commerce in New Netherland fur; illegal trade with Latin America and its Caribbean bases for this activity — Curaçao and Saint Eustatius; and in booty from privateering of Spanish shipping. The other chambers and private investors tended to support Amsterdam's emphasis on quick profit and its support of private agency trade. Yet, these concerns could be found somewhat reversed or less intensified in different areas administered by a particular chamber. The most unifying factors for the Company were the war with Spain, the early success of Dutch privateers in the Caribbean and off Brazil, and the profitable illicit trade with unsupplied Spanish colonists in Latin America. When the war with Spain ended in 1648, the Company went into a gradual decline. Basically, the African slave trade based at Curaçao kept the Company running until its demise in 1674. The growing French and English capacity to supply and defend a national trade monopoly with their New World plantation colonies also contributed greatly to the decline. The West India Company realized far too late the long term profitability of establishing plantation economies. Dutch involvement in Brazil and North America, especially the Company's policy towards and relations with the Indians, will serve to illustrate the paradoxical nature of the causes of early Dutch success, as they eventually became the reasons for failure in most of their American colonies.

There were two main Indian groups living in Brazil during the 1600s: the Tupí and Tapuya. The Tupí were greatly influenced by early Portuguese settlers. Many had been forcibly placed in communities (*aldeias*) which were administered by Jesuit missionaries and local Portuguese officials. This arrangement was common throughout Latin America as it ensured control of the Indians as a labor resource. The Tapuya lived in the interior and were actively hostile toward the Portuguese. As was the case throughout Central and

South America, many Indians were killed in battle; enslaved; died of European diseases from which they had no immunity; and/or consequently, retreated into the tropical rain forest interior.

As early as the 1590s the Dutch had established irregular trading with Indians in the interior, as well as those in the Portuguese enforced villages. Sugar, hides, tobacco, ginger, canafistula, sarsaparilla, cacao (chocolate beans), cochineal and indigo dyes, and dyewoods (e.g. brazilwood), were the products sought. Salt was also a major commodity since the Netherlands operated an extensive salted herring-fish industry. Dutch commerce with Brazil expanded after 1621 and local anti-Spanish Portuguese officials were easily persuaded to trade. In 1624 the Zeeland chamber of the Company started colonization in New Holland (northern Brazil) by planting sugar plantations. The Portuguese were not pleased with this event and so began a thirty year period of guerrilla warfare. Usually the Tupí allied themselves with the Portuguese, and the Tapuya joined with the Dutch. Supposedly, when the Tapuya learned that the Dutch were not Portuguese, this fostered trade and military alliances between them. During this prolonged struggle the Dutch attempted to convince the leader of the Petiqua Indians, Poty, to withdraw his support of the Portuguese; but it was to no avail. Poty was knighted and named Don Felipe Camarao by the Iberians for his help against the Dutch.

From 1637 to 1644 Count Johan Maurits served as the Company's director in New Holland. He emphasized friendly relations with the natives and encouraged their anti-Portuguese sentiment. Because of conflicts with the Company over establishing a plantation colony, he was dismissed. The Zeeland chamber also promoted colonization in northern Brazil; but the prevailing preference for immediate profit via illicit trade and raiding made the building and peopling of colonies a secondary, if not a minor, concern for the controlling Amsterdam chamber. The complaints of the Dutch colonists in Brazil echoed those of the earlier Spanish-American residents — insufficient supplying for their needs. In Brazil the Dutch followed Spain's neglect, which in itself had been what led to the Dutch success in smuggling. This oversight contributed to New Holland being lost to the Portuguese in 1664: a loss of a valuable source of sugar and salt.

The New Netherland colony of the United Provinces provides an excellent example of the problems of Dutch colonization when fighting with Spain was not involved. New Netherland covered much of present day New York, particularly the Hudson Valley and the Delaware Valley. Henry Hudson's early 1600s explorations led to the establishment of Dutch trading posts in the area. It was not until 1623, however, that the West India Company sent any settlers. Most of these people and the earlier colonists were interested primarily in fur trading with the Indians. Individuals licensed as patrons included many Zeelanders. The familiar conflicts of free trade versus Company monopoly together with the Company's inability to administer the area without these individual patrons, were a source of constant disputes in New Netherland. In the final analysis, only one patronship survived and prospered — that of the Rensselaerwyck family. All of the personally sponsored patroonships (the term patroon is not a Dutch word but a term commonly used in discussion of these estates) were in regular conflict with the company, including the lone survivor.

Both individual and Company trading followed the usual Dutch policy of maintaining friendly trading relationships with the Indians. Commerce was their aim, not religious conversion nor Europeanization.

Title of Dutch map printed c. 1671.

The goods traded for furs were steel knives and hatchets, cotton cloth and clothing, and even firearms and powder; although the last two were often considered illegal trade items. In North America the Dutch, as well as the English and French, wanted animal furs for their European markets. In 1634 the Dutch-Indian fur trade was not doing well. Tomassen and Jerronimus de la Croix, along with two other Dutchmen named Harman and Bogaert, went through the Mohawk Valley to establish regular trade with the Oneida Indians and with the other four members of the Iroquois Confederacy: Seneca, Onondaga, Cayuga and Mohawk. Fort Orange, near contemporary Albany, New York, was the site to which the Iroquois would come for trade. Throughout the administrations of the Company's New Netherland directors, Wilhelm Kieft (1638-1647) and Peter Stuyvesant (1647-1664), the fur commerce prospered. The period was characterized by regular protests against patrons who cut into the Company's trade. Individuals were arrested, goods confiscated, and still the illicit trade continued. Patrons emphasized colonization and trade; whereas the Company stressed commercial benefits and neglected non-trade oriented settlements. The Indians, especially the Iroquois, were aware of this situation and felt no obligation to trade with only Company officials or independents. Furthermore, the geographical location of the Iroquois groups between the Dutch and other Indians, such as the Huron, Algonquin, Susquehannah (White Minquas) amd Erie (Black Minquas), permitted them to act as middlemen for the Dutch fur trade. So, too, the Iroquois Confederacy and its expansion was largely due to their growing dependence on European goods obtained by trade. They waged wars to control the fur resource areas.

Dutch-Indian relations were not always smooth. Kieft sent an expedition against the Weckquasgeeks in 1642 and fought with the Mohawks in 1643. In 1663, Stuyvesant waged war with the Esopus Indians. Many of the problems stemmed from dishonest traders. Often, the Dutch had to ally themselves with the English settlers of New England and accept more and more Englishmen in New Netherlands to be able to effectively retalliate Indian attacks. This alliance ultimately proved fatal to Dutch control in the area. Peaceful relations were eventually negotiated with the Mohawks, who then initiated warfare with the Indian allies of the New England English. Except for the disputes with the Mohawks, Dutch-Iroquois relations were good and mutually beneficial. The Iroquois waged wars with other Indians and traded the captured fur to the Netherlanders. It was with the other Amerindian groups that the Dutch were unsuccessful in their relationships.

The Iroquois-Dutch alliance was based upon a mutual interest in maintaining commerce. The alliance was implicit rather than professed. New Netherland never experienced continuous and widespread Indian hostility and an ultimate major Indian uprising, as did the English colonies in 1675. The main reasons stemmed from the West India Company's emphasis upon trade, fostering good relations with the aboriginal populations, and lack of support for permanent colonization based on its own local economy — the same reasons which caused the patroonships to fail and also necessitated growing dependence upon military aid from New England colonists. This brought about the United Provinces' loss of a North American colony.

One of the most impressive results of Dutch policy with the Iroquois was the impetus to the rise of Iroquois military strength and interest in commerce for European goods. The Iroquois-Dutch trade relation was inherited by the English, whose presence was increasingly more evident in New Netherland after 1640. Not only did the Company depend upon the English as allies against hostile Indians; but they also licensed them as independent traders. Further, the colony's loss resulted from the treaty which concluded the Second Anglo-Dutch War of the seventeenth century. It was fought in Europe, Western Africa, the Caribbean and North America. The Dutch ceded New Netherland to keep Surinam (formerly Dutch Guiana) because they considered the latter's sugar plantations as potentially more profitable than the North American fur trade.

JOHN H. PHALEN

DWAMISH belong to the Nisqually dialectic group of the coast division of the Salishan linguistic family.

They are a small group of Salish near Seattle, Washington, a city which was named for the chief of this tribe. They reside at the outlet of Lake Washington.

Their population about one hundred years ago is variously given from 64 to 312. Today they number several hundred.

DWELLINGS. The Western stereotype of the Indian, still featured in movies, is that the original Americans lived only in tipis, wore Sioux war bonnets, and spoke one "Indian language." In point of fact there were and are many Indian tribes differing from each other in regard to their ways of life, and their physical environment.

Their dwellings (just like the food, arts, crafts and clothing of each tribe) depended on the available materials, climates, topography, and flora and fauna. (It is interesting that none of the aboriginal tribes had any domestic animals — except the dog, and of domestic fowls, turkeys were raised only by the Pueblos). In building their homes, the Indians used many different materials and designs: the stone and plaster pueblos of the southwest; the cedar houses of the far northwest with skillful carpentry and elaborate carvings; the earth-covered, log hogans of the Navajos, the skin tipis of the Plains; the bark and pole houses of the Iroquois. Among the highly developed peoples of Middle America and Peru, buildings went much further; stone was used to build spacious and beautiful temples and palaces richly ornamented with carvings.

Most of the region east of the Mississippi was heavily forested. There the Indians lived in villages and

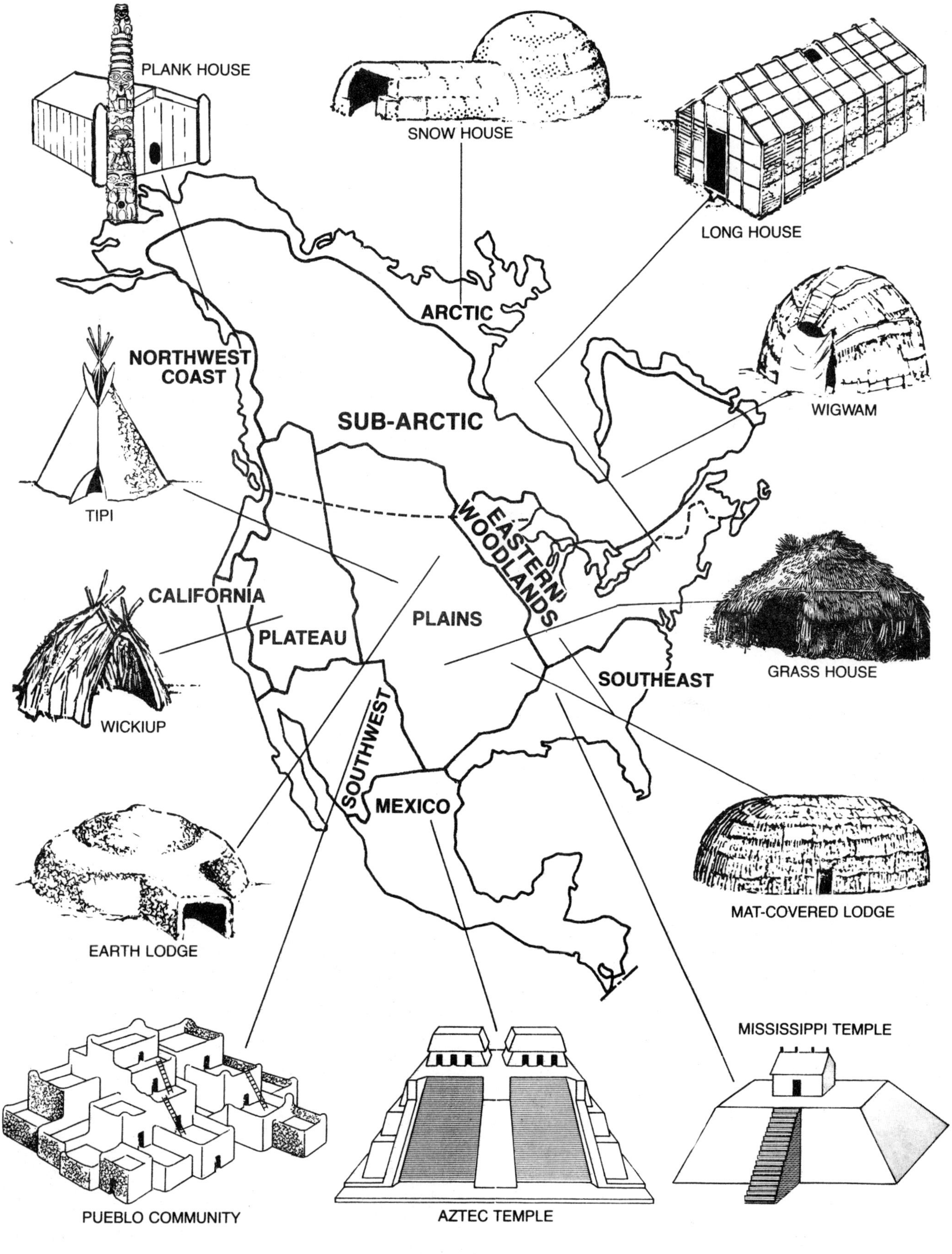

Indian dwellings in the cultural areas of North America.

Reconstruction (1971) of 19th century *"Do-Giagya-Guat-(Tipi of Battle Pictures)."* By Dixon Palmer, (Kiowa).

settlements of substantial houses near streams and rivers, made with a framework of poles covered with mats or bark or plastered with mud mixed with straw. They protected their villages by palisades of closely set poles driven into the ground. Having no metal axes to cut down the trees, they peeled off the bark and used it. In the far north the Indians built a pointed tent of poles and covered it with a wrapping of birch bark. Farther south, they constructed a dome-shaped wigwam, like a frame of bent branches, covered with strips of tough elm bark. In the area which is now New York, they built gabled long frame community houses, covered with strips of bark; they accommodated from 5 to 20 families. In the far north of this area they made a pointed tent of poles and covered it with a wrapping of birch bark. In the extreme southern regions, they constructed shelps covered with neatly woven mats of cane or branches. The Creek settlement typified the economic and social life of the southwestern tribes. At its center were the public buildings, set on terraces in the most important settlements. The "square" consisted of 4 shed-like structures enclosing an open space of hard-packed earth with the sacred communal fire in the center. This public center was surrounded by individual dwellings, composed usually of from one to 4 separate buildings.

While the religious and ceremonial life of the Woodland Indians (from Maine to Florida, from the Atlantic Ocean to the Great Lakes and the Mississippi Valley, and on through most of eastern Canada) was based on the corn, that of the Plains tribes centered around the buffalo and the worship of the sun. The latter tribes hunted buffalo and gathered roots and berries. Needing a movable dwelling, they invented the famous tipi, a cone-shaped tent, usually of dressed skins, mounted on poles meeting near the top. These portable dwelling were usually assembled and erected by the women as the Plains tribes went from place to place following the buffalo. A group of tipis often were placed in a large circle, perhaps around a central council tipi. The existence of the buffalo was here of utmost importance, since the long leaning poles of the tipi were covered with 12 or more buffalo hides sewed together.

In fact, in the Plains, the preparation of the buffalo hides was a whole industry in itself. On the ground near the tipi the women stretched out a large skin of the slaughtered buffalo, pegging it to the earth with wooden stakes. Bent almost double over the hide, they raked the flesh, scraping the skin down to an even thinness. They rubbed oily fat and brains into the surface of the hide with firm, massaging strokes. When the whole skin was covered with the fatty mass, they took a smooth stone, rubbing it slowly up and down until the fat was thoroughly worked in and then hung it in the sun to dry. The tipi provided more than a shelter and a place to sleep. The conception that the abode served the bare essentials of usage still remains. In 1886 the last great herd of buffalo was exterminated. Thereafter, most Indian families had to live in small one room log houses with single (or no) windows and dirt floors.

The basic furnishings were one or two castiron stoves, shifted during the seasons between the house, tent or outdoors, and several beds on which a number of individuals slept closely huddled together; others

Embassy of Venezuela, Information Service.

Community hut of Motilon Indians in Peryá, Zulia, Venezuela.

Bureau of American Ethnology Collection.

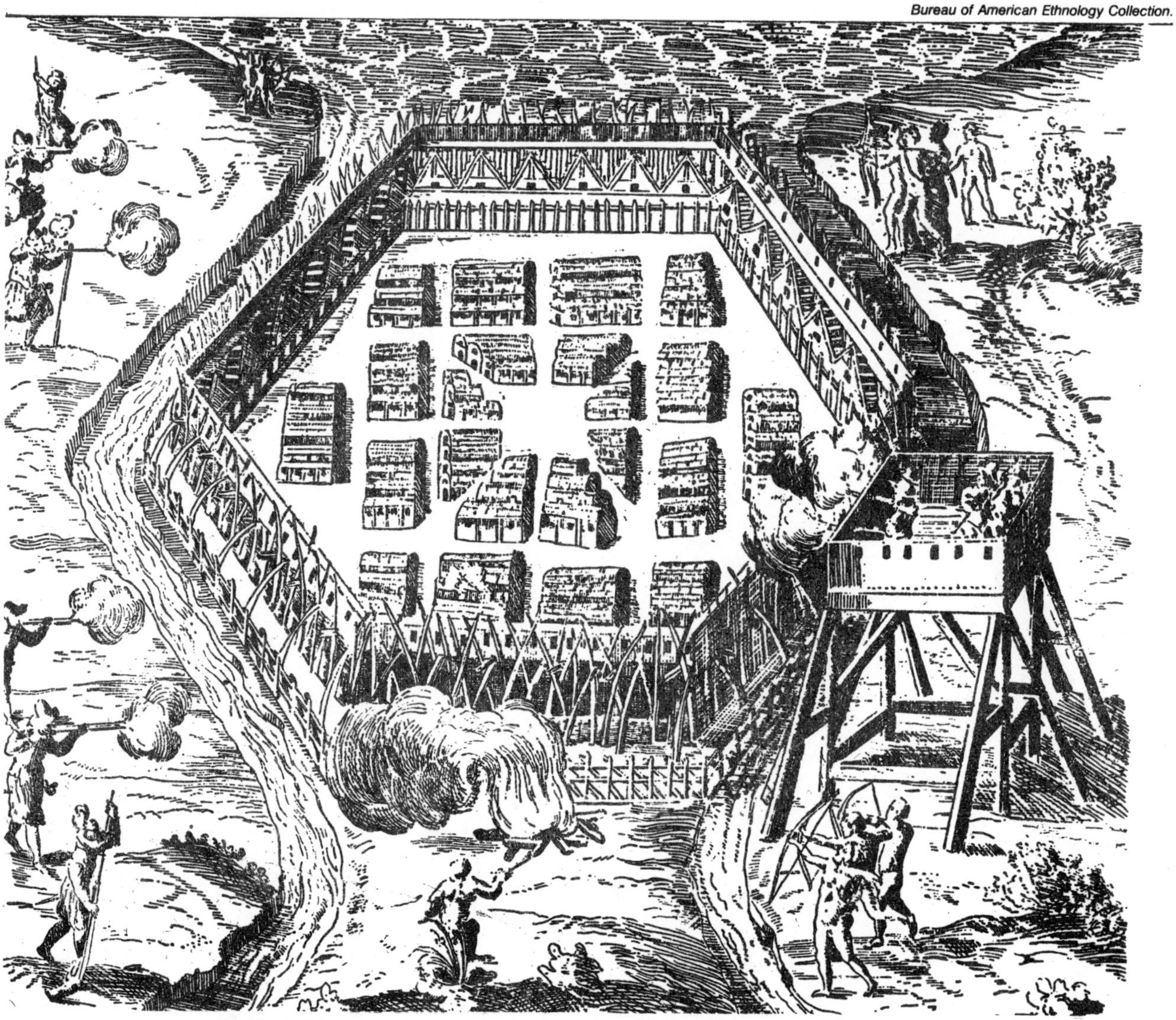

Palisaded Onondaga (Iroquois) town attacked by the French led by Champlain (1615).
It stood in the town of Fenner in the present Madison County, New York.

slept around the sides of the tent. Many families lived permanently in tents.

For the Fox tribe of Iowa life had two distinct phases, a sedentary agricultural aspect in the spring and summer and a nomadic hunting existence in the fall and winter. From April to August, the people lived in permanent villages. Here they had long-rectangular houses covered with elm bark, 50 or 60 feet long. There were openings at either end of the house, and 2 sleeping benches about 3 feet high and 4 feet wide, ran along the side walls. From September to April, these Indians used the small, mat-covered *wickiup,* a grass hut shaped like a beehive, a round or oval dome structure, which was easy to heat and simple to transport. The mat coverings, made of cat-tails, were rolled up and taken to deck the new frame when the family reached the camping site.

Most picturesque of all Indian dwellings were the multistoried houses of stone or adobe in the southwest Pueblos, built by the native Indians of New Mexico and Arizona and of a narrow strip of southern Colorado and Utah, a small portion of southeastern California, and considerable territory of northern Mexico. The word *pueblo* means a village. Southwest, it was once thought to be the work of an extinct people, but it is known now that the buildings perched on mesas and on lodges of canyon walls were built by the ancestors of the Pueblo Indians as defenses against nomadic tribes. Pueblo lands are rich in abnormalities and wonders, and the homes on them are difficult to approach, for they are built on far up the perpendicular walls which have to be climbed, although they are constructed in the vicinity of streams or waterholes. These buildings are erected in nooks and corners of the cliffs. With rough stone implements, the Indians hacked niches for footholes into the faces of the cliffs and climbed up with their loads of adobe earth; for the chief well-making material, they went to the beds of streams and gathered fragments of rock of various shapes and size or broke pieces from the adjoining cliffs and worked them into convenient form; or, from the soft sandstone or the brittle volcanic

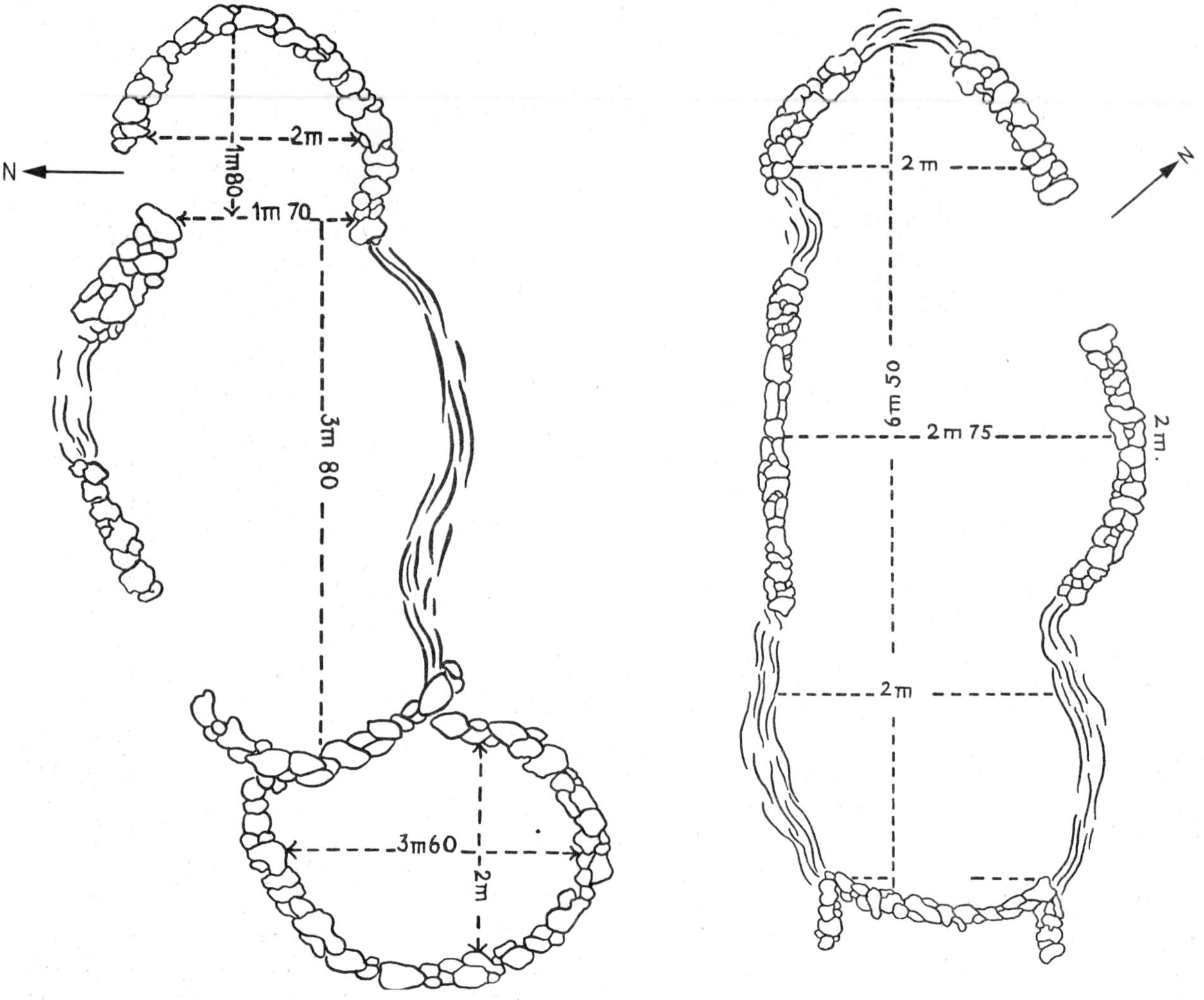

Ground plans of cave dwellings at Intihuasi, Sierra de Comechingones, Province of Córdoba.

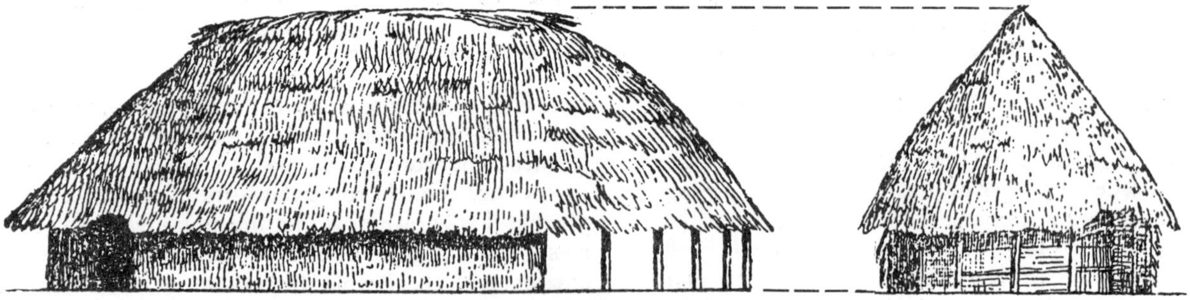

Guahibo dwelling.

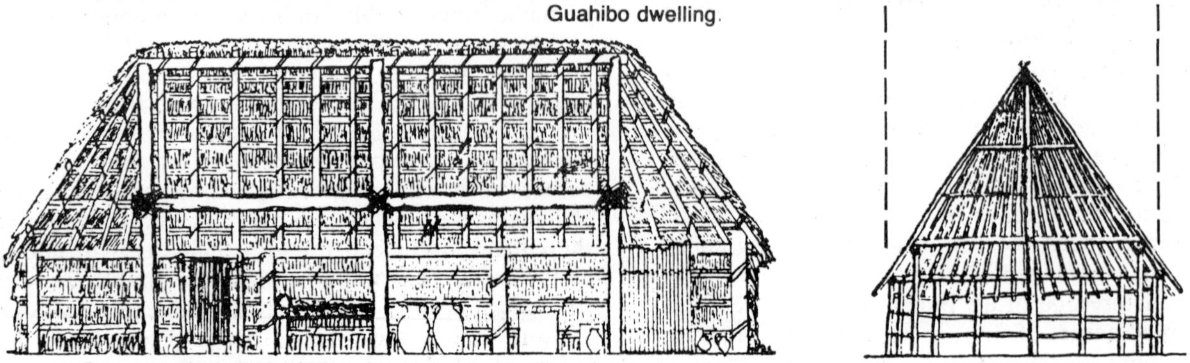

Cross section of the interior of a Mapuche dwelling, or *ruka*.

rock, they fashioned rectangular blocks. If no suitable stones were available, and adobe clay could be easily secured, they made bricks, dried them in the sun, and then carried them up to the shelvy rocks on which the houses were to perch.

In some localities excavations were made into the sides of the cliffs. They hacked into the sandstone or volcanic rock and scooped out their rude cells. Entrances were made from the faces of the cliffs, and were purposely difficult to approach. Beneath the doorways, along the sides of the cliffs, usually ran narrow, irregular, and often times dangerous paths, connecting one cave house with another. Into the rock, directly above the doorways on the outside, deep, narrow, holes were often made, for supporting poles, over the projecting ends of which skins could be thrown for awnings.

The water problem was somewhat solved by building rude cisterns (reservoirs) to catch the snow and rain. In some localities, towers, built of stone and adobe clay, were placed out on projecting rocks, from which an approaching enemy might be detected. Groups of the terraced, many-storied stone and adobe apartments were arranged around a plaza where religious ceremonies were held. The many-roomed houses (of the contemporary apartment houses type), sometimes 4 or 5 stories high, were the types completely different from any other Indian shelter in the Americas. Their style of agriculture was symbolic of their coordinate, orderly, cooperative society, fully integrated into its environment. The object of life for all members was to live harmoniously with each other and with the universe. Only if order and peace prevailed and the spirits of the dead were content would the rain fall, the harvest would be good, and people and animals would be healthy and fertile. The inhabitants of the pueblos tried to assure the harmony of the universe by a cycle of religious ceremonies observed throughout the year, and secret religious societies were responsible for the round of observances. The priests of the societies, who formed the town council, saw to it that the religious ceremonies took place on time; members of the council also decided town policy and sat in judgment on anyone accused of a crime. A warrior society carried out the orders of the council and provided for defense.

In the Southwest the Pueblo people lived in multistoried houses of stone or adobe, remaining in the same location for centuries and growing their crops by irrigation. They obtained their meat by hunting, but raised cotton for their clothing and excelled in pottery. Their ceremonials and artistic decorations stressed — and still stress — the importance of rain. The Indians farther south in this area lived until recently in bog domed-shaped houses made of poles and brush, covered with earth.

A dry and empty land across the southern Rocky Mountains (Utah, Nevada, southern California) was tramped over by the Indian tribes on a regular route each year, living on ripened seeds (acorns, sweet nuts from small pine trees, seeds from wild plants). They built a frame of poles, usually in a round or beehive shape, and tied on bunches of grass or desert bushes. In winter they heaped earth over the house.

The Indians of the Great Basin and the California desert utilized all the resources of their countryside. They wandered over it in small family groups, gathering seeds and nuts, digging roots, and snaring rabbits and other small animals. They made their clothing from the desert plants, weaving strings of sagebrush or desert willow into a sort of mat to serve as a scanty garment and weaving a winter wrap from strips of rabbit fur. Their dwellings were temporary, made of branches covered with bunches of grass or desert bushes; in winter they covered the whole with earth.

In aboriginal times the Puyallup of Washington (the Pacific coast) commanded the water entrance to the

Smithsonian Institution, National Anthropological Archives.

Pueblo of Acoma, New Mexico.

Photo by Antonio Macedo.

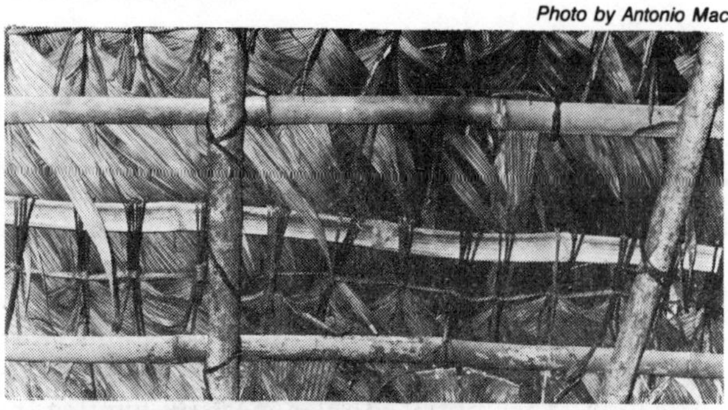

◀ Detail of the thatching of the houses of the acculturated Guarani Indians, São Paulo, Brazil (1971).

House built by the Guarani in the forests off the coast of São Paulo, Brazil (1971).

Photo by Antonio Macedo.

Detail of the construction of a Guarani house.

USDA photo.

Dual houses in the Tabio agricultural community, Colombia. Building at right is used for kitchen and childrens' sleeping quarters, (1944).

southern Sound. Their villages were located either on small streams which tumbled down to the Sound from the highlands of the Kitsap Peninsula, or along the river system which drained the west slope of Mt. Ranier and the country lying between the mountain and Commencement Bay. These streams pointed toward a hub at the mouth of the Puyallup River (today's Tacoma). This was a region with a heavy rainfall, a temperate land of swamps, extensive tide flats, damp, overgrown gullies and sudden floods. It was a land offering food for the taking, fish (salmon), clams, seal and porpoise, and elk and bear. Each village was located at the mouth of a stream above the tide flats. The houses were built of split cedar planks, the ridge pole of the rather high gable roofs following the length of the building. Doorways were located at each end on a line with the roof peak and one door facing upstream toward a narrowing vista of water and clear bank and the other facing the wider expanse where two waters met. The typical "village" suggested a cluster of small houses; it consisted of a single large communal dwelling, occupied by most of its inhabitants over most of the year and seldom left completely alone. The small stream provided the village with salmon, wood was found along its upper reaches and carried back or floated to the back of the house site, while hunting followed the course of the stream. The house was divided into 4 or 6 sections, each serving as the living quarters of a single family group. The house sections were at either side, one in each corner and, in larger

Photo by Arthur Tress. Contemporary Inuit housing.

Houses built entirely by Indians in Methakahtla, Alaska.

Photo by Fred W. Marvel. Sequoya's cabin.

Photo by Linda Bartlett.

Living conditions on Indian reservation.

Photo by Marcia Kay Keegan.
Contemporary Indian housing.

houses, 2 facing each other in the center of the bed platform which ran around the walls of the house, of the storage platforms above, and of the drying racks which extended as high as the roof peak. Each family did its own cooking on fires built on stones let down into the dirt floor or directly on the hardened dirt. They were located along the center passageway in pairs. The central passage was used by all and the area of common recreations (story-telling, the playing of organized children's games). The sense of family privacy was, however, strong and centered around the cooking activities of each fire.

Along the Pacific Coast (from northern California to southern Alaska), the land of trees, the western red cedar was commonly used by the Indians for building material. They burned through the trunks to fell the trees, then split them into planks with wedges of horn or wood. The cross planks were tied with vines to the upright planks; this structure had no chimneys or windows. Some of the houses were more than 500 feet long, holding 8 to 10 families, and divided into compartments by hanging mats.

JOSEPH S. ROUCEK

DYES AND PIGMENTS were used from earliest times by the Indians of the Americas who obtained them from the natural materials available. Sources were used such as blood and a few other animal substances, pollen, fruit, flowers, leaves, and other plant parts, fungi, and a wide variety of clays, earths, and ores. With the great importance of color in Indian culture, dyes and pigments were universally employed for a wide range of purposes, from the decoration of utilitarian articles to the symbolic use of color in religious ceremony. Coloring agents themselves were occasionally given religious significance and ritually gathered and prepared. Many of the large array of natural preparations used aboriginally are now unknown, having fallen into disuse after the Indians' acquisition of European dyes and paints through trade.

Vegetable and other materials which were soluble, usually in water, were extracted or decocted by pulverizing and boiling to produce dyes. These were used to color basketry materials, porcupine quills, textiles, and hide. Some of the sources of black dye were clays, wild grape, sunflower seeds, and hickory or black walnuts. Red dye was obtained from such sources as iron and manganese ores, sumac berries, savoyenne root, buffalo berries, and alder bark; yellow from ochers and lichens; green and blue from copper salts and leaves; purple from chokecherries. Other plant materials and a few minerals were used singly or in combinations to produce other hues and shades. Mordants were also employed; the Navajo, Hopi, and Zuni, for example, commonly using urine or an impure native alum.

Clays, sandstones, and ores as well as many vegetable materials were used as pigments. Sandstones and ochers, for example, were commonly used for red; charcoal, soot, graphite, lignite, and fungi for black; chalk, kaolin, gypsum, diatomite, and limestone for white; sandstone, ochers, lichens, jarosite, and pollens for yellow; copper ores, crushed leaves, serpentine, and jarosite for blue and green; burnt lignite and manganese and iron ores for brown. A wider range of hues and shades was produced by some tribes by mixing or heat treating the more common pigment materials. For kiva wall murals of the Southwest, for example, red and yellow ochers were mixed with various clays to give orange, pink, salmon, and vermilion.

Pigments were usually separated from impurities, ground by mortar and pestle, and combined with water, mucilagenous and glue agents, or oils and fats to form paint for coloring tools, weapons, masks, walls, pottery, textiles, disguise, and other objects and surfaces. They were used in dry powder form for sand-painting in the Southwest, and in many areas were dried in cake or powder form and sealed in containers for storage or trade.

EAGLE. Among the many birds held in regard by the Indians of the Americas, the eagle, by reason of its majestic, solitary, and mysterious nature, became a special object of worship. This is expressed in the use of the eagle by the Indians for religious and esthetic purposes. The wing-bones were fashioned into whistles to be carried by warriors or used in ceremonies, and the talons formed powerful amulets or fetishes, having secondary value as ornaments; the feathers were, however, of greatest importance. The capture of eagles for their feathers was a hazardous branch of hunting, requiring great skill. Among some tribes eagle-killing was delegated to certain men. Owing to the difficulty of getting within bowshot of the bird, it was often trapped or visited to secure the young. Eagles are still kept in captivity by the Pueblo Indians in the time of Coronado, the 16th century.

The striking war-bonnet of the Plains tribes was made of eagle feathers and was highly valued. Warriors of the Plains tribes usually wore the feathers of the golden eagle only, and the customs of many tribes were similar. Many tribes wore one or more eagle feathers in the hair, and these feathers were often cut, colored, or otherwise decorated by the wearer. It was the custom of the Pillager Chippewa to allow a warrior who scalped an enemy to wear on his head two eagle feathers, and the act of capturing a wounded prisoner on the battlefield earned the distinction of wearing five. Fans made of the primary feathers of the eagle formed an accessory to the costume of the Sioux and other tribes. Eagle feathers were also attached as ornaments for the buckskin shirts worn by men, and war costumes and paraphernalia, including shields, were ornamented with them. As one of the prominent totemic animals, the eagle gave its name to many clans and religious fraternities. Nearly every tribe in the United States recognizing clan or gentile organization had an eagle clan or gens at some period in its history.

The eagle held an important place in symbolic art. It was depicted by all the the methods of art expression known to the Indian, appearing on pottery, basketry, textiles, beadwork, quillwork, shields, crests, totem poles, house and grave posts, pipes, rattles, and objects pertaining to cult and ceremony. It was also represented in the primitive drama connected with ceremonies. Many tribes possessed eagle deities, as the Kwahu, the eagle kachina of the Hopi of Arizona, and the Eagle god of the Miwok of California.

Among the Haida, passes made with eagle fans were thought to be effectual in conjuring, and this use reappears in many tribes. The wing-bones were often employed as sucking tubes, with which medicine-men pretended to cure disease. The Tlingit and other North Pacific tribes used eagle down for ceremonial sprinkling on hair, masks, and dance costume; it was also scattered in the air, blown through a tube or sprinkled by hand. The Pawnee and other Plains tribes as well as the Pueblos also used the down in ceremonies, and it was a general custom. Among the Hopi, the eagle is generally associated with the Sky god, and its feathers are used with disks to represent the Sun god.

The use of eagle feathers in religion is nowhere better represented than among the Pueblos, when downy plumes are attached to masks, rattles, prayer-sticks and other cult objects entering into ceremonies. For this purpose a great quantity of feathers were required. The Hopi claimed the eagle nests in the localities where they formerly resided, and caught in traps or took from the nests eaglets, whose down was used in ceremonies. The eaglets, when required for feathers, had their heads washed; they were killed and buried with appropriate rites in special cemeteries, in which offerings of small wooden images and bows and arrows were deposited. The Salish also had property in eagles. Among the Zuni, feathers shed by their captive eagles had special significance, though the feathers were regularly plucked and formed a staple article of trade.

The mythology of almost every tribe is replete with eagle beings, and the wide-spread thunderbird myth relates in some cases to the eagle. In Hopi myth the Man-eagle is a·sky-being who lays aside his plumage after flights in which he spreads devastation, and the hero who slays him is carried to the house in the sky by eagles of several species, each one in its turn bearing him higher. The Man-eagle myth is widely diffused; most tribes regard this being as a manifestation of either helpful or evil power.

South America. Notable for its magnificent size, plumage, bearing, and strength is the famous monkey eagle, harpy eagle, "harpia," "pega macaco" (*Harpia harpyja*) which is found sparsely distributed throughout the forests of the Guiana-Brazilia and Central America.

The prey of this huge eagle is large: namely, sloths, monkeys, and even wild pigs and small deer and calves.

The flight is by rapid wing beats, carrying the bird deep among the trees and foliage, and the short "stoop" to quarry is as sWift and lethal as a bolt of lightning. The imposing size and strength of this king of predators and the appearance of its erected crest, large narrow beak, and glaring eye give it a special place in the culture of any native group. The young were eagerly sought and were raised in captivity; the feathers, plucked or molted from wings and tail, gave special value to arrows or head bands, and were items of wealth for display or trade. The meat, fat and even the excrement had special medical value to some tribes of the Xingu and Araguaya rivers.

Related and similar in appearance, though slightly smaller, are the crsted harpy (*Harpyhaliaetus coronatus*) and the long-tailed harpy (*Morphnus guianensis*). The former is found in extreme southwest Guiana-Brazilia and adjacent Patagonia-Chile region.

Museum of The American Indian.

Pair of Nazca gold effigy ear ornaments, representing a man holding a spear and a woman, beating a drum.

EARLY MAN. *See* PALEO-INDIAN.

EARRING is an ear ornament inserted through a hole pierced in the lobe or rim of the ear.

In mounds built in the Hopewell era (*c.* 200 BC-AD 400, Ohio), many ear-discs and earrings were found. In later Mississippian mounds (*c.* AD 700-1500, southeastern U.S.), large, polished shell discs with pictorial carvings like Mississippian gorgets are believed to be pendants. In 16th century Mexico, Indians wore gold earrings imbedded with colored stones. From the earlier Mexican Toltec culture (*c.* AD 900-1100) came a gold dangle-type earring with a stylized animal figure, probably a butterfly, and three tiny bells suspended beneath it. Modern southwestern Zuni works in silver have a similar style, with abstract designs and long dangling beads and other suspended forms. The first Navajo silver earrings (*c.* 1870) were large hoops of silver, each made from one silver dollar. In the early days when Navajos were learning from Mexican smiths, one pair of earrings was paid for with one sheep.

Stone and pottery ear plugs shaped like spools have been found in California and Arizona; similar ones of shell plated with copper came from Ohio. Long, slender, engraved bird bones to be stuck through pierced ear lobes, like sticks have come from California mounds.

An earring sometimes showed high status or wealth and was given to honor a person. In such cases, the ear-piercing was given to honor a person. The ear-piercing was often accompanied by ceremony, and each procedure cost the donor — usually a parent or relative — a standard price. An ear ornament probably of this origin was the Seminole (Florida) Pendant hanging from a loop inserted in the ear lobe, accompanied by perforations all around the rim of the ear with smaller loops inserted in them.

EARTH LODGE is an Indian dwelling partly underground, circular in form, from 30 ft. to 60 ft. in diameter, with walls about 6 ft. high, on which rested a dome-shaped roof with an opening in the center. The entrance was a projecting passage-way from 6 to 14 ft. long.

The earth lodge was used by the Pawnee, Arikara, Omaha, Ponca, Osage, and other tribes. Similar abodes were used in the Aleutian islands, and in southwest Alaska. There were habitations among some of the California tribes that had features in common with the earth lodge.

The method of construction of an earth lodge was first to draw a circle on the ground and excavate the earth within it from 2 to 4 ft. deep. About 1. ft. within the circle were set crotched posts some 8 or 10 ft. apart, on which were laid beams. Outside these posts were set others, one end of them braced against the bottom of the bank of earth at the periphery of the circle, and the other end leaning against the beams, forming a closed stockade. Midway between the center of the excavation and the stockade were planted 4, 6, or 8 tall crotched posts, forming an inner circle. In the crotches were laid heavy beams to support the roof of long, slender, tapering tree trunks, stripped of bark. The wall and roof were afterward carefully tamped with earth and made waterproof. The long entrance way was built in the same manner as the lodge, and thatched and sodded at the same time. The grass of the sod continued to grow, and wild flowers brightened the walls and roof of the dwelling. Within, the floor was made hard by a series of tampings, in which both water and fire were used. The fireplace was circular in shape and slightly excavated. A curtain of skin hung at the opening from the passageway into the lodge. The outer door was covered with a skin that was stiffened by sticks at the top and bottom, and which was turned to one side to give entrance to the passageway.

More than one family sometimes occupied a lodge. The back part, opposite the entrance, was reserved for the keeping of sacred objects and the reception of guests. In the winter curtains of skin were hung from the beams of the inner circle of posts, making a smaller room about the fireplace. The shields and weapons of the men were suspended from these inner posts, giving color to the interior of the dwelling, which was always picturesque, whether seen at night, when the fire leaped up and flinted on the polished blackened roof and when at times the lodge was filled with men and women in their gala dress at some social meeting or religious ceremony; or during the day when sunlight fell through the central opening over the fireplace, bringing into relief some bit of aboriginal life and leaving the rest of the lodge in shadow. Few large and well-built earth lodges exist today. Even with care a lodge could be made to last only a generation or two.

Ceremonies attended the erection of an earth lodge. Both men and women took part in these rites and shared in the labor of building. To cut, haul, and set the heavy posts and beams was the men's task; the binding, thatching, and sodding that of the women.

The Pawnee had the most elaborate ceremonies and traditions pertaining to the earth lodge. This tribe abandoned the grass house and learned to construct the earth lodge. According to their ceremonies and legends, not only the animals were concerned with its construction — the badger digging the holes, the beaver sawing the logs, the bears carrying them, and all

Smithsonian Institution, Bureau of American Ethnology.

A Pawnee earth lodge in the village on the Loup Fork in Nebraska. The lodge is partly underground, circular in form, covered by a dome-shaped roof made of brush and grass with an opening in the center that allows light to enter and smoke to escape. The erection of an earth lodge was marked by elaborate ceremonies.

obeying the directions of the whale — but the stars also exercised authority. The star cult of the people is recognized in the significance attached to the four central posts. Each stood for a star — the Morning and Evening stars, symbols of the male and female cosmic forces, and the North and South stars, the direction of chiefs and the abode of perpetual life. The posts were painted in the symbolic colors of these stars — red, white, black, yellow. During certain ceremonies corn of one of these colors was offered at the foot of the post of that color. In the rituals of the Pawnee, the earth lodge was made typical of man's abode on the earth; the floor is the plain; the wall the distant horizon; the dome the arching sky; the central opening the zenith, dwelling place of *Tirawa,* the invisible Power which gives life to all created beings.

EASTERN WOODLANDS CULTURE AREA. The Indians that occupied the northeastern woodland areas from the Great Lakes to the Atlantic belonged to two great language families — Iroquoian and Algonquin. Both groups had similar living patterns. The Algonquin tribes who lived along the Atlantic included the Montagnais and Naskapi of Subarctic Canada; the Penobscot, Passamoquoddy, Mahican, Massachuset, Abnaki, Narraganset and Wampanoag of New England and New York; and the Delawares of the mid-Atlantic region.

In the forests to the west around the Great Lakes lived the Ojibwa (Chippewa), Ottawa, Menominee, and Cree tribes, and south of them such Prairie tribes as the Sauk, Fox, Kickapoo, Miami, Illinois, and Shawnee. These Algonquins formed a fringe around the aggressive Iroquois who were probably later invaders of the area, and were especially concentrated in the Mohawk Valley and Finger Lakes region of New York and around lakes Erie and Huron. The best known of these tribes were the Five Nations of the Iroquois League — the Mohawk, Cayuga, Seneca, Oneida, and Onondaga. (Later a sixth nation, the Tuscaroras, joined them.) Other large Iroquoian tribes were the Hurons and Eries.

The lore and traditions of the Woodland Indians are familiar to all Americans, though often in romanticized form, from the Leatherstocking Tales of Cooper, the poems of Longfellow, and the legends of the Pilgrims. It was the Wampanoags who befriended the Pilgrims and shared the first Thanksgiving dinner with them in 1622. (They were virtually exterminated in a war with the settlers in 1676.) The Algonquian words *wigwam, wampum, squaw, papoose, tomahawk, mocassin,* and *powpow* have been adopted into our language.

The Woodland tribes were casual farmers. All of them, except those tribes living too far north, planted corn, beans, and squash. Planting and harvesting were women's work. Only the sacred tobacco plant was tended by men. The ceremonial smoking or burning of tobacco leaves developed among the western Algonquin into the sacred ceremony of the calumet ("peace pipe").

The Algonquins lived in dome-shaped, bark-covered wigwams. Where available, birchbark was used for wigwams, utensils, and canoes. Their clothing was made of buckskin, often handsomely decorated by beadwork or quillwork. Most of their possessions were simple and utilitarian. The women and children gathered berries, nuts, wild onions and potatoes. The men hunted deer, moose, fox and smaller animals and entire families moved in a sort of holiday spirit to gather seasonal foods such as wild rice, maple sugar, or shellfish.

The first corn, first fruits or game were always offered to the *Manitu* (good and bad spirits) that inhabited their world. Manitu existed in the sun, stars, thunder, corn, or animals. Daily life involved many ritual precautions. An animal was never killed without performing certain acts of etiquette so as not to offend its spirit.

Social organization was informal and democratic. *Sachems* (chiefs) were respected but not all-powerful. Shamans, who often had genuine healing skills, functioned as doctors, and to a lesser extent, as sorcerers.

Children were raised indulgently and patiently taught the skills of their parents. A newborn infant was cleverly guarded against the spirits of the dead. It was wrapped in an older person's clothes so that the ghosts would mistake it for a grown-up. Its mocassins were pierced with holes so that it would not be able to travel back to the spirit world. A boy's killing of his first game was accompanied by celebration. Young boys undertook a vision quest for a guardian spirit.

War, raiding, and scalping were common to all the Woodland Indians but the most warlike were the five nations of the Iroquois League who terrorized Algonquins and Iroguois alike. The League (called by its founders the *Great Peace*) was formed before 1600 by the Iroquois prophet Deganawidah and his disciple Hiawatha. Though it was effective in keeping peace among its member nations, it was devastating to the Hurons, Eries, and Algonquians. Though the Iroquois are chiefly remembered now for their cruel practice of torturing captives, historians are impressed with their organization and the political astuteness that enabled them to play off the French, English, Americans, and other Indians against one another.

A small number of Iroquois still exist in small reservations in New York where they were rescued from despair and alcoholism in the early 19th century by a religious revival led by the remarkable Seneca prophet Handsome Lake, brother of the warrior chief Cornplanter. Today the Iroquois religious message is gaining adherents among Indians nationally. Other Iroquois survive in Canada or in western reservations.

Many of the Atlantic Algonquin tribes were virtually wiped out at an early date by disease, or war with settlers or Iroquois. Some Penobscot and Passamoquoddy people remain in Maine on reservations. At the turn of the century the western Algonquians were briefly united to resist white encroachment under the chiefs Pontiac (Ottawa), Little Turtle (Miami), Tecumseh (Shawnee), and Black

Hawk (Sauk). Thereafter they were removed to the West or escaped to Canada, although a few still occupy their traditional lands in the northern Great Lakes regions.

EAST GREENLAND INUIT are famous for two reasons. They were probably the first Eskimos to have contact with whites, and their development of weaponry and tools is the highest of any Eskimo.

East Greenland Inuits consist of two major branches: the *Angmagsalingmiut,* who live in the fiords and around Cape Daniel; and the Southern group living along the southern coast. More than three-fourths of these Inuits are *Angmagsalingmiut,* and are usually isolated from white contact.

They have perfected many types of tools. The most interesting are their harpoons with detachable shafts that float in the water while seals swim off with the line. They also have flexible jointed lances for killing a struggling animal.

For kayaking they developed a special double bladed paddle and cloths that fit snugly around the opening of the boat to prevent water from getting in.

Curiously, except for one isolated northeast band, they have not developed any decorative arts.

Seafood, particularly sea mammals, are their main source of food. During the winter they live in long, narrow sod and stone houses.

Their first contact with whites was the Norsemen in the 11th century. This contact seems to have ended abruptly in the 13th century. But since then they were met off and on until the 1700s when Denmark claimed Greenland and began establishing posts on the island. Today they have regular contact and trade with whites.

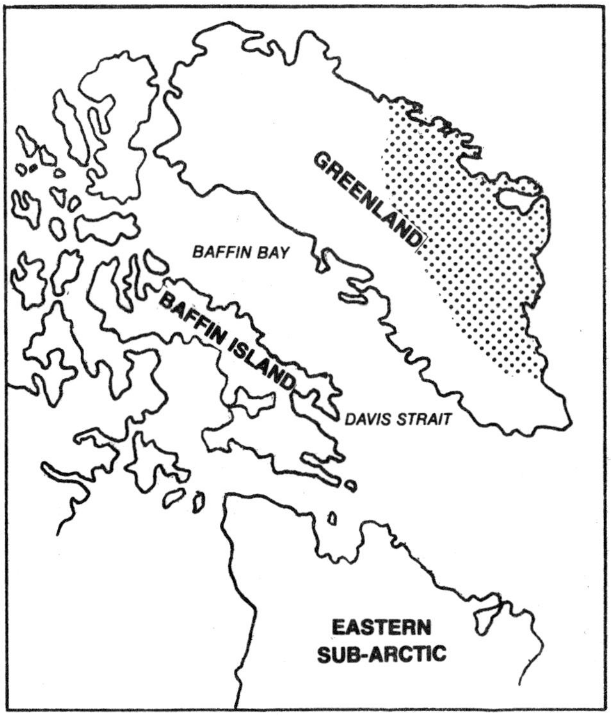

East Greenland Inuit.

EASTMAN, CHARLES ALEXANDER (Santee Sioux; 1858-1939), was a distinguished physician, lecturer, and author. The youngest of five children, he was born in Redwood Falls, Minnesota, to a Sioux Father of the Wahpeton subtribe and a half-blood mother who died when he was an infant. He was named Hakadah ("The Pitiful Last") and renamed Ohiyesa ("The Winner") when he was four years of age.

Ohiyesa was raised by his paternal grandmother and uncle, who were forced to flee with him into Canada after the 1862 Sioux uprising in Minnesota. In 1872 he was claimed by his father, Jacob Eastman ("Many Lightnings"), who took him to the small Santee Sioux farming colony in Flandreau, South Dakota. Renamed Charles Eastman, he began his education at a mission school, graduating from Dartmouth College (1887) and the Boston University medical school (1890).

Eastman's first position was that of government physician at the Pine Ridge Agency in South Dakota. The massacre at nearby Wounded Knee Creek occurred shortly after his arrival. Eastman was in charge of treating the wounded survivors.

Eastman spent three years (1890-93) at Pine Ridge, where he met Elaine Goodale, a white poet and Indian educator whom he married in 1891. He was forced to resign his post after he refused to back down from his charges of official corruption at the agency. He then opened a private medical practice in St. Paul, Minnesota, and later served as official representative of the Sioux in Washington, D.C. He traveled a great deal and lobbied with federal officials in attempts to defend Indian treaty rights. He was active in pan-Indian movements and was one of the founders and the first president of the Society of American Indians, although he later became an inactive member.

Eastman helped the federal government to revise the Sioux allotment roles (1903), and was commissioned (1910) to find and buy rare Indian curios and ethnological specimens. He represented the North American Indians at the First Universal Races Congress in London (1911), and in the 1920s served as a government physician at the Crow Creek Agency, South Dakota. Eastman was active in work for the YMCA, the Boy Scouts, and the Campfire Girls. He wrote for magazines and lectured widely on American Indian life, culture, and history. His publications include two autobiographies, *Indian Boyhood* (1902) and *From the Deep Woods to Civilization* (1917).

EASTMAN, JOHN (Santee Sioux; 1849-?), was a noted Presbyterian minister and a tribal leader. Born at Shakopee, Minnesota Territory, his Indian name was Mahpiyawakankidan ("Sacred Cloud Worshiper"). His father was a full-blooded Sioux of the Wahpeton subtribe who, upon conversion to Christianity in 1864, took the name Jacob Eastman; his mother was the half-blooded daughter Capt. Seth Eastman, a U.S. Army officer; his younger brother was Charles A.

Eastman, John

Eastman (*q.v.*). In 1874 he married Mary J. Fairbault, a half-blood Santee, who bore him six children.

John Eastman was ordained a Presbyterian minister in 1876 and became pastor of the church in the Flandreau Indian colony, Dakota Territory. In 1878 or 1879 he took over the government school for the children of Flandreau and held that position, despite some opposition, until 1885 when he became overseer of the band. He retired as overseer in 1896 to devote his time to ministering to the affairs of his church and running his farm. From 1880 he annually represented his people in Washington, D.C.

ECHOHAWK, BRUMMETT (Pawnee; March 3, 1922-), is an artist, cartoonist, and illustrator, who was a decorated hero in World War II. Born at Pawnee, Oklahoma, he served in the U.S. Army for five years (1940-45), training men in hand-to-hand fighting and seeing heavy combat duty in North Africa, and Sicily, Italy. Following the war he attended the Chicago Art Institute (1945-48) and then began working as a commercial artist and illustrator. He has a comic strip, "Little Chief," which appears in the *Tulsa World.* He is also a popular lecturer and has written articles for various newspapers, including the *London Sunday Mirror.*

ECHOHAWK, JOHN E. (Pawnee; Aug. 11, 1945-), is an attorney and director (since 1973) of the Native American Rights Fund, a publicly supported national legal services program for Indians. He was born in Albuquerque, New Mexico, and attended the University of New Mexico, where he received his bachelor's degree in 1967 and his law degree in 1970. He joined the Native American Rights Fund in 1970, serving as staff attorney (1970-72) and deputy director (1972-73) before becoming director.

ECONOMIC SYSTEMS. European ways had profound economic effects on Indian life virtually from the beginning of the historic period, particularly through the introduction of the horse and the gun.

The horse was first introduced into North America by the Spanish. Although they tried to keep the Indians from learning to ride, individuals learned in secret and taught the skill to others. Eventually, through raids into Spanish territories or rebellions against Spanish overseers, the Indians acquired large numbers of horses. The acquisition of horses in such quantities eased the problems of transportation considerably, and many village dwelling and agricultural peoples soon became nomads. The horse also simplified the pursuit of game, and hunting thereafter became an easier, more profitable, and more widespread activity.

The availability of the gun encouraged hunting activities too, although it also fostered warfare between different tribes. Introduced by the English and the French in the east, the gun was used by such peoples as the Ojibwa and the Cree to push enemies such as the Dakotas further west. Through warfare, raiding parties, and trade, horses and guns quickly spread to tribes all across the continent.

Transportation and weaponry are still two important areas in which native Americans are being influenced by Western culture. For example, among the Indians, Eskimos, and Aleuts of Alaska, motor boats have replaced kayaks and umiaks for fishing, and the rifle has replaced the harpoon for hunting. Telescopes are used to scout for migrating herds of caribou. In many isolated villages, food and other materials are brought in by air. For local transportation, snowmobiles have replaced the dog sled. Malamutes, once working animals, are now bred only for racing. But these changes have not always improved the lives of these native Americans. In the past they had developed cultures that enabled them to live happy and peaceable lives in the often hostile environment in which they live. Today — even with the most modern machines, weapons, and communications systems — poverty, malnutrition, and poor education and health facilities are the rule rather than the exception. And the necessity to fly in supplies from distant places means that the natives pay two to three times as much for some items as do people who live in the "lower 48."

The problem of poverty is widespread among Indians in all regions of North America. In 1968, for example, the Bureau of Indian Affairs estimated the average per capita income for Indians at $900 per year. Family income was set at just over $5,800 in 1969, as compared to nearly $6,200 for all minority groups. For the population as a whole, average family income was about $9,500.

An example of changing economic systems is that of the Cherokee.

By the end of the 18th century, the Cherokee had already begun adopting white economic practices on a large scale. Then as now the aim was economic self-sufficiency that would enable them to retain their own cultural heritage in a country that had become alien. They established mills, black smith shops, schools, looms and spinning wheels, cultivated land, and established sizeable libraries. But their efforts, though eminently successful, ended abruptly a few years after the passage of the Indian Removal Act in 1830. Though only about five thousand out of a population of 20,000 people agreed to move, government troops forcibly evicted the whole tribe. The forced march West that followed is remembered to this day as "the Trail of Tears"; at least four thousand Cherokee died on that march.

Today, the Cherokee are once again building a solid economic structure. Their major sources of income derive from the tourist trade, a few factories, and some lumbering activities. One Cherokee industry produces moccasins, another makes quilted products and babywear, while a third produces women's hair accessories. Total payroll for these three industries, however, comes to only about one million dollars per year. By the 1970s average annual income per family was only about $3,000; but this looks better when compared to the $1,000 average of 1956.

Navajo Indians are operating a number of industrial enterprises, the most successful of which is a large electronics plant that produces transistors and miniaturized circuits. Of nearly 800 employes, nearly all are Navajo. About ninety percent of the supervisory personnel are also Navajo. Interestingly, Navajo women work with the aid of microscopes to wire the miniaturized circuits — their traditional craft of weaving intricately patterned rugs has proved an asset in memorizing the complex structure of these tiny circuits. When the plant first began operations, a turnover rate among employees of 12 percent monthly resulted in a revision of personnel policies, which at first had not recognized that Indian culture does not share the emphasis on clockwork efficiency that characterizes white culture. More relaxed rules on office hours and days off have helped to stabilize the work force. This same looseness of organization characterizes the policies of many Indian business enterprises.

By the mid-1960s nearly sixty industrial sites had been located on Indian reservations. The majority of these have been operating only since 1960. During the last decade, the Bureau of Indian Affairs, the Department of Housing and Urban Development, the Small Business Administration, and the Economic Development Administration have all begun making funds available for building, or offered loans to industries to locate plants on reservations. Although the investment to date has been insufficient to create a truly self-sustaining economic base for the Indians, the first tentative steps in that direction are perhaps discernible.

ECUADOR, the third smallest country in South America with a population of six million and one of the highest birthrates, is a natural geographical extension of Peru, having three major ecological zones: coast (*costa*), highlands (*sierra*), and an extensive eastern tropical forest region known as the *oriente* which is a continuation of the Peruvian *montana,* or *selva.* More than fifty percent of the population, overwhelmingly Quechua-speaking Indians, occupies the temperate highland basins where the capital, Quito, has existed since pre-Inca times. The *costa,* which extends the length of Ecuador from the Pacific coast inland to the Andean foothills, is sparsely populated except for the city of Guayaquil and its environs. There is a nucleus of mixed descendents of African slaves in the northern part of this region as well as remnants of aboriginal peoples such as Esmeraldas, Cayapa, Manta, and Colorado. The total population is probably less than one-half million, even including their mestizo descendents, known as *montuvios.* (*See* CAYAPA and COLORADO).

The *oriente* is even more sparsely populated than the *costa* and is occupied by aboriginal peoples, best known of which are the Jivaro and Canelo, who are essentially monolingual in their native languages and are out of the mainstream of national life. (*See* CANELO). The Jivaro maintain a traditional slash-and-burn horticulture and depend heavily on hunting and fishing. They live in large communal houses made up of members of extended families. Sometimes communities consist of several of these establishments. Although there may be temporary alliances for warfare, each community is politically independent. An interesting result of Spanish colonization in Ecuador may be seen in the group called Yumbos. Not aboriginal, this group grew out of many — Quijos, Canelos, Baezas and others — who were under the influence of Quechua-speaking missionaries and traders. These peoples adopted Quechua as their language and as years passed their tribal identities were forgotten. The modern Yumbos live in typical tropical forest fashion. Although the peoples of the *oriente* were protected to some extent from the ravages of colonization because of the climate, life as they knew it may soon be coming to an end. Recently this area has begun to produce petroleum which will probably have great effects on its inhabitants through the settlement by Spanish-speaking Ecuadorians and the construction of roads and towns which accompany the exploitation.

The political, economic, and overall social and cultural axis in Ecuador runs between the ancient city of Quito and the modern port of Guayaquil. Ten per-

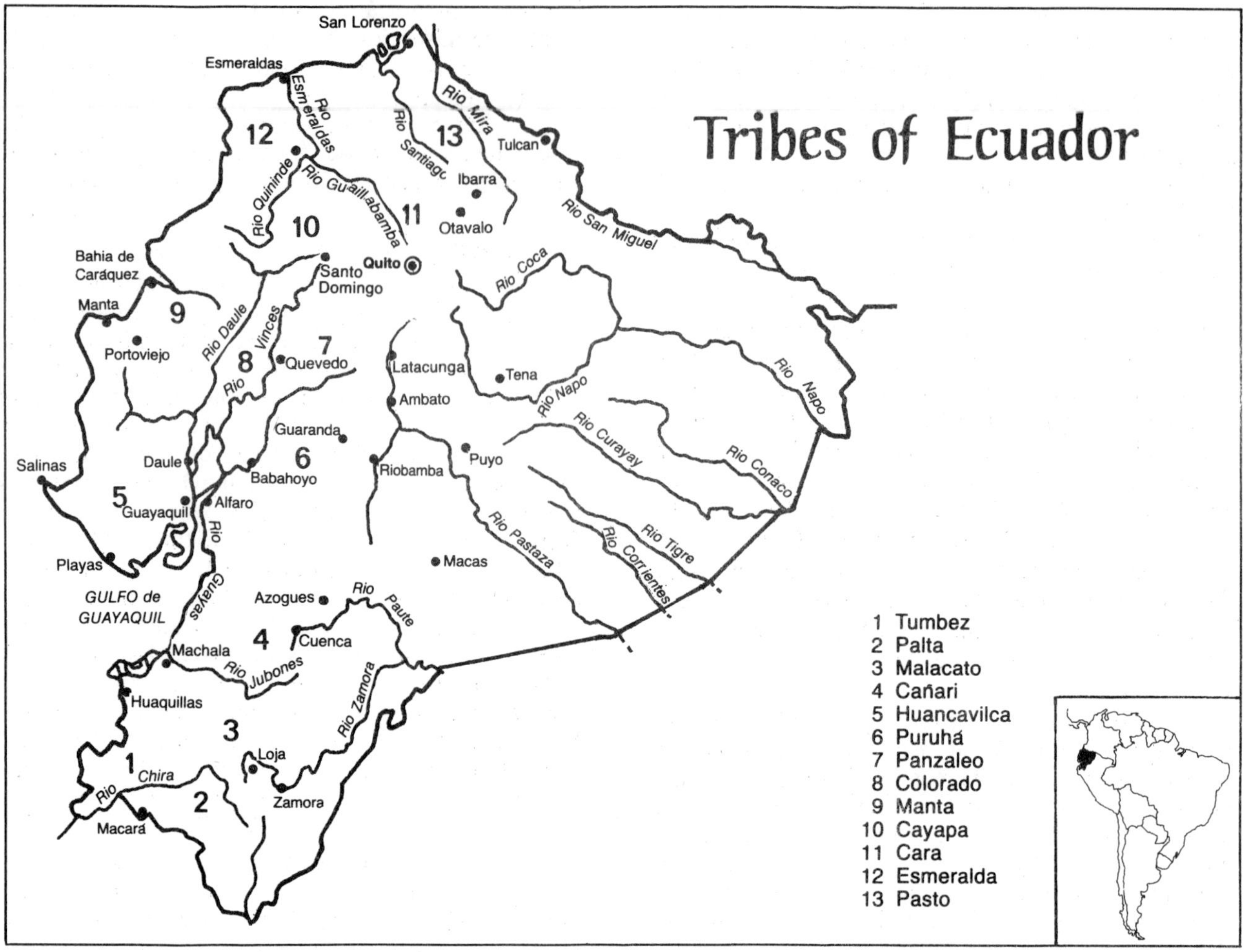

cent of the population, which boasts unmixed Spanish heritage and which itself is polarized along this axis, dominates the country. The descendents of the aboriginal Pasto, Cara, Panzaleo, Canari, and Palta make up the peasant producers who continue to occupy the same inter-montana valleys (*mudos,* or knots) as in pre-Spanish times. They maintain to a high degree the local cultural and social forms which represent a mixture of diverse traditions modified by Inca hegemony in the first decades of the 16th century and, immediately thereafter, by the colonial society imposed by the Spanish conquest beginning in 1532. Such are the historical connections between the Inca Empire and Ecuador that modern Ecuadorians say that Atahuallpa, a contender for the Inca Empire in its troubled years, was the first Ecuadorian, born as he was in Quito. Ecuador and Peru have a great common cultural tradition crystallized by Inca rule, symbolized by the spread of the Quechua language in Inca times and the retention of Quechua as the *lingua franca* of Spanish administrators and clergy, and more recently signalized by the passage of agrarian reform laws in both countries in 1964.

The highland Indians of Ecuador were sedentary agriculturalists who cultivated maize, beans, a large variety of potatoes, sweet potatoes, squashes, chili

An Indian milkmaid in Quito, Ecuador (1952) keeps her child bundled close to her as she tends the early morning milking chores. The Food and Agriculture Organization (FAO) of the United Nations trains health inspectors who make regular visits to milk-producing farms to see that standards of hygiene, sanitation and cleanliness are maintained.

Dirreccion Nacional de Turismo del Ecuador.

Otavalo Indians, Imbabura Province, Ecuador.

Direccion Nacional de Turismo del Ecuador.

A Salasaca Indian from Tungurahua Province, Ecuador.

Direccion Nacional de Turismo del Ecuador.

Ingapirca Indian archaeological ruins in Cañar Province, Ecuador.

peppers, *cabuya* (maguey), and had domesticated dogs and guinea pigs. Women did most of the agricultural labor. Nearly all of these people hunted deer, rabbits, and many kinds of birds. Since highland production depended largely on irrigation of the fields, it may be distinguished from the tropical forest type of rainfall, slash-and-burn horticulture of the lowland peoples, who were known for their cultivation of a variety of fruits including pineapples, *chirimoyas,* and avocados. The highland agricultural base, similar to that of Peru, produced surpluses which allowed the formation of dense, stable village complexes and fostered the increase of population, all of which has served to distinguish the highlanders from the lowlanders for hundreds of years.

Since pre-Conquest times these highland peoples had market centers, the best known of which were Saraguro (in the south), Quito, and Otavalo (in the north) and they also traded with the western coastal and eastern selvatic peoples. Because of this ample subsistence base, many of the highland settlements were very large and densely populated, an example of which may be seen today in the Otavalo, generically Cara, who live in the northern province of Imbabura. Some people, such as the Panzaleo, Puruha, Canari, and Palta, lived in a dispersed settlement pattern, spread out over the terraced and irrigated mountainsides, in substantial houses, many of them made of stone with thatched roofs and enduring for a generation or more.

The social and political organization of these

Direccion Nacional de Turismo del Ecuador.

Village women in rural Ecuador processing a locally grown, tough fiber into thin white strips which they then weave into Panama hats.

Dirreccion Nacional de Turismo del Ecuador.

Otavalo Indian market, Imbabura Province, Ecuador.

peoples were basically the same. The concept of strong chieftainship enabled these highland peoples to form political federations. These were not nearly as complex and solidary as those which crystallized among their southern Peruvian neighbors and in the Chibcha chiefdom to the north in Colombia, but they were sufficient for concerted, though futile, defensive efforts against conquests by the Inca and Spanish empires. (*See* CANARI).

The traditional religion of the Ecuadorian peoples was based on animistic beliefs focused on impressive natural features, such as volcanos, and was handled by shamans rather than by a priesthood, characteristic of their Inca conquerors. As always, the Inca imposed their imperial religion on subjugated peoples. The Spaniards did the same. The result may be seen today in a well-ordered, syncretic Catholicism which co-exists with folk beliefs rooted in shamanism in highland and coastal Ecuador. In the *oriente,* syncretic Catholicism has a less appreciable influence, although in recent years the Jivaro have come under the influence of North American protestant missionaries.

The modern highland Indian, such as the Otavalo, is still primarily Quechua-speaking, reluctant to accept innovation, distrustful of outsiders, having all the characteristics of peasant populations throughout Latin America. Poorly informed and politically powerless, he may eventually benefit from the 1964 agrarian reform law which legally abolished haciendas and the sharecropping system (*huasipunga*) and which was in line with the general liberal political and economic swell throughout Latin America in that decade to improve the conditions and life styles of the multitude.

L.C. and S.R. FARON

Dirreccion Nacional de Turismo del Ecuador.

A Jivaro Indian from the eastern region of Ecuador.

USDA photo.

Sheep breeding at *"Hacienda Pachamama."*

EDENSHAW (Haida; ?-*c.* 1885), was chief of the Stustas kinship on Graham Island in the Queen Charlotte Islands, British Columbia, who is remembered as a skillful treader and friend to the whites. He was one of the wealthiest of the Haida chiefs and shortly after 1860 he erected a large house at the mouth of Naden Harbor. He once saved the crew of a U.S. ship from unfriendly Indians and was responsible for a missionary being sent to the village of Masset on the island.

EDISTO were a small tribe, now extinct, which occupied the area of lower Edisto River, South Carolina. The Huguenots of Ribault's colony were kindly welcomed by them in 1562, and the Spaniards for a time had a mission among them. They were included in the Cusabo group, and were still living in the region named in 1670, when English colonization began. With the Westo and Stono they were possibly driven out by the Shawnee in 1680. It is probable that they spoke the Uchean language.

EDUCATION of the American Indians began with the first mission school founded by the Jesuits for Florida Indians in 1568. The first 300 years of formal education for Indians was dominated by the church, with the goal of "Christianizing" and "civilizing the heathen," especially by missionaries.

While it was not certain that the English would maintain their hold as planters in Virginia, Sir Edwin Sandys, Treasurer of the Bay Company, proposed in 1619 to found a college in the colony for English and Indian youth in common, and received an anonymous gift of L500 for the education of Indian youth in English and in the Christian religion. Other gifts were added. By advice of the King and the Bishops L1,500 were collected in England. The Company appropriated for the purpose 10,000 acres of land at Henrice (near Richmond). But the massacre of the whites by the Indians in 1622 effectively nullified all these plans.

Evidence of early interest in the matter of Indian education was found in Harvard's charter of 1650, which dedicated the college to "the education of English and Indian youth . . . in knowledge and goodliness." The second building at Harvard, erected in 1654, was called "the Indian College" and contained the college press on which John Eliot's Indian Bible and various grammars, tracts, catechisms, etc. were printed. It was built by funds collected in England. Its design was to furnish rooms for 20 Indian youths who, on a level with the English, might pursue a complete academic course, for which they should have been prepared by a "Dame's school," and by "Master

Photo by Paul Conklin.

Indian children in a typical classroom setting.

Corlet's Grammar School." But the results were wholly unsatisfactory. There were some Indian undergraduates at Harvard in those days but only one seems to have been granted the B.A. degree: Caleb Cheeshateaumuch, in 1665.

Dartmouth College was the outgrowth of Wheelock's Indian school at Lebanon (Connecticut). Dartmouth royal charter of 1769 provided that "there would be a college erected in our Province of New Hampshire by the name of Dartmough College, for the education and instruction of youth of the Indian Tribes of this land, in reading, writing and all parts of learning which shall appear necessary and expedient for civilizing and Christianizing children of pagans, as well as in all Liberal Arts and Sciences, and also of English youth and any other." (Dartmouth College started as "Moors' Charity School for Indians," for the education of their youth and of missionaries to them). The motto on the college seal is *Vox clamantis in Deserto.* (A list of subscriptions made in its behalf from 200 places in Great Britain is still preserved, chiefly collected by the preaching there by an ordained Indian Christian minister, Sampson Occum). But the missionaries sent forth from the college were not successful and the whites soon monopolized the advantages of the institution.

There sprung up several other schools in New England. But the success of these various religious efforts was questionable, to say the least. For instance, the general attitude of the Puritans toward the Indian was revealed by an incident in 1637 when the Pequot tribe resisted the migration of settlers into the Connecticut Valley; a Pequot village was burned to the ground and some 500 Indians were burned to death or shot. The surviving Pequots were sold into slavery. The Puritans gave thanks unto the Lord that they had lost only two men and Cotton Mather was grateful to the Lord that "On this day we have sent 600 heathen souls to hell."

Just as the Puritans had ideological difficulties in handling the Indians, so did a Founding Father, Thomas Jefferson, who was so concerned with the concept of liberty that he once raised the question whether the condition of the American Indians, without any government at all, was not the most desirable. On the other hand, quite interestingly, the Declaration of Independence of July 4, 1776, referred to the American Indian as: " . . . the present King of Great Britain . . . has excited domestic insurrections amongst us, and has endeavoured to bring on the Inhabitants of our Frontiers, the merciless Indian Savages, whose known Rule of Warfare, is an indistinguished Destruction of all Ages, Sex and Conditions."

Beginning with President Washington, the stated policy of the federal government was to replace the Indian's culture with that of the white man. This was considered "advisable" as the cheapest and safest way of subduing the Indians, of providing a safe habitat for the country's white inhabitants, of helping the whites acquire a desirable land, and changing the Indian's economy so that he could be content with less land. Education was a weapon by which these goals were to be accomplished. The Indian's lack of "civilization" was the ideological justification used for taking his land, and education was clearly to play a very secondary role to the use of force.

From September 17, 1778, when the first treaty between the United States and an Indian tribe was signed with the Delawares, until 1871, treaties established the main legal bases for the federal policies with respect to Indian education. The earliest treaty containing a specific provision with respect to education was the treaty with the Oneida, Tuscarora, and Stockbridge Indians of December 2, 1794. Through treaties and agreements, the Indian tribes ceded to the U.S. almost a billion acres. Although treaty provisions varied, in general, the Indians retained lands for their own use which were to be inalienable and tax exempt; the government in turn agreed to provide public services such as education, medical care, technical and agricultural training; specific provisions for education were, in fact, included in a substantial number of treaties.

The first gesture establishing congressional responsibility for Indian education was a statutory provision of March 30, 1802, appropriations not to exceed $15,000 annually to "promote civilization among the aborigines." At the request of President Monroe, the Congress passed an act on March 3, 1819, the organic legal bases for most of the educational work of the Indian Service, aiming to "civilize" Indians by converting them from hunters to articulturists. The funds were apportioned among the societies and individuals — usually missionary organizations — prominent in an effort to "civilize" the Indians; the annual appropriation, known as the "civilization" fund, lasted until 1873.

The Office of Commissioner of Indian Affairs was created by Congress as a part of the act on July 9, 1832, although the Bureau itself had been established in 1824. The office was under the direction of the Secretary of War and subject to the regulations prescribed by the President. But in 1849 it was moved to the newly established Department of the Interior, although army officers continued to be employed as agents.

The attitudes of the early Commissioners of Indian Affairs shaped the policies of Indian education for the century that followed; the annual reports of the Commissioners were clear indicators of these attitudes.

As early as 1838, the educational policy of "civilizing" Indians through manual training in agriculture and the mechanical arts became established practice. During the later part of the treaty period, greater concern was expressed over the reluctance of Indian children to attend the white man's schools, and treaty provisions regarding compulsory attendance were developed.

In 1871, the treaty period was ended when Congress decreed that "No Indian nation tribe within the United States shall be acknowledged or recognized as an independent nation, tribe, or power;" but this did not rescind the obligations of the federal government under the nearly 400 established treaties.

In the last three decades of the 19th century, the slaughter of the buffalo herds, the principal source of food for the Indians, reduced the Indians to the point of starvation in the Plains; many Indian tribes were also decimated by epidemics of smallpox, cholera, and other infectious diseases introduced by the U.S. Army and white settlers. A new policy, "The Peace Policy," was introduced by President Grant; reservations were distributed among the major religious denominations, delegating most power to church bodies and giving the right to nominate new agents and direct educational and other activities of the reservations. The missionary dictatorship tried to crush Indian culture and institutions, and the military was frequently called in to reinforce the missionaries' orders. Several severe rebellions were crushed. The completion of the white man's conquest of the Indian was reached in 1890 by the murder of the Sitting Bull and the massacre of a Sioux band at Wounded Knee, South Dakota.

The basic approach of subsidizing various religious groups to operate schools for Indians ended only in 1897. However, the Bureau of Indian Affairs had started building its own educational system in the 1870s, based on the model created by Gen. R.H. Pratt who founded the Carlisle Indian School in Pennsylvania in 1879 in abandoned army barracks, run in a rigid military fashion, and with heavy stress on rustic vocational education. The approach was to provide a maximum rapid coercive assimilation into white society. The Carlisle School set a pattern that was to dominate the federal government's approach to Indian education for half a century — until it came under devastating attack in the Meriam Report of 1928. (The school had been closed in 1918).

The act of Congress in 1882 helped the development of the federal school system by authorizing the use of abandoned Army posts or barracks.

The counterpart of the educational policy whose objective was to "dissolve" the social organization of Indian life on the reservations was the Dawes Severalty Act of 1887, designed to "dissolve" the Indian land base. This legislation ushered in the "Allotment Period" in the history of Indian affairs, and was carried out with a missionary zeal — halted only by the reform legislation of the New Deal; it had diminished the Indian tribal economic base from 140 million acres to approximately 50 million acres of the least desirable land. The interrelationship between the educational policy and the land policy of this period was obvious — coercive assimilation. (Under the Dawes Act of February 8, 1887, purchase money to be paid by the federal government for surplus lands not allotted to individual Indians were to be held in trust in the Treasury of the United States, and was to "at all times be subject to appropriation by Congress for the education and civilization of such tribe or tribes of Indians or the members thereof." Thus the money was to pay the costs of taking Indian children from their homes and placing them in federal boarding schools. Since many Indian families refused to send their children to school, in 1893 Congress legalized the technique of starvation to enfoce compulsory attendance.

The investigation of the Navajo school situation in 1919 by both the Congress and the Board of Indian Commissioners showed that of an estimated 9,613 Navajo children eligible for schools, only 2,089 were actually attending schools. This started a campaign in 1920 to educate Indian children in the now overcrowded schools and the transportation of all Navajo children in and above the 4th grade to other nonreservation boarding schools throughout the West and Southwest, since each agent on the reservation received a quota which he had to fill.

During the 1920s, corruption, exploitation, mismanagement, and the general failure of the Indian programs stimulated a prolonged Senate Indian Affairs Committee's debate (published in the Meriam report in 1928). The call for sweeping changes produced the Indian Reorganization Act of 1934, and President Roosevelt appointed John Collier as Commissionery of Indian Affairs to shape a "New Deal" for American Indians. But the intellectual and financial support of Collier's program lost momentum or had been undermined before the end of World War II. At any rate, the tribal councils had been given more powers for self-government and many more day schools on reservations had been introduced and expected to replace boarding schools. But in the 1950s a reaction in Congress against economic help to Indian tribes resulted in the termination of several reservations, a policy aimed to "get the government out of the Indian business." The division of tribal property among the individual members of the tribe was to encourage Indians to merge into the broader society. But most Indians wanted self determination, as tribes, and did not want to terminate the rights and privileges in their tax-exempt reservation land.

Since the 1960s a "New Policy" emerged. Two major federal government laws put money behind this policy — The Indian Education Act (1972) and Indian Self-Determination and Educational Assistance Act (1975). This led to a policy of local self-determination for Indian tribes and Indian communities, and to a greater responsibility of Indians as teachers and administrators. There has been a rapid expansion of the number of Indian students in colleges, most of them aided by government scholarship funds, a rise of schools on reservations operated by local native school boards with government funds. Basically, the education of the Indians since 1965 has been especially influenced by the acceptance of the broad policy, known as "cultural pluralism," which propounds that minority groups are to be integrated into the economic, political, and social spheres of the society, but could retain their cultural differences without discrimination or deprivation.

In 1978 there were about 275,000 Indians aged 6-17,

Photo by Paul Conklin.

A Navajo community college classroom.

inclusive, and about 90% of them were enrolled in schools in 4 categories or types of schools: (1) schools with practically all-Indian enrollment; the Bureau of Indian Affairs operated boarding and day schools, Indian-controlled School Boards, contracted mission or other private schools and public schools operating on or contiguous to reservations; (2) public schools, contiguous to Indian reservations or in native communities, with 50 to 90% enrollment; (3) public schools with 10 to 50% Indian enrollment (mainly in large cities); and (4) public schools with 1 to 10% Indian enrollment (mainly in large cities). The proportion of Indians graduating from school was approximately the same as the proportions of other ethnic groups having a similar socioeconomic or income background. On standard tests of school achievement, Indian pupils fell below national averages, as a group. But the relatively low academic achievement is not because Indian children are less intelligent than white children. In fact, several studies based on intelligence tests which did not require reading ability showed Indian children to be at or slightly above the level of white children. The difficulty was that the Indian children had lived in a community or neighborhood characterized by poverty.

Since the majority of Indian pupils attend public schools with white children and are taught with white children, both groups have the same teachers. But the schools operated by the Bureau of Indian Affairs (BIA) had about 1,800 teachers who had passed a federal civil service examination and had been assigned to BIA schools. In 1968, there were 1,772 teachers (61% women) and 15% Indians. Salaries ranged from $6,176 to $15,119. (Employment in Alaska was accompanied by a 25% cost of living supplement). Indian teachers have tended to stay longer in service than non-Indians. Of school administrators in BIA schools, 28% were Indian.

Before about 1960, the number who completed high school had been small and most did not go on to college, a substantial number going into a 1- to 2-year vocational training program, such as that of the Haskell Institute maintained by BIA at Lawrence, Kansas, offering secretarial and trade training. In general, there has been, however, a very rapid increase in the number of Indian youth entering a university and finishing a 4-year course.

There is only one Indian college: the Navajo Community College in Arizona (Corsicana), founded in 1968 by the Navajo tribe and supported by the federal government in recent years; it holds that uniquely Indian values, skills, and insights are highly functional in the modern world today and it is possible for Navajos to direct and control their own institutions — and that this is the only way they will ever be able to assume total responsibility and self-support, at least as a group. The institution is ruled by a Board of Regents consisting of 10 Navajos, one from each of the 5 administrative areas of the reservation, 2 members elected at large and appointed by the Tribal Chairman, and 3 ex-officio members: the chairman of the tribe, the chairman of the Navajo Education Committee, and the President of the college student body. The Indian faculty members have organized a Curriculum Committee searching for and formulating a Navajo philosophy of education in which the present and future are rooted in the values of the traditional past.

A further impetus to higher education for Indians came in 1976, when $500,000 was provided for 50 fellowship Indian students accepted for professional study by universities; this grant came from the Indian Education Act, allocating money for the academic year 1976-1977 to cover tuition costs and subsistence for students in engineering, law, medicine, business, forestry, and fields related to one of these areas.

Early in the 1970s, the federal government provided funds to assist Native Americans to reform and direct their educational systems. The Indian Education Act of 1972 and its successor, the Indian Self-Determination and Educational Assistance Act of 1975 provided funds and required Indian direction and Indian responsibility for the design programs. The Bilingual Education Act, part of the Elementary and Secondary Education since 1967, provided funds for the employment of teaching staff speaking the local home language of Indian and Eskimo communities.

The report of the American Indian Policy Review Commission, created in 1975, recommended that all government-aided Indian programs should be brought together under a federal Indian department, or an independent agency reporting to the office of the President; that Congress should enact legislation that would aid tribal governments and Indian communities to take responsibility for control of education according to their desires. Among other objectives was that of recruiting and training Indians to serve as teachers in practically all schools with a predominantly Indian enrollment.

In 1977 initiative was taken by several hundred Indian organizations seeking and receiving money from the federal government for educational programs. (For instance, under the Indian Education Act and for fiscal year 1976, approximately $18 million was granted to school and tribal educational projects in the form of 210 separate grants, aimed to supplement existing education programs and to train Indian personnel for work in the schools). This amplified the program started in the late 1960s, whereby the BIA contracted with a local Indian school board on a reservation to give the money to pay expenses of a BIA-operated school to the Indian Board taking responsibility for the school. By 1975, there were 15 of these Indian-contracted school boards; these have banded into a Coalition of Indian Controlled School Boards.

The Bilingual Education Act has a major application in Indian education, stressing the use of the child's home language in his learning to read. For Indian children speaking English at home, the tribal language is treated as a second language to be learned after the pupil has been using English in the school; the basic aim is to teach respect and familiarity with the native

Photo by Paul Conklin.

The Bilingual Education Act, 1967, provided funds for the employment of elementary and secondary education teachers familiar with the home language of Indian communities.

CARE photo.

Wide-eyed wonder was the natural reaction of these little Indian girls at the village school of Quinchuqui, Ecuador, when the teacher opened the CARE box that contained the score of illustrated volumes of the "Village Library." These are the first reading books the children had ever seen. Though primarily designed for first and second grade students, these books were used in the adult literacy classes which the teacher conducted at night for the parents of these children.

lasting. (The order was suppressed in the late 18th century).

But all the educational efforts on behalf of the Indian were nearly nullified by the socio-economic conditions confronting him.

Spaniards who arrived in America in the 16th century looked for conquests, not settlements, quick returns not steady development, and for resident populations which would do the work for which they were unsuited, disciplined to engage in manual labor or commerce. They found several sedentary, agricultural peoples unprepared for long wars and used to steady and prolonged manual labor. The invaders were militaristic, energetic, and fanatically religious seekers after gold and glory. The outcome of this confrontation was tragic.

The misadministration by the colonial administration resulted in Indian revolts and frequently of Creole native descendants of Spanish conquistadores.

Throughout its period of domination in the Americas the Spanish monarchy was harassed by a difficult juxtaposition of the real and the ideal. The mercantilistic theory propounded that the colony existed primarily for the use and benefit of the mother country; simply, it was supposed to show a profit. As the Spanish crown's financial difficulties and obligations multiplied, the importance of this profit increased. In order to show a profit, the mines, pearl fisheries, and farms had to be worked. While imported Negro slaves partially solved the problem in the hot coastal areas, in the highland mines such as Potosi, Huancavelica, Guanajuato, and Zacatecas, the Indians had to be forced to work; the same was true in all the farming areas of temperate climate. Madrid was caught in a dilemma between its humanistic concern for the welfare of the Indians and its urgent need for the gold and silver. The religious orders, especially the Franciscans, working hard to convert the Indians, saw much of their work frustrated; the Creole entrepreneurs and landowners, who needed the reluctant labor of the Indians, played on the Crown's dire financial straits and the royal administrators. Evolution of the colonial labor system mirrored the twists and turns of these policies. The Crown, under strong religious pressures, abolished widespread enslavement of the Indians; but it also admitted their lack of Catholic religion. The result was the *encomienda* system whereby Indians were "entrusted" to supposed Spaniards for indoctrination and physical care; in return the *encomenderos* were allowed to exact work from them.

Although the system worked efficiently in some areas, it also became soon obvious that many clerics and some administrators were dissatisfied that all exploitation of the Indians had ceased. The famous "News Laws" (1542) called for a gradual but definite abolition of the *encomienda* system and the substitution of wage labor. (These laws caused open rebellion in some cases). A new system emerged. Known variously as the *mita* and *repartimiento,* it provided for forced, paid, Indian labor on a selective service basis. In many cases a certain number of Indians from selected villages were collected in the public square of the principal town on a fixed day of the week or month, and there *repartides* were divided among the local Spanish employers.

The system was abolished only before the end of the colonial period. Many Indians eventually found their way into a free market situation where their exploitation continued on a cultural rather than a formalized basis. Others, especially those in the isolated agricultural areas, soon fell under the labor system known as "debt peonage," whereby, through various devices, they and their children became so hopelessly indebted to the owners or administrators of the *hacienda* or workshop that their departure was impossible. Many also became sharecroppers, which, given their lack of education and their conditioning to a life of servility, tied them effectively to one employer. (These two labor systems exist and coexist in many parts of Highland Latin America to this day).

By the middle of the 17th century, the Indian population continued to decline; this meant that formerly prosperous industries and agricultural areas were abandoned.

This century saw also the first formative era in the colony. A large *mestizo* class was coming into being. Spaniards were being born who had never seen Spain and who thought of themselves as Creoles and Americans. These young, disgruntled, upperclass Creoles, influenced by the European Enlightenment philosophy, supported the wars of independence.. But the turmoil brought few changes. For instance, the Andean Indian certainly did not profit by the wars; in fact his status and level of living actually deteriorated after independence. After all the Creole was his exploiter and traditional enemy. What little protection he had ever obtained had been from the Crown; after the wars the Crown was gone and the exploiters controlled the new societies. (Peru even witnessed a brief Indian revolt which wanted the return of Ferdinand VII of Spain). The new rulers of Peru and Bolivia quickly restored the Indian tribute payments which had been abolished by the Spaniards.

The wars of independence, to the chagrin of Simon Bolivar, hardly transformed Latin American society with regard to the Indian.

From the time of their independence in the 19th century, the policies of the various states south of the border has been strikingly similar: the Indians are viewed as a hindrance or dead weight to racial amalgamation. Any policy of ethnic pluralism makes the ruling classes uneasy, and they want to liquidate all the symptoms that might consider their societies as being "backward." For, after all, 40% to 50% of the continental population are illiterate (and literacy ranges from 30% in Bolivia to 87% in Argentine (as pointed out by UNESCO). When a majority of the population is illiterate and lives in semi-slavery because of caste and language, it is difficult to speak of the enlightened self-interest of the individual. Thus in the school training programs there are evidences of cultural deprivation. The environment and class status appear to be a dominant factor in the people's welfare and the attendance in schools. Often classes are conducted in an alien tongue in which the Indian knows only a smattering. Thus a pupil from the poor and racially different group is discriminated against because of the drawbacks of his environment and social inferiority. This prevents national unification and the spread of democratic institutions. The spirit of national education does not exist. The state refers to the Indians but does not refer to them as Peruvians, for instance, equal to the rest, since they are considered an inferior race. The ruling cliques feel that the entire process of Westernization (whether it is known as assimilation, incorporation, or integration) is good for the Indians, that the Indian problem can be solved only by the Indians forgetting that they are Indians; that they must stop forming component parts of the belts of misery surrounding the great cities, and no longer form a part of the great mass of unemployed migrants, moving about all the time searching for work.

In the various regions within each country, the whites — whether they call themselves *ladinos* (of Spanish descent), *gente de razon* ("civilized people"), or *mestizo* (mixed) — differ only in observing the local guidelines dominating inter-ethnic relations. In the regional metropolises those who exploit the Indians consider themselves a privileged elite (or as they are called in Yucatan, the "divine castes"); together with the local oligarchies, which include departmental and provincial officials, and the wealthy bourgeoisie they sponsor what is called "the national consciousness," by aiming to do away with the Indian cultures. The result is that the Indian is "alienated" — a feeling of noninvolvement in and estrangement from the dominant society and culture; he feels that his own cultural background is without value and thus is oppressed, defensive and isolated. And he is right, since the legal equality which is granted by law in each Latin American country, is a monopoly of the whites, the Creole (whites born in the Americas) and the mestizos (those of mixed white and Indian ancestry). The Indian thus has withdrawn into his communal and ethnocentric survival isolationism.

Only if the Indian learns Spanish and accepts Western clothes and mentality, can he achieve any recognition — as did the 19th century Mexican President Benito Juarez (1806-1872). But then such a successful Indian is no longer viewed as an Indian.

In their efforts to cope with the Indian problem, Latin American nations have run the gamut of sociological approaches. Mexico, formally committed to complete integration of its Indians since the 1910 revolution, has freed them from peonage and settled perhaps 70% of them in agricultural communities where land is held collectively. To ease them into the mainstream of Mexican life, the National Indian Institute (Instituto Nacional Indigenista — INI), under the Ministry of Public Education, which coordinates all Indian agencies, was founded in 1948. It has founded 12 "Coordinating Centers" staffed with men equipped to teach their charges everything from Spanish to how to grow taller corn. The central purpose is, of course, to nationalize the Indian: that the Indians become aware of belonging to the Mexican state. This has continued to be the most important source of directed social change, concentrating on the improvement of realistic educational facilities, health programs, agriculture, and communications, while making no direct effort to manipulate the symbolic and belief structure or social system of the Indians. (The INI has been frequently aided by the UNESCO and the Organization of American States through pilot or training programs).

There have been other general forces encouraging the Indian to acculturate, the favored position of mestizo culture as opposed to the disadvantaged one of the Indian and the incentives offered by the national government. This carrot-and-stick situation has brought increasing numbers of Indians into the national society. Movement is accompanied by "passing" or acquiring some prestigious cultural traits and by separating oneself from close ties with the Indian group. "Passing" is easier for the wealthier Indian with extensive mestizo contacts already formed. He may change to a Spanish surname, adopt Western dress, and marry a mestizo woman. In all cases, "passing" requires speaking Spanish and adopting a mestizo outlook. But, even so, the man himself may not be fully accepted as mestizo, although his children most likely will be.

Government incentives, in addition to the distribution of land — the *ejido* program — have improved educational opportunities in Mexico and have also done something to increase political participation. In 1936, under President Lazaro Cardenas, 1934-1940, the Autonomous Department of Indian Affairs was founded, followed the next year by the Department of Indian Education. Despite opposition, the former group was able to redistribute an additional 45 million acres to the Indians by 1940. In 1942, the government established Indian brigades to instruct communitities in modern agricultural methods to help Indians make full use of their land; the brigades offered instruction in crop diversification, animal husbandry, pest and disease control, and the use of modern agricultural machinery, and helped to organize producer and consumer cooperatives, repair old roads and build new ones and install better telecommunications networks.

Formal education is officially recognized as an important means to integration; it signifies, to a great extent, the transmission and adoption of mestizo culture and values.

Until about 1940 the new educational program of Mexico gave first priority to bringing literacy and primary schooling to the countryside, particularly to the physically isolated Indian villages where Spanish was to many an unfamiliar language, for the self-contained traditional communities had their own cultures to which schools were extrinsic and the goals of the revolution were irrelevant. (At that stage in cultural orientation, the schoolhouse often replaced the church as the center of village life). Yet, in the early 1970s, there were still rural communities with no school or in which the school was still an extrinsic element. And the extension of the primary system in rural areas is still severely handicapped by a shortage of trained and willing teachers. The regular staffs were supplemented by a system of cultural missions, teams of dedicated specialists travelling around villages, teaching, instructing the poorly trained teachers and assisting in community activities. They are still active in the countryside and helped with social brigades of university students on vacation.

At the other end of the spectrum stands Brazil, whose tiny Indian minority is made up of primitive jungle tribes, some 150,000 at the very least. The Brazilian Indian is a descendent of pre-Columbia civilizations who, preserving the beliefs and customs of his tribes, possesses specific socio-cultural characteristics that are quite distinct from those of the rest of society. Even when he is not a pure Indian and lives like any other member of the Brazilian population, he retains a kind of loyalty to his ethnic identity. Since there is no realistic prospect of integrating these "savages" in the foreseeable future, Brazil's Indian Protection Service concentrates on protecting them from the larcenous — or murderous — forays of Brazilian whites.

The lot of Mexican and Brazilian Indians is idyllic when compared with that of the Indians of the Andes. When Francisco Pizarro and his conquistadors destroyed the Inca Empire, they pushed the Indians out of the fertile valleys up into the inhospitable highlands. Ever since, the descendants have led a life so bleak that they ease their misery by dulling their senses with *chicha* (corn beer) and *coca* (cocaine).

Most Aztec girls' education involved domestic tasks. A mother teaches her daughter to grind corn and to use the loom.

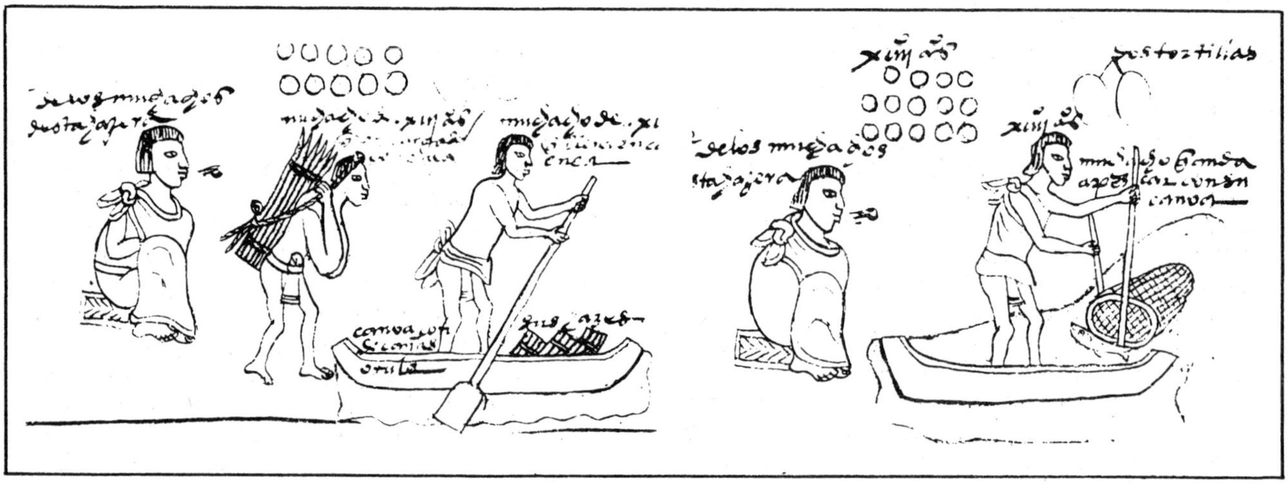

An Aztec father teaches his son how to carry firewood, to load and handle a canoe, and to catch fish with a net.

The Indians living along the shores of Peru's Lake Titicaca delight tourists with their picturesqueness — but they nearly all are illiterate, tuberculosis-ridden and extremely backward. Although Peru abolished serfdom several decades ago, and Ecuador followed suit in 1964, serfdom is still prevalent.

Bolivia was the first of the Andean nations trying to improve the conditions of its Indians; its government, soon after the country's 1952 revolution, outlawed the very word *indigena* (native) and allotted its Indian peasants both land and the vote. A good step was the policy of Bolivia's army drafting brigades of young Indians and setting them to work clearing the lowlands of the mountains. After a year's service, the recruits were offered free land, a grubstake, and transportation for their families. Some accepted immediately and others trickled back later. Some other experiments in resettling Bolivia's Indians in the lowlands have been less successful. By in 1963 Bolivia exported rice and sugar for the first time.

More recently, Peru also launched a drive to bring the country's Indians down from the Andes to the rich eastern slopes and integrate them into Peruvian society. As part of this effort, Peru's first agrarian reform program adopted and, through a kind of domestic peace corps, is striving to modernize Indian farming methods.

Of importance is the contemporary Indian movement *Indigenismo,* aiming to elevate the precarious standard of living of the Indian in Latin America and to incorporate him materially and spiritually into the ordinary civic life of the country in which he resides — while preserving his own culture and without diminishing his specific psychological personality. Today *indigenismo* is considered a policy of change, to be carried out by the state and other institutions, while respecting the human dignity of the Indian, his communities and his traditional culture regardless of its level of development. Its most widely accepted goal is the integration of the Indian into national life while at the same time according his peculiar cultural traits the consideration to which they are entitled. The movement rejects the paternalistic methods of dealing with the Indians; when this approach is used, the Indians merely take what is offered; their spirit of enterprise is undermined, and they are encouraged to become dependent on the handouts confered by public charity. Contemporary *Indigenismo* favors an active methodology that encourages Indian groups to express their needs and desires and to participate in the planning and execution of programs affecting them. The movement recognizes the importance of programs in the fields of health, agriculture, housing, and so on, but it maintains that they must be well coordinated and integrated. In such an integrated endeavor, economic and educational programs will play a key role, education being considered in the broadest sense of the word to embrace efforts to create new habits and change attitudes. In the economic sphere, agrarian reform constitutes one of the most effective means of improving the life of the Indian population, since most of them depend upon agriculture.

Contemporary *Indigenismo* faces many serious problems. Indians continue to be discriminated against in many ways, as is shown by their poverty, by the inadequate services they receive, by their nonparticipation in civic life, and at times by paternalistic legislation and programs that treat them as if they were children. Programs, especially in the educational and economic fields, have been badly focused and inadequately financed; nor have they been available to train the skilled and dedicated technical personnel to carry on this work. Meanwhile, the sectors that exploit the Indian population and benefit from its present plight have offered much resistance, both openly and subtly. In general the non-Indian population has shown no positive attitude towards the integration of the Indian, nor has it acknowledged his values and rights. Political and ideological position have arisen that frequently disorient action or serve as instruments helpful to forces interested in avoiding substantive changes. The experiences with past programs have not changed much the negative attitudes of the Indians, although all the South American nations show the will to improve the living conditions of their Indians, estimated at between 15 and 30 million.

JOSEPH S. ROUCEK

WHERE THE INDIANS ARE

Country	Percentage
Bolivia	63
Guatemala	53.6
Peru	45.9
Ecuador	39
Mexico	30
El Salvador	20
Panama	20
Honduras	6.7
Nicaragua	5
Colombia	2
Venezuela	2
Chile	2
Paraguay	2
Argentina	.4
Costa Rica	.3
Brazil	.2
Uruguay	0

n.a., The Hemisphere; Submerged Dynamite," in *Newsweek*, Vol. LXVI, October-December, 1965, pp. 60-61.

EDWARD I, a Mosquito Indian king who "ruled" in 1740 by accepting British rum and dominance. The first English commissioner of Nicaragua's Mosquito Coast, Robert Hodgson, actually governed under the sponsorship of Edward Trelawny, governor of Jamaica. Edward was about 20 at this time, during the Anglo-Spanish conflict called the War of Jenkins' Ear.

EDWARDS, BRONSON WILBUR (Ottawa; May 22, 1910-), is an artist who concentrates on Indian themes and an Ottawa tribal official. Edwards was born at Miami, Oklahoma. Although he had been interested in art since childhood, he did not take up painting seriously until 1947, the same year he became secretary-treasurer of the Ottawa Tribal Council. Edwards' art is similar to the European wash style, but it gives evidence of the flat technique common in contemporary Indian painting.

EIGHT DEER (in Spanish *Ocho Venado*) was the "calendar name" of an important Mixtec Indian king who in the 11th century ruled a large portion of southern Mexico in the Oaxaca region. His nickname, distinguishing him from a later Mexican ruler called Eight Deer (signifying the day of birth) was "Tiger Claw" (Garra de Tigre). Eight Deer has been the subject of many studies by modern scholars, and was prominent in the pre-Hispanic Mexican Indian sources, which give a remarkable amount of information.

Eight Deer was born in 1011, the son of King Five Alligator, known as Tlachitonatiuh, by Eleven Water, the king's second wife; it is generally agreed that Five Alligator ruled the ancient city of Tilantongo. The prince's career began early, following his father's death in 1030. The next year, Eight Deer began a series of campaigns to expand the kingdom, allied with his half-brother and constant companion Twelve Movement ("Bloody Tiger"), who possibly held the Tilantongo throne before Eight Deer. 1032 saw Eight Deer crowned as lord of the city of Tututepec, an important addition to the Mixtec lands. By 1040 he and Twelve Movement has annexed 26 neighboring towns.

The next decade was the most active of Eight Deer's life, as he brought most of Mixtec Alta under his rule. In 1045 his power was given official sanction when the high priests of the Tula empire honored him as a *tecuhtli* (great lord) in a ceremony marked by piercing his nose with a precious ring. The death of his half-brother in 1048 inspired, as a memorial, the conquest in 1049 of a site known as Xipe Bundle. In 1050 Eight Deer quashed a power struggle in his kingdom by sacrificing his chief rivals. He further strengthened his position by a series of political marriages, including one to the queen of Teozacoalco. By 1053 he had begun a new major series of conquests. The end of Eight Deer's life came in 1063, when he was sacrificed on his 52nd birthday.

Under Eight Deer, the Mixtecs were united into an unusually large kingdom, which after his death eventually reverted to petty chiefdoms. Modern scholarship has corrected earlier errors concerning his life, but a full evaluation of his importance, particularly the extent of his kingdom, has not yet been made.

EIGHT NORTHERN INDIAN PUEBLOS COUNCIL (ENIPC) is a non-profit Association of eight Indian Pueblo governments, all located in Northern New Mexico. The Pueblos are Iatapai-Mu Pahoatel (Taos), Peen Waltah (Picuris), Ohkay-Owingeh (San Juan), Kha Poe (Santa Clara), Powhogeh (San Ildefonso), Te ts'ugeh (Tesuque), P'osuwangeh (Pojoaque) and Nanbe (Nambe), The purpose of ENIPC is to sponsor broad based programs in education, economic development manpower, health, social management.

ENIPC had its beginning in the early 1960s when the governors and their staff met monthly to discuss law and order problems. These meetings planted the seeds for comradeship among the leaders.

1964 was a historic year for all Indians. The Economic Opportunity Act was passed by the United States Congress; through this Act in 1965 the Pueblos jointly sponsored an NYC Program; (Taos Pueblo operated its own program); Santa Clara and Tesuque each received direct funding from OEO, and before the year was out the Northern Pueblos organized a Community Action Agency.

The years between 1965 and 1967 were developmental, and in succeeding years each Council can be credited with at least one major accomplishment. 1967 through 1969, Mr. James Hena, from Tesuque served the Council as its first Indian director and in March of 1969, the governors were successful in establishing the Northern Pueblos Agency, under the Bureau of Indian Affairs in Santa Fe. Under Ed Cata the Council developed an Overall Economic Development Plan and received recognition by the Economic Development Administration. In April 1970, the Council selected Herman Agoyo, as their Executive Director. Since then the Council established the Northern Pueblos Enterprises, Inc.; received funding from other major federal agencies; established the Northern Pueblos Housing Authority; and using Pueblo men constructed a 4,000 sq. foot Council Headquarters in San Juan Pueblo.

The Council has become well-known not only in the United States, but also internationally, especially in South America, as a model of cooperative action.

EL ARBOLILLO, Mexico, is an archaeological site located on the western edge of ancient Lake Texcoco, Valley of Mexico. The site represents an established village of the Middle Formative (*c.* 1000-300 BC). The settlement shows little social differentiation unlike that present in other villages in the valley at this time. El Arbolillo and the related Formative site of Zacatenco stand in contrast to the cultural manifestation present at the neighboring site of Tlatilco. The former two sites exhibited local traditions (tripod vessels and composite silhouettes, banded geometric-incised decorations, and white-on-red painted wares) while at the latter site the local tradition as well as supra-regional cultural traits were present (Olmecoid style).

The Middle Formative village at El Arbolillo was established directly on the sands of a beach fronting an arm of Lake Texcoco. The lake environment as well as a fresh water stream near the site offered a favorable ecological setting for the ancient inhabitants. The site was protected from winter winds by the slopes of a nearby hill. Abundant waterfowl, rich soils and deer and other small mammals were available. The farmers depended on both the products of their fields and from the lake. More than 23 feet of accumulated midden deposits have been found at the site including refuse, the casts of maize leaves, and burned daub from the walls of pole-and-thatch huts. The refuse and its immense quantities of bones from deer and aquatic birds support the fact that hunting was important during this early time. Small lance points chipped from obsidian were used in hunting and hides were cleaned of fat with small obsidian scrappers.

Sixty-three burials were excavated at El Arbolillo including those found under the floors of houses as well as those found together in cemetaries. At El Arbolillo, as well as at other sites in the area during this period, the midden deposits are rich in fragments of clay figurines providing information on the costume of the day or its lack. Some of the figurines represent males, but the greater number are females. Some exhibit exaggerated sexual characteristics or are obviously pregnant. Figurines are most commonly found in household refuse and therefore are usually broken. They are too plentiful to have been luxury objects and this fact, together with their appearance in household refuse, suggests that they were part of a popular household cult and perhaps served as talismans or charms. No recognizable depictions of gods or goddesses have ever been identified in these villages, suggesting the possibility that the only cult was that of the figurines, which may have been objects of household devotion perhaps concerned with the fertility of the crops. So abundant were figurines at El Arbolillo, Zacatenco and Ticoman that George Vaillant based his Preclassic chronology, the first ever devised, on an intricate figurine typology.

In addition to the figurines, clay pottery was made including utilitarian wares, serving wares and wares frequently found in the burials at the site. Other items recovered in the excavation of the site and reflecting social and economic activities include implements of clay (bird faces, human faces, human effigy pots, rattles and whistles, earplugs, beads, spindle whorls, gorgets, ladles, balls), stone objects (metates, manos, balls, quartz tools, flint, obsidian points, tools, blades and flakes), and bone, antler and shell objects (bone tools, antler tools including picks, pounders, awls, shell sequins, shell pendants, disc and cylindrical beads).

The sigificance of the site lies in the fact that it represents a localized tradition, an established village not unlike others in the valley at this early time period and shows social and economic adaptation to a favorable ecological niche for the early Mesoamerican village.
ELLEN R. KINTZ

EL BAUL, Guatemala, is an archaeological site located on the southern slopes of the Pacific coast halfway between Kaminaljuyu and the Pacific Ocean. The location of the site represents a transition from the settlement pattern associated with earlier Preclassic sites found on the coast and those later Classic sites found further inland in the intermontane valleys. El Baul is located on a coffee plantation to the south-east of the Preclassic site of Abaj Takalik in a region which later was to be known for the Classic sites of the Cotzumalhuapa culture.

The significance of the site lies in the fact that the"Herrera Stela," Stela 1, is found here and provides information on early calendrical inscriptions in the Maya area. The stela exhibits a figure in profile with a spear in hand below a cloud-scroll. The lower portion of the face of the figure is covered and the head-dress is attached to a chin strap. Two vertical columns of glyphs are found to the side of the figure. The hieroglyphics on the stela are badly eroded but show that Long Count dates were being recorded. The vital *baktun* glyph which designated the cycle of 144,000 days is missing. However, assuming a baktun 7 a Calendar Round day of 12 Eb is reached which seems to be correct. The series of Long Count numbers have been reconstructed as 7.19.15.7.12, or AD 36.

Furthermore, the El Baul stela is not the only reckoning of dates found in the southern Mexican lowlands and in Guatemala. Monuments of the Late Preclassic period are found in Veracruz, the Isthmus region, Oaxaca, and the Pacific slope area of Guatemala near El Baul. In that the earliest known Long Count date from the lowland Maya area has been interpreted as AD 292 (Stela 1 at Tikal), the origin of the Maya calendrical system is assumed to have been outside the Classic core area of the Peten. In addition, the jungle fauna (crocodiles, monkeys, and jaguars) represented in the glyphs also point out that the origins would probably not lie in the highland areas of Mesoamerica but rather in the tropical climates.

Stela 1 at El Baul may represent the earliest dated monument in the Maya area predating by some 256 years Stela 1 at Tikal, but it is significantly later than the inscriptions found in Chiapas and those on the Veracruz coast.

ELLEN R. KINTZ

EL DORADO is the name of a mystical, mythical kingdom, which legend has endowed with fabulous wealth. Over time its reputed location has changed from the highland plateaus of Colombia first, to an area lying on the southern edge of the Venezuelan *llanos* second, and finally to the Guianas. During the 16th century when the legend formed, it cost the lives of several famous Spanish, Portugese, Dutch, German and English explorers and their men.

The foundation of the legend is based upon practices of the Chibcha tribes on the plateau of Bogota, or as it was then called, *Cundinamarca,* in Colombia. The Chibcha had five sacred lakes around which much of their religious and ceremonial life centered. At the time of the coronation of a new chief, and perhaps at other times as well (early histories are not clear), this individual was coated with sticky resin, and rolled in gold dust until he gleamed like a golden statue. After appropriate incantations to the deities, he then leaped into the lake. Although the Chibcha had ceased performing this ceremony before the Spanish arrived (the last such occasion being about AD 1500), the ceremony had been very impressive, and stories about it were found throughout all of northwestern South America. The gold did not come from the Bogota region; rather the Chibcha traded salt, cloth and highland products with various lowland jungle tribes to get the gold dust.

King Carlos I of Spain wanted to become the Holy Roman Emperor of Europe. When he finally was named Holy Roman Emperor Charles V in 1519, he was heavily in debt to some German banking houses who had helped bankroll his election. It was partly to pay off these debts that Spain became so gold hungry, acquiring great wealth first with the conquest of Mexico by Cortés in 1521, and second with the conquest of Peru in 1533 by Pizarro. Because Cortés and Pizarro had been so successful in finding great wealth, the stage was set for other still undiscovered kingdoms of great wealth. Spain was in control of Panama and the northern shores of Colombia, as well as Ecuador to the south. Carlos I of Spain had given rights for explorations in Venezuela to one of the German banking houses to whom he was in debt. Thus the decade of 1529-1539 is marked by a series of expeditions of Spaniards driving south from Santa Marta on the Colombian Caribbean coast, and north from Quito in highland Ecuador, and German-led expeditions moving west from Venezuela, all in search of the *Cundinamarca* area, all striving to be first to follow the stories of the gilden man or gold-covered chief to its source. It was one of the Spanish expeditions from Ecuador which first coined the term "El Dorado" or "The Gilded One" referring to this kingdom. Three of these expeditions reached the Bogota area, and conquered the Chibcha in the years of 1537-1539. While they initially did obtain some wealth, including more than 200 pounds of gold, and almost 2,000 emeralds (for which Bogota is still a famous producer), the conquerors were much disappointed to discover that unlike Peru and Mexico, there were no gold mines in the Chibcha area, but that all the gold had been obtained in trade from eastern jungle tribes.

During the next thirty years, from 1540-1570, the search for the legendary kingdom shifted eastward, to the area of the Venezuelan llanos, and parts of Northwest Brazil and the Amazonian headwaters, particularly the area of the Omagua tribe, well-known traders in gold dust. The Spanish grant to the German banking house to exploit Venezuela had been revoked in 1550. Thus the search for El Dorado had become a Spanish one, almost as ritualistic a quest as those for the Holy Grail. This area was explored, but El Dorado was not found.

In the last quarter of the 16th century, the search shifted to yet a new location. It is during this period that much of the legend of El Dorado was developed. The new location for search was near the mouth of the Orinoco River, and eastward into the Guianas. Frustrated explorers invented stories to entice their financial backers to give them more time and money to find the elusive kingdom. El Dorado now acquired a capital city, Manoa, and soon Manoa was placed on a great lake, Lake Parima. El Dorado became populated by a number of peoples, including Incas of Peru, reputed to have escaped from Pizarro with all their gold, as well as the original Chibcha gold-covered chief and his people. By the late 1590s, El Dorado was beginning to show up on maps of South America, attracting still more adventurers. This time the focus shifts, and the new searchers are primarily from England and Holland. A number of English and Dutch expeditions were sent into the area between 1595-1620, and we find Dutch expeditions still looking for El Dorado as late as 1740. Sir Walter Raleigh was behind a number of the ill-fated English expeditions, and ultimately was executed for his failures. Of lasting impact from these Dutch and English expeditions were the founding of the colonies of British and Dutch Guiana, now the countries of Guyana and Surinam.

El Dorado typifies the get-rich-quick ethic of the 16th century. It is now a beautiful legend, built around a fantastic golden city in a fabled country, populated by scores of mythical peoples, including (according to recent sources) even escapees from Atlantis and Lemur.

DAVID L. BROWMAN

EL INGA. The archaeological site of El Inga, from which the El Inga cultures derive their name, is located in Pichincha province, about a dozen miles east of Quito, Ecuador, in the valley of the Rio Inga at 8,400 feet. The site was first discovered in 1947, but its importance as an unique example of the earliest known Ecuadorian culture was not realized until it was excavated about a decade later. These excavations revealed two discreet El Inga cultures — one group living at the site around 8,000 to 9,000 years ago, and a subsequent group re-using the same campsite about 4,000 to 5,000 years ago. The major significance of the site is the first group of settlers. Unfortunately mixture of various components at El Inga makes it impossible to clearly specify associations.

The earliest people, El Inga I, were a group of nomadic hunters, who sought many now extinct species, such as the mastodon, paleolama, horse (a different variety of horse than the ones the Spanish reintroduced), and sloth. The tool kit for hunting and butchering included a number of spearpoints, including fluted and non-fluted fishtail points and lanceolate points: bifacial knives, flake and blade scrapers, plano-convex scrapers, and burins. Some of these tool types are important fossils of human interchange, for they have allowed us to demonstrate wide interaction of the El Inga I culture with other South American peoples. Most important are the spearpoints whose constricted neck gives them an appearance of a child's drawing of a fish — thus the name "fishtail" points. Half of these points exhibited a special thinning technique called "fluting." Similar fluted fishtail points have been found running south along the east slopes of the Andes, in Brazil, and as far south as the tip of Patagonia, where they date between 8,500 to 11,000 years old. They usually are associated with hunters of extinct horses, mylodon, mastodons and guanaco-like animals, species adapted to grassland environments. Thus it appears that El Inga I people are members of a group of hunters who were exploiting the lower Andean slopes and moister Atlantic drainage savannahs and grasslands that existed in South America at the end of the Pleistocene.

There are other indicators, however, that the El Inga I people also engaged in extensive interchange with highland and even Pacific coastal peoples of different cultures. One of the most important cultural fossils here is the burin tool, a special tool for working bone and wood, most typical of Pacific coast and highland Andean cultures from somewhat earlier time periods. The presence of this tool at the El Inga campsite on the edge of the paramo indicates late exchange of the El Inga band with other highland groups. Some of the other artifacts also show considerable western influence; El Inga might be considered as a hybrid group of lowland savannah hunters and highland hunters. Many of the spearpoints found with the fluted fishtail points are identical to those being manufactured by another group of Andean hunters in Peru and Bolivia during the period of 8,000 to 11,000 years ago. Such exchange is further supported by the occurrence of one of the El Inga-like fluted fishtail points on the Peruvian coast at the La Cumbre elephant kill of 10,500 to 12,000 years in age.

Our current archaeological reconstructions show two different cultural adaptations for the period ten thousand years ago — one particularly adapted to the animals and environments of the high Andes and their Pacific slopes, and a second focussing on savannah type biomes on the eastern side of the Andes. El Inga I cultures are important not only for Ecuador, but also in the special interrelationships that it preserves for us between these two different cultures.

DAVID L. BROWMAN

EL JOBO. The El Jobo people take their name from a site near the town of Coro, in the state of Falcon, on the Caribbean coast of Venezuela. These people belong to one of the earliest known Paleo-Indian cultures in South America, and were first discovered and reported on in 1956 by Dr. Jose M. Cruxent. Most diagnostic of this culture is a spear point, which is lanceolate in outline, lenticular in cross-section, with a rounded base, and with sometimes also serrated edges. This point is diagnostic of the cultural influence of the El Jobo people. Subsequent to its original discovery, El Jobo materials have been found elsewhere along the Andes in South America, indicating early cultural contact among several areas.

The El Jobo culture was first described based on a series of archaeological materials from a river terrace of the Rio Pedregal in Venezuela. These first artifacts could not be dated well because they came from the surface only. Consequently there was a good deal of controversy surrounding the identification of the people, and the time they dated to. Subsequent work at sites such as Muaco and Taima-Taima in Venezuela has corroborated the first findings, and has revealed some of the lifeways of the period. There are now nearly two dozen radiocarbon age determinations on El Jobo people, ranging from between 11,800 and 14,500 years ago, with most dates falling between 12,600 and 13,600 years ago. The El Jobo people thus lived during a period 12,500 to 13,500 years ago, or 10,500-11,500 BC. They are part of a cultural stage in the New World called "Big-Game Hunters," referring to their successful hunting of such animals as mastodons and glyptodons. Other extinct animals associated with El Jobo sites include two types of ground sloths (Megatherium and Mylodon), two types of horses, Paleolama, Toxodon (which resembles a hippo), Macrauchenia (which looked like a cross between a llama and tapir), two felines (jaguar and lynx), wolf and the spectacled bear.

The El Jobo people lived at a time which was more humid and moister than today, as determined from the habitat of these animals and the plants found around their campsites. The people were nomadic, with only a small inventory of tools, which they carried with them from place to place. These tools included choppers, pounders, mammoth long bones used as anvils, knives, plano-convex scrapers and flake scrapers, and the long lanceolate El Jobo spear points on wooden spears. They hunted by lying in wait around springs and waterholes, or along the edge of rivers, probably making their kills from ambush. A single mastodon or elephant would provide them with food for a week or so, after which time they moved on to another hunting site. Groups were small — there were only small bands of 25 to 35 people at a maximum, living at great distance from the next nearest neighboring band.

DAVID L. BROWMAN

ELKO COLONY, in Elko County, Nevada, is a federal reservation of 195 acres for the Shoshone tribe. It had 140 Indians living on the land in the early 1970s.

The reservation was established in 1918 by executive order. Whites had first come to the area in the 1820s. The influx of traders, miners, and settlers began to rapidly affect the life of the Indians, and by 1850, there was friction. After several major battles, the U.S. government and the Nevada tribes signed a series of treaties in 1863. By 1880, the area was peaceful.

The Indians living on Elko claim to be a segment of Chief Te-Moak's band of Shoshone Indians. Like other Shoshone, who have been called "Digger Indians," these Shoshone are descendents of the Indians who foraged and scraped for their food and survival. They are proud of their heritage, but practice few traditions. The Colony is a member of the Te-Moak Western Shoshone Council, a governing body which has total jurisdiction over all matters concerning lands of member reservations. The council meets monthly. The Elko body is a council of 6 members, elected to 2 year terms.

The tribe has no income, and the land, which is arid and inhospitable, has few resources. The colony provides water and waste disposal, and gas and electricity. Other services are in Elko, 2 miles from the colony.

EL SALVADOR is the smallest nation in the western hemisphere with an area of 8,260 square miles. The 3.5 million populace averages a density of 500 people per square mile. El Salvador is bordered by Guatemala on the west, Honduras to the north, and a ferry service across the Gulf of Fonseca connects the country with Nicaragua to the east. The lowland southern coastal plain lies off the Pacific Ocean. Two mountain ranges, the Sierra Madre and the Coastal Mountains, cross east to west creating valleys and plateaus between them. Currently there are four active volcanoes, which is the largest number in any Central American country. Climate varies from semitropical hot and humid coastal plains to temperate in the rest of the nation. There is separation of church and state although over 80% of the people are Roman Catholic; the remaining segment is mostly Protestant. Spanish serves as the official language; yet, there are still an uncertain number of Indians who speak Nahua dialects and a few Lenca speakers. Another Indian language, Cacaopera (Matagalpan), had been spoken until the 1950s. Unlike the other two Mesoamerican languages, this was a South American tongue. Many Nahua names for local flora and fauna have been adopted by Salvadorean Spanish. The economy is predominantly agricultural with high quality coffee being the major export cash crop. Sugar, cotton, and sesame are also exported. Non-agricultural industry is developing slowly. A government and a private railroad system, as well as trucking, carry the export crops to the major ports of Acajutla and La Libertad on the Pacific and La Union in the Gulf of Fonseca. A few of the country's rivers are navigable, but only in part.

Two ethnic groups comprise the Salvadorean population: *Ladinos* and *Indios*. These terms are cultural and not biological classifications. Most Ladinos are of mixed Spanish and Indian descent to varying degrees. Such a population segment is characteristic of Latin American countries and is often referred to as mestizo. Indios or Indians are more uniformly descended from indigenous pre-Columbian peoples. Unlike the Ladinos, the Indians practice more of a traditional Indian cultural lifestyle and limit contact with the Ladinos. However, acculturation to the predominantly European derived Salvadorean culture is a pervasive outgoing process. Indian population estimates range from 4% (140,000) to 16% (560,000) of the overall national figure. This vagueness results from the difficulty in labeling a group as culturally more Ladino or Indian. Both Indians and rural poor Ladinos share many cultural traits, especially with regard to subsistence. As in the rest of Latin America, the impoverished rural population's agricultural techniques are basically those of pre-Columbian Indians. During pre-Columbian times Central American Indians maintained a cultural distinctiveness together with many relations with Mesoamerica and South America. Archaeological data from El Salvador exhibits these influences.

The Lenca are the first Indians known to have occupied El Salvador. They were a non-Mayan Mesoamerican group who migrated to the area around AD 150. From AD 150 to 600 these migrants flourished without further intrusions. After this time Chorotega Maya from Honduras and Pokoman Maya from highland Guatemala and possibly Nahua speaking Mexican peoples came to the country. The latter would be a very early influx of a *Pipil* population. *Pipil* is a term used to refer to Nahua speaking migrants from the Mexican highlands. Migrations to other parts of Mesoamerica and Central America were made either to establish outposts for the long distance trade of

United Nations.

A vegetable garden in an emergency camp near San Salvador which accommodated the refugees of the May 7, 1951 earthquake that ravaged the central area of El Salvador.

luxury goods, or were Mexican groups fleeing victorious enemies.

Another Pipil incursion occurred in the 11th century. These were Toltecs who are ancestral to the historic and present day Pipil Indians of El Salvador. The contemporary cities of Sonsonate and Ahuachapan originally were established by these people. Many of the then resident Lenca acculturated to Toltec culture, others kept their distance, and some went to Honduras to escape subjugation.

In 1524 Pedro de Alvarado led an expedition of Spanish and Indian troops from Mexico through

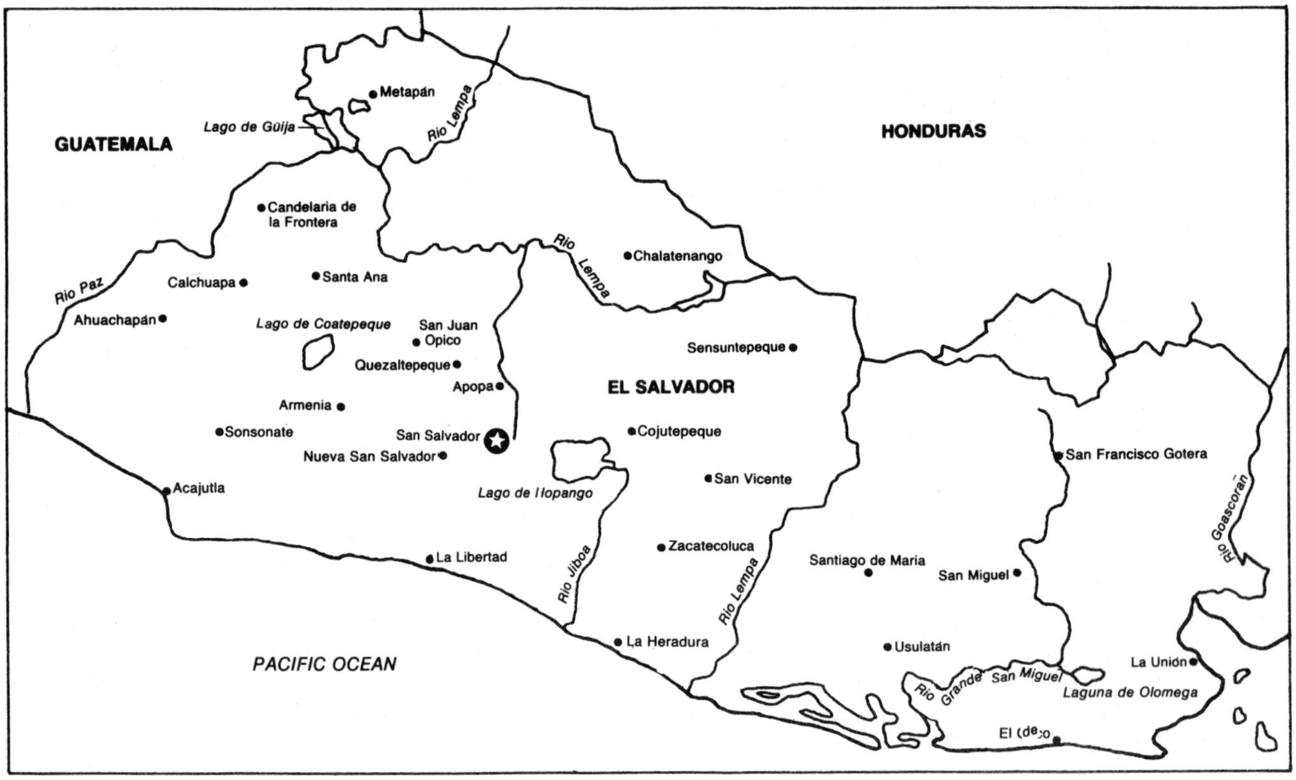

U.S. Department of Agriculture Office of Information.

Plowing land with a yoke of oxen and a wood plow in San Andres, El Salvador.

Guatemala to conquor El Salvador. They met fierce and successful resistance. Along with many of his men, Alvarado was wounded. The force retreated to Guatemala. The Spanish renewed their attack in 1525 and gained a hard won victory. From 1525 to 1821 El Salvador was a Spanish colony governed by the Captaincy General of Guatemala. Not yielding gold, silver, or other mineral wealth the colony spent this period as a neglected and unimportant part of the New World Spanish Empire. Initially there were disputes between the Spaniards from Mexico and Panama over control of the area. When no riches were realized these conflicts subsided. After 200 years of being a backwash, El Salvador slowly developed an important position which ultimately made the city of San Salvador second only to Guatemala City by the year 1800. The population grew gradually, agriculture improved, and a lucrative cattle industry began. Indigo dyes provided an important cash crop for export.

Unsuccessful revolts for independence occurred in 1811 and 1814. These were the first such uprisings in Central America and American nations during the 1820s. After Mexico separated from Spain the Mexicans occupied El Salvador (1821-1823). Salvadorean independence came in 1823 and the country joined the loose federation of the United Provinces of Central America. By 1838 this coalition collapsed. With dissension and open conflict rampant in Central America, El Salvador began its turbulent existence as an independent republic. As in other Latin American countries, a small elite, who owned and controlled most of the best agricultural land, developed. These families have always exerted great indirect and at times direct influence on the government. Military leaders have often become president and have been increasingly influential. From 1838 to 1900 several major political disturbances occurred: ranging from residential assasinations, three interventions by Guatemala in the selection of a president, and four wars. Salvadorean politics of the 20th century have been less chaotic, but similar to the 1800s.

The large number of landless people in an agriculturally oriented country with essentially no vacant land precipitated a massive migration starting around 1940. Thousands of people went to Honduras where much vacant land remains available. During the 1960s, workers with industrial skills also migrated from their homeland where unemployment is chronic. By 1969 approximately 300,000 Salvadorean cultivators and agricultural laborers lived in Honduras. Considerable interethnic tension and conflict developed in Honduras and both governments became increasingly hostile with one another. A riot errupted at a soccer game between El Salvador and Honduras, which was held in San Salvador in July 1969. This sparked a brief but costly war. Many expatriot Salvadoreans fled home, but El Salvador could not accommodate so great an influx and soon made re-entry difficult.

Agricultural production of export cash crops are the backbone of El Salvador's economy. Land is extremely scarce and labor is cheap and seasonal due to the timing of harvest for coffee, sugarcane, sesame, and cotton. Many poor rural agricultural laborers rent small lots to grow a few subsistence crops for their own consumption: corn, beans, sorghum, and rice. The United States, West Germany, Japan and the Central American Common Market countries are the major customers for Salvadorean exports. Imports from the first three nations are usually of machinery, chemical products, and other manufactured goods. In the early 19th century coffee replaced indigo, cacao, and balsam as the most important product. Although there were more than 40,000 coffee growers in the 1960s, the average holding was 7 acres. Only 3% of this number held more than 125 acres on which 60% of the coffee crop was grown. Cattle raising and dairy products remain important industries. Most cattle keepers have small herds. Shrimp fishing has become an increasingly important industry since 1960.

Ladinos and Indians are the two ethnic segments of Salvadorean society. Ladinos are culturally and biologically mestizo. Compared to other regions of Latin America and the Caribbean, few black Africans have been present in El Salvador. Those few that were present in colonial times have been absorbed by the

Ladino ethnic group. As in the rest of Latin America, Ladino (mestizo) culture is a syncretic combination of Spanish and Indian culture. Any attempt to rigidly define and cull a Ladino from an Indian is difficult and often misleading. Noting that very few Indian cultural traits have remained entirely intact from pre-Columbian times, an examination of some traits considered to be Indian is somewhat useful in separating Ladino and Indian peoples.

Most of the contemporary Indian population is located in the southwestern departments of Sonsonate and Ahuachapan: the communities of Panchimalco, Nahuizalco, and Izalco. There is another Indian community in the northeast, Cacaopera. Remnant pre-Columbian cultural traits are predominantly religious. However, certain aspects of local political organization, indigenous crafts, women's clothing and the perpetuation of Indian township exist, but are rather differentially distributed. In Izalco and Panchimalco women use the hip-strap loom to make textile belts. The loom is attached to a tree or some other stationary object and the woman's waist. Both towns make distinctive belts and in Panchimalco the material used for women's skirts is also woven. Manguey fiber mats are produced in Nahuizalco. In Cacaopera string hammocks and bags are made out of locally grown henequen fiber. Indians traditionally carry their wares to regional markets in a bag placed on the back and held with a leather strip looped around the forehead. The weight of the contents hold the bag in place. Ladino mule and ox drawn carts are being used more often by Indians to transport goods.

Within the political and religious cultural sphere Salvadorean Indians maintain an ancient Mesoamerican pattern which is found throughout contemporary Mesoamerica: the civil-religious hierarchy or ladder system. This is an organizational pattern for men wherein all males throughout their life occupy some niche — from boys sweeping the church steps to mayor. Rural dwelling is responsible for the upkeep of the village saint's shrine and officiates at fiestas (festivals). Arable plots are set aside to grow produce which is sold to help finance regular village events such as the fiesta celebrating the town's patron saint, the preparation of fields for planting, or at harvest. Indian dances are enjoyed by both Indian and Ladino participants and elaborate costumes and masks are worn at some of these fiestas.

Nahua is still spoken in Indian villages, but it is increasingly becoming the domain of the elderly, young children and women: i.e., among individuals who have limited contact with Ladinos. Spanish is certainly becoming the single language of El Salvador.

The remaining distinctive Indian cultural traits appear to be evermore rapidly acculturated into the dominant Salvadorean Ladino culture.

JOHN PHALEN

ELY COLONY, in White Pine County, Nevada, is a reservation of only 10 acres. It is home to about three dozen members of the Shoshone tribe.

The Ely Colony was established in 1931, when the land was put in trust to the U.S. Government for some Shoshone Indians, who had no tribal rights on any other reservations for Shoshone. Like all Shoshone in Nevada, the descendants were forced onto reservations by treaties of 1863. They lost their cultural background, and adopted the ways of the whites.

The Shoshone on Ely Colony speak Shoshone, and practice some traditional crafts. They are organized under the bylaws and constitution of 1966. They have few resources. The Colony is connected to the city of Ely, which provides, sewer, gas, and electricity, and has medical facilities open to all Indians. The lone community building on the Colony is the center for tribal activities.

EMBROIDERY was done by Indians who characteristically decorated the articles they used in everyday life. The materials with which they embroidered were animal hair, porcupine and bird quills, beads, and wool. When European glass beads were received in trade by Indians in the early 19th century they supplanted quills for the most part. Some tribes believed in a myth which held that the teacher of embroidery was the spider who sent embroidery designs to women in their dreams.

It is among the Plains Indians that embroidery techniques on hides, chiefly buffalo, were widespread. Plains tribes decorated their clothing, including robes and moccasins, tipi covers and linings, containers, drums, shields, and other utilitarian articles with paint and embroidery of dyed horsehair, porcupine quills, and trade beads. Each tribe embroidered distinctive designs sometimes related to pictographic painting, sometimes abstract or geometric.

In the Great Lakes area dyed moose hair and porcupine quills were embroidered with fine stitching onto a base of deerhide, birchbark, or cloth to make clothing and pouches. Early geometric designs were replaced by curvilinear floral patterns which Huron girls learned in French Canadian convents in the 18th and 19th centuries. Some of this type of embroidery is still being produced today using silk embroidery thread instead of porcupine quills. Floral motifs in Woodland beadwork were also adapted from embroidery taught in convents and observed on clothing of French and English travelers.

Some Eskimo embroidery combined split quills of bird feathers with moose hair. The Tlingit and Tsimshian tribes of the Northwest Coast embroidered on hide with porcupine quills and beadwork in floral designs.

In the Southwest weavings were frequently decorated with embroidery in geometric designs. Today only the Hopi continue this tradition. Among the Hopi, only men embroider with wool on cotton kilts, sashes, shirts, shawls, and ceremonial dresses. The cotton, raised by Hopis until the beginning of the 20th century, is now obtained from commercial sources. Hopi women still wear plain weave white cotton wedding dresses which are embroidered later for other ceremonial uses with bright colored wool yarn.

Formerly wool yarn for embroidery was ravelings from bayeta; today commercial yarn is used. In the mid 19th century Indians of the Rio Grande pueblos developed embroidery on clothing to a high degree including black or white kilts and shawls of cotton or wool embroidered in bright colors. At Acoma, unlike most pueblos, embroidery was done by women who produced richly embroidered shawls, shirts, and dresses first made of cotton, later of finely woven wool.

Related to embroidery is quillwork, a distinctively North American Indian art form. It consists of embroidering or weaving porcupine, or sometimes bird, quills on animal hides in a great variety of articles such as tobacco and tinder pouches, knife cases, cradles, robes, shirts, leggings, belts, moccasins, and horsetrappings and on birchbark containers.

Skillful and patient technique produced smooth, even quillwork. Quills were gathered by men hunting porcupines and worked by women who kept the quills in cases made of buffalo or elk bladders. The quills were sorted, softened in water, then flattened by pulling between the teeth or using a shaped bone tool. Quills were used in their natural colors of white and brown and were dyed yellow, red, blue, green, or black with vegetable dyes. Later aniline dyes of brighter colors were used. Most tribes sewed quills with an awl. Quills are so short that each one made only a few stitches. Designs were usually stencilled, traced, or drawn on hide or birchbark with a brush, knife, or stick although some women worked out their designs as they embroidered. Early designs were geometric and angular. After European contact, designs became more naturalistic with human, animal, and floral forms.

Plains Indians, including the Sioux, Cheyenne, Arapaho, Arikara, and others, applied quills to buffalo and deer hides in elaborate decoration of costumes, pouches, moccasins, and horsetrappings. They decorated pipe stems with intricately braided quills. Among Indians of the Eastern Woodlands, such as the Seneca and Ottawa, quillwork was probably the most widely used decoration of costumes. An important art form among the Micmac Indians of Eastern Canada was quillwork in geometric designs on birchbark made into boxes. Indians of Western Canada, such as the Chipewyan, were technically unsurpassed in their finely split quillwork found in knife cases, pouches, and costumes of elkskin of the 18th and 19th centuries. On the Northwest Coast the Tlingit and Tsimshian tribes, influenced by their inland neighbors, used porcupine quilling on their clothing made of hide. In the early 20th century Karok Indians of Northwest California made finely woven covered baskets in which they worked quills with maidenhair fern stems.

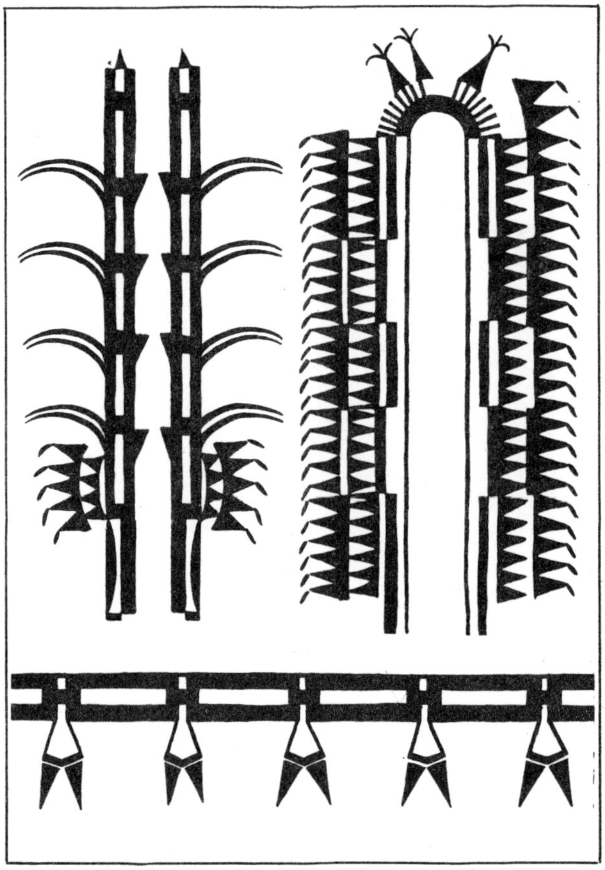

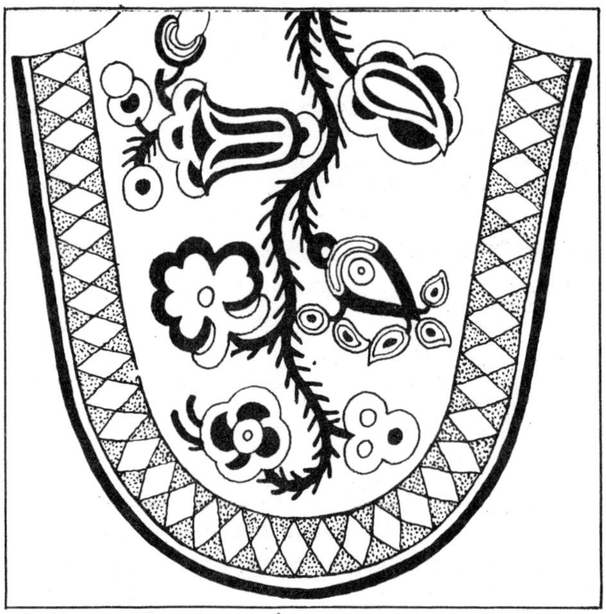

Moose hair embroidery with quillwork border, Kaska.

▲ Quillwork, Blackfoot. ▶

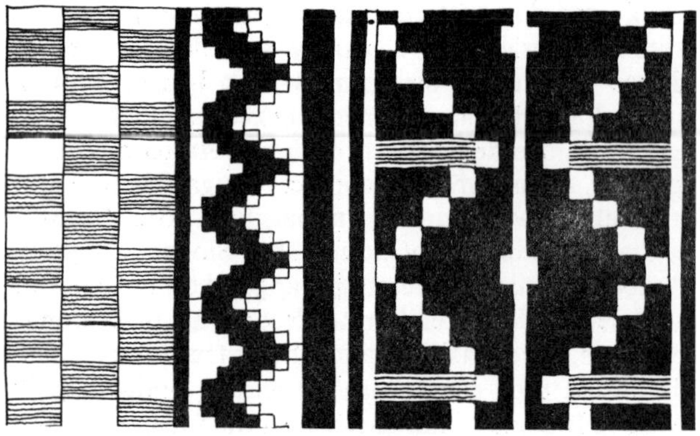

Quillwork, Slavey.

Quillwork, Tinne.

Quillwork, Chipewyan.

Quillwork, Athapascan.

EMERILLON The few surviving Emerillon Indians live along the Oyapock River on the boundary between French Guiana and Brazil. Prior to *c.* 1700, the Emerillon were further south, along the Amazon, but pressures from the intruding Portuguese colonists drove them north. First historic reference to them moving into the Oyapock River drainage is in AD 1736. For the next three-quarters of a century there are occasional historical references to conflicts between various Emerillon-related groups and the Carib-groups that they were displacing.

In the most limited sense, the Emerillon are only a small group of surviving Tupí-speaking natives living along both sides of the Oyapock River in northern Brazil and southern French Guiana. The term "Emerillon" also is sometimes used to refer to a wider grouping, including all of the Tupí-speaking groups which invaded French Guiana in the 18th century. In this sense, it includes the groups of Tupí-speakers of: Apanto, Caliana or Calayua, Camacom or Tamacom, Cusari, Paikipiranga or Parichy, Uara-Guacu, Oyampi (a.k.a. Aipi, Uajapi, Guyapi, Wayapi, etc.), and Emerillon proper, or as they call themselves, the Merignons.

The Emerillon were a semi-nomadic people. Slash-and-burn agriculture provided the major portion of their nutrition, with hunting and gathering of slightly less importance. The single most important food plant was the bitter manioc. Flour cakes cooked on hot griddle stones form the basic daily food. Bitter manioc,

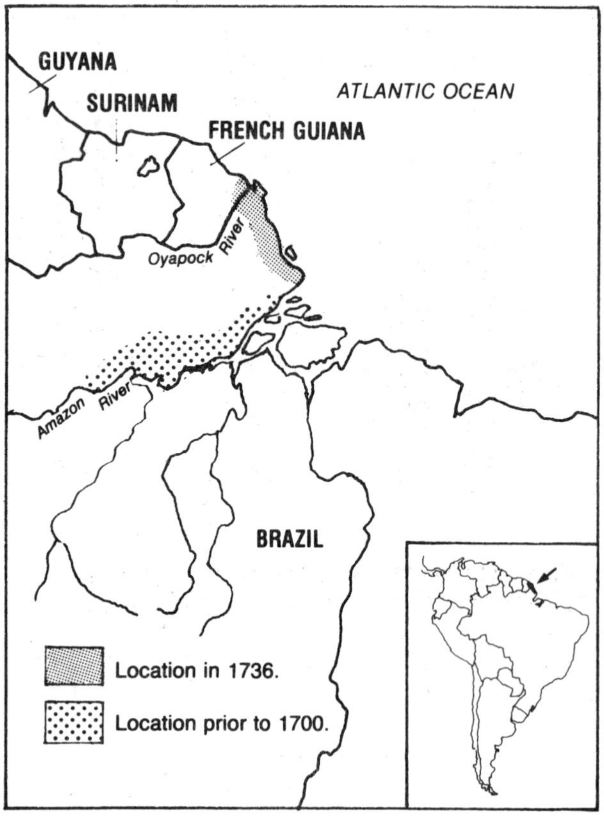

Emerillon

unprocessed, contains poisonous prussic acid. To detoxify the tuber, the plant is first ground on manioc graters, with stone chips or fishbones imbedded to help shred the plant. The processed mass is then squeezed in long basketry tubes (the tipiti or tepitsi) to extract the bulk of the toxins, and the resulting flour baked on stone or pottery griddles into manioc cakes.

Other important cultivated plants utilized by the Emerillon include peppers, corn, sweet potatoes, peanuts, pineapples, gourds, papaya, tobacco, and cotton, and more recently, bananas, plantains, yams, and sugarcane. Because of the low fertility of jungle soils, the Emerillon are constantly preparing new fields. Until recently, clearing was still done using only stone axes and fire, and planting was done using wooden digging sticks. The men clear the fields; the women plant and weed. The cabaya of the surrounding forest finds the new manioc plants to be a delicacy; thus huts are frequently constructing in the field to guard the field. Thus the village itself tends to shift population centers each year as the major field areas shift.

A variety of techniques are used in hunting the tropical animal species. The Emerillon were traditionally skilled in imitating animal cries and did some hunting from blinds. They also used a series of pitfalls and traps historically for larger game, although these have not been reported in use in this century. The Emerillon were among the Amazon groups who did not use the blowgun, but rather used long bows. Bows usually were 180 to 200 cm. in length, and have been reported up to 250 cm. in length. Four different types of arrows were used: a long arrow with a blunt wooden head for birds; an arrow with 2-3 prongs for fishing; and two different sizes stone-tipped (now iron-tipped) arrows for large and small game. Dogs were frequently used in hunting larger game. Animals most frequently taken included deer, wild pigs, monkeys, agouti, armadillos, sloth, tapir, anteaters, cabaya, and various birds.

In fishing, in addition to the 2-3 prong arrow, nets and basket weirs, fish poison, and hook and line fishing were used. Those groups in closest contact with the Caribs also used a kind of spring-hook trap for fish.

The "villages" of the Emerillon were small. Typical sizes for both the 19th and 20th century are no more than 30-40 people, usually living in single family houses grouped into small settlements around a central area. Some of the 18th century villages are said to have as many as 200 people; some of the "villages" reported in the last quarter century have had as few as five people. In most villages there was a large common hut, rectangular and gabled in form, which surrounded by the smaller huts with their 2-3 hammocks each. Villages were always placed on slightly higher ground to avoid wet season flooding, and were always close to a water source—small spring to major river.

The houses were constructed with poles and palm thatch. In most cases they were open, though more important individuals might have partly enclosed elevated platforms. There was little in the way of furnishings beyond the hammocks. Males had wooden seats or benches, usually decorated with zoomorphic effigy heads on either side. The feathers for decoration and other small, rare personal possessions were stored in a variety of baskets hung from the roof poles, or placed on small platforms. Bows and arrows, musical instruments, and other possessions similarly were hung from the poles.

There was little in the way of eating utensils. Gourd dippers were used for spoons and drinking containers. Pottery vessels formerly were used for some liquid storage and food preparation, but the knowledge of making ceramics has been lost by the 20th century group, and today all utensils are traded in enameled iron-ware, or other tin-ware.

Little clothing is worn. The women weave on backstrap looms, making larger pieces of cloth as wraparound skirts for the women and smaller pieces as loincloths for the men. Some of the larger pieces are tinted red or brown, in complex geometric designs; some of these designs are fond on the hammocks, carved in gourds, and on the earlier clay ceramics.

Most of the decoration involves the use of bodypaint or feathers. The body is always decorated in a melange of colored (usually black and red) designs. Feathers are stuck in the hair, in armbands, and also occasionally in wrist-bands and necklaces. Both sexes have a passion for elaborately decorated necklaces of trade beads, seeds, jaguar and peccary teeth, vertebrae of various animals, insect shells, fresh-water pearls, etc.

The technology is basically fairly simple, and oriented along clear sexual division. Basket-making is only a male task; thus men make all the baskets from the manioc-squeezing presses to the various storage baskets. The women do all the weaving of cotton goods. Men carve their own wooden stools or benches, and make the bows, arrows, war clubs, and other wooden items. Women formerly made the ceramics. Since the people were semi-nomadic, moving as each field became exhausted, relatively little in the way of permanent accumulation of material goods was made, and thus crafts were mainly oriented toward producing consumable, expendable items.

Relatively little has been written about the life cycle of the tribe during the early years of contact. Most early observers were most impressed with the elaborate and arduous initiation rites, or rites of passage from youth to adulthood. Individuals underwent this ceremony sometime between 12 and 20 years of age. The ceremony lasts nearly the entire six months of the wet season. It is reported as a severe ordeal, with rites involving the use of stinging ants, and frequent "bad trips" or overdoses of various locally used hallucinogenic infusions.

Political power was relatively slight. Although there was a headman, all the elders in the village had certain political power. The headman's decision did not have the force of law. Rather it can be ignored more or less at will. As marriages and alliances shifted over the years, so too did the particular headman of the village.

The religion of the Emerillon seems to have a fairly elaborate pantheon and a loose hierarchy of religious beings. There were a series of culture heroes or folk heroes typical to each village, which took on quasi-religious features. There were a series of bush spirits and other spirits which could be manipulated. These spirits were organized in a loosely knit ascending order, from local topographic spirits up to more or less deities such as the rain or river spirits; in a couple of cases there was a supreme deity, a creator figure, who resides in the sun.

Curing and religion are closely tied together, since most ailments are believed to be caused by some difficulty with the spirits. Both the religious experience, and curing, involve the use of hallucinogenic snuffs and infusions, which are though to allow the individual to directly commune with the spirits. On these occasions, a variety of bamboo trumpets, ranging in size from only 5-7 cm. up to 3-4 m. may be used.

Since the first contact with the white man, the Emerillon tribe has been fighting a losing battle to survive and maintain its cultural identity. Ceremonial cannibalism was an important part of the basic religious and social order of the Tupí-tribes around the mouth of the Amazon.

Early Christian missionaries felt impelled to change the entire social and religious constructs of Emerillon and other groups. There was a labor shortage on plantations, and the Portuguese frequently raided the Indian tribes for slaves for plantation labor. Even peaceful contact in terms of trade was harmful—for the Indians were not immune to the diseases brought to the New World by the new conquistadores, and tribe after tribe were wiped out by European-introduced epidemics. The century from roughly AD 1650-1750 marks the migration of a number of Tupí tribes, including the Emerillon, from the mouth of the Amazon, north into the Guianas, and west along various Amazonian tributaries in a vain attempt to escape Portuguese Christianization, disease, and slavery. These migrations were into areas already occupied by other Indian groups, and hence this period is marked by a good deal of warfare between various Indian groups. In the year 1597, English and Dutch explorers found only Carib Indian tribes living along the Oyapock River, but by 1736-1740, the Emerillon, Oyampi and other Tupí-speaking groups had appeared and were establishing themselves along the river, pushing the Caribs northward. Continued warfare between the displaced Carib-groups and intrusive Tupi groups continues through the historical record; as recently as 1923 there is a report of a raid by a Carib-speaking tribe on the Emerillon tribe. The magnitude of this disaster may be better appreciated when contrasted to the census made in 1888, which only listed about 100 known surviving Emerillon at that time. By 1950, the population of Emerillon was less than 50, and recent sources indicate that the group is nearly extinct.

As with so many other New World tribes, the Emerillon have fallen victims of "progress." We will be forced to rely upon unpublished archives to reconstruct the full range of the vivid cultural patterns perfected by these groups.

DAVID L. BROWMAN

Handbook of South American Indians.

Emerillon (*Oyampi*) Indians making a bark canoe.

EMISTESIGO (Creek; 1752-1782), ws a principal chief of the Upper Creek who aligned himself with the British during the American Revolutionary War. In 1776 the British arranged a peace agreement between the Creek and the Choctaw. In return Emistesigo (also known as Guristersigo) agreed to aid the British against the Americans. He died in a battle with U.S. forces under Gen. Anthony Wayne near Savannah, Georgia.

EMPLOYMENT AND UNEMPLOYMENT. Today most Indians live on reservations, and the majority — perhaps three fourths — make their entire living through wage work on and off their reservations which range in size from small settlements of a few acres in California up to the 25,000 square miles of the Navajo Reservation. In Canada, the Canadian government has set aside 2,241 similar reserves for its Indians. In the last half of the last century some Indian reservations resembled concentration camps, being closely guarded by the U.S. government — such as the Dakota, Cheyenne, Comanche and various Apache tribes. They were provided with food and clothing and crooked Indian Agents and contractors had their heyday. With the growing demand for the reservation land, many of the reservations were reduced in size, crowding the Indians even more, although during that period the Indian population declined in numbers. The Indians were asked to give up their traditional culture patterns of living and to become farmers instead of becoming hunters, a strange idea to the Indians of the hunting tribes; furthermore, outside Arizona and New Mexico, farming was looked upon as woman's work, and they also resented the requests that they should

U.S. Department of Agriculture Office of Information.

On the Navajo Indian Reservation (1968) encompassing 25,000 square miles in the states of Arizona, Utah and New Mexico, the U.S. Department of Agriculture's Commodity Distribution Program supplements the diet of over 21,000 Indians. Ninety-six thousand Navajo were then members of families at the poverty level with incomes of $3,000 a year or less.

live in wooden or log houses, wear more clothes, and cut their hair short. (The Bureau of Indian Affairs hoped to civilize Indians by cutting off their hair).

But during the last three or four decades, the BIA stated as its objectives: (1) maximum Indian economic self-sufficiency; (2) full participation of Indians in American mainstream of life; and (3) equal citizenship privileges and responsibilities. (More than half of the BIA's regular employees have Indian blood today). Today, thousands of Indians live and work away from the reservations, and most Indian tribes govern themselves through tribal councils elected by the tribe. The Indians have to work for their living, pay taxes (unless exempted by treaty or other arrangements), and only the elderly, the blind and other needy individuals are granted public assistance or welfare, while, on the reservations the government provides education and health services.

Indians attach a great social and symbolic significance to their land, and some of them, in Oklahoma and elsewhere, have become successful farmers; others, like the Western Apaches, are successful cattle raisers. But some are indifferent farmers or cattle raisers, barely managing to get by. Many have chosen to remain on their land as self-employed farmers or livestock growers until economic necessity forces them to abandon agriculture or supplement income from this source through seasonal or temporary wage work. This change mirrors a growing Indian population on a fixed land base, an abandonment of subsistence agriculture, and a desire for a higher standard of living which, in agriculture, can be gained only through an increase in size of land holdings. In spite of this economic shift, the BIA estimates that reservations are "overpopulated," and that farming and livestock raising could support a reasonable standard of living only of one-half to two thirds of the Indian families now trying to make their living by this means.

The 1950 official figures show the heavy percentage of Indians in low income jobs and in types of work which allow periodic and seasonable employment. For instance, the Northwest Coast Indians still live on salmon, but most of them now work in salmon canneries or on fishing boats. In Canada and Alaska Indian and Eskimo hunters and trappers continue to roam their old homelands. Hundreds of Iroquois are famous as structural steel workers on high buildings and bridges from New York to San Francisco.

At any rate, the Indian reservations have had for

decades to endure a rate of unemployment estimated at being almost double on the reservations when compared to the figures for the whole of the United States. In fact, the high rate of self-destruction in the 20 to 34 age group — the group which in American society is one of the most productive — has been attributed to the frustration, the sense of hopelessness which stems from the lack of opportunities on the reservations. In 1973, the Bureau of Indian Affairs estimated that there were approximately 60,000 reservation Indians unemployed.

Between 1957 and 1966, about 50,000 Indians left their reservations and relocated in the cities but most of the jobs they were able to secure were often of a marginal type only. When America's national economy slumped in the late 1950s, these jobs were the first to disappear. At the same time, the Indians were also the victims of race discrimination in the labor market. To these, more arrivals had been added to the World War II veterans (some 25,000 had enlisted) and those who had found jobs in the cities due to the war labor shortages. In the cities, the Indians gravitated to the cheapest, poorest, and most run-down houses; the result was the rise of Indian ghettos with the usual problems of city poverty — poor health, poor education and alcoholism. Not prepared for living in large cities, they had difficulties in getting adjusted to heavy traffic, using public transportation and finding necessary goods and services. The U.S. Census report of 1970 noted that in 30 metropolitan areas with at least 2,500 Indians, median family income ranged from as low as $3,389 in Tucson, Arizona, to not more than $10,000 in Washington and Detroit. Many non-Indian employers still feel that Indians are not reliable or intelligent workers, and the myth that all Indians are lazy drunkards still prevails, especially in Oklahoma. Evidently alcohol is preferable to the accommodation to the white world by many Indians, who find their way to the urban Indian bars — the Ritz in Los Angeles, the Larimer Street barns in Denver, the Shamrock or Sammy in Chicago, where whites are unwelcome, and where they are joined by reservation Indians; drunken reservation Indians can be found any Saturday night on the streets of Gallup, New Mexico, the "Indian Capital of the World." The pressures of urban life in a strange society seem to magnify alcoholism.

While government agents' promised good jobs or education, decent housing, and a life in the cities, and the recruiters were issued one-way tickets to Minneapolis, Cleveland, Dallas, and several California cities, the promised new jobs proved to be only part-time work at substandard wages, and the decent housing failed to materialize; when the initial living allowance ran out, the result was a shift from dependence on the federal government on the reservation to a place on the welfare rolls in the city. The victims eventually became aware that life in the reservation — despite its largely unarable land, its dirt-floor shanties, its patronizing government officials, its

Jan Marie Blackbird (left) of Houston, Texas was lead draftsperson in the central Gulf of Mexico area of Cities Service Oil Company's Gulf of Mexico Exploration Production Region. As lead draftsperson, she supervised several other draftspersons. Jan is an Apache Indian and is shown with one of her draftspersons from India.

boredom — was not as oppressive as the urban slums, simply because the reservation was still open country owned by those inhabiting it. The city always evokes a longing for nature. Compared to the life in urban slums, the reservation still offers the stable values of the tribal heritage — tribal ties, religious concepts and memories, family relationships and loyalties, and attachment to the land.

Thus many Indians, relocated from their family and friends and the security of their home communities, returned to their reservations; others moved back and forth from cities to reservations in a constant quest for work or for some new job opportunity. Some joined seasonal migrations to the reservation to fish, hunt, or harvest wild rice. But this also meant that they were not eligible for government services either in the city or on the reservation. (No minority or other special interest group is so closely tied to the federal government as the American Indian). In fact, some authorities estimate that there are more Indians living in cities and towns than are remaining on the reservations, and of these now dwelling in urban areas, approximately three-fourths are living in poverty, often losing out in the opportunity to participate in the programs designed for disadvantageous groups.

Unfortunately, occasional successes in employment and business have barely made a dent in the massive Indian poverty. The much publicized project of bringing industry to the reservations has made some dent but has been somewhat offset by the fact that the main pitch to industry has been low capital, cheap labor, and has been scarcely conducive to blue-chip

Indian businessman Richard Locklear, second from left, owner of Cherokee Construction Co. in Alexander, VA., directs workers on a building site.

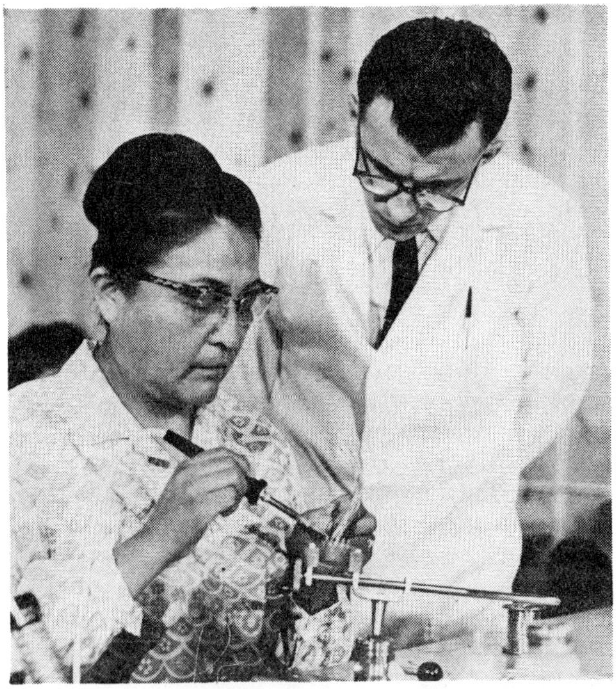

Navajo facility of General Dynamics, Fort Defiance, Arizona, was dedicated in November, 1967. The $800,000 facility was built and is largely staffed by Navajos. Employees are engaged in assembly and fabrication of electronic components for the Standard Missile, a shipboard defense system produced for the United States Navy by the Pomona Division of General Dynamics.

deals. Yet, one of the biggest advantages of industry located on the reservation is the huge pool of available labor, and there are millions in federal training funds available to companies for training, although on many depressed areas the human and physical resources are inadequate to support manufacturing plants. At any rate, in 1964, a total of 56 industrial plants, including those in Alaska, had been located on or near reservations, employing a total of 2,363 people, of which 1,385 were Indians; but as of September 30, 1964, 6 plants had been closed and 7 under construction, leaving 43 in active operation. To cite a few examples: there were cheese and milk products produced at Selfridge, North Dakota, near the Standing Rock Reservation, and by the Sioux Dairy Cooperative at Mission, South Dakota; electronic components made in the Laguna Pueblo, in New Mexico; tufted carpets produced at Anadarko, Oklahoma; electric meters and parts made on the Lac de Flambeau Reservation, Wisconsin; metal products manufactured by the Turtle Mountain Steel and Supply Co., Rolla, North Dakota.

In some reservations, the Indians commute to cities, but many opportunities for seasonal labor have been lost as a result of mechanization of such farm work as potato planting and harvesting. Especially affected are those Indians accustomed to working with seasonal crops like cotton, sugar beets, potatoes, and other vegetables which now require mechanical equipment. Then, especially in isolated reservations with no work available within commuting distance, a desperate need exists for developing a nucleus of economically successful Indian operators of farms, ranches, and small commercial undertakings. Thus welfare payments continue a very important source of Indian income; another source of support is the federal program for distributing of surplus agricultural products. State welfare assistance is also provided in some but not.all states which have assumed responsibility for Indian welfare. At any rate, Indian welfare payments are disproportionately high when compared with those going to the general population. And the need for creating employment and developing Indian property is rendered more imperative than ever before due to the growing reservation population, coupled with a diminishing land base. (Many reservations are unable to solve their economic problems until they can cure the evil of fragmented ownership). And until 2 or 3 decades ago, on most reservations and in other parts of the country, the major dependence upon subsistence agriculture there has been a shift to wage work.

Some of the Indians that have moved to the cities are, of course, doing well financially. Some Indians in the cities have become assimilated — and many war veterans have become leaders in improving Indian conditions, helping to form inter-tribal community centers where they discuss their problems, receive help, organize for action — or simply socialize. In the fiscal year of 1971, the Indian Action Team (IAT) program was established to provide essential training on the reservations without relocation; it includes classroom work, shop application and on-the-job experience which enables the workers to progress toward the journeyman's level of that trade; union officials agreed to credit trainees for the apprenticeship training received through the program.

In 1970, the Bureau of Indian Affairs contracted for an Indian Offender Rehabilitation Program to provide for Indian ex-offenders to work with potential Indian parolees in custody in federal and state institutions; this program gave parolees a chance for gainful employment after release, hoping to reduce the number of repeat offenders (recidivists).

Dorothy Tisdale, Cherokee Indian, employed as secretary-managerial for Exploration-Production Division, Cities Oil Service Co. She majored in computer science/engineering at the University of Tulsa and was a business school graduate. Under the direction of the U. of Tulsa Archeological travel studies, she participated in field work in Yucatan Mexico.

Indian tribes are increasingly aware of the dollar potential of tourism; numerous tribally owned motels have been built; an example is the $2.5 million Bottle Hollow Resort opened on the Uintah and Ouray Reservation by the Ute Tribe of Utah in the summer of

Smithsonian Institution, National Anthropological Archives.

Zuñi Indians making adobe bricks.

1971. The Office of Economic Opportunity is shotgunning poverty funds into the reservations; in 1972 it spent $208,741, to show the Zuni how they could mass-produce their handicraft jewelry for a guaranteed income. Over 5,500 Indians (together with Eskimos and Aleuts) earn part or all of their annual incomes from production and sale of a wide variety of unique craft products; the number of persons involved varies from several individuals in some areas to entire villages which are sustained by production and sale of pottery, silverwork, carving, or numerous other crafts, featuring Indian "specialties." In addition, over 500 individuals are self-employed professional painters, sculptors, or printmakers. The Cherokee Reservation, North Carolina, supports roughly 15% of its population through extensive and craft operations. In the Southwest, sales of Indian art and crafts products (more than an estimated $7 million annually) represent a substantial economic factor for thousands of Indian artisans. In authorizing the establishment of the Indian Arts and Crafts Board within the U.S. Department of the Interior in 1953, Congress gave official recognition to Indian culture, and instructed the Board to encourage Indians to turn certain aspects of their culture to commercial advantage. (A fine, imprisonment, or both, may be imposed on merchants who misrepresent imitation Indian art and craft products as being authentic Indian craft).

There is a small group of professional, middle class Indians in the cities. Some are divorced from their fellow Indians, but many provide leadership in Indian organizations. The last few decades have witnessed a number of young Indian men and women move into professional life — both within and outside the Indian world. A growing number of Indians are employed by the federal, state and even municipal agencies.

The most concrete Indian economic successes have been realized in group terms — tribal cattle herds, or the communal big business of recreation on some reservations (such as the $1.5 million complex built by the Crow in Montana, at Yellowtail Dam on the Bighorn); the financial renaissance of the Cheyenne River Sioux in South Dakota who now operate, among other things, a cattle business, sale pavillion, supermarket; and their telephone company serving Indians and non-Indians in two counties, grew mainly from initial successes with a tribal-consolidation program. The Tribal Land Enterprise Agency of the Rosebud Sioux in South Dakota buys land at a rate reaching a quarter-million dollars a year, and the land-consolidation program of the Crows has reached a million dollars' worth a year.

JOSEPH S. ROUCEK

ENCABELLADO were a group of Amazonian borderland Indians. They received the name *Encabellado* from the early conquistadores, from the archaic Spanish word meaning *one who has grown much hair.* The Encabellado are one of the major members of the Western Tucanoan speaking peoples, who lived primarily on the Napo, Putumayo and Caqueta rivers in Napo Province, eastern Ecuador, and formerly in parts of Putumayo and Caqueta provinces in southern Colombia.

Historical reference to the group is very confused. The question of nomenclature is complicated both by changes introduced during the historic contact period, and by a lack of significant cultural and political divisions among the people themselves. In the strictest sense, the Encabellado are identified with the Western Tucanoan group known as the Pioje, members of the group also including the Coto, Siona, Macaguaje, Icaguate, Correguaje, Secoya, Tetete, Icuene, and Tama. The Encabellado are thus sometimes referred to by one or more of these latter group names. They are also referred to by their own name for local topographical features, and by local mission names. Hence we find them called *Santa Maria* after a mission, or *Ancutere, Campuya, Tarapoto,* or *Cushmas,* almost an endless list. To ascertain the accuracy of any source, one must know both the geography and the language — not only must the reference be to the correct geographical region, but also to the correct linguistic group. The Encabellado or Pioje lived in close proximity to a non-Tucanoan speaking group usually known as the Cofanes. These two groups were frequently confused. Consequently some references to Cofanes are actually *Pioje, Siona, Secoya,* etc., and vice versa.

The major subsistence base of the Encabellado was agricultural. They grew sweet and bitter manioc, bananas and plantains, sweet potatoes and yams, beans, corn, sugar cane and a domesticated palm. Cultivation was with large knives and wooden planting sticks. Villages were not permanently located in any one spot. Rather, after a few years, when the soil closeby was over-used, the game driven away, and other resources near to the village depleted, the villagers simply picked up and moved the village a few miles. This somewhat transient existence led to economic attachment to resources acquired through hunting and collecting activities. The Encabellado hunted with blowgun and poison darts, nets, pitfalls, deadfalls, with the help of trained hunting dogs. Major animals taken were tapir, peccaries, capivaras, deer, monkeys, sloth and armadillo. The group at the time of first contact did not have their camps near rivers because the major highways of the region were the rivers, and it was a period of intense raiding. Once peace was re-established, they returned to the river, fishing by means of net, thorn fishhooks, bow and arrow, and the use of plant poisons such as barbasco. They gathered wild fruits and plants such as cashew nuts, various palm fruits, papaya, lime, and wild honey.

The Encabellado attached great importance to their personal appearance. Although during informal occasions the long hair might fall loose, during formal occasions the hair was carefully braided and wound around the head, bound with a piece of cloth. The face and body were very carefully painted with designs.

Each village had a slightly different inventory of designs. Arm and leg bands, necklaces, bracelets, chest bands of seeds, animal teeth, feathers and beads, were worn in great profusion.

Clothing was limited to an occasional red bark cloth shirt, and some woven cotton and *chambira* fiber fabrics. In more recent times, cotton cloth traded in from other areas has replaced bark cloth. These shirts or "cushma" were also decorated with the same designs painted on the body. "Cushma" were worn both by the Encabellado and the closely related Sioni, though more frequently by the Sioni. Because other neighboring tribes apparently did not wear such shirts, the Encabellado and Sioni were sometimes called the *Cushma* Indians.

Housing was in huts with thatched roofs and cane or pole section walls. Everyone slept in chambira-fiber woven hammocks, but little other furniture existed. The men had logs or carved woodenstools; other members of the family sat or squatted on the ground. The earliest references to the Pioje or Encabellado (1599-1651) refer to rather small huts, each holding no more than one or two nuclear families. By 1750, the Encabellado were living in large, rectangular communal dwellings, accommodating ten families or more. This style of housing continued among the last known Encabellado in the 20th century. The communal houses were divided into separate compartments for each family, each with its own fireplace, food utensils and sparse belongings.

Food preparation was very simple. Vegetable food was ground in wooden troughs and cooked in clay pots. The bitter manioc was ground on thorn-studded ceramic or wooden graters, the prussic acid extracted by use of the woven squeezer or *tipiti,* and the processed meal baked on a clay stove. Extra meat was smoked on rectangular and pyramidal drying racks, which retarded its spoilage in the tropical environment. Eating utensils were spoons and dishes fashioned from the various gourds of the jungle, river shellfish scoops, or wooden spatulas.

Little information has been recorded about the life cycle. At birth both the husband and wife were isolated for several days, to protect the child and to protect the village, since they were religiously impure and dangerous. Twins were bad luck and not allowed to live. There were rites of passage associated with male and female puberty, involving periods of isolation. There was no set age for marriage. The woman must have matured physically, and know the appropriate cooking and household skills. The man must be able to demonstrate hunting skills, proficiency in clearing agricultural patches, and in weaving hammocks. Bride-price was involved in the marriage, with the man making payment to the bride's parents in either goods or services. After death of the man of the house, the indivídiual was wrapped in his hammock and buried under the house floor, and the house burned and abandoned. After the Encabellado shifted to long houses, this practice was modified.

One of the few pleasures of these jungle people were the large fiestas they had. Sometimes these were held in conjunction with trading parties from other villages, and sometimes in concert with important religious ceremonies. For musical instruments, they had drums, panpipes, flutes, rattles, and musical bows.

Little is known about Encabellado religious beliefs. The tribe is now gone, having perished because of European-introduced diseases and extermination policies. Vague reference is made in early accounts to belief in some sort of remote supreme being in the heavens. Various powerful drugs were used both for religious experiences and for curing ceremonies. Among these were snuff powders from *Datura, Banisteriopsis, Ilex,* and *Andanthera* sp plants, and the narcotic coca. A major cause of disease was thought to be soul-loss. The shaman cured this by means of hallucenogenic spells in which they determined the cause of soul-loss by talking with spirits in the next world.

Spears and war clubs were the main weapons used in raids and warfare. The spears frequently had poisoned tips that would break off in the wound. The Encabellado were not notorious warriors, but did engage in both offensive and defensive fighting. They particularly exchanged raids with the neighboring Awishira, who raided them for loot, women and slaves. Villages under frequent attack were defended with trenches having sharpened, poisoned stakes in the bottom. During raids, men took trophy heads, and the successful war parties engaged in ritual cannibalism to celebrate the success of their raid.

Local political structure was transient. The Encabellado, when first contacted by the white man, were suffering a large number of attacks from neighboring groups. As a consequence, early villages were very small, and were located several miles from the nearest river, the major avenue of trade but also attacks. The early villages (between 1599-1651) contained 4-8 houses, each with 1-2 families, with a village population of 50-60. More than 100 such villages are reported for the Encabellado in 1635, with the total population of the group said to have been 6,000-8,000.

The Spanish influence changed the social and political structure of these groups markedly. After the pacification of the area by the Spanish, there is a shift toward larger villages and larger houses. By 1750, the Encabellado are living in long houses having 8-10 families per house, and in villages having 14-15 houses, and with additional feast halls capable of holding 300-400 people. These villages now have moved back to the river side.

Between 1599 and 1739, the Franciscans and Jesuits made more than a dozen attempts to missionize the Encabellado area. Most of these early missions failed after only a few years. At some missions, the priests were killed because they tried to force alien values on the people. At other missions, smallpox and other epidemics wiped out the Indians, forcing abandonment. Still other missions failed because of another

European practice — slavery. Tribes living on the edge of Spanish settlements closer to the Andes discovered they could obtain desired machetes and other trade goods in exchange for slaves. Therefore increasing raids were made on tribes further into Amazonia to obtain captives to trade with the Spanish. Tribes settled in mission villages made ideal candidates for such raids. Some missions were thus closed due to slave raids by other Indian groups. Such raids also led to the breakdown of the large villages, so that by the late 19th century, villages were once again reduced in size to only half a dozen or so scattered houses, each house with no more than 3-4 families. Yet another factor contributing to the failure of the missions was the fact that that the Encabellado were semi-nomadic. After being settled in a mission settlement for a few years, local game was killed out and the soil of local garden plots exhausted. The tribe would then just pick up and leave, looking for a more suitable village site, leaving the mission abandoned, and the missionary now with no flock to missionize.

The Western Tucanoan group is nearly extinct today. In 1635, they were an estimated 8,000 or more of just Encabellado alone. But by the beginning of the 20th century, only a few remnants of several different Tucanoan groups were found collected at Avruiys and Nussuibs. Records from the missions for the first quarter of the century indicated a population of about 2,000 Tucanoan, mainly Siona, with smaller numbers of Pioje, Secoya, Coto, and Macaguaje. Many of these Indians were on the verge of losing their native customs. By 1950, there were only 1,000 Tucanoan spekars, apparently only Siona, Secoya, and perhaps Coto. By 1960, this number had dropped to only 550 Tucanoan speakers, none of whom were of Encabellado-related groups. Recent reports indicate the continuing decline of the few remaining; sources for the mid- 70s report less than 100 known speakers of the language.

The Encabellado no longer exist.

DavidL. Browman

ENCOMIENDA SYSTEM, basically, was a grant of a number of Indians to a Spanish settler in South America who was expected to Christianize and civilize his charges, and in return to exact labor services or tribute from them. But no land was granted to the settler — though eventually land was acquired, usually at the expense of the Indian. The exacting of labor and of tribute was the primary goal, while the "civilizing" factor was of secondary importance, if any at all.

The roots of this system go back to Columbus who decided to force the Indians to do the physical work which the Spaniards would not even consider. His reasoning was that the Indians were subjects to the Queen and should pay taxes of tribute like her other subjects, especially with gold. Those not obeying or unable to pay were subject to the death penalty. Or, instead of paying with gold dust, they could pay 25 pounds of cotton cloth as their tribute. The result of this practical slavery was horrible. Some Indians

Handbook of South American Indians.

The Corregidor's table. (After Guaman Pomo, 1936).

not used to labor in mines and to persistent and systematic toil, committed suicide, by drinking a poison fluid of the cassava plant (which was also a source of meal); others ran off to the hills or woods, or escaped to neighboring islands, or committed infanticide.

The system was inaugurated by Columbus who, on his third trip to Hispaniola, interpreted royal instructions to suppress the possible fratricidal war among the Spaniards. When he came back with his crew of convicts in August 1548, he faced the revolt of one Francisco Roldin, which was splitting the Spanish party. Unable to defeat him or win him over, Columbus made peace with Roldin by agreeing to change the tribute system so that the natives would provide labor for individual Spaniards. The plan was based on the *encomienda* system used by the Spanish armies during the Reconquest in lands won from the infidels. In Hispaniola the system provided that each Spaniard strong enough to make himself respected was placed in charge of a certain number of natives (resembling a system of slavery or feudalism at its worst). A number of the natives were distributed among the Spanish colonists who were holders of concessions. Within a decade this *encomienda* system was to become general in the territories under the jurisdiction of the Spanish crown. At the beginning there was hardly any difference between the workers subject to requisition and simple slaves, although, legally, they were regarded as "vassals," at the express wish of Queen Isabella, who insisted on having the Indians treated humanly. But actually, the *encomiendas* became slave markets and the *encomenderos* slave traders. In theory, only the Indians taken in warfare or who rebelled against Spanish Empire could be legally enslaved, and as a source of labor, slavery was limited in most areas only in the early years of the colonial period; in Brazil Indian slavery was, however, more common and lasted longer.

While tremendous abuses characterized the *encomienda* system, it must, however, be also noted that a small cluster of humanitarian churchmen, especially the Dominican Order, opposed the maltreatment of the Indian, as voiced by the Dominican friar Antonio de Montesinos (December, 1512). The Spanish Crown was rather sympathetic to the appeals of churchmen and made numerous attempts to regulate the workings of the system, working under the license of the Council of the Indies in Seville. In fact, nearly all ecclesiasts tried to alleviate the harshest aspects. Their leader was Fray Bartolome de Las Casas (1474-1566), whose ideology was that the Indian, being a rational being, had the same rights as any other Spanish subject and should be treated accordingly, should not be exploited by the colonizer, but protected by the *encomienda* system. He was opposed by those claiming that the Indians were basically inferior being, "naturally servile" in the Aristotelian sense. The Papacy supported Las Casas; in his Bull *Sublimis Deus* (June 1, 1537), Pope Paul III proclaimed that

"the Indians are truly men and . . . are . . . capable of understanding the Catholic faith . . . The said Indians are by no means to be deprived of their liberty or the possession of their property, even though they be outside the faith of Jesus Christ . . . nor should they be in any way enslaved."

The Crown noted this proclamation, and in 1542, issued "Laws and Ordinances newly made by His Majesty for the Government of the Indies and Good Treatment and Preservation of the Indians" ("New Laws"). But these New Laws were fiercly resented in the colonies, and, in a few years, actually preserved the *encomienda* rather than the Indian. Nevertheless, the Crown succeeded in realizing such changes as that the *encomiendas* could be inherited only for a limited number of generations, and that the stress was on Indian tribute rather than on labor services. In fact, the institution slowly ceased to be of importance in the American Empire, as more and more Indians were placed under normal royal government.

It was the older colonies that provided the basis for the New Laws (especially Mexico, or New Spain), where the abuse of the *encomienda* system, introduced of necessity by Cortés, and continued by the Crown's representatives as the only way of satisfying the labor needs of the settlers, made legislative control essential. In 1565 Governor Garcia Castro founded a special office of *corregidor de indios* to represent the Crown. His successor, Viceroy Toledo ruled that all Indians not living in missions would be responsible to a *corregidor*, and, if possible, would continue residing in their ancient village communities or, in many cases, be forced to move to new settlements established by the Crown; there they would observe their traditional rulers (*carucas*), whose positions were hereditary; they exercised three key functions: the tribute, the *repartimiento* (or forced sale of goods), and the *mita* (or labor draft), the last remaining in use until the end of colonial times — and probably beyond. The tribute was usually the only tax the Indians paid; if he was delinquent, his relatives paid for him or he might become something of a slave until he had worked off his debt. Indian districts were governed by a *corregidor de indios* (Indians' magistrate). The more scandalous malpractices were most common at this level of administration, characterized by corruption, extortion and exploitation. But eventually this old system of the *corregidores* was taken over by a new breed of colonial officials, the *Intendants*, introduced in Havana in 1764, in Buenos Aires in 1728, in Mexico and Chile in 1786, and in the remainder of the empire in 1790.

JOSEPH S. ROUCEK

ENEMAS seem to have been widely applied for medical purposes in the northern half of the South American continent. Their use is reported from the *Arawak, Choco, Jivaro, Canelo, Maina, Omagua, Cacharary*, the *Mura, Maue, Caripuna, Chiriguano* and *Araucanians*.

The Indians of the Amazon region have contributed two important inventions in this area: the rubber-bulbed syringe, brought to Europe by the Portuguese, and the use of narcotic clyster, adopted to anesthetics.

(Nevertheless, the narcotic clysters seldom had strictly medical applications among the Indians. The Indian clysters belong only partly to the medical field; they had also become, as among the Europeans of the 17th and 18th centuries, a kind of social custom.)

ENGLISH, WILLIAM D. (Inuit; Jan. 31, 1923-), is a commercial airline pilot and executive; he has also worked as a radio announcer and is vice president of Northern Television, which operates stations in Anchorage and Fairbanks, Alaska. Born at Wiseman, Alaska, he declined an appointment to the U.S. Military Academy at West Point because he wanted to become an airline pilot. He began working for Wien Airlines in 1946 as a bush pilot and in the mid-1970s he was a member of the board of directors. English was an aerial announcer for the North American Sled Dog Championships, and he broadcast the Eskimo Olympics in Fairbanks.

ENGLISH POLICY. While the Crown was normally the source of agreements between the Europeans and the Indians, those who governed the English colonies in America were considered to be the representatives of the Crown. As such they were authorized to work out practices to govern relationships with the Indians. Under such an arrangement there were bound to be differences in the Indian programs from colony to colony.

One of the basic features of the relationships between Indian and non-Indian was trade. The drive was to secure and keep this trade. There was competition not only between the European powers, but also between the differrent English colonies. Attempts were made to secure uniform practices from colony to colony, but by mid-18th century it was recognized that colonial management had failed. Trade was not adequately controlled. The Englishmen regularly encroached on Indian lands. To show their resentment the Indians periodically attacked the English settlements.

Based largely upon information secured in conferences with the Indians during the Albany Congress of 1754, and because the English learned that more Indians supported the French program than their own, in 1755 steps were taken to remove Indian affairs from the control of separate colonies and place them directly under the British government. To carry out this program Sir William Johnson was appointed superintendent over the Indians in the northern department and in 1756, Edmond Atkin became superintendent in the south. In 1762, Atkin was replaced by John Stuart. The two superintendents were given full responsibility for all relations between the English colonists and the Indians.

By 1763, as a result of their experience, the English had learned that they got along best with the Indians when they were separated some distance from them. Based on this experience, at the close of the French and Indian War, King George III issued the Proclamation of 1763, which established boundaries for the colonies, encouraged colonists to settle in the newly acquired areas east of the proclamation line, and outlined a new policy to govern Indian affairs.

The most revolutionary departure from the previous program in Indian affairs was the recognition of a boundary line that separated Indian lands from non-Indian lands. The result was the creation of an "Indian Country." This area, generally to the west, was reserved for the Indian. The officials of the established colonies were forbidden "for the present, and until our further Pleasure be known," to allow surveys or to grant lands beyond the wateshed of the Appalachians. Any persons who had already established themselves in "Indian Country" were ordered to remove themselves.

In regard to this proclamation time soon made a practice apparent that was to recur again and again in the future. Established lines, with military power to secure those lines, might keep Indians in Indian country, but that military power could not guard the Indians against the political pressures that allowed settlers to invade Indian country. Troops could keep Indians in, but they *would not* be used consistently to keep non-Indians out.

In the controversy that would develop between Great Britain and the Colonies after 1763, the Indian's causes of complaint almost all came from the colonist's abuses of the Indian trade and encroachment on Indian lands. The British officials had a better record in their dealings with the Indians, and they did not fail to remind them of this. As the controversy heightened, the Indians tended to give their support to the British rather than the colonists. Each grew out of similarities and differences between their political systems at home, the Indian groups encountered in the different areas, and the basic nature and character of the four peoples: the way each had learned to interact within the four separate social and political systems.

One thing, however, was common to all four groups: in each case the Crown attempted to act toward the conquered people in such a way that the European states could to their own satisfaction maintain their national credibility; also in each case the frontiersman or neighbor acted toward the native generally in the way that was advantageous to him, in the face of laws to the contrary that may have been issued by the Crown or their representatives. One example was the use of liquor as a trade item. The official position of the Crown was almost always against making liquor available to the Indians. In actual practice the trader or frontiersman found a way to use it when it was to his advantage to do so.

On the English frontiers in particular there seemed to be a general attitude of hostility toward the native Americans. The Englishmen had not experienced as much regular contact with people of other races when the age of discovery, trade, and the establishment of colonies began. Intermarriage and miscegenation seem to have been less desirable to the Englishman than to his Spanish or French counterpart.

Once the Englishman had learned that the Indian was going to maintain a separate identity, and that he would not, by choicc, and by a natural course of events, begin to give up Indian ways and adopt English ways, the Indian became an undesirable creature and a foreigner. As such he became a mere obsticle that stood in the way of securing whatever the Englishman wanted that the Indian had. In the face of laws passed by the Crown to protect the Indian, the frontiersman usually found some way to get around this obstacle.

To some extent, the history of Indian policy is a record of the interaction between the Crown or national governments, and the frontiersmen or local governments, in their relations with Indians. The central governments of European and American nations have developed their policies step by step, in an attempt to govern the relations between the Indians and their neighbors in a way that would protect the Indian until he was able to cope with the more aggressive European or American. Of all the European influences on the Indians, those of the English were the most substantial

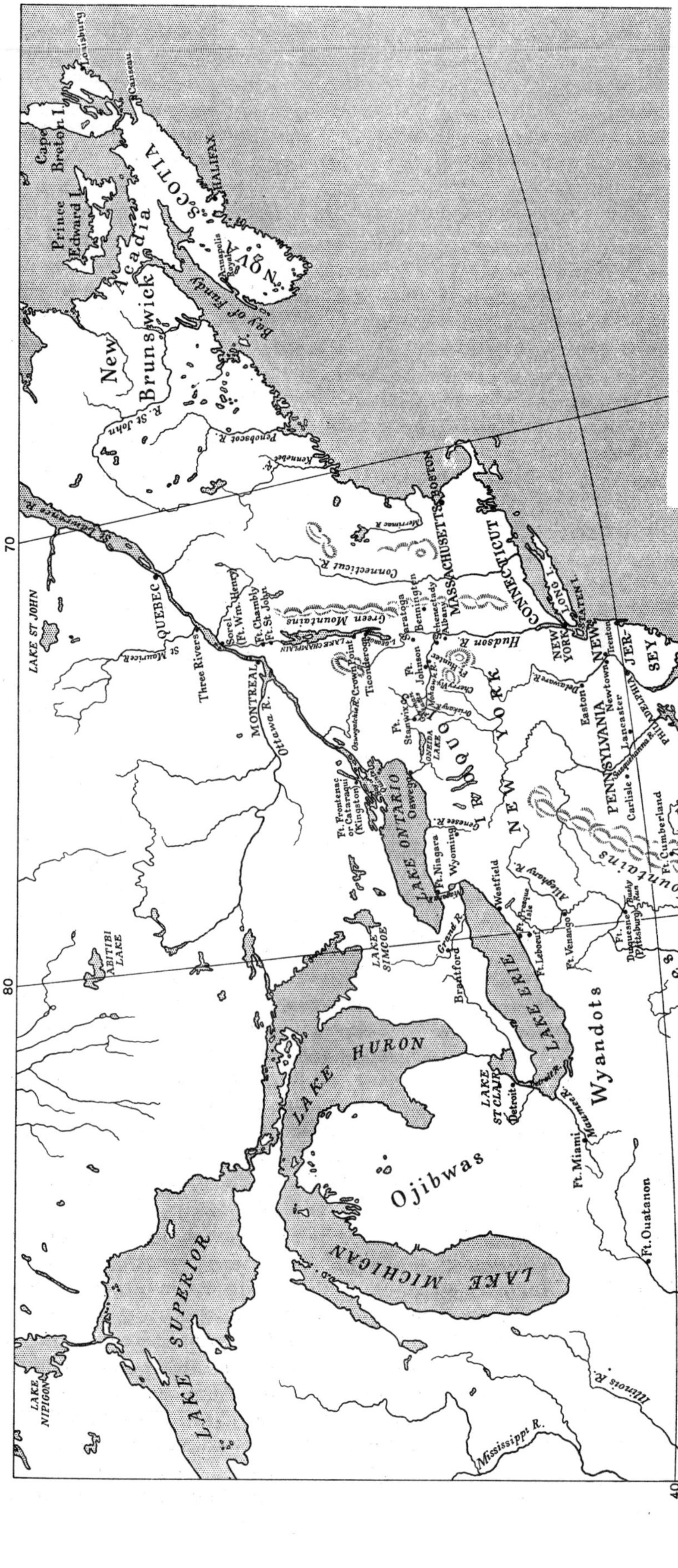

INDIAN TERRITORIES
IN EASTERN NORTH AMERICA
DURING THE TIME OF
THE BRITISH COLONIES
17TH CENTURY

and enduring. British colonials were the basic progenitors of the new nation.

Despite the claim in the New World provided by John Cabot's voyage in 1497, the British were the last of the three major European powers to attempt to settle. Yet, by 1700, they had established substantial colonies all along the Atlantic coast, and changed the lives of countless Indians.

The need of the New England colonies for a common defense resulted in the beginning of conflicts with the Indians. Throughout most of the colonial period, New England faced hostile Indians. The first real trouble began in 1633, when settlers moved into Pequot country in Connecticut and alienated the Indians. Sporadic attacks occurred until 1637, when the Pequot War began with an attack on Wethersfield. Wreaking a terrible vengeance, Massachusetts and Connecticut militia burned the Pequot fort at Mystic and killed most of the 600 or so inhabitants. The militia pursued them, killed many, and captured others and made them slaves of the colonials or sold them into slavery in the West Indies. Others who later surrendered were distrubuted among the Mohegan, the Narragansett, and the Niantic—English allies. Thus the Pequots lost their identity as a separate tribe.

Fear of additional Indian attacks led in 1643 to the formation of the New England Confederation—the first attempt at intercolonial cooperation—consisting of Massachusetts, New Haven, Plymouth, and Connecticut. Each of the four had an equal voice in the council, although Massachusetts outnumbered the others three to one in population and furnished most of the funds. Nevertheless, the confederation was fairly active for about two decades, though theoretically it existed until 1684.

In 1645, the confederation conducted a victorious campaign against the Narragansett Indians; in 1650, negotiated the Hartford Treaty with Peter Stuyvesant of New Netherland; established a system of criminal extradition; insisted that member colonies regulate church membership and exclude Quakers from their jurisdictions; and, finally, led a stumbling but ultimately victorious defense in King Philip's War (1675-76). One of the bloodiest Indian uprisings in colonial history, this war was caused by the increasing encroachment of the Puritans on Indian lands. King Philip (Metacomet), chief of the Wampanoag tribe and son of Massasoit, who originally befriended the Pilgrims, led his allies in a series of raids on New England towns and settlements. They won numerous victories and destroyed 12 towns, but confederation-sponsored troops finally defeated them.

In the 18th century, conflict between France and England, part of the larger European War of the Spanish Succession (1701-1714) resulted in Queen Ann's War. In America bloodshed was concentrated largely on the New England frontier.

For at least a generation England and France had each used their Indian allies to war upon each other. As a new conflict neared, France secured an unofficial truce with the mighty Iroquois of New York (England's most powerful Indian ally). The Marquis de Vaudreuil, Governor of Canada, used the Abnaki Indians of Maine and the Iroquois of the Caughnawaga mission on the St. Lawrence River to war upon the English frontiers. Bands of warriors led by Frenchmen attacked isolated western settlements of the Massachusetts Bay Colony as well as the seacoast villages of Maine and New Hampshire.

In the summer of 1703 about 150 Englishmen died on the frontier. Wells, a village on the Maine seacoast, was attacked by Abnaki in August of that year with the loss of 40 people, killed or captured. On February 29, 1704, Deerfield, a frontier settlement of the Massachusetts Bay Colony, was burned in a surprise attack by 50 Canadians and 200 Indians. Of its 300 inhabitants about 50 died and 100 were taken prisoner. The prisoners were force marched back to Canada in a grueling winter trek and some died enroute.

From 1705-1707 French Canada and the English colonies tried unsuccessfully to come to a peace agreement and ignore the larger European conflict. In 1710 a

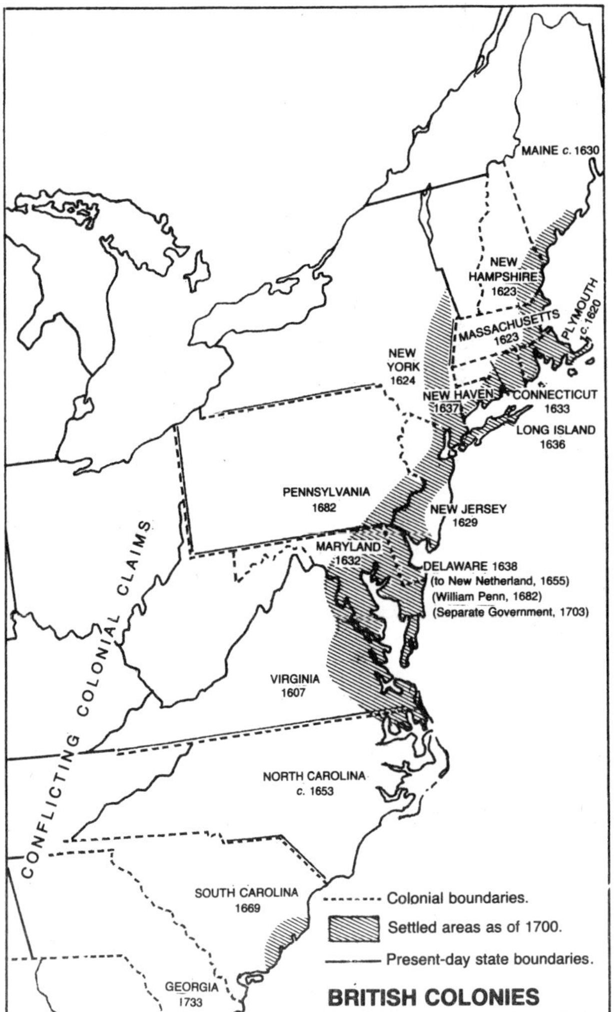

BRITISH COLONIES IN PRESENT UNITED STATES
(WITH DATE OF FIRST PERMANENT SETTLEMENT)

force fo 1,500 colonists and 400 British marines captured Port Royal, Acadia.

During the war the English twice attempted to attack Quebec. In 1708 a land expedition floundered because promised British warships were never sent. Three years later a land force was again stranded when the large British naval force shipwrecked on the St. Lawrence near Isle oux Oeufs with the loss of many lives.

The European fighting was concluded with the Treaty of Utrecht (1713). In North America, Britain had gained Acadia, Newfoundland, and a perimeter of land around Hudson Bay. Although the bloodshed was officially over, the enmity that had been created continued. Trade and frontier hostility eventually culminated in the French and Indian War. (1754-1763).

During the French and Indian War, many Indian nations had fought with the French against the English. In 1760, Pontiac, the Ottawa chief, learned of the French defeat in Canada and began working toward an Indian confederacy to continue the fight against white expansion in the Ohio region and elsewhere. He sensed that the Indian nations would be doomed if they lost their lands. Pontiac's War to drive the English forts and settlers from Indian lands began in May, 1763. Within a month, ten British-controlled forts were lost.

On October 7, 1763, a royal proclamation was issued by King George at the request of the Lords of Trade to calm Indian fears of a white takeover. It stated that all lands beyond the source of the rivers which flowed into the Atlantic Ocean from the west or northwest were closed to white settlement. Furthermore, the proclamation stated, the land belonged to Indians because it had been neither ceded to nor purchased by the English.

The edict said that private individuals could not purchase Indian territory. Purchases of land west of the Appalachians could only be made by the king or one of his colonies at a meeting with the Indians. Late in the 1760's, the British expanded into the Ohio region by receiving permission from the Iroquois, Creeks, and Cherokees—Indian nations whose homelands were elsewhere.

White settlers who had mistakenly moved to the Indian lands would leave, the edict promised. The govenment further guaranteed to restrain white expansion by maintaining a military force to keep the peace between the colonists and the Indians. The colonial army's cost in taxes further embittered white colonists anxious to move to the west.

The Proclamation of 1763 was one of many factors leading to the Revolutionary War. British authorities, determined to enforce the royal edict, removed settlers from the lands in question. Angry frontiersmen attacked both the Indians and the Royal troops.

ENGRAVING AND INCISING. Among the Indians of the Americas, as no definite line can be drawn between the lower forms of relief sculpture and engraving, all ordinary petroglyphs may be classed as engravings, since the work is executed in shallow lines upon smooth, rock surfaces. Point work is common on wood, bone, horn, shell, bark, metal, clay and other surfaces. Each material has its own particular technique, and the designs run the entire gamut of style from graphic to purely conventional representations, and the full range of significance from purely symbolic through esthetic to simply trivial motives.

Perhaps the most artistic and technically perfect examples of engraving are those of the Northwest Coast tribes of North America, executed on slate utensils and on ornaments of metal, yet the graphic productions of the Inuit on ivory, bone, and antler have sometimes a considerable degree of merit. With both of these peoples the processes employed and the style of representation have undergone change because of contact with the white man.

The steel point is superior to the point of stone, and this alone would have a marked effect on the execution. The picture writings on bark of many of the northern tribes, executed with bone or other hard points, are good examples of the native engraver's art, although these are not designed either for simply pictorial or for decorative effect. The ancient mound builders were clever engravers, the technical excellence of their work being well illustrated by examples from the mounds and dwelling sites of Ross County, Ohio and by others from the Turner mounds in Hamilton County, Ohio.Shell also was a favorite material for the graver's point, as is illustrated by numerous ornaments recovered from mounds in the middle Mississippi valley.

In decorating their earthenware, the native people often used the styles with excellent effect. The yielding clay afforded a tempting surface, and in some cases considerable skill was shown especially by the ancient potters of the lower Gulf States, who executed elaborate scroll designs with great precision. The point was used for incising, trailing, and indenting, and among ancient Pueblo potters was sometimes used upon dark-painted surfaces to develop delicate figures in the light color of the underlying paste.

SOUTH AMERICA

Engraving of metal was occasionally used in Peru, but was much less common than embossing. Some of the early sheet gold cut-outs from the Titicaca region (Early Tiahuanaco?) have details added by means of incised lines, but they are poorly done. They are the earliest examples of engraving (about AD 700). Later cups from Cuzco and the Chimu region are carefully engraved in complex designs.

ENMEGABOWH (Ottawa; fl. 19th century) was a Protestant preacher who served as a Methodist and later as an Episcopal clergyman. Born at Ottawa, Enmegabowh was adopted by the Ojibwa (Chippewa) as a youngster. while living in Canada he was converted to the Methodist faith. He attended the Methodist mission school at Jacksonville, Illinois, and was ordained a Methodist preacher upon graduation. At this point he became known as the Rev. John Johnson. Johnson preached to the Ojibwa in Minnesota for five years (1839-44) with Elder T. B. Kavanaugh, but then the Methodist church abandoned the upper Mississippi as a place for missionary work.

Johnson convinced the Episcopal Church to renew religious development in the Ojibwa-Dakota (Sioux) region of Minnesota in 1852, and he served as an assistant and an interpreter for the clergymen. Johnson himself became an Episcopal minister in 1858, and in the following year he was placed in charge of the mission school at Gull Lake, Minnesota. He served there during the Dakota uprising in 1862 when all the other Episcopal missionaries fled from the hostile arena.

In 1869 Johnson moved the Gull Lake mission to the White Earth Reservation, where he attacked a sizable congregation and erected a chapel and parsonage. He helped the Rev. Joseph A. Gilfillan establish a training school for Indian clergy at White Earth in 1873, and he devoted the remainder of his life to religious activity among his Indian brethren. He was still living in 1898 when he was described as the "aged Indian pastor and co-worker of Bishop Whipple."

ENRIQUE, an Arawak Indian chief who was able, in the midst of the Spanish settlement of the island of Hispaniola, to establish an independent Indian community that lasted from the early 16th century to the middle of the 18th. By rising from a condition of slavery, he was a prototype of future Haitian revolutionaries.

Enrique was the son of an Arawak chief ruling in a region known to the Spanish as Barruca, in the Haitian sector of Hispaniola. As a young man he had been educated by Dominican friars, who converted him to Christianity. Enrique was living contentedly among his own people when he was taken as a slave to work on one of the Spanish repartimientos (forced labor farms), operated by a brute named Valenzuela. Not content with reducing the noble Indian to servitude, Valenzuela took Enrique's wife as concubine. This action led to Enrique's revolt in 1522.

The Indian followers of Enrique fought their way off the repartimientos and took refuge in the Bahorucho Mountains, where they were able to resist all Spanish incursions. By 1526, Enrique's movement had won so many followers, the Spanish began the free introduction of African slaves After refusing several offers of peace, Enrique agreed, at the intercession of the famous missionary Bartolome de Las Casas, to sign a treaty in 1533. A free Indian community of 600 members was granted in a village called Boya, where Enrique lived out his life as an independent leader.

The race of Enrique was known as late as 1750, though the influx of black slaves, caused in part by his rebellion, led to such race mixing that modern Haiti can claim no pure Arawaks.

ENSENORE (Secotan?; ?-*c.* 1586), was chief of a tribe near Albemarle Sound in present-day North Carolina who greeted the first English settlers at Roanoke Island with friendship. He protected them from his son Wingina and persuaded his people to plant corn for the starving colonists.

ENTERPRISE RANCHERIA, in Butte County, California, is a small reservation of 33 acres and was home, in the early 1970s, to only 3 members of the Maidu tribe.

The rancheria was established by the Secretary of the Interior in 1906. It lies in northern California, in forested and mountainous terrain. The Maidu speak their language, eat traditional foods and follow traditional ways in this setting. They follow no organized government. On the rancheria, water is piped from a spring, and only electricity is available. For everything else, the Maidu must fend for themselves.

EPANOW (Wampanoag; fl. early 17th century) was kidnapped from Marthas Vineyard, Massachusetts, in 1611 and carried off to England where he was displayed as a curiosity of the New World. Crafty and bold, Epanow managed to return to his Massachusetts home by pretending to guide some English adventurers to a gold mine. He escaped, made his way to Marthas Vineyard, and in 1619 led several warriors in attacking the English who were attempting to land there.

EPIDEMICS among Indians in post-Columbian times, primarily of introduced diseases, were numerous and devastating, but little is known regarding pre-Columbian epidemics. Prior to European contact the Indians apparently enjoyed relatively good health and were free of several major infectious diseases present in European and other societies. Scarlet fever, typhoid, cholera, diphtheria, smallpox, measles, gonorrhea, sylphilis, malaria, and yellow fever were apparently absent in aboriginal America. The Indians' lack of immunity to these introduced diseases and lack of experience in treating them led to many serious epidemics which resulted in widespread suffering and death.

Records of early observers indicate that by the eighteenth century a series of smallpox and other epidemics had decimated most of the Indian communities in contact with colonial settlements. As white traders and settlers penetrated the rest of the hemisphere, the pattern was repeated. Rough fatality estimates reported in early accounts give an indication of the seriousness of the problem for some tribes. One-half of the Cherokee were said to have died of smallpox in a year's time around 1738; 350 Cherokee of malaria in one week of 1779; nine-tenths of the northern Athapaskans of smallpox in 1781-82; two-thirds of the Blackfoot of smallpox in 1837; the inhabitants of about 200 Cheyenne lodges of cholera in 1849. Tuberculosis was apparently rare or absent among Indians aboriginally but after continuous contact with whites became common in many areas, sometimes reaching epidemic proportions. Generally, epidemics were responsible for a significant part of the drastic reduction in the Indian population during the three centuries following the first colonial settlement. Overcrowding, malnutrition, poor health care and hygiene, and other conditions on many reservations and reserves have resulted in continued recurrence of epidemics of diseases such as tuberculosis, influenza, and various intestinal, ear, and other infections to the present day.

ERIE, now extinct, were a populous, sedentary Iroquoian tribe. In the 17th century their territory extended south from Lake Erie to the Ohio river, east to the lands of the Conestoga along the Allegheny river and to those of the Seneca along the Genesee river, and north to those of the Neutral of Lake Erie.

Historically, little is known of the Erie and their political and social organization, but it was similar to that of the Huron. The Jesuits gave a few glimpses of their lives, while describing their last wars with the Iroquois Confederation. The Erie had many towns and villages, were organized into several divisions, and cultivated the soil and spoke a language resembling that of the Huron. It is not known which of the four of five Huron dialects, usually called "Wendat" (Wyandot) by themselves, was actually spoken. From the same sources comes a rough estimate of the population of the Erie at the period of final war. At the taking of the Erie town of Rique in 1654 it is claimed that the defenders numbered between 3,000 and 4,000 but as it is not likely that all the warriors of the tribe were present, 14,500 would probably be a conservative estimate of the population of the Erie at this time.

The years 1655-56 were the last years of the Erie. Thirty ambassadors of the Cat Nation were sent to *Sonontouan,* the Seneca capital, to renew the existing peace. But through an accident, one of the men of the Cat Nation killed a Seneca. This incensed the Seneca; they massacred all except 5 of the ambassadors in their hands. This led to the final war between the Erie and the confederated tribes of the Iroquois, especially the Seneca, Cayuga, Oneida, and Onondaga.

Erie

The Erie were brave and warlike, employing only bows and poisoned arrows. Following the rupture of relations between the Erie and the Iroquois tribes in 1653, the Erie burned a Seneca town, pursued an Iroquois war party returning from the region of the great lakes, and slaughtered 80 men, while the Erie scouts had come to the very gates of one of the Iroquois palisaded towns and seized and carried into captivity Annenraes (Annencraos), "one of the greatest captains." All this, of course, roused the Iroquois, which raised 1,800 men to punish the Erie for these losses. After a stubborn resistance, the Erie were overrun and the Onondaga "entered the fort and there wrought such carnage among the women and children that blood was knee-deep in certain places." This was at the town of Rique, which was defended by between 3,000 to 4,000 Indians, and was assailed by the 1,800 Iroquois. This devastating war lasted until about the close of 1656, when the Erie power was broken and the people were destroyed, dispersed or led into captivity. Six hundred surrendered at one time and were led to the Iroquois country to be adopted as one of the constituent people of the Iroquois tribes. The victory at Rique was won at a loss to the Iroquois, who were forced to remain in the enemy's country for two months to care for the wounded and to bury the dead.

ESCHETEWAURHA. Whites have failed to find the concept of a Supreme Being in the religion of the Chaco Indians of South America. *Peritnalik, Asin,* and the bird Carancho (*Polyborus plancus*) are mythic culture heroes. The Beetle (*escarabajo*), who, according to the *Lengua,* made the universe and peopled it with spirits and men, remains aloof from his creation and is never invoked. The only mythological character who approximates a supreme god is Eschetewaurha of the *Chamacoco* of South America. She is the mother of countless spirits (*guara*); she dominates everything, and makes sure that the Sun does not burn the earth and that mankind obtains water. She expects men to sing every night for her and punishes them if they are remiss in this duty.

ESCORIA (Guaymi; fl. 16th century), was a Indian chief of the Veranaguas region of Panama at the time of the Spanish conquest. He owed his allegiance to the powerful chief Urraca. In January 1517 the Spanish conquistador Gaspar de Espinosa overran Escoria's village, though the chief presumably lived through this first encounter.

ESKEBUGECOSHE (Pillager Chippewa; *c.* 1774-*c.* 1860), was a noted chief, respected by both Indians and whites, who was a leader in the contest with the Dakota (Sioux) for the land at the headwaters of the

Mississippi River but who refused to involve his people in the War of 1812. As a youth, Eshkebugecoshe ("Flat Mouth" or "Wide Mouth") traveled extensively, living among the Cree and the Assiniboine, and visiting in war or peace the tribes of the upper Missouri River. His father, Wasonauneque ("Yellow Hair"), became chief through his knowledge of medicine, and it was said that anyone who incurred his hatred died mysteriously. Eshkebugecoshe, however, was greatly impressed by the teachings of Tenskwatawa (*q.v.*), the "Shawnee Prophet," who denounced many of the witchcraft and medicine practices of his people. Through the influence of Eshkebugecoshe poisoning was halted among the Pillager.

Together with Curly Head and Broken Tooth, he was a leader of the Ojibwa (Chippewa) warriors in their incessant territorial struggle with the Santee Dakota. Eshkebugecoche's territory was in the area around Leech Lake. He was visited by Lieut. Zebulon M. Pike during his journey to the region in 1805-06 and received from him a U.S. flag and medal. Despite enticements from the British, he remained loyal to the U.S. from that time. When encouraged by a political agent to enlist his warriors on behalf of the British in the War of 1812, he suggested that instead the British should join him in his war with the Dakota.

ESKIMINZIN (Aravaipa Apache; fl. 1870s) was a once dangerous chief who is remembered primarily for his influence in bringing his band of about 150 to live in peace near Camp Grant, only to have most of the women and children exterminated in one of the most brutal and senseless massacres in the history of Arizona Territory.

Called Skimmy by soldiers, he and his people arrived at Camp Grant, a small post at the confluence of the Aravaipa Creek and the San Pedro River, in February 1871. They soon became trusted favorites of Lieut. Royal E. Whitman, who found them eager and quick to learn. Kindly ranchers in the immediate vicinity agreed to hire them at fair wages, and soon more Apache joined them.

But a group of unscrupulous businessmen who called themselves the Tucson Committee of Public Safety claimed that the Federal Government had failed to defend Arizona from the savage Apaches. Without proof, they accused the Camp Grant Indians of leaving the post to plunder and kill white men. The mastermind behind the scheme to destroy the Camp Grant Indians was William Sanders Oury, a veteran Indian fighter. Few of the original committee participated in the crime, but they were responsible for recruiting outlaws, Papago Indians, and Mexicans—a total of 140 men. They struck at dawn on Sunday, April 30.

Lieutenant Whitman learned of the plan at breakfast on April 30. The men he sent to warn the Indians returned an hour later with the news that the camp was burning, the ground littered with dead women and children. ("Nits make lice" was the committee's slogan.) No living Indians could be found. Unarmed, they were completely at the mercy of their brutal attackers. A few men escaped, including Eskiminzin, who took to the warpath with vengence.

In may 1872 he returned to Camp Grant with other Apache leaders to confer with a representative of the Department of the Interior, Gen. Oliver Otis Howard, a religious fanatic often called "Bible Quoting" Howard. As Howard neared the assembled Indians, he dropped to his knees, rolled his eyes heavenward, and began to pray.

The alarmed Eskiminzin sought refuge behind a building and refused to rejoin the group until Whitman assured him that Howard was not making bad medicine. A Civil War veteran with a distinguished record, Howard told the Apaches that he once commanded 30,000 men who, if the Indians did not do as he ordered, would come there and exterminate them. He invited the leaders to accompany him to Washington, but Eskiminzin was not among the ten who accepted the invitation.

In 1873 all Indians at Camp Grant were moved to the San Carlos Reservation, where conflicts for leadership soon erupted among major factions, one of which was led by Eskiminzin. Arrested on January 1, 1874, unjustly, according to his followers, he was placed in the guardhouse from which he escaped three days later, taking with him several warriors. Seven other bands then jumped the reservation. Gen. George Crook, then in command of the Department of Arizona, began an all-out campaign to bring the renegades in, dead or alive. Largely because of the skill of his Indian scouts, most of the leaders were soon killed. Eskiminzin surrendered his small, starving band at San Carlos. He was placed in chains until Indian agent John Philip Clum arrived in August. Clum set him free, and the chief soon became his trusted aid.

In 1879 the Aravaipa Apache were given their choice between the San Carlos and Fort Apache reservations. Eskiminzin and about 40 followers chose land near the border of the San Carlos Reservation. They were displaced in 1883 when the reservation line was changed. When Eskiminzin's son-in-law turned outlaw, the old chief was accused of aiding him. Gen. Nelson A. Miles imprisoned him and the whole band, but eventually they were returned to San Carlos.

ESKIMO. *See* INUIT.

ESMERALDA a Chibcha-speaking people of Ecuador, received their name from the emeralds which the Spaniards found in their territory. Their aboriginal name is uncertain. They inhabited the lower course of the Esmeraldas and perhaps the Verde Rivers, and the hilly country between Cojimies and Atacames.

It is probable that the *Esmeralda* occupied a much larger territory along the coast, but at the Conquest they were being displaced by *Manta* colonies, and their older settlements looked like alien enclaves on an otherwise homogenous coast.

Language. The *Esmeralda* language was the only coastal idiom still spoken in the 19th century, when a large vocabulary of it was collected. It is extinct today.

Culture. The *Esmeralda* lived in coastal villages which were quite independent from each other and frequently at war. The *Esmeralda* raised no crops and depended only on fishing and root gathering. Fishing was important; fish were consumed locally and were traded, along with salt, to the peoples of the interior. Other evidence paints them as a folk rich in jewelry of gold and silver with set-in emeralds, skilled weavers of cotton cloth, inspired molders of elaborate ceramics, and agile maneuverers of dugout canoes. The *Esmeralda* were probably poorer than their commercially minded coastal neighbors to the south. The *Esmeralda* deformed their heads, believing it gave them health and endurance. Like other coast groups, they wore earrings, labrets, and nose plugs of gold and silver. Little is known of their social, political and religious organization, and their population numbers in the 1970s are unknown.

See tribes of Ecuador map page 209.

ESMISA, (Guanaca; fl. 16th century), chief of the Guanaca tribe, was an important ally of the Spanish in their conquest during the late 1530s of modern Colombia. With his brother-in-law Anabeima, Esmisa helped the Spanish commander Domingo Lozano defeat the Paez Indians under Abirama; the Guanaca were the first Colombian Indians to submit to the conquistadors.

ESOPUS were a group of *Munsee Delaware* and *Mahican* speaking peoples that lived in the Wallkill, Rondout, Esopus, and Catskill River valleys between the Hudson Highlands and the Catskill Mountains to the west of the Hudson River in southeastern New York State. The seventeenth century *Esopus* consisted of five confederated groups. The *Waoraneck* lived along the shores of the Hudson River and in the mid-Wallkill Valley above the Hudson Highlands. The *Waranawankong* occupied a number of fortified settlements in the lower Wallkill, Rondout, and Esopus River valleys to the south of the Catskill Range. The little known *Mamakating* inhabited the middle reaches of the Rondout River to the west of the Shawangunk Mountains which separated the Rondout from the Wallkill. The *Wawarsing* settlements were located along the upper portion of the Rondout Valley between the Shawangunks and the southern foothills of the Catskill Mountains. The *Catskills* were a *Mahican*-speaking group whose villages lined the banks of the Catskill Creek from its outlet into the Hudson River to the eastern wall of the Catskill Range.

The *Esopus* were a populous people whose large walled villages, often called castles, dotted the fertile bottom lands beside the many broad rivers that coursed through their country. These rich soils yielded abundant harvests of corn, beans, squash, tobacco, and other crops as well as a wide assortment of wild greens, roots, fruits, and berries. The rivers provided freshwater fish in the valley streams as well as saltwater fish and shellfish in the Hudson River Estuary. The gentle uplands and deep sheltered valleys of their mountains were good hunting and trapping grounds where deer, bear, and beaver could be taken in great numbers. Large flocks of geese, ducks, passenger pigeons, turkeys, and other birds were also harvested.

The highly structured and confederated *Esopus* more closely resembled the socio-political organization of their *Iroquoian* neighbors, the *Mohawk*, to the north than the much looser and more flexible social order of their *Delaware*-speaking bretheren to the south. The *Esopus* reckoned descent on the female side. Each *Esopus* group was made up of a number of matri-clans. Each matri-clan was housed in a longhouse that sheltered up to two hundred related women, their children, and their husbands. An *Esopus* husband was expected to move into the home of his wife's relatives following marriage.

Esopus villages consisted of a number of bark longhouses. The larger settlements were enclosed by a wall of closely spaced timbers. Each *Esopus* village was led by a civil chief in peacetime and a war captain during periods of conflict. The office of civil chief was hereditary and descended through a highly ranked matri-clan. War captains were elected and earned their positions through proven success in battle. Both civil chiefs and war captains had their councils. The women

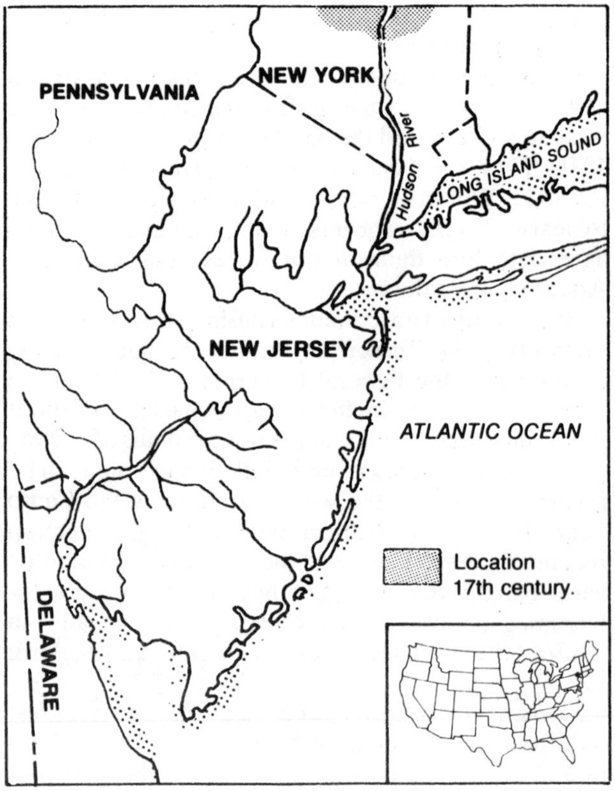

Esopus

and the young warriors also took part in the decision making process. A consensus of all of the interest-groups was necessary before a decision could be made.

Each of the *Esopus* groups consisted of a number of villages. Each group further had its respective civil chief, war captain, councils, and groups of women and young warriors. The five *Esopus* groups acted as a confederacy without a paramount leader when faced with problems that concerned all of the groups.

The *Esopus* first encountered the Europeans during the fall of 1609 when Henry Hudson visited two of their villages along the Hudson River. Later Dutch settlements bypassed the *Esopus* country. The Dutch established their major trade centers north of the *Esopus* at Fort Orange, now Albany, New York and south at Fort Amsterdam on the southern tip of Manhattan Island at the mouth of the Hudson River. The Esopus managed to escape direct involvement in the Governor Kieft War (1640-1645). They did not, however, evade the massive smallpox and measles epidemics that swept away thousands of Native people throughout the region.

Dutch desire for the fertile *Esopus* lands was translated into action during the 1650s. The Dutch established a town at Wiltowyck, now Kingston, New York and a large number of farmsteads soon appeared in the surrounding countryside. Friction soon developed between the settlers and the *Esopus*, but both succeeded in avoiding involvement in the Peach War of 1655-1657. Relations finally reached a flashpoint in September, 1659, and enraged *Esopus* war parties burned the outlying Dutch plantations and besieged Wiltwyck. Supported by their *Minisink, Wappinger, Raritan*, and *Neversink* allies, the Esopus were soon subjected to assaults by the Dutch and their *Western Long Island* and *Hackensack* Native auxilliaries. The Dutch fought a series of skirmishes that resulted in the capture of a number of *Esopus* warriors and leaders. These the Dutch sold into slavery on the West Indian island of Curacao. A peace was signed on July 15, 1660, but its harsh terms called upon the *Esopus* to surrender their territories and remove westward into the interior.

War again broke out when the *Esopus* attacked and burned Wiltwyck on June 10, 1663. The Dutch and their Native allies captured and burned a number of *Esopus* castles and settlements during the summer of 1663. Dispersed and demoralized, the *Esopus* signed a final peace treaty that confirmed both the loss of their land and their subjection by the Dutch on May 15, 1664. The Dutch triumph was short lived, and the English promised better relations with the *Esopus* following their capture of New Netherland on September 6, 1664.

The English continued to reconfirm their friendship with the *Esopus* on a yearly basis. They further proceeded to purchase the *Esopus* lands, and most of their traditional territory was alienated by the 1680s. The *Esopus* moved westward into the mountains and the upper Delaware River valley, though many remained near the Hudson River in small unobtrusive settlements.

A large number of *Esopus* chose to remain in their traditional homeland. Most of them resided in the Catskill Mountain valleys and in a series of settlements near the mouth of Lackawaxen Creek on the upper Delaware River. A document dated August 27, 1743 reported that the Esopus were divided into four "tribes," the *Kighshepax, Mahew, Mogewehogh,* and *Kaghkatewees*. Many of the Lackawaxen *Esopus* were forced from their lands by white settlers during the 1750s, and most moved west to join their *Delawaran* bretheren along the upper Susquehanna River or north among the *Oneida* and Mohawk. Those that joined the *Munsee* along the Susquehanna River also joined their war parties against the English when the Seven Year's War began in 1755. These *Esopus* became assimilated into the *Munsee* following the end of the conflict, and withdrew with them west into the Ohio River valley.

All of the *Esopus* that had settled among the *Oneida* and *Mohawk*, as well as a number from the Susquahanna towns returned to their homeland following the end of the Seven Year's War in 1763. These groups settled along the East Branch of the Delaware River in the heart of the Catskills in the villages of *Coleteyne, Alheepens,* and *Papagonck*. They remained in these towns until 1777, when they rejected colonial overtures and joined the *Munsee* and their English allies during the War of Independence. Many *Esopus* undoubtedly participated in the *Mohawk* Joseph Brant's devastating raid through the Wallkill, Neversink, and Delaware valleys in 1779. The English defeat in 1783 ended the *Esopus* dream of regaining their homeland. Unable to return to their Catskill Mountain towns, the *Esopus* eventually joined the *Delaware* and *Munsee* in their long westward exile. Their descendents today reside in reservations in Ontario, Wisconsin, and Oklahoma.

ROBERT STEVEN GRUMET

ESPEQUE. *See* DIGGING STICK.

ESPINOSA, MANUEL (Yaqui; fl. 1920s), was one of the last Yaqui Indian leaders to yield to the Mexican national forces in Sonora state after the final Yaqui revolts of 1927. In November of that year Espinosa, with 600 soldiers, surrendered to General Francisco R. Manzo.

ESPOGACHE (Guale; ?-1601?), was the leader of an uprising in 1597 against the Spanish missions that had been established on the coast of present Georgia by Franciscan missionaries. The Spanish governor of Florida organized an expedition against the Indians and by spring 1601 they had nearly all submitted. Later that year the Indians who had submitted attacked the remaining hostiles, killing some of them—including, probably, Espogache—and driving the rest into the interior.

ESTES, FRANK CHESTER (Lower Brulé Sioux; March 21, 1933-), is a public health official in the field of Indian health. Estes, whose Indian name is Ounteca ("New Year"), was born at Fort Thompson, South Dakota. While earning degrees at South Dakota State University and the University of California at Berkeley, he worked in various health-related positions in South Dakota, Montana, and Nebraska. After spending one year with the U.S. Office of Economic Opportunity in Vermillion, South Dakota (1965), he returned to the Indian Health Service, working as health educator with Indians in New Mexico and Arizona (1966-69). He has served as director of the Sioux Sanitarium in Rapid City, South Dakota (1969-71), and as director of the Alaska Native Hospital, Alaska (1971-).

ETHNOBIOLOGY of Native American peoples might be discussed under many headings, among them ethnic or racial biology, comparative physiology, human biology, physical anthropology and medical geography. Scholars interested in this topic are found in many different fields. The development of both the biological and the social sciences in the New World has been intimately addressed in such studies have shaped the history of several sciences, especially anthropology. These questions can be organized into three broad groups: *origins and biological diversity* of Indians and Eskimos, *adaptations* to differing ecological, economic, and social conditions in various Native American peoples, and the biological effects of rapid cultural and economic *change* from 1492 to the present.

Origins and diversity

Many general discussions of the biology of Native Americans stress the relative similarity of populations throughout the New World. Most Native Americans are of intermediate height, skin color, and physique, and most have dark, straight hair and dark eyes. Genetic markers in the blood are also rather similar in most Native Americans. This lack of biological diversity as compared with the native peoples of the world's other large land masses has been cited as evidence that people entered the Americas across the Bering Land Bridge only a few tens of thousands of years ago, and that they have thus had less time than the inhabitants of other continents to adapt biologically to local environmental conditions. World-wide studies of the frequency of genetic markers in the blood, for example, the ABO blood group and serum protein polymorphisms, and of genetically controlled characteristics of the teeth and skull show that Native American populations are most similar to the peoples of North Asia, Siberia, and certain coastal regions of South and Central Asia. These areas are the probable source of the small groups of people who crossed the Bering Land Bridge and become the ancestors of Native Americans. Archeological, biological, and linguistic evidence all suggests that there were several such migrations, with the Eskimos and Aleuts representing the most recent movement of people from Asia to North America. While there may have been contributions from other areas of the world, they have left little biological evidence.

Genetic differences among Native American populations can also be related to historical, archaeological, and linguistic connections between various tribes, bands, and language families. Geneticists and physical anthropologists have made a great many studies of this kind in various parts of North and South America, and only a few examples can be discussed here. Patterns of similarity in genetic markers in skulls and measurements of prehistoric skeletons in many cases support archaeological reconstructions of culture history based on pottery and other artifacts. An example of such research is the work on discrete variants in skulls from the Midwest and Great Plains. Using characteristics of the skull that differ among individuals and are genetically controlled—examples of such traits that are visible in living people are brown versus blue eyes, curly versus straight hair—researchers have been able to identify particular archaeological cultures found in Minnesota between 700 and 1400 AD as ancestral to the Dakota, Assiniboin, and Cheyenne.

Language similarities can be used to reconstruct culture history as well, because one can infer that people who speak similar languages have more recent common ancestors than groups who speak very different languages. Reconstructions of culture history based on language similarity can be compared with patterns of biological similarity at several different levels. One researcher made such a study on a very large scale by comparing blood group similarities for twenty-one North and Central American Indian groups with language similarities for the same groups. It was found that geographical distance between groups, rather than the common history reflected in similar language, explained the biological differences he saw. While there are some characteristics of groups of people as geographically distant as the Navajo in Arizona and the Kutchin in Canada, both of whom speak related Athapaskan languages, that reflect in part their common origins and history. Blood group data mainly shows biological resemblances among neighbors, for example the Navajo and Pima, who speak very different languages. It is possible to estimate the amount of time that two related languages have been separated by a process called *glottochronology*. This technique indicates that the language groups that Spuhler studied had been separated from 700 to several thousand years. Over this relatively long period of time, biological similarity ceased to reflect the historical connections expressed in common language. Instead, at this scale, biological similarities reflect long residence in similar environments and opportunity for intermarriage.

On a much more local and more recent scale, others have studied blood groups and other genetic markers in Yanomamo Indians in Venezuela. Genetic differences among villages of a few hundred people correspond closely to small differences in the dialect of Yanomamo spoken in different villages and to historical relationships among villages. The Yanomamo show extremely rapid biological differentiation among villages—detectable in a generation or so—because new villages are formed by groups of closely related men and their families.

These studies are examples of research into patterns of biological diversity that are conducted by geneticists and physical anthropologists in all areas of the world. Research with Native American populations contributes to our understanding of the ways that biological differences among human populations arise. In addition, these studies of biological diversity provide independent evidence for relationships among Native American groups for comparison with histories based on archaeological and linguistic data, and with oral histories passed down by the people themselves.

Adaptations

North and South America offered a wide variety of environments to the people who crossed the Bering Land Bridge a few tens of thousands of years ago, and Native American peoples created for themselves a great diversity of lifeways, differing in ecology, technology, subsistence, social structure, and many other aspects. For this reason, Native American populations present scientists with unusual opportunities to study biological adaptation to differing environmental conditions. A classic study of this kind is the investigation of the extent to which Bergmann's rule accounts for differences in body size in Native American populations. Bergmann's rule is a principle that explains much of the variation in the body size with climate in a wide variety of organisms: animals in cold climates tend to be larger than similar forms in warm climates because they are more efficient in conserving body heat. Data on stature from many Native American populations from the Arctic to the tip of South America was studied, and it was found that contemporary Native Americans are shortest in tropical areas and tallest in cold-temperate climates, in agreement with what one would predict from Bergmann's rule. Prehistoric skeletons, some of them several thousands of years old, from areas where a great deal of archaeology has been done in the United States, Mexico, Guatemala, and Peru were examined, including the stature from the lengths of the limb bones in these skeletons. It was found that the oldest specimens were of moderate height. In the more recent skeletons from each area, stature became more and more variable in directions that correspond to Bergmann's rule—taller in cold climates and shorter in warm ones. Nutritional differences as well as temperature differences contribute to this change. This study is one of the more convincing demonstrations that this principle applies to human populations as well as to other species.

Biological adaptations to some of the more extreme environments successfully inhabited by Native Americans for many thousands of years have been the subject of two recent multi-disciplinary projects conducted as part of the International Biological Program. The first of these concerns, the Quechua Indians of Peru, one of the few human populations able to live successfully at altitudes of 4,000 meters or higher. High-altitude Quechua are relatively short, lean people with quite short limbs, large chests, and well-developed hearts and lungs. They differ from other human populations in many aspects of their physiology, growth patterns, fertility, and lifeways. However, most of these differences do not appear to be the result of genetic adaptations resulting from generations of living at high altitude. Instead, they appear to result for the most part from the influence of scarce oxygen, cold, and limited food supplies, especially on growing children. Some researchers who have worked both the Quechua and other Indians who live at high altitudes are now looking at the same aspects of human biology in Quechua who have migrated to coastal cities in Peru in order to see to what extent the unusual aspects of their biology disappear. Many of the features that are distinctive about their health and physiology are lessened after a few years of residence at low altitude, and others fail to appear in the children of migrants. One of the most striking findings of the I. B. P. study is an appreciation of the careful adjustment that the Quechua have made to the rigorous environment in which they live. Traditional technology, farming practices, work habits, levels of activity, diet, and reproductive cycles are all fine-tuned to conserve the limited resources that their high altitude home offers the Quechua.

The second of the I. B. P. studies concerns Native Americans living in a very different but equally rigorous environment: the Eskimos of the North Slope of Alaska. A very wide variety of investigations were made into the health, physiology, body form, growth, diet, psychology, and behavior of people living in five northwest Alaskan villages. The popular picture of Eskimos as short, stocky, and well-insulated by body fat from the cold was found to be a misconception. North Alaskan Eskimos are of moderate height and build, and are leaner than middle class Americans or Canadians of the same age. They are very physically fit, in keeping with their active way of life. As with the Quechua, many of the biological differences separating them from other human groups can be attributed to growing up and living in a rigorous and unusual environment, rather than to long term genetic adaptations to that environment. However, several interesting aspects of their physiology appear to have a genetic basis. Their diet is rapidly becoming more like that of the general U. S. population, but it remains high in meat protein and fat and low in carbohydrates and vegetable foods. A number of differences in fat and carbohydrate metabolism as well as in bone mineral metabolism appears to be related to both long and short term adjustments to this high meat diet. There is a high frequency of a genetic condition in which one lacks *lactase*, an enzyme that allows the digestion of milk sugar. Lactase deficiency is common in other Native Americans and in other peoples who did not traditionally keep cattle or other animals for milk. A more unusual genetic condition is lack of the enzyme sucrase, which allows the digestion of ordinary sugar. This condition is found in Eskimos, but is extremely rare elsewhere in the world. Both these conditions are adaptations to a low carbohydrate diet, and are part of the biological adjustment of the Eskimos to their environment. Biological adjustments to cold do not seem to be so important for the Eskimos, probably because the elaborate technology they developed many centuries ago is very effective in protecting them from the cold.

Change

The research discussed above has focussed on Native Americans living in ways that resemble their traditional patterns, but it is safe to say that no contemporary Native American group is insulated fully from the cultural, economic, and biological changes that have occurred since Europeans came to the Americas. Many of these changes have important consequences for health and population biology, perhaps the most important of these being population size.

The Indian population of all regions of the Americas decreased drastically after the Conquest, and continues to decrease today in areas where native peoples are only beginning to have substantial contacts with modern society, for example in the more isolated portions of the Amazon Basin. This decrease occurred through a variety of processes: warfare, exposure to new diseases, economic disruption and exploitation, forced acculturation, and gradual assimilation into non-Indian society. In areas with relatively sparse aboriginal populations and heavy European settlement, for example, much of eastern North America, Native American communities continue only as small, relatively isolated entities, and many groups are extinct. In areas where the aboriginal population was large, for example central Mexico, where the city of Tenochtitlán alone had a population at the conquest of about 150,000, and where European immigration was comparatively limited, Native Americans have made substantial contributions to modern national populations, and traditional lifeways, languages, and social groups have persisted despite the influx of elements of European culture. In areas such as the Arctic or the more distant portions of the Amazon Basin, where European settlement has been very limited, aboriginal lifeways may persist almost unchanged, and population decline is less marked, at least until the influences of the outside world are felt. Studies of the population biology of contemporary Native Americans differ accordingly, for instance, and studies of the genetics of bi-racial and tri-racial hybrid groups in the Southeastern United States are an example of the first, while the extensive literature on the population biology of modern Mesoamerican Indians and mestizos are of the second, and the Yanomamo and Eskimo studies discussed above are of the third.

A second important force since the Conquest is the change in health and in diseases experienced by Native American populations. There was a rapid exchange between the Old World and the New following the Conquest—an exchange that included people, diseases, and domesticated animals and plants—and this exchange profoundly altered lifeways and ecology in both areas. In the New World, such diseases as smallpox, measles, cholera, yellow fever, and malaria were introduced by European immigrants, often with catastrophic consequences for Native American populations who had no previous experience with these diseases and no immunity from them. It was once widely believed that the high death rates from these diseases among Native American groups resulted from a genetic lack of resistance to infection. Medical and epidemiological studies of measles epidemics among the Yanomamo and other relatively isolated South American Indian groups demonstrate that some of this apparent greater succeptibility to European diseases results from the collapse of community activities and services when everyone is sick rather than any special hereditary factor in disease resistance.

The early physical anthropologist Hrdlicka made a similar argument in 1909, attributing the high tuberculosis mortality in U. S. reservation Indians to poor living conditions and diet, rather than some special succeptibility to a newly introduced disease. It was widely believed that recently that tuberculosis belonged on the list of European diseases above. However, tuberculosis has been found in pre-Columbian mummies from Peru and in skeletons from the Midwest, supporting Hrdlicka's contention. In the same manner, we can argue that in many contemporary Native American communities, the biological problems are not biological problems at all, but the result of lack of access to economic resources, food, and medical care. In impoverished communities, malnutrition, disease, and mortality interact, each worsening the other, both in Native American communities, and among other groups of people. It is to this point that much of the work in applied physical anthropology, human biology, and medicine is addressed today.

DELLA C. COOK

ETHNOHISTORY. *See* HISTORY.

ETHNOLOGISTS. *See* ANTHROPOLOGISTS AND ETHNOLOGISTS.

ETOWAH MOUND, a prehistoric ceremonial and political center, is on a bottom of the Etowah River in north Georgia. All evidence of human occupation is rigidly limited to the inside of a 1500 by 30,000 foot area defined by the remains of fortifications and the river.

Pottery, changes in which help us to measure other cultural changes and to perceive relationships, was characteristically decorated with complex stamped designs, mostly based on diamonds, when the site was first occupied about AD 1200. As time went on, filfot crosses were added to the Etowah period stamp inventory. They were later supplemented by other complex curvilinear designs. By about AD 1300, the pottery is still stamped, but designs are almost all curvilinear and more heavily stamped, a style called *Wilbanks* after a satellite town a few miles up the river. By 1500-600, Wilbanks pottery had changed further, through sloppy execution, the addition of notched strips at vessel rims, and a few other features, into a style often called *Lamar*. In this area, this particular kind of Lamar is identifiable with the Cherokee. Etowah then is a Cherokee site at the end of its continuous occupation by one ever changing society over some 500 years, at about 1700.

There were many structures at Etowah. All mounds, plazas, houses and graves, in periods from Etowah to Cherokee, were inside the fortifications.

The largest structure, Mound A, is a multiple level temple mound 60 feet high with its access ramp facing the plaza to the east. All stages of construction were completed in the Etowah period. Off its southwest corner is Mound C. It appeared to be another truncated pyramidal temple mound when first recorded. It was the site of mortuary and possibly other ceremonial structures, with multiple interments, from the late Etowah through the Wilbanks periods. Many of the burials were wearing, or were accompanied by, objects such as copper plates and engraved shell gorgets. These were, or bore, symbols of various kinds, particularly winged beings. All of the symbols are representative of a widespread late southeastern phenomenon called the Southeastern Ceremonial Cult. Representations of beings in nearly identical costumes, identical symbols, and nearly identical objects of various kinds have been found in a number of sites, particularly a few large ones such as Moundville and Spiro. Interpretations vary, but certainly the objects and symbols were associated in all instances with a few persons who had great social power. It has been suggested that these persons were officials in similar social-religious systems which practiced related fertility rites and were engaged in warfare to expand their boundaries.

Copper plate from Etowah Mound, Georgia.

Sculpture from the Etowah Mounds, Georgia.

One more mound, B, is at the southeast corner of Mound A. It is a long narrow structure some 12 feet high. Its function is unknown. It was present in late Etowah times, and it may have been used through the Wilbanks period. Along the eastern edge of its base, covered by layers of wash from its slopes, huge pits were found. They were as much as 5 feet in diameter and 6 feet deep. The fill in these Etowah period features consisted of entire loads of broken pottery, shells, or bones. Some sort of ceremony, perhaps of the cyclical renewal type, may be inferred and may have some relationship to the function of Mound C.

Well made houses were mud plastered with thatched roofs. Early specimens were square or rectangular, later ones circular or oval. Central fireplaces were clay lined. Many, perhaps most, burials of the common people were made through the floors of their houses.

There was a large, well defined plaza, about the size of a football field, in front of the Mound A ramp. It was clay paved and edged with stone slabs set on edge during the late, early Cherokee period.

Related sites, with the same pottery sequence, often with the last occupation being a documented 18th century Cherokee town, are found across northern Georgia, western North Carolina, and parts of Tennessee. Most of the sites have one mound which on excavation proves to be a collapsed earth covered town house, or a series of them each built on the ruins of an earlier structure. None of these related towns have any evidence of fortifications. Each one has a few burials in its earlier levels accompanied by objects bearing Southern Cult symbols. The distribution of sites which changed through time in the same way, along with the distribution of earth lodges and cult symbols, has been interpreted as evidence for a nascent state with its capitol and religious center at Etowah.

WILLIAM B. SEARS

ETSOWISH-SIMMEGEE-ITSHIN (Kalispel; ?-April 6, 1854) was a chief in northwestern Montana Territory who was converted to Christianity in 1842 to 1843 by the famous Jesuit missionary Pierre-Jean de Smet. Known to whites as Loyola, the name he took at his baptism, he was noted for his firm adherence to the Roman Catholic religion and his zealous efforts to lead his people to observe the teachings of the missionaries.

EVA, a shell mound some 200 feet in diameter by 8-10 feet high, was on the flood plain of the Tennessee River in Benton County, Tenn. The floodplain location, characteristic of shell midden-mound sites, meant that the community was often flooded while people lived there as well as since, a small price to pay for ready access to the river mussell supply which formed the basic stratum of their economic system.

Internal evidence suggests a life span for the site of several thousand years, estimated to fall in a period between 6,000 and 2,000 BC. Clearly differentiated strata and variation in strata content suggest a number of changes, economic and stylistic, in the life ways of the community during its 3-4,000 years of existence. For example, some significance has been attached to a decrease in shells and an increase in deer bones during the deposition of strata IV and V.

The most significant artifacts, significant in potential for cultural reconstruction, are chipped stone projectile points and knives, a variety of bone tools, and a few classes of heavy, pecked and polished stone tools.

Most of the projectile points recovered are the large, some two to four inch long, stemmed points. These, with minor variations, served as points on darts propelled by spear throwers throughout eastern United States in this "Archaic" time level. Such "atlatl" thrown darts appear to have been the dominant deer hunting weapon. An Eva specialty were unusually well made points with a short stem formed by two notches chipped into the base.

Most of the hundreds of bone tools found were pointed implements of various kinds, "awls," characteristic of most prehistoric Indian cultures. They attest to the vitality of the skin working, mat weaving, and basketry industries. Bone needles with eyes tell us that "tailored" clothing was present. Bone fishooks in all stages of manufacture provide obvious evidence on food gathering as do antler hooks for the spear-throwers.

Heavy stone pestles of various shapes, with hand grinding stones and mortars at least permit the suggestion that seeds were ground for food. Some of them may have been used on nuts, or pigments.

The skeletal remains of 98 inhabitants of the site were found in the midden debris where they had been buried. 18 dogs, medium sized animals used primarily for watchdogs and occasionally for food were present.

There are nearby sites with closely related tools and weapons nearby. On the whole, Eva and its relatives represent a minor variant of the "Archaic" culture or way of life, an American Indian adaptation to the new ecological systems of forested eastern United States after the end of the Pleistocene. From these Archaic cultures, after millennia of evolution, descended most, perhaps all, of the historic Indians of eastern United States.

WILLIAM B. SEARS

EVEA (Commanche; fl. 1770s), was recognized as the leader of his people by the Spanish authorities in Texas during the 1770s. The Spanish governor referred to Evea during 1772 in regard to a treaty he had signed with the Comanche *"capitan"* in June of that year. Other evidence indicates that Evea was still the Comanche chief at least as late as 1778.

EXPLORERS AND CONQUISTADORS. The first known European explorers to the North American continent were Norsemen. Leif Ericson and his brother, Thorvald, were among the Vikings who crossed the Atlantic Ocean (known to them as the *Sea of Darkness*) about AD 1000. Thorvald was slain by one of the natives, whom the Norsemen called *Skrellings*.

Major European exploration and contact with the Indians began late in the 15th century with the arrival of Christopher Columbus. When Columbus landed at San Salvador seeking a short route to India and the Spice Islands (Indonesia), he mistakenly called the inhabitants "Indians." Columbus returned to Spain speaking of gentle people who lived on lush isles. Spain, indeed all of Europe, responded to the challenge of unlimited wealth and conquest.

At about the time Columbus landed there were approximately 800,000 Indians on the continent divided into hundreds of tribes. As a general rule, there were the woodsmen of the East, hunters of the western Plains, fishermen of the North, seed gatherers on the Pacific coast, and the tribes of the Southwest. All of these people were soon to feel the impact of the European explorer.

As in other parts of the world, one of the first things explorers did was to capture native people and return with their prisoners as proof of their discovery and conquest. Some Indians were taken to work in European mines. Relationships between the Indian and the white explorer were as varied as the individuals involved. To some extent it also depended on the nations the white men represented. The land was explored by men from various nations: Spain, Portugal, the Netherlands, England, and France. The Indian's initial attitude was generally one of curiosity and trust. With more contact the Indians witnessed European greed backed up by gunpowder and firearms. Distrust and active hostility in the interest of self-preservation were ultimately the Indian's only alternative.

The Spanish, perhaps the most brutal in their conquests, virtually controlled 16th-century exploration in the New World. Using the West Indies as a base, they fanned out to the north, west, and south. By 1515 they had established 17 mining and farming towns on the island of Hispaniola, all worked by enslaved Indians. The Indian population had shrunk from 250,000 to 14,000. Eventually these Indian people were wiped out.

In 1513 the legend of a "Fountain of Youth" led Ponce de Leon to discover and name Florida. He plundered his way through the peninsula and was followed by slave-catching expeditions. When de Leon returned in 1521, Indians attacked killing most of his men. De Leon himself died in Cuba of wounds inflicted in Florida.

In 1519 the Spaniards landed in Mexico finding Indians rich with gold. A series of conquerors and treasure seekers descended on the "new" land and its peoples determined to find gold and silver with no concern for the Indians. They plundered, enslaved, and demanded tribute.

A Spanish missionary, Bartolome de Las Casas, was appalled by the actions of conquistadors such as Cortés and Pizarro. He recorded the details of their "glorious" conquests and tried to intercede with the king of Spain on behalf of the Indians.

The beleagured Florida Indians drove away a Spanish exploratory and colonizing group in 1528. The Europeans then shipwrecked on the Texas Gulf Coast and were taken care of by poor Indians until an epidemic nearly destroyed them all. When they returned to Mexico, the Spaniards talked of the Seven Cities of Cibola (q.v.) to the northwest. An expedition headed by Francisco Vasquez de Coronado was dispatched and it included a large number of Indians. They captured the Zuñi and tortured some to force them to give up their great wealth. Disappointed, Coronado went further north becoming the first European on the Great Plains. He eventually returned to Mexico in 1542 having failed in his mission.

Hernando De Soto explored the southeastern United States and discovered the Mississippi River beginning in 1538. Equipped with 550 armed men and 200 horses he fought his way up the Florida peninsula. His retinue included ironsmiths who made slave collars and chains. He made his way through the interior by stopping at small, friendly villages where Spaniards were as

"Coronado's March—Colorado" by Frederic Remington.

Spaniards of Hernando De Soto's expedition (1539-43) committing atrocities against the Indians of Florida: a 1598 depiction by the German engraver Théodore de Bry.

yet unknown. He then took their food, women, and riches and used their chief to guide them to the next town.

At the town of *Cufitachiqui* (Cusseta) a Creek queen greeted him with presents only to be kidnapped. He did the same at Coosa. In Chocktaw country, Chief Tuskaloosa resisted his demands. During the battle both sides were severely hit. The Spanish, however, rallied and set fire to the town. He wintered in a Chickasaw town where the Indians killed most of his horses and 11 men when De Soto made his demands for carriers and women.

De Soto reached the Mississippi in May and some Quapaw Indian chiefs brought presents to the shore. As they were withdrawing the Spaniards began to fire, killing several of the chiefs. The De Soto expedition crossed the Mississippi in June and began to plunder its way through Arkansas behind bands of fleeing people. In the spring they returned to the Mississippi at Guachoya. De Soto fell ill and died after he ordered a nearby town destroyed in a sudden attack. His followers went West fighting Indians and taking slaves before their eventual return to Mexico.

For Portugal Gaspar Corte-Real went to Labrador and Newfoundland in 1500. The next year he took two shiploads of natives to be sold as slaves.

While the Spanish were initially mainly interested in gold and silver, other European nations explored the land with trade and settlement in mind. While their eventual colonization drove the Indians off their ancestral lands with hundreds of years of bloody contacts, the initial explorations were often marked by friendliness.

In 1497 England claimed parts of North America based on Cabot's voyage along the Atlantic coast. As settlements began the Indians would share food and teach the colonists how to farm the new crops. Sir Walter Raleigh's explorers declared the Indians on the North Carolina coast to be unspoiled "such as live after the manner of the golden age." Raleigh's "Lost Colony," abandoned while the British fought Spain, might have been assimilated by nearby Lumbee Indians. Francis Drake in 1579 landed to the north of San Francisco where he found the Indians "without guile or treachery." Drake accepted the country for the Queen from the uncomprehending Indians.

Jacques Cartier left France looking for a northwest passage to India and, in 1534, he traveled the St. Lawrence River, claiming the land for France. LaSalle traveled down the Mississippi in 1670 and claimed all the land it drained for the French. The French came to mid-America with missionaries. While the missionary tried to "conquer" his soul, the Indian and the Frenchman had an understanding. By 1800 French traders and explorers had been in mid-America for over 50 years. When the French were defeated in the French and Indian War, many traders and explorers stayed on working with their Indian friends for the English explorers.

In 1793 six Frenchmen and two Indians helped Alexander Mackenzie on his historic trip to the Canadian Pacific. The Shoshoni provided explorers with horses to cross the Rockies.

The Lewis and Clark Expedition was a famous 1804-1806 U.S. exploration of the recently acquired Louisiana Territory. The explorers were dispatched to report on the Indian nations and geographical features of the unknown land between the Mississippi River and the Pacific Ocean. Guided by Sacajawea, a young Shoshoni woman, the explorers reported on dozens of friendly Indian nations in their 28-month journey of 8,500 miles.

On April 30, 1803 President Thomas Jefferson purchased the territory from France and began to organize an expedition to explore the 1 million square miles inhabited by Indians and a few French trappers and traders. Captain Meriwether Lewis, Jefferson's probate secretary, and Lieutenant William Clark prepared for their journey at Wood River, north of the French fur trading post at St. Louis. After their return there in 1806, St. Louis became known as the Gateway to the West.

On May 14, 1804 approximately 40 men in three boats began their adventure traveling the Missouri River to the Platte by July 26. They met the Poncas at the mouth of the Niobrara River and the peaceful Cheyennes while passing through the Black Hills. An Indian baby born on August 30 was wrapped in the U.S. flag and became struck by the *Ree,* a Yankton Sioux chief.

They wintered among the Mandan and Sioux, whom they reached in October, and sent 16 men back to St. Louis with initial reports for the President. That winter they built Fort Mandan, near the present Bismarck, North Dakota, and met Sacajawea, a Shoshoni who had been kidnapped by the Hidatsa people. When the expedition left the following April, they were joined by Sacajawea, her French-Canadian husband and their infant son, Jean-Baptiste.

Lewis and Clark sighted the Rockies in May and soon reached the Shoshoni, Sacajawea's people, who provided the explorers with food and horses for the rigorous mountain crossing. Lewis' journal glowingly speaks of the Shoshoni character. The difficult Rocky Mountain crossing was accomplished by September, 1805, but the expedition was sick and starving when they encountered the Nez Perce nation at the Clearwater River. The Nez Perce, who raised Appaloosa horses, gave the white men food and tended their horses for months as the explorers continued on by canoe.

Following the Columbia River, they triumphantly reached the Pacific on November 15, 1805. Wintering near the present Astoria, Oregon, they built Fort Clatsop and prepared for the return journey. On the trip back, they occasionally split into three groups for more extensive observation. The only unpleasant Indian experience the long exploration faced was when, on meeting some hostile Blackfeet, two of the Indians were killed.

Lewis and Clark's expedition had been given up as lost when they sailed into St. Louis on September 23, 1806. Only one man had been lost on the trip — to disease and not hostile Indians.

Although in mapping the land from North Dakota to the Pacific the adventurers had destroyed the hopes of an easy water crossing of the territory, other plans for Jefferson's purchase soon began. Legislators and speculators happily read the accounts of a vast land and friendly Indian people. A deluge of treaties soon pushed eastern Indian nations onto new land west of the Mississippi River.

MESO AND SOUTH AMERICA

The 15th century Europe was divided among four kings: Louis XI of France, Maximilian of Germany, Henry VII of England, and Ferdinand of Spain. Each wanted to realize a grand policy which would culminate in the conquest of Europe. But each needed arms and finance. After having been turned down by the King of Portugal, Isabelle and Ferdinand of Spain were enticed by the plan of Christopher Columbus to reach Asia by the west, form an alliance with the Great Khan and find enormous gold riches.

Columbus (*c.*1451-1506) was probably born in Genoa; a propagator of the Christian faith, he was probably of Jewish descent. A geographer, he was not sure that the world was round, a mathematician who could barely count, and an admiral who made errors in charting his course and reckoned his sea routes by guesswork. Discoverer of America, he actually thought he was in Asia. Only after 8 years of repeated efforts did he win the backing of Ferdinand and Isabella. He sailed from Palos, Spain, on August 3, 1492, with 88 men in 3 ships. They stopped briefly at the Canary Islands and on October 12, after persisting in the voyage despite fears of the crew, made their first discovery, an island they called *San Salvador,* one of the present Bahamas. The aborigines they called *Indians,* because Columbus thought they had reached the coast of India. Continuing, he sailed along the coast of Cuba and on December 5 reached Haiti. There, after the Santa Maria ship broke up in a storm, Columbus

EXPLORERS AND CONQUISTADORS— NORTH AMERICA

Norse contact.

986 possible first "discovery" of NA by Bjarni Herjolfsson.

11th century-c. 1000 exploration about Hudson Strait and Gulf of St. Lawrence by Leif & Thorvald Ericsson; Thorvald killed by natives.

c. 1020 Thorfinn Karlsefni to NA. Freydis (sister of Leif Ericsson) to NA, but expedition marred by murders by natives. Temporary settlement at Newfoundland—date unknown, but in 11th century, marked by armed clashes with indigenous peoples.

Spanish

1513 Juan Ponce de Leon skirted Florida.

1519 Alonso de Pineda traced entire shoreline of Gulf of Mexico.

1524-25 Esteban Gornes (Portuguese Spanish service) traced NA coast from Grand Banks to Florida.

1528 Panfilo de Narvaez landed in Florida. Expedition included Alvac Nunez Cabeza de Vaca and Esteban. From 1534-36 Cabeza de Vaca explored the Southwest.

1539 Hernando De Soto; Fray Marcos de Niza.

1540 Francisco Vazquez de Coronado.

1542-43 Juan Rodriquez Cabrillo and Bartolome Ferrelo surveyed Pacific coast from lower California beyond 42° N Latitude.

1760-1770s Explorers to S.F. Bay and inland seeking links with Santa Fe and Taos.

1776-77s Silvestre Velez de Escalante went from Santa Fe to NW Utah Lake, SW to Sevier Lake and the upper Virgin River, and back to Santa Fe.

French

1534-42 Jacques Cartier ascended St.Lawrence River.

late 1500s French fished the Gulf of St. Lawrence and began fur trade.

1605 traders founded Port Royal.

1608 Quebec became center of fur trade.

1603-16 Samuel de Champlain; Etienne Brule.

1671-72 Paul Denis, sieur de St. Simon, followed Saquenay and Rupert rivers to James Bay.

1671 Simon Francois Daumont reached Sault Ste. Marie. Daniel Grey solon, sieur Dulhut (Duluth) reached Minnesota and Wisconsin.

1673 Louis Jolliet and Jacques Marquette descended Mississippi almost to Arkansas, returning via Illinois River to Lake Michigan.

1682 Rene Robert Cavelier, sieur de La Salle descended Mississippi to its mouth.

Expeditions of Louis Juchereau de Saint Denis from Natchitoches, La., to San Juan Bautists (Villahermosa), Mexico in 1714; of Bernard de la Harpe along the Red, Arkansas and Canadian rivers between 1719 and 1722; and of Pierre and Paul Mallet. Beginning in the winter of 1738-39 the Mallet brothers followed the Missouri, the Platte and the South Platte into the high plains, angled southwest to Taos and Santa Fe and returned to the Mississippi along the Canadian and Arkansas rivers. In the northern plains Pierre Gaultier de Varennes, sieur de a Verendrye, countered British competition by pushing trading posts beyond Lake Superior, baiting his request for a western trading monopoloy by promising to seek the Western sea. Between 1731 and 1744, Verendrye, and his sons discovered and described Lakes Winnipeg, Winnipegosis and Manitoba and their relation to the major rivers of the region. They reached the Black Hills and mapped the upper Missouri, but decided that the Saskatchewan river provided the best route to the Pacific.

English

1497 John Cabot (Genoese [1461-98] in English service) reached NA.

1578-79 Sir Francis Drake explored Pacific coast to 48°N.

1576-78 Sir Martin Frobisher.

1585-87 John Davis.

1610-11 Henry Hudson.

1673 James Needham reached a Cherokee village on upper Tennessee river and accompanied by braves, went on to Kanawha and Ohio rivers and to junction of the Chattahoochee and Flint rivers.

1690-92 Henry Kelsey ascended Hayes River, crossed Lake Winnipeg and explored beyond Lake Winnipegosis.

1754 Anthony Henday pushed beyond longitude 113° W between major branches of the Saskatchewan.

1770-72 Samuel Hearne reached lower Coppermine River and returned across Great Slave Lake and to Slave River.

1778 James Cook sailed from Oregon to Bering Strait, expedition continuing after his death to 70° 44″ N.

1798 (later Sir) Alexander MacKenzie descended MacKenzie River from Great Slave Lake to the Arctic Ocean.

1793 MacKenzie followed Peace River to Rockies, traversed to the Fraser River and went overland to the Pacific.

1819-20 William Edward Parry sailed from Baffin Bay to Melville Island.

1819-27	Sir John Franklin	explored coastline
1837-39	Thomas Simpson	between Point Bar-
1846-54	John Rae	row and the Melville Peninsula.

1826 Frederick W. Beechey, by sea, explored west of Point Barrow.

1829-33 Sir John Ross explored the Boothia Peninsula and, together with James Clark Ross, located the north magnetic pole.

Dutch

1609 Henry Hudson reached Hudson River.

1610-11 Henry Hudson reached Hudson Bay.

1692-94 Arnout Cornelius Viele descended the Ohio, perhaps to the Mississippi.

Russian.

1728 Vitus Janassen Bering traversed Bering Strait.

1741 Vitus Janassen Bering and Alexei Chirikov reached southern Alaska.

U.S.

1804-06 Lewis and Clark expedition ascended the Missouri River, crossed to the Pacific slope, and reached mouth of the Columbia River.

Norwegian.

1903-06 Roald Armundsen sailed through NW Passage.

Canadian

Villijalmur Stefansson discovered last of the major islands in the northern Canadian archipelago.

started a small colony — and thus became the first conquistador, the first of Spanish conquerors and explorers in the New World during the 16th century. (Among the more important ones of these military adventurers were Cortés, Pizarro, Balboa, and Quwaada; these men, and hundreds of lesser known conquistadores who have left little individual mark on history, seized a great part of the New World — including much of North America — for Spain. Despite the preponderance of favorable historical sources we have for the lives of the conquistadores, many are known to history as the personification of ruthless violence and personal greed).

At any rate, Columbus sailed back to Spain, where he was made the "Admiral of the Ocean Sea" and Governor of the newly discovered lands. His second voyage began September 15, 1493, with 17 ships and 1500 men. Reaching Haiti, he found that the Indians had destroyed his colony. After establishing a new one, he went on exploring the coast of Cuba and discovered Jamaica. On his third voyage, 1498, he visited Trinidad and finally reached the American continent, at the mouth of the Orinoco River in Venezuela. Charges of misrule by Columbus as Governor in the New World induced Ferdinand and Isabella to replace him in 1500, and Columbus was returned to Spain in chains. Eventually he was released but without the honors originally promised to him. In 1502, undertaking another expedition in the hopes of at last reaching Asia, he sailed down the coast of Central America, then turned back to Spain. He died in poverty at Valladolid, Spain, knowing he had touched a continent in his western explorations, but not knowing its identity. (Controversy still is going on as to whether Columbus or Leif Ericson was the first to reach America).

During Columbus' lifetime, other expeditions were sailing the "Dark Sea." Broadly speaking, Columbus had reconnoitered the Greater and Lesser Antilles, the Gulf of Mexico, Yucatan, the coasts of Honduras and Nicaragua, the Isthmus of Panama and the Gulf of Darien, the Venzuelan Coast and the Delta of the Orinoco. These countries were not the Indies, a name actually given to them by a German, Martin Weldseemuller at Saint-Die in 1507, in his work entitled *Cosmographiae Introductio.* The term America, first applied to the territories south of the equator, later designated the whole of the New World. In 1541, 35 years after the death of Columbus, a Dutch geographer, Gerhardus Marcator, drew a map in which, for the first time, *Mundus Novus* was separated from Asia; it bore the name America, the concept originated by Amerigo Vespucci (1451-1512), Italian navigator who reached America on June 16, 1497 and gave his name to it. ("Amerigo" is the Italian form of "Emmerich." His letters are available in translation through Hakluyt Society, 1894).

When the conquerors landed on unknown soil, they eventually were met by strange men whose skin was like bronze or sometimes like red sand. The Spaniards named them "Indians," since the conquistadores thought they were in the Indies.

After Columbus, Haiti and Cuba, the great West Indian Islands, served as the platforms from which the conquistadores took off. A new period of 15 years started in 1506, the year of Columbus' death, and extended to 1521, when Hernan Cortés conquered Mexico. During these 15 years of bloodshed, stand out such names as Alonso de Ojeda, Juan de la Cosa, Ponce de Leon, Vicente Yanez Pinzon, Diego de Nicuesa, Diego Velasquez, and Francisco Piazarro. Especially known was Vasco Nunez de Balboa (1475-1517), the discoverer of the Pacific Ocean (1513), a member of the expedition to Mexico made by the Spanish conqueror Cortés. (Balboa was later executed on a charge of treason, for having usurped command of the smaller expedition during which he made his discovery).

Hernan (or Hernando) Cortés (1485-1547), Spanish conquistador in Mexico, began his career as a public "scrivener" ("intellectuals" were rare in Spain those days, but were needed for administrative details). Educated for the law, he became a soldier. After two trips to the West Indies he was commissioned by Diego de Velasquez, governor of Cuba, to lead an expedition against Mexico. His mission was religious and military, since it was a question of conquering and converting. As his lieutenants, Cortés chose Pedro de Alvarado, Cristobal de Olid, Gonzalo de Sandoval, Juan Velasquez de Leon, kinsman of the Governor, Alonson Hernandez de Puertocarrero, Juan de Escalante, Montejo, Diego de Ordaz, Francisco de Morla — all veterans of the quest; Father Bartolome de Olmedo was simultaneously the military chaplain and the moral adviser. Bernal Diaz del Castillo was chronicler. His six vessels sailed into Trinidad and then Havana, where he made new recruits. Early in February 1519 the army comprised 11 ships, 580 soldiers and captains, 100 sailors, 16 horses, 10 cannons, 4 falconers, 13 arquebuses, and 32 crossbowmen. That year, he landed at Yucatan and defeated the Tarascans and then sailed up the coast to found the settlement (now called Veracruz). Chosen Captain General of the settlement, and thus freed of the authority of Cuba, he sank his fleet to prevent any return to the island, and started his march inland to the Aztec capital, Tenochtitlan, ruled by Montezuma. On the way he defeated and gained as allies the Tlaxcalans. (Cortés' cannon and horses were no match for the Indians). Reaching Tenochtitlan, he pretended to be a descendant of the god Quetzalcoatl and made Montezuma his puppet. In 1520 he was to be arrested on the orders of Velasquez but repelled a fleet sent from Cuba. On his return to Tenochtitlan he found that his lieutenant, Pedro de Alvarado, had massacred about 600 Aztecs. Unable to appease the Aztecs, the Spaniards had to fight their way out of the city. Montezuma succumbed to his wounds — or had the Spaniards killed him? The Aztec capital and empire eventually collapsed. On the ruins of the destroyed capital, Cortés founded Mexico City, and from there carried on the conquest of Mexico into Central America. The Spaniards made slaves of the Indians

Biblioteca Nacional, Madrid.

Cortés' departure from Tenochtitlan to challenge Narvaez was presented by the American historian William Prescott: "Montezuma in his royal litter, borne on the shoulders of his nobles and escorted by the Spanish infantry, accompanied the general to the causeway. There, embracing him in the most cordial manner, they parted...." In the illustration (*right*) of that scene, Cortes bids the Emperor Montezuma farewell.

and destroyed most of the remarkable buildings that the Aztecs had erected.

Of interest is that Cortes felt called upon to preach to the Indians wherever he went, reasoning with them that their gods were worthless; evangelization, however, was the special province of the missionaries who accompanied all expeditions. By a papal decree of Alexander VI, issued in 1493, it became mandatory that the natives of the new lands discovered and taken possession of in the name of the Spanish sovereigns were to be properly instructed in the Catholic faith, "for the salvation of these souls, and so that the barbarous nations may be humbled and converted to the Faith." The conquisador's conscience was thus clear that he was on a sacred mission, although he felt no embarrassment about saying that he wanted to make a fortune. The dispatches of Cortés, addressed to Charles V of Spain, were very soon published abroad and reached a wide audience of Europeans who read avidly of these incredible adventures among exotic peoples. There were 5 dispatches, although there are other letters extant, and are known conventionally as the *Cartas de Relacion* of Hernan Cortes. The second and third of these were published in Seville in 1522 and 1523 respectively, then published in Nuremberg in Latin, the international language of cultivated men, and subsequently appeared in Venice in Italian translation, in Antwerp in a Flemish edition, in Augsburg in a German edition of 1550, and a French translation. Since the 16th century, there have followed numerous other editions and translations of the letters.

At the end of his career, Cortés' main enemy was Spain. Captivated at first by the conquistador's personality and by his gifts, Charles of Spain listened more and more to those of his counselors who disapproved of Cortés' policies — he had more gold and would soon have more soldiers than Charles himself. His powers had to be limited. Commissioners were sent to Mexico, and then inquisitors. Disregarding the dangers around him, Cortés enlarged his conquests. He dispatched his lieutenants to the shores of the Gulf of Mexico from the Rio Panuco to Yucatan, to the shores of the Pacific as far as the present-day San Francisco, and into Michoacan. He went to see the King of Spain and was loaded with honors. But offsetting the honors conferred on him, New Spain became a Vice-Royalty, and thereafter Antonio de Mendoza ruled at Mexico in the name of Charles V. Returning to Mexico, Cortés tried his new role as a planter. Then, after 7 years, he died in an Andulusian village, about 4 miles from Seville, from heart attack at the age of 62.

At the very same time when the Aztec Empire was being destroyed by Cortés, a similar nation of a high degree of civilization existed in South America — the

Inca Empire on the high mountains and plateaus of Peru. The Emperior there was called the *Inca*; he was all-powerful and his word was law; he was worshipped as a god who had come to earth. The Incas built the capital city of Cuzco on a high plateau amidst the towering Andes. Here, they erected enormous temples and palaces, and great forts. They discovered rich beds of gold and silver ore in the mountains and from the bottom of the deep valleys and up the lower mountain slopes, they built broad terraces. (Some exist today). But the story of the fall of the Incas reads much like that of the Aztecs. A dozen years after Cortés had conquered Mexico, Pizarro overcame the Incas.

Francisco Pizarro (1477-1541) was raised as a swineherd, and fought in the Italian wars before going to Santo Domingo. Afterwards, he served successively under Ojeda, Balboa, Pesrarias Davila, and Cortés, changing his "patron" according to circumstances. (Nunez de Balboa had been his chief and companion, but he did not hesitate in arresting and handing him over to the executioner). He was one of the harshest among all conquistadores, and his only soft spot in his heart was his greed for gold.

Born in secret at Trujillo in Estremadura (some 30 miles from Yurta, where Charles V was to die), he was abandoned by his prostitute mother (his father was a Spanish colonel) on the steps of a church; his first nurse was a sow. As a youngster he earned his living as a swineherd. As an adolescent, he enlisted as a simple soldier in Italy's army — and never passed that rank. He did not even know how to sign his name. At the age of 40, at Seville he enrolled aboard a caravel as one of the crew and sailed to Santo Domingo (1509). Ten years after his arrival, while clearing a way for successive leaders, he became one of the richest colonists with the pearls of the Gulf of Paria and the gold of Panama.

He had been with Balboa when the latter discovered the Pacific Ocean, and knew, of course of the success Cortés had had in Mexico. Perhaps there were other similar regions and new sources of wealth along the west coast of South America for him. He sailed down the coast and soon learned of the Inca people. Presently, he was back with a small force of men to conquer them. He reached Inca territory at a time when the Inca Empire was weakening by fighting among its leaders. The Emperor had seized the throne from the rightful ruler and was striving to hold it. Pizarro offered to help him. Instead, when admitted to the capital, he seized the Inca and demanded a vast amount of gold and silver to free him. This was paid. However, Pizarro again broke his word. He brought false charges against the Inca and put him to death. Then, by degrees, the Spaniards conquered the territory. Pizarro was appointed the first Viceroy, or personal representative of the King of Spain. He seized any treasures wherever he could find them, tortured the local leaders to make them tell where treasures were hidden, and where mines were located. But even these steps were not always successful, and Pizarro did not gain the wealth he expected. There was wealth, however, in other natural resources, as Pizarro soon discovered. The forests yielded rich products, and, especially in the south, fertile lands made great crops possible. Cattle and horses and seed for new crops were brought over, and the real development of the land began. Soon Spain owned all of western and southern South America.

Interestingly enough, although Pizarro failed to get all the wealth he had expected, his expedition gave to the world something of great value. Some soldiers sent a few potatoes back to Spain, where the unknown plant was first grown as a garden curiosity. Gradually, its food value was recognized. Today, the potato has become the most valuable vegetable food in the world.

The Inca people certainly suffered under the Spaniards. The Spaniard felt that it was beneath them to work. The great landowners practically made slaves of the natives. The King of Spain appointed his own Council to pass laws for the colonies. For 300 years, this Council did what it pleased, regardless of the welfare of the Incas; it taxed them without mercy and granted them practically no rights. Several revolts were mercilessly put down.

In 1528, at Toledo, the Queen, in the absence of the Emperior of Spain, signed a convention reserving to Pizarro the privilege of conquering Peru, named "New Castile" in anticipation. The bastard from Trujillo

The capture of Atahuallpa after his defeat by Pizarro in 1532.

Courtesy Chicago Historical Society.

The thirteen sovereigns that reigned successively in Peru before the arrival of the Spaniards. From Antonio De Herrera, "The General History of the Vast Continent and Islands of America".

became Captain General for life and Supreme Judge of the new province, and was also rewarded the collar of the Order of Santiago. On his return to Peru he faced a war between the conquistadores headed by Pedro de Alvarado who had landed at Puerto Viejo on the coast of Ecuador, who proclaimed himself Governor of Guatemala; his title was confirmed by Charles V. In 1541, Pizarro was about 65 years old. He had abandoned military expeditions in order to realize his true passion for construction. Lima had become an important city; other cities (Humanga, Chuquisaca, Areguipa) had arisen too. In the middle of the plaza mayor at Lima, Pizarro kept up the appearance of a king, enveloped in his purple cloak or in the marten furs sent to him by Cortés from Mexico. He no longer wished to fight, leaving this matter to his lieutenants, Pedro de Candia at Titicaca, Gonzalo Pizarro in eastern Peru, while Pedro de Valdivia was continuing the conquest of Chile (that Almagro had begun). Pizarro was a victim of a secret conspiracy, led by Diego Almagro, the son of one executed man, who had gathered all the elements hostile to Pizarro. He scorned the warnings of his friends, and had his throat cut.

Among the other conquistadores are noted Alonson de Ojeda, Juan de la Gosa, and Amerigo Vespucci who discovered Venezuela in the spring in 1499. Vincente Yanez discovered the coast of Brazil, while Pedro Alvares Cabral also reached Brazil in 1500. Ponce de Leon discovered Florida in 1513, and two years later Diego Velasquez and Panfilo de Narvaez found Havana. On September 6, 1513, Vasvo Nunez de Balboa set out from the Bay of San Miguel (Panama

Isthmus) to discover the South Seas. In 1517, he landed at Yucatan, and Balboa was executed at Acla on the orders of Pedro Arias de Avila (Pedrarias Davila), his father-in-law. On April 25, 1520, Panfilo de Narvaez landed at San Juan de Ulua. In 1522, the first expedition to Peru was led by Pascual de Andagoya, and a year later Pedro de Alvarado conquered Guatemala. In 1524, Gonzalez Davila landed in Honduras. In 1525, Santa Maria in Colombia was founded by Rodrigo de Bastidas. Between 1527-1531, Diego de Ordaz explored Guiana; and Sebastian Cabot (?-1557), son of John, explored the Rio de la Plata area in SE South America. In 1529, Ordaz, under the mandate for the Welsers, bankers of Augsburg, explored Venezuela. In January, 1535, Pedro de Heredia founded Cartagena in Colombia. In 1535, Diego de Almagro undertook the conquest of Chile. A year later, Pedro de Mendoza founded Puerto de Nuestro Senora del Buen Aire (Buenos Aires). In the spring of 1536, an expedition under Gonzalo Jimenez de Quesada explored the Magdalena River and conquered the Chibcha empire and Bogota. In August, 1537, Juan de Salazar founded Asuncion (later capital of Paraguay). On August 6, 1538, Jimenez de Quesada founded the city of Bogota.

In 1540, Pedro de Valvidia led an expedition into Chile. On February 12, 1541, Pedro de Valdivia founded Santiago Estremadura (the future Santiago of Chile); in June Francisco de Orillana crossed South America from the Pacific to Alvarado. Between 1541-1545 little was done with Venezuela. In 1528 Charles V turned over the area to the Welsers, a banking family of the Germanys; the immediate purpose was to pay off some of his debts, but the Emperor hoped that Germans might succeed where Spaniards had failed. Massacre, rapine, seizures, and violent quarrels among the invaders characterized the whole sad effort; in 1548, Charles V revoked the grant. In 1541, Hernando De Soto who had landed in Florida in 1539, died there. In 1544 Cabeza de Vaca (1490-1557) was deposed as governor of Paraguay. In March 1550, Pedro de Valvidia founded the city of Concepcion and reached the Bio-Bio River; he died in January 1554. In 1560, Francisco Fajardo founded Caracas, capital of Venezuela, and 7 years later, Diego de Losada, officer of Ponce de Leon, again founded Santiago de Leon de Caracas. In 1573, Juan de Garay founded Santa Fe de la Vera Cruz in Argentina, and Jerenimo Luis de Cabrera founded Cordoba.

With the assassination of Pizarro (1541), the age of conquistadors was about to end, with Peru and Chile the furthest outposts of the Spanish colonial empire; and much of the interior of South America still had to wait to be conquered. Especially Central America remained an obscure Spanish colony for nearly 3 centuries. In 1523, Cortés sent his lieutenant, Pedro Alvarado overland into Guatemala where he proceeded to torture, slay and burn. While carrying on his murderous mission in Guatemala, Francisco de Montejo did not succeed in making it a second colony; eventually it was annexed to Guatemala, a region full of refugee Indians and foreigners. In 1527, Pedradias (Pedro Arias de Avila) became Governor of Nicaragua, and during his tenure of office until his death in 1531, he tyrannized Spaniards and abused Indians on a large scale. An independence attempt led by the Contreras brothers (Pedro and Hernando) collapsed in 1550, and Nicaragua was to become a little known appendage of Guatemala. Nuevo Cartage (Costa Rica) saw the traditional difficulties — disease, mutinies, food shortages, Indian hostility — but the Spanish foothold endured and developed into a white settlement with numerous independent landowners. In northern Panama, the colonizing effort proved entirely disastrous.

The key man in the Central American history at that time was Pedro de Alvarado, Governor and Captain-General of Guatemala for 2 decades; but in 1541 he was defeated for once by the despised Indians when trying to help Viceroy Mendoza in putting down the Mixton rebellion, and crushed by a horse. Nominally under the Viceroy of New Spain, Guatemala carried on during the colonial period as a little viceroyalty itself.

JOSEPH S. ROUCEK

Pedro de Valdivia (left) the first governor of Chile, who was killed during an Araucanian uprising in 1553. Francisco de Villagra (center) also a governor of Chile and (right) G. Alderete Adelantando. From Alonso Ovalle, "Historica relacion del reyno de Chile, 1646.

FABRICS. *See CLOTH.*

FACTORY SYSTEM was an official United States program for trading with the fur-trapping Indians of the then Northwest Territory. It operated from 1795 to 1822.

The Indians of the upper Mississippi and Ohio region had long dealt their furs to the white trader. A long association with France diminished after the French and Indian War (1754-1763). Trade for British goods then increased, continuing well after the colonies had gained independence. The Jay Treaty of 1794 between the U.S. and England preserved the Canadian-Indian trade. It allowed for the free border passage of Indians into British Canada with goods of trade.

The United States was eager to diminish the English, French, and Spanish influence on its frontier. The Indians preferred to trade for English goods rather than those of the U. S. trader. In one of his early messages to Congress, President George Washington had recommended the establishment of a government operated and regulated organization for trading with the Indians. He also suggested that its white agents should live among the Indians to maintain peace and protected the Indians from the extortions of private fur traders.

In 1795 the 'factory' system was introduced through a series of trading houses where the U. S. offered a "fair price" for furs. Agents in charge of the houses were appointed by and directly responsible to the President. The system was administered by the superintendent of the United States Indian Trade. In 1816 Colonel Thomas L. McKenney was appointed to the superintendent's post; he later (1824) became the first head of the Bureau of Indian Affairs, then a division of the War Department.

By 1803 official government trade centers had been established at Detroit and Fort Wayne. Other locations included a post at the mouth of the Missouri, the southern tip of Lake Michigan (Fort Dearborn, Chicago), Sandusky (1806), Mackinac, and Fort Madison on the Mississippi (1808).

President Thomas Jefferson hoped to persuade the Indians to farm and raise livestock on the Louisiana Territory (newly purchased from France) instead of hunting for a living. To this end he suggested that spending at the government posts should be encouraged. He believed that eventually the Indian would be forced to cede land to settle his debts to the government.

The factory system was not successful in stemming British frontier influence and, as the War of 1812 approached, the U. S. began to make other economic moves against the British. The factory system was terminated in 1822 as Congress responded to the political force of the fur trading companies.

FADDEN, RAYMOND (Mohawk; 20th century), is a noted author and historian of the Iroquois people. Known also as Aren Arweks, he is director of the Six Nations Indian Museum in Onchiota, New York. Among his publications are *History of the Oneida Nation* and *Migration of the Iroquois* (1972).

FALLEN TIMBERS, BATTLE OF was a 1794 battle in Ohio between Indians of the Northwest Territory and a U. S. military expedition. The Indians were defeated and forced to cede a vast tract of land the following year at the Treaty of Greenville.

The Indians of the Old Northwest, opposed to the white settlement of their homelands, had repelled two U. S. military expeditions in 1790 and 1791 under the leadership of Little Turtle, a Miami chief. The pace of white migration north and west of the Ohio River had slowed, but a third military expedition was being prepared by General Anthony Wayne. His 3,000-man force (2,000 regular and 1,000 mounted militia) advanced slowly in 1793, building and supplying forts along the way.

In July 1793 at a conference at Sandusky the Indians unsuccessfully insisted upon the Ohio River boundary as agreed to at the Treaty of Fort Stanwix in 1768. The conference being a failure, Wayne built Fort Greenville, about 80 miles north of Cincinnati, and camped there for the winter of 1793-94.

In June of 1794 after an unsuccessful attack on Fort Recovery, Little Turtle counseled peace, doubtful of the promised British aid and wary of the powerful military force advancing toward them. As a result Blue Jacket and Black Wolf became the leaders of the approximately 2,000-man Indian force of Shawnee, Delawares, Ottawas, Miamis, and others.

The decisive battle was engaged in August 1794 near the Maumee River rapids, about 12 miles southwest of present-day Toledo. The Indians defended the Ohio region from a forest nearly leveled by a recent tornado. The ground was strewn with a natural barricade of fallen timbers and the Indians hid along a two mile front. On August 20, Wayne ordered a surprise attack, a bayonet charge that quickly routed the Indians. The warriors fled to nearby British-held Fort Maumee (Mims) where they were refused the promised sanctuary.

As disillusioned by empty British promises as by the defeat at Fallen Timbers, the Indians then suffered a winter of freezing and starvation. Wayne had burned every Indian village and cornfield. In August 1795 at Greenville the Indians were forced to cede 25,000 square miles of land in the Ohio Valley.

FALLING, LEROY (Cherokee; June 15, 1926-), was administrator for the Kinlichee Boarding School in Arizona in the mid-1970s. Born in Estella, Oklahoma, he received his master's degree from Arizona State University in 1966. He was president of the Indian Workers Conference (1965) and a member of the National-International Social Concerns Committee (1964-66).

FALLON COLONY AND RESERVATION, over 5,000 acres in Churchill County, Nevada, is home to 200 Shoshone-Paiute Indians.

History. As a result of the General Allotment Act, 196 allotments were made to a band of Paiutes living in the Sink and Stillwater area. In 1906 an agreement was reached between the Bureau of Indian Affairs and the Fallon Indians to trade acreage for water rights. In 1917, 840 acres were added as tribal trust land. After a number of sales and changes, the present reservation acreage was reached. Sixty acres were added in 1917 to establish the Fallon Colony at Rattlesnake Hill.

Fallon Colony Reservation.

Culture. Before the formation of the reservation, bands of Paiute and Shoshone Indians moved about in small bands utilizing natural foods and game in the area. Crafts that have survived include beadwork, cradleboard making, and some basket weaving. Fishing and hunting are now pursued more for recreation than for necessity.

Government. The governing body of the Fallon Paiute-Shoshone tribe, the Fallon Business Council, consists of five members elected by tribal members. They serve a term of two years or until they are replaced. Members elect from within themselves a chairman, vice-chairman, and secretary-treasurer. The constitution and bylaws, approved in 1964, cover the duties and privileges of these members.

FALSE FACE SOCIETY. The false face ceremonies of the Iroquois were held for the purpose of exorcising evil spirits and driving away diseases. In the late fall and spring members of the society went from house to house, wearing masks and trying to behave like persons whom the masks represented. Rattles of horn, of wood splints and of hickory bark or snapping turtle shells were carried.

Highly colored wooden masks depicting mythological and legendary characters, with wry, hideous mouths, are known to have been used by the Seneca as far back as the seventeenth century.

There were many types of masks representing different characters and serving different purposes.

Masks designed to be worn by members of the False Face Society were likenesses or symbols of supernatural beings.

According to ancient tradition a strange creature in the form of a great head with terrible flaming eyes made his home on a huge rock over which his long hair streamed. During storms the howling of the wind was thought to be his voice. Another tradition told of several bodiless spirits with ugly visages that had the power to inflict ailments and send disease among people. Still a third tradition told of two brother heads, one in red, the other in black, and a cousin, one-half red and one-half black. It was these traditional figures that suggested the use of the false face masks. Representations of the bear, the pig and other animals are also seen in the old masks.

Carved masks

The carving of wooden masks was a ceremonial procedure and was usually carried on by artists of exceptional ability. Masks varied according to the style of the artist who carved them. To give it potency and to keep within it the spirit of the tree, a mask was carved on the trunk of a living tree, usually the basswood, willow, cucumber, or other tree of soft wood. A three days' ceremony preceded the carving. Sacred tobacco was burned, a pinch at a time, as a plea for forgiveness to the Tree Spirit for the necessity of mutilating the tree. The tobacco smoke was blown into the roots and among the branches. Because of this offering to tobacco, it was thought the tree would not die, and scars left on the tree would heal over in from two or four years. Today masks are often carved on barm beams.

After the mask had been roughly blocked out, the entire block was cut off the tree, the features carefully carved in high relief, the eyes encircled with wide rings of sheet metal, and the entire face usually painted black or red in solid color. A mask painted half red and half black was known as the whirlwind mask, as it had the power to divert an approaching storm. For this reason it was hung on trees facing the wind. "If he had sought his tree in the morning, the artist painted the mask red, but if he found the tree and commenced carving after noon the mask would be black." Unpainted masks were worn by clowns.

Long strands of horse hair, either black or white, or of basswood, moosewood, or slippery elm, were fastened to the top of the mask and hung down like hair on both sides to the knees. Tiny medicine bags were often attached to the masks to make them more efficacious.

Masks about five by seven inches were made for children. Miniature masks from one to three inches in diameter, made of stone, wood, or corn husks, were attached to the larger masks, hung from the end of the leader's pole, or were used as charms to protect buildings from withcraft. At one time the small mask was sent as a notification of election to candidates for admission to the False Face Society.

FAMILY. The biological family, that is, parents and children, constituted the household for most Indians of the Americas. The household was very nearly a self-sufficient economic unit and as such an independent social and political unit. With the exception of large game, all foods belonged exclusively to the households of the persons acquiring them. Food-gathering activities were conducted largely by independent households under the leadership of the household head.

But, though the household was the most stable social and economic unit, some factors tended to disrupt it and others to enlarge it or to extend obligations beyond it. The main disruptive factors were divorce, which occurred easily and frequently, and wife abduction. These, however, merely realined households.

The household was often enlarged by the inclusion of relatives, especially grand parents, who had no households of their own. It was also temporarily enlarged by the addition of the spouse of one or more of its children. Up to a year of matrilocal residence as bride service was common and, in any event, a young married couple usually remained with one family or the other until they had children or their own house. A household might also be augmented by polygyny or polyandry. These forms of marriage were probably not produced in some area by economic factors, but unusual individual wealth was a condition upon which they rested. A man could not hold one wife, to say nothing of several, unless he were a diligent hunter and brought home many buckskins. Polyandry was usually an extension of hospitality and sex privileges to the husband's brother, who would eventually acquire a wife of his own. But it meant that one woman had to provide an increased amount of seeds. The average household was about 6 persons, according to census data, but additions might bring it up to 10.

These additions to the household, however, were not permitted to threaten the welfare of the biological family. Those who were able-bodied shared the tasks of food seeking. Old or infirm persons, especially grandparents, cared for the children. But when starvation was imminent or the exertion of long treks for food excessive, infirm persons were abandoned to perish. Necessity thus strictly limited expansion of the household.

There were also responsibilities if there were not strict obligations to persons outside the household. Whether a village were large or small, several related families usually lived in the proximity of one another. These were usually the households of parents, their married children, brothers and sisters and their spouses, and other close relatives who, in some localities, were further related through cross-cousin and pseudo cross-cousin marriage. These related family traveled together and camped near one another. Though not obligatory, food was freely shared with them. The male members of these households assisted one another in abducting a wife or in defending a wife against abduction and rendered mutual assistance in other ways.

The nature and extent of the manifold duties and obligations between kinfolk is a rich field for extended inquiry. In order that obligations to a relative shall have significance, there must be assurance that one will see him sufficiently often and under sufficiently well-defined circumstances. Lack of consistency in post-marital residence and frequent change of residence for practical reasons brought certain relatives into close association at some times and widely separated them at other times. There was, for example, no assurance that the maternal or paternal grandparent would be present to care for children, that a sister's son or a brother would be on hand to help build and require a dole of seeds, or that any particular relatives would be able to defend one's wife against abduction.

The more stable social conditions were more favorable to the development of readily definable patterns of bahavior between kin. A person knew when and under what conditions he would see his different relatives. Thus, a man knew that he would see his different relatives. Thus, a man knew that he would be in frequent contact with his father's sister, so that it was possible for him to help support her, to marry her step-daughter, and to have her sons as his closest companions. A man would live near his father's sister so that he could help support her and associate with her son only if the father and his sister had decided to remain in the same locality.

Mesoamerica

The most important social institution among agricultural Indian groups is the family. Marriages are often arranged by the parents of both paties through an intermediary or friend. Mutual consent of the partners, their parents, and important relatives is necessary; if any one of the interested parties resists, the marriage cannot take place. Marriage serves as a means of establishing kinship relationships among families within the group, a device for improving one's social status through marriage into a higher-status family, an arrangement for an economic division of labor, and a means of having children born and reared.

Within the context of the larger group, it is the household (usually made up of husband, wife, and their children) which is accorded social, economic, and political recognition. Unmarried people are not regarded as full-fledged members of the community, and they cannot participate in group decisions. If one's marriage is terminated through divorce or death of one of the partners, the group will not accord original social status to the surviving partner until he remarries. But marriage alone is sufficient to establish the social standing of the couple: they must have children to completely validate their position in the group.

Indian families do not practice primogeniture. At the death of the parents, their assets, including land are divided equally among the surviving children. In order to prevent these assets from falling into the hands of members of other groups there are rigorous rules against marriage outside the particular Indian group itself. The continual division and subdivision of assets produces a communal ownership pattern with the Indian group.

Within the Indian village, much importance is attached to the participation of each household in both private and public religious rituals. The highest religious prestige is accorded to those very old households whose moral ascendancy is great by virtue of years of experience, contribution to the community, and ritual performance. On the private or family level, precolonial Indian rituals and beliefs continue. Publicly, Roman Catholic ceremonies are scrupulously observed.

Within the Indian community, group interests dominate over those of the individual. The community emphasizes adjustment of individual differences in the name of group solidarity. Although the individual is responsible for supporting himself and his immediate household, his goals are expected to be pleasing the gods and contributing to the community rather than accumulating individual wealth.

South America

A state organization on a modern pattern can be ascribed to the higher Andean civilizations, where it was associated with the ayllu system still found in the region. However, stratification occurs on simpler levels. Apart from distinctively political groupings, we must take cognizance of the family, the extended family. The patrilineal house community; the patrilineal band; patrilineal or matrilineal moieties and clans.

The individual family is universal and in some instances figures as the only significant economic and social unit. The *Yahgan* exhibit a much weaker sense of kinship for the larger local group bearing a topographical name and only an attenuated sentiment for fellow members of the same dialectic division. Their far more land-minded *Ona* neighbors attach importance to their 39 territorial groups, which approximate Steward's concept of a patrilineal band. Since they are emphatically exogamous, they might be classed with the autonomous landowning "clans" of the *Southern Diegueño* (California) were it not for a doubt as to the inflexibility of the unilateral reckoning. It appears that even married women did not lose all contact with their native group and that the overwhelming majority of males had a lifelong connection with the hereditary hunting grounds. Nevertheless, men were not precluded from settling in an alien district with the owner's permission; and the precise nature of a female's tie with her native territory is not certain. Hence, the *Ona* system, though hardly definable as "loose," does not quite attain the rigidity of a unilateral organization and may be taken as a borderline case.

The *Witoto* house community, on the other hand, strictly defines the status of its members. Marriage is patrilocal and exogamous, and all those born within the settlement bear the same surname. Here, then, males and females are brought together exactly as in a typical patrilineal clan. The *Yagua* in the same area have similar "clan" malocas.

Definitely unilateral types of aggregation, such as moieties and clans, have a fairly wide but far from preponderant distribution. They are conspicuously lacking in the Chaco and regions southward. In a great many populations of intermediate cultural status, such as the tropical forest areas and coastal Brazil, the extended family prevails—a residential unit comprising the native blood-kindred of a settlement plus the affinities who dwlel with them. Since it does not fix the alinement of members once and for all, it falls under the head of "loose" organizations.

Loose systems, however, may have a distinct bias toward either rule of descent; indeed, without such trends it is impossible to conceive the origin of full-fledged clans. Hence, one should not be surprised to find characteristics of unilateral systems among loosely organized peoples. However, one must be careful not to ascribe a matrilineal or a patrilineal pattern on the basis of such elements: such classification must rest on explicit statements that children are reckoned kin with their mother or their father. To illustrate the danger of not observing this precaution, many tribes of the

Amazon-Orinoco area practice atrilocal residence, a frequent concomitant of and hypothetical condition for matrilineal clans. But it is not an adequate cause of such clans, since the avuncular marriage reported in the same region excludes the possiblity of such a system. Inheritance or succession in either line is a safer index: the nepotic rule of the *Chibcha* certainly makes it plausible that they once had matrilineal clans. Yet there, as well as elsewhere in the world, property and rank of different types have been known to descend according to diverse principles.

The bilateral or conjugal family, consisting merely of father, mother (or mothers), and children, underlies all sociopolitical types. Among the *Guató, Mura,* and *Nambicuara*, it was the only permanent sociopolitical unit, and, though several families might associate with one another seasonally for special activities, they lacked permanent cohesion and had no leader or chief.

The problem of dealing with crime and other offenses was very often the family's responsibility. Indians very frequently considered crimes to be personal matters, and accordingly left judgment, retaliation, or other settlement in the hands of the persons and family involved. Among the Hidatsa, for example, gangs of youth of about twelve years of age frequently harassed the young girls of the tribe. Rape was a common occurrence. In the case of a rape, the boy might be whipped by the girl's brothers, or the boy's sisters might try to restore good relations by expressing regrets or presenting the girl's family with gifts. In any case, the young man lost face, as it ws considered cowardly to force a woman into sexual relations.

One criminal distinction not found in contemporary societies was universally present among the Indians—namely, the distinction between good and bad magic. It was permissible to use witchcraft to harm a recognized criminal, but should witchcraft be used against an innocent person it was considered a crime of unprovoked aggression.

Throughout their history, the Indians had their own methods for dealing with crimes in their communities. Toward the end of the nineteenth century, however, a feud between two Sioux chiefs resulted in the murder of one by the other. The Indians reached their own settlement according to traditional means, but a federal trial was nevertheless held. Public interest was much aroused by the trial, which resulted in a sentence of death for the defendent. But the Supreme Court ruled that, in the absence of related legislation, the federal courts has no jurisdiction in the case. The outraged reaction to this decision led to passage of the Major Crimes Act of 1885. This act, along with later acts of Congress, empowered the federal government to try cases involving Indians that were related to the so-called ten major crimes—including murder, rape, arson, burglary, and incest. Civil matters, however, remained in the hands of tribal courts, except in a few cases where tribal authority has been limited by federal legislation.

FARMER'S BROTHER (Seneca; *c.* 1730-1814), was a chief noted as both a warrior and a peacemaker. Also known as Honanyawus, he ws born near the southeastern shore of Lake Ontario. He signed three treaties between 1794 and 1802, and he recommended peace with the U.S. to the Indian council at Niagara in 1798. He fought with distinction on the side of the French during the French and Indian War, the English during the American Revolution, and the U.S. during the War of 1812.

Farmer's Brother was at least 80 years old at the battle at Fort George, New York, on August 17, 1813, but he is mentioned as a leader in that battle and a warrior as respected as his close compatriot Red Jacket. He died at the Seneca village soon after the Battle of Lundy's Lane in 1814 and was buried with full military honors by the U.S. Army.

FAULKNER CULTURE, which is dated *c.* 9000 BC, refers to the Indians who inhabited some parts of southern Illinois and who used rock shelters as temporary hunting stations. They subsisted mainly on game hunted with flint-tipped spears, and on seeds and acorns which they gathered and ground on stone mortars.

FEASTS AND FESTIVALS for the Indians of the Americas were made possible in most areas by the temporary increased food supply produced by drives, trips, hunts, or other communal economic affairs. The essential motivation of festivals was noneconomic. People desired social intercourse with friends and relatives rarely seen during the remainder of the year. They wished to dance and gamble, and, in some localities, to hold religious observances. Some of these activities, like the dances, were developed individually. Others, like the games, were probably introduced from neighboring areas at a remote time in the Americas.

The size of groups united by festivals rarely exceeded that produced by communal economic undertakings. In some areas festivals could be held only at times of communal hunts or when many families were gathering nuts or other species at a certain locality. They merely provided an additional motive for assembling together. Some held special gatherings for festivals. In providing an extra occasion for band activity, festivals enhanced band solidarity. But, as neighboring bands were often invited, temporary organization greater than the band was sometimes achieved. Among the North American Indians there seems to have been no major festival in aboriginal days. (The Sun Dance is recent.) Round dances served merely to amuse small portions of the bands. Possibly the Bear Dance among the Ute and some mourning ceremonies among Southern Paiute effected some group solidarity, but too little is known of who participated in them.

The sweat house was an integrative factor only in a small portion of festivals, where each village had a large permanent sweat house which served as a meeting house and men's club and dormitory. When villages were not too widely separated all male band members tended to for-gather in a central sweat house.

Feasts and festivals were held by Indians to memorialize a certain event, to seek spiritual aid, or to entertain participants or spectators. Dancing was nearly always part of North American Indian rites and celebrations. The term, "dance," has become the descriptive name for whole feasts or festivals often having many aspects and lasting several days. Dance, song, and instrumental accompaniment were often integral to each other, with the dance embodying the rhythm, and the song expressing the magic that the rite possessed.

Most feasts and festivals were held at a specified time or season. The Cherokee of the southeastern U.S. had rites referring to ghosts and death that were always performed in the winter so they would not harm growing crops.

Certain events could be enacted only by specific groups, societies, or families of a tribe. Others may have belonged to an individual and could be performed only by him or her; still others may be intertribal or open to all present. Dances that belonged to individuals could be bought and sold, together with the songs and objects that were pat of their power. Some ceremonies were only for women, others only for men, some for both.

Feasts and festivals were directed toward many different purposes. Help was sought from spirits for war, farming, hunting, and healing. Thanksgiving was offered when these things were well accomplished. Peace was sealed by formal singing, dancing and ritual smoking. Important milestones in a person's life—birth, puberty, marriage, death— were marked by rituals. Magic power might come to a person during a celebration, making him or her a shaman capable of healing. Sometimes they were for entertainment, as with the social events of the Plains and Prairies tribes. The purpose might be visually or physically portrayed, as in the Buffalo Dance where Plains Indians acted out their hope for a plentiful supply of buffalo by impersonating great throngs of the animals.

Feast and festival dance forms varied by geographical area. In the central part of the continent, from Labrador south through the eastern woodlands to Central America, groups tended to move counter-clockwise in an open circle or oval pattern with the participants facing forward or toward the center. Sometimes the pattern spiraled or was an undulating line. In general, the prodominant dance step went forward with the right foot, sliding the left up beside it. In the Great Basin, Plateau, and Plains, east to the Great Lakes, and sometimes in the Southwest, celebrants moved clockwise in closed circles, often with leaps and dramatic gestures In more sedate events, the left foot led the right. Some circle dances were planned so that the dancers always faced the sun; others were choreographed along the sun's course. In most areas there were events in straight lines; sometimes parallel lines of Indians faced each other, dancing together and then apart.

Religious ceremonies often had to be done in a certain way—the way that the gods had originally directed— if they were to accomplish the desired result and avoid disaster that might result from a mistake or breech in the ritual. But in some rites, they could be improvised.

Participation in a public ceremony was sometimes a requirement for adult status or for claiming inherited or won privileges. Among some Plains tribes the scars of self-torture from the Sun Dance were a necessary sign of adult malehood, and the annual Green Corn Dance in the southeast was the time for Creek warriors to be promoted according to the past year's accomplishments.

In southern California and among some Apache tribes of the Southwest, the principal ceremonies were initiations marking puberty. In California there were men's and women's societies who directed similar initiations for adolescent boys and girls. A vision always resulted from drinking a hot tea made from jimsonweed (Jamestown weed). Generally, the vision was of a supernatural spirit in the form of an animal who gave the initiate a personal song and became the

Photo bv Hilda Harrison.

Indians of San Blas, Panama, wearing their familiar derbies during a festive occasion.

person's special helper through life. Among the Apaches, the girl's puberty ceremony was the main public event, given by one's family soon after menstruation began. Since the U.S. government prohibited public Apache ceremonies except on U.S. Independence Day (the U.S. patriotic season apparently to ward off Indian wars), families have joined to give a single, annual celebration around the fourth of July. The ceremony lasts about four days. Girls are clothed in gold-colored buckskin, imitating the pollen with which their faces are painted by older women who are their sponsors. Games are held during the day, and at night spirit-impersonators dance by firelight. The girls themselves dance inside a ceremonial tipi each evening until midnight. Successful completion of the rite insures that a girl will live a good life and that she, her family, and her world will be protected from evil.

This Apache rite is an exception for southwest tribes, for the ceremonies of their neighbors, the Pueblos, paid little attention to individuals, but were dedicated to well-being of the whole community. The Apaches were immigrants from the north and retained northern customs, but southwestern society depended on rain for life, and at Zuñi, for instance, even personal healing rituals often contained petitions for rain and fertile crops.

The Hopi yearly festival cycle had two parts. The six months from the winter solstice in December until after the summer solstice in June was the time for masked ceremony when the Kachinas lived in the villages and dominated ceremonial life. The other six months, after the Kachinas returned to their homes in the San Francisco mountains, was for unmasked rites. Each major rite had two enactments roughly six months apart.

An unmasked Hopi rite was the Snake Dance, held in August. Eight to sixteen days of ceremony began with the gathering of rattlesnakes, whip snakes and bull snakes, continued through several days of secret rites in the kivas, and ended with the public dance in the plaza where snakes were carried in the mouths of participants. The snakes were released and taken back to the desert below the mesa in the direction of the four quarters of the earth. It was believed that the snakes, whom the Hopi view as their relatives, would intercede with the gods in the underworld to bring rain to the mesa. When the snakes were dropped they moved like lightning—symbolic of the hoped-for rain.

In recent times some Pueblo celebrations have had both Christian and traditional Indian aspects. A costumed dancer may leave the others and enter the village church where rattles and organ music join together.

Festivals were sometimes aimed toward dissipation or prevention of a specific crisis. One example, an eclipse of the moon, was recorded in 1910 by a U.S. photographer. Members of the Kwakiutl tribe on the Northwest Coast celebrated around a smoky fire, brandishing sheaves of sticks to successfully induce a great monster in the sky to cough up the just-swallowed moon.

Other Northwest Coast occasions for rites were the great trading conventions where, similar to 20th century American custom, the merchants and wholesalers, European and Indian, accompanied their business with days of eating, drinking, singing and dancing.

The Ojibwa of the northern Great Lakes celebrated on snowshoes, giving thanks for the first snowfall that made it easier to track and catch animals for food and clothing.

The most important ceremony among the Creeks and other Eastern Woodland peoples was the Green Corn Dance, or Busk. "Busk" is a European corruption of the word *boskita,* to fast. Fasting, as preparation for communication with the supernatural, was a characteristic part of many Indian ceremonies. The Green Corn Dance was held in July or August when the corn was ready to eat. It centered on agriculture, but touched all of life through thanksgiving for past prosperity and prayers for continued growth—both moral and physical. Except for murder, all crimes were forgiven at this time and every person started anew, like each house fire that was extinguished and relit from the new Busk fire.

In the western United States, Indians celebrated the fall festival, which included the circle dance, gambling, and annual mourning observances. It was the only noneconomic motive for large numbers of persons to assemble. There were no other group ceremonies. Small

Jivaro woman in festival attire, Ecuador.

Handbook of South American Indians.

Bringing wild fruit, with music, during a Tuyuca "Yurupary" feast.

groups of people who happened to be in the same vicinity might hold a minor circle dance during the summer, dancing one to several nights. The fall festivals, however, were annual events, enlisting people from a considerable territory. The temporarily increased food supply following the communal rabbit hunt and pine-nut harvest supported these large aggregates for a brief time.

The location of fall festivals depended partly upon the whereabouts of large villages, which acted as hosts, partly upon the annual occurrence of good seed crops, especially pine nuts. There seems to have been considerable reciprocity between certain villages which acted as hosts in alternate years. (It had somewhat crystallized in the institution of the exhibition dance, performed by visitors who were paid by their hosts.)

People participated in these with great enthusiasm as they afforded an opportunity to visit and revel with families seen only rarely or not at all in the course of the year. As new factors introduced by the white man made it possible to travel farther there were fewer but larger festivals. They were abandoned years ago.

Direction of festivals was the most important task of the chiefs.

FEATHERWORK appeared in ceremonial and utilitarian articles made by Indians in most areas. They used feathers of all common species of birds but some, such as the eagle, were especially prized. Among some Indians feathers were thought of as a connection between the spirit world and the everyday world. Myths of creaton incorporate feathers.

Featherwork decoration was a distinctive feature in ceremonies of the Northwest Coast tribes. Red feathers of the woodpecker decorated deerskin headdresses worn in dances, and deerhide carried on poles in wealth-display ceremonies. Plains Indians decorated the stem of the calumet with feathers whose colors varied according to the ceremony in which the pipe was used. War bonnets and trails made of eagle feathers were worn in dances and ceremonies. In the Southwest, Pueblo Indians use feathers of eagles, hawks, turkeys, and parrots on prayersticks and dance wands. The Zuñis and Hopis use featheres on Kachina dolls and masks, headdresses, and costumes worn in Kachina dances. The most dramatic use of feathers appears in the costumes worn by performers in the Shalako cere-

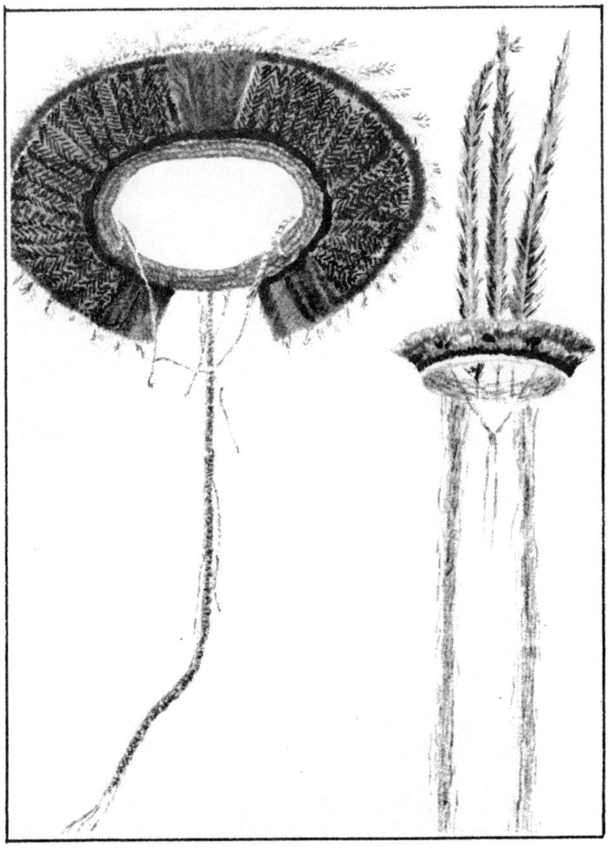

Feather headdresses; (Left) Macusi; (Right) Taruma.

mony. The Pomo Indians of California were unsurpassed in their technique of using feathers in their beautifully woven baskets. In ceremonial belts worn over one shoulder the Pomo wove feathers in symbolic designs believed to have supernatural power.

Feathers were widely utilized in clothing. In the Arctic regions parkas were made of the skins of waterfowl using feathers for warmth. Some Eastern tribes wove strips of birdskin into blankets. Others tied feathers in knots to create beautifully patterned robes. The Iroquois made fans of bird feathers.

Feathering was used on all arrows except on some used for short-range hunting of fish, where it was not needed. Its purpose was to keep the arrow aligned in flight by retarding the butt end. There were two main types of arrow feathering, tangential and radial. Tangential feathering was formed by tying two whole feathers along opposite sides of the shaft. Radial feathering was formed by tying and gluing two to four, usually three, half feathers to the shaft, radiating from its long axis. The feathers on an arrow were taken from the same side of the bird so that their natural curvatures would be aligned. Radial and tangential feathering were both used in some areas, but radial was definitely more effective. Tangential feathering was used in the eastern Arctic, part of the eastern Subarctic, and by a few tribes on the Northwest Coast. Both tangential and radial types were used in the central and western Arctic, the Northwest Coast, and the Southwest. Radial feathering was used throughout the rest of North America north of Mexico.

Mexican feather dance.

Feather shield, Aztec.

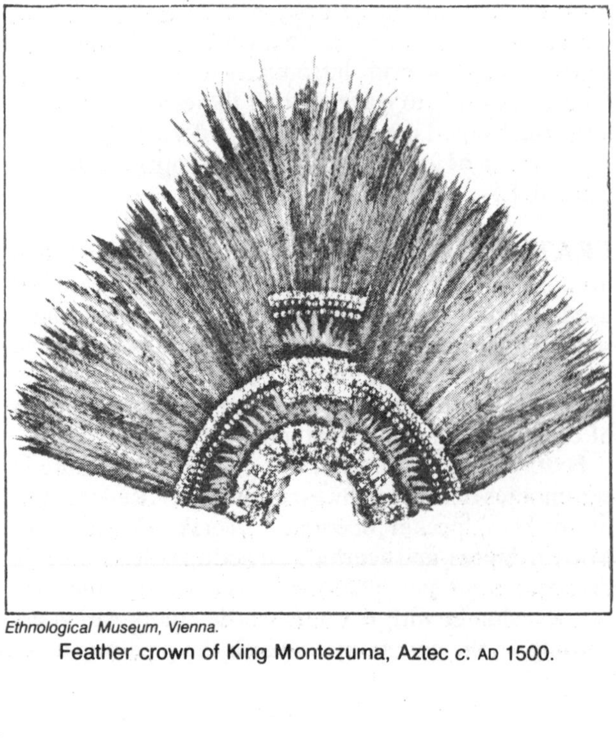

Ethnological Museum, Vienna.

Feather crown of King Montezuma, Aztec *c.* AD 1500.

Lowie Museum of Anthropology.

Yuki Indian wearing feathered headdress and shoulder garment.

FELTS, JACK LEON (Choctaw; Jan. 7. 1921-), is a writer and publisher. Born at Blanchard, Oklahoma, he founded Pan Press in Hollywood, California, in 1953. He has worked as a scenarist (1953-56) and as a literary agent (1953-). He established the Tahlequah Writer's Conference (1961-65), organized historical excavations in Mexico (1963-65), and is director of the Individualist Society.

FERTILIZER in the form of ashes was used widely by North American Indians before the coming of Europeans. Historically, ground shell and fish heads were used in New England and Virginia. The Seneca and Arikara are said to have used manure. Aboriginal use of these fertilizers, however, is not well substantiated.

Most agricultural tribes commonly cleared land of grass, brush, and trees by burning. In addition to clearing the land and making it more workable, this practice served to return nutrients more quickly to the soil. Indians on the northern Missouri River spread brush evenly over the entire area to be planted before burning. In much of California and the Great Basin, wild crops such as grasses, tarweed, and wild tobacco were burned to produce a better yield the next season.

In the Southwest, Indians took advantage of the natural fertilization process of alluvial flood plains. By planting in the river mud deposited seasonally they were able to recultivate the same areas continually without exhausting soil fertility. In most other agricultural areas, however, cultivation of new land was necessary when old fields were exhausted. Throughout the Prairies, Eastern Woodlands, and Southeast generally, fields were abandoned after a maximum of about a decade, and new fertile ones cleared.

FETTERMAN INCIDENT was an embarrassing defeat for the U.S. military during the Sioux War (1865-1868). The government had built a string of forts on the Bozeman Trail, which crossed Sioux territory into the gold-bearing region of western Montana. The trail was vigorously and often successfully opposed by the Sioux nation under Red Cloud. Eventually in 1868 the United States abandoned the route.

In December 1866 Red Cloud and 2,000 Sioux, Cheyenne, and Arapaho warriors moved south toward Fort Phil Kearny and camped nearby. On the morning of December 21, they laid in ambush at Peno Creek while 10 warriors teased and decoyed Captain William J. Fetterman and 81 cavalrymen and infantrymen into the little valley. Indian casualties were heavy but all the soldiers were killed.

The "Fetterman Massacre" was called the "Battle of the Hundred Slain" by the Indians. Captain Fetterman reportedly once said, "Give me 80 men and I'll ride through the whole Sioux nation". Two Cheyennes, two Arapahoes and six Sioux—10 Indian warriors led him to the ambush.

At that time it was the worst defeat the U.S. military had sustained in Indian battles and only the second with no white survivors. Among the decoy party were Little Wolf, Hump, Rain-In-The-Face and Little Horse. Crazy Horse, who led the decoy, later (June 1876) defeated Custer and the Seventh Cavalry at the Battle of Little Big Horn.

FIBERS, NATURAL, including cotton, distinct from the species of the Old World, were domesticated in the Americas. The archaeological record reveals that *Gossypium hirsutum* was the species of ancient Mexico whereas the textiles found in Peruvian graves were made from *G. barbadense.* Both of the American species of cotton are polyploids that arose from hybridization of two species followed by chromosome doubling. At one time it was postulated that one of the ancestral species had been carried to the New World from the Old by man, but more recent investigations do not substantiate this view.

The other important natural fiber plants include various members of the family Agavaceae. Henequen, maguey and sisal belong to various species of *Agave* and were cultivated in Middle America, while various kinds of cabuya, species of *Fucraea,* were grown in South America.

A number of wild plants, particularly palms and bromeliads, also furnished fibers used by the Indians, and bark cloth was made from some trees.

FIESTAS. While most people use the Western calendar for daily and business activities, two other calendars are significant in the lives of Indian groups in Latin America. One, used in parts of Huehuetenango, Guatemala, is the old Maya "vague year" calendar of 365 days divided into 18 months of 20 days each. The extra five days, which come after the end of one year and before the beginning of the next, are the "evil days," or the days of the "five women." The most important event in connection wtih this calendar, and perhaps the oldest Indian rite still practiced, is the Year Bearer's ceremony on the first day of the new year. This ceremony has been best preserved in the *municipio* of Jacaltenango. The old calendar was constructed so that the first day of the new year could fall on only four day names. The deity of the first day of the new year is the Year Bearer. Thus four deities take turns being the Year Bearer. Prayer-makers begin their duties days in advance in anticipation of the ceremony. They burn incense, make offerings of red flowers, and burn candles.

The Tzolkin calendar, which has 260 days divided into thirteen months of 20 days each, is important to the Indians of Momostenango, Totonicapan. Each day of the month has its own name. In addition, each day is numbered from one to 13, so that each month the same name will have a different number from the one that it has in any other month. The ancient Maya used the sacred Tzolkin calendar simultaneously with the "vague year" calendar. The most important celebration in connection with this calendar is also the first day of the year. The occasion is called the Ceremony of Eight Monkeys. Those who live in the village, and those who were born there but live elsewhere, take part in the ceremony, for it is considered very bad luck not to attend.

Towns throughout Latin America celebrate their saint's days, a Spanish contribution, with a characteristic mixture of solemnity and festivity. The emphasis is somewhat different in Indian and *ladino* towns. Among *ladinos* a novena may be held before the feast day. On the day itself, Mass is held, and images of the saint are carried through the town. Social dances, games, cockfights, sports, and comic theatrical performances provide the festive aspects of a *ladino* fiesta.

The saint's day in an Indian town is similar in many ways. Masked dances, however, such as the Dance of the Moors and the Christians, and the Dance of the Conquest, play a prominent role in the Indian town. Sacred *costumbres* (customary religious rituals), sacrifices, and prayers accompany these performances. The flavor of the Indian fiesta is more religious than that of the *ladino.*

The market is usually a relatively local affair, held once or twice a week in the *cabacera* of a *municipio.* Traders are usually residents of the *municipio,* though there may be some itinerant peddlers who come from farther away. The products sold at these frequent markets are necessities such as fruits, vegetables, and locally made textiles.

A fair, usually held in connection with some other occasion such as a fiesta, goes on for several days. It is a larger version of the market and attracts people from many parts of the country. Sections of the marketplace are set aside for particular products. Most Guatemalan *municipios* are known for a particular craft or product. The men from Chinautla, laden down with water jugs, go to the pottery section where they rent space; those from Momostenango carry their woolen blankets to another section. In recent years sections have been set aside for inexpensive factory-made items, such as combs, soap, and flashlights. Goods are usually bought and sold for cash after much bargaining.

FIFE (Creek; fl. early 19th century), was an Upper Creek chief who led his warriors in support of Gen. Andrew Jackson during the Creek War (1813-14) in Alabama. On January 22, 1814, his intervention in the battle on the Tallapoosa River near Emuckfau Creek saved Gen. John Coffee's division from being overrun, although General Jackson was forced to retreat to Fort Strother after the battle, despite Fife's efforts. Known as James Fife, he lived at Talladega, Alabama, and signed the treaty of Indian Springs, Georgia, on February 12, 1825.

FINGER, WALLACE L. (Sioux; Nov. 12, 1902-), was a star runner on the Haskell Indian School track team during the mid-1920s. Finger, whose Indian name is Yellow Horse, was born on Pine Ridge Reservation, South Dakota. He was a member of the two-mile and sprint-medley relay teams at Haskell. The two-mile relay team was recognized as one of the best in the U.S. Finger was inducted into the American Indian Athletic Hall of Fame in 1973.

FINHIOVEN (Kadohadacho; fl. 1770s), was a chief who assisted Athanase De Mézières, the lieutenant governor of Spanish Louisiana, in making peace with the Indian tribes of the northern Red River Valley. Finhioven arranged and helped to conduct De Mézi eres' successful treaty conference in 1770. In October 1771 he guided the Wichita Indians to Natchitoches, Louisiana, to sign a treaty with the Spanish. In August 1777, Finhioven fought a band of Osage near the Arkansas River after they had attacked a party of Spanish hunters. In the course of this campaign he learned of the presence of English traders and was commissioned by De Mézières to plunder the English.

FIRE MAKING. Nearly all Indians of the Americas knew how to make fire. The two chief aboriginal methods of fire making are those of rotary friction and of percussion.

The rotary friction method, with use of a plain hand drill, is by far the more common of the two methods, occurring as it does throughout North America, the southern Middle American and Antillean regions, and almost the whole continental South American region down to the Strait of Magellan.

There are two main methods of fire drilling were the one without, and the other with, complete piercing through the hearth.

Fire making by percussion, or "strike a light" method, was found less so throughout the Americas.

As a general rule, fires once lit were not allowed to die, but were carefully conserved and kept going day and night. Within or near the dwelling, when not in use, they were fed roots, rotten wood or other slow-burning material or may be banked under ashes. The arrangement of the fire logs in star-shaped fashion with the burning ends toward the center was reported and is probably fairly widespread, and easily lends itself to conservation of the fire; as the fire dies down the logs are pushed inward. On journeys by land, fire was commonly carried along—as fire sticks or firebrands, in clay pots or in sections of bamboo, on sherds, and so forth; on journeys by water, through similar means or on an earthen or shell hearth aboard the watercraft.

Torches of many kinds were used: bundles of dry grass stalks, plain bark, resin-rich woods, bark or other plant material dipped in or impregnated with wax, oil, resin, or gum; bark tubes filled with copal resin; and so forth. Candles of various types were recorded, usually among tribes who had a good deal of contact with whites.

FISHHOOK is one of the many devices used by American aborigines for catching fish for food. Though generally not as efficient as the net, weir, and fish spear, it was commonly made in a variety of forms. It was used throughout almost all of the Arctic, Subarctic, Great Lakes region, Northwest Coast, Plateau, and northeastern United States, and in parts of the Great Basin, Plains, California, Southwest, and Southeast in the United States.

The Indians used two basic types of fishhooks, the gorge and the more familiar design incorporating one or more hooked points. The gorge was a straight or slightly curved sliver of wood, bone, stone, shell, or copper with both ends pointed and the line attached in the middle. It was designed to be swallowed with bait and to turn sideways when the line was tightened, lodging in the stomach or throat of the fish. The familiar "J"-shaped type of fishhook was made in several ways. Some were carved or ground from a single piece of bone, ivory, or shell or hammered from naturally occurring copper. In northern areas this type was commonly made from a point of bone, thorn, ivory, or copper lashed to or imbedded in a straight or curved shank of wood, stone, or ivory at an acute angle. The resulting composite hooks were normally a rough "V" shape with the line usually attached at or near the end of the shank. Some were multipointed, and a few had barbed points. Some Eskimo composite hooks had shanks carved in a manner allowing them to be used as lures or jugs rather than as baithooks. In historic times steel fishhooks rapidly replaced the older types.

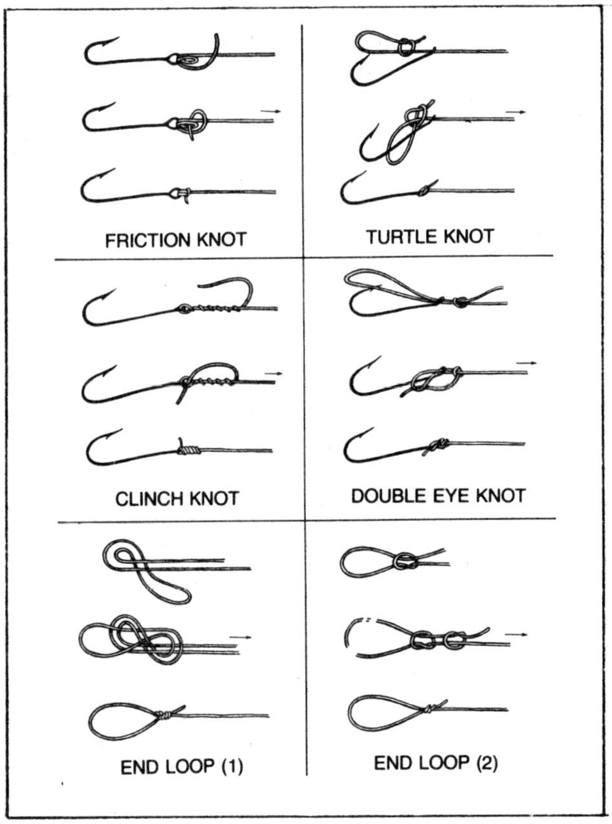

Knots used in attaching hooks.

FISHING. Indians were skillful in fishing, and employed a great variety of methods. Only the Indians of the Prairies, where lakes were absent and the muddy rivers were poorly stocked with fish—and those of inferior quality only—paid little attention to fishing, and instead sought game and wild fruits. Elsewhere the fishhook and the fishspear, the net, trap, and weir, were as indispensable as the bow and arrow; and dried fish was a staple food in nearly every community during the first two months of winter.

The Indians were well acquainted with the barb, which they used on spears and harpoons; but they generally avoided it on fishhooks. Their bait was either some part of a fish—the eye, or the skin from the belly—or else a piece of bright bone, ivory, or even stone. Among the Eskimo and Kutchin it was carved to imitate a fish. The Indians of the Atlantic and Pacific shores fished from canoes in the bays and gulfs, catching mainly cod, halibut, and salmon; the northern Indians and the Eskimo used their canoes for trolling, and fished through the ice of the lakes for whitefish, trout, and salmon trout. For set lines the natives used a gorge—a short pencil of bone or hardened wood sharpened at both ends and inserted inside a piece of meat or fish, with the line attached to the middle. The Eastern Indians captured large numbers of sturgeon, salmon, and eels with torches and spears. Two men would go together in a canoe at night; one sits in the stern and paddles and the other stands with a spear over a flambeau (of birch bark) placed in the head of the canoe. The fish, attracted by the light, come in numbers and the spearman then takes the opportunity of striking them. Some tribes in British Columbia similarly speared (or clubbed) by night the salmon that were migrating up the rivers. By day they often adopted a method common among the Indians and Eskimo of North America: they set lures, such as a bear's tooth at holes in the ice and speared the fish that approached the bait.

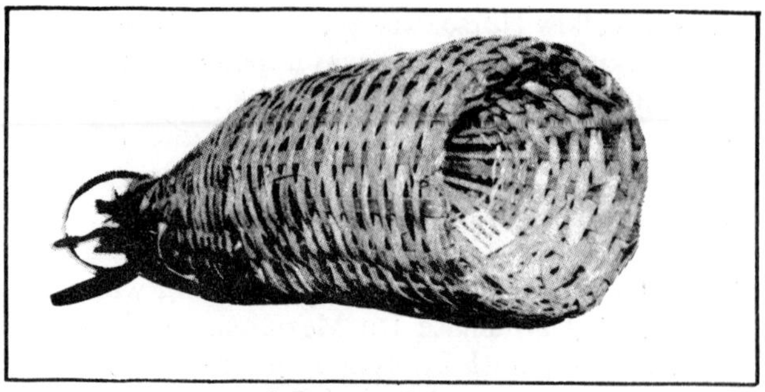

A Catawba fish trap.

Several tribes employed pronged and gaff for hooking salmon. A modification of the instrument—a pole generally about ten feet long armed with a row of bone spikes for two feet from one end—served the Nootka for both herring and oolakan; drawn through a shoal of herring it nearly always impaled three or four fish. Special tools of this kind were not uncommon, for the Indians were quick to conceive or borrow new ideas that related to fishing (and hunting).

Despite their variety, all these methods yielded a small amount of fish compared with the number caught with nets, traps, and weirs. It is curious that the Eskimo, who employed a kind of square seine for capturing seals, never adopted the same method for fish until about the time of the discovery of America, when it was introduced from Siberian tribes into Alaska and spread eastward as far as the Mackenzie Delta in Canada. The Northern, Eastern, and West Coast Indians all used the seine, setting it under the ice during the winter. The Eastern Indians also had bag-nets and dip-nets, which they usually employed in conjunction with weirs. The material of these nets varied considerably: the Pacific Coast Indians generally used nettle, their inland neighbor's hemp, the Eastern Indians nettle or hemp, Northern natives willow-root or caribou thongs, and the Eskimo willow-root.

The Indians turned weirs to full advantage. Certain

Smithsonian Institution, Bureau of American Ethnology.

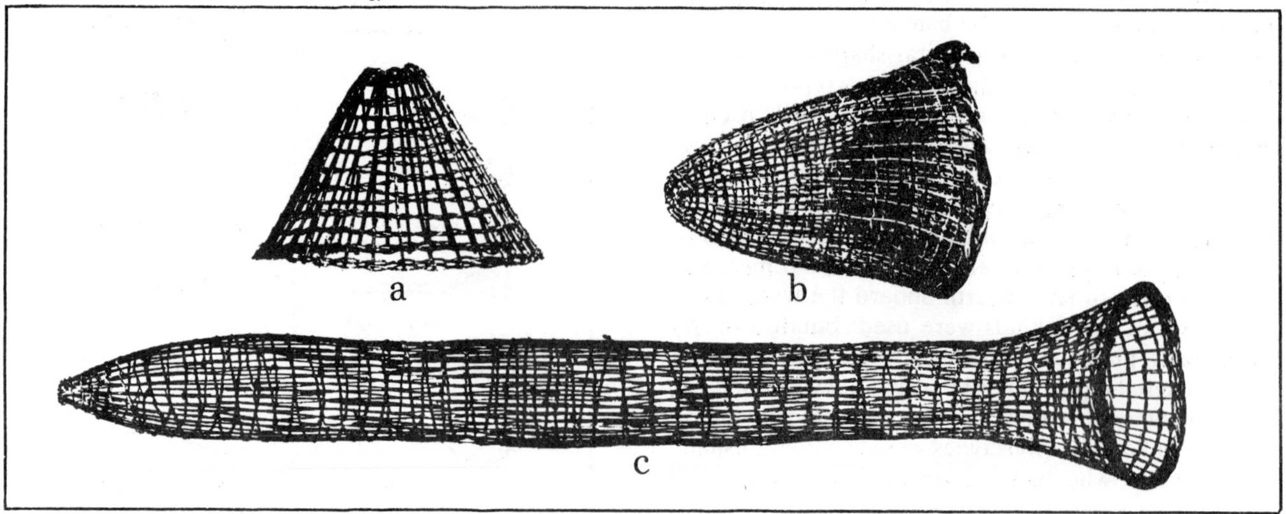

Pomo fish traps: (a) open on top, plunged over small fish; (b) funnel pot, for small fish; (c) a narrow trap which is laid in a current, thus preventing a fish from backing out and too narrow for them to turn.

rocky canyons left only a few narrow openings for the passage of the migrating salmon; there the Indians planted their basket-traps, and plied their nets and spears in the swirling water below them. On the sea-coast, again, the receding tide often left a few fish stranded in pools among the rocks. These natural weirs probably suggested the construction of artificial ones in suitable places. Some Indians built dams of stones in the shape of large horseshoes along the banks of tidal rivers to impound the salmon when the tide went out, and in the Arctic the Eskimo laid straight stone dams across streams that the salmon trout ascended, leaving small openings in the lower rows, but completely closing the uppermost. The Indians of eastern and western Canada had fences of piles and brush, many of them so elaborate and extensive that their construction required the entire community. These log weirs provided many tribes with two-thirds of the yearly food supply, so that their destruction by floods or enemies was a terrible disaster.

The community weir, like the buffalo or caribou pound, was a powerful factor in welding the different families of Indians into a single, social unit. Every man contributed his labor to the building and maintenance of the weir or pound, and every man was entitled to his share of the booty. At the weirs each man retained whatever fish he caught, but allowed no family to remain hungry. The Indians realized that every man had his days of ill-luck when fish seemed to elude his weapons; that accidents and sickness attacked the strongest and ablest hunter, making him dependent for a time on his fellow-men; and they insisted on an equitable division of food, permitting no one to hoard it while his companions starved.

The fishing of the sea-mammals required not only ingenuity but courage. However uncertain the weather the Indians fearlessly went to sea in their dugout canoes (during the months of April and May), to attack the whale. The whaling equipment of the West Coast tribes closely resembled that of the Eskimo, which was adopted by whites until the whaling-gun. One observer described it: "The harpoons which they use to strike the whale or any other sea-animal, except the otter, are contrived with no common skill. The shaft is from eighteen to twenty-eight feet in length; at the end whereof is fixed a large piece of bone, cut in notches, which being spliced to the shaft, serves as a secure hold for the harpoon, which is fastened to it with thongs. The harpoon is of an oval form, and rendered extremely sharp at the sides as well as the point—it is made out of a large muscle-shell, and is fixed into another piece of bone, about three inches long, and to which a line is fastened made of the sinews of certain beasts, of several fathoms in length; this is again attached to the shaft; so that when the fish is pierced, the shaft floats on the water by means of seal-skins filled with wind, or the ventilated bladders of fish, which are securely attached to it. The chief himself is the principal harpooner, and is the first that strikes the whale. He

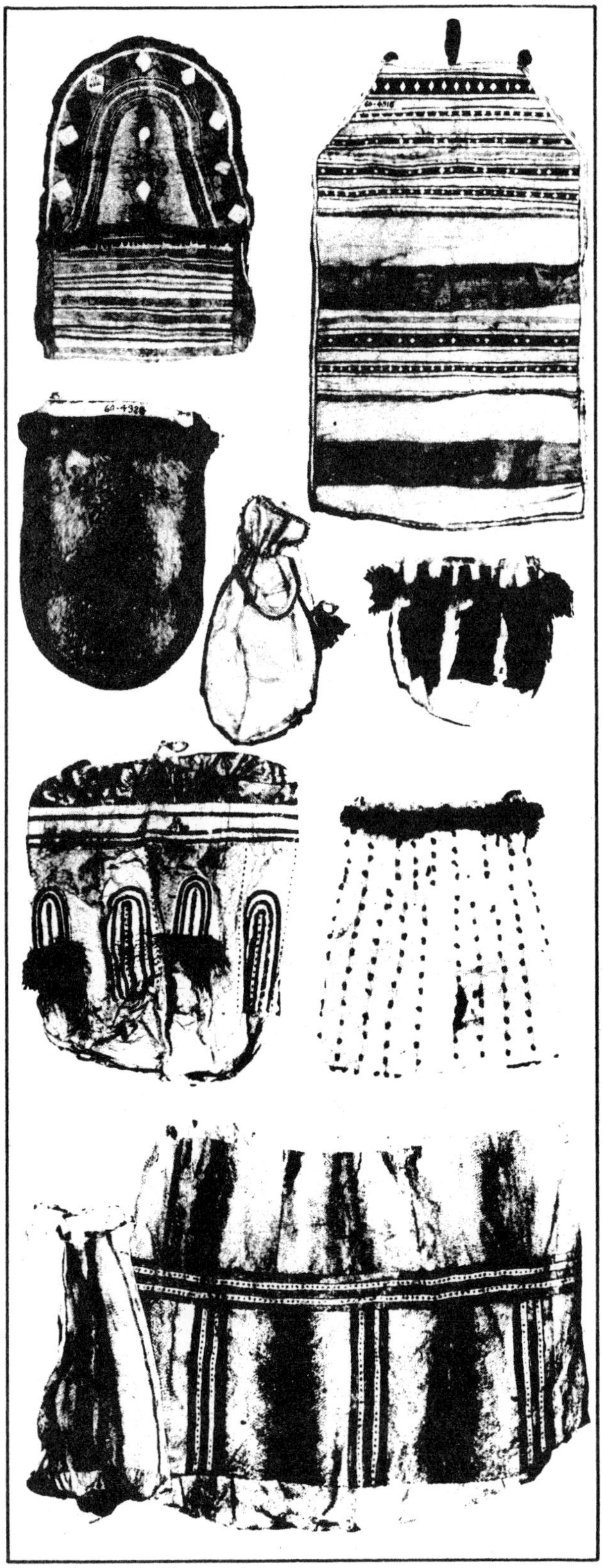

Anthropology Dept., Yale University.
Fish skin and fur bags.

is attended by several canoes of the same size as his own, filled with people armed with harpoons, to be employed as occasion may require. When the huge fish feels the smart of the first weapon, he instantly dives, and carries the shaft with all its bladders along with him. The boats immediately follow his wake, and as he rises, continue to fix their weapons in him, till he finds it impossible for him to sink, from the number of floating buoys which are now attached to his body. The whale then drowns, and is towed to shore with great noise and rejoicings."

Almost as strenuous as whaling was the sea-otter fishing of the Pacific Coast Indians. For this, equipped with light harpoons and with bows and arrows, Indians set out in two very light canoes. If they found an otter sleeping on the surface of the water, the harpooned it and dragged it to one of the boats, where it fought with its claws and teeth. Usually it sighted their approach and dived. The two canoes then followed in its course, separating in order that one or the other might be within bow-shot when it rose for breath; but the otter was swift: the pursuit often lasted several hours before it was killed.

The same Indians lured seals within range of their arrows by wearing wooden masks, covering their bodies with branches and imitating the actions of a seal basking among the rocks. Sea-lions, which were less timid and more frequently came ashore, were attacked with clubs; the Haida Indians killed large numbers of these animals during their spring excursions to the west coast of the Queen Charlotte islands. But the most skillful fishing Indians of sea-mammals were the Eskimo. Like the Pacific Coast Indians they harpooned the whale, the seal, and also the walrus from their boats during the summer months.

FISHING AND HUNTING RIGHTS are the governance of fishing and hunting behavior, included ownership of hunting grounds or fishing sites, and the procedures determining the distribution of game and fish. Fishing spots were privately owned more frequently than hunting grounds, although throughout North America fishing and hunting were, to one degree or another, cooperatively pursued.

Hunting grounds were of two major types, including improved sites, where game fences, traps, or similar devices were constructed to aid in the hunt, and unimproved sites. Territorial boundaries created few disputes among the Eskimos, except where traps or other improvements had been made. Ownership of an improved tract, however, rarely lsted longer than a single season, and quite often less than that. In the western Arctic regions, fishing sites were privately owned by individuals and were ordinarily inherited by the owner's son. In Greenland, fishing sites for seals were owned by families. The nature of inheritance in this region is not known.

The Yurok Indians often owned fishing sites jointly, particularly rich ones. Use of the spots rotated among the owners, usually for a day or two at a time; the length of the shift varied with the share of ownership. A guest owed the owner the bulk of his catch, and if only one fish was caught the owner kept all but the tail end. The Yuroks forbade fishing below an established fishing site, in order to insure the continued value of the already existing site. Hunting lands were privately owned to about one mile inland from the river. Poachers could be, and were, shot, although a wounded animal—belonging to the hunter—could be pursued into neighboring tracts.

Hunting among the Algonquians was pursued cooperatively between several families within a band, ensuring that, in the uncertain Subarctic environment, all would have a sufficient food supply. With the arrival of whites, however, hunting for the fur trade replaced hunting for use, and the older patterns disappeared. Earlier, for example, the band leader allocated lands among the families of his band; now he helped them obtain favorable terms at the white-owned trading post. Entering someone else's territory to fish or to hunt had in the past constituted trespassing. But after the arrival of whites, trespass was committed only if the intruder's intent was to hunt fur-bearing animals.

On the Northwest Coast the most favored sites were owned by kin groups. The wealthiest member of a family or village had direct control over these sites, although in practice he could not refuse a member of his village or kin group the right to hunt or fish on his property.

In the Plains region, during the annual buffalo hunt, special societies were given policing powers over the hunters. The rights of the tribe as a whole were bound up in the hunt, and one who jeopardized its success by some rash action could be severely punished.

FITZGERALD, KENT (Chippewa; Sept. 9, 1911-), is a former official of the U.S. Bureau of Indian Affairs (BIA) who in the mid-1970s was the executive officer for Indian affairs, Executive Council of the Episcopal Church. Born in Chicago, Illinois, he joined the BIA after graduation from Northwestern University. During his long career in government service, he developed procedures related to the Indian Reorganization Act of 1934, directed a revamping of the position structure of the BIA, and designed the Relocation Program (later the Employment Assistance Program), which assisted Indians in finding work in urban areas. Fitzgerald played an important role in establishing guidance and counseling programs for reservations and relocation cities.

FIVE CIVILIZED TRIBES were the Cherokee, Choctaw, Chickasaw, Creek, and Seminole nations. They came to be called "civilized" because of their outstanding accomplishments in self-government in the Indian Territory (Oklahoma). The term, used officially and unofficially, was also meant to distinguish them from the southern Plains tribes who roamed the area directly to the west.

Forced from their homelands in Georgia, Alabama, and Florida after the Indian Removal Act of 1830, more than 60,000 members of the Five Nations were moved west from 1830-1842. They were in a strange land, demoralized, poor, and sometimes a fraction of their former number. During Cherokee removal about 25% of the nation died on the notorious Trail of Tears. The broken tribes were often suspicious of their leaders because some of the cession treaties were accomplished through bribery. Despite suspicion of the government's new assurances, they gathered their hopes and built a new life in the Indian Territory, renaming geographical features for the ancestral homelands they had left behind.

The five tribes were never united or organized as a group, although, since 1874, a special section of the Bureau of Indian Affairs has dealt with them. Their western homeland was directly west of Arkansas. The nations owned the land under patented title. This Indian Territory comprised the present state of Oklahoma except for the panhandle (Oklahoma east of the 100th meridian). A small portion in the northeast belonged to the Quapaws and some Senecas and Shawnees.

The FiveNations settled in the eastern portion of the territory and, within three decades, built individual republics which were more advanced than those they had left behind. The prospering independent governments were complete with executive, legislative, and judicial branches. There were great plantations worked by black slaves, and industry also advanced.

The Cherokees were torn by internal problems for a while, but in 1839 they established a capital at Tahlequah. Other capitals were Nanih Wayah (Choctaw, 1834); Tishomingo (Chickasaw, 1856); and Okmulgee (Creek, 1867). The Seminoles successfully resisted union with the Creeks and, by 1856, they were settled on their own land where they began a tribal government and school system. The Seminole capital was Wewoka.

A government agent lived with each of the tribes to advise them on treaty guarantees and report to the Department of Indian Affairs on their progress. Except for the agent, the Indian nations were relatively isolated from governmental interference as they restructured their lives. Fort Gibson, built in 1824, was followed by other garrisons as the frontier of the Civilized Tribes expanded.

Newspapers, books, and educational pursuits were available in each republic. School systems were established with the aid of missionaries. The Cherokee organized a national school system in December, 1841 and the Choctaw soon followed.

By 1860, without the proximity of white civilization, the Five Civilized Tribes had built stable social organizations capable of dealing with the white system. With the advent of the Civil War, however, the Indians were faced with making a choice beteen competing white groups. U.S. troops had been moved from the territory into Kansas and Confederates occupied their military

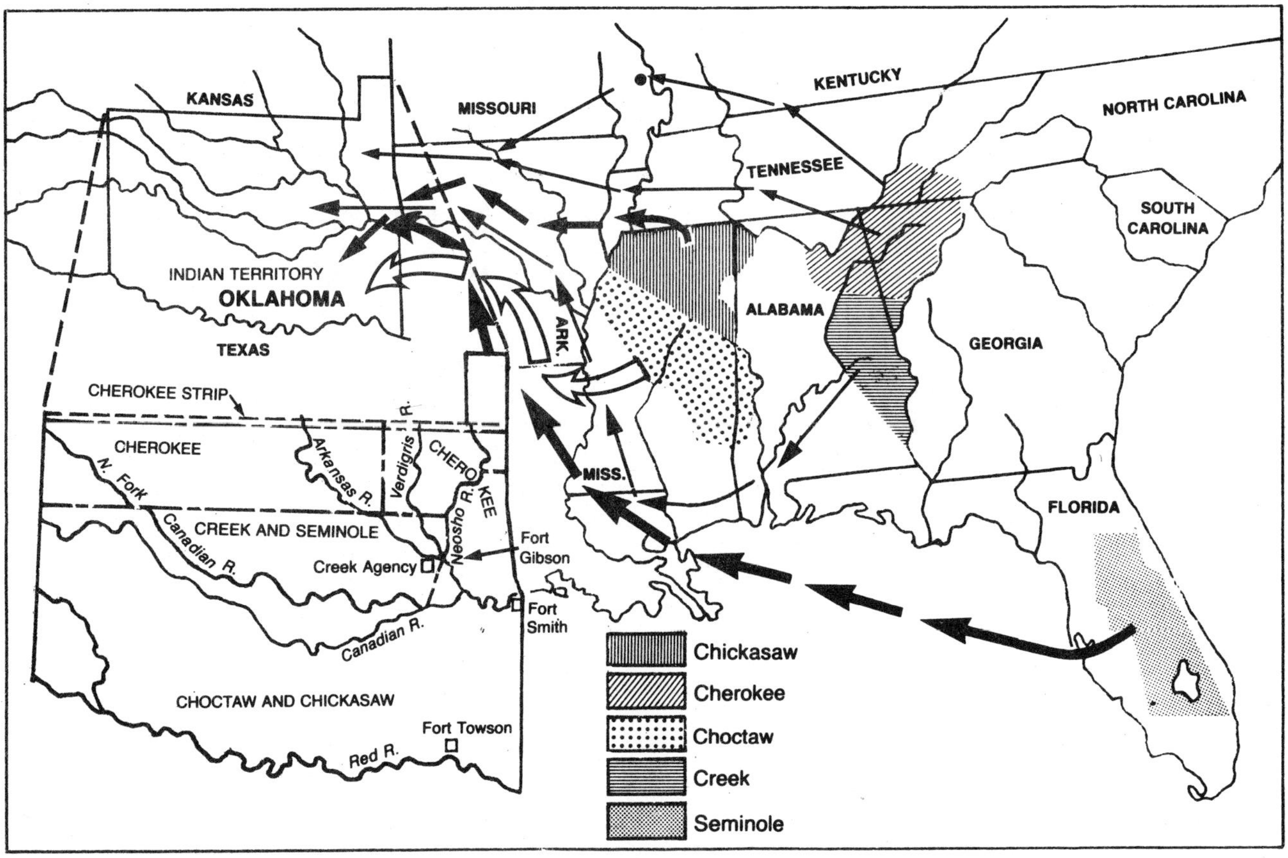

Locations of Five Tribes before and after removal 1830-1842.

posts. While a strong faction argued for neutrality, by 1861 the nations had concluded treaties with the Confederacy. Several Civil War battles were fought on the Indian Territory.

At war's end, the land of the Five Nations was within the grasp of manifest destiny. Reconstruction treaties were forced upon the tribes in 1866 as payment for Confederate collaboration. These treaties ceded the western portion of the territory and granted railroad rights. Indian peoples being relocated from Kansas and Illinois were settled on portions of the ceded lands and the remainder was opened to the white "boomers" who had been lobbying for the unassigned lands.

Oklahoma Territory was organized in 1890 on the ceded western portion of Indian Territory, but the eastern half remained under tribal title of the Five Nations. Although the tribes had been exempted from the Dawes Act (1887) which alloted land in severalty, pressure to force allotment soon began with the Dawes Commission (1893). The Curtis Act of 1898 forced allotment on all. Land was parceled out on an individual basis to tribal members and "freedmen," former slaves. Ignoring a succession of treaties and clear deeds to the land, Indian governments had been abolished and millions of acres were made available to white homesteaders. In 1907 the Oklahoma and Indian territories were admitted to the Union as the State of Oklahoma.

FIVE NATIONS IROQUOIS. When Europeans first encountered the Indian tribes of what is now upstate New York they met the Five Nations Iroquois. Their confederacy was to play an important role in the struggles among Europeans and Americans for control of the northeastern woodlands.

The Iroquois got their name from their Algonquin Indian enemies; Iroquois is thought to mean "real adders." The five tribes call themselves the *Ongwanonhsioni*, meaning "Longhouse builders," or *Hodinonhsioni*, "people of the longhouse," in reference to their confederacy. The five tribes are now known as the *Seneca, Cayuga, Onondaga, Oneida,* and *Mohawk*. These names are descendents of the appelations applied to the tribes by themselves, other Indians, the French, the Dutch, the English, and Americans over several hundred years. Each tribe has a name for itself meaning the "people of" a particular town or place. The Seneca are *Onondewagaono*, the Cayuga are *Gayokwehono*, the Onondaga are *Onontaga*, the Oneida are *Oneyotdehaga*, and the Mohawk are *Kanyengehaga*.

At the time of European contact the Seneca, Cayuga, Onondaga, Oneida, and Mohawk lived in that order from west to east in the region between the Genesee River and Schoharie Creek. Their hunters, traders, and warriors ranged from the Mississippi River to New England. Today the Iroquois lands are reduced to reservations in New York, Quebec, Oklahoma, and Wisconsin.

The Five Nations speak Northern Iroquoian languages. Each tribe's speech is sufficiently distinct to call it a separate language, but there is also enough mutual intelligibility between them that they could be called dialects of a single language. The Iroquois made pictographs, but they did not develop a written alphabet.

The Iroquois believed that the world had many supernatural spirits whose good will was needed for a bountiful life. Therefore, everyday activities were closely interwoven with religious beliefs.

The Iroquois year began in the spring. A festival was held to express gratitude to "The Creator" and "The Maple" for the sweet syrup made from sap. Spawning fish and roosting pigeons were caught. During this season clearings were made in the forests to replace old fields and also for new palisaded villages. Villages had to be moved every ten to twenty years as firewood supplies and fields became exhausted. By May "The Three Sisters," maize, beans, and squash, were planted and a festival was held. These foods were the main sustenance of the people. Elm bark for longhouses, canoes, and containers was then gathered. Wild strawberries appeared in the woods, and a festival was held in thanks for these first fruits.

In the summer most men departed to go trading or on the warpath. Women gathered wild plants for food and medicine, worked in the fields, and harvested and stored the crops. Festivals were held to honor "The Corn Mother" and to celebrate the harvest.

In the fall deer were hunted, nuts were gathered, and fish were caught to help sustain them through the coming winter. Councils were held during this time as snow confined them to their villages for the most part. Winter was a time for socializing, storytelling, and the manufacture and repair of tools and clothing. Raw materials including stone, clay, plant fibers, and animal products were made into knives, axes, drills, bows and arrows, clubs, jars, bowls, mortars, mats, baskets, fishhooks, needles, snowshoes, lacross sticks, dolls, and many other items.

The New Year came after winter solstice, and Midwinter, the most important festival, was held to strengthen "The Creator" after his winter struggle with his evil twin.

Children were free of responsibilities and all played together until the age of eight or nine, when the boys and girls separated and began to acquire adult skills through observation and mimicry. After marriage the husband usually went to live in his wife's longhouse. Their children belonged to the mother's clan. Each longhouse held several families which belonged to a single clan tracing descent through the women.

Villages contained at least three of twelve different clans. The clans had ceremonial duties towards each other in various games and rituals. The clans were the basis of political organization at all levels. Clan chiefs and other elders determined village policy. The clan matrons selected the fifty hereditary sachems representing the tribes at the confederacy's councils. Other leaders, such as war chiefs, were selected on the basis of merit.

Contact with white culture brought many changes. The Iroquois adopted western technology, but their rich cultural traditions survive today, as shown in their art forms, including pottery, basketry, bead and porcupine quill decoration, silver smithing, and carving. They are best known for False Face masks used at curing ceremonies.

The Iroquois were descended from hunters and gatherers who lived for thousands of years in upstate New York. The actual date of the formation of the League of the Iroquois is not known. Most estimates fall between AD 1400 and AD 1600. The Iroquois generally stated that the league was formed before European contact. In Iroquois oral tradition two men, Deganawida and Hiawatha (not Longfellow's Hiawatha), founded the league.

After European contact the Iroquois fell into competition with surrounding Indian groups for hunting territory to obtain the furs needed to trade for French, Dutch, and later English goods, such as cloth, beads, guns, and metal axes, knives, and kettles. Between 1638 and 1675 the Iroquois defeated the Wenro, Huron, Petun, Neutral, Erie, and Susquehannock confederacies. Many of the defeated Indians moved among the victorious Iroquois.

Throughout most of the seventeenth and eighteenth centuries the Iroquois maintained their position between the British and the French by a combination of warfare and skillful diplomacy. French Jesuits began missionary activities among the Iroquois after 1653. Their missions were soon closed, but were resumed in 1668. Relations with the French became strained and the missions were abandoned in the early 1680s. The Iroquois raided the French, who attacked the Seneca in 1687, the Mohawk in 1693, and the Onondaga and Oneida in 1696.

Smallpox and warfare reduced the Iroquois population during the seventeenth century, though some of this loss was made up by the adoption of other Indians. In AD 1660 the Iroquois tribes were believed to have had under 2,200 warriors.

Starting in the latter part of the seventeenth century a number of Iroquois left their traditional homeland. During the 1660s some Cayuga settled on the Bay of Quinté. Mohawks began to settle along the Saint Lawrence River in Canada, and by the mid-eighteenth century they had established large settlements at Saint Regis and Caughnawaga. Cayugas, Onondagas, and Oneidas also moved to the Saint Lawrence area, and in the 1750s a number were living at Oswegatchie (now Ogdensburg, New York).

The Tuscarora of North Carolina began to join the Iroquois in New York during the early eighteenth century. In 1753 the Cayuga adopted the Tutelo and Saponi, who established a village south of Cayuga Lake.

After the British defeated the French at Montreal in 1760 the Iroquois could no longer control the balance of power. When the American Revolution broke out the Iroquois attempted to remain neutral. Eventually most of them were drawn in on the side of the British, though some Oneida sided with the Americans. In 1779 an American army destroyed the homeland of the Iroquois, who fled to western New York and Canada.

The Revolution destroyed the power of the league. The Americans made treaties with the Iroquois forcing them to sell their remaining lands in New York, except for a few reservations. Many Iroquois moved to reserves in Canada and some went west. Two councils were formed, one in Canada, and one in the United States. Since the last major treaty was signed in 1842 land has continued to be sold or leased to whites, sometimes against the wishes of the Indians, as in the case of Kinzua Dam in the 1960s.

The change to reservation life was a difficult one. Drinking and fighting became serious problems. However, the teachings of Handsome Lake, a Seneca, reconciled traditional religious beliefs with white material culture and helped the Iroquois adapt to their new lives. Constitutional governments replaced the hereditary chiefs on the Allegany and Cattaraugus Reservations in 1848, and in 1924 the Canadians forced an elected council on the Grand River Reserve. During the early 1960s the Iroquois population on reservations in Canada and the United States was conservatively estimated at 26,000 people.

Today the Iroquois live both on and off reservations. Except for garden plots farming is generally decreasing in importance, as individuals seek wage labor. For example, Mohawks from the Saint Regis and Caughnawaga Reserves have achieved prominence as high steel workers. On reservations many old practices and beliefs are maintained by traditional members of the community, though most Iroquois are Christians. Ceremonies for traditional foods, curing rituals, and the Midwinter Festival are still held. The League of the Iroquois continues in existence and clan mothers wield their influence in selecting chiefs. The Iroquois genius for survival has kept their cultural heritage alive through the present.

NEAL TRUBOWITZ
WILLIAM ENGELBRECHT

FLANDREAU RESERVATION, in South Dakota, is home to about 100 Santee Indians.

History. In March 1869, 25 families of the most enterprising Indians at Santee Agency left and took homesteads at Flandreau, Dakota Territory, as authorized by the Sioux Treaty in 1868. They had no agent for the first four years, but after that a part-time agent looked after their affairs until they were placed under the Santee Agency in 1879. They had no reservation, and their agency was referred to as the Flandreau Special Agency until 1879. The only government-owned property property was a school, established in

1870. The reservation was established in 1935 through an Act of Congress.

Culture. This group was active in adopting white men's ways and today is fully integrated, economically, and educationally, into the dominant culture. Unemployment, low income, and federal dependency are no longer reported to be problems.

Government. The constitution, under the authority of the Indian Reorganization Act, was approved in April 1936 and revised in November 1967. The tribal charter was ratified in October 1936. The governing body is the executive committee which is elected at large in August of even-numbered years. A president, vice-president, secretary-treasurer, and two trustees form the executive committee.

FLATHEAD is a misnomer for the Indian tribe inhabiting western Montana which never practiced artificially flattening children's heads. The name's origin is obscure. Some authorities believe that surrounding tribespeople so designated them; others state the name (*Têtes Plates*) was applied by early French fur traders. The Shoshoni of east-central Idaho called the Flatheads, *Ootlashoots* or *Red Willow people* of the Tushepaw nation. Other tribesmen called them *Sa'lic* or *Sa'lix*. They called themselves *Salish*, "the people," and are a division of the former large and powerful Salishan linguistic family. One Pacific Coast Salish division was addicted to head flattening. Besides the Flatheads, other Interior Salishan subdivisions included the Spokan in eastern Washington, the Kalispels or Pend d'Oreilles, and Coeur d'Alenes in northern Idaho.

The Salish, or Flatheads, their popular name, occupied the easternmost extreme of the Plateau culture zone, between the Bitter Root Range on the west to east of the Rockies. Their habitat east of the Continental Divide in primitive times was in large detached bands west and south of the Gallatin River Valley extending to the Little Belt ranges on the east. After the horses' introduction, the Flatheads clashed with the Blackfoot over territorial hunting rights to the Plains buffalo. As continual warfare prevailed which decimated their numbers, the scattered Flathead bands drew together for mutual protection. Within the last 200 years, they established their main camp in the Bitter Root Valley of southwestern Montana between present Stevensville upriver to Darby. Previous to the horse complex, Flathead material culture resembled the Plateau area, afterwards it acquired almost all the traits of a typical Plains tribe, rich horse trappings and elaborate beaded regalia. Flatheads had animal legends from Coast Salish and the Plains indicating they were influenced by both culture zones.

The people were noted for possessing all the virtues—well-built, good-looking, friendly, courageous, hospitable, and honest. They lived peacefully with their neighbors the Pend d'Oreille (Kalispel) north of the Bitter Root. In time their culture blended to such a degree that dialectic differences tended to disappear.

Dwellings formerly were long, mat-covered communal lodges similar to the Nez Perce. Flatheads adopted the Plains conical skin tipi after they acquired horses and became more mobile. Later canvas substituted for animal skins, although permanent long houses were used for dance purposes until acculturation began, and are erected today for reservation ceremonials.

Political organization was tribal, ruled by a head chief for usually three familial generations. A council of subchiefs administered petty affairs and acted in an advisory capacity to the high chief. As occasions arose, other chiefs held temporary power for hunting, berrying, scouting, and war. Emblems of the high chief's authority were the tribal pipe and a whip. He punished transgressors with a flogging or a public tongue lashing. Ridicule was the strongest informal means of social control, but the "Grabbers," an internal police corps, assisted the chief in suppressing serious antisocial acts. Although the custom died out in modern times, judicial whipping and reprimand were the most important methods of punishing wrongdoers for nearly 200 years.

Flatheads had many taboos surrounding pregnancy and birth, and elderly midwife services were common. Cradleboards for carrying infants are no longer used. Salish mores indicated that premarital relations were tolerated but had to take place in secret. Parents whipped the erring daughter if she was found out. An unmarried girl's pregnancy was considered disgraceful,

Flathead

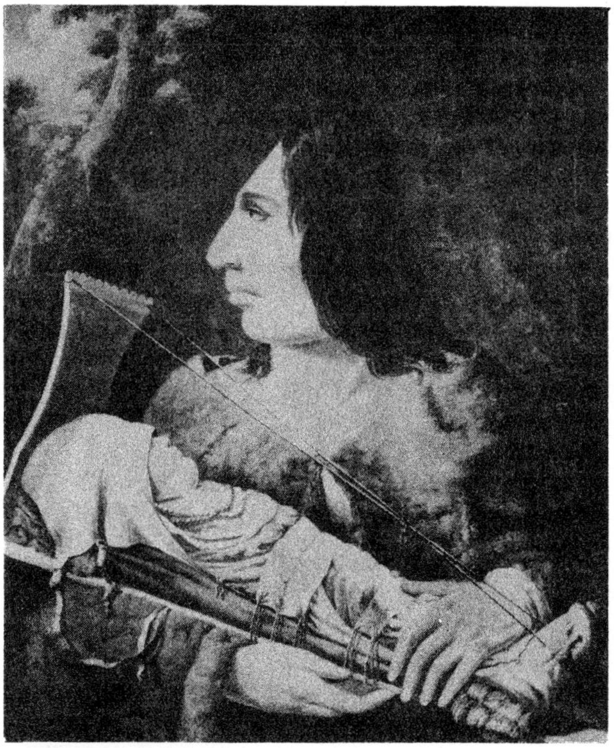

Montreal Museum of Fine Arts.

Flathead woman and child. Painting by Paul Kane, 1847.

although no opprobrium attached to the boy. Marriages were usually arranged by the boy's and the girl's mothers. Elopements were not uncommon, but the Salish proudly proclaimed they "never sold their daughters." Three forms of marriage rites practiced were wedding by public acknowledgment of cohabitation; wedding by parental exhortation; wedding by the marriage Song Dance, the formal type. Polygamy was common until the missionary era.

All household tasks burdened the women who always set up and dismantled the tipis. Their domestic utensils were simple, crude baskets for berry and root gathering, twined grass spoons, and cooking, done in a fire pit.

The horses' introduction had a profound impact on Salish life-style and caused the wealth concept to become an equine complex. A man rich in horses was considered rich in everything else. Tribal tradition indicates horses were acquired from the Shoshoni, estimated between 1600 to 1750. The Flatheads' fine herds became of paramount economic importance for hunting and protection in war. Dogs guarded camp and children, and men used them to hunt bears, deer, and elk.

Other economy included women gathering edible foods in season, men providing meat by fishing and trapping with deadfalls. People traded with friendly tribesmen, especially the Nez Perce for their fine basketry. Gift exchanging within the band bore a slight resemblance to Northwest Coast potlatches, a trait continued into modern times.

Wars were minimal in pre-horse days, but afterwards Blackfoot encounters on the Plains became serious and bloody. Flatheads engaged in war dances preceding a foray and a scalp dance after a successful one. Their greatest coup honor was to capture an enemy without using any weapons. Men and women war captives became slaves. Notched coup-sticks and an eagle feather were the signs of war honors.

Flatheads had a major religious ceremonial at each season as they recognized the soul's existence and survival after death. A Creator called *Amótkan*, a spirit, made the world and lived on high but could be approached with prayer. A goddess, Emtĕp, "She-who-sits-at-the-foot-of-a-tree," occupied the world's bottom. The high chief annually prayed to Amótkan at Midsummer rite. Since the world was not perfect, Creator sent Coyote (a culture hero) to rectify things. All men had a monogenetic origin and racial differences were due to Tricksters.

Religious and magical observances focused on the food quest were very complicated. The First Roots Dance with song-prayers was celebrated in the spring before women dug up camas and bitter roots, the two primary economic plants used as cooked vegetables. An ancient Thanksgiving Dance of men and women, accompanied by song and prayer, was held immediately after the First Roots ceremony, although it could be given at other times. Feasting and prayer also marked the elk fall hunt.

The First Bison ceremony was the most important invariable rite, observed during the tribe's eastward march in winter, but omitted during the brief summer hunt. When hunting was poor, the shamans began bison calling songs, dances to induce a blizzard that would drive a herd toward the encampment. Pre-Christian days' next most important ceremonial was the Midwinter Festival which survived missionizing. It began at New Year, the first crescent moon of Month of Wandering (but held much later in modern times), and was divided into the Camas Dance—primarily a song-prayer in winter for an adequate springtime vegetable supply—and the Bluejay Dance.

When near puberty boys and girls practiced a Guardian Spirit vision quest by fasting alone in the mountains. Usually they acquired at least one song. The Spirit helper gave the votary some object which was made into a medicine (magical power) bundle and preserved through life.

Although Flatheads were free from many contagious diseases, few lived to advanced age partly due to seasonal famines and recurrent smallpox epidemics. Evil spirits caused illness, so people used various charms to frighten them away. Shamans treated most ailments with herbal potions of roots, leaves, flowers, and fir needles. When people died a grave in the earth was prepared with care. Following the wake, a mourning feast was held to give away the deceased's property, and lasted several days to pay mourners and to honor the dead. Abstinence and isolation characterized the

Photo by N. A. Forsyth.

Salish woman,and children, western Montana 1907.

mourning period for a year or longer, but Salish did not practice body mutilation.

Indian-white relations were always peaceable from the Flatheads first contact on September 4, 1805 with Lewis and Clark expedition members. The captains estimated the tribe at 400 persons in thirty-three lodges. Between 1812-1820 the Indians heard of the Christian religion from Catholic Iroquois who accompanied French traders west from near Montreal. After four attempts to petition "Black Robes" in St. Louis to teach them the white man's medicine power, they embraced the new religion when Jesuit Father DeSmet built St. Mary's Mission, September 24, 1841, at the tribe's Bitter Root camp at present Stevensville. Missionary priests taught the Indians agriculture and mechanic arts.

Together with neighboring tribes, Pend d'Oreille (Kalispel), and unlinguistically related Kutenai to the north, Flatheads signed a peace treaty with Washington Territory's Governor I. I. Stevens, July 16, 1855. Head Chief Victor's tribespeople would stay in the Bitter Root; the others would live north of the Salish in Mission Valley near the Mission Ranch southeast of present Arlee. In 1872 part of the tribe led by subchiefs moved to the reservation after signing the James Garfield Treaty. Head Chief Charlot's band, despite their poverty-stricken condition and increasing white settlement in the Bitter Root, passively resisted removal until October 15, 1891, when they located in Jocko Valley. Charlot's people had remained neutral, except for scouts serving with the military, during the 1877 Nez Perce War when retreating bands passed through Salish territory.

Agency headquarters were relocated near Dixon, Montana in 1910 as a more central site. Known today as the Confederated Salish and Kutenai tribes of the Flathead Reservation, the Indians became farmers and stock raisers. Salish tribal law, controls, and customs deteriorated during transition from an aboriginal lifestyle to an alien culture, but they tried to become acculturated. The 1930s Depression left the Flatheads destitute.

To regain socio-cultural indentity, numerous young people today are attending the Indian Studies program at the nearby University of Montana in Missoula and at its other state systems. Educated youth have revived on the reservation traditonal Salish life, ceremonies, dances, and culture. The Flathead Culture Committee is collecting and recording cultural history information from tribal elders to educate the younger children.

However, the committee reports that alcoholism among unemployed reservation residents is a major problem, although the tribe sponsors a federally funded alcoholism program with a detoxification-information center. Housing programs are making strenuous efforts to improve inadequate housing. Health, hospitalization, and dental care "is one of the best that the Public Health Service can offer." Medical facilities in adjacent Missoula are available to Indians. Child education "is taking on a new aspect" by concerned parents and the tribe placing more emphasis on the learning process. Poverty income levels, however, plague the majority of reservation adult members, though some educated Indians have succeeded very well. In general, progress is being made in improving modern tribal conditions.

Flathead population has fluctuated through the years. Gibbs gave their probable number in 1853 as 325, in 1909 it had risen to 598, and exploded in the 1960s to an estimated 2500. Together with a small group of Kutenai, Pend d'Oreille, Kalispel, Spokan, the combined tribes in the mid-1970s had a reported 5400 members with 2800 residing on the reservation. The others are scattered throughout the United States and in various foreign countries.

HELEN ADDISON HOWARD

april 6/82
X